The Blackwell Handbook of Mentoring

To my fascinating husband Mark and my extraordinary son Ethan,
who fill my life with inspiration, joy, and love
Tammy D. Allen

To my supportive and loving family, especially Craig and Turner Alexis
Lillian T. Eby

The Blackwell Handbook of Mentoring

A Multiple Perspectives Approach

Edited by

Tammy D. Allen

Department of Psychology, University of South Florida

Lillian T. Eby

Department of Psychology, University of Georgia

© 2007 by Blackwell Publishing Ltd

BLACKWELL PUBLISHING
350 Main Street, Malden, MA 02148-5020, USA
9600 Garsington Road, Oxford OX4 2DQ, UK
550 Swanston Street, Carlton, Victoria 3053, Australia

The right of Tammy D. Allen and Lillian T. Eby to be identified as the Authors of the Editorial Material in this Work has been asserted in accordance with the UK Copyright, Designs, and Patents Act 1988.

First published 2007 by Blackwell Publishing Ltd

2   2008

Library of Congress Cataloging-in-Publication Data

The Blackwell handbook of mentoring : a multiple perspectives approach / edited by Tammy D. Allen, Lillian T. Eby.
    p. cm.
  Includes bibliographical references and index.
  ISBN: 978-1-4051-3373-9 (hardcover: alk. paper)
  1. Mentoring. I. Allen, Tammy D. II. Eby, Lillian T.

  BF637.M45B56 2007
  158'.3—dc22

                                                    2006025795

A catalogue record for this title is available from the British Library.

Set in 10/12pt Galliard
by Graphicraft Limited, Hong Kong
Printed and bound in Singapore
by COS Printers Pte Ltd

The publisher's policy is to use permanent paper from mills that operate a sustainable forestry policy, and which has been manufactured from pulp processed using acid-free and elementary chlorine-free practices. Furthermore, the publisher ensures that the text paper and cover board used have met acceptable environmental accreditation standards.

For further information on
Blackwell Publishing, visit our website:
www.blackwellpublishing.com

Contents

Notes on Contributors

Editors

Tammy D. Allen is Professor of Psychology at the University of South Florida. Her research interests include mentoring relationships, work–family issues, organizational citizenship behavior, and occupational health psychology. Her mentoring research has focused on factors that relate to both formal and informal mentorship effectiveness and on understanding mentoring relationships from the viewpoint of the mentor. Her research has been published in journals such as *Journal of Applied Psychology*, *Personnel Psychology*, and *Journal of Vocational Behavior*. She is currently Associate Editor of the *Journal of Occupational Health Psychology* and serves on the editorial boards of several other leading journals.

Lillian T. Eby is Professor of Psychology and Fellow at the Institute for Behavioral Research at the University of Georgia. Her research program focuses on career-related issues such as workplace mentoring, job-related relocation, career success, the work–family interface, and gender issues in organizations. For the past 9 years she has systematically investigated both the positive and negative aspects of mentoring relationships from the perspective of the protégé, mentor, and organization. She has published over 50 research articles and book chapters and her work appears in such outlets as *Personnel Psychology*, *Journal of Applied Psychology*, and the *Journal of Vocational Behavior*. Lillian is also co-editing a special issue of the *Journal of Vocational Behavior* on multidisciplinary approaches to mentoring research and was recently awarded a grant by the National Institute on Drug Abuse to study the relationship between mentoring relationships and employee turnover in substance abuse treatment centers.

Contributors

Steve Bearman is a social psychology doctoral student at the University of California, Santa Cruz. His work integrates the perspective that people are not self-contained entities, but rather are distributed across networks of interactions, with research on interventions to diminish racism and other forms of oppression. Bearman is also a counselor and the founder of Interchange, a San Francisco based training program in Radical Counseling.

Eric Benjamin is a Professor of Psychology at Montgomery College in Rockville, Maryland. He is also an adjunct professor in the Counseling and Human Services Department at Johns Hopkins University and at Bowie State University. He has published several articles and manuscripts investigating the development and role of cultural and racial identity. Additionally he has served on the editorial board of the *Journal of Counseling and Student Development.* He is currently consulting with secondary educational institutions in order to utilize noncognitive predictors of academic success to promote student retention and matriculation.

Stacy Blake-Beard is an Associate Professor of Management at the Simmons College School of Management and Research Faculty in the Center for Gender in Organizations. She holds a BS in Psychology from the University of Maryland and an MA and PhD in Organizational Psychology from the University of Michigan. Her research focuses on the impact of changing workforce demographics on mentoring relationships. She has published research on gender, diversity, and mentoring in several publications including the *Journal of Career Development*, the *Academy of Management Executive*, *Psychology of Women Quarterly*, and the *Journal of Business Ethics.*

Lynn Blinn-Pike is currently a Professor of Sociology, Indiana University-Purdue University. She received her doctorate from the Ohio State University. Her research interests include examining how to prevent or ameliorate the effects of high-risk behaviors such as gambling, unsafe sex, and substance use among youth. She has developed, directed, and evaluated community-based mentoring programs for pregnant and parenting adolescents in over 15 states.

Marcus M. Butts is a doctoral student in Applied Psychology at the University of Georgia. His research interests include careers, mentoring, organizational commitment, and research methods.

Clark D. Campbell is a Professor of Psychology and Director of Clinical Training in the Graduate Department of Clinical Psychology at George Fox University in Newberg, Oregon. He is also Adjunct Associate Professor of Psychiatry and Family Medicine at Oregon Health and Sciences University. In addition to mentoring graduate students in clinical psychology, he maintains a small private practice in a rural community and enjoys outdoor activities with his family.

Faye J. Crosby is a social psychologist specializing in issues of social justice. She has written, co-written, edited, or co-edited 14 books and over 150 articles and chapters. Crosby is the recipient of numerous awards including the Carolyn Wood Sherif Award (bestowed by Division 35 of the APA), the Lewin Award (bestowed by the Society for the Psychological Study of Social Issues), and an honorary doctorate from Ball State University. Crosby's most recent book, published by Yale University Press, is *Affirmative Action is Dead; Long Live Affirmative Action*. Crosby also writes about and attempts to put into practice good mentoring.

Thomas W. Dougherty is the Hibbs/Brown Chair of Business & Economics and Professor of Management at the University of Missouri-Columbia. He is currently doctoral program coordinator for the Department of Management. He received his PhD in Industrial/Organizational Psychology from the University of Houston. His research interests are diverse and have included mentoring/networking relationships and linkages to career success, employment interviewer decision-making, and role stress and burnout.

George F. Dreher is a Professor of Business Administration in the Kelley School of Business at Indiana University-Bloomington. He recently was a visiting scholar at Hong Kong University of Science and Technology. He received his PhD in Industrial/Organizational Psychology from the University of Houston. His current research addresses the role of race, ethnicity, age, and gender in accounting for selection, promotion, and retention decisions in organizational settings (with a focus on managerial and executive talent pool management). His research has been published in journals such as the *Academy of Management Journal*, the *Academy of Management Review*, the *Journal of Applied Psychology*, *Personnel Psychology*, *Human Relations*, and the *Journal of Vocational Behavior*. He has also co-authored three books and numerous other papers and book chapters.

Jaime R. Durley is a doctoral student in Applied Psychology at the University of Georgia. Her primary research interests include mentoring, career development, and gender issues.

Sarah Carr Evans is a doctoral student in Applied Psychology at the University of Georgia. Her research interests include workplace mentoring, dysfunctional relationships at work, career development, learning in organizations, and the relationship between work and family life.

Lisa M. Finkelstein is an Associate Professor and Coordinator of the Social-Industrial/Organizational Area in the psychology department at Northern Illinois University in DeKalb, IL. She received her PhD in Industrial/Organizational Psychology in 1996 from Tulane University in New Orleans. Her current central research interests include mentoring, age and generation issues in the workplace, and humor at work. She is currently serving as Secretary of the Society for Industrial and Organizational Psychology.

Jennifer M. Grossman, Post-Doctoral Fellow, Harvard Medical School/Massachusetts General Hospital, has been involved in a variety of research projects focusing on adolescent development and diversity. Her recent research focuses on the impact of ethnic identity and racial discrimination in Asian American youth. She has published several articles and book chapters related to socio-cultural influences on adolescent development.

Dana L. Haggard is currently pursuing her PhD in Management at the University of Missouri-Columbia. Her research interests include mentoring, psychological contracts, and interpersonal relationships in the workplace. She has benefited greatly from the encouragement of her mentors at Missouri, and she hopes someday to be as inspiring to others as her mentors have been to her.

Laurie Hunt is a management consultant, executive coach, and principal of Laurie Hunt & Associates. She is a consulting affiliate with the Center for Gender in Organizations (CGO) at Simmons College. Her research, writing, and consulting interests include mentoring, diversity, women of color entrepreneurs, and leadership communication. She works with Fortune 500 and non-profit organizations to design and implement customized formal mentoring programs to support the advancement of women and people of color. Laurie has over 20 years of international marketing, communications, and human resources experience in the high-tech industry. She has an MA in Gender & Cultural Studies from Simmons College in Boston and a Bachelor of Business from Wilfrid Laurier University in Waterloo, Canada.

Hazel-Anne M. Johnson is an Industrial/Organizational Psychology doctoral candidate at the University of South Florida. She is an active member of the Mentoring Research Group, which is conducting a cross-cultural examination of diversity and workplace mentoring. She also serves as a mentor to both graduate and undergraduate students in the Psychology Department. Her research interests involve emotions in the workplace as well as mentoring and diversity in organizations.

W. Brad Johnson is an Associate Professor of Psychology in the Department of Leadership, Ethics, and Law at the United States Naval Academy. He is also a Faculty Associate in the Graduate School of Business and Education at Johns Hopkins University. He received a PhD in Clinical Psychology and an MA in Theology from Fuller Theological Seminary in 1991. He is a Fellow of the American Psychological Association (APA) and the current president of the Society for Military Psychology (division 19) within APA. Research interests include mentorship, professional ethics, and leadership.

Thomas E. Keller is the Duncan and Cindy Campbell Professor for Children, Youth and Families with an Emphasis on Mentoring in the Graduate School of Social Work at Portland State University. His research on the development and influence of mentoring relationships in Big Brothers Big Sisters community-based and school-based programs has been supported by the National Institute of Mental Health and The Spencer Foundation. Prior to earning his doctorate in Social Welfare at the University of Washington, he worked for several years with a Big Brothers Big Sisters affiliate in Seattle as a case manager, supervisor, and program director.

Elizabeth Lentz is a doctoral candidate at the University of South Florida, where she also received her Master of Arts degree in Industrial/Organizational Psychology. Research interests include mentoring relationships, leadership development, selection, and performance appraisal. Her work has appeared in journals such as the *Journal of Applied Psychology*, *Personnel Psychology*, and *Journal of Career Development* and national conferences such as the *Society for Industrial Organizational Psychology*, *American Psychological Association*, and *Academy of Management*.

Belle Liang, Assistant Professor, Counseling and Developmental Psychology, Boston College, has been a practicing licensed psychologist for the past decade. Her research and clinical work focus on developing cross-culturally and developmentally appropriate relational approaches to clinical and community interventions among high-risk and ethnic minority youths. In addition, she has developed theory and assessment instruments that reflect the underlying beneficial and potentially harmful qualities of mentor relationships. Her recent work developing a youth version of relational mentoring (Relational Health Indices-Mentor) is being funded by the Robert S. and Grace W. Stone Primary Prevention Initiatives Grant Program, Wellesley College.

Angie L. Lockwood is a doctoral candidate in the Applied Psychology Program at the University of Georgia. She completed her Bachelors in Psychology from the University of Virginia. Her primary research interests are mentoring, interaction of work and family experiences, and managing change in organizations.

Andrew Miller is Professor of Mentoring & Active Citizenship and Director of the Institute for Community Development and Learning at Middlesex University in London, England. He is currently also a Director of the Aimhigher National Mentoring Scheme and the HE MentorNet, a network for 130 universities in England. In 2002, *Mentoring Students and Young People* was published by Kogan Page in the UK and Stylus Publishing in the US. Since then he has undertaken evaluations for the UK government on its Mentoring Fund strategy 2001–2004 and for IBM on their e-mentoring program. He is part of a European Union funded research program examining mentor training in vocational education and training.

Carol A. Mullen is Associate Professor in the Department of Educational Leadership & Policy Studies, University of South Florida, Tampa, FL 33620-5650. Dr Mullen has authored over 140 works, including 8 books, and many refereed journal articles, in addition to 11 special issues of journals. Her most recent book is *A Graduate Student Guide: Making the Most of Mentoring* (Rowman & Littlefield Education, 2006). She is editor of the refereed international journal *Mentoring & Tutoring: Partnership in Learning* (Carfax Publishing/Taylor & Francis).

Kimberly E. O'Brien is an Advanced Industrial/Organizational Psychology doctoral student at the University of South Florida. She has developed, introduced, and evaluated a university-wide peer mentoring program for graduate students at her current institution, and serves as a mentor for several undergraduates in the department. Her research interests include methodology and antecedents to organizational citizenship behavior and counterproductive work behavior.

Ekin K. Pellegrini is an Assistant Professor at the University of Missouri-St. Louis business school. Her primary research interests are leader–member exchange, cross-cultural management, organizational justice, and mentoring.

Mark L. Poteet, PhD, is founder and president of Organizational Research & Solutions, a consulting firm specializing in employee selection, executive/managerial assessment and coaching, performance management, and training design and delivery. He has worked with many companies, both as an employee and consultant, in industries such as government, education, aerospace, electronics, insurance, and utilities. He has published and presented numerous articles on the subjects of training, mentoring, and performance management. He lives in Tampa, Florida.

Belle Rose Ragins is Professor of Management and the Research Director of the Institute for Diversity Education and Leadership (IDEAL) at the University of Wisconsin-Milwaukee. She is co-author/editor of *Mentoring and Diversity: An International Perspective* (with David Clutterbuck), *Exploring Positive Relationships at Work* (with Jane Dutton), and *The Handbook of Mentoring* (with Kathy Kram). Her national research awards include the AOM Mentoring Legacy Award, the Sage Award for Scholarly Contributions to Management, the ASTD Research Award, the APA Placek Award, and five Best Paper Awards from the Academy of Management. She is a fellow of the Society for Industrial-Organizational Psychology, the American Psychological Society, the Society for the Psychology of Women, and the American Psychological Association.

Aarti Ramaswami is a doctoral student majoring in Organizational Behavior and Human Resources Management in the Kelley School of Business at Indiana University-Bloomington. She completed her Masters in Industrial and Organizational Psychology from the University of Mumbai, India, and her Bachelors in Psychology, with Sociology honors, from St. Xavier's College, Mumbai. Her research interests include cross-cultural organizational behavior and human resources, person–environment fit, mentoring, life satisfaction, and job satisfaction.

Jean E. Rhodes, Professor of Psychology at the University of Massachusetts in Boston, has researched both natural and assigned mentoring relationships within different social contexts. Professor Rhodes is a Fellow in the American Psychological Association and the Society for Research and Community Action, a Distinguished Fellow of the William T. Grant Foundation, and a member of the John D. and Catherine T. MacArthur Foundation Research Network on Transitions to Adulthood. She sits on the Board of Directors of the National Mentoring Partnership, the advisory boards of many mentoring and policy organizations, and the editorial boards of several journals in community and adolescent psychology. Professor Rhodes has published widely in developmental and community psychology journals. Her book, *Stand by me: The Risks and Rewards of Mentoring Today's Youth* (Harvard University Press), was recently issued in paperback.

Ozgun B. Rodopman is a doctoral student in the Industrial/Organizational Psychology program at the University of South Florida. She is a member of the Mentoring Research Group, which is currently involved in cross-cultural research in mentoring relationships. She also serves as a mentor in the peer mentoring program for new graduate students. Her research interests include mentoring, stress, and voluntary workplace behaviors.

Gail Rose is a Research Assistant Professor of Psychiatry at the University of Vermont. She received her PhD in Clinical Psychology from the University of Iowa in 1999. Her research and scholarly interests include mentoring, leadership and professional development, academic medicine, health behavior change, quantitative research methods, and alcoholism prevention and treatment.

Terri A. Scandura is Professor of Management and Psychology at the University of Miami. Her research interests are leadership, mentoring, international organizational behavior, and applied research methods.

Lewis Z. Schlosser is an Assistant Professor of Counseling Psychology in the Department of Professional Psychology and Family Therapy at Seton Hall University. He received his PhD in Counseling Psychology from the University of Maryland in 2003. His research and scholarly interests include advising and mentoring relationships, multicultural psychology, religion, and Jewish issues.

William E. Sedlacek is Professor of Education, Assistant Director of the Counseling Center, and Adjunct Professor of Pharmacy at the University of Maryland. He earned Bachelor's and Master's degrees from Iowa State University and a PhD from Kansas State University. His latest book is *Beyond the Big Test: Noncognitive Assessment in Higher Education* and he has published extensively in professional journals on a wide range of topics including racism, sexism, college admissions, advising, and employee selection. He has received research awards from the American College Personnel Association, the American Counseling Association, and the National Association for College Admission Counseling.

Hung-Bin Sheu is a doctoral candidate in the Counseling Psychology program and received two master's degrees in Counseling and Statistics & Measurement from the University of Maryland, College Park. He has served as a counselor in college settings and as a consultant in business settings. His research interests include multicultural counseling, subjective well-being, and career development; and he has presented papers in these areas at national and international conferences. He has received research awards from the American Psychological Association and the Association for Assessment in Counseling and Education.

Renée Spencer, Ed.D, LICSW, is an Assistant Professor at the Boston University School of Social Work. She received her masters in Social Work from the University of Texas at Austin and her doctorate in Human Development and Psychology from the Harvard Graduate School of Education. Her research focuses on youth mentoring relationships, adolescent development, and gender.

Daniel B. Turban is the Stephen Furbacher Professor in the Department of Management at the University of Missouri-Columbia. He received his PhD in Industrial/Organizational Psychology from the University of Houston. His research interests include mentoring relationships, employee recruitment and applicant attraction, motivation, and role perceptions. He is blessed to have married Patricia White, and they live with their two children, Kathryn (16 years old) and Stephen (12 years old), who provide them with many opportunities to learn about mentoring.

Xian Xu grew up in Hangzhou, China and completed her BA at Fudan University in Shanghai. She obtained her MA from and is pursuing her PhD in Industrial/Organizational Psychology at the University of South Florida. Her interests include mentoring, organizational citizenship behavior (OCB), emotions, and cross-cultural studies. Her research has focused on the moderating effect of cultural values on the relationship between personality and OCB, a new measure of discrete emotions at work, and mentoring across cultures.

Foreword: The Maturation of Mentoring Research

With this *Handbook*, mentoring comes of age as a subject of scientific inquiry. This maturation occurs in part because the chapter authors generally concur on the linguistic explication of mentoring, an accomplishment not to be overlooked. They agree on mentoring's universal core attributes, delimit its meaning by excluding overlapping constructs, and accept operational definitions based on local knowledge appropriate to particular domains and specific situations. From their shared perspective, the *Handbook* authors provide an up-to-date review and synthesis of research and theory on the antecedents, correlates, and consequences of mentoring. More than a survey, the *Handbook* provides critical analyses of that literature and then reflection on these appraisals. In addition to evaluating the validity of theoretical assertions and empirical findings, the authors determine the usefulness of various conceptual schemata in accounting for them.

In accomplishing these goals, which are noteworthy in themselves, the *Handbook* does even more. It codifies inquiry into mentoring by imposing discipline and order on it. The editors systematically and coherently organize the research on mentoring by delineating the scope of scientific inquiry into a framework consisting of three domains: the workplace, the academy, and the community. The 20 years of accumulated research in these three domains has been disparate and fragmented, having been the product of several disciplines, each with a unique orientation. The plan of the *Handbook* codifies the field of inquiry and the assembly of chapters integrates what had been different substantive areas into a unified whole.

While reading this *Handbook* I kept asking myself "Why has it appeared now?" Many of the chapter authors indirectly addressed this question by reporting the same history. They narrate mentoring's creation myth by explaining why Odysseus, as he was preparing to leave for battle, asked Mentor to guide his son Telemachus during his absence. This accounts for the construct's name and root metaphor. These authors then report that the book entitled *Seasons of a Man's Life* (Levinson, Darrow, Klein, Levinson, & McKee, 1978) aroused contemporary interest in mentoring research and initiated the modern study of developmental relationships. And finally, they tell us that Kram's (1985) seminal book entitled *Mentoring at Work: Developmental Relationships in Organizational Life* provided the core concepts for the next two decades of research and reflection on mentoring.

This agreement that mentoring became a special interest of many researchers about 20 years ago aroused my curiosity because it explains only when, not why. To me, the why merits attention because it involves a societal response to the reorganization of the work world occasioned by the global economy. In today's information era, the typical worker encounters numerous transitions across occupational positions. During the agricultural era, workers grew up on the farm and, if they remained there, they knew what to do. If they wanted to leave the farm, they could take advantage of advice from a "friendly visitor." When the industrial era replaced the agricultural era, a new discipline called vocational guidance emerged. Guidance personnel succeeded friendly visitors as they adopted the modern perspective of science as the solution to life's problems. They believed that guidance occurs when science touches an individual. Street youth, immigrants from other nations, and migrants from the farm to the factory often felt lost in the city and tempted by urban ills. They sought and received vocational guidance, based on scientific ability tests and interest inventories, about where they fit into the work world. This guidance happened once, and then the worker having selected an occupation was expected to retire from it 30 years later. Following World War II, with the advent of international corporations characterized by bureaucratic hierarchies, vocational guidance personnel reformed themselves into career counselors who advised individuals about how to both choose an occupation and then develop a career in it by climbing the corporate ladder.

Today the ground is shifting under our feet as we experience the most rapid economic transformation in history. The global economy has prompted a seismic shift in the social arrangement of work. Occupations now lack the stability that they once had and, as large corporations flatten, downsize, and outsource, they are less available as a medium in which to develop a career. Today we rarely view careers as unfolding or developing in a hierarchical corporation. Instead, we talk about managing transitions and constructing careers. At the heart of the new boundaryless career with its postmodern psychological contract is the core concept of repeated transitions. The fragmentation, tentativeness, and discontinuity of 21st-century jobs leave workers rife with tension, ambiguity, and insecurity. Rather than seeking stability, they must become flexible and mobile. Rather than developing in an occupational position, they must adapt to a long series of different assignments. The models of friendly visiting, vocational guiding, and career counseling are inadequate societal responses to the momentous changes in work life wrought by digitalization and globalization.

So, in a world where workers are insecure, contingent, and temporary and where assignments and projects are replacing permanent jobs, negotiating transitions becomes the central mechanism producing work success and satisfaction. The single friendly visit or three sessions of vocational guidance and career counseling must give way to lifelong learning and a continuous progression of developmental relationships and mentoring mosaics. In an uncertain world, workers must construct certainty within the self and then attach themselves to significant others who can assist them to adapt to the series of tasks, transitions, and traumas that they will encounter. Essentially, mentoring involves the secure attachment of a protégé to an individual who eases transitions and prompts adaptation. Thus, for me, mentoring has emerged as the prime form of career assistance for the information age, one rooted in a helping relationship that provides visiting, guiding, and counseling yet much more as the chapter authors duly discuss.

At age 21, counting from Kram's 1985 book, mentoring research has reached its majority. The *Handbook* signals this new status and consolidates it by comprehensively chronicling the accumulated research and reflection on mentoring. By design, the 24 chapters systematically and coherently examine five major themes across the three domains of workplace mentoring, faculty–student mentoring, and youth mentoring. The cross-disciplinary, and almost "team science," approach takes multiple perspectives to provide a penetrating view that has been missing in prior attempts to structure the literature on mentoring and extract meaning from it.

The editors and authors are to be congratulated for publishing a book that organizes and critiques the mentoring literature in a way that identifies key issues and prompts heuristic hypotheses. Their accomplishments anticipate the next generation of mentoring research that will investigate process dimensions, identify causal mechanisms, examine theories with testable hypotheses, and more fully attend to issues of diversity and cultural context. In so doing, the editors and authors may serve as guides, if not vicarious mentors, for the wide audience of researchers in several disciplines who will structure collaborative studies using the framework codified in the *Handbook of Mentoring*.

Mark L. Savickas
Northeastern Ohio Universities College of Medicine

References

Kram, K. E. (1985). *Mentoring at work: Developmental relationships in organizational life.* Glenview, IL: Scott, Foresman and Company.

Levinson, D. K., Darrow, C. N., Klein, E. B., Levinson, M. H., & McKee, B. (1978). *The seasons of a man's life.* New York: Ballantine.

Acknowledgments

As with any edited volume, this has been a multi-year journey. The journey began with the conviction that it was important to bring together the vast body of research that had accumulated concerning mentoring relationships across the lifespan. The process required us to broaden our understanding of all forms of mentoring relationships. Thus, this has been a true developmental experience for us as editors. We have learned a tremendous amount in putting together this volume. The process has strengthened our own collaborative bond and has allowed us to make some wonderful new colleagues.

We would like to thank the many people that made this volume possible. We were fortunate to assemble a group of superb scholars who contributed excellent work and did so in a timely fashion. They deserve our heartfelt appreciation for the time that they took to contribute their unique and varied insights. Special thanks go to Brad Johnson. Brad was the first contributor to whom the idea for this book was proposed and he became a wonderful source of support throughout the project. Early words of encouragement from Jean Rhodes also inspired confidence that a volume of this nature would be a welcome addition to the mentoring literature.

Our respective academic institutions, University of South Florida and University of Georgia, are appreciated for their support of this project. We also thank the students at our respective universities for giving us the opportunity not only to conduct and collaborate with them concerning research on mentoring, but to practice as mentors as well.

We are privileged to have directly experienced the power of mentoring. We are grateful for the excellent guidance through the years that we have received from our own mentors including Kim Buch, Greg Dobbins, Larry James, Tom Ladd, Ron Riggio, Mike Rush, and Garnett Stokes. A special thank you to Joyce Russell for her mentorship and for nurturing our interest in the academic study of mentoring.

Each of these individuals has made a difference in our lives and we sincerely thank them.

We thank Senior Acquisitions Editor, Christine Cardone, for believing in this project and shepherding us through the process. We also thank her editorial assistant, Sarah Coleman, for never failing to respond quickly to our many questions.

Finally, we thank our families for their love, support, and encouragement.

Part I
Introduction

Chapter 1

Overview and Introduction

Tammy D. Allen and Lillian T. Eby

Interest in mentoring as a means to foster individual growth and development continues to flourish among researchers, practitioners, policymakers, educators, and the public at large. An impressive body of research has developed that has yielded insight into many aspects of the mentoring process. The majority of mentoring research has concentrated on three different focal points, mentoring of youth, student–faculty mentoring relationships, and mentoring within the workplace. Research has been conducted primarily within each of these three defined areas with limited consideration of similar research on mentoring found across areas. The isolated nature of mentoring research to date inspired the development of the current volume.

For the first time, the efforts of leading mentoring scholars focusing on different types of mentoring relationships are organized together to provide a comprehensive review of the broad field of mentoring research and practice. This book is designed as a cross-disciplinary volume that incorporates multiple perspectives on mentoring research. By bringing together several perspectives within one volume, researchers from various disciplines and areas of focus can readily become familiar with one another's work. Comparisons across areas of mentoring scholarship and the subsequent integration of knowledge gained from these varied perspectives can help advance the overall state of mentoring theory, research, and practice.

Objectives for the Handbook

There is a growing realization among scientists from all disciplines that multidisciplinary work is critical to answering the major research questions of the day. One objective of this handbook is to break down the disciplinary silos that exist in the field of mentoring. This is important because different areas of scholarship have unique perspectives and there is much to be learned by integrating existing knowledge across youth, student–faculty, and workplace mentoring. A second objective is to provide a single source for scholars interested in state-of-the-art reviews and critical analysis on mentoring. By bundling scholarship together in one comprehensive multidisciplinary volume, we enable researchers and practitioners to obtain a richer and more inclusive perspective on the primary themes in mentoring research and practice today than has been available in the past. Finally, we aim to provide practitioners with empirically based, yet accessible information on the practice of mentoring. With the proliferation of formal mentoring programs and initiatives in community, educational, and organizational settings this volume is an important resource for those charged with developing, implementing, and evaluating mentoring programs.

Overview of Handbook Structure and Chapters

After this introduction, Part I of the handbook continues with a chapter on the evolution and definition of mentoring. This is important in that one common denominator across mentoring areas is the struggle to define the term (e.g., Applebaum, Ritchie, & Shapiro, 1994; Friday, Friday, & Green, 2004; Garvey, 2004; Gibb, 2003; Jacobi, 1991). It could be said that much of the empirical research concerning mentoring has focused primarily on substantive validity versus construct validity (Schwab, 1980). That is, the literature has been more concerned with understanding the relationship between mentoring and other constructs, rather than defining the nature of mentoring itself. More work is needed toward the development of comprehensive theoretical explanations of the mentoring construct. Eby, Rhodes, and Allen provide some initial advancement toward this goal and outline some of the ways that mentoring relationships differ from other types of relationships. Chapter 2 also provides the reader with an overview of the three types of mentoring relationships that are the focus of the handbook, youth mentoring, student–faculty mentoring, and workplace mentoring. We recommend that readers begin with chapter 2 as an overview for the entire volume.

Parts II–VI form the bulk of the book and their format is unlike typical edited volumes. Rather than bring together disconnected chapters from the three areas of mentoring focus, we identified five fundamental themes that were common to all areas of mentoring research. Authors from each of the three perspectives contributed chapters on each of the five themes. To minimize overlap, authors were asked to refer to literature and findings relevant only to their specific form of mentoring. For example, authors of the workplace mentoring chapters were careful not to use research regarding student–faculty mentoring. Our intent is for readers to be able to discern what research is generalizable across areas of study and what findings are unique to certain areas of study. The theme for Part II is mentoring theory and methodological issues, the theme for Part III is naturally occurring mentoring relationships, the theme for Part IV is benefits of mentoring relationships, the theme for Part V is diversity and mentoring, and the theme for Part VI is best practices for formal mentoring programs. At the end of each part is a "reflection" chapter. The reflection chapters provide a brief summary of the similarities and differences across the three areas of mentoring within each theme. For example, the first reflection chapter (chapter 6) integrates the information contained in the chapters on theoretical and methodological issues in youth (chapter 3), student–faculty (chapter 4), and workplace (chapter 5) mentoring.

Theme	Youth	Student–faculty	Workplace	Reflection
	Chapter			
Theoretical and methodological issues	3	4	5	6
Naturally occurring mentoring	7	8	9	10
Benefits of mentoring	11	12	13	14
Diversity and mentoring	15	16	17	18
Formal mentoring practices	19	20	21	22

Figure 1.1   Matrix of themed chapters

The chapters contained in Parts II–VI may be thought of in terms of a 5 × 4 matrix that considers the five themes and the various perspectives (see Figure 1.1). For example, a reader interested in focusing on youth mentoring relationships should turn to chapters, 3, 7, 11, 15, and 19. A reader interested in the benefits of mentoring across all areas would turn to chapters 11, 12, 13, and 14.

The final section of the handbook (Part VII) provides integrative ideas for viewing mentoring and suggestions for future research. In chapter 23, Bearman, Blake-Beard, Hunt, and Crosby discuss cross-cutting future directions for mentoring research. Their chapter raises provocative research ideas for scholars interested in better understanding mentoring relationships and integrating knowledge across the three types of mentoring discussed in this volume. They also challenge commonly held assumptions about mentoring in an effort to promote critical thinking on the topic. The volume concludes with chapter 24. Allen and Eby develop an integrative perspective of mentoring that considers multiple levels of development and multiple levels of analysis as applied to all types of mentoring relationships. They propose that fulfillment of the need to belong plays a central role in explaining why mentoring relationships are a powerful tool for individual growth and development.

The audience for this volume includes a wide range of scholars who are conducting research on all forms of mentoring relationships across a variety of contexts and disciplines. Professionals engaged in the design and delivery of formal mentoring programs will also benefit from this handbook, as will policy makers who have a stake in the successful delivery of mentoring programs. We hope that this handbook will be a useful resource to all interested in mentoring and serve as a guide for charting new directions in mentoring research, theory, and practice.

References

Applebaum, S. H., Ritchie, S., & Shapiro, B. T. (1994). Mentoring revisited: An organizational behaviour construct. *International Journal of Career Management*, 6, 3–10.

Friday, E., Friday, S. S., & Green, A. L. (2004). A reconceptualization of mentoring and sponsoring. *Management Decision*, 42, 628–644.

Garvey, B. (2004). The mentoring/counseling/coaching debate: Call a rose by any other name and perhaps it's a bramble? *Development and Learning in Organizations*, *18*, 6–8.

Gibb, S. (2003). What do we talk about when we talk about mentoring? Blooms and thorns. *British Journal of Guidance & Counselling*, *31*, 39–49.

Jacobi, M. (1991). Mentoring and undergraduate academic success. A literature review. *Review of Educational Research*, *61*, 505–532.

Schwab, D. P. (1980). Construct validity in organizational behavior. In L. L. Cummings & B. M. Staw (Eds.), *Research in organizational behavior* (Vol. 2, pp. 3–43). Greenwich, CT: JAI Press.

Chapter 2

Definition and Evolution of Mentoring

Lillian T. Eby, Jean E. Rhodes, and Tammy D. Allen

The concept of mentoring dates back to Homer's *Odyssey* and is discussed in many other literary works including Mary Shelley's *Frankenstein*, F. Scott Fitzgerald's *The Great Gatsby*, and Shakespeare's *Much Ado about Nothing*. Famous mentor–protégé pairs can be found in almost every profession, including science (e.g., Sigmund Freud mentored Carl Jung, Harry Harlow mentored Abraham Maslow), literature (e.g., Gertrude Stein mentored Ernest Hemingway, Saul Bellow mentored Phillip Roth), politics (e.g., George Wythe mentored Thomas Jefferson), the arts (e.g., Haydn mentored Beethoven), athletics (e.g., Phil Jackson mentored Michael Jordan, Dale Earnhardt Sr. mentored Michael Waltrip), and entertainment (e.g., Duke Ellington mentored Tony Bennett, Tina Turner mentored Mick Jagger). Mentoring has also made its way into popular culture. It is depicted in sitcoms, reality television shows, and featured in print media stories. In short, mentoring is everywhere, everyone thinks they know what mentoring is, and there is an intuitive belief that mentoring works (Rhodes, 2005; Wrightsman, 1981).

The prevalence of mentoring in our daily lives and our vernacular use of the term is a mixed blessing. On the positive side, it has generated considerable interest in the topic of mentoring. Scholars from various disciplines study the phenomenon and mentoring initiatives abound in educational, community, and business settings. Mentoring is discussed as a way to help reduce school dropout rates, increase academic achievement, promote self-identity and positive self-image, reduce risky behaviors, and facilitate career development (DuBois, Holloway, Valentine, & Cooper, 2002; Jacobi, 1991; Kram, 1985; Levinson et al., 1978). However, the application of mentoring to diverse settings and its broad scope of potential influence has created definitional and conceptual confusion about what is mentoring (Garvey & Alred, 2003; Hall, 2003; Jacobi, 1991; Peper, 1994). The purpose of this chapter is to provide a brief overview of pioneering and influential research that has shaped how scholars view mentoring, offer a definition of mentoring and differentiate it from other similar types of interpersonal relationships, and present an overview of three types of mentoring that are the focus of this book: youth mentoring, student–faculty mentoring, and workplace mentoring.

Pioneering and Influential Research on Mentoring

Scholarly interest in the role of mentoring in adult development is often traced to Levinson's (Levinson et al., 1978) seminal study of human development. Levinson and colleagues provided a chronology of the lives of 40 men, focusing on developmental transitions and milestones that they experienced throughout the lifespan. Descriptive accounts of these men's life experiences highlighted the important role that relationships play in human development: specifically, the relationship with a mentor. A mentor is described as a guide, teacher, counselor, and developer of skills who "facilitates the realization of the Dream" (p. 98), the vision that one has about the sort of life one wants as an adult. Levinson goes on to discuss the influential role of a mentor, elevating it to that of a parent when noting that not having a mentor or having poor mentoring is "the equivalent of poor parenting in childhood" (p. 338). Ainsworth (1989) also notes the powerful role of emotional attachments beyond childhood, suggesting that relationships with parent surrogates (e.g., teachers, coaches) play a critical role in healthy human development and psychological adjustment.

The important role that mentoring can play in adult development is supported by several other influential studies in the late 1970s and early 1980s. Vaillant (1977) studied some of the nation's most outstanding men and found that those who were most successful tended to have a mentor in young adulthood. Likewise, Roche's (1979) highly publicized *Harvard Business Review* article reported that two thirds of nearly 4,000 executives listed in the *Who's News* column of the *Wall Street Journal* reported having a mentor. Moreover, executives with mentors reported earning more money at an early age, attaining higher levels of education, following a specific career plan, and feeling more satisfied with their careers. Kanter (1977) also discusses how those who make it to the top of an organization typically have a "rabbi" or "Godfather" to guide them along the way. These descriptive accounts of mentoring led the way for Kram's (1985) pioneering qualitative study of 18 mentor–protégé dyads. This was the first in-depth study of mentoring in the workplace in which Kram delineated several key aspects of mentoring relationships such as the functions of mentoring, phases of a mentoring relationship, and complexities of cross-gender relationships. Kram's study created a flurry of research on mentoring in the fields of education, psychology, and management.

Other streams of research during this same time period supported the important role that relationships with nonfamilial adults can have on individuals, especially college students. Educational research focused on how interactions with faculty outside the classroom influenced academic and affective outcomes among college students. Chickering's (1969) conceptual model of college impact posited that informal student–faculty interaction positively influenced students' intellectual development, academic achievement, career aspirations, and academic self-image. Empirical research supported these links, finding that informal contact with faculty related positively to a wide range of student outcomes (see Jacobi, 1991; Pascarella, 1980, for reviews). Two particularly influential works include a longitudinal study by Astin (1977) and another one by Wilson, Gaff, Dienst, Wood, and Bavry (1975). Both studies concluded that student–faculty interaction has a positive influence on a wide range of personal, career, and educational outcomes.

Similarly, the literature on at-risk youth identified the important role of relationships with adult role models on the emotional, academic, and personal development of youth (for a historical review of the youth mentoring literature see Keller, this volume). Forty years ago, psychiatrist Gerald Caplan (1964) discussed the psychological benefits of intimate, nonprofessional caregivers or "extra familial helping figures such as older people with a reputation for wisdom" (p. 64). He argued that such people are much closer to the individuals in need, both "geographically and sociologically," (p. 64) than professional caregivers. They occupy a position between the latter and the family member and are generally far more likely than the professional to be called on for support. Sociologists reached similar conclusions. In their classic study *Growing Up Poor*, the sociologists Williams and Kornblum (1985) followed 900 low-income urban youth, and identified mentors as an extremely important factor in predicting the youth's healthy outcomes. Similarly, the sociologist Lefkowitz (1987) recognized supportive adults as a vital protective influence on low-income at-risk youth. Developmental psychologists who study the concept of resilience have also provided evidence for the importance of mentors (Masten & Garmezy, 1985). For example, Werner and Smith (1982) conducted a 30-year study of 700 high-risk children and found that those who succeeded showed an ability to locate an adult in addition to their parents for support. Similarly, Rutter (1987) noted that at-risk children with "one good relationship" (p. 237) were less likely than others to develop conduct disorders.

Along with these classic works, several reviews have assimilated existing research and provided directions for the field of mentoring. This includes Merriam's (1983) review of mentoring in adult development, business, and academic settings, Jacobi's (1991) review of mentoring in academic contexts, Pascarella's (1980) review of student–faculty informal contact, DuBois et al.'s (2002) meta-analysis of the effects of youth-based mentoring programs, and Allen and colleagues' meta-analysis of the benefits of mentoring for protégés in the workplace (Allen, Eby, Poteet, Lentz, & Lima, 2004).

Taken together, these descriptive accounts, empirical studies, and reviews of mentoring have shaped the way that we think about mentoring and mentoring relationships. However, this work also raises difficult issues with respect to what mentoring is and the role of mentoring in individuals' growth and development. We now turn our attention to some of these definitional issues and offer a way to think about mentoring that builds on existing research, while also creating some much-needed boundary conditions for this complicated and often elusive construct.

Definitional Issues

What is mentoring?   Jacobi (1991) identified 15 different definitions of mentoring in the educational, psychological, and management literature. Other scholars (e.g., Burke, 1984; Merriam, 1983) make similar observations, noting that these varying definitions create problems in drawing conclusions across research studies. Even *within* a given discipline there is often a lack of consensus on a definition of mentoring (e.g., Jacobi, 1991; Peper, 1994; also compare Johnson, Rose, & Schlosser, this volume, to Sedlacek, Benjamin, Schlosser, & Sheu, this volume). Further, within some fields there is heated debate about what mentoring is and what it is not (Hall, 2003). Some of the conceptual looseness relates to the degree of emotional intimacy associated with a mentoring relationship. While some authors conceptualize mentoring as an intense, emotionally deep relationship (e.g., Kram, 1985; Levinson et al., 1978; Shapiro, Haseltine, & Rowe, 1978), others define it in much less emotionally-rich terms (e.g., Lester & Johnson, 1981; Phillips-Jones, 1982; Schmidt & Wolfe, 1980). Additional areas of disagreement include the age difference between mentor and protégé, duration of the relationship, and the specific functions provided by mentors (compare Kram, 1985; Lester & Johnson, 1981; Levinson et al., 1978; Moore & Amey, 1988; Phillips-Jones, 1982; also see Jacobi, 1991). Notwithstanding these issues, it is possible to identify several attributes of mentoring that provide a common frame of reference for understanding the phenomenon.

First, mentoring reflects a unique relationship between individuals (Austin, 2002; Garvey & Alred, 2003; Jacobi, 1991). No two mentorships are the same; distinct interpersonal exchanges and idiosyncratic interaction patterns define and shape the relationship. As Levinson et al. (1978) chronicle, some mentoring relationships can be life-altering, whereas others may be superficial, short-lived, or even destructive (Eby, McManus, Simon, & Russell, 2000; Grossman & Rhodes, 2002; Levinson et al., 1978; Rhodes, 2002b). Second, mentoring is a learning partnership (Garvey & Alred, 2003; Jacobi, 1991; Peper, 1994; Roberts, 2000). Although the goals of the mentoring relationship may differ across both settings and relationships, nearly all mentorships involve the acquisition of knowledge. In fact, learning can occur in mentorships that are highly effective as well as in relationships that fail to live up to one or both individuals' expectations. Third, mentoring is a process, defined by the types of support provided by the mentor to the protégé (Jacobi, 1991; Kram, 1985). While the specific functions that characterize mentoring vary, they are broadly classified as emotional or psychosocial (e.g., friendship, acceptance, support) and instrumental or career-related (e.g., coaching, information, advocacy, sponsorship) (Jacobi, 1991; Kram, 1985). Fourth, a mentoring relationship is reciprocal, yet asymmetrical. Although the mentor may benefit from the relationship, the primary goal is protégé growth and development (Jacobi, 1991; Kram, 1985; Levinson et al., 1978). Fifth, mentoring relationships are dynamic; the relationship changes over time (Garvey & Alred, 2003; Kram, 1985; Roberts, 2000) and the impact of mentoring increases with the passage of time (Grossman & Rhodes, 2002; Kram, 1985).

Owing to the definitional issues that plague mentoring, it is important to discuss how it is distinct from other types of similar relationships. Table 2.1 compares mentor–protégé relationships to role model–observer, advisor–advisee, teacher–student, supervisor–subordinate and coach–client relationships. Comparisons are made in terms of the context in which the relationship occurs, primary scope of influence, degree of mutuality, relationship initiation (formal–informal), relational closeness, power difference between individuals, and whether or not interaction is required for the relationship. The shaded cells in Table 2.1 illustrate how mentoring relationships are similar to, and distinct from, the other types of relationships considered.

Table 2.1 Comparison of mentoring to similar types of interpersonal relationships

Type of relationship	Relational dimension						
	Context	Primary scope of influence	Degree of mutuality	Relationship initiation	Relational closeness	Interaction required	Power difference
Mentor–protégé	Academic, community, workplace	Academic, social, career, personal	Low–high	Informal or formal	Low–high	Yes	Large–small
Role model–observer	Academic, community, workplace	Academic, social, career, personal	None	Informal or formal	None	No	Large–small
Teacher–student	Academic	Academic, career	Low–moderate	Formal	Low–moderate	Yes	Moderate–small
Advisor–advisee	Academic	Academic, career, personal	Low–moderate	Formal	Low–moderate	Yes	Large
Supervisor–subordinate	Workplace	Career	Low–moderate	Formal	Low–moderate	Yes	Large–moderate
Coach–client	Workplace	Career, personal	Low	Formal	Low–moderate	Yes	Large

Note. Shading indicates where mentor–protégé relationships are similar to other types of relationships.

As illustrated in Table 2.1, mentoring is similar to the other types of relationships depicted, yet distinct in one or more respects. The mentor–protégé relationship appears most similar to the role model–observer relationship. This is consistent with discussions of how one aspect of mentoring is being a role model to protégés (see Johnson, this volume; Keller, this volume; Scandura & Pellegrini, this volume). Mentor–protégé and role model–observer relationships can exist in a wide range of contexts, have a similarly broad potential scope of influence, may be initiated formally or informally, and may be characterized by a small to large power difference between individuals. However, these two types of relationship differ in important ways. This includes the degree of mutuality (mentoring runs the gamut from low to high whereas role modeling involves no mutuality whatsoever), relational closeness (mentoring varies from low to high whereas there is no relational closeness in role modeling), and interaction required (essential for mentoring but not for role modeling).

It is also instructive to compare mentor–protégé relationships to the other types of relationship displayed in Table 2.1. While mentor–protégé, student–teacher, advisor–advisee, supervisor–subordinate, and coach–client relationships all require interaction between relational partners, mentoring is unique. Mentor–protégé relationships can exist in a wide range of contexts, have a broad scope of potential influence, display variability in mutuality and relational closeness, can be formal or informal, and can involve small to large power differences between individuals (see Table 2.1).

What is formal versus informal mentoring?   Another source of confusion in the literature on mentoring is the distinction between formal and informal mentoring. Sedlacek et al. (this volume) argue that within academia, most student–faculty relationships are formalized and tend to start out as advisor–advisee relationships. Johnson (this volume) concurs, but notes that while student–faculty mentoring relationships often start out as formal advising relationships, research on academic mentoring either tends to assume that mentorships develop informally or does not specify the context of relationship formation. In this volume, both Johnson and Mullen define formal academic mentoring as relationships where the protégé is assigned to the mentor. In contrast, Campbell (this volume) does not define formal academic mentoring but his descriptions refer to institutionalized academic mentoring programs.

Informal mentoring is not consistently defined in the chapters on academic mentoring contained in this volume. In contrast, those studying youth mentoring (e.g., Keller, this volume; Miller, this volume; Spencer, this volume) and workplace mentoring (e.g., Dougherty, Turban, & Haggard, this volume; Finkelstein & Poteet, this volume) tend to make a clear distinction between formal and informal mentoring. Relationships where mentor and protégé are matched by a third party (e.g., organizational member, mentoring program staff) and are part of an officially sanctioned mentoring program are typically considered formal mentoring. Relationships that develop naturally or spontaneously without outside assistance are considered informal mentoring.

The distinction between formal and informal mentoring is not trivial. Within the workplace literature, research finds important differences between formal and informal mentoring in terms of the amount of mentoring provided and the impact of mentoring on relevant protégé outcomes (e.g., Chao, Walz, & Gardner, 1992; Ragins & Cotton, 1999). Likewise, Cavell, Meeham, Heffer, and Holliday (2002) discuss how informal mentoring has a greater positive impact on youth compared to formal mentoring. Perhaps more importantly, the general practice of making gross distinctions between formal and informal mentoring solely in terms of relationship initiation masks substantial and potentially important variability *within* formal and informal mentoring. In particular, there is considerable variability in the "formality" associated with formal mentoring (cf. Eddy, Tannenbaum, Alliger, D'Abate, & Givens, 2001). Therefore, we suggest that it is important to consider two different aspects of formality: *relationship initiation* and *relationship structure*, since both may influence relational processes and outcomes.

Relationship initiation.   This refers to whether or not a third party is involved in encouraging, facilitating, or matching mentors and protégés. At one extreme a third party may determine who is matched in a mentoring relationship with no input from mentor or protégé. This other-party matching process can range from random assignment to deliberate pairing based on one or more attributes. This type of matching occurs in workplace settings where mentor and protégé are paired up by program staff on the basis of demographic characteristics, job function, interests, hobbies, etc. (cf. Finkelstein & Poteet, this volume). Likewise, program representatives often create mentor–protégé matches in youth mentoring based on specific criteria (e.g., mentor and protégé gender, mentor and protégé race) (cf. Liang & Grossman, this volume; Miller, this volume). However, youth mentoring programs do not always have the luxury of custom matching since in many cases there are more protégés available than mentors to serve them (Sherman, 1999). At the other extreme are some academic mentoring programs where the program is simply a venue for potential mentors and protégés to come together; the program neither identifies specific participants nor matches individuals (cf. Campbell, this volume). In between these extremes are situations where a third party brings together a pool of potential mentors and protégés, yet allows mentors and protégés to self-select into mentoring relationships or have some input into the match (cf. Finkelstein & Poteet, this volume).

Relationship initiation is important to consider because the extent to which individuals have personal choice and voice in determining their relational partner is likely to influence subsequent relational processes (Allen et al., 2006). For example, perceived similarity and liking are probably greater when mentor and protégé have input into the mentoring match since these perceptions influence partner attraction and relationship initiation in other types of close relationships (cf. Graziano & Musser, 1982). Relationships built on a foundation of perceived similarity and liking may foster the development of important relational processes such as trust, disclosure, and commitment (Levinger, 1979). This may be particularly important in settings where "at risk" individuals are targeted for mentoring, as is the case with youth mentoring, and to some extent student–faculty mentoring.

Relationship structure.   A different aspect of formality is the extent to which there are predetermined guidelines for one or both persons' roles in the mentorship, implicit or explicit relationship goals, parameters on when and how to interact in the mentorship, and a prearranged length for the mentoring relationship. These aspects of relationship structure can be communicated in training prior to the start of the relationship as well as through program materials such as recruitment brochures and program mission statements. Pre-relationship training appears most common in youth mentoring programs (cf. Miller, this volume), sometimes offered in workplace programs (cf. Finkelstein & Poteet, this volume), and uncommon in educational programs (cf. Campbell, this volume). Mentoring programs in all three areas may also have specific program objectives which influence mentor–protégé interactions. For example, youth programs may target behaviors such as juvenile delinquency, drug use, academic performance, etc. (Keller, this volume). Workplace programs may target diversity enhancement, managerial succession, or new employee socialization, among other things (Eddy et al., 2001). Academic programs are often developed to increase minority student retention or involvement in research (cf. Campbell, this volume). Finally, relationship timelines are often explicitly stated in workplace mentoring programs (Finkelstein & Poteet, this volume) and implicit in academic programs since a student's educational journey is time bound.

The formality in relationship structure is important to consider since it places boundaries on *when*, *how*, and *how much* mentors and protégés interact with one another, which in turn affects relational processes and outcomes. For example, Huston and Burgess (1979) discuss how interpersonal closeness is a function of the breadth, intensity, and duration of interactions among individuals. If patterns of behaviors are prescribed in a way that limits contact to a particular context (e.g., school, work) or focuses exchanges on specific goals (e.g., reducing drug use, developing research skills), this may limit relational depth and reduce the likelihood that the mentorship will lead to mutual learning and growth. Goal setting and relationship contracting may also limit the scope of relational behaviors and create specific expectations for the mentoring relationship from the outset. While this may help in clarifying mentor and protégé roles, it can reduce relationship spontaneity and lead to antiseptic exchanges between mentor and protégé. It is also likely that the contracting process will focus primarily on protégé goals, which may influence the mentor's commitment to the mentoring relationship. Likewise, with clearly stated guidelines on relationship length there may not be adequate time for the mentorship to develop into one marked by both instrumental and psychosocial support (Kram, 1985).

Areas of Mentoring Scholarship

Being cognizant of these thorny definitional issues, we now turn our attention to three relatively independent streams of mentoring research that are the focus of the present book: youth mentoring, student–faculty mentoring, and workplace mentoring. Each area is briefly described below.

Overview of youth mentoring.   Youth mentoring represents a sustained relationship between a caring, supportive adult and youth (Jekielek, Moore, Hair, & Scarupa, 2002). The term has generally been used in the human services field to describe a relationship between an older, more experienced adult and an unrelated, younger protégé. In this relationship the adult provides ongoing guidance, instruction, and encouragement aimed at developing the competence and character of the protégé. Over the course of their time together, the mentor and protégé often develop a special bond of mutual commitment, respect, identification, and loyalty which facilitates the youth's transition into adulthood (Rhodes, 2000).

Youth mentoring is based on the premise that supportive adult relationships are important for personal, emotional, cognitive, and psychological growth (Ainsworth, 1989; Rhodes, 2002b). A mentor provides guidance and support in various areas of life, such as academics, career-planning and decision-making, and social interactions. Blinn-Pike (this volume) provides a review of the known benefits of mentoring for youth. Interactions between mentor and youth may revolve around leisure activities, academic assistance, and personal concerns (e.g., peer relationships, parental relationships). Mentors can fulfill the role of teacher, role model, friend and ally, and in some cases they serve as surrogate parents for youth (Hamilton & Darling, 1989; Jekielek et al., 2002). Youth mentors can provide both emotional and instrumental support in an effort to help youth effectively navigate through predictable yet difficult developmental transitions (Grossman & Rhodes, 2002). However, given the emotional and psychological vulnerability of adolescents, youth mentoring can also have negative or detrimental effects on adolescents, particularly if the relationship terminates shortly after formation (Grossman & Rhodes, 2002). In such situations, youth may feel abandoned and the premature ending of the mentorship may exacerbate existing concerns that they are not worthy of loving attachments with adults (Downey & Feldman, 1996; Grossman & Rhodes, 2002).

Youth mentoring relationships can develop spontaneously (see Spencer, this volume) or with the assistance of others (see Miller, this volume). Caring, informal relationships may develop among youth and religious leaders, family friends, teachers, and relatives. Some youth, especially those from disadvantaged social and economic backgrounds, may have limited access to informal mentors or adult role models (Rhodes & Roffman, 2002). This has led to the proliferation of formal youth mentoring programs such as the community-based program, Big Brothers Big Sisters. Currently there are over 4,000 agencies and youth-based mentoring programs serving an estimated two and a half million youth each year (Rhodes, 2002b). In addition, there are many state-based and federal youth mentoring programs, which often target youth from at-risk backgrounds (e.g., single parent families, economically disadvantaged youth). Formal programs include on-site youth interventions (e.g., school, church, work, or agency based) and community-based efforts that are not confined to a specific context (Rhodes, 2002b). Programs also vary widely in their goals and philosophies. Some focus on youth development very broadly, whereas others focus more specifically on education, employment, or reducing specific risky behaviors (e.g., drinking, drug use, gang activity) (Sipe, 2005).

Overview of student–faculty mentoring.   Student–faculty mentoring exemplifies the apprentice model of education (Jacobi, 1991). It is viewed as an essential part of a student's educational experience because student–faculty interaction provides a venue for learning beyond the classroom (Pascarella, 1980). Johnson (this volume) provides a review of the benefits of student–faculty mentoring. In this context a more experienced and knowledgeable mentor provides support and guidance to a less experienced protégé (Jacobi, 1991). The faculty member imparts knowledge, provides support, and offers guidance on academic (e.g., classroom performance, academic skill-building) as well as nonacademic (e.g., personal problems, identity issues) issues (Chickering, 1969; Pascarella, 1980; Pascarella, Terenzini, & Hibel, 1978). These interactions can help students develop a sense of belonging in their institution and chosen profession (Austin, 2002; Nagda, Gregerman, Jonides, von Hippel, & Lerner, 1998). Student–faculty mentoring includes relationships between undergraduates and faculty members as well as those between graduate students and faculty members.

Undergraduate mentoring can include both planned (e.g., scheduled meetings, advising, formal mentoring program participation) and unplanned (e.g., impromptu conversations, unscheduled lunches) interactions between students and faculty. Particularly for undergraduates, college is an important socializing agent and represents an important transition into adulthood (Levinson et al., 1978). Developing a faculty mentoring relationship may help students navigate this transitional period and increase their chance of academic success, although most of the evidence is indirect (Jacobi, 1991; for an exception see Nagda et al., 1998). Interactions with faculty outside the classroom can also sharpen critical-thinking skills and help undergraduates develop self-confidence and positive attitudes about learning (Pascarella, 1980). In fact, several universities have instituted mentoring programs for undergraduates, such as the Undergraduate Research Opportunities Program (UROP) at the University of Michigan (Nagda et al., 1998).

Mentoring in graduate education is viewed as an essential component of graduate student professional development (Clark, Harden, & Johnson, 2000). Faculty mentors are a primary mechanism for indoctrinating students into a professional field and the relationship can have profound effects on students' professional identity and career plans (Austin, 2002). Faculty mentors serve as role models and can provide students with a realistic preview of their chosen profession (Austin, 2002). Graduate school mentoring experiences are highly idiosyncratic since guidelines do not typically exist for mentoring relationships and faculty have substantial latitude in how they interact with their students. Variability in student–faculty mentoring relationships is also due to competing role demands on faculty – teaching, conducting research, service activities – which can detract from a mentor's ability to provide high-quality, organized, developmental experiences for a graduate student (Austin, 2002). This opens the door to potential relational problems between faculty mentors and student protégés, such as mentor neglect, relational conflict, and mentor exploitation (Johnson & Huwe, 2002).

As with youth mentoring, student–faculty mentorships may be informal (Mullen, this volume) or formal (Campbell, this volume). Formal mentoring for undergraduates is increasingly popular in educational contexts and has a wide range of goals, including student retention, academic success, career development, and leadership development (Jacobi, 1991). Often those early in their academic career and/or minority students are targeted for participation (Cosgrove, 1986; Nagda et al., 1998). Formal mentoring programs also exist in graduate education as a means to enhance the graduate education experience (Boyle & Boice, 1998; Clark et al., 2000).

Overview of workplace mentoring. Workplace mentoring involves a relationship between a less experienced individual (the protégé) and a more experienced person (the mentor), where the purpose is the personal and professional growth of the protégé (Kram, 1985). The mentor may be a peer at work, supervisor, someone else within the organization but outside the protégé's chain of command, or even an individual in another organization (Eby, 1997; Kram & Isabella, 1985; Scandura & Schriesheim, 1994). Organizational mentors provide two primary types of support to protégés. Career-related support prepares protégés for career advancement and helps them learn to navigate within the organization. This includes mentor actions such as sponsorship, exposure and visibility, and coaching. Psychosocial support helps protégés develop a sense of competence and identity as a professional and occurs through the provision of acceptance and confirmation, counseling, role modeling, and friendship to protégés (Kram, 1985; Noe, 1988).

Organizational mentoring is often discussed as a critical early career experience with lasting career and personal effects on protégés (Noe, Greenberger, & Wang, 2002; Phillips-Jones, 1982; Stumpf & London, 1981). The outcomes of mentoring for protégés include both objective (e.g., compensation, promotion) and subjective (e.g., career satisfaction, organizational commitment) career success (for a review see Allen et al., 2004; also see Ramaswami & Dreher, this volume), although research also identifies a host of potential problems associated with mentoring (Eby & Allen, 2002; Eby, Butts, Lockwood, & Simon, 2004; Eby et al., 2000). Many workplace mentoring relationships develop spontaneously, typically based on mutual attraction and interpersonal comfort (Dougherty et al., this volume). However, organizations also implement formal mentoring programs in an effort to capitalize on the positive benefits of mentoring (Finkelstein & Poteet, this volume) In such programs protégés are matched with mentors by a third party. Formal programs have various goals such as talent development, improvement of employee knowledge, skills, and abilities, employee retention, and diversity enhancement (Eddy et al., 2001). Formal mentorships tend to have contracted goals, a specific timeline, and offer guidelines on how often and in what context mentor and protégé should meet (Eddy et al., 2001; Ragins, Cotton, & Miller, 2000). Generally speaking, formal workplace mentoring appears to be less effective in promoting personal and career growth than spontaneously developed mentor–protégé relationships (Chao et al., 1992; Fagenson-Eland, Marks, & Amendola, 1997; Ragins & Cotton, 1999).

Concluding Thoughts

Mentoring is a broad and complicated construct that has been applied to many areas of study. Although definitions of mentoring have been scrutinized, debated, and criticized by scholars, it is possible to identify several key features of mentoring relationships and to place some loose boundaries on what is often a fairly fuzzy construct. It also allows us to see similarities and differences between mentor–protégé relationships and other types of similar relationships. This provides a useful vantage point for subsequent chapters and foreshadows more specific discussions of the similarities and differences among youth, student–faculty, and workplace mentoring.

References

Ainsworth, M. D. S. (1989). Attachments beyond infancy. *American Psychologist, 44*, 709–716.

Allen, T. D., Eby, L. T., & Lentz, E. (2006b). Mentoring behaviors and mentorship quality associated with formal mentoring programs: Closing the gap between research and practice. *Journal of Applied Psychology, 91*, 567–578.

Allen, T. D., Eby, L. T., Poteet, M. L., Lentz, E., & Lima, L. (2004). Career benefits associated with mentoring protégés: A meta-analysis. *Journal of Applied Psychology, 89*, 127–136.

Astin, A. W. (1977). *Four critical years: Effects of college on beliefs, attitudes, and knowledge.* San Francisco: Jossey-Bass.

Austin, A. E. (2002). Preparing the next generation of faculty. *Journal of Higher Education, 73*, 94–122.

Boyle, P., & Boice, B. (1998). Systematic mentoring for new faculty teachers and graduate teaching assistants. *Innovative Higher Education, 22*, 157–179.

Burke, R. J. (1984). Mentors in organizations. *Group and Organization Studies, 9*, 353–372.

Caplan, G. (1964). *Principles of preventive psychiatry.* New York: Basic Books.

Cavell, T. A., Meeham, B. T., Heffer, R. W., & Holliday, J. (2002). The natural mentors of adolescent children of alcoholics (COAs): Implications for preventative practices. *Journal of Primary Prevention, 23*, 23–42.

Chao, G. T., Walz, P. M., & Gardner, P. D. (1992). Formal and informal mentorships: A comparison on mentoring functions and contrast with nonmentored counterparts. *Personnel Psychology, 45*, 619–636.

Chickering, A. (1969). *Education and identity.* San Francisco: Jossey-Bass.

Clark, R. A., Harden, S. L., & Johnson, W. B. (2000). Mentor relationships in clinical psychology doctoral training: Results of a national survey. *Teaching of Psychology, 27*(4), 262–268.

Cosgrove, T. J. (1986). The effects of participation in a mentoring-transcript program on freshman. *Journal of College Student Personnel, 27*, 119–124.

Downey, G., & Feldman, S. I. (1996). The implications of rejection sensitivity for intimate relationships. *Journal of Personality and Social Psychology, 70*, 1327–1343.

DuBois, D. L., Holloway, B. E., Valentine, J. C., & Cooper, H. (2002). Effectiveness of mentoring programs for youth: A meta-analytic review. *American Journal of Community Psychology, 30*, 157–197.

Eby, L. T. (1997). Alternative forms of mentoring in changing organizational environments: A conceptual extension of the mentoring literature. *Journal of Vocational Behavior, 51*, 125–144.

Eby, L. T., & Allen, T. D. (2002). Further investigation of protégés negative mentoring experiences: Patterns and outcomes. *Group and Organization Management, 27*, 456–479.

Eby, L. T., Butts, M., Lockwood, A., & Simon, S. A. (2004). Protégés' negative mentoring experiences: Construct development and nomological validation. *Personnel Psychology, 57*, 411–447.

Eby, L. T., McManus, S. E., Simon, S. A., & Russell, J. E. A. (2000). The protégé's perspective regarding negative mentoring experiences: The development of a taxonomy. *Journal of Vocational Behavior, 57*, 1–21.

Eddy, E., Tannenbaum, S., Alliger, G., D'Abate, C., & Givens, S. (2001). *Mentoring in industry: The top 10 issues when building and supporting a mentoring program.* Technical report prepared for the Naval Air Warfare Training Systems Division (Contract No. N61339-99-D-0012).

Fagenson-Eland, E. A., Marks, M. A., & Amendola, K. L. (1997). Perceptions of mentoring relationships. *Journal of Vocational Behavior, 51*, 29–42.

Garvey, B., & Alred, G. (2003). An introduction to the symposium on mentoring: Issues and prospects. *British Journal of Guidance and Counselling, 31*, 1–9.

Graziano, W. G., & Musser, L. M. (1982). The joining and parting of ways. In S. Duck (Ed.), *Personal relationships 4: Dissolving personal relationships* (pp. 75–106). London: Academic Press.

Grossman, J. B., & Rhodes, J. E. (2002). The test of time: Predictors and effects of duration in youth mentoring. *American Journal of Community Psychology, 30*, 199–219.

Hall, J. C. (2003). *Mentoring and young people: A literature review.* Glasgow, Scotland: The SCRE Centre, University of Glasgow.

Hamilton, S. F., & Darling, N. (1989). Mentors in adolescents' lives. In K. Hurrelmann and U. Engle (Eds.), *The social world of adolescents* (pp. 121–139). New York: DeGruyter.

Huston, T. L., & Burgess, R. L. (1979). Social exchange in developing relationships: An overview. In R. L. Burgess & T. L. Huston (Eds.), *Social exchanges in developing relationships* (pp. 3–28). New York: Academic Press.

Jacobi, M. (1991). Mentoring and undergraduate academic success. A literature review. *Review of Educational Research, 61,* 505–532.

Jekielek, S. M., Moore, K. A., Hair, E. C., & Scarupa, H. J. (2002, February). Mentoring: A promising strategy for youth development. Washington, DC: *Child Trends Research Brief.*

Johnson, W. B., & Huwe, J. M. (2002). Toward a typology of mentorship dysfunction in graduate school. *Psychotherapy: Theory/research/practice/training, 39,* 44–55.

Kanter, R. M. (1977). *Men and women of the corporation.* New York: Basic Books.

Kram, K. E. (1985). *Mentoring at work: Developmental relationships at work.* Glenview, IL: Scott, Foresman and Company.

Kram, K. E., & Isabella, L. A. (1985). Mentoring alternatives: The role of peer relationships in career development. *Academy of Management Journal, 28,* 110–132.

Lefkowitz, B. (1987). *Tough change: Growing up on your own in America.* New York: Free Press.

Lester, V., & Johnson, C. (1981). The learning dialogue: Mentoring. In J. Fried (Ed.), *Education for student development. New directions for student services: No. 15* (pp. 49–56). San Francisco: Jossey-Bass.

Levinger, G. (1979). A social exchange view on the dissolution of pair relationships. In R. L. Burgess & T. L. Huston (Eds.). *Social exchange in developing relationships* (pp. 169–196). New York: Academic Press.

Levinson, D. J., Darrow, D., Levinson, M., Klein, E. B., & McKee, B. (1978). *The seasons of a man's life.* New York: Knopf.

Masten, A. S., & Garmezy, N. (1985). Risk, vulnerability, and protective factors in developmental psychopathology. In B. B. Lahey & A. E. Kazdin (Eds.), *Advances in child-clinical psychology* (pp. 1–52). New York: Plenum.

Merriam, S. (1983). Mentors and protégés: A critical review of the literature. *Adult Education Quarterly, 33,* 161–173.

Moore, K. M., & Amey, M. J. (1988). Some faculty leaders are born women. In M. A. D. Sagaria (Ed.), *Empowering women: Leadership development strategies on campus. New directions for student services: No. 44* (pp. 39–50). San Francisco: Jossey-Bass.

Nagda, B. A., Gregerman, S. R., Jonides, J., von Hippel, W., & Lerner, J. S. (1998). Undergraduate student–faculty research partnerships affect student retention. *Review of Higher Education, 22,* 55–72.

Noe, R. (1988). An investigation of the determinants of successful assigned mentoring relationships. *Personnel Psychology, 41,* 457–479.

Noe, R. A., Greenberger, D. B., & Wang, S. (2002). Mentoring: What we know and where we might go from here. In G. R. Ferris & J. J. Martocchio (Eds.), *Research in personnel and human resources management* (Vol. 21, pp. 129–173). Greenwich, CT: Elsevier Science/JAI Press.

Pascarella, E. T. (1980). Student–faculty informal contact and college outcomes. *Review of Educational Research, 50,* 545–595.

Pascarella, E. T., Terenzini, P. T., & Hibel, J. (1978). Student–faculty interactional settings and their relationship to predicted academic performance. *Journal of Higher Education, 49,* 450–463.

Peper, J. B. (1994, April). *Mentoring, mentors, and protégés.* Paper presented at the annual meeting of the American Educational Research Association, New Orleans, Louisiana.

Phillips-Jones, L. (1982). *Mentors and protégés.* New York: Arbor House.

Ragins, B. R., & Cotton, J. L. (1999). Mentor functions and outcomes: A comparison of men and women in formal and informal mentoring relationships. *Journal of Applied Psychology, 84,* 529–550.

Ragins, B. R., Cotton, J. L., & Miller, J. S. (2000). Marginal mentoring: The effects of type of mentor, quality of relationship, and program design on work and career attitudes. *Academy of Management Journal, 43,* 1177–1194.

Rhodes, J. E. (2000). Mentoring programs. In A. E. Kazdin (Ed.), *Encyclopedia of psychology* (pp. 198–200). Washington, DC: American Psychological Association.

Rhodes, J. E. (2002b). *Stand by me: The risks and rewards of mentoring today's youth.* Cambridge, MA: Harvard University Press.

Rhodes, J. E. (2005). A theoretical model of youth mentoring. In D. L. DuBois & M. A. Karcher (Eds.), *Handbook of youth mentoring* (pp. 30–43). Thousand Oaks, CA: Sage.

Rhodes, J. E., & Roffman, J. G. (2002). Nonparental adults as asset builders in the lives of youth. In R. J. Lerner & P. Benson (Eds.), *Developmental assets and asset-building communities. Implications for research, policy, and practice* (pp. 195–209). New York: Kluwer Academic Publishers.

Roberts, A. (2000). Mentoring revisited: A phenomenological reading of the literature. *Mentoring and Tutoring, 8,* 145–170.

Roche, G. R. (1979). Much ado about mentors. *Harvard Business Review, 57,* 14–28.

Rutter, M. (1987). Psychosocial resilience and protective mechanisms. *American Journal of Orthopsychiatry, 57,* 316–331.

Scandura, T. A., & Schriesheim, C. A. (1994). Leader–member exchange and supervisor career mentoring as complementary constructs in leadership research. *Academy of Management Journal, 37,* 1588–1602.

Schmidt, J., & Wolfe, J. (1980). The mentor partnership: Discovery of professionalism. *NASPA Journal, 17,* 45–51.

Shapiro, E. C., Haseltine, F. P., & Rowe, M. P. (1978). Moving up: Role models, mentors, and the "patron system". *Sloan Management Review, 19*(3), 51–58.

Sherman, L. (1999). *Reaching out for diversity: Recruiting mentors requires multiple strategies and long term commitment.* National Mentoring Centre Bulletin 2.

Sipe, C. L. (2005). Toward a typology of mentoring. In D. L. DuBois & M. A. Karcher (Eds.), *Handbook of youth mentoring* (pp. 65–80). Thousand Oaks, CA: Sage.

Stumpf, S. A., & London, M. (1981). Management promotions: Individual and organizational factors affecting the decision process. *Academy of Management Review, 6,* 539–550.

Vaillant, G. (1977). *Adaptation to life.* Boston: Little, Brown, & Company.

Werner, E. E., & Smith, E. S. (1982). *Vulnerable but invincible: A study of resilient children.* New York: McGraw-Hill.

Williams, T., & Kornblum, W. (1985). *Growing up poor.* Lexington, MA: Lexington Books.

Wilson, R. C., Gaff, J. G., Dienst, E. R., Wood, L., & Bavry, J. L. (1975). *College professors and their impact on students.* New York: Wiley.

Wrightsman, L. S. (1981, August). *Research methodologies for assessing mentoring.* Paper presented at the annual meeting of the American Psychological Association, Los Angeles, CA (ERIC Document Reproduction Service No. ED 209 339).

Part II

Theoretical Approaches and Methodological Issues

Chapter 3

Youth Mentoring: Theoretical and Methodological Issues

Thomas E. Keller

Youth mentoring is characterized by a personal relationship in which a caring individual provides consistent companionship, support, and guidance aimed at developing the competence and character of a child or adolescent (MENTOR, 2003). The practice of mentoring youth has a long history, and in contemporary society it is experiencing widespread popularity and rapid growth. On one hand, mentoring corresponds with the intuitive understanding that youth learn about themselves and their world in the context of relationships with the significant adults in their lives. On the other hand, mentoring is an approach that resonates with mainstream cultural values because it is viewed as simple, direct, individualized, inexpensive, and effective (Freedman, 1993).

The potential benefits of a close, enduring relationship with a mentor are suggested by research indicating that children and adolescents who feel a sense of connection with a supportive adult engage in fewer health-risk behaviors (DuBois & Silverthorn, 2005b). Similarly, studies consistently find that youth who show healthy adjustment despite environmental adversity are distinguished by the reliable presence and support of at least one caring adult (Masten, Best, & Garmezy, 1990). Support for youth mentoring as an intervention has been provided by rigorous evaluations demonstrating improvements in youth competencies and reductions in problem behaviors (Tierney, Grossman, & Resch, 1995) and by meta-analytic results substantiating the general effectiveness of mentoring across a range of programs and studies (DuBois, Holloway, Valentine, & Cooper, 2002). However, research also points to the potentially harmful consequences of short-lived mentoring relationships characterized by conflict and disappointment (Grossman & Rhodes, 2002; Rhodes, 2002b).

Despite longstanding interest in mentoring as a means to influence children's lives, a solid theoretical and empirical literature addressing important issues involved in youth mentoring has only begun to emerge. This chapter reviews several important conceptual frameworks and theoretical perspectives that have been proposed to better understand youth mentoring. A broad view of the field is taken to illustrate many areas worthy of investigation. To provide background and context, the chapter begins with a brief description of features that define and distinguish youth mentoring. Next, the discussion of significant theoretical perspectives is framed by four fundamental questions: What purpose is youth mentoring meant to serve? Why do individuals become mentors? How do mentoring relationships develop? How do mentoring relationships influence youth development? Because these four themes are integrally related and reciprocally informative, important interconnections are highlighted. Each thematic section also includes consideration of directions for future research and discussion of relevant methodological issues.

Context of Youth Mentoring

A mentoring relationship may evolve naturally between a youth and an older, more experienced member of his or her existing social network. Alternatively, a mentor may be introduced into the youth's life through a formal intervention program. The inclusive definition of youth mentoring encompasses a wide array of relationships that may be differentiated by context (e.g., school, workplace, community), special population (e.g., gifted, disabled, at-risk youth), and developmental period (e.g., children, adolescents) (DuBois & Karcher, 2005). This diversity is further multiplied because mentors may adopt a variety of potential mentoring roles (e.g., tutor, coach, counselor), emphasize particular aspects of child development and functioning (e.g., academics, physical health, emotional well-being), and maintain differing levels of contact and length of involvement in their relationships (Sipe, 2005). Given the heterogeneity represented in youth mentoring, the conceptual issues discussed below must rely on generalizations that may or may not apply in specific situations. The traditional model of the Big Brothers Big Sisters program, in which a volunteer establishes a one-to-one relationship with activities occurring in community settings, is prominent in much of the existing theoretical and empirical work on youth mentoring (Rhodes, 2002b; Sipe, 2002). Although this work may translate across mentoring programs, important distinctions may exist between formal and informal mentoring.

Beyond the diversity in youth mentoring, a developmental perspective suggests important features that add layers of complexity to the relationships. For example, significant differentials are likely in the basic capacities of the mentor and protégé based on the youth's level of physical, cognitive, social, and emotional development. The mentor must adapt as the youth exhibits advances in complex reasoning, social skills, level of responsibility, and competencies in multiple domains (Keller, 2005a). Another consideration is that the protégé's participation in the relationship may be instigated and facilitated by another significant adult in the child's life, such as a parent or teacher. Consequently, the mentor is likely to interact with other adults who have roles in supporting and monitoring the mentoring relationship (Keller, 2005b). Each individual involved in the mentoring intervention (mentor, youth, parent, agency worker) may hold different opinions about the aims of the mentoring relationship and the best way to promote those objectives.

What Purpose is Youth Mentoring Meant to Serve?

The word mentor derives from a character in Homer's *Odyssey*. Before his voyage, Odysseus charged Mentor, his wise and faithful friend, to look after and educate Telemachus, Odysseus' only son. In this case, mentoring entailed substantial responsibility for raising a youth at the request of an absent parent. Without relinquishing their own roles, parents in many cultures routinely share much of the care, education, and socialization of their children with extended family and other members of the community (Garcia Coll, Meyer, & Brillon, 1995; Whiting & Whiting, 1975). Similar forms of informal but influential care have been common through different historical periods and within numerous cultural communities in the US (Haraven, 1989). Youth today are most likely to refer to a relative or kin when asked which nonparental adult has an important influence, makes a significant difference, or otherwise acts as a mentor (Beam, Chen, & Greenberger, 2002; DuBois & Silverthorn, 2005a; Zimmerman, Bingenheimer, & Notaro, 2002). However, substantial numbers indicate someone acting in a professional capacity (e.g., teacher, counselor, minister, social worker) or with whom they have other forms of contact (e.g., coach, employer, neighbor) (DuBois & Silverthorn, 2005a). These relationships are commonly characterized as natural mentoring.

The origins of formal youth mentoring programs in the US were situated within major social movements of the late 19th and early 20th centuries (Baker & Maguire, 2005; Freedman, 1993). Owing to displacements associated with industrialization, immigration, and urbanization, many children and families lived in impoverished, overcrowded, and stressful circumstances. Freedman (1993) suggests that youth mentoring had its roots in the Friendly Visiting movement that saw middle-class volunteers personally reach out to poor families to provide neighborly support, moral uplift, and role modeling. Baker and Maguire (2005) link the beginnings of youth mentoring more directly to the efforts of social reformers, such as Jane Addams, who viewed rising juvenile delinquency as the consequence of deleterious urban environments. Addams and her colleagues provided the impetus for establishing the nation's first juvenile court, attended the court to serve as guardians and advocates for the youth, and raised funds for other socially minded individuals to serve as probation officers. Seeking to provide caring guidance and support to their young charges, these probation officers have been considered among the first mentors to disadvantaged youth (Baker & Maguire, 2005). Just a few years later a judge of the juvenile court in New York City sought 90 influential men to befriend youth brought before the court. This cause was taken up by the court clerk, Ernest Coulter, who is credited with establishing the Big Brothers movement in 1904 with his passionate appeal to business and civic leaders to act as big brothers for youth otherwise destined for the reformatory (Beiswinger, 1985).

As this history illustrates, the initiation of formal youth mentoring drew on the charitable impulses of volunteers and focused on disadvantaged youth whose behavior had brought them to the attention of the authorities. This reliance on volunteer mentors and emphasis on children in need remains at the core of most structured programs. Although some programs still focus on youth in the juvenile justice system, both the rationale and the practice of youth mentoring have evolved with the emergence of new paradigms for intervention with youth. The growth of applied social sciences, government funding for social issues, and professionalization in social services resulted in interventions targeting specific youth problems and populations (e.g., substance abuse, teenage pregnancy). Prevention-oriented approaches that came into prominence tended to be categorical in nature, attempting to identify and reduce risk factors associated with specific problem behaviors (Catalano, Hawkins, Berglund, Pollard, & Arthur, 2002). A corresponding prevention strategy is to reinforce protective factors that buffer the impact of psychosocial risks and promote coping and resilience in the face of adversity. Following this strategy, many youth mentoring programs have been designed to serve youth at risk for difficulties, such as school failure or teenage pregnancy, and evaluations of mentoring programs frequently focus on the prevention or reduction of negative outcomes.

An alternative perspective is provided by proponents of the expanding positive youth development field. Following the premise that "problem-free is not fully prepared," positive youth development programs focus on promoting personal competencies, enhancing psychological well-being, and preparing youth to be healthy and productive members of society (Roth & Brooks-Gunn, 2003). Youth mentoring that espouses this orientation promotes the development of life skills and fosters the talents and abilities of youth, including their artistic, athletic, and vocational pursuits.

Still other youth mentoring initiatives have been prompted by the desire to address community-level concerns. Social trends such as single parenthood, residential mobility, and patterns of labor force participation have resulted in disrupted relationships and limited contact for children and the adults in their lives (Haraven, 1989). Many youth spend their time in age-graded settings or home alone. Forging connections between adults and youth through mentoring programs has been advocated as a way to rebuild a sense of caring, civic engagement, and intergenerational commitment within communities (Freedman, 1993; Rauner, 2000). For example, some programs encourage mentors from businesses and organizations to expose youth to adult roles and sponsor involvement with adults in the workplace and various community settings.

Youth mentoring also can represent a mechanism for implementing social policy. In Britain, for example, large-scale mentoring programs have been designed to reengage socially excluded youth with the formal labor market by influencing their attitudes, values, and beliefs about work and employment (Colley, 2003). Colley (2003) voices concern that such programs with narrowly focused goals may place more emphasis on molding youth to the needs of the economy than on encouraging the development of their individual personhood.

Summary

This brief review suggests that the practice of mentoring youth has been enlisted to serve a variety of purposes. The diversity seen in youth mentoring is a function of the many possible interstices between individualized helping relationships, larger social conditions, and philosophies of intervention. A question raised in connection with formal youth mentoring, like many other social interventions, is the extent to which it reflects a form of social control, a way to support vulnerable youngsters, a means to provide personal opportunity and empowerment, or an approach to repairing a social fabric threatened by the gulf between rich and poor (Freedman, 1993). On a practical level, however, at least three possible aims for natural or program mentors are apparent: 1) preventing the emergence or continuation of psychosocial difficulties or problem behaviors; 2) promoting positive adjustment through the development of individual competencies; and 3) fostering integration with the community through opportunities for involvement. The function that mentoring is meant to serve may strongly influence what motivates mentors, how mentoring relationships develop, and what they accomplish.

Research Directions and Methodological Issues

Possibilities abound for investigating how organizational philosophy (for formal mentoring) and community-level factors (for formal and natural mentoring) affect the nature of youth mentoring. The necessity of program infrastructure (e.g., procedures for screening, matching, monitoring) is commonly emphasized (Freedman, 1993; Rhodes, 2002b), and research indicates that programs providing greater structure and support to participants are more effective (DuBois et al., 2002). Yet, a fundamental question is how the mission of an agency may be transmitted through its program policies, staffing, and volunteer recruitment and training practices. These structural factors may communicate implicit messages to program participants that permeate the mentoring relationships that are established. For instance, programs with a positive youth development orientation may promote leadership by giving youth a voice in setting policy. On the other hand, programs targeting risk factors could be stigmatizing by signaling to youth that they have deficits in their families and social networks. Other issues arise at the community level. Some communities may be rich with mentors, whereas the communities with greatest need are almost by definition those lacking the presence or active involvement of adult role models. How do programs indigenous to a community differ from those attempting to span geographic and social boundaries? How do community factors such as size, population demographics, residential stability, and economic vitality affect base rates of formal and informal mentoring?

Several methodological approaches could be employed to investigate issues such as these. For example, in-depth comparative case studies of several agencies could trace links between agency philosophy and program practice by incorporating data as diverse as agency literature, job shadowing, and interviews with people at all levels of the agency (Lock, 2002; McLaughlin, Irby, & Langman, 1994). Increasingly sophisticated techniques for community-mapping and spatial analysis could be used to investigate correspondences between neighborhood characteristics and the prevalence of natural mentoring or the predominant orientation of formal mentoring programs located within them. For formal programs, aggregation of uniform youth outcome measures across numerous programs would permit multi-level modeling that partitions sources of variance in nested designs with individuals within programs within communities. Alternatively, meta-analyses of mentoring effectiveness could examine program philosophy and other organizational and community factors that moderate developmental outcomes achieved through mentoring.

Why do Individuals Become Mentors?

Youth mentoring exists because some individuals voluntarily commit themselves to improving the well-being of youth outside their immediate families. Although the history and logic of mentoring provide some insights into reasons for assuming this role, conceptual frameworks developed to explain volunteerism are being introduced to understand what inspires and sustains mentors, particularly program mentors with no previous connection to a particular youth (Karcher & Lindwall, 2003; Stukas & Tanti, 2005). Because many programs contend with a chronic imbalance between the need for mentors and their actual availability (Freedman, 1993; Rhodes, 2002b), understanding the motivations of volunteers is a critical issue in the field of youth mentoring. Models of volunteerism typically point to the individual attributes of volunteers, their personal values and motives, the salient features of the situation or setting, and the interaction of these individual, motivational, and contextual factors (Penner, 2002; Wilson, 2000).

Individual Attributes

Individual factors in models of volunteering generally represent either the capacity or inclination to become involved. For example, variables indicating possession of human capital, particularly level of education, tend to predict volunteering (Wilson, 2000). Individuals with higher education may have greater awareness of social issues, more skills to offer, and more resources to support their involvement. On the other hand, greater human capital presumably would correlate with higher opportunity costs, a possible deterrent to participation. Being embedded in an extensive social network also corresponds to greater volunteerism, perhaps because the probability of a direct invitation increases or because trusting, extroverted individuals are more likely to join a cause (Wilson, 2000). In fact, Penner (2002) proposes that personal disposition does contribute to volunteering, and cites work on prosocial personality, identifying two personality traits, other-oriented empathy and helpfulness, associated with voluntary behavior. Consistent with these expectations, research suggests that both being a mentor and having a longer mentoring relationship are associated with college education and family income (Grossman & Rhodes, 2002; McLearn, Colasanto, Schoen, & Shapiro, 1999). Also, high-school mentors tend to be more socially connected than their counterparts who do not volunteer, and the mentors who persist in their relationships score higher on traits indicating empathy and cooperation (Karcher & Lindwall, 2003).

Motives

Defining motives as goal-directed forces to obtain a valued outcome, Batson and colleagues (Batson, Ahmad, & Tsang, 2002) conceptualize four broad types of motives to explain community involvement: *egoism*, the goal of increasing one's own welfare; *altruism*, the goal of increasing the welfare of one or more specific individuals; *collectivism*, the goal of increasing the welfare of a group; and *principlism*, the goal of upholding a moral principle, such as justice. Importantly, each type of motive may be transitory, and the different types of motives may be in conflict or coopera-tion. A convergence of self-oriented and other-oriented motivations during adult-hood is apparent in Erikson's concept of *generativity*, which has been invoked by authors pointing to fundamental motivations for mentoring (Freedman, 1993; Rhodes, 2002b; Taylor, LoSciuto, & Porcellini, 2005). Generativity is manifested in actions demonstrating a commitment to improving society and providing for the survival and well-being of future generations (McAdams, Hart, & Maruna, 1998). According to theory, generativity is impelled by inner desires to feel needed and cap-able of providing valuable assistance to others, combined with the desire to leave a lasting legacy. In addition, generativity is motivated by the cultural demands of adulthood, with expectations of responsibility for transmitting social customs and knowledge through roles such as parent, teacher, and mentor.

A functional approach to discerning volunteer motivations provides additional and more detailed insights. A basic premise of this approach is that a particular behavior, like volunteering, may serve various psychological or adaptive functions for particular individuals during certain periods in their lives (Clary et al., 1998). Accordingly, researchers (Clary et al., 1998; Omoto & Snyder, 1995) have devel-oped scales assessing several theoretically relevant motivations for volunteering: a) values (acting on humanitarian values); b) career (exploring career options, gaining experience; c) understanding (learning about self and others); d) enhancement (increasing own self-esteem, feeling needed/important); e) protective (distracting from own problems by helping others); f) social (meeting expectations of others); and g) community (demonstrating investment in a community).

Reflecting this functional approach, a qualitative study by Philip and Hendry (2000) identified four general explanations for why adults had become natural mentors to youth: 1) enabling mentors to make sense of their own past experiences; 2) gaining insight into another person's life; 3) establishing a different type of relation-ship (cross-generational); and 4) building skills in providing a helping relationship. Presumably, the motivations of individual volunteers also could correspond to the functions mentoring may serve, such as helping youth to stay out of trouble, promoting positive development, and strengthening community connections with youth.

Situation or Setting

Features of the volunteer opportunity, such as the cause, nature of the task, and reputation of the organization, may influence the decision to engage in a particular form of voluntary action (Penner, 2002). According to the "matching hypothesis" of the functionalist approach, these features are important to the extent that they correspond to, and provide the ability to fulfill, the particular functions that motivate the volunteer (Clary et al., 1998). The same principle applies after volunteering has been initiated. Actual experiences that meet volunteer goals and that promote pos-itive feelings about involvement with the organization result in higher satisfaction and greater retention (Clary et al., 1998; Omoto & Snyder, 1995; Penner, 2002). Experiences that foster development of role-identity as a volunteer and affiliate of a particular organization also encourage continued commitment (Grube & Piliavin, 2000).

Summary

Reference to conceptual frameworks of volunteerism and corresponding research can advance understanding of why individuals become mentors and also generate several practical recommendations for encouraging, recruiting, and sustaining mentors (Stukas & Tanti, 2005). Drawing on established social psychological theories, such as Fishbein and Ajzen's (1975) theory of reasoned action, may yield additional value by providing coherent, process-oriented models of decision-making that account for the relative strength of multiple motives and determinations of their likely fulfillment within a particular setting. According to the theory of reasoned action, intention to volunteer would depend on the individual's attitude toward volunteering and on perceived social norms about volunteering. Attitudes would be based on beliefs about the consequences of volunteering: enumerating possible costs and benefits, and how likely each is to occur. Evaluation of individual variables bearing on success, such as personality, experience, and resources, could enter into this calculation. Similarly, perceived social norms would be based on beliefs about the social consequences of volunteering: whether particular people approve or disapprove of volunteering, and the relative importance of their opinions. Again, individual factors relating to social standing could influence these assessments. Actually becoming a volunteer would affect subsequent behavior (i.e., continuing to volunteer) by providing information that circles through the model again as beliefs about likely outcomes and beliefs about the opinions of others are modified with experience.

Formal and informal mentors are likely to become involved in mentoring under very different circumstances. Formal mentors choose to volunteer and deliberately enter into a relationship with an unfamiliar youth. Natural mentors, such as teachers and relatives, may simply perform their jobs or fulfill family obligations without even realizing that a youth considers them particularly influential. When a natural mentor does purposely invest extra time or effort with a youth, the decision is informed by prior knowledge and experience with the youth, and the reasons may differ from those discussed for volunteers. Among relatives, for example, evolutionary theory would predict greater investment in youth with closer genetic relationships. Teachers or coaches may work with a promising youth with the expectation of noteworthy successes that fulfill their own professional ambitions.

Research Directions and Methodological Issues

Several avenues of research may yield clues regarding the processes leading to the decision to become a mentor. Given the potential importance of social norms and expectations, it may be informative to survey the general public or specific populations regarding knowledge of and attitudes about both formal and informal mentoring. Quasi-experimental designs, such as interrupted time-series, could provide evidence about how initiating public service announcements, opening community-based programs, or changing recruitment strategies affects the number or type of individuals who become mentors. At the individual level, researchers could address the calculus of the decision-making process by investigating both the variety of functional motivations and the relative weight given to each. Studies inquiring about the decision process likely will be retrospective, after a volunteer has contacted the program, so the necessary reliance on self-report data may bias responses toward socially acceptable explanations. However, creative experimental designs could be used to isolate recruitment messages and program factors that increase the probability of initiating or sustaining mentor participation.

Questions related to volunteer retention could be studied with prospective designs that determine whether and how the motivations of mentors change as a result of their involvement. These studies might examine the goodness-of-fit between volunteer expectations and the program reality or investigate whether mentors identify reasons for volunteering they had not originally considered. Following the rationale of service-learning programs, for example, the volunteer may become increasingly engaged because the experience of mentoring reveals the extent of social needs in the community and gives the mentor a sense of making a difference (Youniss, McLellan, & Yates, 1997).

How do Mentoring Relationships Develop?

A mentoring relationship, like any interpersonal relationship, is complex because each person is simultaneously thinking, feeling, behaving, and pursuing goals. The relationship emerges from a series of interdependent, reciprocal interactions over time in which each individual influences the other through exchanging information, expressing emotions, regulating behavior, and negotiating goals (Reis, Collins, & Berscheid, 2000). These experiences with the other person are interpreted and organized into mental representations of the particular thoughts, emotions, actions, and accomplishments that characterize the relationship (Hartup & Laursen, 1999). The expectations, emotional resources, patterns of behavior, and motivations that each person brings to the new relationship represent the starting conditions in this process. Consequently, examination of how mentoring relationships develop should include consideration of these initial, person-oriented factors as well as process-oriented factors reflecting the nature of interactions between the individuals over time (Keller, 2005a).

Despite its importance, the topic of relationship development in youth mentoring has received relatively little attention. The existing literature tends to emphasize how the development of relationships is shaped by the initial beliefs and motivations of mentors, especially their ideas about the role of a mentor. One perspective, associated with the inductive research of Morrow and Styles (1995; Styles & Morrow, 1992) and incorporating principles from counseling and psychotherapy, places priority on creating a trusting, emotionally close relationship. Another perspective, associated with inductive research by Hamilton and Hamilton (1990, 1992) and drawing on concepts about learning and education, stresses engagement in instrumental activities that build the competence of the youth. The mentor's initial sense of self-efficacy with respect to the mentoring role also seems to influence relationship development (Parra, DuBois, Neville, Pugh-Lilly, & Povinelli, 2002). On the other side of the equation, recognition of the youth's part in forming the relationship has prompted consideration of the youth's experiences in previous relationships (Grossman & Rhodes, 2002; Rhodes, Haight, & Briggs, 1999).

Relational Perspective

A relational perspective suggests that the first task of the mentor is to foster a trusting, emotionally close connection that makes the youth feel understood, valued, and respected (Rhodes, 2002b). Having established a strong and caring relationship, the mentor can offer meaningful support and constructive challenge that will be well received by the youth. A primary emphasis on relationship-building is congruent with many prevailing concepts regarding effective counseling and psychotherapy (Spencer & Rhodes, 2005). Research on the therapeutic alliance suggests a phase during which the relationship is developed, followed by a phase when the therapist begins more active intervention to challenge the client toward change (Horvath & Luborsky, 1993). The conceptual model of the therapeutic alliance focuses on three elements of the relationship: goals, tasks, and affective bond (Bordin, 1979). Emphasizing the importance of flexible negotiation and collaboration, a well-functioning alliance entails agreement about the goals of the relationship, and both parties must perceive the relevance and purpose of the tasks and behaviors that make up the relationship. The therapeutic bond encompasses aspects of the relationship such as trust, acceptance, and interpersonal regard. A strong therapeutic alliance develops when the helper is perceived as caring, attentive, interested, understanding, respectful, and experienced, and these impressions are formed very early in the relationship (Henry & Strupp, 1994; Horvath & Luborsky, 1993). Research on common factors contributing to therapeutic success across diverse treatment strategies signals the importance of a client-centered approach, highlighting the therapist's empathy, positive attitude, warmth, and authenticity (Spencer & Rhodes, 2005). Youth likewise value mutuality and empathy in their relationship with helping adults, emphasizing that both individuals must actively participate in constructing the relationship by being open, respectful, understanding, and responsive in their interactions (Spencer, Jordan, & Sazama, 2004).

Qualitative studies by Morrow and Styles (1995; Styles & Morrow, 1992) have provided support for the relational perspective by identifying and tracing the course of different types of mentoring relationships. These researchers found that the goals and expectations of mentors distinguished between relationships characterized as "developmental" and "prescriptive." Mentors in developmental relationships believed their purpose was to meet the needs of the youth. These mentors were flexible and supportive, allowing the youth time to gain trust in the relationship as a reliable source of support. Demonstrating a "youth-driven" approach, mentors in developmental relationships identified the needs and interests of the youth and included the youth in selecting mutually enjoyable activities. Mentors in developmental matches also provided consistent reassurance and kindness, responded to requests for help in a non-judgmental manner, offered problem-solving suggestions, and avoided criticizing and lecturing. As developmental relationships solidified, the youth began to voluntarily disclose their difficulties at home or school, allowing the mentor to provide advice and guidance. Likewise, as their relationships strengthened, the mentors started to address objectives beyond relationship-building, such as encouraging the youth to become more responsible.

In contrast, Morrow and Styles (1995) described very different trajectories for prescriptive relationships. Some mentors viewed their role as being an authority figure, with responsibility for regulating the youth's behavior. These mentors initiated their matches with goals for transforming the youth and attempted to address the youth's difficulties early in the relationship. From the outset, these mentors tended to set the goals, determine the pace, select the activities, and establish the ground rules for the relationship with little regard for the youth's preferences. A common approach of prescriptive volunteers was to point out the youth's mistakes, state expectations for change, and express displeasure if they were not met. Consequently, the youth resisted the mentor's efforts to focus on problems areas by avoiding contact with the mentor and withdrawing from the relationship. Because frustrations increased quickly on both sides, these matches were typically short-lived (Morrow & Styles, 1995; Styles & Morrow, 1992). In other prescriptive relationships, the mentor expected that the youth would take an equal responsibility for maintaining the relationship by initiating contacts and planning activities. When the youth did not initiate contact or show sufficient appreciation, the mentor often became disappointed and gave up on the relationship. Thus, prescriptive relationships suffered because the mentors established and maintained unrealistic expectations.

Instrumental Perspective

An instrumental perspective suggests that the driving force in relationship development is the mentor's ability to engage the youth in challenging, goal-directed activities (Darling, Hamilton, & Niego, 1994). The youth comes to appreciate the mentoring relationship as a means to mastering skills, exploring opportunities, and attaining instrumental goals that the youth values. According to this perspective, a mentor is differentiated from a coach or teacher, who promotes the acquisition of skills in a particular domain, when the mentor also addresses personal development, social competence, and character development (Hamilton & Hamilton, 2004). This perspective is embodied in an oft-cited definition of mentoring by Bronfenbrenner that highlights the intentionality of the mentor, the focus on activities and skill development, and the resulting personal bond (Darling, Hamilton, & Shaver, 2003):

> A mentor is an older, more experienced person who seeks to further the development of character and competence in a younger person by guiding the latter in acquiring mastery of progressively more complex skills and tasks in which the mentor is already proficient. The guidance is accomplished through demonstration, instruction, challenge, and encouragement on a more or less regular basis over an extended period of time. In the course of this process, the mentor and young person develop a special bond of mutual commitment. In addition, the young person's relationship to the mentor takes on an emotional character of respect, loyalty, and identification. (Bronfenbrenner, personal communication, cited in Hamilton & Hamilton, 1990, p. 358)

The instrumental perspective has been informed by research indicating that adolescents describe their relationships with nonparental adults primarily with reference to the functional benefits they provide, in contrast to the primarily affective terms used to characterize their relationships with family and friends (Darling et al., 1994; Darling et al., 2003). Also influential were findings from a qualitative study of a university-initiated mentoring program by Hamilton and Hamilton (1990, 1992). Mentors were classified into four levels based on comments about their aims for their matches: Level-1 mentors focused primarily on developing a relationship; Level-2 mentors spoke of introducing opportunities; Level-3 mentors stressed developing character; and Level-4 mentors saw their task as developing the youth's competence. Importantly, the four levels were hierarchical – mentors at higher levels talked about the importance of lower-level purposes, but lower-level mentors did not mention higher-level purposes.

According to Hamilton and Hamilton (1992), mentors whose primary focus was building a relationship were susceptible to relationship worries and disappointments (e.g., Were they liked? Were they choosing the right activities? Were they appreciated?). In general, Level-1 mentors were the least likely to persist in their matches. In contrast, the more purposeful focus of the higher-level mentors seemed to sustain them through the early phases of their relationships. Consequently, they spent more time with their protégés and had more positive and productive relationships. As an example, the researchers described the perseverance and creativity of a Level-4 mentor. Because his protégé did not offer suggestions for outings, the mentor generated ideas for various activities that would teach new skills, provide new experiences and challenges, and inspire new pursuits for the youth. He carefully monitored the youth's reaction during this process of experimentation, attempting to identify activities that sparked the youth's interest.

Mentor Self-efficacy

A perspective that complements the preceding attention to the goals and strategies of the mentor suggests that the self-efficacy of the mentor also contributes to the development of the relationship (Parra et al., 2002). According to social cognitive theory (Bandura, 1982, 1989), perceptions of personal self-efficacy strongly influence behavior. Self-efficacy reflects a belief that one has the ability to exercise control over events and to successfully meet challenges. In general, a healthy sense of self-efficacy promotes greater effort and perseverance, higher standards for performance, and higher expectations for positive outcomes. Accordingly, individuals whose past experiences have resulted in positive perceptions of their capacity for mentoring youth would be more likely to strive for success and to persevere despite inevitable challenges in actually establishing a relationship. In a path model using prospective data from Big Brothers Big Sisters (BBBS) matches, Parra and colleagues found that mentor-perceived self-efficacy at the beginning of the match was associated with greater mentor–youth contact, greater involvement in program-relevant activities, and fewer mentor-reported obstacles to relationship development. These factors were associated in turn with higher ratings of relationship closeness and relationships of longer duration.

Youth Psychosocial History

A perspective acknowledging the youth's contribution to building the mentoring relationship suggests that experiences in previous relationships may influence how the youth approaches interactions with the mentor (Rhodes, 2002b). Mentoring programs often serve youth who have experienced difficult or disrupted relationships with parents, and natural mentors may take youth under their wing for similar reasons. These youth may be particularly vulnerable to, or feel responsible for, any problems in the mentoring relationship (Rhodes, 2002b). In particular, they may harbor fears about whether others will accept and support them, and they may have heightened sensitivity to rejection by a mentor (Downey, Lebolt, Rincon, & Freitas, 1998). Consequently, these youth may interpret even minor or ambiguous difficulties in the relationship as indicators of intentional rejection by the mentor. Research has not examined whether rejection sensitivity could lead youth to be overly tentative and guarded with a mentor or make youth withdraw from a mentoring relationship over misinterpreted slights. However, research does indicate that early termination of BBBS matches is associated with identified youth difficulties at the outset of the relationship, particularly being overly dependent upon adults and having psychological problems (Grossman & Rhodes, 2002). On the other hand, youth in foster care, who very likely have experienced rejection and separation from parents, generally derive greater benefits than other youth when mentoring relationships do last (Rhodes et al., 1999).

Summary

The relational perspective proposes that youth-centered relationship-building is an important precursor to promoting youth development and transformation, whereas the instrumental perspective suggests that challenging and rewarding activities that build youth competence are the vehicle for developing a meaningful interpersonal relationship. Despite differing in emphasis, these perspectives are not mutually exclusive. In descriptions of positive mentoring from each perspective, mentors aspired to the dual goals of ensuring a solid relationship and developing competence and positive attributes in the youth. This combination is consistent with developmental theories emphasizing the importance of promoting relatedness *and* autonomy (Ryan, Deci, & Grolnick, 1995). In short, establishing a positive mentoring relationship may require a hybrid approach, merging lessons from both perspectives (Keller, 2005a). Because mentoring relationships are voluntary, a mentor who wants to teach skills and develop character may have limited success with an authoritarian or prescriptive approach. Instead, the mentor must adopt a youth-centered strategy that incorporates the youth's interests and preferences in selecting activities that provide learning opportunities. Conversely, a mentor who wants only a mutual friendship may be disappointed. As the adult in the relationship, the mentor may need to assume greater responsibility and provide enough structure for the youth's productive participation in activities, especially those providing a sense of accomplishment. Effective mentors find opportunities to simultaneously build the relationship and promote youth development through activities that are mutually enjoyable, challenging and engaging, and aligned with youth interests (Keller, 2005a).

Mentors with greater levels of self-efficacy may succeed in establishing stronger relationships because they have high expectations, have confidence in their ability to influence the youth, and persevere until they identify approaches that generate positive responses from the youth. Greater patience and interpersonal skill may be necessary when the youth has a history of troubled relationships or psychosocial difficulties. Similarly, the appropriate balance between the relational and instrumental aspects of a relationship may depend on several other factors, such as whether it is natural versus program mentoring, the reasons the youth sought a mentor, and the gender and age of the youth. For instance, interpersonal issues may be especially salient for females, and adolescents may have more instrumental goals than younger children (Darling et al., 1994). The process of negotiating these aspects of the relationship is likely to be more intentional, and awkward, for two strangers introduced through a formal mentoring program than for a youth and adult whose informal mentoring relationship evolves out of natural opportunities for contact.

Further understanding of interpersonal processes in the development of mentoring relationships may be achieved by application of theories from developmental, cognitive, and social psychology. For example, attachment theory provides insights into relationships between children and other nonparental adults, such as school teachers (Pianta, 1999), and into therapeutic relationships between clients and clinicians (Dozier & Tyrrell, 1998). Attachment theory asserts that children's early experiences with parents will influence their later capacity to form close, affectional bonds with others (Bowlby, 1973; Sroufe & Fleeson, 1986). Based on interactions with parents, children develop expectations regarding the availability and sensitivity of attachment figures. These expectations are incorporated into mental models of relationships that influence strategies for eliciting support from others, making use of emotional cues, and attributing intentions to others in social interaction (Bowlby, 1973; Bretherton & Munholland, 1999). Thus, a child's attachment history has potential implications for establishing a relationship with a mentor and using this relationship as a resource (Sroufe & Fleeson, 1986). Likewise, an adult's mental models of attachment and caregiving influence the capacity to attend to, interpret, and respond appropriately to children's emotional cues (George & Solomon, 1996). Owing to asymmetries in the power and competence of adult and child, relationship development is biased toward input from the adult (Pianta, 1999). Presumably, formation of a new relationship would depend more heavily on the adult's model of relationships, which would be more firmly established and resistant to change than that of the child (Bretherton & Munholland, 1999).

Research Directions and Methodological Issues

Given the relatively limited knowledge about the formation of youth mentoring relationships, research is needed to address their normative development over time, individual and contextual factors resulting in diverse relationship trajectories, and dyadic processes contributing to change and continuity over the course of the relationship (Keller, 2005a). Progress in this area will require attention to several methodological issues involving assessment, design, and analysis. For example, many variables may be used as indicators of the nature and course of relationships, such as the tone of interactions, types of activities, communication, reciprocity, support, closeness, commitment, and satisfaction. Researchers could trace growth and decline along a single dimension or incorporate several in a holistic view of overall relationship functioning. Ideally, studies would be prospective in design and include multiple and frequent assessments of the relationship from the perspective of each participant. Reporting by both participants on structured assessments or in qualitative interviews provides opportunities to investigate relationship attunement and congruence. In addition, cross-informant designs are important in studies that rely on self-report data for investigating whether individual factors measured at the outset contribute to the partner's later perception of the relationship. Innovative approaches that may shed additional light on momentary experiences in interactive processes include direct observation of the pair (Keller, Pryce, & Neugebauer, 2004) and use of the experience-sampling method (Csikszentmihalyi & Larson, 1987). Relationship data pose several analytical challenges concerning conceptual models, units of analysis, nonindependence of data with dyads, types of predictor variables, and covariance components (Malloy & Albright, 2001). These issues are being addressed in newer hierarchically nested dyadic designs for analyzing individual-level dyadic actor and dyadic partner effect models as well as mutual influence models examining reciprocal processes (Kenny, 1996). With the dyad as the unit of analysis, longitudinal data at intervals over the course of the relationship permit growth curve analyses of relationship trajectories or latent transition analyses evaluating different stages of relationship development. Other analytic strategies for time-series data, such as nonlinear modeling, could prove valuable for understanding dynamic developmental processes within relationships.

How do Mentoring Relationships Influence Youth Development?

Assuming that mentoring is intended to serve a helpful function in a youth's life, that the mentor is motivated to support the youth, and that developing a relationship is the mode of intervention, attention turns to the particular mechanisms by which the relationship may influence youth development. As noted, youth mentoring may vary in its aims and the context in which activities between mentor and youth occur. Furthermore, mentoring is an individualized intervention, and every relationship is distinguished by the developmental needs, interpersonal capabilities, and social circumstances of mentor and youth. Thus, in any given case, the mentor may contribute to a particular aspect of the youth's development or may become involved in various life domains and exercise a broad and pervasive influence.

Several theoretical perspectives have been invoked to explain interpersonal processes involved in youth mentoring. For example, Darling et al. (1994) employ concepts from symbolic interactionism, social learning theory, and Vygotstky's zone of proximal development to propose three mechanisms by which significant, unrelated adults promote youth development: providing feedback incorporated into the adolescent's self-concept; sharing normative beliefs/expectations and role modeling appropriate behaviors; providing direct instruction to develop skills and abilities. Similarly, Hamilton and Hamilton (2004) discuss the implications of social learning theory and the creation of social capital to highlight a mentor's potential contributions to youth development through socialization and expansion of social networks. Drawing on theories of motivation and achievement, Larose and Tarabulsy (2005) present a model describing how mentor involvement, structure, and perspective-taking could promote youth relatedness, competence, and autonomy, respectively.

Reflecting the wide range of developmental processes that may operate in mentoring relationships, Rhodes (2002b) presented an influential framework proposing that mentors promote youth development in three interrelated ways: a) enhancing social skills and emotional well-being, b) improving cognitive skills through instruction and dialogue, and c) fostering identity development by serving as role model and advocate. With its focus on three central domains of youth development, this framework flexibly accommodates many theories regarding specific interpersonal mechanisms, including those noted above. To continue themes developed in previous sections and to draw freely from the various perspectives represented in the literature, the following selective review is organized according to three complementary avenues for influencing youth development: protecting from psychosocial risk, enhancing personal competence, and promoting social integration.

Protecting from Psychosocial Risk

As noted earlier, youth may be connected to mentors, whether formal or informal, because they have experienced strains or losses in their relationships with parents or because they have been exposed to high levels of psychosocial adversity. As a form of preventive intervention, these mentors may emphasize the development of a caring, emotionally supportive relationship following the more therapeutic, relational perspective described above. The rationale for this approach is provided by research on resilience and social support suggesting the protective effect of positive relationships when individuals are confronted with stress (Masten et al., 1990; Thoits, 1995). For example, a supportive relationship may protect against stress by preventing or minimizing its occurrence, buffering its effect, or counteracting its effects by strengthening compensatory variables that contribute to adjustment (Sandler, Miller, Short, & Wolchik, 1989).

Attachment theory offers a conceptual framework for understanding how a relationship with an older, caregiving adult can have implications for psychosocial adjustment (Bowlby, 1969/1982). According to theory, a youth who feels threatened or stressed will become anxious and distressed, which signals to an attachment figure a need for comfort and protection. The ability of the attachment figure to interpret these signals and to alleviate the distress becomes the basis for the youth's working model of the relationship (Bretherton & Munholland, 1999). Over numerous interactions, the youth develops expectations regarding the availability and attentiveness of the attachment figure and identifies strategies for eliciting support when needed. There may be several important implications when a mentor proves to be consistent and responsive in resolving the youth's distress. First, the relationship provides an effective means of coping with the immediate source of stress. Second, the youth recognizes that the mentor is trustworthy and reliable, thereby introducing or reinforcing models of relationships as valuable and supportive. For a youth who has been disappointed in previous relationships, this may represent an important change in the working model of relationships. Third, when the mentor demonstrates genuine concern by being sensitive and responsive, the youth is more likely to view the self as valued and worthy of care. Finally, knowing that the mentor is a dependable source of support in case of problems may permit more confident exploration of the environment to develop knowledge, skills, and competence.

Enhancing Personal Competence

A focus on enhancing personal competence corresponds to the philosophy of positive youth development and is consistent with an instrumental perspective on mentoring relationships. A basic premise is that the mentor, as someone older and more experienced, will introduce the youth to knowledge, skills, and practices that will enable the youth to pursue his or her interests and become a more effective member of society (Darling et al., 1994; Hamilton & Hamilton, 2004; Rhodes, 2002b). Several theories have been referenced to explain how this learning might occur in a mentoring relationship. According to Vygotsky (1978), development is driven by the very process of learning through social interaction. Through guidance and instruction, the adult creates a "zone of proximal development" which stimulates achievement beyond the youth's current level of ability. The adult provides structure and support in joint activities, and this scaffolding enables the youth to attain and consolidate higher levels of competence and performance than could be reached without assistance. Vygotsky's theory emphasizes both the active role of the learner and the role of the teacher in establishing an instructional environment providing an appropriate level of challenge (Vygotsky, 1978).

Processes of learning beyond direct instruction are specified by social learning/social cognitive theory (Bandura, 1982, 1989). This theory is highly relevant for mentoring because it explicitly addresses the observation of a model as an important mode of learning. According to theory, an individual's perception of self-efficacy promotes the development of competencies by fostering greater confidence, greater effort, more perseverance, higher standards for performance, and higher expectations for positive outcomes. Judgments of self-efficacy are based upon several sources of experiential evidence. Successfully mastering situations and achieving goals enhances self-efficacy. Appraisals of self-efficacy also can be influenced vicariously by social comparison to a model performing a particular task. An experienced model demonstrates effective strategies for dealing with challenge and achieving success. Finally, verbal persuasion that one is capable of success can influence a person's perception of self-efficacy. In other words, a mentor may promote self-efficacy and competence by providing the youth opportunities for successful learning and accomplishment, role modeling the appropriate behaviors for the youth to observe, and by providing encouragement that demonstrates confidence in the youth. Learning through structured guidance and observation is proposed to operate across multiple domains of functioning, including academic, vocational, and recreational pursuits. In addition, a mentor or role model may demonstrate how to interact with others in various social situations. Likewise, a mentor may carefully structure conversations about emotionally sensitive topics and coach a child in strategies for managing emotions (Rhodes, Spencer, Keller, Liang, & Noam, 2006).

Promoting Social Integration

In addition to providing instruction and social support, a mentor may play an important function in enriching and expanding the system of relationships that constitute the social network of a youth. A family systems perspective suggests that individuals are embedded in a matrix of interdependent relationships, and experiences in one relationship can have repercussions for interactions in another relationship (Cox & Paley, 1997). Consequently, a mentoring relationship may influence development by altering the dynamics of the youth's relationship with parents and other important people in the youth's life (Keller, 2005b; Rhodes, 2002b; Rhodes, Grossman, & Resch, 2000). As described above, one possibility is that a sensitive and consistent relationship with a mentor provides a "corrective experience" that changes the youth's working model of attachment relationships (Rhodes et al., 2006). Alternatively, the mentor may affect a stressful parent–child relationship by providing occasions of respite, helping each to understand the other's perspective, providing advice on how to resolve difficulties, and offering each a more hopeful view of the youth's future (Keller, 2005b).

A mentoring relationship also offers many prospects for influencing the nature and extent of the youth's social network outside the family. Serving as a guide who introduces the youth to a variety of new settings, the mentor may facilitate opportunities for involvement in activities that promote bonds to new individuals and institutions. To the extent that these new contacts share the norms and values of the mentor, they provide a form of informal social control that multiplies and reinforces the socializing influence of the mentor (Catalano & Hawkins, 1996). When the youth becomes familiar and conversant with settings different from his or her typical experience, the result may be a form of bicultural competence that expands the youth's repertoire (Blechman, 1992). For example, the youth may accompany the mentor to the workplace and learn about expectations and conventions in this context.

This ability of the mentor to expand the social network of the youth is most often conceptualized in terms of building the youth's social capital (Hamilton & Hamilton, 2004; Rhodes, 2002b). Social capital refers to the benefits that accrue to individuals by virtue of their participation in relationships or membership in groups (Portes, 1998). The concept of social capital often is invoked to explain differential access to educational and occupational mobility and economic success (Coleman, 1988). For example, it is through social connections that individuals, particularly adolescents, gain information about and initial entrée to education (e.g., learning about scholarships, admission procedures) and employment (e.g., informal referrals) (Granovetter, 1974). In this regard, the relationship with the mentor represents social capital to the extent that the mentor can open up opportunities for the youth. The mentor also may mediate the acquisition of social capital by fostering relationships to others in the community who become advocates for the youth. Beyond the actual benefits to human or financial capital derived from a widening social network, this exposure to the larger community of adults may provide the youth with a sense of direction for the transition to adulthood.

Summary

As suggested by this brief review, mentors may contribute to youth development through a variety of interpersonal processes, and the literature on youth mentoring has drawn from existing theories of adult–child interaction to propose numerous routes of potential influence. A framework that organizes the functions of mentors in terms of protecting from psychosocial risk, enhancing personal competence, and promoting social integration points to correspondences with particular aims of mentoring and certain types of relationship development. Mentors employing a relational approach may be sensitive to psychosocial risks facing the youth and prevent negative consequences by providing direct assistance to reduce stress or providing emotional support to buffer the effects of adversity. Mentors adopting an instrumental approach may promote positive youth development by structuring activities, providing instruction, and role modeling. Mentors aiming to foster intergenerational ties and connections with the larger community could develop the social capital of youth by introducing them to new settings and creating opportunities for them to explore adult roles. As noted earlier, mentors may focus their efforts narrowly on a particular purpose or may integrate several approaches to exert a more comprehensive influence on a youth's life. Furthermore, the mechanisms of influence discussed above would seem equally relevant to program and natural mentors.

Another lens for summarizing the lasting influence of mentoring on youth is the process of identity development (Darling et al., 1994; Rhodes, 2002b). In some ways, the three domains outlined above are consolidated in the evolving self-concept of the youth. According to Harter (1988), a youth's determination of global self-worth is based primarily on two assessments: 1) their perception of acceptance, support, and positive regard from significant others; and 2) their evaluation of their competence in the activities they consider to be important. In addition, self-concept often incorporates a sense of future identity, or the "possible selves" that one may want to become (Markus & Nurius, 1986). A mentoring relationship may contribute to the youth's self-concept in each of these ways. This is consistent with Rutter's (1987) claim that a secure and supportive personal relationship promotes a youth's feelings of self-worth, perceived self-efficacy, and ability to plan for the future.

Any discussion of the influence of mentoring on youth must also point to the very real potential for the consequences of the relationship to be negative (Rhodes, 2002b). Depending upon the nature of the interaction, the youth may receive implicit or explicit messages that he or she is not valued by the mentor, is not considered competent, or has poor prospects for the future. As with any effort to provide assistance, a guiding principle must be to do no harm, and mentoring programs must make every effort to prevent iatrogenic experiences.

Research Directions and Methodological Issues

Although several theoretical perspectives have been incorporated into explanations for the beneficial effects of youth mentoring, few of the proposed mechanisms have been examined empirically. In fact, very little research has systematically investigated what really happens in mentoring relationships. The distinctive nature of each mentoring relationship, based on the individual characteristics and circumstances of mentor and protégé, poses several methodological challenges. As in other research on social support, for example, the type and extent of assistance provided by the mentor may be conditioned on the needs of the youth. Thus, research must account for a variety of individual and contextual factors and strive for specificity in linking particular mentor behaviors to conceptually relevant youth outcomes. In-depth qualitative studies will be valuable for identifying the range of developmental processes encompassed within mentoring relationships and evaluating the plausibility of theoretical models that have been proposed. Deductive studies focusing explicitly on theoretically based constructs and process models also hold great potential for advancing knowledge regarding the developmental influence of mentoring. Ideally, studies examining mediating processes and moderating factors would employ longitudinal, multimethod, multiple informant designs. Longitudinal studies with assessment of youth status prior to initiation of the mentoring relationship can evaluate whether variability in relationship quality, perhaps in interaction with contextual factors, translates to expected changes in process and outcome variables relative to baseline. Program evaluation studies employing random assignment present excellent opportunities to measure intervening, process-oriented variables as well as outcomes to determine whether youth with mentors report more instrumental support, more experiences for developing competence, and greater access to social capital. Unfortunately, methodological approaches for research on formal mentoring are less suitable for natural mentoring because assessment prior to the relationship is unlikely, making it difficult to disentangle factors that might contribute to both the presence of a mentor and to youth outcomes.

Conclusion

Youth mentoring is many things to many people. An understanding of its multidimensional nature involves consideration of the purpose mentoring is meant to serve, the reasons individuals become mentors, the manner in which mentoring relationships develop, and the processes by which mentoring relationships influence youth development. Although distinct perspectives have emerged to provide insight into each of these issues, the perspectives certainly are not incompatible. In fact, youth mentoring may offer its best when multiple approaches converge. Increasingly, for example, it is recognized that the most effective prevention and positive development programs share common features, such as holistic approaches addressing multiple aspects of the child's experience in the natural contexts of family, school, and community (Catalano et al., 2002). Similarly, the most resourceful and committed volunteers may be those with a combination of both egoistic and altruistic motives for mentoring a youth. Likewise, there is strong evidence that the most effectively engaging adults provide an appropriate balance of structure and challenge with enjoyment and support (Larson, 2000). In addition, investigations of the nature of social support suggest the potential for cumulative benefits of perceived emotional support, received instrumental support, and being embedded in a network of social relationships (Thoits, 1995).

As noted at the outset, youth mentoring is characterized by a personal relationship in which a caring individual provides consistent companionship, support, and guidance aimed at developing the competence and character of a child or adolescent. Mentors may employ many approaches and strategies to accomplish this aim. Ultimately, an effective mentor is an adult who will enter into the world of the youth and gradually bring the youth into the world of adults.

Author Note

The writing of this chapter was supported in part by a grant from NIMH (1RO3MH067129-1A1).

References

Baker, D. B., & Maguire, C. P. (2005). Mentoring in historical perspective. In D. L. DuBois & M. J. Karcher (Eds.), *Handbook of youth mentoring* (pp. 14–29). Thousand Oaks, CA: Sage.

Bandura, A. (1982). Self-efficacy mechanism in human agency. *American Psychologist, 37*(2), 122–147.

Bandura, A. (1989). Human agency in social cognitive theory. *American Psychologist, 44*(9), 1175–1184.

Batson, C. D., Ahmad, N., & Tsang, J. A. (2002). Four motives for community involvement. *Journal of Social Issues, 58*(3), 429–445.

Beam, M. R., Chen, C., & Greenberger, E. (2002). The nature of adolescents' relationships with their 'very important' nonparental adults. *American Journal of Community Psychology, 30*(2), 305–325.

Beiswinger, G. L. (1985). *One to one: The story of the Big Brothers/Big Sisters movement in America.* Philadelphia: Big Brothers/Big Sisters of America.

Blechman, E. A. (1992). Mentors for high-risk minority youth: From effective communication to bicultural competence. *Journal of Clinical Child Psychology, 21*(2), 160–169.

Bordin, E. S. (1979). The generalizability of the psychoanalytic concept of the working alliance. *Psychotherapy: Theory, Research and Practice, 16*(3), 252–260.

Bowlby, J. (1969/1982). *Attachment and loss: Vol. 1. Attachment* (2nd ed.). New York: Basic Books.

Bowlby, J. (1973). *Attachment and loss: Vol. 2. Separation, anxiety and anger.* New York: Basic Books.

Bretherton, I., & Munholland, K. A. (1999). Internal working models in attachment relationships: A construct revisited. In J. Cassidy & P. R. Shaver (Eds.), *Handbook of attachment: Theory, research, and clinical applications* (pp. 89–111). New York: Guilford Press.

Catalano, R. F., & Hawkins, J. D. (1996). The social development model: A theory of anti-social behavior. In J. D. Hawkins (Ed.), *Delinquency and crime: Current theories* (pp. 149–197). New York: Cambridge University Press.

Catalano, R. F., Hawkins, J. D., Berglund, L. M., Pollard, J. A., & Arthur, M. W. (2002). Prevention science and positive youth development: Competitive or cooperative frameworks? *Journal of Adolescent Health, 31,* 230–239.

Clary, E. G., Snyder, M., Ridge, R. D., Copeland, J., Stukas, A. A., Haugen, J., & Miene, P. (1998). Understanding and assessing the motivation of volunteers: A functional approach. *Journal of Personality and Social Psychology, 74*(6), 1516–1530.

Coleman, J. S. (1988). Social capital in the creation of human capital. *American Journal of Sociology, 94*(Suppl.), S95–S120.

Colley, H. (2003). Engagement mentoring for "disaffected" youth: A new model of mentoring for social inclusion. *British Educational Research Journal, 29*(4), 521–542.

Cox, M. J., & Paley, B. (1997). Families as systems. *Annual Review of Psychology, 48,* 243–267.

Csikszentmihalyi, M., & Larson, R. (1987). Validity and reliability of the Experience-Sampling Method. *Journal of Nervous and Mental Disease, 175*(9), 526–536.

Darling, N., Hamilton, S. F., & Niego, S. (1994). Adolescents' relations with adults outside the family. In R. Montemayor, G. R. Adams, & T. P. Gullotta (Eds.), *Personal relationships during adolescence* (Vol. 6, pp. 216–235). Thousand Oaks, CA: Sage.

Darling, N., Hamilton, S. F., & Shaver, K. H. (2003). Relationships outside the family: Unrelated adults. In G. R. Adams & M. D. Berzonsky (Eds.), *Blackwell handbook of adolescence* (pp. 349–370). Malden, MA: Blackwell.

Downey, G., Lebolt, A., Rincon, C., & Freitas, A. L. (1998). Rejection sensitivity and children's interpersonal difficulties. *Child Development, 69*(4), 1074–1091.

Dozier, M., & Tyrrell, C. (1998). The role of attachment in therapeutic relationships. In J. A. Simpson & W. S. Rholes (Eds.), *Attachment theory and close relationships* (pp. 221–248). New York: Guilford.

DuBois, D. L., Holloway, B. E., Valentine, J. C., & Cooper, H. (2002). Effectiveness of mentoring programs for youth: A meta-analytic review. *American Journal of Community Psychology*, *30*(2), 157–197.

DuBois, D. L., & Karcher, M. J. (Eds.). (2005). *Handbook of youth mentoring*. Thousand Oaks, CA: Sage.

DuBois, D. L., & Silverthorn, N. (2005a). Characteristics of natural mentoring relationships and adolescent adjustment: Evidence from a national study. *Journal of Primary Prevention*, *26*(2), 69–92.

DuBois, D. L., & Silverthorn, N. (2005b). Natural mentoring relationships and adolescent health: Evidence from a national survey. *American Journal of Public Health*, *95*(3), 518–524.

Fishbein, M., & Ajzen, I. (1975). *Belief, attitude, intention, and behavior*. Reading, MA: Addison-Wesley.

Freedman, M. (1993). *The kindness of strangers: Adult mentors, urban youth, and the new voluntarism*. San Francisco: Jossey-Bass.

Garcia Coll, C. T., Meyer, E. C., & Brillon, L. (1995). Ethnic and minority parenting. In M. H. Bornstein (Ed.), *Handbook of parenting: Vol. 2. Biology and ecology of parenting* (pp. 189–209). Mahwah, NJ: Lawrence Erlbaum.

George, C., & Solomon, J. (1996). Representational models of relationships: Links between caregiving and attachment. *Infant Mental Health Journal*, *17*(3), 198–216.

Granovetter, M. S. (1974). *Getting a job: A study of contacts and careers*. Cambridge, MA: Harvard University Press.

Grossman, J. B., & Rhodes, J. E. (2002). The test of time: Predictors and effects of duration in youth mentoring relationships. *American Journal of Community Psychology*, *30*(2), 199–219.

Grube, J. A., & Piliavin, J. A. (2000). Role identity, organizational experiences, and volunteer performance. *Personality and Social Psychology Bulletin*, *26*(9), 1108–1119.

Hamilton, S. F., & Hamilton, M. A. (1990). *Linking up: Final report on a mentoring program for youth*. Cornell University: Department of Human Development & Family Studies.

Hamilton, S. F., & Hamilton, M. A. (1992). Mentoring programs: Promise and paradox. *Phi Delta Kappan*, *73*(7), 546–550.

Hamilton, S. F., & Hamilton, M. A. (2004). Contexts for mentoring: Adolescent–adult relationships in workplaces and communities. In R. M. Lerner & L. Steinberg (Eds.), *Handbook of adolescent psychology* (2nd ed., pp. 395–428). New York: Wiley.

Haraven, T. K. (1989). Historical changes in children's networks in the family and community. In D. Belle (Ed.), *Children's social networks and social supports* (pp. 15–35). New York: Wiley.

Harter, S. (1988). Developmental processes in the construction of the self. In T. D. Yawkey & J. E. Johnson (Eds.), *Integrative processes and socialization: Early to middle childhood* (pp. 45–78). Hillsdale, NJ: Lawrence Erlbaum.

Hartup, W. W., & Laursen, B. (1999). Relationships as developmental contexts: Retrospective themes and contemporary issues. In W. A. Collins & B. Laursen (Eds.), *Relationships as developmental contexts* (Vol. 30, pp. 13–35). Mahwah, NJ: Lawrence Erlbaum.

Henry, W. P., & Strupp, H. H. (1994). The therapeutic alliance as interpersonal process. In A. O. Horvath & L. S. Greenberg (Eds.), *The working alliance: Theory, research, and practice* (pp. 51–84). New York: Wiley.

Horvath, A. O., & Luborsky, L. (1993). The role of the therapeutic alliance in psychotherapy. *Journal of Consulting and Clinical Psychology*, *61*(4), 561–573.

Karcher, M. J., & Lindwall, J. (2003). Social interest, connectedness, and challenging experiences: What makes high school mentors persist? *Journal of Individual Psychology*, *59*(3), 293–315.

Keller, T. E. (2005a). The stages and development of mentoring relationships. In D. L. DuBois & M. J. Karcher (Eds.), *Handbook of youth mentoring* (pp. 82–99). Thousand Oaks, CA: Sage.

Keller, T. E. (2005b). A systemic model of the youth mentoring intervention. *Journal of Primary Prevention*, 26(2), 169–188.

Keller, T. E., Pryce, J. M., & Neugebauer, A. (2004). *Observational methods for assessing the nature and course of mentor–child interactions.* Unpublished manuscript.

Kenny, D. A. (1996). Models of non-independence in dyadic research. *Journal of Personal and Social Relationships*, 13, 279–294.

Larose, S., & Tarabulsy, G. M. (2005). Academically at-risk students. In D. L. DuBois & M. J. Karcher (Eds.), *Handbook of youth mentoring* (pp. 440–453). Thousand Oaks, CA: Sage.

Larson, R. W. (2000). Toward a psychology of positive youth development. *American Psychologist*, 55(1), 170–183.

Lock, E. (2002). *Examining the relationship between organizational ideologies and technology: The case of urban youth development programs.* Unpublished manuscript, University of Chicago.

Malloy, T. E., & Albright, L. (2001). Multiple and single interaction dyadic research designs: Conceptual and analytical issues. *Basic and Applied Social Psychology*, 23(1), 1–19.

Markus, H., & Nurius, P. (1986). Possible selves. *American Psychologist*, 41, 954–969.

Masten, A. S., Best, K. M., & Garmezy, N. (1990). Resilience and development: Contributions from the study of children who overcome adversity. *Development and Psychopathology*, 2, 425–444.

McAdams, D. P., Hart, H. M. H., & Maruna, S. (1998). The anatomy of generativity. In D. P. McAdams & E. de St. Aubin (Eds.), *Generativity and adult development: How and why we care for the next generation* (pp. 7–43). Washington, DC: American Psychological Association.

McLaughlin, M. W., Irby, M. A., & Langman, J. (1994). *Urban sanctuaries: Neighborhood organizations in the lives and futures of inner-city youth.* San Francisco: Jossey-Bass.

McLearn, K. T., Colasanto, D., Schoen, C., & Shapiro, M. Y. (1999). Mentoring matters: A national survey of adults mentoring young people. In J. B. Grossman (Ed.), *Contemporary issues in mentoring* (pp. 66–83). Philadelphia: Public/Private Ventures.

MENTOR (2003). *Elements of effective practice* (2nd ed). Alexandria, VA: MENTOR/ National Mentoring Partnership.

Morrow, K. V., & Styles, M. B. (1995). *Building relationships with youth in program settings: A study of Big Brothers Big Sisters.* Philadelphia: Public/Private Ventures.

Omoto, A. M., & Snyder, M. (1995). Sustained helping without obligation: Motivation, longevity of service, and perceived attitude change among AIDS volunteers. *Journal of Personality and Social Psychology*, 68(4), 671–686.

Parra, G. R., DuBois, D. L., Neville, H. A., Pugh-Lilly, A. O., & Povinelli, N. (2002). Mentoring relationships for youth: Investigation of a process-oriented model. *Journal of Community Psychology*, 30(4), 367–388.

Penner, L. A. (2002). Dispositional and organizational influences on sustained volunteerism: An interactionist perspective. *Journal of Social Issues*, 58(3), 447–467.

Philip, K., & Hendry, L. B. (2000). Making sense of mentoring or mentoring making sense? Reflections on the mentoring process by adult mentors with young people. *Journal of Community & Applied Social Psychology*, 10, 211–223.

Pianta, R. C. (1999). *Enhancing relationships between children and teachers.* Washington, DC: American Psychological Association.

Portes, A. (1998). Social capital: Its origins and applications in modern sociology. *Annual Review of Sociology*, 24, 1–24.

Rauner, D. M. (2000). *"They still pick me up when I fall": The role of caring in youth development and community life.* New York: Columbia University Press.

Reis, H. T., Collins, W. A., & Berscheid, E. (2000). The relationship context of human behavior and development. *Psychological Bulletin, 126*(6), 844–872.

Rhodes, J. E. (2002b). *Stand by me: The risks and rewards of mentoring today's youth.* Cambridge, MA: Harvard University Press.

Rhodes, J. E., Grossman, J. B., & Resch, N. L. (2000). Agents of change: Pathways through which mentoring relationships influence adolescents' academic adjustment. *Child Development, 71*(6), 1662–1671.

Rhodes, J. E., Haight, W. L., & Briggs, E. C. (1999). The influence of mentoring on the peer relationships of foster youth in relative and nonrelative care. *Journal of Research on Adolescence, 9*(2), 185–201.

Rhodes, J. E., Spencer, R. A., Keller, T. E., Liang, B., & Noam, G. G. (2006). A model for the influence of mentoring relationship on youth development. *Journal of Community Psychology, 34*(6), 691–707.

Roth, J. L., & Brooks-Gunn, J. (2003). Youth development programs: Risk, prevention and policy. *Journal of Adolescent Health, 32*, 170–182.

Rutter, M. (1987). Psychosocial resilience and protective mechanisms. *American Journal of Orthopsychiatry, 57*, 316–331.

Ryan, R. M., Deci, E. L., & Grolnick, W. S. (1995). Autonomy, relatedness, and the self: Their relation to development and psychopathology. In D. Cicchetti & D. J. Cohen (Eds.), *Developmental psychopathology: Vol. 1. Theory and methods* (pp. 618–655). New York: Wiley.

Sandler, I. N., Miller, P., Short, J., & Wolchik, S. A. (1989). Social support as a protective factor for children in stress. In D. Belle (Ed.), *Children's social networks and social support* (pp. 277–307). New York: Wiley.

Sipe, C. L. (2002). Mentoring programs for adolescents: A research summary. *Journal of Adolescent Health, 31*, 251–260.

Sipe, C. L. (2005). Toward a typology of mentoring. In D. L. DuBois & M. J. Karcher (Eds.), *Handbook of youth mentoring* (pp. 65–80). Thousand Oaks, CA: Sage.

Spencer, R. A., Jordan, J. V., & Sazama, J. (2004). Growth-promoting relationships between youth and adults: A focus group study. *Families in Society, 85*(3), 354–362.

Spencer, R. A., & Rhodes, J. E. (2005). A counseling and psychotherapy perspective on mentoring relationships. In D. L. DuBois & M. J. Karcher (Eds.), *Handbook of youth mentoring* (pp. 118–132). Thousand Oaks, CA: Sage.

Sroufe, L. A., & Fleeson, J. (1986). Attachment and the construction of relationships. In W. Hartup & Z. Rubin (Eds.), *Relationships and development* (pp. 51–71). Hillsdale, NJ: Erlbaum.

Stukas, A. A., & Tanti, C. (2005). Recruiting and sustaining volunteer mentors. In D. L. DuBois & M. J. Karcher (Eds.), *Handbook of youth mentoring* (pp. 235–250). Thousand Oaks, CA: Sage.

Styles, M. B., & Morrow, K. V. (1992). *Understanding how youth and elders form relationships: A study of four Linking Lifetimes programs.* Philadelphia, PA: Public/Private Ventures.

Taylor, A. S., LoSciuto, L., & Porcellini, L. (2005). Intergenerational mentoring. In D. L. DuBois & M. J. Karcher (Eds.), *Handbook of youth mentoring* (pp. 286–299). Thousand Oaks, CA: Sage.

Thoits, P. A. (1995). Stress, coping, and social support processes: Where are we? What next? *Journal of Health and Social Behavior, 35*, 53–79.

Tierney, J. P., Grossman, J. B., & Resch, J. (1995). *Making a difference: An impact study of Big Brothers/Big Sisters.* Philadelphia: Public/Private Ventures.

Vygotsky, L. S. (1978). *Mind in society: The development of higher psychological processes.* Cambridge, MA: Harvard University Press.

Whiting, B. B., & Whiting, J. W. M. (1975). *Children of six cultures: A psycho-cultural analysis.* Cambridge, MA: Harvard University Press.

Wilson, J. (2000). Volunteering. *Annual Review of Sociology, 26,* 215–240.

Youniss, J., McLellan, J. A., & Yates, M. (1997). What we know about engendering civic identity. *American Behavioral Scientist, 40*(5), 620–631.

Zimmerman, M. A., Bingenheimer, J. B., & Notaro, P. C. (2002). Natural mentors and adolescent resiliency: A study with urban youth. *American Journal of Community Psychology, 30*(2), 221–243.

Chapter 4

Student–Faculty Mentoring: Theoretical and Methodological Issues

W. Brad Johnson, Gail Rose, and Lewis Z. Schlosser

Although research on mentor relationships is more than three decades old (Crosby, 1999), the vast majority of theoretical and methodological advances in this area arise from business and organizational environments. Universities and academic programs frequently extol the benefits of mentoring and most assume that undergraduates and graduate students alike benefit substantially from a mentor relationship (mentorship) with a faculty member (Tenenbaum, Crosby, & Gliner, 2001). Yet, 20 years after Merriam (1983) cautioned that the literature on mentoring was biased in favor of the phenomenon and recommended both greater clarification of the construct and more effective assessment of mentoring outcomes, research on student–faculty mentorships remains comparatively sparse, marginally sophisticated, and focused nearly exclusively on positive outcomes.

In this chapter, we review theoretical issues and methodological approaches unique to studying mentorships between students and faculty in both undergraduate and graduate settings. Although students often find mentors in peers, external professionals, and family members (Grant-Vallone & Ensher, 2000), our review is limited to the student–faculty mentorship. We begin by addressing definitional issues and conceptual problems in mentoring research. We then consider salient theories undergirding mentoring in academe and offer some analysis and critique of the extant literature on student–faculty mentoring. We conclude with several recommendations for subsequent elucidation of theory and refinement of research methods.

Definitional Clarity in Student–Faculty Mentoring Research: Still Searching After all These Years

Perhaps the most frequent criticism of student–faculty mentoring literature is the enduring absence of a widely accepted operational definition of the mentoring construct

(Crosby, 1999; Jacobi, 1991; Merriam, 1983; Mertz, 2004). In both theoretical writing and research on the topic, scholars use widely disparate definitions of the mentorship construct and the boundaries between mentoring and other relationship forms are poorly articulated. Such definitional dysfunction in the mentoring literature has led to confusion, and questions about the cumulative value of this research.

A salient theme in these criticisms is the tendency for researchers to label nearly any supportive or developmentally oriented relationship as mentoring (Mertz, 2004). Although much of the literature emphasizes *traditional* mentorships, intense personal relationships between a faculty member and student of long duration, other strands of research in academe focus on role models (Erkut & Mokros, 1984; Gibson, 2004; Gilbert, 1985; Speizer, 1981) and advisors (Schlosser & Gelso, 2001). Although role models may positively affect students, modeling does not require a relationship. Consider the following operational definition of role model from a large study of undergraduates:

> After you have thought about all the professors that you have known, select the one professor who has had the greatest impact on you by demonstrating the kinds of commitments, skills, and qualities that you see as important for yourself. (Erkut & Mokros, 1984, p. 403)

Although it is possible that many of the subjects in this study had mentoring relationships with the professor identified, this cannot be assumed. Because researchers have frequently used terms such as advisor, sponsor, role model, and mentor interchangeably within a survey on mentoring (e.g., Turban, Dougherty & Lee, 2002), it is likely that the current body of mentoring literature subsumes several distinct kinds of interpersonal relationships.

To Define or Not to Define

In some student–faculty mentoring research, no operational definition of mentoring is provided so that respondents are left to interpret the construct idiosyncratically (e.g., Cochran, Paukert, Scales, & Neumayer, 2004; Cronan-Hillix, Gensheimer, Cronan-Hillix, & Davidson, 1986; Kring, Richardson, Burns, & Davis, 1999). This method has the advantage of allowing for flexibility on the part of the respondent, but the disadvantage of making the interpretation of results ambiguous.

In other cases, researchers supply a precise definition for respondents to ensure a common response frame (e.g., Aagaard & Hauer, 2003; Busch, 1985; Clark, Harden, & Johnson, 2000; Wilde & Schau, 1991). One of the most comprehensive definitions emerges from the work of O'Neil and Wrightsman (2001):

> We propose that mentoring exists when a professional person serves as a resource, sponsor, and transitional figure for another person (usually but not necessarily younger) who is entering that same profession. Effective mentors provide mentees with knowledge, advice, challenge, and support as mentees pursue the acquisition of professional competence and identity. The mentor welcomes the less experienced person into the profession and represents the values, skills, and success that the neophyte professional person intends to acquire someday. (p. 113)

Definitions used by these researchers indicate that the relationship is formed between an experienced or senior person and a student or less experienced person. However, the more specific aspects of these definitions differ in important ways. For example, only Wilde and Schau's (1991) definition includes the aspect of the student assisting the mentor with various activities, while Aagaard and Hauer's (2003) definition indicates that the relationship is sustained and ongoing. Furthermore, Busch's (1985) unique definition emphasized "the parameters of mutuality, comprehensiveness and congruence" (p. 258).

It is apparent that students can easily differentiate mentoring from other relationship forms. Paludi, Waite, Roberson, and Jones (1988) administered a survey of open-ended questions to 46 female graduate students at a Midwestern university to assess their definitions of role model and mentor. Results indicated that these respondents differentiated the two terms. Specifically, relationships with mentors were perceived to be longer in duration and to involve career advancement. Mentors were described as supportive and caring for others. Role models, on the other hand, were individuals the respondents admired and wished to emulate.

In another study designed to elucidate protégés' definitions of mentoring, Rose (2003, 2005) developed the Ideal Mentor Scale (IMS) to assess graduate students' definitions of the "ideal mentor." The scale was administered to PhD students at three universities. Item frequencies indicated that two universal qualities were central to graduate students' definitions of a mentor: communication skills and the provision of feedback. Principal factor analysis of the IMS indicated that students' importance ratings could be represented by three individual difference dimensions. The *Integrity* dimension defines as ideal a mentor who exhibits virtue and principled action and can be emulated as a role model. The *Guidance* dimension describes a mentoring style characterized by helpfulness with the tasks and activities typical of graduate study. Finally, the *Relationship* dimension describes ideal mentoring as the formation of a personal relationship involving sharing such things as personal concerns, social activities, and life vision or worldview. This study suggests that there is substantial agreement on the core functions the ideal graduate student mentor would serve, namely effective communication and feedback, and also there are individual differences among students about the additional qualities or functions that person would embody.

Toward Common Components of Mentorship

Although a majority of college and graduate school students can differentiate mentoring from some other faculty advisor roles, many respondents interpret mentoring questions idiosyncratically (Clark et al., 2000; Crosby, 1999). It is therefore prudent to supply a reasonably detailed operational definition when studying mentorships in academe. Here are some of the most distinctive components of mentoring relationships for consideration when defining the construct (Johnson, 2006): a) mentorships are enduring personal relationships, b) mentorships are increasingly reciprocal and mutual, c) compared to protégés, mentors demonstrate greater achievement and experience, d) mentors provide direct career assistance, e) mentors provide social and emotional support, f) mentors serve as models, g) mentoring results in an identity transformation in the protégé, h) mentorships offer a safe environment for self-exploration, i) mentorships generally produce positive career and personal outcomes.

Theoretical Issues in Student–Faculty Mentoring Research

Many studies on student–faculty mentoring are void of theoretical discussion or any attempt to make theoretical ties between mentoring and student outcomes (Jacobi, 1991). With a few notable exceptions, many of the frequently cited studies in this area utilize surveys to simply gauge the frequency of and satisfaction with mentorships. Fewer studies work to link method with theory; the most highly refined theoretical models of student–faculty mentoring have rarely been researched. In this section we briefly survey the most influential theoretical models in this area.

Mentoring and the Life Structure

It was Daniel Levinson and colleagues (Levinson et al., 1978) who launched modern interest in mentoring research. Levinson's theory of the evolution of an individual *life structure* gave rise to a few interview-based ("Levinsonian Method") studies of adults (Roberts & Newton, 1987). According to Levinson's theory, the early phase of adulthood – and more specifically the *novice phase* of early adulthood (age 17–23) – is a life period during which: "the individual is an apprentice adult, facing several large tasks in his efforts to move from the world of childhood and its quandaries to life as a fully hatched adult. These novice-phase tasks are (a) forming a dream, (b) forming a mentor relationship, (c) forming an occupation, and (d) forming an enduring love relationship" (Roberts & Newton, 1987, p. 155). Levinson's life structure theory is often cited by researchers as a rationale for studying mentorships. The theory itself has rarely been scrutinized empirically.

Kram's Mentor Functions

It was Kathy Kram's model of *mentor functions* (Kram, 1985) that brought theoretical clarity and programmatic research efforts to the field of mentoring. By systematizing the wide range of mentoring concepts, most notably the mentor's behaviors and roles (functions), Kram helped both practitioners and researchers begin to effectively differentiate mentoring from other kinds of developmental relationships (Crosby, 1999). A rather substantial body of research has generally confirmed the distinction between Kram's career (mentor behaviors aimed at preparing and promoting a protégé for career development) and psychosocial (mentor behaviors aimed at helping and supporting a protégé on personal/emotional levels) functions. For example, Tenenbaum et al. (2001) administered a measure of mentor functions to 189 graduate students. Factor analysis confirmed Kram's primary factors, socio-emotional (personal) and instrumental (career), among the mentor functions. They further identified a third factor which they labeled "networking" (making professional connections).

Hunt and Michael's Model of Mentoring

Some researchers refer to Hunt and Michael's (1983) comprehensive framework for research on mentoring. The model depicts reciprocal relationships among five major categories or factors in mentoring. The authors created the model to help researchers think intentionally about the primary domains of research variables in mentorships. These include: a) contextual or environmental factors (how do differing institutional contexts affect mentoring?); b) mentor characteristics (what impact docs personality, career or life stage of the mentor have on mentorships?); c) protégé characteristics (how does protégé gender, age, and personality impact selection by a mentor?); d) stage and duration of the mentorship (what events or changes bring about new stages in a mentorship?); and e) outcomes for mentor, protégé, and organization (how do the various parties benefit and how can mentoring be facilitated?).

O'Neil and Wrightsman's Sources of Variance Theory

In the early 1980s, O'Neil and Wrightsman (2001) proposed what is arguably the most complex and comprehensive model of student–faculty mentoring. Their Sources of Variance Theory of mentoring incorporates mentorship factors, parameters, correlates, and tasks. Primary factors underlying the mentoring construct include roles occupied by the mentor, personality characteristics, situational/environmental variables, and diversity variables. Relationship parameters include degree of mutuality or reciprocity, comprehensiveness or breadth of the relationship, congruence (degree of match between mentor and protégé's needs, values, and goals), and diversity sensitivity. Six correlates of mentoring then define, in interpersonal terms, what actually transpires between mentors and protégés (O'Neil & Wrightsman, 2001). Correlates of mentoring relationships include interpersonal respect, professionalism–collegiality, role-fulfillment, power, control, and competition. Finally, the authors identify six tasks of student–faculty mentorships. These are critical activities that define the working relationship and include making the critical entry decision, building mutual trust, taking risks, teaching skills, learning professional standards, and dissolving or changing the relationship.

Although there is little doubt that the Sources of Variance Model is among the most comprehensive and thoughtfully developed theories of mentorship in academe, the only empirical assessment of the model was a study by Busch (1985) of 537 education professors. In this study, two of O'Neil and Wrightsman's four components of mentoring were confirmed in factor analysis of a mentoring questionnaire. Specifically, mutuality and comprehensiveness emerged as distinct factors as well as a third factor labeled "career planning."

Other Theories

At least one study of student–faculty mentoring was based on the social psychological theory of perceived similarity. Turban, Dougherty, and Lee (2002) found that doctoral students were more likely to be in helpful mentorships with faculty advisors who were similar to them in both race and gender. Although race and gender did not influence the amount of career and psychosocial mentoring received, perceived similarity between mentor and protégé did. The authors concluded that identification and attraction are heightened between students and faculty members who are perceived as similar along demographic and personal dimensions. These findings support Byrne's Similarity-Attraction Paradigm (Byrne, 1997). Byrne's theory might offer an excellent foundation for research on initiation and formation of student–faculty mentorships. Finally, several authors refer to Bandura's (1977) social learning theory when offering a rationale for research on mentoring (Gibson, 2004; Jacobi, 1991; Speizer, 1981). These researchers often emphasize the salience of modeling in producing mentoring outcomes.

Methodological Approaches and Issues in Student–Faculty Mentoring Research

Mentoring in academic settings has been studied predominately from the protégé's perspective, via self-report questionnaires of unknown reliability and validity. These studies almost always use cross-sectional designs with small samples, making generalizability of findings questionable (Merriam, 1983; Noe et al., 2002). As in business settings, early research on student–faculty mentoring relied heavily on retrospective testimonials – rarely guided by a coherent theory of mentorship (Merriam, 1983). Most of this research has been quantitative in design, entailing the administration of a mailed questionnaire or survey (e.g., Atkinson, Neville, & Casas, 1991; Busch, 1985; Clark et al., 2000; Cronan-Hillix et al., 1986; Luna & Cullen, 1998; Wilde & Schau, 1991).

Notably, there has been little standardization of the questionnaires used in this research. Investigators have typically designed their own surveys for one-time use, often based solely on practical criteria and relying exclusively on content validity to guide item development or modification (e.g., Cochran et al., 2004; Cronan-Hillix et al., 1986). Most instruments have been modifications of existing surveys (e.g., Sprague, Roberts, & Kavussanu, 1997). The resulting heterogeneity of item sets across surveys makes generalizability of findings difficult. A few surveys have been based in a specific theory of mentoring (e.g., Busch, 1985; Luna & Cullen, 1998), or have been created using established principles of scale development (e.g., Rose, 2003; Wilde & Schau, 1991), but these efforts are the exception. Response rate for survey research in this area has been another source of concern in interpreting results. Survey return rates range from 9% (Young & Perrewé, 2000b) to 79% (Clark et al., 2000) with rates of 50% the norm (Atkinson et al., 1991; Cronan-Hillix et al., 1986; Tenenbaum et al., 2001). Arguably, such unsophisticated designs are appropriate for a field of study that is relatively young and whose conceptual basis is still being refined.

Existing research on mentoring has relied almost exclusively on protégé descriptions of mentors, rather than on individual self-reports of protégés' or mentors' behaviors (Crosby, 1999; Grant-Vallone & Ensher, 2000; Young & Perrewé, 2000b). Tapping a single perspective when researching a dyadic relationship poses obvious conceptual problems; we know comparatively little about how academic mentors experience mentorships with students. It is not clear whether protégé descriptions are objectively accurate portrayals of the actual behaviors exhibited by the mentor, or the extent to which the protégé's subjective perspective matches the mentor's perception of the relationship.

Two exceptions to this one-sided design are notable. Boyle and Boice (1998) reported results of an assigned mentoring program for graduate teaching assistants who were paired with experienced professors. The participants were asked to keep weekly logs of their meetings, and to submit to regular interviews with the program director. The logs and verbal descriptions of the relationship were rated by the director as to reciprocity in the conversation and the extent to which each member of the pair complied with program expectations. Another example of research involving more than just protégé report is Busch's (1985) survey of professors in education departments. Respondents were asked to rate their own mentoring behaviors and also those of their graduate students. Having self- and other-report offers the opportunity for comparisons in style and expectations, and enables investigations of mentor–protégé match and its impact on outcomes.

In addition to problems with measurement and perspective, the extant research on student–faculty mentoring suffers from problems with sampling, self-selection bias, and the probability of social desirability and halo effects in student responses. Sampling concerns were most evident in early surveys of graduate students regarding experience of the mentoring relationship (Cronan-Hillix et al., 1986; Kirchner, 1969). These studies were limited to graduates of one department in a single institution. Obviously, the results may be more reflective of specific academic cultures and institutions than mentorship broadly. Researchers are increasingly inclined to include students from a variety of departments and programs (e.g., Tenenbaum et al., 2001).

Another source of bias in mentoring survey research is the tendency to limit sampling frames to graduates or those students who were successful in a program. For example, the largest survey of mentoring experiences among graduate students to date sampled 787 recent clinical psychology doctorates, all of whom had successfully completed the doctoral degree (Clark et al., 2000). The sample did not include graduate students who attrite prior to degree completion. It is quite probable that unsuccessful students are less likely to be mentored, and when they are, less likely to report a positive mentoring experience.

Survey nonresponse is another source of bias in mentoring research (e.g., Merriam, 1983). It is reasonable to assume that the majority of those who respond to a questionnaire on mentoring are those with positive experiences to report. Thus satisfied protégés are likely to be over-represented in research samples (Atkinson et al., 1991). In fact, self-selection is likely to be at work in multiple ways (Baker, Hocevar, & Johnson, 2003). First, students who understand the value of mentoring are most likely to actively seek out faculty and initiate mentorships. Second, these same proactive students are most likely to respond to surveys and report positive experiences with faculty mentors: an outcome largely facilitated by their own initiative. For example, Thile and Matt (1995) noted that only a fraction of eligible minority students who received an invitation to participate in a formal mentoring program elected to participate. Ironically, those students who chose to participate may be the very ones least in need of additional guidance and those most prone, based on personal traits (e.g., self-efficacy, internal locus of control, achievement motivation), to achieve positive outcomes in a formal program. Finally, we are aware of no student–faculty mentoring research that has attempted to account for the effects of social desirability or halo effects in survey responses. Most studies asking students to rate mentor functions achieve universally positive function ratings – a positive cognitive halo effect may be stimulated by requests to consider one's "mentor." It may be preferable to clearly define mentoring, but then ask respondents to describe salient mentor behaviors or mentoring experiences in their own terms.

Student–faculty mentoring research has also suffered with lack of construct clarity and problematic assumptions about the nature of relationships between students and faculty based upon formal assigned roles. As noted earlier in this chapter, researchers have defined the *mentor* concept in widely divergent ways (Merriam, 1983; Ragins, 1999). Too frequently, respondents are asked to respond to a series of questions following a statement such as, "if you had a mentor," although no formal definition of the construct is offered (e.g., Atkinson et al., 1991). As Merriam (1983) cautioned, "to continue surveying the extent of mentoring without clarification as to what is being surveyed seems futile" (p. 171). In addition, researchers too often assume that a primary advisor or a dissertation chair is necessarily a mentor for a graduate student (Tenenbaum et al., 2001; Young & Perrewé, 2000b). In fact, only one half to two thirds of doctoral students report ever being mentored by a faculty member (Clark et al., 2000; Cronan-Hillix et al., 1986). Future research on student–faculty mentoring must avoid implicit assumptions about the nature of relationships stemming from assigned departmental roles.

A related set of methodological and definitional problems emerge when attempting to evaluate the outcomes of formal mentoring programs (cf. Thile & Matt, 1995). These institution-sponsored programs are often designed to promote student–faculty relationships and reduce attrition among students. Problematically, these programs often contain numerous components (e.g., formal orientations, personal invitations, training workshops, peer group meetings, individual meetings with an assigned faculty member, episodic evaluation), which differ across institutions, making it quite difficult to compare outcomes or assign effect to specific program ingredients.

Basic research on the prevalence, parameters, and satisfaction with student–faculty mentoring has been an important foundation for further questions about correlates of mentoring. The most common variables examined as correlates of mentoring are demographic, such as age, gender, and other personal variables (e.g., Aagaard & Hauer, 2003; Cronan-Hillix et al., 1986; Rose, 2005; Wilde & Schau, 1991), yet we know very little about the connection of salient diversity variables (e.g., race, ethnicity, sexual orientation) and mentorship experiences and outcomes (Erkut & Mokros, 1984; Crosby, 1999; Ragins, 1999).

Student developmental stage is another student variable rarely evaluated in student–faculty mentorship studies. Recently, Rose (2005) looked at the relationship between graduate students' developmental stages and their definitions of mentoring. The sample contained 537 doctoral students from varied disciplines at two Research I Universities. The study defined developmental stage according to Tinto's (1993) theoretical classification. Students in their first year were categorized as Stage 1 [Tinto's *Transition and Adjustment* stage, $n = 102$ (19%)]. Students from second year through attainment of candidacy (usually the result of passing comprehensive exams or a qualifying paper) were classified as Stage 2 [Tinto's *Attaining Candidacy* stage, $n = 170$ (32%)]. Those who were between candidacy and defense of the dissertation were classified as Stage 3 [Tinto's *Completing the Dissertation* stage, $n = 265$ (49%)]. Study results indicated that, contrary to expectation, no significant differences in ratings on the three Ideal Mentor Scale subscales (mentioned earlier in the chapter) were observed between students at different stages of progress toward the doctorate. Although it is likely that students at varying developmental stages benefit from different mentor functions, and though mentor functions are likely to manifest different characteristics at different stages, it appears that student views of ideal mentor characteristics remain steady over time.

A few researchers have examined relationships between mentoring received and career objectives or academic characteristics such as academic standing, academic discipline, educational climate in a department, productivity, or stage of training (e.g., Cronan-Hillix et al., 1986; Rose, 2005; Sprague et al., 1997; Tekian, Jalovecky, & Hruska, 2001). Preliminary findings suggest that subspecialties within a field (e.g., clinical versus experimental psychology) may predict differences in mentoring frequency and satisfaction (e.g., Cronan-Hillix et al., 1986; Johnson, Koch, Fallow, & Huwe, 2000). One particularly clever study examined the relationship between the quality of poster presented at a regional or national conference, and presence or absence of mentoring received in preparing the poster (Kring et al., 1999).

Cross-sectional correlational studies such as those cited above are a critical stepping-stone toward longitudinal research designs, which would enable more definitive conclusions about the predictors and outcomes of mentoring. One such study was conducted regarding academic advising. Green and Bauer (1995) studied 233 entering doctoral students at three time points over 2 years. They measured student academic potential at entry into the program, mentoring functions used by the faculty advisor at the end of the first year and the end of the second year, and student research productivity and commitment at the end of the second year. Results indicated that student potential predicted the amount of mentoring and collaboration provided by the advisor, but mentoring and collaboration were not related to later productivity or commitment on the part of the student once the students' entering abilities and attitudes were controlled. This result supports the idea that mentors are more inclined to informally mentor those who show "potential," and that it is the observed potential, rather than the mentoring provided, that predicts success outcomes. More studies like Green and Bauer's will help to elucidate the cause–effect relationships between protégé potential, informal mentoring, and positive outcomes.

Where to Go from Here I: Promising Theoretical Innovations

As the forgoing review of the state of student–faculty mentoring research suggests, there is clear need for more solid theoretical grounding and more thorough methodological rigor in explorations of mentoring in academe. In this section, we focus on several promising theoretical innovations in the field of developmental relationships. We encourage readers to clearly link research efforts to an established theoretical framework for both mentorship and other helping relationships in academic settings.

The Role-model–advising–Mentoring Continuum

Perhaps the most pressing conceptual/theoretical need in the field is more careful delineation of the kind of student–faculty relationship one is actually studying. We refer here to the distinctions between the often-mentioned roles of role model, advisor, and mentor. At least one author has suggested that these faculty roles exist on a continuum defined by degree of *intent* to shape and develop a student (Mertz, 2004). One might also place these faculty roles on a continuum defined by degree of involvement, relational reciprocity, level of emotional connection, or the extent to which the faculty member is deliberate in delivering role functions to a student. In the balance of this section, we briefly highlight the contours of each of these salient faculty roles. We encourage both faculty members and prospective researchers to think carefully about which role they occupy with specific students.

Nearly all undergraduate and graduate students can easily identify one or more *role models* among faculty in their program (Speizer, 1981). Role models display skills, techniques, career commitment, and professional behavior, but role modeling does not require a relationship. In fact, a faculty member may very well be unaware he or she is serving in this capacity for a student. Gibson (2004) conceptualized a role model as, "a cognitive construction based on the attributes of people in social roles an individual perceives to be similar to him or herself to some extent and desires to increase perceived similarity by emulating those attributes" (p. 136). When a faculty member becomes a role model, he or she may or may not know that students are intently observing and adopting many of the role model's behaviors, values, and attitudes. Gibson hypothesizes that role modeling is a healthy process during which students may selectively adopt and reject attributes of numerous faculty members.

In contrast to role modeling, which may or may not be intentional on the part of a faculty member, *advising* is a structured and assigned role in nearly every academic department (undergraduate and graduate) the country over. Expected to perform technical guidance functions (e.g., providing information on programs and degree requirements, monitoring advisee progress), the academic advisor (it is hoped) facilitates a student's progress through a program and serves as the student's primary contact point with the larger faculty (Johnson, 2006; Schlosser et al., 2005; Weil, 2001). Mertz (2004) notes that advising requires intent and some attentiveness to the academic needs of students.

Schlosser points out that most student–faculty relationships (especially those formally assigned) are most accurately described as advising relationships and that not all advising assignments develop into mentorships. "Advisors and mentors are not synonymous. One can be an advisor without being a mentor and certainly one can be a mentor to someone without being that person's advisor. It appears that far more students have advisors than mentors" (Schlosser & Gelso, 2001, p. 158).

The advisor is simply the faculty member who has the greatest responsibility for helping guide the advisee through the educational program. But while mentoring nearly always refers to a positive relationship focused on the faculty member's strong commitment to the protégé's broad development and success, advising refers to a relationship that may be positive, negative, or insignificant and which may or may not include guidance and skill development (Schlosser, Knox, Moskovitz, & Hill, 2003). Advising relationships that are successful, and in which the advisor and advisee become closer, more committed, and find the relationship more important, are most likely to evolve into mentorships.

Excellent mentoring relationships (mentorships) in graduate settings are dynamic, reciprocal, personal relationships in which a more experienced faculty mentor acts as a guide, role model, teacher, and sponsor of a less experienced student (protégé). Mentors provide a range of crucial career and relational functions to students and mentoring signifies intentional and generative career development in the context of an increasingly bonded and reciprocal relationship (Johnson, 2002). O'Neil and Wrightsman (2001) offered this summary of the distinctive components of the mentor role:

> A mentor is much more than an academic advisor. The mentor's values represent idealized norms that can have considerable influence on how mentees see themselves and the profession. . . . Mentees have various emotional responses to their mentors, including admiration, awe, fear, and idealization. Experiences with mentors can be impactful and remembered for many years. The mentor's power and influence on the mentee approximates the intensity that parents and children have with each other. (p. 112)

In sum, mentoring can be differentiated from other relatively discrete roles of the graduate school advisor (e.g., teaching, supervising, research oversight, advice-giving) in that mentoring signifies a strong relationship characterized by intentional and generative career development (Johnson, 2002; Schlosser et al., 2005). Mertz (2004) adds that mentors often provide deliberate brokering and advocacy in the service of the protégé's career development and occupational success.

Finally, D'Abate, Eddy, and Tannenbaum (2003) recently offered a *Taxonomy of Characteristics of Developmental Relationships*, as a broad model for conceptualizing any developmental interaction. Certainly, the taxonomy could incorporate role modeling, advising, and mentoring, but it offers even greater specificity along six distinct categories or dimensions. These include: a) participant demographics (e.g., age, knowledge level, career experience of participants), b) interaction characteristics (e.g., duration, frequency, medium, content), c) organizational distance (e.g., hierarchical distance, reporting relationship), d) purpose of interaction (e.g., object of development, beneficiaries of the development), e) degree of structure (e.g., formality, assignment, presence of a coordinator, choice to participate, matching process, provision of support or preparation), and f) behaviors exhibited (e.g., teaching, supporting, protecting, guiding, advocating). Whether researchers choose to specify and operationally define role modeling, advising, or mentoring for respondents, or whether they elect to elucidate some of the more specific characteristics of developmental relationships in academe using D'Abate et al.'s (2003) taxonomy, it is crucial that research efforts focus on highly defined relational forms.

Relationship Quality

Several authors have recently called for less focus on mere mentor functions, and greater emphasis on the quality and strength of student–faculty relationships. Liang, Tracy, Taylor, and Williams (2002) hypothesized that relational quality would be just as significant as discrete functions rendered when it came to influencing mentoring outcomes. In a sample of undergraduate women, the authors found that relational quality, defined by the presence of empathy, engagement, authenticity, and empowerment, significantly predicted lower levels of loneliness and higher levels of self-esteem. Liang et al. (2002) concluded that relational quality may be more meaningful than quantity or structure when it comes to psychosocial value for students.

In the area of advising relationships, Schlosser and Gelso (2001, 2005) created and validated a new measure designed to assess the advisor–advisee relationship in graduate school using the *working alliance* construct. The working alliance, first articulated for the therapist–client relationship in psychotherapy, was theorized to apply to all change-inducing relationships such as teacher–student, supervisor–trainee, and so forth (Bordin, 1983). Bordin theorized that the working alliance in therapy was composed of three parts: a) the agreement on the goals of therapy, b) the agreement on the tasks to be used to achieve said goals in therapy, and c) the emotional bond between therapist and client. Bordin also emphasized two other key aspects of the working alliance. First, the alliance was different from other relationships in that the alliance was formed around the *work* to be done. Second, mutuality was seen as an important aspect of the working alliance; thus, both members of the dyad co-construct their alliance.

Using this framework, Schlosser and Gelso developed two forms of their scale, the Advisory Working Alliance Inventory – Student Version (AWAI-S), and the Advisory Working Alliance Inventory – Advisor Version (AWAI-A). The results indicated that the advisory working alliance was related to a number of theoretically consistent outcomes (e.g., advisee research self-efficacy, advisee interest in science and practice, advisor costs and benefits for advising). The net result of this research was two scales with good initial estimates of reliability and validity with empirically derived subscales that fit well into Bordin's tripartite conceptualization of working alliance.

Relationship Constellations

Although nearly all student–faculty mentoring research focuses on what is termed the *traditional* or *primary* mentoring relationship (Merriam, 1983; Noe et al., 2002; Russell & Adams, 1997), many authors have recently called for a broader conceptualization of helping relationships in college or graduate school. While the traditional mentorship is an intense interpersonal helping relationship of long duration, these authors call for attention to the variety of developmental relationships, some traditional and others not, likely to be experienced by a student. Termed *relationship constellations* or *developmental networks* (Higgins & Kram, 2001; de Janasz & Sullivan, 2004; Kram, 1985), this cluster of helping relationships is described as, "the set of people a protégé names as taking an active interest in and action to advance the protégé's career by providing developmental assistance" (Higgins & Kram, 2001, p. 268). Because it is unlikely that any single mentor can adequately deliver every mentoring function or operate effectively in every critical role with a student, students should be open to the notion of benefiting from multiple faculty role models, advisors, mentors, supervisors, and peers. The concept of multiple mentoring appears to be supported by work relationship theories such as social support theory (Wills, 1991), social network theory (Morgan, Neal, & Carder, 1997), and social capital theory (Arthur & Rousseau, 1996). If students maintain developmental networks, then researchers must ask about a range of helpers and not assume that a protégé has but a single mentoring relationship. It is particularly important to understand networks and constellations when attempting to evaluate mentoring outcomes.

Student Development Models

A notable omission from existing writing and research on mentoring in academe is mention of specific theories of student or human development. Although there has been much discussion of the phases of mentorships (Kram, 1985), there is almost no mention of the developmental stages, tasks, and needs of students in relation to their mentors. Ironically, one of the most comprehensive and frequently cited models of development for young adults, Chickering's vector model of development, was published in 1969. Still, there has been little effort to understand or study student–faculty mentorship in light of student developmental factors. Chickering (1969) identified seven distinct factors or vectors of development for young adults. Each is a vector because it has a distinct magnitude and direction in the life of a student. These vectors include: a) achieving competence, b) managing emotions, c) becoming autonomous, d) establishing identity, e) experiencing freeing personal relationships, f) clarifying purpose, and g) developing integrity. Because each protégé might occupy different locations on each vector, it is reasonable to hypothesize that one's unique vector location might dictate which specific mentor traits and functions are most likely to aid in growth and development.

As one example of how Chickering's model might be explored, Rice and Brown (1990) looked at the relationship between autonomy and perceived readiness to be mentored among undergraduate students. They discovered a curvilinear relationship between these two variables. Students low in autonomy and high in autonomy reported the greatest readiness to be mentored while those at moderate levels appeared to turn inward or rebel in an effort to achieve autonomy.

Social Exchange Theories

Several theories broadly under the umbrella of social exchange bear greater attention in future student–faculty research efforts. Typically mentioned in organizational or business settings, these theories may have relevance for developmental relationships in academe. For example, leader–member exchange theory (Dansereau, Graen, & Haga, 1975) suggests that subordinates become members of either the supervisor's in-group (enjoying high-quality extra-work social exchange) or out-group (the relationship is limited to work-role interactions). In academe, this might be termed "advisor–advisee exchange theory" with in-group status equated with mentoring. Likewise, we expect that effective student–faculty mentorships will be characterized by high-quality and comprehensive exchanges.

Transformational leadership is another theory worth extrapolating to the mentor–protégé dyad (Sosik & Godshalk, 2004). It appears that transformational leadership includes several behaviors characteristic of good mentoring. These include: a) building trust by exhibiting idealized influence behaviors, b) striving to develop followers through individualized consideration, c) promoting protégé's independence and critical thinking, and d) inspirational motivation. Not only would transformational leaders appear to be strong mentors, but Sosik and Godshalk (2004) discovered that the most effective leaders were also humble – those who underestimated their own transformational behaviors were evaluated as most effective by followers.

Another area meriting attention in student–faculty mentorship theory and research is organizational citizenship behavior (cf. McManus & Russell, 1997; Noe et al., 2002). Because mentors are typically committed to helping their protégés, and because this commitment is not a job requirement (perhaps beyond the essential tasks of advising), mentoring can be construed as a form of prosocial or positive organizational citizenship behavior. Research in this area would be concerned with why college professors engage in mentoring; what motives drive this altruistic behavior in relationships with students? Allen (2003) has initiated such a line of research in organizational settings. In her study of dispositional and motivational factors predicting mentoring among managers, Allen found that prosocial personality characteristics predicted mentorship behavior, and that mentors often had a variety of motivations for being mentors, and that these motivations influenced specific functions delivered.

Computer-mediated Mentoring

A final area requiring greater attention in subsequent scholarship on student–faculty mentoring has to do with the changing modalities of mentor–protégé interaction. Increasingly, students and faculty are engaging in extensive e-mail dialogue – either to augment or in some cases replace traditional face-to-face interaction. Termed "e-mentoring" by some authors, such mentoring is defined as: "a computer mediated, mutually beneficial relationship between a mentor and a protégé" (Bierema & Merriam, 2002, p. 214). With the advent of numerous online mentoring services, an increase in distance learning opportunities for students, and the emergence of e-mail as a primary method of communication in academe, it will be essential for researchers to consider the implications (e.g., effects on relational intimacy, commitment, and frequency of misunderstanding) of increasing use of computers in mentorships (Bierema & Merriam, 2002; Ensher, Heun, & Blanchard, 2003).

Where to Go from Here II: Methodological Recommendations

Our review of the student–faculty mentoring literature shows that the field exists in a state of developmental adolescence. Although many of the characteristics, qualities, and outcomes of mentoring in academe are similar to those in other organizations, there are unique contextual factors requiring careful attention and theoretical elaboration. Nearly all of the research on student–faculty mentorships involves retrospective survey-based self-reports from the perspective of former undergraduate or graduate students; efforts to explore existing mentor–protégé relationships are nonexistent (Clark et al., 2000). The extant research on role modeling, advising, and mentoring in academe has largely been mono-method and cross-sectional in nature. Research that incorporates multimethod and longitudinal approaches is sorely needed. This is particularly true in light of the influence of relationship duration on advising and mentoring outcomes (Schlosser & Gelso, 2001). In this final section of the chapter, we offer several brief but salient recommendations for researchers of student–faculty developmental relationships. As this field continues to develop, we hope to spur advances in the sophistication of research design and methodology.

Define Constructs

Researchers must settle on a uniformly accepted definition of mentoring. Because there is such a range of developmental relationships in academe, researchers must clarify the type of relationship they are studying. Whatever construct or term is employed, it is imperative that research participants have a definition of the term in order to reduce idiosyncratic interpretations (Ragins, 1999). It is also important to assume that participants have had multiple mentorships and therefore to ask them to focus in on a particular relationship versus mentoring in the abstract.

Evaluate Academic Mentorships from Multiple Perspectives

Because nearly all of the extant research considers mentoring experiences exclusively from the protégé's perspective, we join researchers in organizational settings in calling for greater attention to other data sources (Noe et al., 2002; Ragins, 1999). Not only should researchers consider the perspective and experience of faculty advisors and mentors, but data from other members of the academic community (other students and faculty) might also illuminate these relationships. Multilevel designs and cross-over analyses would allow consideration of mentor and protégé perspectives within a single study. Tapping multiple perspectives is particularly important because students, faculty, and administrators may hold disparate views about the frequency and quality of mentorships. At least one survey showed that program directors tend to offer inflated estimates of the frequency of mentoring in doctoral programs (Dickinson & Johnson, 2000) when compared with recent program graduates (Clark et al., 2000).

Although advisors and mentors are frequently viewed as pivotal to a student's graduate school experience (Clark et al., 2000; Schlosser & Gelso, 2001; Schlosser et al., 2003), advising and mentoring relationships have not been found to be uniformly central to the experience of faculty (Knox, Schlosser, Pruitt, & Hill, 2006). One reason for this disparity in perceived importance is the fact that not all faculty serve as advisors or mentors. This distinction makes sense given that the purpose of the advising relationship is to facilitate the advisee's progress through the graduate program; any benefits accrued to the advisor as a result, while probably relationship enhancing, are secondary. However, this difference might also affect aspects of research methodology (e.g., response rate) and results (e.g., smaller correlations between advising relationship and relevant outcomes when rated by advisors than by advisees).

It is further recommended that researchers focus on active mentoring dyads so that more useful information regarding relationship variables can be obtained. As research moves beyond simple outcome variables to process and exchange variables, we will better understand the dynamics of mentorship (Young & Perrewé, 2000b). Evidence for the salience of these factors comes from studies showing that the interpersonal dimensions of research mentoring carry significantly more meaning than the instructional dimensions (cf. Gelso, Mallinckrodt, & Judge, 1996). As such, it would be particularly useful to employ matched-pairs designs. For example, Campbell and Campbell (1997) matched 339 undergraduate participants in a formal mentoring program with control students matched on the basis of gender, year in school, race, and grade point average (GPA).

Recognize that Mentorships are Context-specific

It is essential to acknowledge that developmental relationships are context-specific (Green & Bauer, 1995; Schlosser et al., 2003). As such, advising and mentoring relationships will look different across levels of education (i.e., undergraduate versus graduate). Research on academic developmental relationships (Knox et al., 2006; Schlosser & Gelso, 2005, 2001; Schlosser et al., 2003) has focused on the doctoral-level experience because advisors are typically more invested in doctoral students than master's students or undergraduates. Since advisors work with their doctoral advisees for the longest period of time and the most intensively, it follows that they are likely to invest the greatest energy in these students. Greater attention to the mentoring experiences of undergraduates, master's degree, professional school, and other nontraditional and nondoctoral populations is required.

Even within doctoral programs, context variations can dramatically shape advising and mentoring experiences and outcomes. For example, Clark et al. (2000) found that clinical psychologists from traditional PhD programs were significantly more likely to be mentored than graduates of practitioner (PsyD) programs, and those from university-based programs enjoyed higher levels of mentoring than those from free-standing professional schools. Further, even within a specific field, students in various subspecialties might experience distinctly different kinds of advising and mentoring. For example, experimental psychologists are significantly more likely to have a faculty mentor than clinical psychologists during graduate school (Cronan-Hillix et al., 1986; Johnson et al., 2000).

Employ Innovative Sampling Techniques and Research Designs

Most student–faculty mentoring research is limited to protégé perspectives. When mentors are included, researchers generally make the implicit assumption that all faculty in a program, or all faculty who advise students, are active in the mentoring enterprise. Of course, this is not true, nor is it true that all faculty are particularly competent in the mentor role. Alternative sampling approaches might help narrow our research focus to outstanding or *exemplar* mentors. For example, Jennings and Skovholt (1999) used a purposeful sampling strategy called snowball sampling to identify and interview 10 exemplar "master psychotherapists." Using this technique, people in a community are asked to identify information-rich key informants. Individuals who are repeatedly named by a variety of informants constitute the core subject pool. Extending this sampling technique to mentoring would involve asking members of a professional organization or students within a university to identify gifted or excellent "master mentors." In a similar vein, Zuckerman (1977) focused her study of developmental relationships between eminent scientists by limiting her sample to Nobel Prize winners. Seeking mentoring exemplars should offer stronger representation of the construct of interest; studying the attitudes, behaviors, and knowledge of clearly successful mentors would help to increase the validity of ideal mentor profiles. Such exemplar techniques should also reduce the number of respondents required for drawing valid conclusions.

Few researchers have taken advantage of analogue designs in mentoring research. Analogue designs present vignettes, cases, or descriptions of hypothetical mentors and ask respondents to offer ratings or reactions. In a series of three experimental studies regarding the factors making a mentor attractive to a student, Olian, Carroll, Giannantonio, and Feren (1988) provided undergraduates with vignettes involving hypothetical mentors. Variables such as gender, age, and interpersonal competence were varied and showed that interpersonal competence was consistently viewed as more important to students than other demographic factors. Analogue designs help to minimize confounding effects due to the idiosyncrasies of real-life mentors, protégés, and organizations; they offer an efficient means to explore new research questions.

Finally, qualitative research designs are largely ignored in research on student–faculty mentoring. An exception is the work of Schlosser and colleagues on advising relationships. These authors employed Consensual Qualitative Research (CQR; Hill, Thompson, & Williams, 1997) in two research projects undertaken to examine the advising relationship in graduate school (Knox et al., 2006; Schlosser et al., 2003). The advantage of qualitative methods is that they allow participants to share their thoughts on these important and complex relationships in their own words.

CQR represents a newer, yet methodologically rigorous approach to qualitative research in that it employs several judges and at least one auditor; this is done to reduce the influence of any one researcher on the data analysis. In addition, CQR uses a consistent, yet flexible approach to the interview (i.e., participants are all asked the same core set of questions, while the interviewer is free to probe based on the participants' responses). Given the relative infancy of the research on mentoring relationships, CQR and other qualitative approaches can and should be used to facilitate theory development, which can then be tested empirically.

Control Variables and Covariate Analyses

A final recommendation for researchers is that there be greater attention to both accounting for and controlling potentially confounding covariates of mentoring relationships and their outcomes (Noe et al., 2002; Ragins, 1999). Such variables might include age, race, gender, rank, experience in the mentor or protégé role, relationship duration, context for relationship formation (formal versus informal), status or tenure of mentor, size and type of educational institution, and number of prior developmental relationships. Obviously, each of these variables could confound both prevalence and outcome findings relative to mentoring. By matching participants, or eliminating the effects of these control variables statistically, future mentoring research might offer more robust and meaningful findings.

Conclusion

Practiced for millennia, student–faculty mentorships have only recently become the focus of research efforts. Mentoring has not been clearly differentiated from other common faculty roles, such as role modeling and advising, and few studies are rooted in a coherent theory of mentor relationships. The modal student–faculty mentoring study is based on a retrospective survey of mentoring experience from the protégé's perspective. The survey is typically constructed subjectively from an amalgam of previous questionnaires (of unknown reliability and validity) and the mentoring construct is rarely defined consistently across studies. In order to move this area of research forward, we recommend that researchers clearly differentiate mentoring from other student–faculty roles and remain cognizant of relationship quality, multiple sources of mentoring, student development variables, and existing theories bearing on social exchange. Methodologically, we encourage future researchers to operationally define mentorship, evaluate mentorships from multiple perspectives, consider contextual variables, employ a wider range of sampling techniques and research designs, and consider the value of including control variables and covariate analyses.

References

Aagaard, E. M., & Hauer, K. E. (2003). A cross-sectional descriptive study of mentoring relationships formed by medical students. *Journal of General Internal Medicine, 18*, 298–302.

Allen, T. D. (2003). Mentoring others: A dispositional and motivational approach. *Journal of Vocational Behavior, 62*, 134–154.

Arthur, M. B., & Rousseau, D. M. (Eds.). (1996). *The boundaryless career: A new employment principle for a new organization era.* New York: Oxford University Press.

Atkinson, D. R., Neville, H., & Casas, A. (1991). The mentorship of ethnic minorities in professional psychology. *Professional Psychology: Research and Practice, 22*, 336–338.

Baker, B. T., Hocevar, S. P., & Johnson, W. B. (2003). The prevalence and nature of service academy mentoring: A study of navy midshipmen. *Military Psychology, 15*, 273–283.

Bandura, A. (1977). *Social learning theory.* Englewood Cliffs, NJ: Prentice-Hall.

Bierema, L. L., & Merriam, S. B. (2002). E-mentoring: Using computer mediated communication (CMC) to enhance the mentoring process. *Innovative Higher Education, 26*, 211–227.

Bordin, E. S. (1983). A working alliance based model of supervision. *The Counseling Psychologist, 11*, 27–34.

Boyle, P., & Boice, B. (1998). Systematic mentoring for new faculty teachers and graduate teaching assistants. *Innovative Higher Education, 22*, 157–179.

Busch, J. W. (1985). Mentoring in graduate schools of education: Mentors' perceptions. *American Educational Research Journal, 22*, 257–265.

Byrne, D. (1997). An overview (and underview) of research and theory within the attraction paradigm. *Journal of Social and Personal Relationships, 14*, 417–431.

Campbell, T. A., & Campbell, D. E. (1997). Faculty/student mentor program: Effects on academic performance and retention. *Research in Higher Education, 38*, 727–742.

Chickering, A. W. (1969). *Education and identity.* San Francisco: Jossey-Bass.

Clark, R. A., Harden, S. L., & Johnson, W. B. (2000). Mentor relationships in clinical psychology doctoral training: Results of a national survey. *Teaching of Psychology, 27*, 262–268.

Cochran, A., Paukert, J. L., Scales, E. M., & Neumayer, L. A. (2004). How medical students define surgical mentors. *American Journal of Surgery, 187*, 698–701.

Cronan-Hillix, T., Gensheimer, L. K., Cronan-Hillix, W. A., & Davidson, W. S. (1986). Students' views of mentors in psychology graduate training. *Teaching of Psychology, 13*, 123–127.

Crosby, F. J. (1999). The developing literature on developmental relationships. In A. J. Murrell, F. J. Crosby, & R. J. Ely (Eds.), *Mentoring dilemmas: Developmental relationships within multicultural organizations* (pp. 3–20). Mahwah, NJ: Lawrence Erlbaum.

D'Abate, C. P., Eddy, E. R., & Tannenbaum, S. I. (2003). What's in a name? A literature-based approach to understanding mentoring, coaching, and other constructs that describe developmental interactions. *Human Resource Development Review*, *2*, 360–384.

Dansereau, F., Graen, G., & Haga, W. J. (1975). A vertical dyad approach to leadership within formal organizations. *Organizational Behavior and Human Performance*, *13*, 46–78.

Dickinson, S. C., & Johnson, W. B. (2000). Mentoring in clinical psychology doctoral programs: A national survey of directors of training. *The Clinical Supervisor*, *19*(1), 137–152.

Ensher, E. A., Heun, C., & Blanchard, A. (2003). Online mentoring and computer-mediated communication: New directions in research. *Journal of Vocational Behavior*, *63*, 264–288.

Erkut, S., & Mokros, J. R. (1984). Professors as models and mentors for college students. *American Educational Research Journal*, *21*, 399–417.

Gelso, C. J., Mallinckrodt, B., & Judge, A. B. (1996). Research training environments, attitudes toward research, and research self-efficacy: The revised Research Training Environment Scale. *The Counseling Psychologist*, *24*, 304–322.

Gibson, D. E. (2004). Role models in career development: New directions for theory and research. *Journal of Vocational Behavior*, *65*, 134–156.

Gilbert, L. A. (1985). Dimensions of same-gender student–faculty role-model relationships. *Sex Roles*, *12*, 111–123.

Grant-Vallone, E. J., & Ensher, E. A. (2000). Effects of peer mentoring on types of mentor support, program satisfaction and graduate student stress: A dyadic perspective. *Journal of College Student Development*, *41*, 637–642.

Green, S. G., & Bauer, T. N. (1995). Supervisory mentoring by advisers: Relationships with doctoral student potential, productivity, and commitment. *Personnel Psychology*, *48*, 537–561.

Higgins, M. C., & Kram, K. E. (2001). Reconceptualizing mentoring at work: A developmental network perspective. *Academy of Management Review*, *26*, 264–288.

Hill, C. E., Thompson, B. J., & Williams, E. N. (1997). A guide to conducting consensual qualitative research. *The Counseling Psychologist*, *25*, 517–572.

Hunt, D. M., & Michael, C. (1983). Mentorship: A career training and development tool. *Academy of Management Review*, *8*, 475–485.

Jacobi, M. (1991). Mentoring and undergraduate academic success: A literature review. *Review of Educational Research*, *61*, 505–532.

de Janasz, S. C., & Sullivan, S. E. (2004). Multiple mentoring in academe: Developing the professorial network. *Journal of Vocational Behavior*, *64*, 263–283.

Jennings, L., & Skovholt, T. M. (1999). The cognitive, emotional, and relational characteristics of master therapists. *Journal of Counseling Psychology*, *46*, 3–11.

Johnson, W. B. (2002). The intentional mentor: Strategies and guidelines for the practice of mentoring. *Professional Psychology: Research and Practice*, *33*, 88–96.

Johnson, W. B. (2006). *On being a mentor: A guide for higher education faculty*. Mahwah, NJ: Lawrence Erlbaum.

Johnson, W. B., Koch, C., Fallow, G. O., & Huwe, J. M. (2000). Prevalence of mentoring in clinical versus experimental doctoral programs: Survey findings, implications, and recommendations. *Psychotherapy*, *37*, 325–334.

Kirchner, E. P. (1969). Graduate education in psychology: Retrospective views of advanced degree recipients. *Journal of Clinical Psychology*, *25*, 207–213.

Knox, S., Schlosser, L. Z., Pruitt, N., & Hill, C. E. (2006). A qualitative study of the graduate advising relationship: The advisor perspective. *The Counseling Psychologist*, *34*, 489–518.

Kram, K. E. (1985). *Mentoring at work: Developmental relationships in organizational life*. Glenview, IL: Scott, Foresman and Company.

Kring, J. P., Richardson, T. R., Burns, S. R., & Davis, S. F. (1999). Do mentors influence the appearance and content of student posters at regional and national conferences? *College Student Journal*, *33*, 278–280.

Levinson, D. J., Darrow, C. N., Klein, E. B., Levinson, M. H., & McKee, B. (1978). *The seasons of a man's life*. New York: Knopf.

Liang, B., Tracy, A. J., Taylor, C. A., & Williams, L. M. (2002). Mentoring college-age women: A relational approach. *American Journal of Community Psychology, 30*, 271–288.

Luna, G., & Cullen, D. (1998). Do graduate students need mentoring? *College Student Journal, 32*, 322–330.

McManus, S. E., & Russell, J. E. A. (1997). New directions for mentoring research: An examination of related constructs. *Journal of Vocational Behavior, 51*, 145–161.

Merriam, S. B. (1983). Mentors and protégés: A critical review of the literature. *Adult Education Quarterly, 33*, 161–173.

Mertz, N. T. (2004). What's a mentor anyway? *Educational Administration Quarterly, 40*, 541–560.

Morgan, D. L., Neal, M. B., & Carder, P. (1997). The stability of core and peripheral networks over time. *Social Networks, 19*, 9–25.

Noe, R. A., Greenberger, D. B., & Wang, S. (2002). Mentoring: What we know and where we might go from here. In G. R. Ferris & J. J. Martocchio (Eds.), *Research in Personnel and Human Resources Management* (Vol. 21, pp. 129–173). Greenwich, CT: Elsevier Science/JAI Press.

Olian, J. D., Carroll, S. J., Giannantonio, C. M., & Feren, D. B. (1988). What do protégés look for in a mentor? Results of three experimental studies. *Journal of Vocational Behavior, 33*, 15–37.

O'Neil, J. M., & Wrightsman, L. S. (2001). The mentoring relationship in psychology training programs. In S. Walfish & A. K. Hess (Eds.), *Succeeding in graduate school: The career guide for psychology students* (pp. 113–129). Mahwah, NJ: Lawrence Erlbaum.

Paludi, M. A., Waite, B., Roberson, R. H., & Jones, L. (1988). Mentors vs. role models: Toward a clarification of terms. *International Journal of Mentoring, 2*, 20–25.

Ragins, B. R. (1999). Where do we go from here, and how do we get there? Methodological issues in conducting research on diversity and mentoring relationships. In A. J. Murrell, F. J. Crosby, & R. J. Ely (Eds.), *Mentoring dilemmas: Developmental relationships within multicultural organizations* (pp. 227–247). Mahwah, NJ: Lawrence Erlbaum.

Rice, M. B., & Brown, R. D. (1990). Developmental factors associated with self-perceptions of mentoring competence and mentoring needs. *Journal of College Student Development, 31*, 293–299.

Roberts, P., & Newton, P. M. (1987). Levinsonian studies of women's adult development. *Psychology and Aging, 2*, 154–163.

Rose, G. L. (2003). Enhancement of mentor selection using the Ideal Mentor Scale. *Research in Higher Education, 44*, 473–494.

Rose, G. L. (2005). Group differences in graduate students' concepts of the ideal mentor. *Research in Higher Education, 46*, 53–80.

Russell, J. E. A., & Adams, D. M. (1997). The changing nature of mentoring in organizations: An introduction to the special issue on mentoring in organizations. *Journal of Vocational Behavior, 51*, 1–14.

Schlosser, L. Z., & Gelso, C. J. (2001). Measuring the working alliance in advisor–advisee relationships in graduate school. *Journal of Counseling Psychology, 48*, 157–167.

Schlosser, L. Z., & Gelso, C. J. (2005). The Advisory Working Alliance Inventory – Advisor Version: Scale development and validation. *Journal of Counseling Psychology, 52*, 650–654.

Schlosser, L. Z., Knox, S., Moskovitz, A. R., & Hill, C. E. (2003). A qualitative study of the graduate advising relationship: The advisee perspective. *Journal of Counseling Psychology, 50*, 178–188.

Schlosser, L. Z., Lyons, H. Z., Talleyrand, R. M., Kim, B. S. K., & Johnson, W. B. (2005). *Advisor–advisee relationships in counseling psychology doctoral Programs: Toward a multicultural theory.* Manuscript submitted for publication.

Sosik, J. J., & Godshalk, V. M. (2004). Self-other rating agreement in mentoring: Meeting protégé expectations for development and career advancement. *Group and Organization Management, 29,* 442–469.

Speizer, J. J. (1981). Role models, mentors, and sponsors: The elusive concepts. *Journal of Women in Culture and Society, 6,* 692–712.

Sprague, R. L., Roberts, G. C., & Kavussanu, M. (1997). *Sources of ethical beliefs in their discipline: Faculty vs. graduate students.* Paper presented at the annual meeting of the Association for Practical and Professional Ethics, St. Louis, MO.

Tekian, A., Jalovecky, M. J., & Hruska, L. (2001). The impact of mentoring and advising at-risk underrepresented minority students on medical school performance. *Academic Medicine, 76,* 1264.

Tenenbaum, H. R., Crosby, F. J., & Gliner, M. D. (2001). Mentoring relationships in graduate school. *Journal of Vocational Behavior, 59,* 326–341.

Thile, E. L., & Matt, G. E. (1995). The ethnic minority undergraduate program: A brief description and preliminary findings. *Journal of Multicultural Counseling and Development, 23,* 116–126.

Tinto, V. (1993). *Leaving college: Rethinking the causes and cures of student attrition* (2nd ed.). Chicago: University of Chicago Press.

Turban, D. B., Dougherty, T. W., & Lee, F. K. (2002). Gender, race, and perceived similarity effects in developmental relationships: The moderating role of relationship duration. *Journal of Vocational Behavior, 61,* 240–262.

Weil, V. (2001). Mentoring: Some ethical considerations. *Science and Engineering Ethics, 7,* 471–482.

Wilde, J. B., & Schau, C. G. (1991). Mentoring in graduate schools of education: Mentees' perceptions. *Journal of Experimental Education, 59,* 165–179.

Wills, T. A. (1991). Social support and interpersonal relationship. *Review of Personality and Social Psychology, 12,* 265–289.

Young, A. M., & Perrewé, P. L. (2000b). What did you expect? An examination of career-related support and social support among mentors and protégés. *Journal of Management, 26,* 611–632.

Zuckerman, H. (1977). *Scientific elite: Nobel laureates in the United States.* New York: The Free Press.

Chapter 5

Workplace Mentoring: Theoretical Approaches and Methodological Issues

Terri A. Scandura and Ekin K. Pellegrini

Although mentoring relations can be traced back to Greek mythology (i.e., the relationship between Mentor and Telemachus), organizational mentoring has gained the attention of academicians and practitioners only within the past two decades. The majority of the research on mentoring in the workplace has been published in the past 25 years following the seminal works of Levinson, Darrow, Klein, Levinson, and McKee (1978) and Kram (1983, 1985). These early studies suggested that mentoring plays a key role in successful career development (Kram, 1985; Roche, 1979; Vertz, 1985).

The purpose of this chapter is to provide mentoring scholars with a review of key theories and methods used in organizational mentoring research. While reviewing existing approaches, we will discuss both the limitations associated with current research and new directions for future research. First, we will review the key streams of thought in mentoring theory that have guided research, including the traditional definition of mentoring and other theories related to mentoring. This is followed by discussions of potential problems in mentoring relationships (e.g., marginal mentoring, dysfunctional mentoring) and new forms of mentoring (e.g., team mentoring, e-mentoring). Next, we will address the theoretical limitations in the study of mentoring and suggest new directions for future mentoring research. Lastly, we will review major methodological approaches in the study of workplace mentoring, followed by a discussion of their limitations.

Streams of Thought in Mentoring Theory

Traditional Mentoring Theory

Levinson et al. (1978) described the mentor's function as guide, counselor, and sponsor. Ragins and Scandura (1999, p. 496) referred to mentors as "influential individuals with advanced experience and knowledge who are committed to providing upward mobility and support to their protégés' careers." These early definitions distinguished traditional mentoring relations from other developmental relationships in the workplace by incorporating dimensions such as the power of the mentor, the emotional intensity of the relationship, the hierarchical distance between the mentor and the protégé, and the amount and focus of assistance provided by the more senior person (Wanberg, Welsh, & Hezlett, 2003).

More recently, new theoretical models of mentoring have emerged such as team and network mentoring. As evident in these new models, the definition of the mentoring construct has evolved considerably from the original face-to-face, single, dyadic, hierarchical relation suggested by Levinson et al. (1978) and Kram (1983, 1985) to online relationships sustained primarily through electronic means (Hamilton & Scandura, 2003), team mentoring relations where the team leader mentors members and team members mentor each other (Williams, 2000), multiple mentoring with one protégé having multiple sequential mentoring relations (Baugh & Scandura, 1999), and mentoring where one protégé has a constellation of different mentors at one point in time (Higgins & Kram, 2001).

Mapping the Domain of the Mentoring Construct

Much early theoretical work was devoted to articulating the functions and roles of mentors. For example, the types of assistance provided by the mentor that contribute to the protégé's development were referred to as *mentoring functions.* In her study of 18 developmental relationships in a large public utility, Kram (1983) identified two broad categories of mentoring functions: career development and psychological support. Career functions aid career advancement and may include sponsorship, coaching, exposure, visibility, protection, and providing challenging assignments. Psychosocial functions enhance the protégé's sense of competence, clarity of identity, and effectiveness in the job through role modeling, counseling, and friendship. In effect, career development functions focus on the protégé's career advancement whereas psychosocial functions help a protégé's personal development by relating to him or her on a more personal level. Kram (1985) suggested that the greater the number of functions provided by the mentor, the more beneficial the relationship will be to the protégé. Thus, mentoring is not an all or none phenomenon; rather, a given mentor may provide just some of these functions (Ragins & Cotton, 1999).

Kram's conceptualization of mentoring as a two-dimensional (career and psychosocial) construct received empirical support in later studies (Ensher & Murphy, 1997; Noe, 1988; Tepper, Shaffer, & Tepper, 1996). However, some researchers conceptualize mentor functions slightly differently. While Kram described role modeling as a form of psychosocial support, in subsequent studies conducted by Burke (1984) and Scandura and colleagues (Scandura, 1992; Scandura & Ragins, 1993; Scandura & Viator, 1994) role modeling emerged as a distinct mentoring function. In addition, Ragins and McFarlin (1990) suggested 11 mentor roles, including coaching, protection, sponsorship, exposure and visibility, challenging assignments, role modeling, acceptance and confirmation, counseling, friendship, social role, and parent role. To date, only one published study tested the factor structure of the 11-dimension scale (Ragins & McFarlin, 1990), and according to Castro and Scandura (2004) minimal support exists for the concurrent validity of this measure.

Integration of Mentoring and Leadership Theory

Prior to examining the nomological network of mentoring functions (career, psycho-social, and role modeling), it is important to clarify the construct and study how mentoring differs from other developmental relationships in the workplace, such as supervision and leadership. For example, according to leader–member exchange (LMX) theory, leaders differentiate among followers rather than enacting one leadership style with all members (Dansereau, Graen, & Haga, 1975; Graen, Liden, & Hoel, 1982). Some employees enjoy high-quality exchanges with their manager, characterized by a high degree of mutual trust, respect, and obligation ("in-group"), whereas others experience low-quality exchanges, where the employee fulfills job description requirements, but contributes nothing extra; the relationship remains within the bounds of the employment contract ("out-group") (Graen & Uhl-Bien, 1995). Research has determined that LMX quality is related to an array of positive outcomes, including satisfaction with work, satisfaction with supervision, promotion, salary, performance, organizational commitment, and willingness to contribute (Gerstner & Day, 1997; Keller & Dansereau, 1995; Liden, Sparrowe, & Wayne, 1997; Scandura & Schriesheim, 1994; Wakabayashi, Graen, & Uhl-Bien, 1990).

According to Liden, Wayne, and Stilwell (1993), in-group and out-group membership is determined quite early in supervisor–subordinate relationships whereas mentoring relationships may take longer to develop. Thus, as Graen and Scandura (1987) suggested, obtaining in-group status may be a prerequisite for subordinates to receive mentoring from their supervisors (McManus & Russell, 1997). While in-group status may be necessary for mentoring to occur, Scandura and Schriesheim (1994) found LMX and supervisory career mentoring (i.e., Kram's career-related mentoring) to be different constructs. Schriesheim and Castro (1995) also found that protégés were able to differentiate between leader–member exchange (LMX) and mentoring relationships. Scandura and Schriesheim (1994) concluded that exchange relationships (LMX) focus on providing the positional resources necessary for positive short-term career outcomes, such as performance appraisal ratings. However, mentoring relationships are developmental and therefore may be more related to long-term outcomes, such as salary and promotion.

In further differentiating LMX and mentoring, Scandura and Schriesheim (1994) conceptualized LMX relations as being transactional and mentoring relations as transformational, with the latter involving mutual commitment to the protégé's long-term development. According to Yukl (1989), transformational leaders transform or change followers by using personal resources, such as time, knowledge, and experience. They are involved in "serving as a coach, teacher, and mentor" (Yukl, 1989, p. 211). Transactional leaders, on the other hand, pursue a cost–benefit exchange approach that does not change subordinates and uses positional (organizational) resources in return for contracted services rendered by the subordinate (Bass, 1985). Scandura and Schriesheim (1994) suggest that high ratings on LMX quality may not necessarily imply that a supervisor is committed to the long-term development of a subordinate. Further, Scandura and Williams (2004) found that mentoring mediated the relationship between transformational leadership and career expectations. This finding supports Sosik and Godshalk's (2000a) suggestion that transformational leadership behaviors displayed by mentors may facilitate mentoring via building the protégé's self-confidence.

Another leadership construct which should be differentiated from mentoring is paternalistic leadership. Paternalism is an emerging area in leadership research and refers to managers' personal interest in workers' off-the-job lives and attempts to promote workers' personal welfare (Pasa, Kabasakal, & Bodur, 2001). In paternalistic cultures, people in authority assume the role of parents and consider it an obligation to provide protection to others under their care. Subordinates, in turn, reciprocate by showing loyalty, deference, and compliance. Following Graen and Uhl-Bien's (1995) taxonomy, the primary distinction between paternalism and mentoring may be conceptualized as differences in leader-based versus follower-based leadership domains. The leader-based domain studies the appropriate behavior of the person in the leader role. Paternalistic leadership is an example of the leader-based approach as it examines leader behaviors such as being interested in every aspect of employees' lives, making decisions on behalf of employees without asking for their approval, and participating in employees' special days (e.g., weddings, funerals). The follower-based domain studies "ability and motivation to manage one's own performance" (Graen & Uhl-Bien, 1995, p. 224). Mentoring illustrates this approach through its focus on protégé skill development. Another distinction between mentoring and paternalism is that paternalism is a dyadic relationship between a more powerful leader and a follower, whereas mentoring relations may be dyadic, team, or network relations. Finally, with respect to the employee's freedom in making decisions, in paternalistic leadership, decision-making is directive rather than empowering (Uhl-Bien & Maslyn, 2005). In contrast, in a mentoring relationship, the decision-making is participative whereby the protégé learns the ropes of the organization and/or attains management skills through participating in the decision-making process alongside the mentor.

Temporal Theories of Mentoring

Since the inception of mentoring theory, the concept of time has been considered to be an important component of mentoring relationships. According to Kram (1983), although developmental relations such as mentoring vary in length, they generally proceed through four predictable phases. The relationship gets started in the *initiation* phase during which the mentor and the protégé start learning each other's personal style and work habits. Kram (1983) suggested that this stage lasts 6 months to 1 year. If the relationship matures into a mentorship, it then progresses to the *cultivation* phase. During this stage, which may last anywhere from 2 to 5 years, the protégé learns from the mentor and advances in his or her career. The mentor promotes the protégé through developing the protégé's performance, potential, and visibility within the organization (Chao, 1997). The protégé gains knowledge while the mentor gains the loyalty and support of the protégé along with a sense of well-being from passing on knowledge to the next generation (Levinson et al., 1978). This is considered to be the stage of mentorship during which most benefits accrue to the mentor and the protégé (Scandura & Hamilton, 2002). As noted by Scandura (1998), mentoring research has largely focused on issues in the cultivation phase.

As the protégé outgrows the relationship and becomes more independent, the structure of the relation begins to change. This signifies the *separation* phase which involves a structural and/or psychological disconnection between the mentor and the protégé and may last anywhere from 6 months to 2 years. Often, the reason for separation is geographical separation (Kram, 1985; Ragins & Scandura, 1997). The protégé may move on to another position, either through job rotation or promotion, which begins to limit opportunities for continued interaction (Ragins & Scandura, 1999). Indeed, Eby and McManus (2004) found that in their sample of 90 mentors, only 6 (7%) of them gave relationship problems as the reason for termination. The majority of these mentors mentioned protégé resignation, protégé termination, or transfers from the organization as the reason for separation.

The separation phase may be emotionally stressful as either one or both members perceive it with anxiety or defiance (Chao, 1997). After the separation phase, the existing mentoring relationship is no longer needed. In the final *redefinition* phase, a new relationship begins to form where it may either terminate or evolve into a peer-like friendship characterized by mutual support and informal contact (Chao, 1997; Scandura, 1998).

Criterion Variables in Mentoring Theory

Mentoring theory has adopted several distinct approaches to outcome, or criterion, variables. The first is to take a career theory perspective and examine the career outcomes of mentoring for protégés. Mentoring research has examined the career progress of protégés in terms of performance, salary, and promotions (Dreher & Ash, 1990; Scandura, 1992; Scandura & Schriesheim, 1994). Mentoring relations may also support protégé career development through positive effects on protégé learning. The development of a successful relationship reinforces the protégé's confidence in his or her ability to learn and may support risk-taking and innovation (Lankau & Scandura, 2002). Hall (1996) suggests that the ability to regularly grow and change by learning is indispensable for successful careers. Lankau and Scandura (2002) found the presence of mentoring functions to be antecedents of the protégé's learning, which positively related to job satisfaction and negatively associated with role ambiguity, intentions to leave (turnover intentions), and actual leaving (turnover behavior).

The second major approach to criterion variables in mentoring research employs variables that are typically studied in organizational research. Several studies relate mentoring to role stress, an extensively studied variable in organizational behavior. For example, Baugh, Lankau, and Scandura (1996) found mentoring to be negatively related to role stress and Nielson, Carlson, and Lankau (2001) examined mentoring in relation to a specific form of role stress – work–family conflict. Similarly, Kram and Hall (1991) found support for mentoring as a stress reducer during organizational turmoil. Other organizational behavior outcomes examined in relation to mentoring include justice perceptions (Scandura, 1997; Williams & Scandura, 2001), withdrawal intentions (Scandura & Viator, 1994), and withdrawal behavior (Lankau & Scandura, 2002).

Mentoring theory has also addressed benefits at the organizational level of analysis. Organizations are increasingly recognizing the value of mentoring relationships and attempt to reap the advantages through launching formal mentoring programs as part of their career development initiatives. In addition to outcomes for protégé career development and work attitudes, the benefits of mentoring relationships may accrue at the organizational level as well as the management level. Some theorists have suggested that mentoring benefits organizations by improving competencies

(Clutterback, 2004). There is little theoretical development, however, for outcomes associated with mentoring at the organizational level. For example, institutional theory might be applied to better understand whether mentoring occurs more frequently in certain types of organizational settings (Meyer & Rowan, 1977).

Outcomes for mentors have also been examined as criterion variables in mentoring theory and research. Mentoring a less experienced junior person may provide a creative and rejuvenating life experience to the adult mentor (Levinson et al., 1978). By contributing to future generations, mentors may also get a sense of immortality (Erikson, 1963). Second, mentors may obtain valuable, work-related information from their protégés (Mullen, 1994). Kram (1985) suggests that protégés can provide a loyal base of support which may help improve the mentor job performance. The benefit that mentors derive is yet another area that is in need of further theoretical development. For example, theories of upward influence and/or power sharing might be applied to better understand how protégés might influence powerful mentors in the organization by providing loyalty and other benefits. It can be expected that mentoring relationships follow norms of reciprocity and mentoring theory might examine the ways in which mentors and protégés influence one another.

Potential Problems in Mentoring Relationships

Marginal Mentoring

Mentoring is likely to be marked by both positive and negative experiences over time. Recently, Ragins, Cotton, and Miller (2000) proposed the potential for the existence of marginal mentoring relationships which do not involve serious dysfunction, but reduce relationship effectiveness. Marginal relationships may be limited in the scope or degree of mentoring functions provided. They fall midway on a continuum anchored with highly satisfying relationships on one end and highly dissatisfying relations on the other. Ragins et al. (2000) found that the attitudes of protégés who reported marginal satisfaction or dissatisfaction with their mentor were equivalent to or even sometimes worse than those of individuals without mentors. Ragins et al. (2000) refer to marginal mentors as "good enough mentors" (p. 1178) and suggest that although truly dysfunctional mentoring relations are likely to terminate (Ragins & Scandura, 1997), relationships that are marginally effective may endure.

Marginally effective relationships involve problems that minimize the potential of the relationship to meet important needs, but there is no malice involved and the relationship is likely to remain intact (Eby & McManus, 2004). For example, according to Eby and McManus (2004), the protégé's unwillingness to learn and performing below expectations may represent two broad problems that characterize marginally effective relationships since they limit the benefits that can be realized from the relationship but do not cause serious harm to the mentor or the relationship.

Dysfunctional Mentoring

Dysfunctional mentoring relations are those in which the relationship is not beneficial for either the mentor, protégé, or both (Scandura, 1998). Kram (1985) warned that under certain conditions, a mentoring relationship can become destructive for one or both individuals. Her assertion was supported by subsequent research and dysfunctional mentoring relations are reported in both the empirical (Eby et al., 2000; Eby et al., 2004; Ragins & Scandura, 1997) and practitioner literature (Myers & Humphreys, 1985). Scandura (1998) emphasized that most mentoring relationships are positive and productive; however, when dysfunction occurs, it may have negative effects on the performance and work attitudes of the protégé, and the result may be increased stress and employee withdrawal in the form of absenteeism and turnover (Scandura & Hamilton, 2002). Moreover, the negative emotions resulting from mentoring problems may be detrimental to both the protégé's career progress and the organization (Hunt & Michael, 1983).

Scandura (1998) provides a theoretical discussion of the various dysfunctions that may occur in a mentoring relationship. Building upon Scandura's theoretical foundation, Williams, Scandura, and Hamilton (2001) developed a measure of dysfunction in mentoring (DIM) measuring four dimensions of dysfunctionality. *Negative relations* involve psychosocial problems with bad intent (bullying, intimidation, overly aggressive behavior, abuse of power, and provoking diversity issues). *Difficulty* involves psychosocial problems with good intent (different personalities, different work styles, unresolved conflicts, disagreements, placement of binds by the mentor, mentor on the wrong career track, and over-dependence). *Spoiling* reflects changes in the relationship that make a previously satisfying relationship disappointing. It involves vocational issues with good intent (vocational issues with the absence of malice, betrayal, and regret). Eby and McManus (2004) provide an example of spoiling where a mentor discusses poor judgment when a protégé became romantically involved with a senior manager who was married. The protégé's actions disappointed the mentor and strained the relationship. Finally, *submissiveness* reinforces the balance of power (the protégé is submissive, over-dependent, accommodating, meek, and passive). Employing this scale, Williams et al. (2001) found that perceived dysfunction had a negative effect on protégé performance and an even stronger negative effect on self-esteem.

Eby and McManus (2004) suggested *malevolent deception* as another dimension of dysfunctionality. This reflects overt acts of deceit on the part of the protégé. Given the essential role of trust in close relationships (Lewicki & Bunker, 1995; Scandura & Pellegrini, 2003), perceptions of protégé deception may lead to mentor's psychological and/or physical withdrawal from the relationship. Eby and McManus (2004) also discuss *jealousy* and *competition* as dimensions of dysfunctional mentoring relationships since they can lead to suspicion, reduced trust, and counterproductive behavior. New measures of the negative aspects of mentoring have recently emerged (Eby et al., 2004); however, more work is necessary to determine the construct validity of these measures.

New Forms of Mentoring

Multiple Mentoring

The literature on mentoring suggests that individuals develop more than one mentoring relationship in the course of their careers. Kram (1983) originally proposed that individuals rely upon not just one but multiple mentors for developmental support. A protégé may maintain a peer-like relationship with a former mentor, while at the same time developing a new mentoring relationship with a different mentor. Henderson (1985) found both male and female protégés to have two to three mentors in the course of their careers. Baugh and Scandura (1999) also supported the existence of multiple mentoring relationships and proposed that having multiple mentors may enhance mentoring outcomes. Their results suggest that experiencing multiple mentoring relations may result in greater organizational commitment, job satisfaction, career expectations, increased perceptions of alternative employment, and lower ambiguity about one's work.

Recently, Higgins and Kram (2001) reconceptualized the traditional single dyadic relationship definition of a mentoring relationship into a multiple relationships phenomenon in which the protégé has a network of concurrent mentoring relationships. Network mentoring is a multiple mentoring model capturing the existence of a constellation of different mentors at one point in time rather than a sequential existence of single mentoring relations.

Team Mentoring

Team mentoring occurs when the leader serves as a team mentor and develops the team through career coaching, psychosocial support, and role modeling (Williams, 2000). In team mentoring the expertise resident in one individual is made available to multiple protégés at the same time (Ambrose, 2003). Williams (2000) notes that team mentoring also involves a responsibility for each team member to support the learning being promoted by the team mentor through peer mentoring. Thus, team mentoring is both dyadic and group focused, with mentoring ties between both the team leader and each team member and among team members themselves. Kaye and Jacobson (1996) suggest that in team mentoring, a formal mentor does not always lead members, rather members usually provide mentoring to each other. This aspect of team mentoring may be used for corrective feedback and building shared expectations and understanding (Knouse, 2001).

e-Mentoring

e-Mentoring uses electronic means as the primary channel of communication between the mentor and the protégé (Hamilton & Scandura, 2003). e-Mentoring relationships are maintained through various electronic media, including e-mail, chat, or the Web, whereas the traditional mentoring relationships are created and nurtured by frequent face-to-face contact between the mentor and the protégé. According to Ensher, Huen, and Blanchard (2003), electronic mentoring is not different from traditional mentoring in terms of its ability to provide vocational support and friendship. However, they propose that e-mentoring relations have added risks including greater chance of miscommunication, longer time to develop the relationship, and concerns with privacy and confidentiality. e-Mentoring literature is still evolving and there is yet to be an empirical analysis that compares face-to-face and computer-mediated mentoring relationships.

Needs-driven Mentoring

Higgins and Kram (2001) conceptualized mentoring as a network of relationships that span a protégé's entire career. Mezias and Scandura (2005) integrated this perspective with the research on international mentoring and developed a theory of expatriate mentoring as a network of relationships. This "needs-driven" approach focuses on the changing developmental needs of expatriate protégés and on the type of mentoring necessary during the different stages of an international assignment (pre-departure, expatriation, repatriation). Mezias and Scandura (2005) argue that there are different socialization needs during the different stages of an international assignment and as a consequence expatriate protégés may need multiple, concurrent developmental relationships due to the increasing ambiguity, uncertainty, and pressure stemming from the challenges of international assignments.

Theoretical Limitations

Based on the preceding sections, several theoretical limitations are identified. These limitations include: definitional issues, lack of integration from other disciplines, and limited range of criteria examined. These limitations are discussed, followed by directions for future research.

Definitional Issues

A major theoretical limitation in mentoring research pertains to construct clarification. Almost four decades ago, Levinson et al. (1978) described the mentor's function as guide, counselor, and sponsor. Contemporary research is still yet to discriminate among coaching, mentoring, and sponsoring. Future research should address this definitional confusion and distinguish how mentoring offers benefits above and beyond coaching or sponsoring.

Further, despite flourishing research in the new forms of mentoring (e.g., team mentoring, network mentoring, e-mentoring), research is still yet to empirically assess the dynamics in mentoring relationships that take place in virtual space. Ensher et al. (2003) and Hamilton and Scandura (2003) suggest that the traditional mentoring functions (career-related, psychosocial, and role modeling) are still present in e-mentoring and therefore the electronic relationship may be referred to as another type of mentoring relationship that relies on computer-mediated communication. However, Kram's (1985) original conceptualization of career-related functions involves protection and providing exposure and visibility, neither of which can be easily provided when the mentor reaches the protégé only through electronic means. In fact, the only vocational function that may easily be provided in an e-mentoring relation is coaching. Further, Kram (1985) proposed that the psychosocial functions are provided through an interpersonal relationship that fosters increasing intimacy. This level of relating, however, may not easily develop without frequent face-to-face interaction. Finally, the role modeling function may not occur in a virtual environment since it is mastered through direct observation of the mentor's behavior. More research is needed on the mentoring functions provided through e-mentoring before referring to these as "mentoring relationships."

Lack of Theoretical Integration from Other Disciplines

Research on mentoring has largely advanced independent of research in other fields of management and organizational psychology. McManus and Russell (1997) noted that mentoring research could benefit from integration with other psychological research, such as social support and stress. According to Wanberg et al. (2003), integration with other areas of research will enhance the understanding of the nomological network in which mentoring is embedded. Some studies have integrated mentoring with the literature on organizational justice (Scandura, 1997), organizational citizenship behavior (McManus & Russell, 1997), socialization (Chao et al., 1992; Feldman, Folks, & Turnley, 1999b), leader–member exchange (Scandura & Schriesheim, 1994), perceptions of trust (Bouquillon, Sosik, & Lee, 2005), and transformational leadership (Scandura & Williams, 2004; Sosik, Godshalk, & Yammarino, 2004).

Despite these attempts, additional theoretical integration might be developed. For example, research on abusive supervision (Keashly, Trott, & MacLean, 1994; Tepper, 2000; Zellars, Tepper, & Duffy, 2002) appears to be relevant to the study of problems in mentoring relationships. For example, the question of whether mentoring is less likely to be abusive than supervisor–subordinate relationships is an interesting research question. Theories from clinical and counseling psychology also seem relevant to the development of mentoring relationships. For example, Scandura and Pellegrini (2004) employed attachment theory as a theoretical framework to better understand initial relationship development between mentor and protégé. Similarly, theories of interpersonal attraction (Berscheid & Walster, 1969) might be employed to better understand why some mentoring relationships flourish and others wane. Educational research has also examined the development of mentoring relationships (Bierema & Merriam, 2002; Johnson, 1989; Ugbah & Williams, 1989). Theories of mentoring in the academic context may provide insights into the development of workplace mentoring.

Limited Range of Criteria Examined

As discussed previously, existing research typically examines how mentoring influences protégé career outcomes, including promotion, compensation, career satisfaction, career commitment, job satisfaction, and turnover intentions (Allen et al., 2004). Research on mentoring needs to go beyond these variables to expand the nomological network of mentoring. For example, Kram's definition of mentoring involves "exposure and challenging assignments" which may imply increased empowerment and delegation. However, to date the mentoring literature has almost been silent on the issue of participative decision-making. As another example, Scandura (1997) argues that mentoring may relate to justice perceptions. Of particular relevance are interpersonal and informational justice perceptions, neither of which has been examined to date in relation to mentoring. Interpersonal justice reflects the degree to which people are treated with politeness, respect, and dignity whereas informational justice focuses on the explanations provided to the employees that convey information about why procedures were used in a certain way or why outcomes were distributed in a certain fashion (Colquitt, 2001).

Cross-cultural Mentoring

Another area that warrants attention is cross-cultural research on mentoring relations. The impact of mentoring in the international context is an area where research is just beginning (Scandura & Von Glinow, 1997). The majority of mentoring research has been conducted with Western samples; however, globalization increasingly challenges today's managers to become more cross-culturally adept. Societal culture is a superordinate determinant of a person's values, perceptions, and expectations (Shweder & LeVine, 1984), and given the vast cultural differences among different regions of the world, we may find significant differences in the way protégés respond to various mentoring functions. For example, recently Pellegrini and Scandura (2006) found that employees in the Middle East may be disinterested in delegation. Thus, international mentoring research may find divergent results concerning the effectiveness of certain mentoring functions, such as fair treatment (i.e., justice perceptions) and participative decision-making (i.e., delegation).

Directions for Future Research

Kram (1985) initially conceptualized mentoring relations as being parental, emotional, and intense. However, Kram and Isabella (1985) defined mentor–protégé relationships as being in the middle way between intense paternalistic relations and peer-like friendships. Given the increasing interest in research on paternalism, we need empirical research to clarify how mentoring relations differ from paternalistic ones. Paternalistic managers assume the role of parents and consider it an obligation to provide protection to others under their care (Pellegrini & Scandura, 2006). In a paternalistic relationship, the follower voluntarily depends on the leader, which is similar to the "loyal base of support" conceptualized by Kram (1985). It is important to empirically discriminate between mentoring and paternalism for various reasons. First, both literatures are still evolving and prior to developing advanced theoretical frameworks we need to establish construct validity for both of these constructs. Further, paternalism is perceived negatively in the Western context, which has been reflected in metaphors regarding paternalistic leadership, such as "benevolent dictatorship" (Northouse, 1997, p. 39), "cradle to grave management" (Fitzsimons, 1991, p. 48), "country club management style" (Winning, 1994), and "noncoercive exploitation" (Goodell, 1985, p. 252). Thus, we need to empirically examine if and how psychosocial mentoring differs from paternalistic leadership.

Mentor and/or protégé characteristics that may influence the creation and maintenance of mentoring relations will also inform our understanding of the development and process of mentoring relationships (Wanberg et al., 2003). From a practitioner perspective, this information may be useful in identifying employees who will flourish as protégés and/or mentors. Previous research has identified various personality correlates of mentoring. For protégés, these personality characteristics include extraversion and Type A personality (Aryee, Lo, & Kang, 1999), self-monitoring and self-esteem (Turban & Dougherty, 1994), and the need for affiliation and achievement (Fagenson, 1992). The personality characteristics that are found to influence effective mentoring include positive affectivity and altruism (Aryee et al., 1999), self-monitoring (Mullen & Noe, 1999), and upward striving (Allen, Poteet, Russell, & Dobbins, 1997). These studies suggest some antecedents to effective mentoring relationships; however, there is still not sufficient information regarding how mentoring relations develop in early phases. With the exception of diversity variables (cf. Ragins, 1997), theoretical frameworks to guide research on personality and other individual differences are needed. As an illustration, Scandura and Pellegrini (2004) delved into attachment theory and the issues of dependency and counterdependency from both mentor and mentee perspectives. They propose that mentoring may mediate the relationship between attachment styles and work outcomes such that mentoring relations involving counterdependent (avoidant attachment) or dependent (anxious/ambivalent attachment) people either as protégés or mentors will become either marginal or dysfunctional. They suggest that an interdependent stance (secure attachment) is most likely to result in functional mentoring relationships.

Major Methodological Approaches and Limitations

In this section, major methodological approaches to the study of mentoring are discussed, along with methodological limitations. This includes a discussion of both measurement and research design issues.

Measurement

The debate over whether mentoring relationships involve two or three independent functions is reflected in the most commonly used mentoring instruments. Noe (1988) suggests that mentors provide career and psychosocial functions and he measures these two functions with 21 items. Dreher and Ash (1990) also developed a two-dimensional scale involving 18 items. On the other hand, Scandura and Ragins (1993) developed the three-dimensional Mentoring Functions Questionnaire (MFQ) which measures the career, psychosocial, and role modeling functions with 15 items. Recently, Castro and Scandura (2004) reduced the measure to 9 items using multiple samples and analyses. The MFQ is the only three-dimensional mentoring instrument with sufficient evidence supporting its three-dimensional factor structure (Scandura & Ragins, 1993), concurrent validity (Baugh et al., 1996; Nielson, Carlson, & Lankau, 2001), and convergent and discriminant validity (Castro & Scandura, 2004).

Recently, Pellegrini and Scandura (2005) concluded that an accepted measure of mentoring has not emerged. There are a number of commonly used scales (Dreher & Ash, 1990; Noe, 1988; Scandura & Ragins, 1993), but there is still insufficient information regarding their psychometric properties. However, one recent construct validation study is noteworthy. Pellegrini and Scandura (2005) used multiple confirmatory factor analyses to investigate the factorial stability of the MFQ across two groups: protégés who are satisfied with their mentor and those who are not. The results suggested partial measurement invariance indicating that the mentoring relationship might be fundamentally different across satisfying and dissatisfying relationships, and this may affect the way the items are interpreted. Overall, the MFQ-9 demonstrated excellent psychometric properties when used in dissatisfying relationships. The results of this study also show that measuring the mentoring construct with adequate validity may require more items in satisfying relationships. Pellegrini and Scandura (2005) conclude that by identifying invariant items and improving those that are nonequivalent, research on mentoring should be improved. In addition to basic psychometric work, more research is needed that examines the most commonly used mentoring instruments by careful comparison. For example, Castro and Scandura (2004) examined two commonly-used mentoring measures and found that both are useful, but perhaps for different purposes.

Another measurement concern is that research has typically examined the quality of the mentoring relationship from the protégé's perspective. However, the correlation between mentor and protégé ratings of the mentoring relationship is low enough to raise questions about scale validity for one or both sources. For example, Raabe and Beehr (2003) found that mentors believed they were giving more career support than mentees believed they were getting, but mentees perceived greater psychosocial support and role modeling than mentors indicated providing. Measurement perspective is an important issue because it may act as a moderator of the relationship between mentoring and its correlates. For example, the association between mentoring functions and the protégé's job satisfaction might be stronger when mentoring functions are measured from the protégé's perspective as compared with the mentor's point of view. Therefore, future research should examine mentoring from both perspectives to identify whether measurement perspective acts as a moderator, and, if so, among which mentoring functions and outcomes.

Research Design

Qualitative research.   Research on mentoring has flourished over the past 25 years owing primarily to the seminal works of Kram (1983, 1985), who studied 18 mentor–protégé relationships via in-depth interviews. Allen, Poteet, and Burroughs (1997) also conducted a qualitative study examining factors that influence an individual's decision to mentor others. As a result of their in-depth interviews with 27 mentors, they suggested 13 influential factors such as the desire to pass information on to others, the desire to help others succeed, personal desire to work with others, and the desire to increase personal learning. Recently, Eby and Lockwood (2005) interviewed mentors and protégés in two formal mentoring programs. They concluded that the benefits included learning, coaching, career planning, and psychosocial support for protégés, and learning, developing a personal relationship, personal gratification, and enhanced managerial skills for mentors. Qualitative research is important in understanding the dynamics involved in mentoring relationships. Research in mentoring is in need of more qualitative field studies to have a more holistic and an in-depth understanding of mentoring relations.

Time horizon of research.   In order for mentoring research to go beyond showing associations with career outcomes, it is important to demonstrate that mentoring precedes career success outcomes. To date, mentoring research has largely relied on cross-sectional field studies and is in need of more longitudinal studies in order to establish causal directions among mentoring and career success outcome variables.

Initial research on the temporal sequencing of mentoring and outcomes is promising (Wanberg et al., 2003). For example, Donaldson, Ensher, and Grant-Vallone (2000) found that high-quality mentoring relationships were related to organizational commitment and organizational citizenship behaviors reported 6 months later. Silverhart (1994) found that new insurance agents who reported having a mentor were more likely to be with the organization at the end of the first year and to have sold more policies. In a longitudinal study of the careers of lawyers, Higgins and Thomas (2001) found that the organizational level of a protégé's set of developmental relationships was related to promotion to a partner position 7 years later. More recently, Payne and Huffman (2005) found that mentoring was positively related to affective and continuance commitment and negatively related to turnover behavior one year later in a sample of 1,000 US Army officers.

Experimental research. While mentoring research tends to use cross-sectional designs, there are several examples of field experiments. For example, Seibert (1999) found that one year after a formal mentoring program was initiated, protégés participating in the mentor program reported higher job satisfaction, but did not differ from their nonmentored counterparts in terms of work role stress or self-esteem at work. While providing some experimental control, it is important to note that this study is a quasi-experiment because it lacked random assignment.

Experimental laboratory research involving both random assignment and high experimental control could contribute greatly to our understanding of mentoring. As an illustration, the field experiment by Olian, Carroll, and Giannantonio (1993) provided interesting insights about the establishment phase of mentoring. Their sample, which consisted of 145 managers in the banking industry, revealed that mentors were more willing to engage in mentoring when the protégé had a good past performance record, if male protégés were married and female protégés were single.

Experimental and longitudinal comparative research. It is perhaps most surprising that there have been no attempts to examine the efficacy of formal mentoring programs using field experimental designs or longitudinal designs. Yet, as far back as Kram (1985), the suggestion that assigned (i.e., formal) mentoring relationships may not be as beneficial as mentoring relations that develop informally has been asserted. Formal programs are those which are implemented and overseen by the organization, directed by written policy and guidelines (Burke & McKeen, 1989b). Studies comparing formal mentoring to informal mentoring have typically found informal mentoring to be more effective. For example, Allen, Day, and Lentz (2005) found that individuals in informal mentoring relations reported higher levels of career mentoring and higher-quality mentoring relationships than individuals in formal relationships. Chao et al. (1992) also found that protégés in formal mentoring relationships reported receiving fewer career mentoring functions than protégés in informal relationships. Regarding psychosocial mentoring functions, Fagenson-Eland, Marks, and Amendola (1997) found that formal protégés reported lower levels of psychosocial functions than informal protégés. With respect to specific mentoring functions, Ragins and Cotton (1999) found that in comparison to informal protégés, formal protégés reported lower levels of mentoring on almost every mentoring function (e.g., sponsoring, coaching, protection, challenging assignments, exposure, friendship, social support, role modeling, and acceptance). Formal protégés also reported lower compensation than individuals with informal mentors.

The need for experimental and longitudinal research on formal and informal mentoring is a critical area for future research, since many authors have called into question the effectiveness of formal mentoring (Chao, Walz, & Gardner, 1992; Noe, 1988; Ragins & Cotton, 1999). In the formal mentoring context, processes that need to be examined include the mentor's motivation and the protégé's openness to mentoring. Also, formal mentoring may result in feelings of coercion and set up an evaluation agenda which may put individuals in the program on the defensive (Kram, 1985). Nonetheless, organizations are increasingly seeking to formalize mentoring relationships as a career development strategy, despite lack of sufficient empirical evidence supporting the value of formal mentoring initiatives. Scandura (1998, p. 451) suggests that notwithstanding continued practitioner interest "the jury is still out on the efficacy of formal mentoring programs."

Conclusions

The field of mentoring has had a unique stream of development over the past 25 years. Unlike other areas of management research, clear models emerged relatively early in the theoretical development of the field due to the insightful work of Levinson et al. and Kram. These frameworks guided research on mentoring and career outcomes for many years. Also, diversity issues were well integrated with mentoring theory (cf. Ragins, 1997). This careful attention to theoretical issues provided clear guidance for research. In the late 1990s, new models of mentoring emerged such as multiple, team, and network mentoring. Some of these ideas were part of the original work of Kram, such as the idea of developmental networks. These areas of research need further theoretical development and empirical attention.

In our review of methodological issues, we highlighted several areas that are in need of further attention. In particular, there is a need for more attention to the measurement of mentoring and a broader array of research designs. A standard measure of mentoring has not emerged, yet there are similarities among all mentoring measures because most are derived from the original work of Kram. A comparison of the psychometric properties of mentoring measures would be a useful study. For example, Castro and Scandura (2004) compared two measures, but a more comprehensive review is clearly needed. Also, more recent research has sought to carefully define mentoring for respondents and this is a recommended practice. Finally, as have many previous authors, we suggest more longitudinal research on mentoring to better understand how the process unfolds over time.

We also suggest that a broader set of processes and criterion variables be examined. For example, Sosik et al. (2004) examined the learning goal orientations of protégés. The learning goal orientations approach is consistent with Lankau and Scandura's (2002) theory of personal learning as an integral part of the mentoring process. Protégé learning within the mentoring relationship is a potentially important new direction for the examination of mentoring outcomes. Also, there has been recent attention to what mentors learn from the relationship (Germain, 2004). Traditionally, outcomes of career mobility have been studied; however, with organizational downsizing and the changes in careers, a focus on skill development and learning may be more meaningful.

The field of mentoring appears to be flourishing as new theoretical perspectives emerge and empirical research continues to employ a variety of research methods. Some theories were well grounded in qualitative work and resulted in empirical research that has opened up even more avenues for research. Currently, mentoring theory enjoys continued interest and the development of new theoretical perspectives such as mentoring networks and needs-driven approaches. Despite continued theoretical and practitioner interest in mentoring, we feel that mentoring needs to address key issues in the areas of measurement and longitudinal as well as experimental designs. There are yet many unanswered questions for mentoring theorists and researchers to explore. In this chapter, we reviewed the major theoretical streams of research, methodological issues, and developed some suggestions for future theory and research.

References

Allen, T. D., Day, R., & Lentz, E. (2005). The role of interpersonal comfort in mentoring relationships. *Career Development Quarterly, 31*, 155–169.

Allen, T. D., Eby, L. T., Poteet, M., Lima, L., & Lentz, E. (2004). Career benefits associated with mentoring protégés: A meta-analysis. *Journal of Applied Psychology, 89*, 127–136.

Allen, T. D., Poteet, M. L., & Burroughs, S. M. (1997). The mentor's perspective: A qualitative inquiry and future research agenda. *Journal of Vocational Behavior, 51*, 70–89.

Allen, T. D., Poteet, M. L., Russell, J. E. A., & Dobbins, G. H. (1997). A field study of factor related to willingness to mentor others. *Journal of Vocational Behavior, 50*, 1–22.

Ambrose, L. (2003). Multiple mentoring. *Health Executive.* Retrieved June 30, 2005, from www.ache.org/newclub/CAREER/MentorArticles/Multiple.cfm.

Aryee, S., Lo, S., & Kang, I.L. (1999). Antecedents of early career stage mentoring among Chinese employees. *Journal of Organizational Behavior, 20*, 563–576.

Bass, B. (1985). *Leadership and performance beyond expectations.* New York: The Free Press.

Baugh, S. G., Lankau, M. J., & Scandura, T. A. (1996). An investigation of the effects of protégé gender on responses to mentoring. *Journal of Vocational Behavior, 49*, 309–323.

Berscheid, E., & Walster, E. H. (1969). *Interpersonal attraction.* Reading, MA: Addison-Wesley.

Bierema, L. L., & Merriam, S. B. (2002). E-mentoring: Using computer mediated communication (CMC) to enhance the mentoring process. *Innovative Higher Education, 26*, 211–227.

Bouquillon, E. A., Sosik, J. J., & Lee, D. Y. (2005). It's only a phase: Examining trust, identification and mentoring functions received across the mentoring phases. *Mentoring and Tutoring, 13*(2), 241–260.

Burke, R. J. (1984). Mentors in organizations. *Group and Organization Studies, 9*, 353–372.

Burke, R. J., & McKeen, C. A. (1989b). Mentoring in organizations: Implications for women. *Journal of Business Ethics, 9*, 317–333.

Castro, S. L., & Scandura, T. A. (2004, November). *The tale of two measures: Evaluation and comparison of Scandura's (1992) and Ragins and McFarlin's (1990) mentoring measures.* Paper presented at the Southern Management Association Meeting, San Antonio, TX.

Chao, G. T. (1997). Mentoring phases and outcomes. *Journal of Vocational Behavior, 51,* 15–28.

Chao, G. T., Walz, P. M., & Gardner, P. D. (1992). Formal and informal mentorships: A comparison on mentoring functions and contrast with nonmentored counterparts. *Personnel Psychology, 45,* 619–636.

Clutterback, D. (2004). What about mentee competences? In D. A. Clutterback & G. Lane (Eds.), *The situational mentor: An international review of competences and capabilities in mentoring* (pp. 72–82). Aldershot, England: Gower Publishing.

Colquitt, J. A. (2001). On the dimensionality of organizational justice: A construct validation of a measure. *Journal of Applied Psychology, 86,* 386–400.

Dansereau, F., Graen, G., & Haga, W. J. (1975). A vertical dyad approach to leadership within formal organizations. *Organizational Behavior and Human Performance, 13,* 46–78.

Donaldson, S. I., Ensher, E. A., & Grant-Vallone, E. (2000). Longitudinal examination of mentoring relationships and organizational commitment and citizenship behavior. *Journal of Career Development, 26,* 233–248.

Dreher, G. F., & Ash, R. A. (1990). A comparative study of mentoring among men and women in managerial, professional, and technical positions. *Journal of Applied Psychology, 75,* 539–546.

Eby, L. T., Butts, M., Lockwood, A., & Simon, S. A. (2004). Protégés' negative mentoring experiences: Construct development and nomological validation. *Personnel Psychology, 57,* 411–447.

Eby, L. T., & Lockwood, A. (2005). Protégés' and mentors' reactions to participating in formal mentoring programs: A qualitative investigation. *Journal of Vocational Behavior, 67,* 441–458.

Eby, L. T., & McManus, S. E. (2004). The protégé's role in negative mentoring experiences. *Journal of Vocational Behavior, 65,* 255–275.

Eby, L. T., McManus, S. E., Simon, S. A., & Russell, J. E. A. (2000). The protégé's perspective regarding negative mentoring experiences: The development of a taxonomy. *Journal of Vocational Behavior, 57,* 1–21.

Ensher, E. A., Huen, C., & Blanchard, A. (2003). Online mentoring and computer-mediated communication: New directions in research. *Journal of Vocational Behavior, 63,* 264–288.

Ensher, E. A., & Murphy, S. E. (1997). Effects of race, gender, perceived similarity, and contact on mentor relationships. *Journal of Vocational Behavior, 50,* 460–481.

Erikson, E. H. (1963). *Childhood and Society* (2nd ed.). New York: W. W. Norton & Co.

Fagenson, E.A. (1992). Mentoring – Who needs it? A comparison of protégés' and non-protégés' needs for power, achievement, affiliation, and autonomy. *Journal of Vocational Behavior, 41,* 48–60.

Fagenson-Eland, E. A., Marks, M. A., & Amendola, K. L. (1997). Perceptions of mentoring relationships. *Journal of Vocational Behavior, 51,* 29–42.

Feldman, D. F., Folks, W. R., & Turnley, W. H. (1999b). The socialization of expatriate interns. *Journal of Managerial Issues, 10,* 403–418.

Fitzsimons, D. J. (1991). From paternalism to partnership. *Journal of Compensation and Benefits, 6,* 48–52.

Germain, M. (2004, August). *Mentor learning: New constructs for mentoring research.* Southern Management Association Meeting, San Antonio, TX.

Gerstner, C. R., & Day, D. V. (1997). Meta-analytic review of leader–member exchange theory: Correlates and construct issues. *Journal of Applied Psychology, 82,* 827–844.

Goodell, G. E. (1985). Paternalism, patronage, and potlatch: The dynamics of giving and being given to. *Current Anthropology, 26,* 247–257.

Graen, G. B., Liden, R. C., & Hoel, W. (1982). Role of leadership in the employee with-drawal process. *Journal of Applied Psychology, 67,* 868–872.

Graen, G. B., & Scandura, T. A. (1987). Toward a psychology of dyadic organizing. *Research in Organizational Behavior, 9,* 175–208.

Graen, G. B., & Uhl-Bien, M. (1995). Relationship-based approach to leadership: Develop-ment of leader–member exchange (LMX) theory of leadership over 25 years: Applying a multi-level multi-domain perspective. *Leadership Quarterly, 6,* 219–247.

Hall, D. T. (1996). *The career is dead – long live the career.* San Francisco: Jossey-Bass.

Hamilton, B. A., & Scandura, T. A. (2003). E-Mentoring: Implications for organizational learning and development in a wired world. *Organizational Dynamics, 31,* 388–402.

Henderson, D. W. (1985). Enlightened mentoring: A characteristic of public management professionalism. *Public Administration Review, 15,* 857–863.

Higgins, M. C., & Kram, K. (2001). Reconceptualizing mentoring at work: A developmental network perspective. *Academy of Management Review, 26,* 264–288.

Higgins, M. C., & Thomas, D. A. (2001). Constellations and careers: Toward under-standing the effects of multiple developmental relationships. *Journal of Organizational Behavior, 22,* 223–247.

Hunt, D. M., & Michael, C. (1983). Mentorship: A career training and development tool. *Academy of Management Review, 8,* 475–485.

Johnson, C. S. (1989). Mentoring programs. In M. L. Upcraft & J. Gardner (Eds.), *The freshman year experience: Helping students survive and succeed in college* (pp. 118–128). San Francisco: Jossey-Bass.

Kaye, B., & Jacobson, B. (1996). Reframing mentoring. *Training & Development, 50,* 44–47.

Keashly, L., Trott, V., & MacLean, L. M. (1994). Abusive behavior in the workplace: A preliminary investigation. *Violence and Victims, 9,* 341–357.

Keller, T., & Dansereau, F. (1995). Leadership and empowerment: A social exchange perspective. *Human Relations, 48,* 127–145.

Knouse, S. B. (2001). Virtual mentors: Mentoring on the internet. *Journal of Employment Counseling, 38,* 162–169.

Kram, K. E. (1983). Phases of the mentor relationship. *Academy of Management Journal, 26,* 608–625.

Kram, K. E. (1985). *Mentoring at work: Developmental relationships in organizational life.* Glenview, IL: Scott, Foresman and Company.

Kram, K., & Hall, D. (1991). Mentoring as an antidote to stress during corporate trauma. *Human Resource Management, 28,* 493–510.

Kram, K. E., & Isabella, L. A. (1985). Mentoring alternatives: The role of peer relationships in career development. *Academy of Management Journal, 28,* 110–132.

Lankau, M., & Scandura, T. A. (2002). An investigation of personal learning in mentoring relationships: Content, antecedents, and consequences. *Academy of Management Journal, 45,* 779–790.

Levinson, D. J., Darrow, C. N., Klein, E. B., Levinson, M. A., & McKee, B. (1978). *The seasons of a man's life.* New York: Knopf.

Lewicki, R. J., & Bunker, B. B. (1995). Trust in relationships: A model of trust development and decline. In B. B. Bunker & J. Z. Rubin (Eds.), *Conflict, cooperation, and justice* (pp. 133–173). San Francisco: Jossey-Bass.

Liden, R. C., Sparrowe, R. T., & Wayne, S. J. (1997). Leader–member exchange theory: The past and potential for the future. *Research in Personnel and Human Resources Management, 15,* 47–119.

Liden, R. C., Wayne, S. J., & Stilwell, D. (1993). A longitudinal study on the early develop-ment of leader–member exchanges. *Journal of Applied Psychology, 78,* 662–674.

McManus, S. E., & Russell, J. E. A. (1997). New directions for mentoring research: An examination of related constructs. *Journal of Vocational Behavior*, *51*, 145–161.

Meyer J. W., & Rowan B. (1977). Institutional organizations: Formal structure as myth and ceremony. *American Journal of Sociology*, *83*, 343–363.

Mezias, J. M., & Scandura, T. A. (2005). A needs-driven approach to expatriate adjustment and career development: A multiple mentoring perspective. *Journal of International Business Studies*, *36*, 519–538.

Mullen, E. J. (1994). Framing the mentoring relationship as an information exchange. *Human Resource Management Review*, *4*, 257–281.

Mullen, E. J., & Noe, R. A. (1999). The mentoring information exchange: When do mentors seek information from their protégés? *Journal of Organizational Behavior*, *20*, 233–242.

Myers, D. W., & Humphreys, N. J. (1985). The caveats of mentorship. *Business Horizons*, *28*, 9–14.

Nielson, T. R., Carlson, D. S., & Lankau, M. J. (2001). The supportive mentor as a means of reducing work–family conflict. *Journal of Vocational Behavior*, *59*, 364–381.

Noe, R. A. (1988). An investigation of the determinants of successful assigned mentoring relationships. *Personnel Psychology*, *41*, 457–479.

Northouse, P. G. (1997). *Leadership: Theory and practice*. Thousand Oaks, CA: Sage.

Olian, J. D., Carroll, S. J., & Giannantonio, C. M. (1993). Mentor reactions to protégés: An experiment with managers. *Journal of Vocational Behavior*, *43*, 266–278.

Pasa, S. F., Kabasakal, H., & Bodur, M. (2001). Society, organizations, and leadership in Turkey. *Applied Psychology: An International Review*, *50*, 559–589.

Payne, S. C., & Huffman, A. H. (2005). A longitudinal examination of the influence of mentoring on organizational commitment and turnover. *Academy of Management Journal*, *48*, 158–168.

Pellegrini, E. K., & Scandura, T. A. (2005). Construct equivalence across groups: An unexplored issue in mentoring research. *Educational and Psychological Measurement*, *65*, 323–335.

Pellegrini, E. K., & Scandura, T. A. (2006). Leader–Member Exchange (LMX), paternalism and delegation in the Turkish business culture: An empirical investigation. *Journal of International Business Studies*, *2*, 264–279.

Raabe, B., & Beehr, T. A. (2003). Formal mentoring versus supervisor and coworker relationship: Differences in perceptions and impact. *Journal of Organizational Behavior*, *24*, 271–293.

Ragins, B. R. (1997). Diversified mentoring relationships in organizations: A power perspective. *Academy of Management Review*, *22*, 482–521.

Ragins, B. R., & Cotton, J. (1999). Mentor functions and outcomes: A comparison of men and women in formal and informal mentoring relationships. *Journal of Applied Psychology*, *84*(4), 529–550.

Ragins, B. R., Cotton, J. L., & Miller, J. S. (2000). Marginal mentoring: The effects of type of mentor, quality of relationship, and program design on work and career outcomes. *Academy of Management Journal*, *43*, 1177–1194.

Ragins, B. R., & McFarlin, D. B. (1990). Perceptions of mentor roles in cross-gender mentoring relationships. *Journal of Vocational Behavior*, *37*, 321–339.

Ragins, B. R., & Scandura, T. A. (1999). Burden or blessing? Expected costs and benefits of being a mentor. *Journal of Organizational Behavior*, *20*, 493–509.

Roche, G. R. (1979). Much ado about mentors. *Harvard Business Review*, *57*, 14–28.

Scandura, T. A. (1992). Mentorship and career mobility: An empirical investigation. *Journal of Organizational Behavior*, *13*, 169–174.

Scandura, T. A. (1997). Mentoring and organizational justice: An empirical investigation. *Journal of Vocational Behavior*, *51*, 58–69.

Scandura, T. A. (1998). Dysfunctional mentoring relationships and outcomes. *Journal of Management, 24*, 449–467.

Scandura, T. A., & Hamilton, B. A. (2002). Enhancing performance through mentoring. In S. Sonnentag (Ed.), *The psychological management of individual performance. A handbook in the psychology of management in organizations* (pp. 293–308). Chichester, England: Wiley.

Scandura, T. A., & Pellegrini, E. K. (2003, November). *A multidimensional model of trust and LMX.* Southern Management Association Meeting, Clearwater Beach, FL.

Scandura, T. A., & Pellegrini, E. K. (2004). Competences of building the developmental relationship. In D. Clutterback & G. Lane (Eds.), *The situational mentor: An international review of competences and capabilities in mentoring* (pp. 83–93). Aldershot, England: Gower Publishing Limited.

Scandura, T. A., & Ragins, B. R. (1993). The effects of sex and gender role orientation on mentorship in male-dominated occupations. *Journal of Vocational Behavior, 43*, 251–265.

Scandura, T. A., & Schriesheim, C. A. (1994). Leader–member exchange and supervisor career mentoring as complementary constructs in leadership research. *Academy of Management Journal, 37*, 1588–1602.

Scandura, T. A., & Viator, R. (1994). Mentoring in public accounting firms: An analysis of mentor–protégé relationships, mentoring functions, and protégé turnover intentions. *Accounting, Organizations & Society, 19*, 717–734.

Scandura, T. A., & Von Glinow, M. A. (1997). Development of the international manager: The role of mentoring. *Business and the Contemporary World, 9*, 95–115.

Schriesheim, C. A., & Castro, S. L. (1995, November). *A structural modeling investigation of leader–member exchange (LMX) and mentoring as complementary concepts.* Paper presented at the annual meeting of the Southern Management Association, Orlando, FL.

Seibert, S. (1999). The effectiveness of facilitated mentoring: A longitudinal quasi-experiment. *Journal of Vocational Behavior, 54*, 483–502.

Shweder, R., & LeVine, R. (1984). *Culture theory: Essays on mind, self, and emotion.* New York: Cambridge University Press.

Silverhart, T. A. (1994). It works: Mentoring drives productivity higher. *Managers Magazine, 69*, 14–15.

Sosik, J. J., & Godshalk, V. M. (2000a). Leadership styles, mentoring functions received, and job-related stress: A conceptual model and preliminary study. *Journal of Organizational Behavior, 21*, 365–390.

Sosik, J. J., Godshalk, V. M., & Yammarino, F. J. (2004). Transformational leadership, learning goal orientation, and expectations for career success in mentor–protégé relationships: A multiple levels of analysis perspective. *Leadership Quarterly, 15*, 241–261.

Tepper, B. J. (2000). Consequences of abusive supervision. *Academy of Management Journal, 43*, 178–190.

Tepper, K., Shaffer, B. C., & Tepper, B. J. (1996). Latent structure of mentoring function scales. *Education and Psychological Measurement, 56*, 848–857.

Turban, D. B., & Dougherty, T. W. (1994). Role of protégé personality in receipt of mentoring and career success. *Academy of Management Journal, 37*, 688–702.

Ugbah, S., & Williams, S. A. (1989). The mentor–protégé relationship: Its impact on Blacks in predominantly White institutions. In J. C. Elam (Ed.), *Blacks in higher education: Overcoming the odds* (pp. 29–42). Lanham, MD: University Press of America.

Uhl-Bien, M., & Maslyn, M. (2005). *Paternalism as a form of leadership: Differentiating paternalism from Leader–Member Exchange.* Academy of Management Meeting, Honolulu, Hawaii.

Vertz, L. L. (1985). Women, occupational advancement, and mentoring: An analysis of one public organization. *Public Administrative Review, 45*(3), 415–423.

Wakabayashi, M., Graen, G. B., & Uhl-Bien, M. (1990). The generalizability of the hidden investment process in leading Japanese corporations. *Human Relations, 43*, 1099–1116.

Wanberg, C. R., Welsh, E. T., & Hezlett, S. A. (2003). Mentoring research: A review and dynamic process model. *Research in Personnel and Human Resources Management, 22*, 39–124.

Williams, E. A. (2000). *Team mentoring: New directions for research on employee development in organizations.* Paper presented at the Academy of Management Meeting, Toronto, Canada.

Williams, E. A., Scandura, T. A., & Hamilton, B. A. (2001, November). Dysfunctional mentoring relationships and negative social exchange: Uncovering some unpleasant realities in mentoring relationships. *Southern Management Association Proceedings* (pp. 62–66). New Orleans: Southern Management Association Meeting.

Winning, E. A. (1994). *Pitfalls in paternalism.* Retrieved February 22, 2005, from www.ewin.com/articles/paternal.htm.

Yukl, G. (1989). *Leadership in organizations.* Englewood Cliffs, NJ: Prentice Hall.

Zellars, K. L., Tepper, B. J., & Duffy, M. K. (2002). Abusive supervision and subordinates' organizational citizenship behavior. *Journal of Applied Psychology, 87*, 1062–1076.

Chapter 6

Reflections on the Theoretical Approaches and Methodological Issues in Mentoring Relationships

Marcus M. Butts, Jaime R. Durley, and Lillian T. Eby

The previous three chapters have reviewed the theory and methods employed in youth mentoring, student–faculty mentoring, and workplace mentoring. Broadly examining these chapters reveals the aspects unique to and similar across each area of mentoring scholarship. Highlighting the common theoretical and methodological issues across chapters allows speculation about how the three areas of study may contribute to one another.

Unique Aspects

Workplace mentoring has generally been conceptualized as providing both career and psychosocial functions for protégés. However, the orientation in youth mentoring toward increasing the social, personal, and psychological support of the protégé (e.g., befriending the youth, helping the youth avoid trouble, promoting personal development, and serving as a source of support) suggests that psychosocial functions may be more important than career functions for youth mentoring relationships. In contrast, academic mentors provide integral direction for teaching, research, career advice, and advocacy for the protégé and may be relied upon less for psychosocial functions than career functions.

Mentors' motives may also differentiate mentoring in these three types of relationships. Youth mentoring hinges on mentors volunteering time to children in need and making a difference in their community. Underlying this behavior may be a fundamental altruistic drive that is not as prevalent in other mentoring contexts. Although self-centered motivations for youth mentoring may exist, these relationships tend to be more other-focused, often fueled by the desire to help vulnerable youth. There may be relatively more self-focused mentor motives in student–faculty and workplace mentoring relationships. For example, a workplace or an academic mentor may be motivated by the desire to fulfill others' expectations or enhance their own achievements. Academic administrators may expect faculty to mentor students, and managers may be expected to mentor high-potential employees in the organization. In either situation, mentors may initiate the relationship because of self-focused motives, such as the expectation that their own productivity and career success will be enhanced by cultivating mentoring relationships.

The intended impact of mentoring also varies across areas of study. Youth mentoring may have more far-reaching societal effects. Providing youths with opportunities for greater community involvement and personal growth may cause them to feel empowered and confident. Thus, mentoring may not only improve the lives of individual youths but also on a grander scheme may achieve the implicit objective of mitigating rifts between social classes and improve society as a whole. The impact of academic mentoring is less grandiose but still potentially widespread. Success of the student–faculty mentorship can change an academic department's climate, and effective student–faculty mentorships may gradually impact the entire institution or profession. Workplace mentoring primarily affects the personal lives and careers of those involved, although it may also have broader ramifications for the entire organization (e.g., reduced employee withdrawal intentions, enhanced perceptions of fairness).

Similar Aspects

One of the overarching themes of this section is the acknowledgment that mentoring is a two-way street. The literature on youth mentoring emphasizes mutuality between participants; both parties must be willing to participate in the relationship and be open and responsive to the other person's needs. Student–faculty and workplace mentorships also center on the idea that mentoring is an exchange relationship between two people. Although few investigations of mentoring attempt to decipher the nature and development of this dyadic exchange, as discussed by Eby, Rhodes, and Allen (this volume) the existence of two people engaged in a "give and take" relationship is a basic tenet defining mentoring and differentiating it from other types of relationships.

Another notable similarity among the three types of mentoring relationships is the acknowledgement of mentoring as a developmental process. In youth mentoring, the mentor attempts to increase self-efficacy and competence by providing the youth with repeated opportunities for learning and accomplishment. Thus, the mentor develops the youth's self-concept over time by building a perception of acceptance and support from others and by facilitating development of an attainable self-concept. In student–faculty relationships, specific factors (e.g., establishing identity, managing emotions, developing integrity) have been proposed to understand student development. The literature on workplace mentoring has taken a more descriptive approach and proposes that mentoring relationships progress through specific temporal phases marked by unique developmental issues.

All three areas of study also warn against potentially negative outcomes of mentoring. Dysfunctional youth mentoring relationships occur when the youth perceives that the relationship is not important to the mentor, that s/he is viewed as incompetent by the mentor, or that the relationship has little potential for future personal growth. From a student–faculty context, mentorships may fail when mentors with-hold guidance or skill enrichment opportunities, display incompetence in the mentor role, or lack empathy and authenticity when dealing with protégés. The possibility of mentoring problems is also discussed in workplace mentoring from the perspect-ive of both mentor and protégé. As an illustration, protégés can behave deceptively toward mentors, and mentors can sabotage the success of protégés or ignore pro-tégés' developmental needs.

Methodological Issues

Measuring any type of mentoring relationship poses many challenges, and research in each of the three areas recommends both similar and unique approaches to over-coming these obstacles. Research in all three areas faces some difficulty concep-tualizing and operationalizing mentoring as well as distinguishing it from other relationships such as coaching, advising, and role modeling (also see Eby, Rhodes, & Allen, this volume). The area of youth mentoring is perhaps least affected by this problem because most research focuses on formal mentorships, resulting in clearer definitions of "mentor" and "protégé." Johnson et al. (this volume) reports that some researchers avoid this problem entirely by failing to define mentoring, allowing par-ticipants to use their own personal meaning of the term, while others define the term so specifically that it may cause important aspects of the relationship to be overlooked if they are not incorporated into the definition. Descriptions of mentoring that are too vague or too specific limit the generalizability of the study by creating results that are either too ambiguous or too constrained.

All three chapters also discuss how mentoring relationships are inherently dyadic and underscore the importance of collecting multi-source data. As noted by Scandura and Pellegrini (this volume), data may be biased if collected only from the protégé or the mentor. Thus, obtaining information from outside observers may provide a more objective perception of the relationship. Research in youth mentoring explicitly recog-nizes the need for alternative perspectives from parents, teachers, and case workers (see Keller, this volume). Program directors who observe student–faculty mentorships may also provide important insight into academic mentorships. Little discussion of alternative sources exists in workplace mentoring contexts but may include ratings provided by supervisors and/or colleagues who are familiar with the mentorship.

Assessing mentorships over time is also discussed as vital to understanding men-toring relationships. All three areas appropriately cite the need for more longitudinal designs, which would be useful for the generation of comprehensive theories rele-vant to mentoring relationships. While each area has its own perspective of mentor-ship development, a more global description of the process may contribute to the richness of general theory about how mentorships change over time.

New Horizons in the Field of Mentoring

While considering theoretical and methodological development in these three areas of mentoring scholarship, it is important to identify emerging research areas. First, future research should account for the impact of technological advances that may limit the amount of face-to-face interaction between mentor and protégé (e.g., distance learning, flexitime, e-mail, and telework). Second, because individuals are embedded in multiple social relationships simultaneously and over time, a topic of theoretical interest may be how the presence of multiple mentors influences a person across the lifespan. Lastly, while some work has been done on problems in mentoring relationships, there is still much to learn about the negative aspects of mentoring and how one may overcome, or even learn from, such setbacks. Future theoretical and methodological advances in these areas would contribute to the quality and understanding of mentoring relationships across areas of study.

Part III

Naturally Occurring Mentoring Relationships

Chapter 7

Naturally Occurring Mentoring Relationships Involving Youth

Renée Spencer

When successful adults who have overcome difficult life circumstances are asked to reflect on the major influences in their lives, many recall a caring adult whose presence during their youth made all the difference. These familiar stories of what have come to be called natural mentor relationships are receiving increasing attention by researchers of child development and practitioners working to intervene in the lives of vulnerable and troubled youth. This interest is fueled in part by the decades of accumulated research on resilience that links one good relationship with an adult to a host of positive outcomes for children and adolescents, including better overall psychological and academic adjustment (e.g., Masten & Coatsworth, 1998). Today, rapidly proliferating formal mentoring programs are seeking to create for youth the kinds of relationships with naturally occurring adults that have been identified in the research on resilience as providing such significant protection in childhood and adolescence.

Natural mentoring relationships may evolve out of a range of roles that adults play in the lives of youth, including extended family members, family friends, neighbors, teachers, coaches, after-school program staff, and religious group leaders. These relationships may be longstanding, spanning many years, or more short-term with brief encounters at critical junctures leaving a lasting impression on a young person. Some relationships are more focused on the achievement of specific goals, such as developing athletic skills or getting into college, while other natural mentors are integral parts of the many different aspects of the youth's life and offer a range of ever-changing support and guidance as the young person grows and develops.

Natural mentor relationships appear to be far more prevalent than formal ones. For example, in one survey conducted by the Commonwealth Fund (McLearn, Colasanto, & Schoen, 1998), 83% of respondents reported that their mentoring relationships with youth were established through informal connections, such as neighborhood and family ties, whereas 17% indicated involvement in mentoring relationships established through formal programs. Yet, natural mentor relationships have received relatively scant attention in the developmental literature to date. Darling, Hamilton, and Shaver (2003) suggest several reasons for this, including stereotypes about adolescents being overly focused on peer relationships and invested in rebelling against adult norms – notions that have begun to be dispelled (Arnett, 1999), and the tendency for relationships with adults outside the family to be less emotionally salient to adolescents than relationships with parents and peers.

Increasingly, the significant contributions that nonparent adults make to youth as they move through childhood and adolescence and on into adulthood are being recognized. This interest reflects a larger trend in developmental research toward understanding the social ecology of youth development and the many contextual factors that play a role in shaping youths' experiences and developmental pathways (Cicchetti & Aber, 1998; Greenfield, Keller, Fuligni, & Maynard, 2003; Seidman et al., 1998). Natural mentors, whose influence becomes more evident when the scope of inquiry is widened from the more traditional focus on parents and peers, are thought to fulfill a variety of youth's needs in ways that may complement the support provided by parents and in other cases may compensate for deprivations in these relationships (Darling et al., 2003; Zimmerman, Bingenheimer, & Behrendt, 2005).

The research literature on natural mentors is diffuse, as the topic has been approached from a variety of angles. The literature on youth's relationships with unrelated adults, work that has grown out of social network research, has served as the foundation for the consideration of natural mentoring relationships. More recently, focused attention has been paid to what are being called adult *very important people* (VIPs) in the lives of youth. The growing interest in mentoring more generally has contributed to an increase in these studies of adults who serve as a guide or role model to young people in some fashion. As these adults are often family members the use of the term nonparental rather than unrelated adult has been increasing. Other studies use the term natural mentors to refer to influential adults, related and unrelated, in the lives of youth.

In this chapter, research from each of these traditions is synthesized to present a picture of our current understanding of natural mentoring relationships between youth and adults. First, what is known about the prevalence of natural mentoring relationships is reviewed. This is followed by discussions of the development of natural mentoring relationships, the types of support these relationships offer, and what are thought to be some of the key psychological processes occurring in these important connections. Individual differences that appear to contribute to the formation of natural mentoring relationships are then considered and, finally, the conclusion of this chapter is devoted to detailing areas for further research.

Who are Natural Mentors?

No single agreed-upon definition of a natural mentor currently exists in the empirical literature. Rhodes (2002b) has offered a general definition of a mentoring relationship as one "between an older, more experienced adult and an unrelated, younger protégé – a relationship in which the adult provides ongoing guidance, instruction, and encouragement aimed at developing the competence and character of the protégé" (p. 3). Others have defined a natural mentor as an adult who "you can go to for support and guidance if you need to make an important decision or who inspires you to do your best" (Zimmerman, Bingenheimer, & Notaro, 2002, p. 226). The use of the term VIP is growing in the empirical literature on children's relationships with nonparental adults. These VIPs have been defined as an adult at least 21 years old who has had a significant influence on a young person and who can be relied on for support during a time of need (Greenberger, Chen, & Beam, 1998). DuBois and Karcher (2005) noted that most definitions of mentor relationships share three core elements: a) a mentor is someone with greater experience or wisdom, b) the mentor offers guidance or instruction intended to promote the protégé's development, c) there is a trusting emotional bond between the mentor and protégé (p. 3).

The decline of available adults to fill the role of natural mentor has been lamented (Scales, 2003). Shifting family and marital patterns, overcrowded schools, and less cohesive communities have been cited as forces that have restricted the opportunities for informal contact between youth and unrelated adults and reduced the opportunities for caring adults to develop natural mentoring relationships with youth (Furstenberg, 1994; Putnam, 2000). Some have noted that the problem is particularly acute in urban centers where community ties have loosened and many of the middle-class adults who once served as respected authority figures in their communities have moved to the suburbs, leaving far fewer adults in these communities who are able to pass along vital information and resources to youth who are striving educationally and economically (Anderson, 1990; Wilson, 1987). Additionally, the tendency for youth, particularly adolescents, to spend much of their time in peer-focused social contexts is thought to have contributed to a diminishment in opportunities to form close relationships with unrelated adults (Darling et al., 2003).

Despite these trends, a variety of studies have reported that anywhere from approximately 53% to 85% of youth surveyed indicate having a natural mentor (Beam, Chen, & Greenberger, 2002; Chen, Greenberger, Farruggia, Bush, & Dong, 2003; Sanchez & Reyes, 1999; Zimmerman et al., 2002). A range of adults have been identified as serving in this capacity; however, youth commonly report having these kinds of relationships with extended family members, such as aunts, cousins, or grandparents (Chen et al., 2003; Zimmerman et al., 2002). Other research has found that about half of young people's relationships with important nonparental adults are with relatives and half are with nonfamilial adults (Beam et al., 2002; Cavell, Meehan, Heffer, & Holladay, 2002; Greenberger et al., 1998; Rhodes, Ebert, & Fischer, 1992). Nonfamilial adults may include those in professional roles, such as teachers, coaches, counselors, and ministers, and adults who are connected with the family in more informal ways, such as godparents and god-siblings, the boyfriends and girlfriends of family members, friends' parents and friends' siblings, and neighbors (Chen et al., 2003; Zimmerman et al., 2002). These studies suggest that although the opportunities to form connections with adults outside the family may have diminished in recent years, such relationships continue to be an integral part of youths' lives.

Development of Natural Mentor Relationships

Little is known about how natural mentoring relationships between youth and adults begin and develop over time as almost no research to date has attempted to address these issues. This is not surprising in light of how little attention has been paid to these issues in the study of formal mentoring relationships (Keller, 2005a), which have much more clearly defined beginning and end points.

Keller (2005a) has proposed a model for the development of youth mentoring relationships based on Kram's (1983) model for natural mentorships between adults in the workplace. It is intended to be a general model, applicable to a wide range of relationships including those with peers and with both formal and natural adult mentors, and consists of five stages: a) contemplation, b) initiation, c) growth and maintenance, d) decline and dissolution, and e) redefinition (Keller, 2005a, p. 86). Further, changes in a mentoring relationship over time may be the result of several factors and processes, such as the developmental changes in the youth and adult, how interpersonal exchanges shift over time (e.g., increases in self-disclosure, management of conflict), and events and circumstances in the lives of each participant, which may include moves, illnesses, job changes, or other significant life events (Keller, 2005a). These stages generally reflect a model for relationships as having some form of beginning, middle, and end to them. However, not all relationships progress through each of these stages in an orderly or universal way. A relationship with a teacher may pass through each of the five stages over the course of one school year. On the other hand, the contemplation and initiation phases of a natural mentoring relationship with a family member, such as an uncle or grandparent, may be less clear or circumscribed. These relationships may be characterized largely by gradual and lengthy growth and maintenance.

Indeed, natural mentoring relationships tend to serve as an extension to, and arise out of, youths' existing support structures (Freedman, 1994; Rhodes & Davis, 1996; Sullivan, 1996). Beam et al. (2002) in their study of ethnically diverse urban adolescents found that most natural mentor relationships developed gradually over time rather than suddenly in response to a significant event or problem. Through regular ongoing contact a relationship formed that became important to the adolescents.

In one of the few studies that examines natural mentoring relationships over time, Klaw, Rhodes, and Fitzgerald (2003) found that among African American adolescent mothers many had natural mentoring relationships that endured over the 2-year course of the study. Further, these relationships were central to the adolescents' lives in that they received a range of support from these mentors (i.e., loaning them things, encouraging them to stay in school) and had regular and frequent contact with them – the majority interacting with their mentors at least once a week and more than half reporting having daily contact. It is also notable that adolescents who reported having long-term mentors formed these relationships in early childhood and most expected to maintain the relationship forever. In another study of adolescent mothers (Rhodes, Contreras, & Mangelsdorf, 1994), in this case Latina, among those who identified having a natural mentor, almost half had known their mentors most of their lives and expected to maintain the relationship for the rest of their lives. Unfortunately, given that it is rare for studies of natural mentors to inquire about the length of these relationships, it is unclear whether there is something particular to the great need for support among youth who are parenting that solidifies an existing natural mentor relationship, or whether youth who are not parenting would report having such longstanding and significant relationships with their natural mentors.

Finally, whereas frequent contact has been stressed as critical to the development of formal mentoring relationships (DuBois & Neville, 1997; Herrera, Sipe, & McClanahan, 2000), the amount of time youth spend with adults identified as natural mentors varies widely. In many cases, the visits may be infrequent and the time spent together brief (Scales & Gibbons, 1996). For others contact can be quite frequent. Latina and African American girls have reported seeing their mentors at least one time a week (Rhodes et al., 1992, 1994). Similarly, a study with college-aged children of alcoholics who were asked to reflect back on their experiences with a natural mentor when they were growing up found that almost half reported having had daily contact with their mentors (Cavell et al., 2002).

Dimensions of Natural Mentoring Relationships

Adults who serve as natural mentors play a role in the lives of youth that is distinct from both parents and peers while at the same time sharing features that are common to both of these types of relationships. Mentors are freed from the direct responsibilities for sanctioning misbehavior and are often not in the position of structuring youths' day-to-day lives. Mentors may also have the opportunity to engage in more social activities with youth, offering companionship in the way that peer relationships often do. Yet, like a parent, natural mentors are able to provide guidance, counsel, opportunities for learning and access to resources that peers cannot.

It has been suggested that strong and positive relationships with mentors can support overall positive development in youth (Spencer, 2006; Hamilton & Darling, 1989). Hamilton and Darling (1989) base this assertion on Vygotsky's (1978) ideas that engaging in joint activities with others is the central mechanism of human development. Mentors tend to engage in activities with youth and through these activities promote their competence in multiple arenas. The two key dimensions of Vygotsky's (1978) social theory of development, a) participation in activities and b) in the context of interpersonal relationships, have become two aspects of mentoring relationships that have received significant theoretical attention.

Recently, the interpersonal bond in mentoring relationships has begun to be examined more closely (Herrera et al., 2000; Liang, Tracy, Taylor, & Williams, 2002; Parra, DuBois, Neville, & Pugh-Lilly, 2002; Rhodes, 2002b; Spencer, 2006). Rhodes (2002b, 2005) in her model of mentoring relationships has suggested that interpersonal processes such as trust, mutuality, and empathy create a context within which development-enhancing processes unfold. Other specific dimensions of this interpersonal bond have begun to be delineated. For example, Liang and colleagues (2002) found that natural mentoring relationships distinguished by a higher composite score on measures of perceived authenticity, engagement, and empowerment were associated with lower reported levels of loneliness and higher reported levels of self-esteem among college-aged women. Together, these relational dimensions of mentoring were better predictors of outcomes than were some structural aspects of relationships, such as frequency of contact and length of relationship. Some recent research on assigned or formal mentoring relationships has indicated that a close and enduring connection must form in order for youth to be more likely to reap the benefits of a mentoring relationship, such as improvements in self-concept, improvements in interpersonal relationships, decreases in substance use, and improved school attendance (DuBois, Neville, Parra, & Pugh-Lilly, 2002; Parra et al., 2002; Rhodes, 2002b).

However, others (Darling, Hamilton, & Niego, 1994; Darling et al., 2003) have suggested that a close interpersonal bond may not be a critical feature of natural mentoring relationships. Rather, the instrumental aspects of the relationship, or the extent to which the adult engages in challenging and goal-directed joint activities, are what are most salient to the young person and what make the relationships influential. Mentors may challenge youth by pushing them to do their best and also pointing out possibilities they may not have imagined for themselves (Hamilton & Darling, 1989).

In one study examining youths' relationships with adults in Japan and the United States, Darling and colleagues (Darling, Hamilton, Toyokawa, & Matsuda, 2002) found that unrelated adults served as mentors to adolescents even in the absence of strong positive emotional bonds. These researchers conclude that adolescents are able to recognize the important influence that unrelated adults have on them and accept mentoring from them, regardless of how much they "like" the unrelated adult. When an emotional bond does develop, it is thought to grow out of the adult's validation of the youth's efforts and abilities (Darling et al., 1994). Such experiences can be powerful. For example, feeling liked by a teacher for doing well in class may motivate a young person to work harder in school and may eventually contribute to more broad positive perceptions of the self as smart or capable. Positive feedback from adults whose role is primarily instrumental may also be less easy to dismiss than such feedback from a parent or other adult whose praise may be expected or experienced as obligatory.

It is likely that both the interpersonal bond and the degree to which the adult challenges the youth are important components of many natural mentoring relationships. However, depending on the needs of the youth, the qualities of the adult, and the nature of the relationship, one or the other aspect may play a more central or salient role. For example, there may be differences in the importance of the affective and instrumental components in relationships with unrelated adults who fill more prescribed social roles, such as teacher or coach, as compared to relationships with extended family members, where the affective bond may be more critical. Beam et al. (2002) note that sociological study of kin and nonkin social networks more generally has found that relationships with members of kinship groups tend to be more longstanding, have a stronger affective component, and provide a wider array of support whereas relationships with nonkin tend to be more temporary, more instrumental in nature, and fulfill a specific function.

Functions and Psychological Processes

Much of the research to date has focused on whether or not youth have natural mentoring relationships and the associations between the presence of these relationships and youth outcomes, yielding limited insight into the mentoring process itself. Some studies have queried youth about the types of support they receive from their natural mentors; however, little is currently known about the qualities of natural mentoring relationships, such as the amount and kinds of interactions or the nature and range of the support provided. There has been some discussion of the roles that natural mentoring relationships play in the lives of youth and the ways that mentoring may support or enhance positive youth development.

Hamilton and Darling (1989) have noted an important distinction between the social and functional roles of mentors, with the former referring to who the mentor is and the latter to what the mentor and protégé do. The social role of a mentor may be arranged but this does not insure that the functional role will follow. Natural mentoring relationships tend to be defined in terms of the functional role the adult serves – what he or she does for the young person. An adult in a variety of social roles (teacher, coach, or neighbor) may become a mentor in the functional sense, in some cases perhaps without the adult even being fully aware that he or she is being viewed in this way. The primary functional roles cited by Hamilton and Darling (1989) were teaching – formal (music teacher) and informal (working on a project together, such a fixing a bicycle), challenging youth to set high goals for themselves (immediate and long-term) while also working with them to develop a plan for how to achieve these, and serving as a positive role model.

Other early work on youth mentoring by Flaxman, Ascher, and Harrington (1988) delineated two central roles that mentors fulfill. In their view, mentors engage in the instrumental functions of teacher, coach, and advisor (activities that are clearly linked with tangible goals) as well as the psychosocial functions of role modeling, counseling, and providing emotional support. Recent work (Beam et al., 2002) has indicated that that natural mentors provide a wide range of support that is meaningful to youths from their perspective, such as showing respect, serving as someone to talk to, supporting the youth's activities, helping with school, and serving as a companion and role model.

Most of the research has focused on the supportive functions of natural mentoring relationships, specifically employing models of social support in how youth are questioned about the nature of their relationships with natural mentors. Others have begun to develop more comprehensive models of the mentoring process and the many ways that mentoring relationships may influence youth's development in several domains. Each of these approaches to understanding the mentoring process is discussed below.

Social Support

It is generally thought that one of the reasons why important adults are likely so significant for positive youth development is because of the various forms of social support they provide (Barrera & Bonds, 2005; DuBois et al., 2002; Scales & Gibbons, 1996). However, there is less clarity about what kinds of support may be most important or effective. The following major forms of support have been identified and discussed in the literature and are detailed below: a) instrumental support, b) emotional support, and c) companionship. Instrumental support generally connotes the provision of concrete assistance in some way, such as teaching new skills or providing material resources (Cohen & Wills, 1985). It is sometimes also referred to as tangible support. Emotional support is typically thought of as providing a listening ear during times of stress and conveying acceptance and validating the worth of the person (Cohen & Wills, 1985). Companionship support is spending time engaging in leisure or recreational activities (Cohen & Wills, 1985).

Youth tend to report that natural mentor relationships provide a combination of these forms of support. In most studies, the majority of youth report receiving emotional support from their natural mentors. For example, Greenberger et al. (1998) found that among adolescents of diverse ethnic backgrounds, support for personal development and for dealing with interpersonal problems was the most commonly cited function of an important nonparental adult. In a study of Latino adolescents, Sanchez and Reyes (1999) also found that most of these youth (78%) reported receiving emotional support from their mentors. However, natural mentors provide many other types of support as well. African American teen mothers who reported having long-term natural mentors indicated that these adults had provided them with a range of support, both emotional and instrumental, over time, including talking about personal issues, helping them with school, giving them advice, and loaning them things (Klaw et al., 2003). Beam et al. (2002) found that 80% of the adolescents in their study cited interpersonal support, such as showing respect and serving as someone to talk to, as the reason their identified adult was important to them. About half of these youth also indicated that the adult provided other forms of support considered to be important to them, such as helping with school, offering assistance with personal and financial issues, and serving as a companion and a role model.

The nature of the support provided by natural mentors appears to be somewhat different from that experienced by youth in their relationships with their parents. In studies of parenting adolescent girls of color (Klaw et al., 2003; Rhodes et al., 1994), these youth reported experiencing more intangible forms of support, such as emotional support and positive feedback, and greater satisfaction with this support from their natural mentors as compared to their mothers, whom these youth also experienced as being supportive of them. Other youth have reported disclosing personal feelings and concerns to their natural mentors that they were reluctant to share with either their parents or their peers, as they perceived their mentors to be less judgmental and punitive (Beam et al., 2002).

Companionship support has received less attention in the literature to date. Mentoring researchers have noted this dimension of mentoring relationships in passing (Morrow & Styles, 1995; Sipe, 2002; Styles & Morrow, 1992) but few have looked closely at the influence on youth development of simply spending time with an important adult engaging in leisure activities that are pleasurable to both. Social support researchers have come to view companionship as distinct from either instrumental or emotional support. Rook (1995) asserts that companionship may be motivated by the desire to share in "purely enjoyable interaction, such as the pleasure in sharing leisure activities, trading life stories and humorous anecdotes, and engaging in playful spontaneous activities," while other forms of social support are typically sought out during a time of emotional distress or when assistance with a problem is needed (p. 440). Rather than buffering stress, companionship is thought to contribute to feelings of overall well-being in everyday life.

Having fun together is a theme that has been emphasized by youth when they identify what is meaningful to them about their relationships with important adults (Parra et al., 2002; Spencer, Jordan, & Sazama, 2004). In a study by Greenberger et al. (1998), youth indicated that the important adults in their lives were a source of fun and companionship, although this was the case for more boys than girls (12% vs. 6%). Cavell and colleagues (2002) found that a majority (72%) of adolescent children of alcoholics indicated that their natural mentor served as a companion to them when they were growing up. For some youth, companionship experiences may provide a welcome respite from the difficult life circumstances with which they are faced (Morrow & Styles, 1995; Spencer, 2006). This could be an important dimension of some natural mentoring relationships that is being overlooked. The tendency to focus on how strong relationships with adults create opportunities for learning or guidance and provide emotional support during times of stress, or what we might consider to be "real support," may be resulting in us overlooking the potential contribution that simply spending time in the company of an adult whom you like and enjoy spending time with and who feels the same about you may make to positive youth development.

Promoting Psychological Development

It is widely assumed that natural mentoring relationships hold the potential to support and promote positive psychological development in youth but almost no attention has been paid to delineating the processes through which this may occur. Rhodes (2002b, 2005; Rhodes, Spencer, Keller, Liang, & Noam, 2006) has proposed the most comprehensive model of the mentoring process to date, asserting that mentoring affects youth through three interrelated processes: 1) by enhancing youth's social relationships and emotional well-being; 2) by improving their cognitive skills through instruction and conversation; and 3) by promoting positive identity development through serving as role models and advocates. There is some research to support each of these components; however, this research has largely been conducted on formal mentoring relationships.

In this model, mentoring relationships are thought to potentially promote youth's social and emotional well-being and development in several ways. By offering youth genuine care and support, mentors can challenge negative views that youth may hold of themselves or of relationships with adults. Mentors may also demonstrate that positive relationships with adults are possible. This experience may then generalize, enabling youth to perceive their proximal relationships as more forthcoming and helpful (Coble, Gantt, & Mallinckrodt, 1996). Rhodes, Grossman, and Resch (2000) found evidence that volunteer formal mentoring relationships contributed to improvements in adolescents' perceptions of their parental relationships, including levels of intimacy, communication, and trust. The potential for a strong relationship with a natural mentor to contribute to improvements in youth's other relationships has not yet been examined empirically. However, Zimmerman et al. (2002) did find evidence that having a natural mentor may help protect youth from the deleterious effects of negative peer influences.

Mentoring relationships may also enhance youth's ability to regulate affective experiences (Spencer, 2006). Effective emotion regulation is increasingly thought to be an outgrowth of a strong attachment relationship and a central feature of healthy social and emotional development (Cowan, 1996). Some mentors may be promoting the development of good emotion regulation skills in the same ways that effective parents do – by validating and verbally labeling the youth's feelings, viewing their negative emotions as an opportunity for intimacy or learning, and engaging in limit-setting, problem-solving, and discussions of goals and strategies for dealing with situations that lead to negative emotions (Gottman, Katz, & Hooven, 1996).

In addition to these social-emotional supports, it has also been suggested that mentoring relationships can have a range of positive influences on cognitive developmental processes. Mentors may employ a variety of strategies to encourage youth's cognitive development, including scaffolding, tutoring, questioning, and dialogue (Rogoff, 1998). Youth may also facilitate the learning process through observation (which the mentor may or may not be aware of) and initiating activities of interest to them with their mentor (Rogoff, 2003). A trusting relationship with a mentor can thus provide a framework in which youth acquire and refine new thinking skills. In a qualitative interview study of formal mentoring relationships (Spencer, 2006), adolescents and their adult mentors narrated numerous examples of times when the two worked together to help the youth complete a task or achieve some goal. The scaffolding provided by these mentors, whether in the form of assistance with a research project or helping the young person prepare for a school musical audition, appeared to offer important opportunities for developing new skills and learning new approaches to problem-solving.

Finally, mentors may also promote positive identity development through role modeling, identification, and the provision of exposure to expanded social and educational opportunities and information about how to access these. Identity development has long been considered to be one of the major developmental tasks of adolescence (Erikson, 1950/1963). Inherently a social process, adolescents are most likely to model themselves in the fashion of those around them, for better or for worse (Jaffee, Moffitt, Caspi, & Taylor, 2003). The development of a positive and prosocial sense of identity depends on the active encouragement of positive and prosocial adults. However, such support is likely to be more powerful when it is rooted in a genuine knowledge and understanding of the child. As Erikson (1950/1963) notes, "children cannot be fooled by empty praise and condescending encouragement" (p. 95). A highly regarded mentor's positive appraisal may become incorporated into the youth's sense of self and, in turn, modify the way the young person thinks that parents, peers, teachers, and others see him or her.

In a few studies, youth have reported that their natural mentors serve as role models for them (Beam et al., 2002; Chen et al., 2003; Hamilton & Darling, 1989). The assumption is typically that mentors serve as positive role models. However, Sanchez, Reyes, Potashner, and Singh (2006) have also noted that mentors, particularly those who are family members, may sometimes serve as examples for what not to do. In their qualitative study of Mexican American college students' natural mentoring relationships, these important adults were sometimes cited as providing lessons in life's challenges and how choices, such as not continuing with higher education, can compound the difficulties one faces in life.

Individual Differences

There has been limited discussion and examination of the relationship between individual differences and whether a youth is more likely to have a natural mentor and also whether there are differences in the nature of the relationships formed. Factors such as gender, race and ethnicity, age, and parental support have each received some degree of consideration thus far. The empirical literature addressing each of these is summarized below.

Gender

The evidence with regard to whether girls or boys tend to be more likely to have a natural mentor is mixed. Some studies indicate that females are more likely than males to have a natural mentor. For example, Greenberger et al. (1998) found that among adolescents of diverse ethnic backgrounds, girls were more likely than boys (83% vs. 68%) to report having an important nonparental adult in their lives and both boys and girls also tended to report that this was a same-sex adult. Sanchez and Reyes (1999) in their study of Latino youth in an urban high school also found that more females than males (68% and 33%) reported having a natural mentor and that most reported having a same-sex mentor. Among these youth, most (71%) of the mentor relationships were with family members (aunts, uncles, and siblings). However, in another study (Zimmerman et al., 2005) of over 700 African American and White high school seniors, males and females were equally likely to report having a natural mentor. Hamilton and Darling (1989), on the other hand, found that males were more likely than females to report having a natural mentor (8th and 11th graders in a small town and 3rd-year university students).

Same-gender natural mentor relationships appear to be more common than cross-gender relationships. Among the Latino adolescent participants in the study by Sanchez and Reyes (1999) who had a natural mentor, most indicated that this person was of the same gender (68% of males and 70% of females). Similarly, in a study by Chen and colleagues (2003), 65% of the American adolescent males surveyed reported that their mentor was also male and 73% of females reported having a female mentor.

There has also been some discussion about whether the mentoring process may differ for males and females. It has been suggested that the more traditional conception of mentoring as the provision of advice, skill-building, and challenge may be more applicable for males than for females (Bogat & Liang, 2005; Liang et al., 2002; Sullivan, 1996). This assertion is rooted in relational views of girls' and women's development that hold that females tend to respond better in relationships where there is a mutual exchange rather than a more unidirectional provision of support and guidance (Bogat & Liang, 2005).

Consequently, one of the more common conclusions drawn is that girls may benefit more from relationships with women characterized by self-disclosure and empathy whereas boys are more likely to benefit from engagement in shared activities with adult men (Rhodes, 2002b). However, recent research on the effectiveness of formal mentoring programs has indicated that feelings of closeness and emotional support are key ingredients of mentoring relationships that are associated with improvements in youth functioning, even among those that are focused on promoting school success – for both boys and girls (DuBois et al., 2002; Herrera et al., 2000). Still, gender-specific processes have been little explored empirically as yet.

Racial and Ethnic Background

What little consideration there has been of the role that race and ethnicity play in mentoring relationships has largely focused on formal rather than natural mentoring relationships. In formal mentoring relationships youth of color tend to be matched with White mentors (Grossman & Tierney, 1998; Sipe, 1996), mainly due to the fact that otherwise many youth of color would remain on waiting lists for lengthy periods of time (Rhodes, Reddy, Grossman, & Lee, 2002). However, the study of natural mentors has demonstrated that youth tend to have mentors who share similar racial, ethnic, and class backgrounds (Cavell et al., 2002; Klaw & Rhodes, 1995; Rhodes et al., 1992, 1994; Sanchez & Reyes, 1999) and that more youth of color report having a natural mentor than do White youth (Zimmerman et al., 2005). Further, youth of color tend to report having a natural mentor who is a relative or extended family member, such as an older sibling, aunt, uncle, or cousin, rather than an unrelated adult in their schools or larger communities (Bryant & Zimmerman, 2003; Klaw et al., 2003; Rhodes et al., 1994). Sanchez and Colon (2005) have argued that this may be due in part to the cultural values of collectivism (placing greater importance on the needs, interests, and objectives of the reference group than that of individuals) and familism (an emphasis on immediate and extended family members' responsibilities and obligations to one another), which tend to be more prominent among youth of color.

Similarities in backgrounds may make it easier for some youth to identify with their mentors and to benefit from their guidance. Unfortunately, more process-oriented questions, such as whether youth receive differential support from natural mentors with similar or dissimilar racial and ethnic backgrounds and how such support is received and experienced by youth, have not been addressed in the literature to date. Adults who live or work in the youth's communities and who are directly familiar with the circumstances confronting them are likely to be better able to give advice that is consistent with the cultural norms of a given setting and that is also realistic and takes into account existing opportunities and constraints within their specific community context.

These issues have just begun to be taken up by researchers studying formal mentoring relationships and the findings have been mixed thus far. For example, one study found no differences in the benefits to youth of same- versus cross-race matches (DuBois et al., 2002) whereas another reported some differences but these were not of a robust or consistent nature (Rhodes et al., 2002). A third study found no differences in the level of benefits youth derive from same- versus cross-race matches when youth and adults are matched on the basis of shared interests and the relationship endured at least 11 months, although cross-race relationships were more likely to end prematurely (Grossman & Rhodes, 2002). It is important to note that all of these studies have focused largely on White mentors who are paired with youth of color, rather than mentors of color and White youth or mentors and youth of color who have dissimilar racial and ethnic backgrounds (Sanchez & Colon, 2005).

Age

Adolescence is a particularly critical time for youth to have a close connection with an adult, as they "need to acquire the attitudes, competencies, values, and social skills that will carry them forward to successful adulthood . . . and avoid choices that will limit their future potential" (Eccles & Gootman, 2002, p. 1). The developmental challenges posed by the adolescent years can create an opening for unrelated adults to have a positive impact on teens as they explore their changing relationships and sense of self (Rhodes, 2002b). As such, relationships with unrelated adults may increase in number and significance as youth grow older.

The findings from one study indicate that youth's relationships with natural mentors, particularly unrelated adults, may indeed increase in number as they move through adolescence. Beam et al. (2002) found that among 11th graders, these youth reported that their relationships with nonkin important adults tended to have developed within the previous 4 years whereas their relationships with extended family members had been more longstanding. These adolescents also reported having more frequent contact, in most cases weekly, with the nonkin adults. In another study, Hamilton and Darling (1989) found that the proportion of youth who named an unrelated adult as a significant person in their lives grew larger with age across three cross-sectional samples of 8th graders, 11th graders, and 3rd-year college students. Similarly, Benson's (1993) cross-sectional study of 6th through 12th graders found that the older adolescents in this sample relied on nonparent adults with greater frequency and also tended to report having more in-depth conversations with these adults than did the younger adolescents. However, Blyth, Hill, and Thiel (1982) found no difference in the number of relationships with nonfamilial adults among 7th through 10th graders.

A cross-sectional qualitative study of natural mentoring relationships among youth in middle school, high school, and college suggests there may be differences in the relational processes of mentoring relationships during these different developmental time periods (Liang, Brogan, Corral, & Spencer, 2005). The youth in all three age groups identified their mentors as role models. However, the younger adolescents tended to idealize their mentors whereas the high-school and college participants tended also to stress the value of being able to learn from their mentors' struggles and even failures. In addition, the participants in the two older groups also talked about the importance of mutuality in relationships with mentors, particularly with regard to honesty, respect, and being open to learning from one another. Interestingly, sharing pleasurable companionate experiences, or spending time simply having fun together, was something identified by all three age groups as being an important component of their mentor relationships.

Mentoring relationships may also play a somewhat different role during late adolescence or young adulthood for several reasons (Liang et al., 2005). Unrelated adults may possess certain skills, knowledge, or perspectives that are unlike those attained at home. Older adolescents, as they strive for greater autonomy and develop personal value systems, may be more receptive to the influence of adults other than their parents. Older adolescents may also seek out a mentor because it provides them with an opportunity to build a relationship with an adult who shares their interests or from whom they can learn desired skills.

Parental Support

Some youth, particularly as they move through middle and late adolescence, may be seeking nonparent adults to supplement or expand on the support provided by their families. Other youth, whose parents are unable to provide consistent support because of factors such as illness, divorce, persistent poverty, and violence, may turn to other adults within and outside the family for the support they need (Garmezy, 1987; Rutter, 1987).

Zimmerman et al. (2005) found that youth with both high and low levels of parental support may be most likely to seek out natural mentors. In their view, high levels of parental support may enable youth to seek out support from nonparental adults, by providing a secure base and a sense of confidence. Low levels of support may contribute to youth being highly motivated to seek support from other adults to compensate for the lack of support they experience in relationships with parents. Some further empirical evidence for the former hypothesis is apparent as a couple of studies, one examining college undergraduates and the other urban Latino adolescent mothers, found that youth who report having higher levels of parental support were also more likely to have a natural mentor (Hamilton & Darling, 1989; Rhodes et al., 1994). Rhodes and colleagues (Klaw et al., 2003; Rhodes et al., 1994), based on their findings that many of the natural mentor relationships of adolescent mothers of color were formed in early childhood, have speculated that supportive relationships with caregivers early in life may make youth more responsive to, or even more inclined to seek out, the support and guidance of nonparental adults.

Conclusion

Natural mentoring relationships occupy a special position in the lives of youth. These connections with adults who are not parents and not peers can offer some of the benefits of both of these other types of influential relationships. The importance of strong relationships with a variety of adults for positive youth development has been well established (Masten & Coatsworth, 1998; Resnick et al., 1997; Scales & Gibbons, 1996). What is now needed is a better understanding of the nature of these relationships. The research reviewed in this chapter represents what is in fact only an initial base from which to build a more complete picture of the rich array of natural mentoring relationships between youth and adults and how these relationships yield the significant benefits widely cited in the child development literature. Such efforts would not only improve our knowledge of natural mentoring but could also guide adults in the growing arena of after-school programs as they strive to build strong and effective relationships with youth, and inform best practices for formal mentoring programs, which in many ways seek to mimic natural mentoring relationships.

Specifically, research that looks closely at how natural mentoring relationships work is needed. Most of the current research is descriptive, although there has been an increasing examination of the associations between natural mentoring relationships and specific youth outcomes. Still, these studies tell us little about the nature of these associations or the particular processes through which natural mentoring relationships influence youth development. Existing hypotheses about the relative contribution of supportive versus instrumental aspects of these relationships could be tested along with other possible pathways suggested by theories such as attachment and resiliency. Such research would be further enriched by consideration of how the developmental stage of the youth may differentially shape these pathways and processes. Attention to how similarities and differences in racial and ethnic backgrounds between youth and their natural mentors may influence the mentoring process is needed, as is further study of the potential role that gender plays.

The potential differences between natural mentoring relationships with related and with unrelated adults also need further examination. The bias toward conceptualizing natural mentors as adults outside the family has been challenged by studies with ethnic minority youth (e.g., Rhodes, Contreras, & Mangelsdorf, 1996; Sanchez & Reyes, 1999) and subsequent research has demonstrated that adults in a variety of social roles are considered by youth to be natural mentors. However, many questions remain about whether there are qualitative differences in the relationships formed with the adults in differing social roles and whether and how these various relationships may be differentially related to youth outcomes.

Unfortunately, to date almost no studies of natural mentor relationships between youth and adults have included the mentors. Thus, we have little information about the qualities of adults who become important people in the lives of youth or about what motivates adults to become involved with youth in this way. When mentors have been included in studies, their perspectives are typically used to confirm or supplement that provided by youth rather than being the focus of study themselves (Beam et al., 2002; Sanchez et al., 2006). Scales (2003) details some of the barriers to adults getting involved in the lives of youth, particularly unrelated adults, including perceptions that the well-being of children is primarily if not solely the responsibility of their parents, the increased reliance on professionals to provide developmental supports to children, negative images of youth presented in the media, and the general trend toward civic disengagement in the United States. Focused study of natural mentors of the kind evidenced in the literature on organizational and academic mentoring (e.g., Allen, 2003; Johnson, 2002) is greatly needed in order to understand the motivations and qualities of adults who become natural mentors to youth and the conditions under which they are most likely to do so.

Research on child development is increasingly emphasizing the importance of strong, growth-promoting relationships with adults for healthy psychological development throughout childhood and adolescence (Steinberg, 2001). Natural mentors appear to offer youth a distinct and significant type of relationship as they grow, develop, and move toward adulthood themselves. A deeper, more nuanced understanding of the natural mentoring process would greatly enhance our ability to more fully tap into this important natural resource for youth, including how best to promote the development of these critical connections for youth who do not already have such a relationship in their lives.

References

Allen, T. D. (2003). Mentoring others: A dispositional and motivational approach. *Journal of Vocational Behavior, 200*, 134–154.

Anderson, E. (1990). *Street wise: Race, class, and change in an urban community*. Chicago: University of Chicago Press.

Arnett, J. J. (1999). Adolescent storm and stress reconsidered. *American Psychologist, 54*(5), 317–326.

Barrera, M., & Bonds, D. D. (2005). Mentoring relationships and social support. In D. L. DuBois & M. J. Karcher (Eds.), *Handbook of youth mentoring* (pp. 133–142). Thousand Oaks, CA: Sage.

Beam, M. R., Chen, C., & Greenberger, E. (2002). The nature of adolescents' relationships with their "very important" nonparental adults. *Journal of Community Psychology, 30*(2), 305–325.

Benson, P. L. (1993). *The troubled journey: A portrait of 6th–12th grade youth*. Minneapolis, MN: The Search Institute.

Blyth, D. A., Hill, J. P., & Thiel, K. S. (1982). Early adolescents' significant others: Grade and gender differences in perceived relationships with familial and nonfamilial adults and young people. *Journal of Youth and Adolescence, 11*(6), 425–450.

Bogat, G. A., & Liang, B. (2005). Gender in mentoring relationships. In D. L. DuBois & M. J. Karcher (Eds.), *Handbook of youth mentoring* (pp. 205–217). Thousand Oaks, CA: Sage.

Bryant, A. L., & Zimmerman, M. A. (2003). Role models and psychosocial outcomes among African American adolescents. *Journal of Adolescent Research, 18*(1), 36–67.

Cavell, T. A., Meehan, B. T., Heffer, R. W., & Holladay, J. J. (2002). The natural mentors of adolescent children of alcoholics (COAs): Implications for preventive practices. *Journal of Primary Prevention, 23*(1), 23–42.

Chen, C., Greenberger, E., Farruggia, S., Bush, K., & Dong, Q. (2003). Beyond parents and peers: The role of very important non-parental adults (VIPs) in adolescent development in China and the United States. *Psychology in the Schools, 40*(1), 35–50.

Cicchetti, D., & Aber, L. (1998). Contextualism and developmental psychopathology. *Development and Psychopathology, 10*, 137–141.

Coble, H. M., Gantt, D. L., & Mallinckrodt, B. (1996). Attachment, social competency, and the capacity to use social support. In G. R. Pierce, B. R. Sarason, & I. G. Sarason (Eds.), *Handbook of social support and the family* (pp. 141–172). New York: Plenum.

Cohen, S., & Wills, T. A. (1985). Stress, social support, and the buffering hypothesis. *Psychological Bulletin, 98*(2), 310–357.

Cowan, P. A. (1996). Meta-thoughts on the role of meta-emotion in children's development: Comment on Gottman et al. (1996). *Journal of Family Psychology, 10*(3), 277–283.

Darling, N., Hamilton, S. F., & Shaver, K. (2003). Relationships outside the family: Unrelated adults. In G. R. Adams & M. D. Berzonsky (Eds.), *Blackwell handbook of adolescence* (pp. 349–370). Oxford: Blackwell Publishing.

Darling, N., Hamilton, S. F., & Niego, S. (1994). Adolescents' relations with adults outside the family. In R. Montemayor, G. R. Adams & T. P. Gullotta (Eds.), *Personal relationships during adolescence* (pp. 216–235). Thousand Oaks, CA: Sage.

Darling, N., Hamilton, S., Toyokawa, T., & Matsuda, S. (2002). Naturally occurring mentoring in Japan and the United States: Social role and correlates. *American Journal of Community Psychology, 30*(2), 245–270.

DuBois, D. L., & Karcher, M. J. (2005). Youth mentoring: Theory, research, and practice. In D. L. Dubois & M. J. Karcher (Eds.), *Handbook of youth mentoring* (pp. 2–11). Thousand Oaks, CA: Sage.

DuBois, D. L., & Neville, H. A. (1997). Youth mentoring: Investigation of relationship characteristics and perceived benefits. *Journal of Community Psychology, 25*, 227–234.

DuBois, D. L., Neville, H. A., Parra, G. R., & Pugh-Lilly, A. O. (2002). Testing a new model of mentoring. In J. E. Rhodes (Ed.), *A critical view of youth mentoring* (Vol. 93, pp. 21–57). San Francisco: Jossey-Bass.

Eccles, J., & Gootman, J. A. (Eds.). (2002). *Community programs to promote youth development*. Washington, DC: National Academy Press.

Erikson, E. H. (1950/1963). *Childhood and society* (2nd, reissued ed.). New York: W. W. Norton & Co.

Flaxman, E., Ascher, C., & Harrington, C. (1988). *Youth mentoring: Programs and practices*. New York: ERIC Clearinghouse on Urban Education, Institute for Urban and Minority Education, Teachers College, Columbia University.

Freedman, M. (1994). *The kindness of strangers: The movement to mentor young people in poverty*. Berkeley, CA: Public/Private Ventures.

Furstenberg, F. F. (1994). How families manage risk and opportunity in dangerous neigh-borhoods. In W. J. Wilson (Ed.), *Sociology and the public agenda* (pp. 231–258). Newbury Park, CA: Sage.

Garmezy, N. (1987). Stress, competence, and development: Continuities in the study of schizophrenic adults, children vulnerable to psychopathology, and the search for stress-resistant children. *American Journal of Orthopsychiatry*, 57(2), 159–174.

Gottman, J., Katz, L. F., & Hooven, C. (1996). Parental meta-emotion philosophy and the emotional life of families: Theoretical models and preliminary data. *Journal of Family Psychology*, 10(3), 243–268.

Greenberger, E., Chen, C., & Beam, M. R. (1998). The role of "very important" nonparental adults in adolescent development. *Journal of Youth and Adolescence*, 27(3), 321–343.

Greenfield, P. M., Keller, H., Fuligni, A., & Maynard, A. (2003). Cultural pathways through universal development. *Annual Review of Psychology*, 54, 461–490.

Grossman, J. B., & Rhodes, J. E. (2002). The test of time: Predictors and effects of duration in youth mentoring programs. *American Journal of Community Psychology*, 30(2), 199–219.

Grossman, J. B., & Tierney, J. P. (1998). Does mentoring work? An impact study of the Big Brothers/Big Sisters program. *Evaluation Review*, 22, 403–426.

Hamilton, S. F., & Darling, N. (1989). Mentors in adolescents' lives. In K. Hurrelmann & U. Engel (Eds.), *Social world of adolescents: International perspectives* (pp. 121–139). Oxford, England: Walter DeGruyter.

Herrera, C., Sipe, C. L., & McClanahan, W. S. (2000). *Mentoring school-age children: Relationship development in community-based and school-based programs*. Philadelphia: P/PV.

Jaffee, S. R., Moffitt, T. E., Caspi, A., & Taylor, A. (2003). Life with (or without) father: The benefits of living with two biological parents depend on the father's antisocial behavior. *Child Development*, 74(1), 109–126.

Johnson, W. B. (2002). The intentional mentor: Strategies and guidelines for the practice of mentoring. *Professional Psychology: Research and Practice*, 33(1), 88–96.

Keller, T. E. (2005a). The stages and development of mentoring relationships. In D. L. DuBois & M. J. Karcher (Eds.), *Handbook of youth mentoring* (pp. 82–99). Thousand Oaks, CA: Sage.

Klaw, E. L., & Rhodes, J. E. (1995). Mentor relationships and the career development of pregnant and parenting African-American teenagers. *Psychology of Women Quarterly*, 19(4), 551–562.

Klaw, E. L., Rhodes, J. E., & Fitzgerald, L. F. (2003). Natural mentors in the lives of African-American adolescent mothers: Tracking relationships over time. *Journal of Youth and Adolescence*, 32(3), 223–232.

Kram, K. E. (1983). Phases of the mentoring relationship. *Academy of Management Journal*, 26(4), 608–625.

Liang, B., Brogan, D., Corral, M., & Spencer, R. (2005). *Youth mentoring relationships across three developmental periods: A qualitative analysis*. Unpublished manuscript.

Liang, B., Tracy, A. J., Taylor, C. A., & Williams, L. M. (2002). Mentoring college-age women: A relational approach. *American Journal of Community Psychology*, 30(2), 271–288.

Masten, A. S., & Coatsworth, J. D. (1998). The development of competence in favorable and unfavorable environments: Lessons from research on successful children. *American Psychologist*, 53(2), 205–220.

McLearn, K. T., Colasanto, D., & Schoen, C. (1998). *Mentoring makes a difference: Findings from The Commonwealth Fund 1998 Survey of Adults Mentoring Young People*. The Commonwealth Fund. Retrieved March 23, 2005, from the World Wide Web: www.cmwf.org/publications/publications_show.htm?doc_id=230658

Morrow, K. V., & Styles, M. B. (1995). *Building relationships with youth in program settings: A study of Big Bothers/Big Sisters*. Philadelphia: Public/Private Ventures.

Parra, G. R., DuBois, D. L., Neville, H. A., & Pugh-Lilly, A. O. (2002). Mentoring relationships for youth: Investigation of a process-oriented model. *Journal of Community Psychology*, *30*(4), 367–388.

Putnam, R. (2000). *Bowling alone: The collapse and revival of American Community*. New York: Simon & Schuster.

Resnick, M., Bearman, P., Blum, R., Bauman, K., Harris, K., Jones, J., et al. (1997). Protecting adolescents from harm: Findings from the National Longitudinal Study on Adolescent Health. *Journal of the American Medical Association*, *278*(10), 823–832.

Rhodes, J. E. (2002b). *Stand by me: The risks and rewards of mentoring today's youth*. Cambridge, MA: Harvard University Press.

Rhodes, J. E. (2005). A model of youth mentoring. In D. L. DuBois & M. J. Karcher (Eds.), *Handbook of youth mentoring* (pp. 30–43). Thousand Oaks, CA: Sage.

Rhodes, J. E., Contreras, J. M., & Mangelsdorf, S. C. (1994). Natural mentor relationships among Latina adolescent mothers: Psychological adjustment, moderating processes, and the role of early parental acceptance. *American Journal of Community Psychology*, *22*(2), 211–227.

Rhodes, J. E., & Davis, A. B. (1996). Supportive ties between nonparent adults and urban adolescent girls. In B. J. Leadbeater & N. Way (Eds.), *Urban girls: Resisting stereotypes, creating identities* (pp. 213–225). New York: New York University Press.

Rhodes, J. E., Ebert, L., & Fischer, K. (1992). Natural mentors: An overlooked resource in the social networks of young, African American mothers. *American Journal of Community Psychology*, *20*(4), 445–461.

Rhodes, J. E., Grossman, J. B., & Resch, N. R. (2000). Agents of change: Pathways through which mentoring relationships influence adolescents' academic adjustment. *Child Development*, *71*(6), 1662–1671.

Rhodes, J. E., Reddy, R., Grossman, J. B., & Lee, J. M. (2002). Volunteer mentoring relationships with minority youth: An analysis of same versus cross-race matches. *Journal of Applied Social Psychology*, *32*(10), 2114–2133.

Rhodes, J. E., Spencer, R., Keller, T. E., Liang, B., & Noam, G. (2006). A model for the influence of mentoring relationships on youth development. *Journal of Community Psychology*, *34*, 691–707.

Rogoff, B. (1998). Cognition as a collaborative process. In D. Kuhn & R. S. Siegler (Eds.), *Cognition, perception, and language* (5th ed., pp. 679–744). New York: Wiley.

Rogoff, B. (2003). *The cultural nature of human development*. New York: Oxford University Press.

Rook, K. S. (1995). Support, companionship, and control in older adults' social networks: Implications for well-being. In J. F. Nussbaum & J. Coupland (Eds.), *Handbook of communication and aging research* (pp. 437–463). Mahwah, NJ: Lawrence Erlbaum.

Rutter, M. (1987). Psychosocial resilience and protective mechanisms. *American Journal of Orthopsychiatry*, *57*(3), 316–331.

Sanchez, B., & Colon, Y. (2005). Race, ethnicity, and culture in mentoring relationships. In D. L. DuBois & M. J. Karcher (Eds.), *Handbook of youth mentoring* (pp. 191–204). Thousand Oaks, CA: Sage.

Sanchez, B., & Reyes, O. (1999). Descriptive profile of the mentorship relationships of Latino adolescents. *Journal of Community Psychology*, *27*(3), 299–302.

Sanchez, B., Reyes, O., Potashner, I., & Singh, J. (2006). A qualitative examination of the relationships that play a mentoring function for Mexican American older adolescents. *Cultural Diversity and Ethnic Minority Psychology*, *12*, 615–631.

Scales, P. C. (2003). *Other people's kids: Social expectations and American adults' involvement with children and adolescents*. New York: Kluwer Academic.

Scales, P. C., & Gibbons, J. L. (1996). Extended family members and unrelated adults in the lives of young adolescents: A research agenda. *Journal of Early Adolescence*, *16*(4), 365–389.

Seidman, E., Yoshikawa, H., Roberts, A., Chesir-Teran, D., Allen, L., Friedman, J., et al. (1998). Structural and experiential neighborhood contexts, developmental stage, and anti-social behavior among urban adolescents in poverty. *Development and Psychopathology, 10,* 259–281.

Sipe, C. L. (1996). *Mentoring: A synthesis of the P/PV's research: 1988–1995.* Philadelphia: Public/Private Ventures (ERIC Document Reproduction Service No ED 404 410).

Sipe, C. L. (2002). Mentoring programs for adolescents: A research summary. *Journal of Adolescent Health, 31,* 251–260.

Spencer, R. (2006). Understanding the mentoring process between adolescents and adults. *Youth and Society, 37,* 287–315.

Spencer, R. A., Jordan, J. V., & Sazama, J. (2004). Growth-promoting relationships between youth and adults: A focus group study. *Families in Society, 85*(3), 354–362.

Steinberg, L. (2001). We know some things: Parent–adolescent relationships in retrospect and prospect. *Journal of Research on Adolescence, 11*(1), 1–19.

Styles, M. B., & Morrow, K. V. (1992). *Understanding how youth and elders form relationships: A study of four linking lifetimes programs.* Philadelphia: Public/Private Ventures.

Sullivan, A. M. (1996). From mentor to muse: Recasting the role of women in relationship with urban adolescent girls. In B. J. R. Leadbeater & N. Way (Eds.), *Urban girls: Resisting stereotypes, creating identities* (pp. 226–249). New York: New York University Press.

Vygotsky, L. S. (1978). *Mind in society: The development of higher psychological processes.* Cambridge, MA: Harvard University Press.

Wilson, W. J. (1987). *The truly disadvantaged.* Chicago: The University of Chicago Press.

Zimmerman, M. A., Bingenheimer, J. B., & Behrendt, D. E. (2005). Natural mentoring relationships. In D. L. DuBois & M. J. Karcher (Eds.), *Handbook of youth mentoring* (pp. 143–157). Thousand Oaks, CA: Sage.

Zimmerman, M. A., Bingenheimer, J. B., & Notaro, P. C. (2002). Natural mentors and adolescent resiliency: A study with urban youth. *American Journal of Community Psychology, 30*(2), 221–243.

Chapter 8

Naturally Occurring Student–Faculty Mentoring Relationships: A Literature Review

Carol A. Mullen

This literature review examines the prevalence and role of informal student–faculty mentorships, focusing on the formation, development, and dissolution of such relationships within graduate education, with reference to the undergraduate context. Empirical research on the graduate level more clearly distinguishes informal from formal mentoring, giving it priority attention here. Content is organized around seven topics: clarification of informal mentoring; benefits and drawbacks of spontaneous relationships; personality characteristics of mentor and protégé; functions of mentoring; frameworks of informal mentoring phases; formation, development, and termination; and new types of mentoring relationships.

Critics appraise mentoring studies as methodologically flawed for the reason that most are either strictly anecdotal or too limited in sample size (e.g., Tenenbaum, Crosby, & Gliner, 2001; Waldeck, Orrego, Plax, & Kearney, 1997). In fact, Merriam (1983) observed that "no distinct line of research can be traced with respect to mentoring in academic settings" (p. 169), but progress has been reflected in the literature over the last 20 years. Indeed, there is now enough empirical research addressing the emergent topic of informal student–faculty mentoring relationships – from the perspectives of both mentor (e.g., Johnson & Ridley, 2004; Mullen, 2005) and protégé (e.g., Dorn, Papalewis, & Brown, 1995; O'Neil & Wrightsman, 2001) – to fill that gap.

Clarification of Informal Mentoring

Researchers examining student–faculty mentoring describe naturally occurring mentoring relationships as *informal*, that is, spontaneous and gradual (Johnson, 2002). These relationships are not managed, structured, or officially recognized; further, they are often not sanctioned by the institution, can last longer than most other organizational relationships, and have a closer interpersonal bond (Mullen, 2005).

In contrast, *formal mentorship* is a one-on-one mentor–protégé arrangement based on assignment to the relationship (e.g., Johnson & Ridley, 2004). Formal mentoring also occurs within institutionalized groups and cohorts led by qualified, official mentors (Twale & Kochan, 2000). Informal mentoring relationships in graduate school are considered deeper and more effective than such assigned mentorships (Johnson & Ridley, 2004). However, informal mentoring involves greater commitment and risk, as the promised assistance does not always occur (Mullen, 2003, 2005).

The issue of formation is key to clarifying that informal refers to how the relationship itself has been initiated, not the extent that it may have become structured or institutionalized over time and hence formalized. In this context, third-party assignment to the relationship by an academic advisor, departmental chair, or program coordinator (Clark, Harden, & Johnson, 2000) falls outside the range of informal mentorship and hence this review.

Benefits and Drawbacks of Spontaneous Mentoring

Both benefits and drawbacks of spontaneous mentoring have been reported in educational studies, with protégé satisfaction surfacing as the pivotal issue.

Protégé Satisfaction

Researchers in leadership and psychology have found that informal mentoring can actually yield greater benefits for protégés than formal mentoring (e.g., Johnson, 2002; Mullen, 2003). Protégés in informal relationships "receive more career and psychological functions from mentors and report greater effect from, and satisfaction with, the mentorship" (Johnson, 2002, p. 89).

Satisfaction tends to be higher for protégés and mentors alike when mentorships have started out informally, largely because mutual understanding, respect, and trust will have had the chance to evolve (Johnson & Ridley, 2004). Waldeck and colleagues' (1997) survey of 234 doctoral students at 12 major American universities found that master's students characterized their mentoring relationships as "extremely positive and satisfying" and that doctoral students were "highly satisfied." Similarly, Wilde and Schau's (1991) solicitation of evaluative information on the mentoring relationship from the perspective of the protégé reported gains in such areas as mutual support, comprehensiveness, and student professional development (i.e., O'Neil's [1981] originating schema).

A related benefit of spontaneous mentoring is its availability relative to formal mentoring as a resource to graduate students. In fact, studies indicate that the majority of student–faculty mentoring relationships are nonassigned, that is, informal. For example, graduate faculty in psychology who were surveyed have identified that 87% of their mentorships were informal (Dickinson & Johnson, 2000).

Protégé Dissatisfaction

In direct contrast with studies that report satisfaction on the part of protégés in informal mentoring relationships, studies highlighting dissatisfaction in this context support the need for cultural change. As much as 50% of the respondents surveyed by various studies have not received any mentoring in graduate school (e.g., Bigelow & Johnson, 2001), and many doctoral graduates claim that they have not been prepared for their profession (Clark et al., 2000). Providing specifics, Nyquist and Woodford's (2000) large-scale US study found that more than 375 doctoral students reported ineffectual mentoring from their dissertation supervisors. Furthermore, an international study of 139 new graduates indicates that career support from mentors concerning the publication of their doctoral research was lacking (Dinham & Scott, 2001). In higher education, while doctoral students relay that the most important element in graduate education is their mentoring (and advising) relationship, many have also appraised it as their most disappointing one (Henrich, 1991).

Personality Characteristics of Mentor and Protégé

Research on personality and its effect on the mentoring relationship and quality of mentoring received (e.g., Johnson, 2002; Johnson & Huwe, 2003) has resulted in a call for professors and students to prepare well for their respective roles.

Rising to the occasion, exemplary protégés "communicate clearly, work hard, demonstrate loyalty, and accept new challenges" (Johnson, 2002, p. 92). Outstanding mentor qualities and attributes (as judged by protégé feedback) include ethical behavior, emotional balance, intentional role modeling, kindness, and competence, as well as scholastic and professional recognition (Johnson, 2002; see also Mullen, Cox, Boettcher, & Adoue, 2000a).

Other individual difference variables that may influence mentors' availability for mentoring and the quality of the relationship underscore protégés' talent and career potential. Graduate faculty are most receptive to mentoring students who show strong academic promise and whose scholarly and/or professional interests are aligned with their own; furthermore, they gravitate toward working with those who remind them of themselves. Protégé personality characteristics that prove conducive to initiating mentorships with graduate faculty include communication skills and emotional stability, initiative, intelligence, and loyalty (Johnson & Ridley, 2004). Potential protégés are also attractive if independent as well as interdependent, self-monitoring, and, importantly, willing to share with other students and receptive to constructive criticism (Mullen, 2003).

In their study of 144 undergraduate students, Rice and Brown (1990) examined freshmen's perceptions of their own readiness to perform as protégés and of those characteristics they wanted mentors to have. They concluded that protégé readiness and mentor competence are associated with three predictor variables: autonomy, interpersonal skills, and purpose. Undergraduates who actively seek out mentoring also tend not to be those who are most in need of it (Rice & Brown, 1990). For this reason, proactive graduate program faculty offer orientations, retreats, and seminars to expedite the mentoring process for incoming students (Mullen, 2006).

From the research on informal mentoring we can conclude that protégé readiness and mentor competence are key characteristics of faculty mentors and student protégés. While mentors choose protégés with particular profiles, protégés with certain personality types are also prone to soliciting faculty mentors for quality mentoring.

As is probably apparent, the issues addressed in this section have been based primarily on the initiation phase of the mentoring relationship. This is a function of the state of the educational research on mentor and protégé individual differences. That is, the effects of individual differences on other phases of the student–faculty relationship have not been studied.

Protégé Functions of Mentoring

Career and Psychosocial Functions

According to Rose (2003), mentoring "may theoretically encompass a broad array of behaviors or functions" (p. 474). Based on Kram's (1985) well-established workplace model, researchers of graduate mentoring validate two major functions of student–faculty developmental or informal mentoring: career-related and psychosocial. *Career-related functions* include sponsorship, exposure and visibility, coaching, protection, and challenging work assignments. To this list Johnson (2002) adds "transmission of applied professional ethics" (p. 89). *Psychosocial functions* incorporate role modeling, acceptance and confirmation, counseling, and friendship (Clark et al., 2000). Waldeck and colleagues (1997) affirm that "taken together, these personal and professional tools assist in the career advancement of protégés" (p. 3).

As tangible examples of the career function, faculty mentors may aid students in publication productivity and research presentations, developing professional skills, gaining employment in quality institutions, and networking, in addition to providing advice concerning college politics and cultural mores (e.g., Dinham & Scott, 2001; Mullen et al., 2000a; Young, Alvermann, Kaste, Henderson, & Many, 2004).

Protégés judge the psychosocial function of informal mentoring as crucial, so much so that they have assigned it a greater value than the career dimension (e.g., Young et al., 2004). Psychosocial mentoring, when nurtured, increases personal satisfaction in the relationship (e.g., Tenenbaum et al., 2001; Waldeck et al., 1997) and, specifically, "the protégé's sense of competence, identity, and work-role effectiveness" (Waldeck et al., p. 89).

Variations within the categories of career and psychosocial mentoring are evident in studies of informal mentoring. For example, Tenenbaum and coauthors (2001), who surveyed 189 graduate students across disciplines, focus on three, not two, functions: socioemotional (feelings of respect conveyed by the mentor), instrumental (help from the mentor with improving writing skills), and networking (mentor's assistance with meeting other people and becoming savvy about the political environment). Tenenbaum's team (2001) found that "socioemotional mentoring increases student satisfaction, whereas instrumental help increases student productivity" (p. 339). Reflecting gender differences, this study reports that the male mentors offered as much practical help as the female mentors but less psychosocial support; conversely, male students published more with their primary advisors than the female students.

The psychosocial function *friendship* is now seen as an essential, if not liberating, part of the mentoring role (e.g., Anderson & Shannon, 1988; Beyene, Anglin, Sanchez, & Ballou, 2002; Gallimore, Tharp, & John-Steiner, 1992; Young et al., 2004), as well as a benefit to academic partners (e.g., Busch, 1985). Young and colleagues

(2004), who studied mentors' professional friendships with protégés, explain that "intensity of interdependence," together with "relational knowing" and other catalysts, informs the processes of befriending (p. 25). Gallimore and coauthors (1992) believe that attraction and attachment (i.e., intellectual and interpersonal chemistry) underlie all synergistic informal mentorships. Johnson (2002) concurs, referring to how enduring mentoring relationships are rooted in "relational attraction," which includes "shared interests, similarity, frequent contact, and enjoyment of interactions" (p. 89).

Alternative models of professional friendship, emotional intimacy, and authentic communication (Gallimore et al., 1992; Young et al., 2004) support this view. Zajonc (as cited in Thorpe, 2005) says that mentors who fulfill the friendship function might have coffee with their students, a friendly interchange that promotes reciprocity while reducing distance for students. What one individual would identify as friendship, another might consider friendly professional compatibility, a subtle but important difference among faculty mentors. "Kathy," a mentor participating in a study of doctoral literacy, seeks to establish "a comfortable relationship where [my protégés] can come and talk to me, but [not one where] we hang out all the time" (Bean, Readence, Barone, & Sylvester, 2004, p. 374).

Despite the recorded gains, friendship or mutuality is a controversial idea among researchers. Mentors need to be aware that this mentor function, which is associated with intimacy, is a stimulus that encourages closeness (Johnson, 2002; Johnson & Ridley, 2004). Herman and Mandell (2004) argue that because friendship promotes "psychotherapeutic learning," the intellectual and cultural aspects of mentoring can become compromised.

Advising versus Comprehensive Functions

The role of faculty mentor should not be confused with that of academic advisor. Nor is mentoring interchangeable with advising, even though it is a closely related function (Galbraith, 2003; Johnson & Zlotnik, 2005; Mullen, 2005). Unlike advisors who are assigned to direct students' programs of study, mentors fulfill important functions of teaching and learning beyond this, with social and personal elements (e.g., Waldeck et al., 1997). As O'Neil and Wrightsman (2001) explain, a faculty mentor's influence extends far beyond that of advisor, approximating the intensity of a parental relationship, as the mentor's "values represent idealized norms" that can influence "how protégés see themselves and the profession" (p. 112). Because faculty mentors are a scarcer resource than advisors, "more students have advisors than mentors, and one can clearly be an advisor without forming a mentoring relationship" (Johnson & Zlotnik, 2005, p. 98).

A different view of function. Emerging conceptions of *function* in the academic mentoring relationship advance critical, feminist, phenomenological, postmodern, and social justice perspectives. Some researchers believe that institutional barriers in status, role, and title perpetuate distance between the mentor and the protégé. Importantly, these barriers are challenged as mutual learning takes place and critical pedagogical frameworks for shared inquiry are adopted (see, e.g., Bona, Rinehart, & Volbrecht, 1995; Mullen, 2005).

While mentoring relationships of any type are about learning, conversations that occur between professors and protégés can be of a political or critically reflective nature. Some mentoring dyads have managed to confront the pedagogies of indoctrination that are inherent in institutionally embedded relationships (e.g., Franke & Dahlgren, 1996; Mullen et al., 2000a; Young et al., 2004). Student–faculty mentoring that brings together different races, for example, may heighten the need for trust and respect over a same-race dyad.

Johnson-Bailey and Cervero's (2004) informal doctoral mentoring relationship originated when Johnson-Bailey, "a black woman associate professor," approached Cervero, "a white male professor" (p. 7), after having completed a course with him. Such cross-cultural mentoring relationships are, they explained, "affiliations that exist between unequals" that force mentors and protégés to conduct their relationship "on a hostile American stage with a societal script contrived to undermine the success of the partnership" (p. 110). As coauthors, they produced a narrative of inquiry on the topic of their mentoring relationship, concluding that cultural mores will need to change if new possibilities for mentoring across races are to be realized.

Frameworks of Informal Mentoring Phases

Academic graduate mentoring occurs in phases, specifically initiation, cultivation, separation, and redefinition, as well as variations thereof.

Validation of Kram's Model

Kram's (1985) groundbreaking stage theory, derived from the study of 18 mentor–protégé pairs, identifies four overlapping mentoring phases: initiation, cultivation, separation, and redefinition. Johnson and Ridley (2004) support this general model but also caution that these phases should be interpreted as a guide only, not as a literal or chronological manifestation of all graduate student–faculty mentorships. Moreover, Bouquillon, Sosik, and Lee (2005) also give credence to Kram's theoretical framework and observe that empirical research has yet to "fully unveil how mentoring phases influence the dynamics and functions of mentoring relationships" (p. 24).

Higher education researchers who study phases of mentoring typically use Kram's (1985) model and apply it to particular situations. They also examine specific dynamics from either the mentor's or the protégé's perspective, or both (e.g., Johnson & Ridley, 2004; Kochan & Trimble, 2000; Mullen et al., 2000a). Kochan and Trimble (2000) similarly adapted the mentoring phases to their own situation. As a graduate student, science teacher Trimble solicited an informal mentoring relationship with Kochan, the leader of her university laboratory school and a college of education faculty member. Their mentoring relationship, which focused on leadership issues, was characterized as having these phases: "groundwork, warm-up, working, and long-term status" (p. 21). For the groundwork phase, the protégé met with the mentor after engaging in self-assessment. During the warm-up phase, the two "worked at developing a relationship" (p. 22), establishing confidentiality, trust, and other norms. They then moved to the working stage and for 2 years grappled with their agenda, transforming the hierarchical relationship into one of comentoring. During the long-term status stage, the comentors dealt with the changes impacting their significant relationship.

Well-known for his research on mentoring phases, O'Neil (e.g., 1981; O'Neil & Wrightsman, 2001) identifies six stages focusing on interaction: a) making a critical decision and entering a relationship, b) building mutual trust, c) taking risks, d) teaching skills, e) learning professional standards, and f) dissolving or changing the relationship. Busch (1985), who supported O'Neil's theory while noting that it had not been empirically substantiated, summarized his mentoring model in this way: "High degrees of mutuality, comprehensiveness, gender sensitivity, and congruence produce positive and functional mentoring relationships; low degrees of these dimensions produce dysfunctional mentoring relationships" (p. 258).

Bigelow and Johnson (2001) highlighted that within O'Neil's mentoring stages, effective mentors are expected "to remain flexible and adjust to changing protégé needs and expectations, offering distinct functions at each stage" (p. 3). The Mullen mentoring model supports this perspective, underscoring that relationships themselves, not just individuals, change and that interaction is indispensable to the health of the mentoring relationship, particularly as a way of weathering "halted or dissolving communication" (Mullen, Whatley, & Kealy, 2000b, p. 55).

Regarding interaction, one university research team reported a high level of this dynamic occurring within their own informal doctoral student–faculty mentoring group (Mullen et al., 2000a; Mullen et al., 2000b). Through narratives elicited from support group members, the researchers came to view phases not as discrete stages, but as a human system that "brings mentors and mentees close together, but not always. While intensity of contact is part of the experiential basis of learning, so too are halts and even ruptures in communication" (p. 53). In their holistic life-system of mentoring phases and cycles model of informal mentoring, initiation, cultivation, separation, and redefinition work contextually and simultaneously rather than serially, with the following results:

1. Ebb and flow of mentoring occurs as the specific needs of mentors and protégés change over time.
2. Constant communication characterizes short- and long-term mentoring relationships. Emerging stories and mentoring mosaics are manifestations.
3. Density of experience refers to constant communication and what evolves from this. Relationships that deepen can take different forms, such as collegiality, comentorships, and formal mentorships.
4. Peak in contact represents heightened interpersonal dynamics (e.g., dissertation writing, coauthored writing, bureaucratic obstacles), resulting from toil and tensions.
5. Halted or dissolving communication, or even severed communication, stems from communications-related problems.

In concert with the findings described in this section, Johnson and Ridley's (2004) research on informal mentoring phases endorses the viability of Kram's model of initiation, cultivation, separation, and redefinition within graduate school settings. Additionally, Johnson and Ridley (2004) concur with the research cited that interaction is of vital importance, in that "protégés are drawn to emotionally skilled mentors" (p. 56) and "interpersonally competent mentors" learn ways to "maximize the health and productivity of the relationship" (p. 55).

Formation, Development, and Termination

The selection process leads to the formation of naturally occurring mentoring relationships, as well as to their development, dissolution, and possible rebirth.

Forming Mentoring Relationships

The initiation phase or entry stage, wherein mentor and protégé get to know each other and undertake cooperative work (Johnson & Ridley, 2004; Kram, 1985), can last up to 1 year. In the cultivation phase, Johnson and Ridley (2004) indicate that idealizations held about the other and the relationship itself need to be relinquished. Because ideals cannot be met and constraints on the mentoring relationship are inevitable, reality will overtake fantasy; consequently, the relationship will change.

The research on forming academic mentoring relationships is still somewhat limited (Bigelow & Johnson, 2001). Using a psychological model applied to graduate education, Bigelow and Johnson (2001) identify four perspectives that explain the bearing of protégés when forming mentoring relationships: self-psychology (involves transfer of need and image); biological dimorphism (activates the mating process); interpersonal attraction (acknowledges the need for intimacy and affection); and social learning (selection of a role model who is an expert). As initiators, students will identify faculty in response to shared interests, a similar working style, interpersonal chemistry, or other criteria (Gallimore et al., 1992). Students may also be drawn to a professor's proven advisory or mentoring capacity, practical experience, expert knowledge base, interest in their research topic (Bennouna, 2003), or, quite simply, availability and willingness to help (Mullen, 2006).

However, graduate students typically lack familiarity with mentor relationships and specifically the initiation and maintenance of mentorship. Hence, Waldeck and colleagues (1997) encourage potential graduate mentors to understand that students perceive initiation with professors to be intimidating. Many face difficulty establishing "developmental advising" (relationships) with their faculty mentors and thus report higher satisfaction with "prescriptive advising" (guidance). Rose's (2003) survey-based study of 712 doctoral students studying at several Research I universities in the United States reinforces this finding.

Communication issues have also been highlighted in research that examines or accommodates behavioral and psychological processes. A survey of 145 mentored protégés' initiation strategies identified 10 "communication strategies" that graduate students use to initiate mentoring with faculty (Waldeck et al., 1997). "Ensure contact with target," the strategy used most frequently, makes students accessible to their "target mentor" through courses and other forms of contact. Used less often but still frequently is "search for similar interests," whereby students discover shared academic, professional, or personal interests, perhaps even research ideas. In descending order, from the next most frequently used strategy, are the following eight categories: seek counsel from target, appeal to target directly, provide work assistance, present a competent self, assume it will "just happen," concede control, venerate the target, and disclose personal self (pp. 7–11).

Regarding the communicative behavior *assume it will "just happen,"* students saw their primary relationship as naturally evolving, yet these were not recognized as mentorships by the protégé. Waldeck and colleagues (1997) urge university students to select more proactively from the set of communicative behaviors (initiation strategies) in order to increase the chance for success. It is not advisable to just wait for mentoring to happen or to "rely on one generic approach" (p. 14).

Fewer than expected doctoral students initiate mentoring dyads that are informed by their knowledge of the professor's academic expertise and record (Mullen, 2006). In a recent study of 79 doctoral graduates in education, only 10% had chosen their chairs using this academic measure (Bennouna, 2003). Recent graduates selected their chairs based on the personal interest shown in their topic (86%). Others made their choices after having completed a course with the faculty member (47%), or upon receiving a professor's (30%) or another student's (19%) recommendation (Bennouna, pp. 113–115).

An outstanding example of a highly intentional approach to informal mentoring on the part of protégés at the formative stage is that of the Nobel laureates. From Zuckerman's (1977) interviews with 41 (of the 46) laureates working in the United States, she learned that, as apprentices (not yet Nobel winners), they had chosen their dissertation supervisors "*before* the master's important work was conspicuously 'validated' [by] a Nobel prize" and that they "had a discriminating eye," not only for seeking out "scientific stars" but also "for the major universities and departments doing work at the frontiers of the field" (pp. 108–109). Just as these laureates-to-be carefully appraised the professors' achievements in their discipline, so too were the faculty (also future laureates) searching to mine young talent.

Developing Mentoring Relationships

Informal mentoring presents mentors and protégés with the opportunity to get to know one another before deciding whether they will continue nurturing the relationship. Johnson and Ridley (2004), writing from the mentor's perspective, add that graduate faculty–protégé informal relationships must be carefully arranged. "Intentional consideration of a match assumes first an informal period of mentoring," whereby the two individuals get the chance to "work together without the pressure of a commitment to a formal relationship" (Johnson & Ridley, 2004, p. 65). Parties involved in this type of "well-matched mentorship" (Johnson & Ridley, 2004, p. 65) are believed to derive greater value and satisfaction.

Relationships are cultivated as the partners learn more about each other's capacities and the potential of the relationship to realize benefits. Typically lasting 2 to 5 years, the cultivation phase involves "active and intensive mentoring" focused on a wide "range of mentor functions beginning with career functions (coaching, teaching, sponsoring) and also including psychosocial functions (support, encouragement, and friendship)" (Johnson & Ridley, 2004, p. 81). Through the mentor's efforts to affirm, promote, and protect, the protégé's academic study should develop, along with his or her performance and visibility. Completers and noncompleters (individuals experiencing program attrition) alike of the doctorate degree have insight into what it takes for an informal mentoring relationship to develop successfully (e.g., Bennouna, 2003; Stripling, 2004). From the protégé's perspective, expert support, participatory decision-making about crucial matters (e.g., who the committee members will be), and access to a support group can make a significant difference to the candidate's ability to persevere and hence complete.

Comentoring. Comentorship, a critical and expansive treatment of mentorship, refers to "individuals or groups that proactively engage in reciprocal teaching and learning and that transform power structures to honor egalitarianism" (Mullen, 2005, p. 25; see also Bona et al., 1995). Rymer (2002) identifies three significant characteristics of comentoring: "co-mentors are close colleagues in a mutual mentorship"; "co-mentors engage in dialogue"; and "co-mentors form a network" (pp. 347–348). The notion of comentoring is relevant to both a mentorship between a student and a faculty member and a group consisting of a professor(s) and students. A defining feature of comentoring is that the relationship is one of mutuality and reciprocity; although that has always been part of the definition of a traditional mentoring relationship, mutuality and reciprocity are not necessarily realized in every situation.

To elaborate, comentoring practices ideally promote egalitarianism in the forms of shared power and learning between and among mentors and protégés. Each is situated as a comentor or learner and teacher, so learning and teaching become two-way, which changes the entrenched belief that teaching is the exclusive domain of the mentor, and learning, that of the protégé.

Feminist critics, reacting strongly to authoritarian, power-based mentorships, believe that the idea of a mentor as separate from or above the individual or group that follows one's charge is considered outdated (e.g., Banks, 2000). Comentoring is therefore seen as a catalyst for changing traditional practices, hierarchical systems, and homogeneous cultures (Bona et al., 1995; Mullen, 2005, 2006). Specifically, comentoring, also collaborative mentoring, seeks to promote diversity by bringing women and minorities into the network (Bona et al., 1995; Mullen, 2005, 2006). Interdependency and relational knowing, as well as sharing, encouragement, and support, are all elements of comentoring. While these elements not always identified as comentorship in studies of informal mentoring in education (e.g., Young et al., 2004), feminist research nonetheless provides strong support.

Comentoring fits well with the relational model that Beyene and coauthors (2002) describe because the "roles of teacher/student and student/teacher are reciprocal, fluid, and synergistic" (p. 89). As Beyene and colleagues acknowledge, relational/cultural theory (also comentoring theory) is valuable for enhancing diversity and multicultural goals, as well as the psychosocial functions of mentoring, in higher education. These outcomes emerged from their study of 133 multiethnic, undergraduate protégés, some of whom were being mentored informally, from six American universities. Although several had negative mentoring experiences with faculty mentors, most affirmed these as mutual learning experiences that extended "beyond merely instrumental, one-way advice-giving" (p. 97). "Relationship matters" (p. 100) was the strong message sent.

When comentoring is practiced effectively, democratic community-building occurs, and productive synergy is released in such forms as social justice agendas and cross-cultural, informal mentoring relationships (Johnson-Bailey & Cervero, 2004). The familiar practice of collaborative learning among adults calls for trust on the part of university faculty to allow "students to govern themselves" so they can learn to cope with disagreement and difference (Bruffee, 1999, p. 89). Comentors are, at least in theory, grounded in relational mutuality and equality, even though they may be hierarchically unequal. Moreover, comentoring models make a unique contribution by linking the vision and work of mentoring researchers with that of relational theorists (e.g., Beyene, 2002) and liberation educators (e.g., Freire, 1997). Mentors are encouraged to develop feelings of connection, an attitude of equality, and an ethnic consciousness in all of their relationships, and protégés are urged to adapt social justice agendas to guide their decisions (Johnson-Bailey & Cervero, 2004; Mullen, 2005).

Multiple mentoring.   Graduate students and faculty alike who have joined or developed a collegial network of multiple mentors and opportunities for growth are engaged in *multiple mentoring.* Notably, *mentoring constellations* (Johnson & Ridley, 2004) and *mentoring mosaics* (Tharp & Gallimore, 1988/1999) are types of multiple mentoring networks. Both are described as consisting of the primary mentorship (student–faculty dyad) and secondary mentorships (faculty and/or peers). The latter are "typically shorter in duration," "characterized by less emotional bonding," and "focus on specific functions," such as learning about a new idea or field (Johnson & Ridley, 2004, p. 61).

Protégés who have multiple mentors maximize the benefits of the learning relationship (e.g., Wilde & Schau, 1991). They have access to specialized knowledge and skills that may be lacking in their primary mentor, may suddenly be exposed to individuals who are a cultural or emotional match for them, or may experience deeper satisfaction from developing friendships with peer mentors (Johnson & Ridley, 2004; Mullen et al., 2000a). In addition, even outstanding faculty who work exclusively as primary mentors may find it challenging to independently incorporate a range of support for their protégés (e.g., Johnson & Zlotnik, 2005).

Within the mentoring constellation or mosaic, the individual ideally taps the strengths and qualities of his or her partners. Members interchange roles as mentors and protégés through a synergistic, flexible structure. This kind of network is indispensable for cultivating peer mentors; compensating for the dissatisfactions of traditional mentoring relations; and facilitating larger, team-oriented projects. Those who engage in multiple mentoring also transcend the implicit contract of one-to-one faculty–student mentoring, which makes ownership or exclusivity a by-product of mentorships (Mullen, 2005).

Regarding the graduate context, research on multiple mentoring is in an early stage. For example, one student–faculty group in curriculum intentionally borrowed from Tharp and Gallimore's (1988/1999) tenets of mentoring mosaic, lifelong mentoring, and activity-setting to create and implement a network that made available to each member one primary mentorship and numerous secondary ones (Mullen et al., 2000a). Each doctoral member's participation within the constellation had a positive effect on morale, retention, and self-efficacy, as well as on networking, productivity, and success (Mullen et al., 2000a).

Terminating Mentoring Relationships

Like other personal relationships, mentorships change over time. The separation (or termination or dissolution) stage occurs when the mentoring functions are discontinued – either mentor or protégé may believe that there no longer exists a need for the relationship. Perhaps the student has completed his or her thesis/dissertation or moved on to another significant relationship, or perhaps the mentor has changed (Young & Wright, 2001) by choice, due to retirement, or for any other reason. Mentoring relationships that continue beyond separation enter the redefinition stage. Less intense and more collegial (Johnson & Ridley, 2004), such relationships can assume a number of forms, including significant comentorships, coauthorships, and friendships.

Mentorships can also end prematurely or suddenly (Johnson & Ridley, 2004), in which case termination can prove dysfunctional, particularly when either partner feels unprepared for or anxious about the break-up. Separation that is timely for both parties enables a feeling of closure; protégés can claim their independence as confident and capable professionals, and mentors can start new and perhaps more beneficial relationships.

Faculty and students engaged in doctoral mentoring may experience misconceptions at one time or another, especially as the mentoring process intensifies, tensions mount, and concerns surface (Mullen et al., 2000a; Mullen et al., 2000b). Stripling (2004) recommends that students correct any misconceptions in a timely manner, otherwise dissonance or even termination can result. Empirical studies that include negative aspects of informal mentoring typically do not report whether a respondent's complaints have led to dissolution of the relationship, even though this outcome may seem self-evident. Take, for example, a study described earlier wherein 11% of the 133 participants – typically single, undergraduate females – described negative encounters with faculty who became overly parental, asked personal questions, or made sexual overtures (Beyene et al., 2002) – it does not reveal whether or how the protégés terminated these relationships.

In a rare look at termination in graduate school, issues of dissolution were built into a national survey that, overall, reported positive effects (Clark et al., 2000). However, among the 787 recent clinical psychology doctorate participants (70% were women, mostly White American), 17% had terminated their mentoring relationship. Other graduates (11%), both male and female, reported discomfort. Concerns of an ethical nature arose regarding mentors taking credit for protégés' work, exhibiting questionable research behavior and implicating the student, and sexualizing the relationship or exercising poor boundaries (Clark et al., 2000).

New Types of Mentoring Relationships

Naturally occurring mentorships can take such different forms as support groups and mentoring cohorts. Strategies used for developing these new twists on mentoring relationships include, as previously discussed, comentoring and multiple mentoring.

Gains from Alternative Mentoring

The alternative forms and strategies just cited help offset the limitations of traditional and one-to-one mentoring, wherein both protégés and mentors can experience restricted access to multiple mentoring opportunities and artificial barriers in status and power. In addition, the varied options enable protégés to gain invaluable academic and career-related skills, as well as satisfaction, more rapidly than in traditional and dyadic relationships. The expanded options also benefit mentors whose professional development and capacity for mentoring may be enhanced; they may experience some relief from the "professional requirements and emotional demands" of one-to-one mentoring, thereby avoiding disillusionment and burnout (Johnson & Ridley, 2004, p. 4).

Both types of group mentoring (support groups and mentoring cohorts) have been responsible for increasing student satisfaction, retention, and accomplishments, as well as graduation rates (Mullen, 2005, 2006). In fact, cohort members, including disadvantaged students (e.g., Mullen, 2003), benefit at a higher rate than noncohort students (e.g., Horn, 2001; Twale & Kochan, 2000; Witte & James, 1998).

Support groups and mentoring cohorts alike are invaluable motivational strategies, not only for those students who have joined them but also by many who have regretted not doing so. A sample group of noncompleters wished that they had participated in some type of group mentoring (Stripling, 2004). Further, these participants (minority and nonminority males and females, averaging 48 years old) stressed "the advantages of having an additional support structure to augment the institutional systems in place" (p. 229). Even those noncompleters who saw themselves as too independent to work within a group recognized that their cohort-integrated peers had moved ahead; they knew more about the available resources, displayed better coping strategies, had stronger relationships with their colleagues, and made programmatic progress, usually completing their degrees.

Support Groups

Support groups are "temporary, transitional structures for satisfying human needs and meeting goals, with potential for more established and sustaining forms" (Mullen, 2005, p. 99). As Bruffee (1999) explains, people who "want to undergo the same sort of change" and who "depend on one another to help fulfill [similar] needs and solve [similar] problems" constitute these "transition communities" (p. 74). At one end of the support group spectrum, such configurations reflect a casual or cooperative model of learning. Peers who meet on a regular basis for the purpose of preparing for qualifying examinations, discussing the reading of selected authors, or critiquing one another's dissertation material constitute a support group. While this approach fosters expedient ends, only short-term goals are satisfied (Bruffee, 1999). At the other end of this spectrum are intentionally formed support groups that operate informally and experiment with challenging scholarly agendas and ideas. Some groups might tackle issues of authority, freedom, and friendship (e.g., Herman & Mandell, 2004), whilst others grapple with qualitative research methodology, nonlinear thinking, and collaborative inquiry (e.g., Piantanida & Garman, 1999).

While support groups may not be typically considered a form of mentoring relationship, they fit the definition of mentoring. *Mentorship* is "an educational process focused on teaching and learning," whether this occurs within dyads, groups, or cultures (Mullen, 2005, p. 1; see also Bruffee, 1999; Merriam, 1983). Highly effective mentoring within support groups involves "a powerful and passionate interaction, whereby the mentor and protégé experience personal, professional, and intellectual growth and development" (Galbraith, 2003, p. 2). Other elements of mentoring that can be satisfied within this context include professional networking, modeling, instruction, and guiding, as well as new awareness and even "identity transformation" (Galbraith, p. 3). Mentoring groups are considered potentially more empowering than traditional dyads as a type of informal learning relationship, yet these attract less research and institutional attention and hence are undervalued in comparison (Horn, 2001; Mullen, 2005, 2006).

However, not only graduate but also undergraduate populations gain from membership in support groups. In order to succeed, most freshmen need transitional assistance (Bruffee, 1999; Rice & Brown, 1990). Scaffolds for college success include a focus on study group skills and time management, life skills and problem-solving strategies, and personal and family support (Jaffee, 2004). Jaffee (2004) warns that the support groups to which many freshmen belong throughout their undergraduate program may be unruly and immature. Strongly bonded cohorts have been known to initially ignore or even ostracize newcomers, seeing them as potential threats (Mullen, 2005).

Mentoring Cohorts

Mentoring cohort, a concept coined by Mullen (2005), is a "faculty–student support group that brings together learners with an academic instructor or dissertation chair" (p. 98). Some students and faculty especially value cohorts with a dissertation focus. Such cohorts confront the perennial problem of disillusionment and academic failure, as well as writing and inquiry challenges (Dorn & Papalewis, 1997; Horn, 2001). Moreover, cohort mentoring can address the integration of theory and practice through such informal processes as group dialogue and inquiry writing (Harris, 2005; Mullen, 2005; Piantanida & Garman, 1999).

Furthermore, informal cohort mentoring occurs electronically in online environments. Packard, Walsh, and Seidenberg (2004) argue that women and minorities in particular benefit from electronic modalities that encourage learning through structured discourse but that also facilitate the more informal components of chat rooms and threaded conversations.

Generally, cohorts counter the perceived deficits of traditional mentoring by fostering collaboration between protégés and their faculty mentors, as well as self-governance and ownership of the work and process (Bruffee, 1999). Ideally, doctoral mentoring cohorts increase student capacity in such areas as research, writing, and problem-solving. Research on mentoring cohorts indicates that these networks have the great potential to dramatically enhance students' cognitive and affective experience in their graduate programs (Horn, 2001).

Educators assert that mentoring cohorts support many other positive outcomes for students as well. Notably, as Bruffee (1999) indicates, mentoring cohorts stimulate higher-order critical thinking and encourage intellectual development. Doctoral students practice thinking and research skills in a "safe" environment of one's peers (Johnson & Hume, 2003) and, as a result, are more likely than noncohort students to complete their degree program (Dorn & Papalewis, 1997; Mullen, 2005, 2006).

In fact, participating in a cohort group can support individuals professionally, personally, and academically (Johnson & Huwe, 2003). Close collaboration with colleagues helps instill a sense of scholarly and professional identity. Likewise, working closely with others – especially those with similar interests and goals – forms the bonds necessary to build *and* sustain a community of learners (Horn, 2001).

As Burnett (1999) asserts, students belonging to cohorts "felt less isolated" because they could converse with peers about "common issues and concerns" within the context of "a collaborative framework" (p. 48). Academic and professional development occurs as alliances are formed within the group. Recognizing the importance of establishing such peer relationships by embracing diversity in the academic community and promoting social justice, some researchers have particularly stressed the value of mentoring cohorts to minority and female graduate students and faculty (e.g., Horn, 2001; Mullen, 2005).

Mentoring cohorts also allow doctoral supervisors to simultaneously monitor and advise multiple students (Witte & James, 1998). Many university faculty are now expected to fulfill the double (but controversial) agenda of providing support to doctoral students not only as scholars but also as practitioners preparing for the professions. Graduate students majoring in educational leadership, for example, will need proficiency in a range of skills, including the promotion of diversity within school populations and curricula (Mullen, 2005).

Recognizing the myriad of challenges facing doctoral students and the associated low rate of program completion, Burnett (1999) states that "the provision of support, particularly during the dissertation phase of a doctoral program, may be one way to increase completion rates" (p. 46). By studying the draft papers produced by individuals, for instance, cohort members can gain critical insight into their discipline, as well as confidence in their own writing, editing, and critiquing skills (Bruffee, 1999; Mullen, 2003). Members who become self-assured in assessing student work grow into peer mentors and contribute to the intellectual life of the group itself (Horn, 2001).

The graduate cohort mentoring model is a precious but insufficiently tapped resource. Little is known about the development of informal cohorts, as the institutionalized option is more visible and much better documented. Reflective learning that values scholarship is typically a goal for graduate cohorts (Horn, 2001).

A cohort illustration.   The Writers in Training (WIT) program, an informal cohort consisting of doctoral students in education, has received state-level recognition. Carol Mullen, its creator and leader, received the 2005 FASCD [Florida Association for Supervision and Curriculum Development] Excellence Award for this program. Since 2000, the WIT group has been producing quality scholarship on topics related to educational leadership, meeting regularly and discoursing via a listserv (Mullen, 2003, 2006). Because the university calendar does not dictate when and where these students meet – one draw of a more informal structure – sessions are flexibly arranged over the duration of an individual's program. Each meeting is student-driven and has an agenda onto which individuals can opt to add their work, on a rotational, as-needed basis. For students who join early, support continues from program entry to graduation; regardless, students who are invited can join informal cohorts at any time during their programs (Mullen, 2003).

The flexibility, inventiveness, and negotiation afforded to informal mentoring cohorts contrast starkly with formal arrangements. These latter structures are closely regulated through bureaucratic protocols; for example, student members are assigned depending upon the timeframe of their admittance to a program. Importantly, doctoral models like the WIT program work most effectively when the best attributes of an informal cohort are combined with the structured components found in formal heuristics. Scheduled meetings, agendas, turn-taking, and guidelines for producing work, in addition to established routines, rituals, and celebrations, all contribute to the effectiveness and sustainability of informal cohorts (Mullen, 2005).

Such hybrid cohort models illustrate a contemporary dimension of naturally occurring mentoring. They are informal – students (future members) will have initiated the relationship, seeking out the faculty member for guidance and mentorship, and institutions will not recognize or reward their value. All in all, the rhythms of the hybrid cohort model and its developmental processes are in concert with informal mentoring.

Closing Reflections

From this review we take away the message that informal mentoring relationships, where mentors and protégés somehow find each other, are complex and abundant, if not ubiquitous. These situations have clearly outpaced the ability of researchers to thoroughly document such salient aspects as their formation, development, and termination. Researchers could help to remedy this situation by collectively committing to intensifying the study of spontaneous mentoring relationships and by adopting a variety of theoretical frameworks and empirical approaches for doing so. Faculty mentors are also encouraged to experiment with different mentoring forms to help supplement, extend, and, where appropriate, transform their one-to-one mentorships.

We have also learned that we simply do not know the extent that graduate students derive benefit from their informal mentoring relationships, since situations vary and the research is conflicting. We do know that while informal mentors may fulfill the demands associated with guidance, doctoral students often yearn for more comprehensive relationships (Rose, 2003). However, faculty delivery of the holistic mentoring model is less common than might be expected (e.g., Henrich, 1991; Mullen et al., 2000a; Murray, 2000; Nyquist & Woodford, 2000; Rose, 2003). While researchers urge faculty mentors to provide better career development and psychosocial support, a vocal minority (e.g., Head, Reiman, & Thies-Sprinthall, 1992; Mullen et al., 2000b; Rose, 2003) encourage students as well as faculty to be more proactive and creative, supplementing the traditional mentoring dyad with multiple, secondary mentors.

Finally, the success of graduate education depends on the willingness of faculty to go above and beyond to mentor students, a commitment that university systems are not inclined to recognize officially. Without the necessary support for assisting protégés throughout their programs and doctoral candidacy, faculty carry out this mission relying solely (or mostly) on the intrinsic rewards of doing so. These dynamics are often compounded for mentors when protégés are assigned to them, heightening appreciation for the alternative, that is, informal mentoring relationships. Greater organizational support is needed for this type of mentoring; for example, informal mentorship in academic institutions could be built into promotional criteria (Berk, Berg, Mortimer, Walton-Moss, & Yeo, 2005). Better understanding of and recognition for the invisible work of informal mentoring within our institutions will in turn provide support to faculty to carry out this work, enhancing the satisfaction of protégés.

References

Anderson, E. M., & Shannon, A. L. (1988). Toward a conceptualization of mentoring. *Journal of Teacher Education, 39*(1), 38–42.

Banks, C. (2000). Gender and race as factors in educational leadership and administration. In Jossey-Bass Publishers (Ed.), *The Jossey-Bass reader on educational leadership* (pp. 217–256). San Francisco: Jossey-Bass.

Bean, T. W., Readence, J. E., Barone, D. M., & Sylvester, T. (2004). An interpretive study of doctoral mentoring in literacy. *Mentoring and Tutoring, 12*(3), 371–381.

Bennouna, S. (2003). *Mentors' emotional intelligence and performance of mentoring functions in graduate doctoral education.* Unpublished doctoral dissertation, University of South Florida, Tampa.

Berk, R. A., Berg, J., Mortimer, R., Walton-Moss, B., & Yeo, T. P. (2005). Measuring the effectiveness of faculty mentoring relationships. *Academic Medicine, 80*(1), 66–71.

Beyene, T., Anglin, M., Sanchez, W., & Ballou, M. (2002). Mentoring and relational mutuality: Protégés' perspectives. *Journal of Humanistic Counseling, Education and Development, 41*(1), 87–102.

Bigelow, J. R., & Johnson, W. B. (2001). Promoting mentor–protégé relationship formation in graduate school. *The Clinical Supervisor, 20*(1), 1–23.

Bona, M. J., Rinehart, J., & Volbrecht, R. M. (1995). "Show me how to do like you": Comentoring as feminist pedagogy. *Feminist Teacher, 9*(3), 116–124.

Bouquillon, E. A., Sosik, J. J., & Lee, D. (2005). It's only a phase: Examining trust, identification and mentoring functions received across the mentoring phases. *Mentoring and Tutoring, 13*(2), 239–258.

Bruffee, K. A. (1999). *Collaborative learning: Higher education, interdependence, and the authority of knowledge* (2nd ed.). Baltimore: Johns Hopkins University Press.

Burnett, P. C. (1999). The supervision of doctoral dissertations using a collaborative cohort model. *Counselor Education and Supervision, 39*(1), 46–52.

Busch, J. W. (1985). Mentoring in graduate schools of education: Mentors' perceptions. *American Educational Research Journal, 22*(2), 257–265.

Clark, R. A., Harden, S. L., & Johnson, W. B. (2000). Mentor relationships in clinical psychology doctoral training: Results of a national survey. *Teaching of Psychology, 27*(4), 262–268.

Dickinson, S. C., & Johnson, W. B. (2000). Mentoring in clinical psychology doctoral programs: A national survey of directors of training. *The Clinical Supervisor, 19*(1), 137–152.

Dinham, S., & Scott, C. (2001). The experience of disseminating the results of doctoral research. *Journal of Further and Higher Education, 25*(1), 45–55.

Dorn, S. M., & Papalewis, R. (1997). *Improving doctoral student retention.* Paper presented at the Annual Meeting of the American Educational Research Association, Chicago, IL.

Dorn, S. M., Papalewis, R., & Brown, R. (1995). Educators earning their doctorates: Doctoral student perceptions regarding cohesiveness and persistence. *Education, 116*(2), 305–310.

Franke, A., & Dahlgren, L. O. (1996). Conceptions of mentoring: An empirical study of conceptions of mentoring during the school-based teacher education. *Teaching and Teacher Education, 12*(6), 627–641.

Freire, P. (1997). A response. In P. Freire, with J. W. Fraser, D. Macedo, T. McKinnon, & W. T. Stokes (Eds.), *Mentoring the mentor: A critical dialogue with Paulo Freire* (pp. 303–329). New York: Peter Lang.

Galbraith, M. W. (2003). Celebrating mentoring. *Adult Learning, 14*(1), 2–3.

Gallimore, R. G., Tharp, R. G., & John-Steiner, V. (1992). *The developmental and socio-cultural foundations of mentoring.* Columbia University, New York: Institute for Urban Minority Education (ERIC Document Reproduction Service No. ED 354292).

Harris, S. (2005). *Changing mindsets of educational leaders to improve schools: Voices of doctoral students.* Lanham, MD: Rowman & Littlefield Education.

Head, F. A., Reiman, A. J., & Thies-Sprinthall, L. (1992). The reality of mentoring: Complexity in its process and function. In T. M. Bey & C. T. Holmes (Eds.), *Mentoring: Contemporary principles and issues* (pp. 5–34). Reston, VA: Association of Teacher Educators.

Henrich, K. T. (1991). Loving partnerships: Dealing with sexual attraction and power in doctoral advisement relationships. *Journal of Higher Education, 62*(5), 514–538.

Herman, L., & Mandell, A. (2004). *From teaching to mentoring: Principle and practice, dialogue and life in adult education.* London: RoutledgeFalmer.

Horn, R. A. (2001). Promoting social justice and caring in schools and communities: The unrealized potential of the cohort model. *Journal of School Leadership, 11*, 313–334.

Jaffee, D. (2004, July 9). Learning communities can be cohesive – and divisive. *Chronicle of Higher Education, 50*(44), B16.

Johnson, W. B. (2002). The intentional mentor: Strategies and guidelines for the practice of mentoring. *Professional Psychology: Research and Practice, 33*(1), 88–96.

Johnson, W. B., & Huwe, J. M. (2003). *Getting mentored in graduate school.* Washington, DC: American Psychological Association.

Johnson, W. B., & Ridley, C. R. (2004). *The elements of mentoring.* New York: Palgrave MacMillan.

Johnson, W. B., & Zlotnik, S. (2005). The frequency of advising and mentoring as salient work roles in academic job advertisements. *Mentoring and Tutoring, 13*, 95–107.

Johnson-Bailey, J., & Cervero, R. M. (2004). Mentoring in black and white: The intricacies of cross-cultural mentoring. *Mentoring and Tutoring, 12*(1), 7–21.

Kochan, F. K., & Trimble, S. B. (2000). From mentoring to co-mentoring: Establishing collaborative relationships. *Theory Into Practice, 39*(1), 20–28.

Kram, K. E. (1985). *Mentoring at work: Developmental relationships in organizational life.* Glenview, IL: Scott, Foresman and Company.

Merriam, S. B. (1983). Mentors and protégés: A critical review of the literature. *Adult Education Quarterly, 33*(3), 161–173.

Mullen, C. A. (2003). The WIT cohort: A case study of informal doctoral mentoring. *Journal of Further and Higher Education, 27*(4), 411–426.

Mullen, C. A. (2005). *The mentorship primer.* New York: Peter Lang.

Mullen, C. A. (2006). *A graduate student guide: Making the most of mentoring.* Lanham, MD: Rowman & Littlefield Education.

Mullen, C. A., Cox, M. D., Boettcher, C. K., & Adoue, D. S. (Eds.). (2000a). *Breaking the circle of one: Redefining mentorship in the lives and writings of educators* (2nd ed.). New York: Peter Lang.

Mullen, C. A., Whatley, A., & Kealy, W. A. (2000b). Widening the circle: Faculty–student support groups as innovative practice in higher education. *Interchange: A Quarterly Review of Education, 31*(1), 35–60.

Murray, B. (2000, November). The growth of the new PhD. *Monitor on Psychology, 31,* 24–27.

Nyquist, J. D., & Woodford, B. J. (2000). *Re-envisioning the Ph.D.: What concerns do we have?* Seattle, WA: Center for Instructional Development and Research and the University of Washington.

O'Neil, J. M. (1981). Toward a theory and practice of mentoring in psychology. In J. M. O'Neil & L. S. Wrightsman (Chairs), *Mentoring: Psychological, personal, and career developmental implications.* Symposium presented at the American Psychological Association Annual Convention, Los Angeles.

O'Neil, J. M., & Wrightsman, L. S. (2001). The mentoring relationship in psychology training programs. In S. Walfish & A. Hess (Eds.), *Succeeding in graduate school: The career guide for the psychology student* (pp. 113–129). Hillsdale, NJ: Lawrence Erlbaum.

Packard, B. W-L., Walsh, L., & Seidenberg, S. (2004). Will that be one mentor or two? A cross-sectional study of women's mentoring during college. *Mentoring and Tutoring, 12*(1), 71–85.

Piantanida, M., & Garman, N. B. (1999). *The qualitative dissertation: A guide for students and faculty.* Thousand Oaks, CA: Corwin.

Rice, M. B., & Brown, R. D. (1990). Developmental factors associated with self perceptions of mentoring competence and mentoring needs. *Journal of College Student Development, 31,* 293–299.

Rose, G. L. (2003). Enhancement of mentor selection using the Ideal Mentor Scale. *Research in Higher Education, 44*(4), 473–494.

Rymer, J. (2002). "Only connect": Transforming ourselves and our discipline through co-mentoring. *Journal of Business Communication, 39*(3), 342–363.

Stripling, L. (2004). *All-But-Dissertation: Non-completion of doctoral degrees in education.* Unpublished doctoral dissertation, University of South Florida, Tampa.

Tenenbaum, H. R., Crosby, F. J., & Gliner, M. D. (2001). Mentoring relationships in graduate school. *Journal of Vocational Behavior, 59,* 326–341.

Tharp, R. G., & Gallimore, R. (1988/1999). *Rousing minds to life: Teaching, learning, and schooling in social context.* Boston: Cambridge University Press.

Thorpe, J. (2005, January). *APS Observer, 18*(1), 1–3. (Published interview with Robert Zajonc, Stanford University.) Online at http://www.psychologicalscience.org/observer.

Twale, D. J., & Kochan, F. K. (2000). Assessment of an alternative cohort model for part-time students in an educational leadership program. *Journal of School Leadership, 10*(2), 188–208.

Waldeck, J. H., Orrego, V. O., Plax, T. G., & Kearney, P. (1997). Graduate student/faculty mentoring relationships: Who gets mentored, how it happens, and to what end. *Communication Quarterly, 45*(3), 93–110.

Wilde, J. B., & Schau, C. G. (1991). Mentoring in graduate schools of education: Mentees' perceptions. *Journal of Experimental Education, 59,* 165–179.

Witte, J. E., & James, W. B. (1998). Cohort partnerships: A pragmatic approach to doctoral research. *New Directions for Adult and Continuing Education, 79,* 53–62.

Young, C. Y., & Wright, J. V. (2001). Mentoring: The components for success. *Journal of Instructional Psychology, 28*(3), 202–206.

Young, J. P., Alvermann, D., Kaste, J., Henderson, S., & Many, J. (2004). Being a friend and a mentor at the same time: A pooled case comparison. *Mentoring and Tutoring*, *12*(1), 23–36.

Zuckerman, H. (1977). *Scientific elite: Nobel laureates in the United States*. New York: The Free Press.

Chapter 9

Naturally Occurring Mentoring Relationships Involving Workplace Employees

Thomas W. Dougherty, Daniel B. Turban,
and Dana L. Haggard

After receiving her MBA, Kim accepted employment with the consumer products division of a large corporation. As part of the firm's orientation of new managers, she attended a 2-week management orientation program at the division's training center. This program included a variety of orientation and information sessions devoted to understanding the firm, its history, culture, and career opportunities. These sessions included presentations and discussions with top executives in the division.

At a luncheon on the second day of the program, Kim was seated next to Mary, one of the division vice-presidents. As they struck up a conversation, Kim and Mary discovered that, although they were separated by 20 years in terms of age, they had attended the same MBA program and shared similar family backgrounds. They liked each other and soon both perceived that they were "kindred spirits" of some sort. After that initial encounter Kim and Mary found themselves seeking each other out at receptions and lunches over the next 2 weeks of the program. As the program concluded, Mary promised to make herself available to Kim for advice or assistance at any time – emphasizing that "I'm only a phone call away."

Six months later Kim and Mary have regular telephone, e-mail, and personal interactions. The two continue to get together for lunch on a regular basis. Kim finds these interactions to be extremely valuable, not only in the advice she gets from Mary on work and career issues in the firm, but also in the receipt of support and friendship. Kim also appreciates Mary nominating her for a special task force to formulate marketing innovations in the firm. This task force is providing Kim with the opportunity to work with many managers representing several levels of management, including top executives. Mary finds it personally rewarding to have the chance to pass on some of her hard-earned wisdom and share "war stories" with Kim about work and career issues. But she also feels energized by Kim's curiosity, drive, and commitment to her career – which is progressing quite well. Mary has even benefited from Kim's sharing her cutting-edge expertise about computers and information technology.

By most definitions, Mary and Kim would be considered to be in a mentoring relationship. This informal workplace relationship between a senior manager and a more junior manager was naturally formed, is mutually beneficial, and is maintained on a voluntary basis. Mary and Kim's relationship would also be labeled as a *primary* mentoring relationship in the *initiation* phase, concepts we will discuss later.

In this chapter, we provide the reader with an overview of scholarship on this type of mentoring. Our discussion includes a brief introduction to the concept of mentoring, a description of mentoring functions provided to protégés, their receipt of job/career outcomes from mentoring, and phases of the informal mentoring relationship. We then turn to the formation and development of mentoring relationships, beginning with perceived costs and benefits by mentors and protégés. We then devote attention to motivational and individual difference factors – on the part of both mentors and protégés – that play a role in the formation and continuation of mentoring relationships. Next we provide some discussion of the dissolution of mentoring relationships. Finally, we turn to organizational and contextual factors that facilitate effective mentoring relationships, before offering some concluding comments. Our goal is to provide the reader with a broad understanding of key concepts, findings, and issues, as reflected in the literature of naturally occurring workplace mentoring relationships.

Overview of Mentoring: Functions, Outcomes, and Phases

Many have noted that the term *mentor* is adapted from Greek mythology. Mentor was a friend of Odysseus who served as a tutor to Odysseus's son, Telemachus, as Odysseus fought in the Trojan War and then struggled to return home. The term mentor now typically refers to a senior individual who provides guidance and assistance to a more junior individual, typically referred to as a protégé (or mentee). Although the term mentor is derived from Greek mythology, most organizational scholars view Kathy Kram's (1985) book as the seminal source on mentoring at work, although some earlier work can also be acknowledged (e.g., Hunt & Michael, 1983; Levinson, Darrow, Klein, Levinson, & McKee, 1978; Zey, 1984). Kram's (1985) book is cited in most scholarly mentoring articles, and, even when not cited, her conceptualization of mentoring functions has been widely adopted by researchers. Thus, to provide a brief historical overview of mentoring we describe her initial work in some detail, in order to understand her conceptualization of mentoring and how the area has developed over the years.

Kram (1985) conducted her qualitative study by interviewing managers of a public utility. She interviewed both parties of a mentoring dyad (i.e., mentors and protégés) for 18 different relationships; these 18 relationships consisted of 15 junior managers and 16 senior managers. Kram noted (p. 4) that because the word "mentor" had various connotations she decided that, from a research point of view, it was best not to use that term. Thus, she examined what she termed *developmental relationships* at work. Kram initially interviewed a random sample of 15 managers, and found that only 3 (20%) were involved in developmental relationships with senior managers, suggesting that such relationships were relatively rare, at least in this organization. Kram subsequently relied upon internal staff to help her identify individuals involved in developmental relationships.

A few notable features of Kram's sample: First, it appears that all of her participants were managers, and all mentor–protégé pairs worked (or had worked) in the same organization. Protégés were at relatively early stages of their career and were relatively young (between the ages of 26 and 34). Mentors were considerably older and typically were higher in the hierarchy. Notably, in 10 of the 18 dyads the mentor was only one level above the protégé and apparently was the protégé's direct supervisor (Kram, 1983). Finally, given the paucity of female mentors, most female protégés were involved in cross-gender mentoring relationships, although none of the male protégés had female mentors.

Mentoring Functions

Kram's qualitative data led her to define mentoring as a type of developmental relationship in which mentors provide two broad categories of mentoring functions to a protégé: career and psychosocial mentoring functions. *Career mentoring functions* involve specific mentor behaviors supportive of the protégé's career progress, which directly enhance the likelihood of the protégé becoming successful in his or her career. The broad range of career mentoring functions includes sponsorship, exposure-and-visibility, coaching, protection, and challenging work assignments. Sponsorship involves nominating (sponsoring) the protégé for promotions, lateral moves, and other beneficial career opportunities (e.g., awards, research projects, fellowships, etc.). Exposure-and-visibility involves creating opportunities for the protégé to interact with senior colleagues who may be able to provide developmental opportunities. The coaching function involves suggesting strategies for the protégé in terms of how to accomplish certain work-related goals – "showing the ropes." Because some individuals and situations can be harmful to a junior person, the mentor may have to provide protection for the protégé by shielding the person. Finally, challenging work assignments help the protégé develop the knowledge and skills needed to succeed as a professional.

Whereas career functions focus on aspects of the relationship that help the protégé succeed in his or her career, *psychosocial functions* are more personal aspects of a relationship that tend to enhance a protégé's sense of professional competence and identity. Thus, whereas career functions are somewhat dependent on the mentor's ability to provide and create opportunities for the protégé, psychosocial functions tend to depend on the quality of the relationship between the mentor and protégé. Psychosocial mentoring includes the following functions: role modeling, acceptance-and-confirmation, counseling, and friendship. In general, a mentor serves as a role model to the protégé who will frequently emulate the mentor's attitudes, values, and behaviors. An acceptance-and-confirmation of another person provides support, encouragement, and nurturance of the other individual and can be helpful in creating a safe environment for the protégé to learn and attempt new behaviors. A mentor who provides counseling provides a safe environment for the junior person to explore personal concerns and issues that may impede the protégé's development.

Finally, friendship involves mutual liking and enjoyable interactions both inside and outside of the work context.

The vast majority of mentoring research in the context of work organizations has adopted the Kram framework discussed above, although there is some evidence suggesting that *role modeling* is not a sub-dimension of psychosocial mentoring but a third distinct function (Scandura, 1992). Further, Ragins and McFarlin (1990) added two additional psychosocial functions: social and parent. Notably, Kram (1985) indicated that all of the 18 developmental relationships she examined provided career functions, although three of the relationships did not provide any psychosocial functions.

To summarize, Kram's (1985) book is seen as the seminal work for organizational mentoring research and is probably the most widely cited piece by mentoring scholars, with over 275 citations to date. She articulated a categorization of mentoring functions that has been widely adopted by mentoring scholars. Notably, Kram had some difficulty in finding many "mentoring" relationships and elected not to use the term mentoring. Kram's work reflected what might be called traditional mentoring relationships – relationships in which the mentor is older than the protégé and one to two levels higher in the organization than the protégé. Finally, these relationships reflected *primary* mentoring, which is a strong individual relationship with one mentor. Kram also acknowledged that some mentoring is *secondary* mentoring, which involves less intense relationships, often with multiple mentors. The mentoring literature includes studies of both primary and secondary mentoring. Some researchers, for example, have asked protégés to respond to scales measuring mentoring functions received from multiple mentors, over some period of time (e.g. Turban & Dougherty, 1994).

Job/Career Outcomes from Mentoring and Protégé Access to Mentors

Since Kram's seminal work, considerable research has examined mentoring relationships at work (see Noe, Greenberger, & Wang, 2002, and Wanberg, Welsh, & Hezlett, 2003 for recent reviews). A notable and valuable portion of the early mentoring research (subsequent to Kram's) examined relationships between mentoring received by protégés and their career success. For example, several studies investigated whether mentoring received (from both primary and secondary mentors) was related to compensation and promotion progress (Dreher & Ash, 1990; Scandura, 1992; Whitely & Coetsier, 1993; Whitely, Dougherty, & Dreher, 1991). In general, such research indicated that individuals who reported receiving more mentoring also reported receiving more promotions and higher compensation than individuals who received less mentoring. Scholars also soon acknowledged that the construct of career success includes more than salary and promotion rates, and identified subjective outcomes linked to protégés' receipt of mentoring. These outcomes included, for example, protégés' perceived career success, career expectations, organizational justice, job satisfaction, organizational commitment, job burnout, and organizational power, among other outcomes (Fagan & Walter, 1982; Fagenson, 1988; Scandura, 1997; Turban & Dougherty, 1994). A recent meta-analysis confirmed that mentoring relationships are related to objective and subjective measures of career success (Allen,

Eby, Poteet, Lentz, & Lima, 2004). For example, individuals who were mentored reported higher compensation, more promotions, and greater career satisfaction, career commitment, and job satisfaction than those who were not mentored (Allen et al., 2004).

Thus, in some of the earlier mentoring research scholars provided evidence that mentoring is related to important objective and subjective career outcomes, such as salary, promotions, and perceived career success. Perhaps because of such evidence, considerable research examined whether men or women have differing access to mentoring relationships and reap differential benefits from such relationships. Although the evidence is mixed, in general women and men report receiving similar amounts of mentoring and mentoring appears to be equally beneficial for men and women (see Ragins, 1999b, for a review). Similarly, although the evidence is mixed, gender does not appear to be an important influence on willingness to mentor others or on becoming a mentor. However, although gender may not influence the decision to mentor others, scholars have suggested that not all mentors provide equal benefits to protégés. For example, mentors who have more power in the organization may be better able to provide sponsorship, exposure-and-visibility, and other career-related mentoring functions than mentors with less power. As noted by Ragins and colleagues (Ragins, 1997a; Ragins & Sundstrom, 1989), in general White men have more power in organizations than do women or non-White men. In this vein, Dreher and Cox (1996) investigated mentoring relationships of MBA graduates and found that although neither gender nor race was related to mentoring, White men were more likely to have a White male mentor than were females, Blacks, or Hispanics. Notably, individuals with a White male mentor had a large compensation advantage compared to individuals whose mentors were not White men. Dreher and Dougherty (1997) subsequently suggested that organizations consider implementing "substitutes" for informal mentoring in the form of career systems equally available to all employees. Dreher and Cox's (1996) evidence also supports the proposition that not all mentors are created equal and suggests that there is value in examining mentoring *relationships*, rather than asking participants to report on mentoring received from unspecified sources. Further, such evidence suggests the importance of examining mentor characteristics, beyond demographics, that influence the quality of mentoring received by protégés.

Phases of the Mentoring Relationship

Based upon her initial qualitative work, Kram (1983/1985) outlined four phases of the mentoring relationship: initiation, cultivation, separation, and redefinition. These phases are considered to be distinct but somewhat overlapping in nature. Although alternative conceptual models of the phases of the mentoring relationship have been proposed (e.g., Missirian, 1982), Kram's model has received some support in the literature (Chao, 1997; Pollock, 1995) and is a well-accepted framework. Thus, we describe her model here.

Initiation. The first phase of the mentoring relationship is initiation. According to Kram (1985), this phase is approximately six to twelve months in duration, and is characterized by both individuals having positive, often idealized, thoughts about one another. In her book Kram goes on to say that the events of the first year transform initial fantasies into concrete, positive expectations based on the interactions over the past twelve months. The questions of who initiates the mentoring relationship and why are addressed in greater detail later in this chapter.

Cultivation.   Initiation is followed by the cultivation phase. According to Kram this phase is approximately 2 to 5 years, and the range of career functions and psychosocial support peaks during this phase. The positive expectations from the initiation phase are continuously tested against reality. This phase is also described as the one with the least amount of conflict or uncertainty and the phase where boundaries are clarified.

Separation.   The third phase of the mentoring relationship outlined by Kram is separation. Separation can occur both structurally (one of the individuals leaves the organization) and/or psychologically. This phase involves the loss of the original relationship. It is a transitional period in the relationship with uncertainty about how each individual will relate to one another in the future. Either member or both have outgrown the relationship and the time has come for the protégé to step out on his or her own. Kram reported that this phase is where the most dysfunction in the relationship is likely to occur as it is a time when both members may be looking to end the relationship as it has existed.

Redefinition.   Redefinition is the fourth stage of the mentoring relationship. In the redefinition phase, the mentor and protégé look to find new ways to relate to each other. Sometimes it is possible for both parties to feel as if they are peers. Friendship and continued contact would be functional redefinition of the relationship. However, when separation occurred due to unresolved conflict or irreconcilable differences, the redefinition phase is less likely to include friendship.

Research findings on phases.   Although support has been found for the existence of Kram's phases, very few studies have been devoted to investigating the phases of mentoring relationships at work, and those that have are retrospective rather than longitudinal in nature (Chao, 1997; Pollock, 1995). Wanberg and colleagues also noted a dearth of empirical investigation about mentoring phases (Wanberg et al., 2003). Nonetheless, in a study of 178 current and former protégés, Chao (1997) found support for Kram's conceptualization of the four mentoring phases. In addition to confirming the phases, Chao also looked at potential differences in protégé outcomes in each phase. Results showed that protégés in the initiation phase reported lower levels of mentoring functions than did protégés in other phases; however, no significant differences across these phases were found for a variety of job/career outcomes. Pollock's (1995) study, though not on traditional mentoring relationships, showed some support for Kram's phases as well. Participants in this study did not self-identify as protégés, but instead completed a scale reporting mentoring behaviors exhibited by supervisors. Pollock found that all functions were displayed early in the relationship, though psychosocial functions were most predominant, and that all functions were most frequent during the middle rather than the early part of the relationship.

Thus, some evidence supports Kram's (1983/1985) conceptualization of the phases of mentoring relationships, although more research is needed. For example, although Kram provided a detailed discussion of psychological and organizational factors that influence movement from one phase to another, little research has investigated such factors. Furthermore, it would be useful to track relationship development over time, although we acknowledge that such research is quite difficult. Nonetheless, some evidence does support the assertion that mentoring relationships go through certain phases, although we know little about what influences transition through such phases.

Formation and Development of Naturally Occurring Mentoring Relationships

A variety of variables have been studied in examining the formation and development of naturally occurring workplace mentoring relationships, including both protégé and mentor variables. The variables of interest have changed over time. The vast majority of the workplace mentoring literature has taken the protégé perspective; however, some more recent literature has also taken the perspective of mentors, especially in examination of perceived costs and benefits and motivation to mentor. In this section we provide an overview of this literature. Note that diversity issues (e.g., gender and race) relevant to workplace mentoring will not be a focus here, because these issues are discussed by Ragins (this volume). In the following discussion we give some extra emphasis to the role of personality in the formation and development of mentoring – an area that has received surprisingly little attention in the literature on naturally formed mentoring relationships.

Costs and Benefits to Mentors and Protégés

Because mentoring relationships are conceptualized as mutually beneficial relationships, scholars have suggested that these relationships can be conceptualized as social exchange relationships (Allen, 2004; Allen, Poteet, & Russell, 2000; Ensher, Thomas, & Murphy, 2001). In general, in social exchange relationships the benefits of being involved in the relationships must equal or exceed the costs (Blau, 1964; Homans, 1958). Thus, both mentors and protégés are expected to initiate and remain in relationships when the expected benefits from the relationship are equal to or exceed the costs of the relationships.

As noted earlier, there is considerable evidence that mentoring relationships provide benefits for protégés in terms of career success and work attitudes (Allen et al., 2004). Although Kram (1985) postulated that mentoring relationships provide benefits for both protégés and mentors, only recently have researchers begun to investigate the benefits of mentoring relationships for the mentor (Allen & Eby, 2003; Allen, Poteet, & Burroughs, 1997; Bozionelos, 2004). The benefits for mentors include personal satisfaction and gratification, building a support network, learning from the protégé, increased job performance, and objective and subjective measures of career success (Allen & Eby, 2003; Allen et al., 1997; Bozionelos, 2004; Ragins & Scandura, 1999).

There can also be costs for both protégés and mentors, although more research has investigated costs to protégés than to mentors. Nonetheless, studies indicate that mentoring relationships are not always beneficial for protégés (Eby & Allen, 2002; Eby, Butts, Lockwood, & Simon, 2004; Eby, McManus, Simon, & Russell, 2000; Ragins, Cotton, & Miller, 2000) or, for that matter, for mentors (Eby & McManus, 2004; Ragins & Scandura, 1999). Costs for the mentor may include time and the energy drain as well as the possibility that a poorly performing protégé can reflect negatively on the mentor (Ragins & Cotton, 1993; Ragins & Scandura, 1999). Mentoring relationships can also be costly to protégés who become too reliant upon one mentor, who then provides unsound advice or "falls out of favor" in the organization, with subsequent negative consequences for the protégé. In addition, both protégés and mentors may be subjected to blatantly negative behaviors such as exploitation and sexual harassment (Eby & McManus, 2004; Eby et al., 2000; Ragins & Scandura, 1999). More broadly, researchers have suggested that mentoring relationships fall along a continuum from highly satisfying to highly dissatisfying (Eby & McManus, 2004; Ragins et al., 2000). Similarly, Eby and McManus (2004) suggested that there is a continuum of dysfunctional relationships ranging from marginally effective relationships, which provide limited benefits to protégés and/or mentors, to highly dysfunctional relationships, which can involve harassment, exploitation, and sabotage.

We suggest that both protégés and mentors assess the potential benefits and costs of getting involved in a mentoring relationship. Currently, we know little about how mentors or protégés influence the value of the relationship, since little research has investigated *processes* through which mentoring influences career success (Day & Allen, 2004). More broadly, little is known about how individual differences of protégés or mentors influence the quality of mentoring relationships. Research clarifying what leads to effective or ineffective mentoring relationships will be a valuable contribution to the literature. We now provide an overview of literature on factors leading to the formation of mentoring relationships and the development of such relationships.

Mentor Willingness to Provide Mentoring

As Wanberg et al. (2003) pointed out in their review, an understanding of key mentor characteristics in the mentoring process offers not only scholarly but also practical value, such as helping protégés to identify the most effective mentors, assisting experienced employees to assess their likelihood of being effective at mentoring, and providing guidance to firms in how to select and develop mentors. However, it is still true that not much of the mentoring literature has examined mentor characteristics. Of the studies that exist, researchers have examined a variety of variables linked to mentor willingness to serve as a mentor, including demographics, job/career history, and personality.

Some evidence suggests that individuals who have previously been in a mentoring relationship (as protégé or mentor) are more willing to serve as mentors than those who have not (Allen, Russell, & Maetzke, 1997; Ragins & Scandura, 1999). More specifically, individuals who have no experience in a mentoring relationship report greater costs and fewer benefits of such relationships than individuals who have experience as a mentor and protégé (Ragins & Scandura, 1999). However, the Ragins and Scandura study also found that for those with no mentoring experience, perceived costs were not a factor in their willingness to mentor others. Thus, costs may be a factor only for those who have experienced costs. Expanding the mentor variables examined, Allen, Poteet, Russell, and Dobbins (1997) studied a large sample of first-line supervisors, finding that a mentor's education level, experience as a protégé, experience as a mentor, and quality of relationship with one's own supervisor were related to willingness to mentor others. Similarly, Allen, Russell, and Maetzke (1997) found that MBA students' willingness to serve as peer mentors was linked to their gender (female) and to satisfaction with their current mentoring relationships. There is also some evidence that those who are older and have more organizational tenure are somewhat less likely to intend to serve as mentors (Allen et al., 2000; Allen, Poteet, et al., 1997; Ragins & Cotton, 1993). However, Ragins and Cotton (1993) found that employees at higher organizational levels are more likely to intend to mentor others, and report fewer barriers to mentorship.

Research results from several studies also confirm the idea that mentor personality plays a role in willingness to initiate a relationship with a protégé (Allen, Poteet, et al., 1997; Allen, 2003). For example, Allen, Poteet, et al. (1997), in the study of supervisors mentioned above, also found that locus of control and upward striving (e.g., the desire to increase one's job level) were related to intentions to mentor others. In another study Allen (2003) found that willingness to mentor others was related to helpfulness and other-oriented empathy. And in a qualitative study by Allen, Poteet, and Burroughs (1997), mentors reported engaging in mentoring relationships both to help others and for the personal satisfaction gained by mentoring another person.

We should also acknowledge that Wanberg et al. (2003) pointed out that studies of willingness or intentions to mentor tend to implicitly assume that this willingness is, in fact, a determinant of mentoring assistance provided to protégés. However, Tepper, Brown, and Hunt (1993) found no relationships between superiors' willingness to mentor and subordinates' reports of receipt of mentoring. Wanberg and colleagues emphasized that future research should examine the generalizability of this finding and whether willingness to mentor mediates the linkage between individual differences of experienced employees and the provision of mentoring assistance to protégés.

Mentor Characteristics and Amount of Mentoring Assistance Provided

Similar to research on willingness to serve as a mentor, a few studies have examined how various characteristics of mentors relate to the mentoring assistance they provide. Although a number of studies have looked at mentor demographic characteristics, the studies do not appear to provide many consistent results. For example, Wanberg et al. (2003) reported that there are mixed findings as to whether mentor age and education are related to serving as a mentor, although a few studies have found that older mentors provide less psychosocial assistance. But most studies have found no relationships of mentor age and other mentoring functions. Similarly, a number of studies have looked at senior managers' career and job history, with few consistent findings. More specifically, it appears that job, career, and organizational tenure are not related to serving as a mentor, or to mentoring assistance provided. Mentors' organizational rank has also not been consistently linked to serving as a mentor or to the provision of mentoring functions. Wanberg and colleagues also provided the noteworthy suggestion that the lack of observed relationships between mentor demographics and mentoring could be a result of restriction of range on demographic variables (e.g., education and age).

In contrast, some of the recent mentoring studies taking the *mentor's* perspective have provided insight into mentor characteristics that predict the amount of career and psychosocial assistance provided to protégés. Allen (2003) found that mentors provided more career-related mentoring when they had higher self-enhancement motives and motives toward benefiting others, and more psychosocial mentoring when they had higher motives toward benefiting others and intrinsic satisfaction motives. Such results indicate that mentor motives influence the mentoring provided to protégés. Further, it seems likely that mentors may have different reasons (motives) for selecting protégés for developing relationships, an issue we will discuss in greater detail shortly.

Allen and Eby (2004) in a study of male and female professionals found that female mentors provided less career mentoring and more psychosocial mentoring than did males. Also, female mentors provided more psychosocial mentoring to female versus male protégés, but male mentors provided similar mentoring to both genders. Experience as a mentor and duration of relationships were related to career but not psychosocial mentoring. However, in multivariate analyses, only mentoring experience and duration of relationships were correlated with career mentoring, and only experience to psychosocial mentoring. Mullen (1998) reported that mentors reported providing more mentoring when the mentor had greater organizational-based self-esteem. And in Godshalk and Sosik's (2003) study of mentors and protégés, they found that both mentor and protégé learning orientation were related to protégé mentoring received.

The trend in research examining mentor characteristics related to mentoring provided has resulted in additional insight into dynamics of mentoring relationships, although we still know relatively little about why individuals choose to mentor others and how mentoring relationships are formed. Nonetheless, some evidence suggests that mentor motives and personality characteristics influence the type and amount of mentoring provided. Thus, we encourage additional research examining deeper-level variables, such as personality and motives, in addition to surface-level variables such as demographics.

Protégé Characteristics in Formation and Development of Mentoring Relationships

A number of studies have examined protégé characteristics in the formation and development of mentoring relationships (see Wanberg et al., 2003, for a comprehensive review). Not surprisingly, most of the data come from the protégés themselves. Wanberg and colleagues pointed out that knowledge of how protégé characteristics influence mentoring may have practical value in identifying those who would flourish as protégés or in providing help to newer employees who find it a challenge to establish mentoring relationships.

Although numerous studies of protégés' motivation to be mentored have invest-igated protégés' demographic, career, and job history variables, such as marital status, education, age, firm tenure, rank, and work experience, the evidence is incon-sistent. We note the words of Wanberg and colleagues who summarized the demo-graphic studies by saying "Based on this body of research, it is difficult to firmly connect many demographic characteristics of employees with their motivations to have mentors" (p. 65). Their conclusion relevant to career and job history variables was similar.

Another larger set of studies has examined protégé variables related to the amount of mentoring received or frequency of mentor–protégé contact. We again direct the reader to Wanberg and colleagues' (2003) review for a more detailed delineation of these studies than we are able to provide in a chapter such as this. First, researchers have examined protégé competence and protégé attitudes (e.g., job involvement, work centrality) for relationships with mentoring functions received – with mixed results. Second, a larger body of work has focused on protégé demographic characteristics as correlates of mentoring received, including marital status, education, age, and socio-economic status (SES). These results are also mixed and remain unclear, although (based on a few studies) a case might be made that higher SES protégés receive more mentoring. Third, some studies have examined variables reflecting protégés' job and career history for linkages to mentoring functions received. Once again, studies of organizational tenure, organization rank, work experience, continuous (versus interrupted) work history, and average hours worked per week have produced inconsistent results. We agree with Wanberg and colleagues that differences in range restriction across studies (e.g., education, age, and work experience for studies of MBA graduates) may account for some of these differences in research findings. More attention to sampling procedures and their effects on range restriction could con-tribute to our understanding of how demographic and job/career history variables relate to mentoring received by protégés.

Fortunately, some researchers have identified more promising avenues relevant to protégé characteristics and the receipt of mentoring. The Allen and Eby (2004) study of mentoring assistance from the *mentor*'s perspective (mentioned earlier) found that mentors reported giving more psychosocial assistance to female protégés, and that female mentors provided less career and more psychosocial mentoring (to all protégés) than did male mentors. Also, female mentors provided more psychosocial mentoring to female versus male protégés, while male mentors provided equal men-toring to both genders. These relationships did not hold up, however, in a multi-variate analysis.

Another potentially relevant set of protégé characteristics in seeking and receiving mentoring is protégé personality. It is somewhat surprising, given the resurgence of personality research in behavioral management research, that little systematic research has investigated the role of personality characteristics in the formation and mainten-ance of mentoring relationships. For example, Wanberg et al. (2003) noted that it is striking that mentoring research has not examined current models of personality such as the five-factor model of personality (although see Bozionelos, 2004, and Waters, 2004, published after that review). Research into the role of protégé and mentor personality characteristics on mentoring relationships should be a research priority. There is, however, at least some research to review.

Although the implicit assumption of much of the mentoring research has been that protégés are chosen by mentors, there is some evidence that protégés' personality characteristics influence the extent to which they attempt to *initiate* developmental relationships with others. In this vein, Turban and Dougherty (1994) argued that protégés with certain personality characteristics – those indicative of proactive behaviors toward others – might be more likely to initiate relationships and to receive mentoring assistance. Results of their study of managers and professionals in diverse industries and occupations indicated that individuals with an internal locus of control, higher emotional stability, and high self-monitoring initiated, and received, more mentoring. Similarly, in a study conducted in Hong Kong, Aryee, Lo, and Kang (1999) found that extraversion, self-monitoring, and Type A behavior were related to initiation of mentoring, but work locus of control was not.

A few additional studies have investigated protégé personality characteristics related to *mentoring functions received*, although, in general, the authors did not specify whether or how the personality characteristics influenced mentoring. For example, Day and Allen (2004) reported that career motivation was related to both psychosocial and career mentoring received; career self-efficacy was related to career mentoring and marginally related to psychosocial mentoring. They theorized, however, that mentoring may have influenced motivation and self-efficacy. However, since they used a cross-sectional design they noted that the causal flow could be in the opposite direction. More broadly, evidence suggests that mentors provide more mentoring to competent versus less competent protégés (Mullen, 1998; Mullen & Noe, 1999). Bozionelos (2004) examined the role of the big 5 personality characteristics in both mentoring received and mentoring provided. Mentoring received was correlated positively with extraversion and openness and, somewhat surprisingly, was correlated negatively with conscientiousness. Interestingly, Bozionelos (2004) also found that mentor reports of mentoring provided were correlated positively with their own openness to experience and, again surprisingly, were correlated negatively with mentor agreeableness. Godshalk and Sosik (2003) investigated learning goal orientation, the extent to which an individual focuses on learning and developing competencies. They found that both mentor and protégé learning goal orientation were correlated with protégés' reported career and psychosocial mentoring. In addition, when both the protégé and the mentor had a higher learning goal orientation, protégés reported receiving more psychosocial mentoring. Such results suggest that protégés may benefit when they and their mentors are more focused on learning and developing competencies.

Some research has taken a slightly different perspective, examining the characteristics of individuals "with and without mentors." Again, the evidence for demographic and job/career history variables tends to be mixed. For example, there is mixed evidence as to whether individuals with and without mentors differ on variables such as marital status, education, age, socioeconomic status, organizational tenure and rank, work experience, and hours worked per week. Such results suggest, again, that demographic and job and career history variables are not consistently related to employees' status as a protégé or non-protégé.

In contrast, similar to research on mentoring functions received, there is some evidence that individuals who are, or have been, protégés differ in terms of personality characteristics from individuals who have not been protégés. For example, some evidence indicates that protégés have a higher need for power and for achievement and are more masculine and more feminine than non-protégés, although there are no differences in needs for affiliation and autonomy (Fagenson, 1989, 1992). In addition, protégés with high need for achievement, need for dominance, and self-esteem were more likely to be involved with *multiple* developmental relationships (Fagenson-Eland & Baugh, 2001). Such results suggest, as noted by Fagenson (1992), that becoming a protégé is not a random process and that personality characteristics may differentiate who becomes a protégé and who does not.

In summary, the evidence seems to suggest that protégé personality characteristics influence formation of a mentoring relationship as well as mentoring received in the relationship. The evidence is mixed, however, concerning protégé demographic characteristics and job and career history variables. Again, we suggest that researchers might focus on deeper-level variables, such as personality, needs, and motives, rather than more superficial-level variables such as demographic characteristics.

Mentor–Protégé Similarity and Mentoring Received

The amount of mentoring assistance provided to protégés may also be affected by the intersection of mentor and protégé characteristics – mentor–protégé similarity. For example, some evidence suggests that protégés' and mentors' *perceived* similarity may have stronger effects on mentoring relationships than *demographic* similarity (Allen & Eby, 2003; Ensher & Murphy, 1997; Turban, Dougherty, & Lee, 2002). For example, a recent study examined both surface-level variables (the demographic variables sex and race) and deeper-level variables (perceived similarity). The study found that protégé perceived similarity to the mentor had a strong relationship to mentoring received whereas gender and race similarity had no relationship or a weaker relationship with mentoring received (Turban et al., 2002). Similarly, Allen and Eby (2003) found no relationship between gender similarity and mentor learning and relationship quality, yet a positive relationship between perceived similarity to the protégé and these same outcomes. Kram (1985) suggested that mentors seek out potential protégés who remind them of themselves when they were younger. Protégés are thought to seek out potential mentors who will serve as role models, also suggesting that perceived similarity may be important. As noted, recent research indicates that perceived similarity is related to mentoring outcomes, although little is known about how perceptions of similarity are formed. In general, demographic similarity is unrelated or only weakly related to measures of perceived similarity (Allen & Eby, 2003; Ensher & Murphy, 1997; Turban et al., 2002; Turban & Jones, 1988), suggesting that perceived similarity results from deeper-level variables than similarity on demographic characteristics.

The duration of the relationship may influence the effects of similarity on mentoring outcomes. Turban et al. (2002) theorized that surface-level characteristics, such as gender, are important early in a mentoring relationship. However, as the relationship continues over time and individuals learn more about each other, similarity on surface characteristics such as demographics becomes less important and similarity on deeper-level characteristics becomes more important. Interestingly, their results indicated that gender similarity was actually *detrimental* early in the relationship but was beneficial for long-term relationships. Contrary to their hypothesis, however, perceived similarity was more important for shorter duration than longer duration relationships, a finding that was replicated by Allen and Eby (2003). Notably, however, Allen and Eby (2003) did not find a gender similarity by duration of relationship interaction.

To summarize, some evidence suggests that perceived similarity influences the initiation and formation of mentoring relationships, although the effects of demographic similarity tend to be weak or non-existent. In addition, duration of the relationship may be an important moderating variable when examining the effects of demographic and perceived similarity on mentoring outcomes. We agree with Allen (2004) who suggested that it may be useful to consider mentoring as a two-step process involving the initiation of the relationship (regardless of whether the mentor chooses the protégé or vice versa) and the receipt of mentoring. It seems likely that the role of perceived and demographic similarity on outcomes may vary in those two steps, although more research is needed.

Protégé Characteristics Sought by Mentors

Given the potential costs of being a mentor, one might expect mentors to seek out protégés from whom they will obtain more rewards than costs. In general, the limited results support this proposition. For example, in an early experimental study, mentors reported greater willingness to mentor others with higher versus lower work performance (Olian, Carroll, & Giannantonio, 1993). Similarly, Allen, Poteet, and Russell (2000) found that mentors reported selecting protégés based on protégé ability more than on their need for help, and this effect was stronger for female mentors compared to males. In a recent laboratory study with undergraduates, Allen (2004) focused on protégé characteristics seen as important by potential mentors. Both protégé ability and willingness to learn influenced willingness to mentor. There was also an interaction, such that willingness to learn compensated for a protégé's lack of ability. A second study (also reported in Allen, 2004), using a field survey of professionals, found that mentors were more likely to report selecting protégés based on willingness to learn than on ability.

Finally, a qualitative study reported that mentors selected protégés who were motivated, competent, with a strong learning orientation, and with certain personality indicators such as people-oriented, honest, confident, and dependable (Allen, Poteet, & Burroughs, 1997). In summary, it appears that both protégé ability and motivation are seen as desirable traits by potential mentors. But at least some mentors seek protégés who have a need for help, and those who possess certain personality traits or a willingness to learn.

Mentor Characteristics Sought by Protégés

Most studies investigating mentoring relationships have obtained information about protégés as opposed to mentors. Thus, less is known about mentor characteristics than protégé characteristics. Nonetheless, a series of three experimental studies that manipulated the interpersonal competence of a potential mentor found that mentor interpersonal competence was related to protégé attraction to the potential mentor (Olian, Carroll, Giannantonio, & Feren, 1988). Although they did not investigate the mechanisms leading to this relationship, Olian et al. (1988) suggested that potential mentors with greater interpersonal competence are seen as better able to provide the psychosocial benefits of mentoring, and because they are better liked and respected may be better able to promote the career of the protégé than are mentors with less interpersonal competence.

Dissolution of Naturally Occurring Mentoring Relationships

The separation and redefinition stages of the mentoring relationship can be considered the phases in which dissolution of the mentoring relationship occurs. As mentioned before, separation takes place because one or both of the dyad members have outgrown the existing relationship or because one or both of the dyad members are physically relocated or leave the firm.

As outlined by Kram (1985), the separation can be either functional or dysfunctional in nature. A functional separation occurs when both parties acknowledge that the protégé is ready to move on to a new stage in his or her development and the separation occurs with little or no hostility. In general, a functional redefinition happens years after separation when the relationship between the mentor and protégé evolves to one of friendship and peer status. A dysfunctional separation might be characterized by jealousy on the part of the mentor or overdependence on the part of the protégé. Such a separation is likely to end in acrimony and unlikely to result in positive redefinition of the relationship at a later time.

Research on the dissolution of mentoring relationships is rather limited. Other than Kram's qualitative study, not many other researchers have investigated this process. An exception to this is Ragins and Scandura's (1997) study on gender and the termination of mentoring relationships. The researchers examined theoretical reasons for why men and women might differ in their reasons for termination (psychological and physical) and the length of their mentoring relationships. Psychological reasons for termination examined in this study included jealousy on the part of the mentor, dependency on the part of the protégé, issues of support for the relationship, and outgrowing the relationship. After controlling for structural factors (e.g., rank and tenure), Ragins and Scandura found that contrary to assumptions about possible differences between men and women, female ex-protégés did not differ from males in the duration or reason for termination of mentoring relationships. Thus, they found no support for the assertion that women are less likely to terminate the mentoring relationship once it has served its purpose.

Although the dissolution of the mentoring relationship is a natural, necessary, and pivotal part of the mentoring process, little empirical work has been conducted on it. Next, we turn to the organizational and structural factors that might facilitate naturally occurring mentoring relationships.

Organizational and Contextual Factors that Facilitate Mentoring

In this chapter we focus on informal relationships. Although some have recommended strategies for creating an environment conducive to developing mentoring relationships, very little empirical work has linked environmental factors to the development of mentoring relationships. These few studies have looked at how organizational factors are related to individuals' willingness or motivation to mentor (e.g., Allen, 2004; Allen, Poteet, & Burroughs, 1997; Aryee, Chay, & Chew, 1996). Here we will briefly summarize the recommendations outlined by Kram (1985) and review research findings on organizational and contextual variables that may facilitate mentoring.

Organizational Factors

In her book on mentoring at work, Kram (1985) devoted a chapter to conditions that encourage mentoring. The first organizational factor she reported is the need for organizations to provide opportunities for frequent and open interactions between managers at different career stages and hierarchical levels. Without *access* to managers higher in the organizational hierarchy it is impossible to form traditional, hierarchical mentoring relationships. Supporting Kram's recommendation, Aryee and colleagues (1996) looked at "opportunity to interact" from the mentors' perspective and found that these opportunities were positively related to an individual's motivation to mentor.

The second organizational factor for Kram revolved around the organization's reward system, culture, and norms. If the reward system does not encourage developmental relationships, and the culture of the organization is not conducive to the development of supportive relationships, it is unlikely that mentoring relationships will develop. Again, results from Aryee and colleagues' (1996) study support the notion that the reward system is important to an individual's motivation to mentor. The degree to which an organization rewarded the development of junior employees had a positive connection to individuals' motivation to mentor. Allen (2004) also found support for the importance of organizational rewards. However, instead of looking at the direct effect of organizational rewards on willingness to mentor, Allen examined how rewards for developing others related to mentor preferences regarding choice of a protégé. She found that organizational rewards for developing others were related to the extent that protégé willingness to learn influenced selection, and marginally related to the extent to which protégé ability influenced selection.

Other studies that examine willingness to mentor in informal relationships do so in terms of perceived barriers to mentoring (e.g., Allen, Poteet, & Russell, 2000) rather than identifying a specific organizational factor. Though the scale used (Allen et al., 2000; Ragins & Cotton, 1991) to measure perceived barriers contains a dimension labeled "access to mentor," the remaining dimensions are not truly organizational per se, i.e., "fear of initiating a relationship" and "approval of others." These remaining dimensions are similar to individual differences, making it difficult to make organizational recommendations based on these studies. We are unaware of any studies that test the relationship between an organization's culture and individuals' willingness to mentor or the number of individuals reporting involvement in mentoring relationships.

Contextual Factors

As Kram (1985) suggested and Aryee and colleagues (1996) supported, opportunity to interact is an important factor in developing mentoring relationships. Thus, it should not be surprising that in studies of mentoring relationships, often the supervisor is indicated as the mentor (e.g., Day & Allen, 2004; Eby & McManus, 2004; Ragins & Cotton, 1999). Supervisors not only have the opportunity to interact with subordinates but also to assess their subordinates' abilities and desire to learn. In addition, supervisors appear to provide different mentoring functions than non-supervisory mentors (Burke, McKenna, & McKeen, 1991; Ragins & McFarlin, 1990; Tepper, 1995).

Concluding Comments

In this chapter we have attempted to communicate to the reader the essential flavor of the literature on naturally occurring mentoring relationships in the workplace. Our discussion included an overview of key aspects of a literature that has grown over more than 20 years.

We first provided some introduction to the concept of informal mentoring relationships at work, a description of mentoring functions provided to protégés, the connection of mentoring with protégé job/career outcomes, and phases of the informal mentoring relationship. In this section (and throughout) we included some mention of the benefits of mentoring and diversity (e.g., gender, race) issues. But we note that these topics are the focus of other chapters in this volume. However, we have devoted considerable attention to scholarly literature on the formation and development of mentoring relationships. This discussion included costs and benefits of mentoring for both mentors and protégés, and a variety of motivational and individual difference factors that play a role in the formation and continuation of mentoring relationships. Our review acknowledged a number of areas of mixed or inconclusive findings in the literature – especially research on "surface-level" variables such as demographic variables, and job/career history variables – as correlates of mentoring. We have also emphasized what we believe to be a more promising avenue of investigation – the study of deeper-level variables in mentoring relationships, such as personality, needs, and motives. Finally, after some discussion of the limited work on the dissolution of mentoring relationships, we reviewed organizational and contextual variables that may facilitate naturally occurring workplace mentoring.

Throughout this chapter we have attempted to stimulate the reader's thinking about key issues in the study of mentoring relationships, and to underscore the most promising avenues for future work.

References

Allen, T. D. (2003). Mentoring others: A dispositional and motivational approach. *Journal of Vocational Behavior*, 62, 134–154.

Allen, T. D. (2004). Protégé selection by mentors: Contributing individual and organizational factors. *Journal of Vocational Behavior*, 65, 469–483.

Allen, T. D., & Eby, L. T. (2003). Relationship effectiveness for mentors: Factors associated with learning and quality. *Journal of Management*, 29, 469–486.

Allen, T. D., & Eby, L. T. (2004). Factors related to mentor reports of mentoring functions provided: Gender and relational characteristics. *Sex Roles, 50*, 129–139.

Allen, T. D., Eby, L. T., Poteet, M. L., Lentz, E., & Lima, L. (2004). Career benefits associated with mentoring for protégés: A meta-analysis. *Journal of Applied Psychology, 89*, 127–136.

Allen, T. D., Poteet, M. L., & Burroughs, S. M. (1997). The mentor's perspective: A qualitative inquiry and future research agenda. *Journal of Vocational Behavior, 51*, 70–89.

Allen, T. D., Poteet, M. L., & Russell, J. E. A. (2000). Protégé selection by mentors: What makes the difference? *Journal of Organizational Behavior, 21*, 271–282.

Allen, T. D., Poteet, M. L., Russell, J., & Dobbins, G. H. (1997). A field study of factors related to supervisors' willingness to mentor others. *Journal of Vocational Behavior, 50*, 1–22.

Allen, T. D., Russell, J. E. A., & Maetzke, S. B. (1997). Formal peer mentoring: Factors related to protégés' satisfaction and willingness to mentor others. *Group & Organization Management, 22*, 488–507.

Aryee, S., Chay, Y. W., & Chew, J. (1996). The motivation to mentor among managerial employees. *Group & Organization Management, 21*, 261–277.

Aryee, S., Lo, S., & Kang, I. L. (1999). Antecedents of early career stage mentoring among Chinese employees. *Journal of Organizational Behavior, 20*, 563–576.

Blau, P. M. (1964). *Exchange and power in social life.* New York: Wiley.

Bozionelos, N. (2004). Mentoring provided: Relation to mentor's career success, personality, and mentoring received. *Journal of Vocational Behavior, 64*, 24–46.

Burke, R. J., McKenna, C. S., & McKeen, C. A. (1991). How do mentorships differ from typical supervisory relationships? *Psychological Reports, 68*, 459–466.

Chao, G. T. (1997). Mentoring phases and outcomes. *Journal of Vocational Behavior, 51*, 15–28.

Day, R., & Allen, T. D. (2004). The relationship between career motivation and self-efficacy with protégé career success. *Journal of Vocational Behavior, 64*, 72–91.

Dreher, G. F., & Ash, R. (1990). A comparative study of mentoring among men and women in managerial, professional and technical positions. *Journal of Applied Psychology, 75*, 539–546.

Dreher, G. F., & Cox, Jr., T. H. (1996). Race, gender and opportunity: A study of compensation attainment and the establishment of mentoring relationships. *Journal of Applied Psychology, 81*, 297–308.

Dreher, G. F., & Dougherty, T. W. (1997). Substitutes for career mentoring: Promoting equal opportunity through career management and assessment systems. *Journal of Vocational Behavior, 51*, 110–124.

Eby, L. T., & Allen, T. D. (2002). Further investigation of protégés' negative mentoring experiences: Patterns and outcomes. *Group & Organization Management, 27*, 456–479.

Eby, L. T., Butts, M., Lockwood, A., & Simon, S. A. (2004). Protégés' negative mentoring experiences: Construct development and nomological validation. *Personnel Psychology, 57*, 411–447.

Eby, L. T., & McManus, S. E. (2004). The protégé's role in negative mentoring experiences. *Journal of Vocational Behavior, 65*, 255–275.

Eby, L. T., McManus, S. E., Simon, S. A., & Russell, J. E. A. (2000). The protégé's perspective regarding negative mentoring experiences: The development of a taxonomy. *Journal of Vocational Behavior, 57*, 1–21.

Ensher, E. A., & Murphy, S. E. (1997). Effects of race, gender, perceived similarity, and contact on mentor relationships. *Journal of Vocational Behavior, 50*, 460–481.

Ensher, E. A., Thomas, C., & Murphy, S. E. (2001). Comparison of traditional, step-ahead, and peer mentoring on protégés' support, satisfaction and perceptions of career success: A social exchange perspective. *Journal of Business and Psychology, 15*, 415–438.

Fagan, M. M., & Walter, G. (1982). Mentoring among teachers. *Journal of Educational Research*, *76*, 113–118.

Fagenson, E. A. (1988). The power of a mentor: Protégés' and non-protégés' perceptions of their own power in organizations. *Group and Organization Studies*, *13*, 182–194.

Fagenson, E. A. (1989). The mentor advantage: Perceived career/job experiences of protégés versus non-protégés. *Journal of Organizational Behavior*, *10*, 309–320.

Fagenson, E. A. (1992). Mentoring – Who needs it? A comparison of protégés' and non-protégés' needs for power, achievement, affiliation, and autonomy. *Journal of Vocational Behavior*, *41*, 48–60.

Fagenson-Eland, E. A., & Baugh, S. G. (2001). Personality predictors of protégé mentoring history. *Journal of Applied Social Psychology*, *31*, 2502–2517.

Godshalk, V. M., & Sosik, J. J. (2003). Aiming for career success: The role of learning goal orientation in mentoring relationships. *Journal of Vocational Behavior*, *63*, 417–437.

Homans, G. C. (1958). Social behavior as exchange. *American Journal of Sociology*, *63*, 597–606.

Hunt, D. M., & Michael, C. (1983). Mentorship: A career training and development tool. *Academy of Management Review*, *8*, 475–485.

Kram, K. E. (1983). Phases of the mentor relationship. *Academy of Management Journal*, *26*(4), 608–625.

Kram, K. E. (1985). *Mentoring at work: Developmental relationships in organizational life*. Glenview, IL: Scott, Foresman and Company.

Levinson, D. J., Darrow, C. N., Klein, E. B., Levinson, M. H., & McKee, B. (1978). *The seasons of a man's life*. New York: Knopf.

Missirian, A. K. (1982). *The corporate connection: Why executive women need mentors to reach the top*. Englewood Cliffs, NJ: Prentice Hall.

Mullen, E. J. (1998). Vocational and psychosocial mentoring functions: Identifying mentors who serve both. *Human Resource Development Quarterly*, *9*(4), 319–339.

Mullen, E. J., & Noe, R. A. (1999). The mentoring information exchange: When do mentors seek information from their protégés? *Journal of Organizational Behavior*, *20*, 233–242.

Noe, R., Greenberger, D. B., & Wang, S. (2002). Mentoring: What we know and where we might go from here. In G. R. Ferris & J. J. Martocchio (Eds.), *Research in Personnel and Human Resources Management* (Vol. 21, pp. 129–173). Greenwich, CT: Elsevier Science/JAI Press.

Olian, J. D., Carroll, S., & Giannantonio, C. M. (1993). Mentor reactions to protégés: An experiment with managers. *Journal of Vocational Behavior*, *43*, 266–278.

Olian, J., Carroll, S., Giannantonio, C. M., & Feren, D. (1988). What do protégés look for in a mentor? Results of three experimental studies. *Journal of Vocational Behavior*, *33*, 15–37.

Pollock, R. (1995). A test of conceptual models depicting the developmental course of informal mentor–protégé relationships in the workplace. *Journal of Vocational Behavior*, *46*, 144–162.

Ragins, B. R. (1997a). Diversified mentoring relationships in organizations: A power perspective. *Academy of Management Review*, *22*, 482–521.

Ragins, B. R. (1999b). Gender and mentoring relationships. In G. N. Powell (Ed.), *Handbook of gender in organizations* (pp. 347–370). Thousand Oaks, CA: Sage.

Ragins, B. R., & Cotton, J. L. (1991). Easier said than done: Gender differences in perceived barriers to getting a mentor. *Academy of Management Journal*, *34*, 939–951.

Ragins, B. R., & Cotton, J. L. (1993). Gender and willingness to mentor in organizations. *Journal of Management*, *19*, 97–111.

Ragins, B. R., & Cotton, J. L. (1999). Mentor functions and outcomes: A comparison of men and women in formal and informal mentoring relationships. *Journal of Applied Psychology*, *84*, 529–550.

Ragins, B. R., Cotton, J. L., & Miller, J. S. (2000). Marginal mentoring: The effects of type of mentor, quality of relationship, and program design on work and career attitudes. *Academy of Management Journal, 43,* 1177–1194.

Ragins, B. R., & McFarlin, D. B. (1990). Perceptions of mentor roles in cross-gender mentor relationships. *Journal of Vocational Behavior, 37,* 321–340.

Ragins, B. R., & Scandura, T. A. (1999). Burden or blessing? Expected costs and benefits of being a mentor. *Journal of Organizational Behavior, 20,* 493–509.

Ragins, B. R., & Sundstrom, E. (1989). Gender and power in organizations: A longitudinal perspective. *Psychological Bulletin, 105,* 51–88.

Scandura, T. A. (1992). Mentorship and career mobility: An empirical investigation. *Journal of Organizational Behavior, 13,* 169–174.

Scandura, T. A. (1997). Mentoring and organizational justice: An empirical investigation. *Journal of Vocational Behavior, 51,* 58–69.

Tepper, B. J. (1995). Upward maintenance tactics in supervisory mentoring and non-mentoring relationships. *Academy of Management Journal, 38,* 1191–1205.

Tepper, B. J., Brown, S. J., & Hunt, M. D. (1993). Strength of subordinates' upward influence tactics and gender congruency effects. *Journal of Applied Social Psychology, 23,* 1903–1919.

Turban, D. B., & Dougherty, T. W. (1994). Role of protégé personality in receipt of mentoring and career success. *Academy of Management Journal, 37,* 688–702.

Turban, D. B., Dougherty, T. W., & Lee, F. K. (2002). Gender, race, and perceived similarity effects in developmental relationships: The moderating role of relationship duration. *Journal of Vocational Behavior, 61,* 240–262.

Turban, D. B., & Jones, A. P. (1988). Supervisor–subordinate similarity: Types, effects and mechanisms. *Journal of Applied Psychology, 73,* 228–234.

Wanberg, C. R., Welsh, E. T., & Hezlett, S. A. (2003). Mentoring research: A review and dynamic process model. *Research in Personnel and Human Resource Management, 22,* 39–124.

Waters, L. (2004). Protégé–mentor agreement about the provision of psychosocial support: The mentoring relationship, personality, and workload. *Journal of Vocational Behavior, 65,* 519–532.

Whitely, W. T., & Coetsier, P. (1993). The relationship of career mentoring to early career outcomes. *Organization Studies, 14,* 419–441.

Whitely, W., Dougherty, T. W., & Dreher, G. F. (1991). Relationship of career mentoring and socioeconomic origin to managers' and professionals' early career success. *Academy of Management Journal, 34,* 331–351.

Zey, M. G. (1984). *The mentor connection.* Homewood, IL: Dow Jones-Irwin.

Chapter 10

Reflections on Naturally Occurring Mentoring Relationships

Elizabeth Lentz and Tammy D. Allen

The objective of this chapter is to briefly identify similarities and differences across the mentoring areas of study with regard to naturally occurring mentoring relationships. In doing so, we discuss the concept of naturally occurring mentoring relationships, mentoring phases, mentoring functions, mentoring benefits, individual characteristics, and the mentor's perspective.

The Concept of Naturally Occurring Mentoring Relationships

Consistent throughout each area of study is the recognition that spontaneously developed mentorships are distinct from other developmental influences and that they are significant and powerful to those involved. For relationships involving youth, the mentor is an influential adult, whose role is unique from parents and peers. The mentor may be an extended family member, teacher, coach, neighbor, or other nonparental adult. The mentor's responsibility typically does not include structuring the youth's life, but includes providing guidance and opportunities to learn. The mentor may also participate in social activities and offer companionship. The goal of the relationship may vary from the achievement of a specific task to being a source of continual support as the protégé develops into an adult.

Student–faculty mentoring relationships extend beyond the relationship that a student may share with an academic advisor or major professor. The faculty mentor is a source of learning, guidance, and influence. For the student, the faculty mentor may represent how the student perceives the profession and how he or she fits into it. The goal of the relationship may vary, from meeting program requirements to helping the student develop professionally in his or her area of specialization.

A workplace mentoring relationship can be described as a senior employee providing guidance and assistance to a more junior-level employee on a voluntary basis. Although the mentor may be the employee's direct supervisor, all supervisors are not necessarily mentors. The workplace mentor is a unique source of power and support that facilitates the professional development of the protégé within the organization. Similar to youth and student–faculty mentorships, the relationship may be targeted toward completing a specific work task or involve a broader goal of achievement in the organization.

Mentoring Phases

Despite the uniqueness of each type of relationship, all mentoring relationships are thought to follow an orderly pattern of progression through distinct phases. These phase models are fairly similar across areas. The most popular phase model appears to be based on the work of Kram. Based on qualitative research, Kram described how a relationship develops, evolves, and later dissipates. Kram's framework highlighted the distinct, yet overlapping, phases of developmental relationships in the workplace. These phases include initiation, cultivation, separation, and redefinition.

Keller (2005) developed a general framework for relationships involving youth that includes naturally occurring mentoring relationships as well as youth relationships with peers and formal adult mentors. Keller's phases include contemplation, initiation, growth and maintenance, decline and dissolution, and redefinition. For the most part, this framework is similar to Kram's, with the exception of an early focus on contemplation before initiation of the mentorship.

Kram's framework is often adapted for the academic setting in the study of student–faculty mentoring relationships. However, O'Neil developed a model that focuses on student–faculty interaction. Specifically, O'Neil identified six stages of interaction, including: a) making a critical decision and entering a relationship, b) building mutual trust, c) taking risks, d) teaching skills, e) learning professional standards, and f) dissolving or changing the relationship. O'Neil's model is unique in that specific activities and goals of the relationship are highlighted in addition to describing the general process of how the relationship develops and changes. This model offers a more descriptive approach regarding how student–faculty relationships interact and evolve than does Kram's model.

A consistent gap across areas includes limited empirical research regarding mentoring phases. Few studies have examined how mentoring relationships develop across time. Specifically, little is known about how relationships progress through each of these phases, as well as specific factors and outcomes associated within each phase.

Mentoring Functions

Although the functions associated with mentoring may have different names and dimensions across areas, all involve mentor behaviors that are supportive of academic goals or career progress, as well as personal aspects such as emotional support and friendship. Additionally, all three emphasize that mentors serve as role models to their protégés.

Social support is especially critical for youth mentorships. The major forms of social support include instrumental (i.e., tangible support), emotional (i.e., providing a listening ear), and companionship (i.e., spending time in leisure activities). Mentors may also promote identity development by serving as positive role models for protégés.

With regard to student–faculty and workplace employee relationships, research has been primarily based on the career and psychosocial functions described by Kram (1985). Career-related mentoring focuses on the advancement of the protégé, including sponsorship, exposure, coaching, protection, and providing challenging assignments. Psychosocial mentoring focuses on personal aspects such as instilling a sense of competence and identity in the protégé and includes role modeling, acceptance, counseling, and friendship.

Mentoring Benefits

Research consistently suggests that informal mentoring relationships are beneficial to protégés. For youth, research suggests that these relationships are a fundamental part of youth's lives that can promote overall development. Research on student–faculty relationships characterizes informal relationships as positive and satisfying. There is also considerable research on workplace relationships that suggests protégés reap benefits related to career success and work attitudes.

A common research gap across areas is a lack of empirical research documenting the benefits that mentors accrue from engaging in mentoring relationships. Given the benefits for youth involved in mentoring relationships, it is surprising that more research has not addressed the benefits that adult mentors receive by serving in this pivotal role. Similarly, intrinsic rewards associated with being a faculty mentor are recognized, but research on this topic is limited. Recent research does suggest that mentors benefit from workplace mentoring relationships, including increased levels of personal satisfaction and learning from the protégé, as well as objective and subjective measures of career success.

Individual Characteristics

Research suggests that individual characteristics are important considerations, but outside of race and gender, issues that are comprehensively reviewed elsewhere in this volume, only a handful of studies have investigated protégé and mentor characteristics. Different characteristics have been the focus of study across areas. For relationships involving youth, developmental stage appears to be a key focal variable as there are different relational processes among youth in middle school, high school, and college. Additionally, parental support has been studied, finding that youth with both high and low levels of parental support appear more likely to engage in mentoring relationships than are youth with moderate parental support.

Research on student–faculty relationships suggests that protégé readiness and mentor competence are important. Protégé characteristics, such as emotional stability, initiative, and intelligence, are also related to seeking out a mentor. Additionally, faculty members are more likely to mentor students whose professional interests are similar to their own and remind them of themselves.

Within the workplace research suggests that protégé extraversion, self-monitoring, and Type A behavior are related to initiating mentoring. Similarly, mentoring received has been related to emotional stability, self-monitoring, career motivation, career self-efficacy, learning-goal orientation, extraversion, and openness to experience. With regard to mentors, evidence suggests that characteristics such as mentoring experience, helpfulness, other-oriented empathy, locus of control, and upward striving relate to willingness to mentor. Further research indicates that mentor motives, self-esteem, and learning-goal orientation are related to mentoring provided. Similar to research from other areas, workplace research suggests that protégés have a tendency to seek out mentors who are competent and will serve as role models, whereas mentors seek out protégés based on ability, willingness to learn, and the extent that he or she reminds them of themselves.

Mentor Perspective

Although mentorships are dyadic, the majority of research reviewed in each chapter focused on the protégé rather than the mentor. An exception to this includes research that investigated barriers to being a youth mentor. Potential barriers that might limit adult involvement have been identified, such as negative images of youth in the media and perceptions that the well-being of the child is the responsibility of the parents. For student–faculty relationships, research from the mentor's perspective has primarily focused on co-learning, suggesting a reciprocal learning relationship between the student and faculty member. More recent research on workplace mentoring relationships has focused on the mentor perspective, utilizing interviews and surveys to collect data directly from the mentor. The focus of this research has included the costs and benefits associated with being a mentor, as well as the motivation and willingness to provide mentoring to others.

Part IV
Benefits of Mentoring

Chapter 11

The Benefits Associated with Youth Mentoring Relationships

Lynn Blinn-Pike

Youth mentoring is a social phenomenon that has attracted a great deal of attention since the 1970s. Community leaders, educators, parents, politicians, and program directors have rallied around this program type at the local, state, and national levels, although there is a lack of clear evidence concerning the outcomes that mentoring can provide. It appears to make sense intuitively that when an older and wiser adult befriends an at-risk child, the child will benefit. The conventional wisdom is that when youth who live in high-risk environments spend time with caring adults, the negative impacts of their environments on their development will be lessened. The outcomes to youth who have mentors in their lives have been described as a changed life course, decreased substance use, and improved academic performance (Beier, Rosenfeld, Spitalny, Zansky, & Bontempo, 2000).

The positive impacts on youth and mentors appear to be reciprocal. The outcomes to youth mentors have been described as: a) mutual and long-lasting friendships, b) enhanced creativity, c) redefinition of personal values, and d) increased passion and energy (Levinson, Darrow, Klein, Levinson, & McKee, 1978). Hall (2003) summarized that the outcomes afforded to youth mentors include self-esteem, social insight, and improved social and interpersonal skills. Through mentoring, mid-life adult mentors may experience greater feelings of generativity and leave their personal marks on future generations.

The purpose of this chapter is to describe the state of the field of youth mentoring in terms of benefits to both youth and mentors. This includes a review of literature on informal and formal youth mentoring, discussion of the outcomes of mentoring programs to youth and mentors, original review of literature on youth mentoring programs that meet the criteria for strong program validity, and a list of recommendations that will provide the field of youth mentoring with valuable information on which to base future programmatic decisions.

For this chapter, youth mentoring is defined as an informal (naturally occurring) or formal (not naturally occurring), volunteer, one-to-one relationship between an adult and an at-risk child, adolescent, or young adult. Informal mentors may include family members, relatives, coaches, teachers, religious leaders, etc. Other forms of mentoring such as e-mentoring and group mentoring are evolving and existing research is almost exclusively focused on the one-to-one adult–youth relationship or the adolescent–child relationship. The outcomes of both informal and formal mentoring relationships are reviewed below, although there are fewer studies on the outcomes of informal mentoring.

Origins of Informal Youth Mentoring Relationships

In the 1990s, it was suggested that a close and informal relationship with an adult other than a caregiver or paid professional provides youth with exposure to an additional source of support beyond the family (Gilligan, 1999). It was also accepted that having an informal mentor in his or her social network helps the youth benefit from naturally occurring resources and relationships (Dubowitz, Feigelman, & Zuravin, 1993).

Informal mentoring relationships may have greater potential for positively impacting youth, compared to formal or arranged relationships, because a) they are more common; b) the duration of contact is generally longer; c) mentors are typically a part of the social or kinship networks; d) mentors are more likely to be similar to youth in gender, ethnicity, and socioeconomic background; e) mentors may already be familiar with the life circumstances of the youth; and f) mentors are more likely to have access to and participate with youth in religious services, family celebrations, and family rituals (Cavell, Meeham, Heffer, & Holliday, 2002). However, Cavell et al. (2002, p. 25) stated that informal mentoring has been overlooked as a possible intervention for high-risk youth. Few studies have carefully explored how these relationships originate, develop, and are maintained over time. In addition, little is known about the functions such relationships play in the lives of the youth or mentors.

The two studies summarized below make a unique contribution by delineating the process of informal mentoring in different ways: cross-cultural and descriptive. Sanchez and Reyes (1999) explored informal mentoring as described by 162 Latino adolescents. They reported that 71% of the identified relationships were familial (e.g., aunt, uncle, or sibling), which confirms the Latino value of familism. This was described as different from informal mentoring relationships described in the primarily Anglo-dominated literature. Rychener (2003) conducted qualitative interviews with 10 adolescents from low-income families. Findings indicate that youth were more likely to choose male mentors, regardless of their gender, that the duration of the mentoring relationship was between 3 and 4 years, and that mentor contact occurred weekly in one-to-one and group activities. The reasons that adolescents gave for being involved with their informal mentors included the mentor's expertise, personality, intelligence, education, and willingness to help and sacrifice for others (Rychener, 2003).

Outcomes of Informal Mentoring

Studies on the outcomes of informal mentoring are lacking, compared to the number available on the outcomes of formal mentoring programs. Within the field of informal mentoring, one Scottish study was found that examined the impact on mentors. Philip and Hendry (2000) asked what adult mentors get out of informal youth mentoring relationships. They conducted qualitative interviews with 30 adult mentors and found that mentors believed that mentoring provided them with the opportunity to a) develop their own understanding of the realities of youth's lives which may be hidden to them without being mentors, b) redefine adult–youth relationships, c) experience relationships with youth as equals, and d) make sense of their own past experiences as youth.

Outcome measures for youth in informal mentoring relationships have typically covered academics, feelings about self and school, social and emotional functioning, and behavioral conduct. Rhodes, Contreras, and Mangelsdorf (1994) found that informal mentors served as protective factors in the lives of 54 adolescent Latina mothers. The adolescent mothers with informal mentors showed decreased depression, increased satisfaction with the support in their lives, and improved ability to cope with relationship problems.

Schoeny (2001) examined the influence of three groups (family, peers, and informal mentors) on the risk behaviors of 1,592 African American adolescents. He found that the presence of an informal mentor moderated the negative effects of peer influences on substance use and contraceptive use. More specifically, peer pressure had a greater influence on youth risky behaviors related to substance use and contraceptive use if mentor support was perceived to be low. No such moderating effect was found for delinquent behaviors. Zimmerman, Bingenheimer, and Notaro (2002) surveyed 770 adolescents from a Midwestern city and reported both positive and neutral effects from having an informal mentor. On the positive side, having such a mentor predicted decreased likelihood of smoking marijuana, decreased likelihood of being involved in nonviolent delinquency, and increased likelihood of having positive attitudes toward school. On the neutral side, having an informal mentor had no effect on anxiety or depression.

Greig (2004) examined the presence of informal mentors in the lives of 566 middle-school students. She found that having an informal mentor was not related to mental health (depression/anxiety, angry/irritable mood, somatic complaints), even when the qualities of the mentoring relationships (duration of relationship, frequency of visits, length of visits, level of trust) were taken into consideration.

Freedman (1993) cautioned that youth can incur negative effects from mentoring relationships. Failed relationships can lead to disappointment and mental health issues. A poor relationship with a mentor can reinforce preconceived ideas on the part of high-risk youth that adults are not to be trusted. The study described below is one of the few empirical reports that illustrate that, in some cases, informal mentoring has been shown to reveal mental health issues in youth. Cavell et al. (2002) examined if having an informal mentor could improve the emotional and social functioning of 50 children of alcoholics (COAs). He reported that, compared to the COAs who did not identify informal mentors in their lives, COAs with informal mentors failed to show greater adjustment, had more psychiatric symptoms, and reported greater shame over having alcoholic fathers. In addition, the higher the quality of the mentoring relationship with the informal mentor, the more psychological distress reported by the COA. Cavell and colleagues suggested that perhaps youth who reported having an informal mentor were insecurely attached to their own fathers and sought out and idealized their mentors in inappropriate ways. Alternatively, COAs with informal mentors may more openly express their emotional needs and pull adults into mentoring roles.

Finally, Greenberger, Chen, and Beam (1998) asked 200 adolescents about non-parental adults who served as "very important people" or VIPs in their lives. The most nominated VIPs were siblings, aunts/uncles, and teachers. The findings showed that while the youth perceived the VIPs as providing support for dealing with personal problems, academic problems, and personal development, having a VIP had no impact on whether youth participated in problem behaviors such as driving under the influence of alcohol, cheating in school, substance use, status offenses, physical aggression, vandalism, or theft. Perceived warmth of the mentor and willingness to talk openly with their VIP had no effect on involvement in problem behaviors or depression.

Schoeny (2001) stated that informal mentors can play compensatory but not preventive roles related to problem behaviors. The integration of the six studies described above points out that it is unclear if informal mentoring can prevent serious behavioral problems such as delinquency, and mental health problems such as depression, anxiety, personality disorders, and attachment disorders. Perhaps more serious behavioral problems are beyond the scope of nonclinically-trained, informal mentors.

Origins of Formal Youth Mentoring Relationships

More attention has been paid to formal versus informal youth mentoring relationships. Formal mentoring relationships occur when mentors and youth are matched on criteria such as common interests, gender, race, etc. Aseltine, Dupre, and Lamlein (2000, p. 12) labeled formal youth mentoring relationships as "programmatically facilitated."

Recent Literature Reviews on Formal Youth Mentoring

What do recent reviews of the literature reveal about the outcomes of formal youth mentoring? Since 2000, there have been several reviews of the literature on the outcomes of formal youth mentoring. Four of these are summarized below. The first two are narrative reviews of the research literature and the last two are meta-analyses.

Narrative reviews. The first narrative review identified current trends in youth mentoring. Foster (2001), in a report for the California Research Bureau, reviewed the literature on the effectiveness of youth mentor programs from 1995 to 2000. She summarized three themes that have evolved in youth mentoring since 1995. This includes a change in focus from addressing specific risk behaviors (e.g., alcohol use) to a broader youth development approach that considers individual youth assets, greater consideration of the quality of the mentoring program infrastructure on the outcomes for youth, and greater recognition of the need for additional and better program evaluation.

The second narrative review provided a summary of the impact of youth mentoring across a group of studies. Jekielek, Moore, and Hair (2002) reviewed 10 mentoring programs (5 experimental and 5 nonexperimental/quasi-experimental) for their impacts on academics, substance use, delinquent behavior, social and emotional well-being, and self-sufficiency. They summarized that mentoring has a slight impact on youth academic grades, reduces the initiation of substance use among younger youth, reduces some delinquent behaviors, such as hitting others, yet does not consistently or directly improve youth self-perceptions or feelings of self-esteem. In addition, they reported that it is unclear if mentoring influences self-sufficiency among young adults.

Meta-analyses.   Meta-analysis is a statistical technique for summarizing, integrating, and interpreting empirical research. The key metric is the "effect size" statistic that standardizes and represents the findings in a set of research reports in such a way that comparisons can be made across studies (Lipsey & Wilson, 2001). Cohen (1988) suggested that the following general conventions be considered when interpreting effect sizes: a) small effect size is $\leq .20$, b) medium effect size $\cong .50$, and c) large effect size $\geq .80$.

The two meta-analytic studies described below were conducted on an overlapping set of studies covering slightly different time periods. Both reported similar and modest effects for formal youth mentoring programs. DuBois, Holloway, Valentine, and Cooper (2002) conducted a meta-analysis of 55 articles on the effectiveness of youth mentoring that were published between 1970 and 1998. DuBois and colleagues described the average estimated effect size of .18 in their analysis as "modest" or "small" (p. 157). This was interpreted as meaning that participation in the mentoring programs that were included in the meta-analysis had only a small effect on the average youth. However, the effect size increased significantly when the programs were classified as using best practices, when strong relationships were shown between adult mentors and youth, and when participating youth were identified as from risky environments.

Smith (2002) conducted a meta-analysis of 43 articles on the effectiveness of youth mentoring that were published between 1975 and 2001. Given the considerable overlap with the research articles selected by DuBois et al. (2002), it is not surprising that Smith found the average effect size from her analysis as .20. This was described as "small" but typical of those found in social and clinical psychological research (p. 57). Smith reported larger effect sizes in the areas of academics and career preparation and smaller effect sizes in the areas of violence and delinquency.

Outcomes of Formal Youth Mentoring Program for Youth

What do youth gain from their formal relationships with mentors? While more attention has been paid to evaluating formal mentoring relationships than to informal relationships, the evidence that formal mentoring is beneficial to youth has been described as scant (McPartland & Nettles, 1991), not consistent (Abbott, Meredith, Self-Kelly, & Davis, 1997), unknown (Aseltine et al., 2000), not firmly evident (Tierney & Grossman, 2000), sobering (DuBois et al., 2002), and varied (Sipe, 2002). In addition, there have been positive, neutral, negative, and mixed effects found with formal youth mentoring programs, depending on the variables being measured and the quality of the mentoring relationships. The study most often described as providing evidence of the positive effects of youth mentoring was an evaluation of a Big Brothers Big Sisters program in which 959 protégés were compared with a randomly assigned control group that did not receive mentoring. After 18 months, the protégés were significantly less likely to have started using substances, less likely to have hit someone or skipped school, more likely to report getting along with their families, and more likely to be confident about school. However, it is often not reported that this same study showed that the mentored group was not different from the control group in the likelihood of stealing or damaging property (Grossman & Tierney, 1998). The studies below are grouped according to outcomes related to school, attitudes, and behavioral and psychological functioning.

School

Improvements in academic grades, attitudes toward school, school behavior, absenteeism, and preparation for college have been common targets in educationally oriented mentoring programs.

The Career Beginnings program involved a multifaceted intervention for 1,574 high-school seniors who were randomly assigned to the mentored or control group in each of 24 national sites. Mentoring was one component of this program, along with academic preparation, counseling, and job-related services. The results showed that those students who had mentors were more likely to attend a 2- or 4-year college course. In addition, among the mentored group, those who received more career-related services were also more likely to attend college. The authors concluded that mentoring enhances the effectiveness of other career services (Cave & Quint, 1990).

The Sponsor-a-Scholar program involved 434 protégés in a quasi-experimental design with 36 months of mentoring and a 24-month follow-up to determine the effectiveness of academic preparation for college success among high-risk youth. Compared to the comparison group, at posttesting, the mentored youth showed significant improvements in academics in 10th and 11th grades (but not 12th grade), and more involvement in college preparation courses. At follow-up, more of the protégés had successfully completed their freshman year in college (Johnson, 1997, 1999).

When the effects of 9 months of mentoring on 61 mentored and 61 matched comparison high-risk adolescents were compared in the areas of academics, standardized test scores (reading, math, and language), school attendance, and school behavior, the results showed that there were significant improvements among the mentored group in reading, language, grade point average, and school attendance. However, there were no significant group differences in standardized math scores or the number of disciplinary referrals (Starks, 2002).

Finally, another study involved the evaluation of an 18-month Big Brothers Big Sisters program that targeted the self-competence, academic performance, behavior, and parent–child relations of 22 boys being raised in mother-headed households. Compared to 22 boys who were placed on a waiting list to join the program, the mentored group showed no significant changes in the variables of interest. In fact, the mentored boys showed a significant decrease in grade point average compared to no change in the comparison group (Abbott et al., 1997).

The four studies summarized above all targeted improvements in academics, although three were school-based and one was a community-based mentoring program. It appears that mentoring was successful in preparing high-risk youth for success in college and in improving competence in some academic subjects. The one community-based study showed the least positive results. This may have been because it targeted a particular group of young males from single-parent households who had emotional issues other than those related to academics. It could also have been the fact that it was not school-based, with mentoring not provided by or guided by professional educators.

Attitudes

Formal mentoring programs often have attitudinal changes as goals for youth. Attitudes toward others and risky behaviors are most common. The studies described below targeted attitudes toward the elderly, alcohol/drugs, and family.

In an intergenerational mentoring program called Across Ages, 562 youth were matched with older mentors for 9 months to improve attitudes toward the elderly and prevent drug use. Posttest results showed that the protégés scored significantly better on measures of a) attitudes toward school, future, and elders; b) well-being; c) knowledge about older people; and d) reactions to situations involving drug use (LoSciuto, Rajala, Townsend, & Taylor, 1996). Aseltine et al. (2000) tested the effects of an intergenerational mentoring program with 85 middle school students in the mentored group and 138 in the control group. The variables of interest included attitudes toward self and family, as well as drug use. After 8 months of mentoring, the mentored group showed significantly more positive scores on attitudes toward self, family, and school, and less positive attitudes toward drugs. However, 6 months post-mentoring, the authors reported that the significant mentoring effects were no longer evident. A comparison of the effect sizes between pretest/posttest and pretest/6-month follow-up showed a substantial decline in the extent of group differences. The program effects were described as "moderate" and "short lived" (p. 18).

Behavioral and Psychological Functioning

Included in the category of behavioral and psychological functioning are measures of behavioral conduct, feelings about self, interpersonal relationships, and mental health. DuBois, Neville, Parra, and Pugh-Lilly (2000) conducted a study of the impact of participation in a Big Brothers Big Sisters program on 67 youth. The matched comparison group ($n = 67$) was selected from local schools in the same city as the Big Brothers Big Sisters program. The results showed no significant group differences in behavioral or psychological functioning as rated by parents and teachers or on measures of self-esteem and coping ability over a 1-year period. As a result, DuBois and colleagues proposed that there is not a straight line between providing mentoring and improving the emotional and psychological functioning of youth. They suggested a new model that would take into account both program-level initiatives and efforts to support and monitor the development of mentor–protégé relationships to a greater degree than is generally done.

In the Abbott et al. (1997) study described above under the heading of "school," the mothers of the 22 mentored boys reported no changes in parent–child relationships, while the control group mothers reported improved relationships with their sons. The authors described these results as inconsistent with the social support literature and suggested further research with a larger sample and longer timeframe.

Slicker and Palmer (1993) asked if 32 mentored youth, compared to a matched group of 32 nonmentored youth, had a reduced dropout rate, and had improved self-concept over a six-month time period. The initial results showed no significant group differences on any of the variables of interest. However, when comparisons were made between two subgroups of the mentored group (ineffective mentoring and effective mentoring), the effectively mentored group had a significantly lower dropout rate but had no difference in self-concept.

The integration of the findings from the studies described above points to greater ease in improving academic performance and attitudes, compared to intervening to prevent some delinquent behaviors and improve psychological functioning and mental health. Although the small sample sizes in the studies described above are a limitation, all three bring into question whether formal mentoring can have a significant and positive impact on outcomes discussed in this section without also taking into consideration the quality of the mentoring program infrastructure and the quality of the dyadic relationship.

Outcomes of Formal Youth Mentoring for Mentors

What do mentors gain from their formal relationships with youth? No large-scale empirical studies have measured changes in mentors over time in such areas as altruism, world view, generativity, or self-worth. While the research on youth mentors is limited, the four studies summarized below illustrate that studies on the outcomes for mentors have generally been qualitative and anecdotal, and revealed that mentors vary in their reactions to the mentoring experience based on their age (adolescent, adult, and elderly).

First, Karcher and Lindwall (2003) explored the outcomes to cross-age mentors when 27 adolescents volunteered to mentor young children. They asked if adolescents experienced more school connectedness as a result of serving as mentors. The comparison of pretest and posttest scores over six months of mentoring showed that the adolescent mentors had significant declines in connectedness to school. It was proposed that working with challenging children may be a deflating, but temporary, experience for adolescents. However, in the long run, it may be a growth experience and the struggle may make the adolescents stronger. The authors concluded that understanding indirect growth experiences such as this may contribute to the effectiveness of future mentoring programs.

Second, Diversi and Mecham (2005) reported on a program in which Latino students were matched with adult Caucasian mentors in an after-school program. The mentors expressed both satisfaction and tension as a result of their relationships. The satisfaction came from establishing strong relationships with the youth across age, social class, and culture. An ongoing concern among the mentors had to do with a debate over "spoon-feeding" the youth as opposed to empowering them through guidance (e.g., doing their math homework with them versus teaching them the math principles). Finally, Rogers and Taylor (1997) explored intergenerational mentoring and asked about the experiences of elder mentors (51–93 years) when they mentored high-risk youth (9–20 years). The most prevalent stresses for the mentors were a) the length of time it took for youth to trust and relate to them, if at all; b) coming to terms with the protégés' backgrounds; c) fear of the neighborhoods in which the protégés lived; and d) balancing relationships with the protégés' families. Some elders reported direct opposition from protégés' families. Other mentors reported that the families desired relationships with them that were too close emotionally. They wanted the mentors to serve as their personal confidants. This may have been because the family members perceived the mentors as older and wiser.

The Outcomes of Formal Mentoring for Youth: An Additional Literature Review

Purpose

Given the lack of consensus on the outcomes of youth mentoring, and the fact that the findings from some of the studies described so far in this chapter are questionable because of small sample sizes and research designs with weak validity, an additional review of the literature was undertaken. The goal was to contribute to this ongoing discussion by identifying and examining the findings from those mentoring programs that met the highest standards in evaluation. The key questions asked: Would the outcomes be similar to those reported in the existing literature if a more stringent set of criteria were applied that resulted in the selection of a group of more valid studies? In which research findings from youth mentoring research can we have the most faith?

Validity

The majority of the thousands of youth mentoring programs in the United States are small, locally controlled efforts with limited funding. Program administrators are often faced with the difficult decision of whether to use scarce funds for program evaluation or for services for additional youth. If mentoring programs do have sufficient resources for evaluation, the results are often included in reports to funders and are rarely shared in peer-reviewed journals or made available to the public. Owing to scarce resources and limited staff, local mentoring evaluations often have questionable validity because they a) are atheoretical, b) lack randomization in assignment of youth to mentored and control groups, c) lack comparison or control groups, d) include small samples, e) show high rates of attrition of mentors and youth from both program services and evaluation, f) are not longitudinal, and g) are more anecdotal than empirical in their findings. In addition, mentoring programs often include such services as career preparation, tutoring, and counseling, which make it difficult to sort out the unique outcomes provided by the mentoring component alone.

Internal validity.   How can professionals, with reasonable certainty, attribute youth outcomes to the specific mentoring programs in which they participate? Campbell and Stanley (1966) discussed internal validity as the researcher's ability to make causal inference about the impact of an intervention on the changes measured in the sample before and after the intervention. Extraneous variables are those confounding influences that lead to questionable validity. Extraneous variables that may be of particular interest in studying youth mentoring include maturation and development of children or adolescents over the course of the study, statistical regression of scores to the mean where particular groups have been selected because of their high-risk status, and differential attrition of youth from one of the groups over the course of the program. To be better able to control threats to internal validity, the true experimental design is recommended. In the true experimental design, equivalence of groups is achieved by randomization of membership in the mentoring and control groups according to the laws of probability. With randomization, threats such as maturation and attrition are controlled because they are more likely to be present in both groups. However, in many instances a true experimental study is not feasible and program evaluators must assign youth to nonequivalent mentored and comparison groups.

Even in a true experimental study, threats to internal validity can exist. Threats that are particularly relevant to study of youth mentoring programs include reactions of youth to the knowledge that they are part of a research study, and reactions of youth to being assigned to the mentored group versus the control group. This could include being placed in a control group that is on a waiting list to receive mentoring until the program evaluation is completed. It could also involve a youth being placed in a control group that never receives mentoring after he or she has expressed a strong interest in participating in the mentoring program. These reactions could influence youth behaviors during the receipt of mentoring or bias pretest/posttest scores so that their answers are different from youth in mentoring programs without similar features.

External validity.   How can professionals know, with reasonable certainty, that the outcomes observed from a study of one mentoring program are generalizable to other similar mentoring programs? Campbell and Stanley (1966) discussed external validity as the researcher's ability to describe to what populations, settings, treatments, and measurements the reported results can be generalized. The external validity of a study is directly related to the sample size. DuBois (2005, p. 49) stated that a "relatively large sample (and hence expenditure of resources) therefore often is likely to be required to ensure sensitivity to effects of mentoring programs or relationships."

Methodology

A systematic review and analysis of the literature was undertaken to address questions related to the validity of mentoring program evaluations. Two methods were used to identify mentoring programs that illustrated best practices in program evaluation. First, computer searches were conducted using PsychINFO, ERIC, Medline, and Dissertation Abstracts from 1970 to 2005. And second, the reference list of each study was reviewed to identify additional studies. Strict criteria were applied to determine the final selection of studies: a) publication in a peer-reviewed journal or a doctoral dissertation from an accredited college or university; b) involvement of a matched comparison group, random assignment to mentored and control groups, or random assignment of intact classes to mentored and control groups; c) a data-producing sample of at least 50 protégés in the mentored group; and d) empirical and quantitative results.

Results – Posttest

The results yielded 17 studies that met the stringent criteria listed above. The 17 studies are summarized in Table 11.1. Even though the studies were similar in all meeting the predetermined criteria, they showed great diversity. Table 11.1 shows that a) the dates ranged from 1975 to 2004; b) sample sizes ranged from 50 to 487 protégés; c) research designs included random assignment by classes (2 studies), quasi-experimental studies with matched or nonequivalent comparison groups (9 studies), and true experimental studies with random assignment of youth to mentored and control groups (6 studies); d) the duration of the mentoring intervention varied from 3 months to 36 months; and e) only three studies were longitudinal and followed the youth for up to 24 months post-mentoring. In addition, the foci of the studies were categorized according to the following topics: a) school (12 studies); b) self (10 studies); c) interpersonal relations with family and peers (6 studies); d) alcohol/drugs (4 studies); and e) delinquency (6 studies). The "school" category included grades, attendance, attitudes toward school, and bonding with school. The "self" category included self-control, self-esteem, self worth, self-concept, and self and the future. Interpersonal relationships with family included family bonding, parental communication, and parental trust. Interpersonal relations with peers included support, level of conflict, and improved relations with peers. The category involving alcohol and drugs included attitudes toward substance use, likelihood of initiation of substance use, reactions to situations involving potential use of substances, and frequency of use. The delinquency category included high-risk behaviors, minor and major judicial offenses, and violence. The posttest and follow-up results from these 17 studies are presented below, according to the categories a–e listed above. The studies are referenced in parentheses according to the numbering shown in Table 11.1. Only five studies that were mentioned earlier in this chapter also met the criteria to be included in this additional review (1, 4, 5, 8, 16).

School.   Overall, nine studies with school success as a focus showed positive outcomes at posttesting. Compared to control or comparison groups, significant improvements were evident in attitudes toward school, confidence in school success, bonding with school (1, 3, 4, 5, 8, 13, 17), attendance (1, 4, 9, 13, 16), academic grades (5, 9, 16), and involvement in college preparation activities (5). Five reported no significant group differences in academic grades (6, 13, 14) or standardized test scores (9, 10). One reported no improvements in the value of school (13). One found improvements in academic achievement in grades 10 and 11 but not 12 (5), and one found improvements in subjects other than math (16).

Self.   Overall, five studies in this category showed significant positive outcomes. Protégés had significantly higher scores on measures of self-control (1), well-being

Table 11.1 Review of mentoring programs meeting selective criteria

Author(s)	Date	Sample size*	Design**	Duration of mentoring (months)	Longitudinal follow-up post-mentoring (months)	Focus	Significant findings for mentored group compared to comparison or control group (effect sizes***)
1. Aseltine, Dupre, & Lamlein	2000	85	1	8	6	School, self, relationships, alcohol/drugs	**Posttest:** Protégés had better: school bonding, self-control, attendance, family bonding, cooperation, attitudes toward drug use **Follow-up:** None of the significant effects were maintained
2. Fo & O'Donnell	1975	264	3	12	NA	Delinquency	**Posttest:** Protégés with histories of prior serious offenses had fewer serious offenses during mentoring intervention; protégés without histories of serious offenses had more offenses after being mentored than the control group (.27)
3. Foster	2001	67	2	9	NA	School, self, relationships	**Posttest:** Higher risk protégés had improved: scholastic self-confidence (.39), global self-worth (.17), parental relationships (.31)
4. Grossman & Tierney	1998	487	3	12	NA	School, self, relationships, alcohol/drugs, delinquency	**Posttest:** Protégés were less likely to: lack confidence about school, skip school, not get along with families, have started using substances, hit someone. No group differences in how often they stole something or damaged property in the previous year

	Year	N				Domain	Findings
5. Johnson	1997	434	2	36	24	School, self	**Posttest:** Protégés had improved: grades in 10th and 11th but not 12th grade, attitudes toward school, confidence in school, bonding with school, involvement in college prep activities. No group differences in self-esteem. **Follow-up:** More college attendance during 1st year after high school
6. Langhout, Rhodes, & Osborne	2004	378	3	18	NA	School, self, relationships	**Posttest:** Protégés had: higher self-worth (.23), less parental alienation (.22), more parental communication (.22), more parental trust (.20), improved relations with peers (.12), more support from peers (.12), less conflict with peers (.12). No group differences in grades, or behavioral conduct
7. Lee & Cramond	1999	130	2	12	NA	Self	**Posttest:** Protégés mentored more than 12 months showed higher aspirations (.54). No significant group differences in self-efficacy or perceptions of possible selves
8. LoSciuto et al.	1996	180	1	9	NA	School, self, alcohol/drugs	**Posttest:** Protégés had better: attitudes toward school, future and elders, attitudes toward older people, well-being, knowledge about older people, reactions to situations involving drug use. No group differences in frequency of substance use

Table 11.1 (*Continued*)

Author(s)	Date	Sample size*	Design**	Duration of mentoring (months)	Longitudinal follow-up post-mentoring (months)	Focus	Significant findings for mentored group compared to comparison or control group (effect sizes***)
9. McPartland & Nettles	1991	311	2	24	NA	School	**Posttest:** Protégés had better: attendance (.18), grades in English (.14). No significant differences in standardized test scores compared to school district data
10. Moon & Callahan	2001	273	2	12 (1st grade) 24 (2–3 grade)	NA	School	**Posttest:** No group differences on language, arts, math, reading, or vocabulary measures
11. O'Donnell, Lydgate, & Fo	1979	335	3	12–36	0–24	Delinquency	**Posttest/Follow-up:** Protégés with histories of prior serious offenses had fewer serious offenses at follow-up; protégés without histories of serious offenses had more after mentoring than the control group (.15)
12. Rhodes, Haight, & Briggs	1999	90	3	9–12	NA	Self, relationships	**Posttest:** Protégés had improvements in peer support (.24). No group differences in self-esteem

Study	Year	N	Design**	Grades	Sample*/Follow-up	Outcomes	Posttest Results
13. Rhodes, Grossman, & Resch	2000	378	3	9–12	NA	School, self, relationships	**Posttest:** Protégés had improved: perceptions of school competence (.20), attendance (.27), parental relations (.07). No group differences in global self-worth, value of school, or grades
14. Roberts & Cotton	1994	76	2	3	NA	School, self	**Posttest:** No group differences in school grades or levels of self-esteem
15. Sheehan et al.	1999	50	2	18	NA	Delinquency	**Posttest:** Protégés had less acceptance of violence (.80)
16. Starks	2002	61	2	9	NA	School, delinquency	**Posttest:** Protégés had improved: grades (.38), language scores (.48), reading scores (.72), attendance (.54). No significant differences in math scores or disciplinary referrals
17. Valentine et al.	1998	337	2	8 – M.S. 10 – H.S.	NA	School, alcohol/drugs, delinquency	**Posttest:** Protégés had: increased school involvement, decreased alcohol/drug use, decreased violence

NA = Not applicable.

*   Sample size for protégés available for posttest/follow-up data analysis.

**   1 = Random assignment of classes to mentored and control groups.

     2 = Quasi-experimental with matched or nonequivalent comparison groups.

     3 =True experimental with random assignment of subjects to mentored and control groups.

*** Small effect size is ≤ .20, medium effect size ≅ .50, and large effect size ≥ .80.

(8), and self-worth/self-esteem/self-concept (3, 6), as well as higher aspirations for the future (7). Five studies reported no group differences in feelings of self-esteem (5, 12, 14), self-efficacy (7), perceptions of the self (7), or global self-worth (13).

Interpersonal relationships. In terms of interpersonal relationships, all six studies showed significantly improved relationships with families/parents (1, 3, 4, 6, 13) and peers (6, 12) at posttesting.

Alcohol/drugs. A review of the alcohol/drug prevention studies showed that all four reported positive outcomes. Protégés were significantly less positive about drug use (1), showed significantly better reactions when presented with situations involving drug use (8), and were significantly less likely to start or continue using alcohol or drugs (4, 17). One study reported no significant group differences in frequency of substance use (8).

Delinquency. Four of the six studies that dealt with delinquency showed positive outcomes. One study reinforced that higher-risk youth often show better outcomes as a result of mentoring (2). In this study, protégés with histories of prior serious offenses had significantly fewer serious offenses during mentoring. Protégés without prior serious offenses had more offenses after receiving mentoring than the control group. The authors interpreted this finding as follows:

> For the youths with no major offenses in the preceding year, participation in the [mentoring] project resulted in a greater number of youth committing serious offenses as compared with nonparticipation. It is possible that, as a result of their participation in the Buddy System, youngsters with no major offenses in the preceding year formed relationships with those with major offenses. . . . The results raise the spectre of possible iatrogenic treatment effects of the Buddy System approach with youngsters with no record of prior major offenses. (p. 524)

The protégés involved in the three studies targeting violence prevention reported less acceptance of violence (15) and decreased rates of violence (4, 17). One study each reported no significant group differences in behavioral conduct (6) or number of disciplinary referrals (16). Another set of authors reported no significant group differences in how often youth stole something or damaged property in the previous year (4).

Results – Longitudinal Follow-up

Three studies conducted measurements of youth outcomes beyond posttests. One study showed that at posttesting protégés had higher self-control, family bonding, cooperation, and school bonding, as well as fewer absences and less positive attitudes toward drug use. However, none of the significant results were maintained at 6 months follow-up (1). One study reported significantly more college enrollment among protégés at 24 months follow-up (5). Finally, in a follow-up to a previously described study (2), protégés with histories of prior serious offenses had fewer serious offenses; protégés without histories of serious offenses had more offenses after receiving mentoring than the control group (11).

Discussion

Were the findings from this review similar to those reported in the previous literature? What are the findings when a more stringent set of criteria were applied to the
selection of a group of studies? One way to answer these questions is to compare
effect sizes across studies. According to Meline and Wang (2004), researchers should
routinely include estimates of effect size, and interpret effect-size metrics within
the context of their experiments. These outcomes will strengthen the conclusion
validity in research reports and help to bridge the research to practice divide and
benefit the scientific base.

Effect sizes. Little is known about the impact that evaluation design has on
effect size in mentoring research. It is assumed that more tightly controlled studies
would come closer to having the internal and external validity necessary for placing
greater value on the findings and their generalizability. The results of the two
meta-analyses reported here differed in their findings on this question. DuBois et al.
(2002) reported that the type of research design (e.g., quasi-experimental versus
true experimental) was not a significant moderator of effect size. On the other hand,
Smith (2002) reported that more tightly controlled studies (e.g., those with greater
fidelity to best practices in programs and evaluated using true experimental designs)
revealed smaller effect sizes. Smith's finding would lead to the conclusion that the
outcomes attributed to youth mentoring programs in the past may have been
inflated as an artifact of the research design employed.

In addition, both Smith (2002) and DuBois et al. (2002) examined effect sizes
based on the source of the study being reviewed. Smith reported that the largest
effect sizes were seen in research described in dissertations, then peer-reviewed
journals, and finally, nonpeer-reviewed publications. DuBois reported no differences
in effect sizes if the study was published (journal or book) versus nonpublished (dissertation or report).

Table 11.1 shows that standardized effect sizes could be calculated on 10 of 17
studies described in this chapter (2, 3, 6, 7, 9, 11, 12, 13, 15, 16). Two were dissertations (3, 16) and the rest were research reports in peer-reviewed journals. Effects
were not able to be calculated if the researchers did not provide sufficient data from
their results by groups. No effect sizes could be calculated for alcohol/drug use or
delinquency. Using Cohen's (1988) scale (small effect size is ≤ .20, medium effect
size ≅ .50, and large effect size ≥ .80.), it appears that the effect sizes for the 10
studies were small (8 effect sizes), medium (15 effect sizes), and large (1 effect size),
although there were differences within several categories. In terms of arrest rates,
two reports from the same study revealed effects sizes of .27 at posttest and .15 at
follow-up (2 and 11). Effect sizes for academic grades/test scores ranged from .14
(9) to .72 (16); for self, .17 (3) and .23 (6); for improved perceptions of school
competence, .20 (13) and .39 (3); and for peer support, .12 (6) and .24 (12). In
terms of improved school attendance, the three effect sizes ranged from .18 (9) to
.54 (16). Within the category of parental relations, the five effects varied from .07
(13) to .31 (3). The effect size for future aspirations was .54 (7). The largest effect
size (.80) was for decreased support for violence (15).

Ten of the effect sizes ranged from .20 to .39 and were primarily in the areas of
relations with parents, self-worth, and perceived scholastic competence. As the two

previous meta-analyses pointed out, it remains to be determined which categories garner the highest effect sizes. Smith (2002) reported that the largest effect sizes were in studies addressing academic/career variables and the smallest were addressing aggression and delinquency. DuBois et al. (2002) reported greater effects for problem behaviors, academics, and career/employment outcomes compared to social competence and emotional/psychological adjustment. Too few studies addressed alcohol and drug use to draw meaningful conclusions from the effect sizes calculated here or from the two meta-analyses. Likewise, there are too few longitudinal studies to determine if the effects of mentoring were sustained after the mentoring programs had ended.

Limitations

Although the small number of studies was a limitation in this review, this sample of 17 studies may come the closest to demonstrating "best practices" in mentoring evaluation, meeting stringent criteria related to peer review, study design features, and adequate sample size. These strict criteria were imposed to rule out confounding variables or alternative explanations for results, such as nonequivalent groups of youth, peer-reviewed versus nonpeer-reviewed findings, and lack of attention to pretest/posttest strategies. It is noteworthy that so few such studies were identified as meeting these criteria. Barriers to conducting high-quality evaluations of youth mentoring programs, worthy of being published in peer-reviewed journals, often include lack of funding, lack of commitment to program evaluation, and lack of standardized measurement tools.

As with any literature review, the criteria imposed by the researcher serve as an arbitrary filter through which decisions are made about the inclusion of specific studies. Had the filter applied here been even more stringent, the number of studies included would have been even fewer. If the sample had been limited to true experimental evaluation designs, only six would have been discussed. If sample size had been limited to 100 protégés or more, only 11 studies would have been identified. If the duration of mentoring had been limited to 9 months or greater (one school year), only 13 studies would have been identified. The limited number of studies found in this review points to the fact that the empirical evaluation of youth mentoring programs is in its infancy. The limited number of studies may also be attributable to the fact that unsubstantiated claims about the effectiveness of youth mentoring have resulted in a "patina of superficiality" that has discouraged social scientists from conducting quality research on the topic (Rhodes, 2002a, p. 6).

The 17 studies were selected because they met the identified criteria for "best practices" in evaluation. The studies that are selected to receive serious attention in the future need to demonstrate strong validity through best practices in both program administration and program evaluation. The quality of program administration and infrastructure was difficult to determine in the articles describing the 17 studies (for further discussion see Miller in this volume). However, studies involving samples from Big Brothers Big Sisters programs have been described as displaying the standard for quality administration of youth mentoring programs because of adherence to national mentoring standards (Tierney & Grossman, 1995). In the current review, four of the 17 studies involved Big Brothers Big Sisters samples (Grossman & Tierney,

1998; Langhout, Rhodes, & Osborne, 2004; Rhodes, Grossman, & Resch, 2000; Rhodes, Haight, & Briggs, 1999). All four studies used subsamples of the data collected in a large evaluation study conducted with Big Brothers Big Sisters participants by Tierney, Grossman, and Resch (1995). Technically, these studies are not considered to be independent.

Conclusion

In 1992, Blechman described the mentoring field as lacking articulated underlying scientific principles or specified program operations at a level of detail needed for effective program evaluation. The results reported and discussed in this additional literature review point to the need for two actions to be taken in the field. First, another large-scale study of the effects of participation in Big Brothers Big Sisters programs is needed that is informed by the literature reported since the original data were gathered in 1992. And second, additional reports of effect sizes are needed. The meta-analyses described earlier by DuBois et al. (2002) and Smith (2002) have taken the field of youth mentoring in a new quantitative direction. These data can inform youth mentoring program design, administration, and evaluation.

The results of this review were similar to the findings reported by other researchers because the effect sizes were generally small to medium. The exceptions were effect sizes of .72 for reading scores (Starks, 2002) and .80 for attitudes toward violence (Sheehan, DiCara, LeBailly, & Christoffel, 1999). These two areas warrant further examination in future mentoring evaluations. The conclusion can be drawn that mentoring has a low to moderate impact on youth.

In addition to confirming what others have reported regarding effect sizes for mentoring programs, this review was valuable because it identified those youth outcomes that should be examined in greater detail and taken seriously because of the strong internal and external validity in the design of the research on which they are based. These appear to be positive changes in three areas: attitudes toward school and violence, some academic outcomes, and parental relationships.

Chapter Recommendations

There has been little firm evidence that mentoring, by itself, can be a positive experience for youth (Tierney & Grossman, 2000). Over its relatively short history as a popular social program, mentoring has come to be regarded as more complex than first recognized. It has become clear that mentoring alone will not help high-risk youth solve all of their problems. The following are recommendations that were generated based on the information gained while writing this chapter.

First, pay closer attention to specific targeted goals when conceptualizing new mentoring programs. From an ecological perspective, outcomes to all stakeholders need to be identified and addressed. These could include mentor, youth, parents, families, community, mentoring organization/institution, schools, etc. Little attention has been paid to the impact of either informal or formal youth mentoring relationships beyond the youth and mentor. Rarely do researchers point to community-level outcomes when describing how mentoring reduces violence, substance use, or school failure. Grineski (2003) evaluated a university–community collaborative mentoring program and described the outcomes to the community as reduced juvenile crime, and increased recognition by community members that the university can be a trusted partner in addressing the needs of high-risk youth.

Second, pay closer attention to the role of both informal and formal mentoring in the lives of adolescents. Researchers tend to concentrate on only one type of mentoring at a time. No studies were found that examined the possibility that youth could have both informal and formal mentoring relationships in their lives, either simultaneously or sequentially. Such patterns of mentoring could impact youth development in as yet undetermined ways. Third, although informal and formal mentoring relationships are most often studied in isolation, pay closer attention to mentoring within the network of other adolescent relationships (e.g., peer, family, teachers) and the connections between them. Fourth, pay closer attention to the developmental impact (positive, neutral, negative, mixed) of being a mentor. Systematic studies that involve longitudinal surveys of changes in mentors would provide information that could be applied to better understand mentor recruitment and retention. Fifth, conduct additional meta-analytic studies of the effectiveness of youth mentoring programs periodically as the literature continues to grow.

Conclusion

In closing, the present chapter outlined the wide range of potential benefits of informal and formal youth mentoring, for both mentors and youth. The original review of the empirical literature on youth mentoring programs adds to the growing body of scholarship on youth mentoring by isolating the extent to which youth mentoring programs that have been evaluated using strong research designs yield positive outcomes. It also brings to the forefront recommendations for future research aimed at understanding how youth mentoring relationships can benefit mentors and youth alike.

References

Abbott, D. A., Meredith, W. H., Self-Kelly, R., & Davis, M. E. (1997). The influence of a Big Brothers program on the adjustment of boys in single-parent families. *Journal of Psychology, 131*, 143–156.

Aseltine, R. H., Dupre, M., & Lamlein, P. (2000). Mentoring as a drug prevention strategy: An evaluation of *Across the Ages. Adolescent & Family Health, 1*, 11–20.

Beier, S. R., Rosenfeld, W. D., Spitalny, K. C., Zansky, S. M., & Bontempo, A. N. (2000). The potential role of an adult mentor in influencing high risk behaviors in adolescents. *Archive of Pediatric and Adolescent Medicine, 154*, 327–331.

Blechman, E. A. (1992). Mentors for high-risk minority youth: From effective communication to bicultural competence. *Journal of Clinical Child Psychology, 21*, 160–169.

Campbell, D. T., & Stanley, J. C. (1966). *Experimental and quasi-experimental designs for research.* Boston: Houghton Mifflin.

Cave, G., & Quint, J. (1990). *Career beginning impact evaluation.* New York: Manpower Demonstration and Research Corporation.

Cavell, T. A., Meeham, B. T., Heffer, R. W., & Holliday, J. (2002). The natural mentors of adolescent children of alcoholics (COAs): Implications for preventive practices. *Journal of Primary Prevention, 23,* 23–42.

Cohen, J. (1988). *Statistical power analysis for the behavioral sciences* (2nd ed.). Hillsdale, NJ: Erlbaum.

Diversi, M., & Mecham, C. (2005). Latino(a) students and Caucasian mentors in a rural after-school program: Towards empowering adult–youth relationships. *Journal of Community Psychology, 33,* 31–40.

DuBois, D. L., Neville, H. A., Parra, G. R., & Pugh-Lilly, A. O. (2000). Testing a new model of mentoring. In J. Rhodes (Ed.). *New directions for youth development: A critical view of youth mentoring* (pp. 21–55). San Francisco: Jossey-Bass.

DuBois, D. L., Holloway, B. E., Valentine, J. C., & Cooper, H. (2002). Effectiveness of mentoring programs for youth: A meta-analytic review. *American Journal of Community Psychology, 30,* 157–196.

DuBois, D. L. (2005). Research methodology. In D. L. DuBois & M. J. Karcher (Eds.), *Handbook of mentoring* (pp. 44–64). San Francisco: Sage.

Dubowitz, H., Feigelman, S., & Zuravin, S. (1993). A profile of kinship care. *Child Welfare, LXXII,* 153–169.

Fo, W. S., & O'Donnell, C. R. (1975). The Buddy System: Effect of community intervention on delinquent offenses. *Behavior Therapy, 6,* 522–524.

Foster, L. (2001). *Effectiveness of mentor programs: Review of the literature from 1995 to 2000.* Sacramento, CA: California Research Bureau.

Freedman, M. (1993). *The kindness of strangers.* San Francisco: Jossey Bass.

Gilligan, R. (1999). Enhancing the resilience of children and young people in public care by mentoring their talents and interests. *Child and Family Social Work, 4,* 187–196.

Greig, R. (2004). *Natural mentors, ethnic identity, and adolescent mental health.* Unpublished doctoral dissertation, University of Florida.

Greenberger, E., Chen, C., & Beam, M. R. (1998). The role of "very important" nonparental adults in adolescent development. *Journal of Youth and Adolescence, 27,* 321–343.

Grineski, S. (2003). A university and community-based partnership: After-school mentoring for low income youth. *School Community Journal, 13,* 101–114.

Grossman, J. B., & Tierney, J. P. (1998). Does mentoring work? An impact study of the Big Brothers Big Sisters program. *Evaluation Review, 22,* 403–426.

Hall, J. C. (2003). *Mentoring and young people: A literature review.* University of Glasgow: The SCRE Centre.

Jekielek, S., Moore, K. A., & Hair, E. C. (2002). *Mentoring programs and youth development: A synthesis.* Washington, DC: Child Trends.

Johnson, A. W. (1997). *Mentoring at-risk youth: A research review and evaluation of the impacts of the Sponsor-A-Scholar Program on student performance.* Unpublished doctoral dissertation, University of Pennsylvania.

Johnson, A. W. (1999). *An evaluation of the long-term impact of the Sponsor-a-Scholar (SAS) Program on student performance.* Princeton, NJ: Mathematica Policy Research.

Karcher, M. J., & Lindwall, J. (2003). Social interest, connectedness and challenging experiences: What makes high school mentors persist? *Journal of Individual Psychology, 59,* 293–315.

Langhout, R. D., Rhodes, J. E., & Osborne, L. N. (2004). An exploratory study of youth mentoring in an urban context: Adolescents' perceptions of relationship styles. *Journal of Youth and Adolescence, 33,* 293–306.

Lee, J., & Cramond, B. (1999). The positive effects of mentoring economically disadvantaged students. *Professional School Counseling, 2,* 172–178.

Levinson, D. J., Darrow, C. N., Klein, E. B., Levinson, M. H., & McKee, B. (1978). *The seasons of a man's life.* New York: Alfred A. Knopf.

Lipsey, M. W., & Wilson, D. B. (2001). *Practical meta-analysis*. Thousand Oaks, CA: Sage.

LoSciuto, L., Rajala, A. K., Townsend, T. N., & Taylor, A. S. (1996). An outcome evaluation of *Across Ages*: An intergenerational mentoring approach to drug prevention. *Journal of Adolescent Research, 11*, 116–129.

McPartland, J. M., & Nettles, S. M. (1991). Using community adults as advocates or mentors for at-risk middle school students: A two-year evaluation of Project RAISE. *American Journal of Education, 99*, 568–586.

Meline, T., & Wang, B. (2004). Effect-size reporting practices in AJSLP and other ASHA journals, 1999–2003. *American Journal of Speech-language Pathology, 13*, 202–207.

Moon, T. R., & Callahan, C. M. (2001). Curricular modifications, family outreach, and a mentoring program: Impacts on achievement and gifted instruction in high-risk primary students. *Journal for the Education of the Gifted, 24*, 305–321.

O'Donnell, C. R., Lydgate, T., & Fo, W. S. O. (1979). The Buddy System: Review and follow-up. *Child Behavior Therapy, 1*, 161–169.

Philip, K., & Hendry, K. L. (2000). Making sense of mentoring or mentoring making sense? Reflections on the mentoring process by adult mentors with young people. *Journal of Community and Applied Social Psychology, 10*, 211–223.

Rhodes, J. E. (2002a). Mentoring has become an extremely important aspect of youth program planning. In J. E. Rhodes (Ed.), *New directions for in youth development* (pp. 5–8). San Francisco: Jossey-Bass.

Rhodes, J. E., Contreras, J. M., & Mangelsdorf, S. C. (1994). Natural mentor relationships among Latina adolescent mothers: Psychological adjustment, moderating processes, and the role of early parental acceptance. *American Journal of Community Psychology, 22*, 211–227.

Rhodes, J. E., Haight, W. L., & Briggs, E. C. (1999). The influence of mentoring on the peer relationships of foster youth in relative and nonrelative care. *Journal of Research on Adolescence, 9*, 185–201.

Rhodes, J. E., Grossman, J. B., & Resch, N. L. (2000). Agents of change: Pathways through which mentoring relationships influence adolescents' academic adjustment. *Child Development, 71*, 1662–1671.

Roberts, A., & Cotton, L. (1994). Note on assessing a mentor program. *Psychological Reports, 75*, 1369–1370.

Rogers, A. M., & Taylor, A. S. (1997). Intergenerational mentoring: A viable strategy for meeting the needs of vulnerable youth. *Journal of Gerontological Social Work, 28*, 125–140.

Rychener, S. R. (2003). *The relationship between adolescent characteristics and the quality of their natural mentors*. Unpublished doctoral dissertation, Texas Tech University.

Sanchez, B., & Reyes, O. (1999). Descriptive profile of the mentor relationships of Latino adolescents. *Journal of Community Psychology, 27*, 299–302.

Schoeny, M. E. (2001). *An ecological model of adolescent risk and resilience: The influence of family, peers, and mentors*. Unpublished doctoral dissertation, DePaul University.

Sheehan, K., DiCara, J. A., LeBailly, S., & Christoffel, K. K. (1999). Adapting the gang model: Peer mentoring to prevent violence. *Pediatrics, 104*, 50–54.

Sipe, C. L. (2002). Mentoring programs for adolescents: A research synthesis. *Journal of Adolescent Health, 31*, 251–260.

Sipe, C. L., & Roder A. E. (1999). *Mentoring school-age children: A classification of programs*. Philadelphia: Public/Private Ventures.

Slicker, E. K., & Palmer, D. J. (1993). Mentoring at-risk high school students: Evaluation of a school-based program. *School Counselor, 40*, 327–334.

Smith, A. (2002). *Does mentoring really work? A meta-analysis of mentoring programs for at-risk youth*. Unpublished doctoral dissertation, Texas A&M University.

Starks, F. I. (2002). *Mentoring at-risk youth: An intervention for academic achievement*. Unpublished doctoral dissertation, Alliant International University.

Tierney, J., & Grossman, J. B. (2000). In M. P. Kluger, G. Alexander, & P. A. Curtis (Eds.), *What works in child welfare* (pp. 323–326). Washington, DC: Child Welfare League of America.

Tierney, J., Grossman, J. B., & Resch, N. L. (1995). *Makes a difference. An impact study of Big Brothers/Big Sisters.* Philadelphia: Public/Private Ventures.

Valentine, J., Griffith, J., Ruthazer, R., Gottleib, B., & Keel, S. (1998). Strengthening causal inference in adolescent drug preventions studies: Methods and findings from a controlled study of the Urban Youth Connections program. *Drugs & Society, 12,* 127–145.

Zimmerman, M. A., Bingenheimer, J. B., & Notaro, P. C. (2002). Natural mentors and adolescent resiliency: A study with urban youth. *American Journal of Community Psychology, 30,* 221–243.

Chapter 12

Student–Faculty
Mentorship Outcomes

W. Brad Johnson

Are mentorships in academe efficacious? Do they really make a difference in the life of a protégé? And what about those who mentor and the institutions in which they function? What benefits accrue when a college or graduate school faculty member develops a strong helping relationship with a student? In this chapter I review existing outcome literature bearing on student–faculty mentor relationships in undergraduate and graduate settings.

Daniel Levinson's developmental theory of the *life structure*, and his in-depth qualitative study of 40 adult men (Levinson, Darrow, Klein, Levinson, & McKee, 1978), initiated modern study of mentorship. On the significance of establishing a mentorship in young adulthood, Levinson concluded:

> The mentor relationship is one of the most complex, and developmentally important, a [person] can have in early adulthood . . . No word currently in use is adequate to convey the nature of the relationship we have in mind here . . . Mentoring is defined not in terms of formal roles, but in terms of the character of the relationship and the functions it serves. (pp. 97–98)

Nonetheless, early reviews of the mentoring literature revealed only a handful of studies on mentorships in academe (cf. Merriam, 1983), most of which explored prevalence rates or offered narrative self-reflections while ignoring salient outcome issues. Several years later, Jacobi (1991) lamented that although formal mentoring programs had become commonplace in academic settings, there was very little empirical basis or theoretical rationale for such programs; their efficacy remained largely unknown. Still, leaders in graduate education continued to promote the vital importance of mentoring as a core component of student development. The comments of Henry Ellis in a widely read *American Psychologist* article are representative of this perspective among educators:

> I am convinced that the success of graduate education depends on a student–faculty relationship based on integrity, trust, and support. I believe that quality graduate

programs have some sort of faculty mentor system in which students can obtain advice, counseling, and helpful direction in their training . . . Good mentoring represents one of the important factors in graduate training, fosters long-term competence, and promotes effectiveness for both scientists and professionals. (Ellis, 1992, p. 575)

More than 20 years after Merriam's (1983) caution regarding lack of evidence for the utility of student–faculty mentorship, research efforts in this area remain sparse and quite heterogeneous with regard to populations of interest, sampling techniques, variables employed, and general empirical rigor. In contrast, research on mentorships in business and organizational settings has accumulated comparatively rapidly, leading the authors of one review to assert that: "the benefits to the protégé can be so valuable that identification with a mentor should be considered a major developmental task of the early career" (Russell & Adams, 1997, p. 3).

Mentoring in postsecondary education involves a close personal relationship between a supervising professor and a student. Merriam (1983) noted that the faculty mentor, "seeks advancement for the student in order to enhance the field and the student's role in it" (p. 167). The faculty mentor acts as a guide, role model, teacher, and sponsor of a less experienced (usually younger) student. A mentor provides the protégé with knowledge, advice, challenge, counsel, and support in the protégé's pursuit of becoming a full member of a particular profession (Johnson & Huwe, 2003; Kram, 1985). Erdem and Ozen (2003) emphasized that the intellectual and emotional bond between a senior academic and a junior student is a foundational element of university life; they observed that mentorships often last longer in graduate school settings than in other types of organizations.

Before considering the benefits of student–faculty mentoring, it is essential to note that interpreting and comparing research outcomes is hampered by conflation of several closely allied but nevertheless distinct relational constructs. Johnson, Rose, and Schlosser (this volume) suggest the need to distinguish between *role modeling*, *advising*, and *mentoring*. These developmental relationship forms can be construed as existing on a continuum of relational intensity, depth, or intent, with role modeling comprising less relational connection and mentoring suggesting greater relationship development.

A faculty role model might display salient professional attitudes, values, and behaviors, leading to demonstrable personal and professional benefits for a student. But a significant interpersonal relationship between the faculty role model and student is not required. In fact, role modeling may exist largely in the internal cognitive experience of the student (Gibson, 2004). Only when the student is asked to provide a retrospective account of the role model's influence can benefits be assessed.

Farther along the continuum of academic developmental relationships comes advising. Nearly every undergraduate and graduate degree program requires the assignment of a faculty advisor and advisors are expected to provide guidance and assistance relevant to degree requirements and student progress. The advisor's engagement with an advisee need not extend beyond these assigned roles; frequency of contact and depth of relationship may range widely (Schlosser & Gelso, 2001, 2005).

When an advisor–advisee relationship evolves into a more connected, active, and reciprocal relationship and when the advisor begins to offer a range of both career-enhancing and emotional or psychosocial functions, the advising relationship has become a mentorship (Johnson & Huwe, 2003; Johnson, Rose, & Schlosser, this volume; Schlosser & Gelso, 2001). Although some academic mentorships evolve between students and faculty members outside of formal advising assignments, this appears to be a less common scenario. Mentorships constitute more bonded and mutual relationships in which the faculty mentor is deliberate about both facilitating the student's personal and professional development and promoting his or her career.

In this chapter, I review available outcome research relevant to the benefits of mentoring in college and university settings. I do not consider the substantial research arising from nonacademic settings (see Blinn-Pike, this volume and Ramaswami & Dreher, this volume). After first summarizing current prevalence data, I consider student–faculty mentorship outcomes including functions received, academic achievement, scholarly productivity, professional skill development, networking, initial employment, confidence and identity development, career eminence, satisfaction, and personal health outcomes. I also highlight distinctions between informal and formal mentorships. I then briefly review the sparse research relevant to benefits for faculty mentors and academic institutions themselves. I further consider research on the efficacy of group or team mentoring, some of the salient variables likely to influence the benefits of mentoring in academe, and negative outcomes of student–faculty mentoring. I conclude with several recommendations for subsequent research on mentoring in academia.

Prevalence of Student–Faculty Mentoring

Research bearing on the proportion of students who are mentored by a faculty member is sparse and focused nearly exclusively on graduate students – primarily in the field of psychology. Kirchner (1969) found that 50% of psychology graduate program alumni from Pennsylvania State University reported experiencing a close mentorship with a faculty member. Cronan-Hillix, Gensheimer, Cronan-Hillix, and Davidson (1986) surveyed 90 graduate students enrolled in various psychology doctoral programs at one large Midwestern university. Although 53% reported having a mentor, the authors found striking differences in the prevalence of mentoring based on specialty. A full 100% of experimental and social psychology students were mentored while the rate among developmental and industrial/organizational students was 75%, and only 43% of clinical students enjoyed a mentorship. More recently, Johnson, Koch, Fallow, and Huwe (2000) confirmed this discrepancy in mentoring prevalence among subdisciplines within psychology. Although 60% of their sample of 292 psychology doctorates reported being mentored in graduate school, experimental/research psychologists were significantly more likely to report a graduate school mentor than graduates of clinical degree programs. Although it is possible that some clinical doctoral students are mentored by external clinical supervisors, no existing evidence supports this hypothesis.

The largest study of mentoring experiences among recent graduate students to date involved a sample of 787 (79% response rate) recent clinical psychology doctorates (Clark, Harden, & Johnson, 2000). Sixty-six percent reported having a mentorship with a faculty member. The rate was significantly higher for PhD graduates (71%) versus PsyD graduates (56%). In a follow-up study of PsyD (professional program)

graduates, this rate was confirmed; 54% of recent clinical psychology PsyD graduates ($N = 658$) reported having a graduate school mentor (Fallow & Johnson, 2000).
Fallow and Johnson also found that rates of mentoring were equivalent in secular
and sectarian graduate programs.

Three studies specifically surveyed prevalence rates of mentoring among ethnic minority graduate students. Atkinson, Neville, and Casas (1991) found that among 101
ethnic minority psychologists, 73% were mentored during graduate school. This finding
is congruent with other research showing no significant difference in the mentoring
prevalence of minority and majority group students (Clark et al., 2000). Two studies
focusing exclusively on African American students offered markedly incongruent
prevalence data. While Smith and Davidson (1992) found that among 182 African
American graduate students at a single university only one third were mentored,
Dixon-Reeves (2003) surveyed 34 recent sociology doctorates and found that 97%
reported having a graduate school mentor.

Research on the prevalence of undergraduate student mentoring is nearly nonexistent. Jacobi (1991) reported that 67% of undergraduate students report difficulty
finding a mentor; however, research on the proportion of undergraduates who do
experience a faculty mentorship is sorely lacking. Erkut and Mokros (1984) surveyed
723 undergraduate students who identified a faculty role model. It was not clear
how many students in the population were unable to identify a role model, nor was
it clear how many of those in the sample were mentored by the identified role model.
The only research on mentoring prevalence in undergraduate samples comes from
a military sample. Baker, Hocevar, and Johnson (2003) found that 47% of midshipmen
at the Naval Academy report having a mentor; however, in many cases, the mentor
was a senior student. Further, it is unclear whether service academy samples can reasonably be extrapolated to other institutions. It is quite likely that undergraduate
mentoring will range widely depending on the size and mission of the institution.
For example, one might hypothesize higher rates of undergraduate mentoring in smaller
teaching-oriented colleges and lower rates of mentoring in larger research-oriented
universities.

Student–Faculty Mentoring: Benefits to Protégés

Literature focused on student–faculty mentoring outcomes is sparse, and the variables
of focus less clearly defined than is true in organizational settings (Russell & Adams,
1997). Early studies of student protégés asked simply whether the relationship had
a "good effect" on their development (Kirchner, 1969). Although designs have
increased in sophistication, many studies continue to rely exclusively on subjective
personal reflections by protégés – typically after the active phase of mentorship has
ended. In this section, I highlight the documented benefits of mentoring for student
protégés.

Mentor Functions Received

By and large, Kram's (1985) career and psychosocial functions are regarded by
graduate students as both important and present in their mentoring relationships

with faculty. In samples of recent doctorates in psychology, protégés generally rate each of Kram's primary career and psychosocial functions as descriptive of the mentor's behavior (Atkinson, Neville, & Casas, 1991; Clark et al., 2000; Fallow & Johnson, 2000; Johnson et al., 2000). For example, in the largest of these samples, Clark et al. (2000), the most common mentor functions included direct training and instruction, acceptance, support and encouragement, role modeling, sponsorship for desirable positions, and opportunities to engage in research. A strikingly similar pattern was discovered in the mentor function ratings of undergraduate protégés (Baker, Hocevar, & Johnson, 2003).

Among school psychologists, mentorships are most defined by the presence of advising, instruction, and emerging collegiality (Swerdlik & Bardon, 1988). Among recent doctorates in sociology, specific career functions appear more descriptive of mentorships than psychosocial functions. Dixon-Reeves (2003) reported that letters of recommendation (83%), advice on career matters (79%), and critiques of work (76%) were more prevalent than emotional support (59%). Similarly, among undergraduates who identified a salient role model (Erkut & Mokros, 1984), the most notable function present was encouragement to pursue further academic work (versus emotionally focused encouragement)

Some research suggests that academic mentorships require some time to develop, perhaps as they evolve from advising relationships to mentorships (Johnson et al., this volume; Schlosser & Gelso, 2001), and that academic career functions are most evident early on while psychosocial functions evolve more slowly (Erdem & Ozen, 2003). As psychosocial functions increase, satisfaction with the mentorship increases (Tenenbaum, Crosby, & Gliner, 2001). Further, it appears that career or instrumental functions are most prone to increase student productivity while psychosocial functions are most likely to increase satisfaction – both with the mentorship and the graduate program (Clark et al., 2000; Tenenbaum et al., 2001). It is interesting that in academe, strong support and encouragement define the psychosocial side of mentorships while friendship and counseling are less descriptive. This may indicate a salient difference between academic and business settings. Owing to the hierarchical nature of academic mentorships, friendship, personal counseling, and genuine collegiality may be seen as inappropriate or ethically troubling (Johnson & Nelson, 1999) early on and may only develop fully (if ever) after the protégé exits the academic program.

Academic Outcomes

The few studies bearing on mentorship and academic outcomes utilize exclusively undergraduate samples. It appears that undergraduates' out-of-class experiences with faculty – including mentoring activities – result in positive correlations on various measures of academic achievement, and that freshman students who have more personal contact with faculty are significantly more likely to return to college for their sophomore year (Terenzini, Pascarella, & Blimling, 1996). In the most rigorous study of mentoring and academic outcomes, Campbell and Campbell (1997) compared the academic outcomes of 339 undergraduates who were assigned to mentors with 339 students not assigned to mentors. Experimental and control group students were matched on gender, ethnicity, and entering grade point average (GPA). All mentors were faculty volunteers, and the target population during recruitment included underrepresented minority group students. Results showed that after one year, mentored students earned higher GPAs (2.45 vs. 2.29), completed more credit units per semester (9.33 vs. 8.49), and were less prone to attrite (14.5% vs. 26.3%) than non-mentored students. Similar findings were reported by Thile and Matt (1995) in a sample of 32 minority group undergraduates. After one year in a formal mentoring program (including meetings with faculty, peers, and workshop attendance), mentored freshmen were significantly less likely to attrite and earned significantly higher GPAs. In contrast, Baker et al. (2003) found no correlation between mentoring experiences and either GPA or class ranking among 568 undergraduate students.

A criticism of studies linking mentoring with academic success is the potential for self-selection bias to better account for academic gains. It is quite likely that students with strong aptitude for achievement and students with achievement-oriented personality features are those most likely to volunteer for mentoring programs, and most likely to initiate contact with professors outside of class (Jacobi, 1991; Johnson et al., this volume). Further, when mentoring does correlate with academic success, it is unclear what mechanism or function best accounts for these gains. For example, one study of medical school students revealed that medical school advisors/supervisors tend to give their own students higher marks on scales of knowledge and technical skill (Coulson, Kunselman, Cain, & Legro, 2000). Finally, although narrative and retrospective accounts of graduate school mentorship suggest that mentored students enjoy better academic outcomes – including more rapid dissertation and degree completion (Johnson & Huwe, 2003) – there is little objective evidence to support these claims.

Scholarly Productivity

Protégé scholarly productivity may well be the most consistently demonstrated outcome of academic mentorship. Further, the connection between mentoring and production of scholarly products appears to hold up both during graduate school and long after a student graduates. Utilizing samples of graduate students, several studies show that being mentored is positively correlated with presenting papers at conferences, publishing articles and book chapters, and securing predoctoral grant funding (Cronan-Hillix et al., 1986; Hollingsworth & Fassinger, 2002; Reskin, 1979). Similar findings are evident in two studies sampling exclusively African American samples. Among African American graduate students, having a mentoring relationship was associated with higher rates of scholarly submissions, actual publications, and conference presentations (Dixon-Reeves, 2003; Smith & Davidson, 1992). In a recent study of 194 counseling psychology doctoral students from several universities, students' experiences with a mentor served as one of the strongest predictors of predoctoral research productivity (Hollingsworth & Fassinger, 2002). The authors suggested that mentoring mediated the relationship between a research training environment and actual productivity. These studies consistently support the hypothesis that active mentorship facilitates preparation for careers in academe. The impact of being trained and mentored by a productive scholar appears to be substantial.

Perhaps even more fascinating is the ongoing manifestation of mentoring effects well into a protégé's own academic career. Long (1978), in a sample of biochemists, found that it was not a new professor's own early career publications, presentations, or citations that predicted prestige of first job, but the sponsorship of a highly prolific mentor. Similarly, Williamson and Cable (2003), in a study of junior management faculty, found that one's early career productivity was significantly correlated with the productivity and reputation of the faculty mentor. Because collaboration with a mentor afforded them more predoctoral scholarly products, these faculty enjoyed more opportunities and productivity later in their own careers. Several other studies of early-career professionals in research-oriented universities confirm that having a mentor is strongly correlated with publication productivity (Bode, 1999; Cameron & Blackburn, 1981; Peluchette & Jeanquart, 2000).

Finally, two studies by Dohm and Cummings (2002, 2003) show that having a research mentor during graduate school predicts whether one will continue to engage in research following graduation. In samples of 519 men and 616 women with doctorates in clinical psychology, 68% reported having a mentor who coached and supported them through the research process. Those with mentors were significantly more likely than those without mentors (Men: 49% vs. 17%; Women, 39% vs. 12%) to be doing research (at least part-time) in their own careers. Perhaps not surprisingly, research collaboration between mentors and protégés is highly correlated with provision of career functions but only moderately correlated with psychosocial mentor functions (Green & Bauer, 1995).

Professional Skill Development

Mentors are often credited with helping student protégés develop requisite attitudes and skills for appropriate functioning within a profession. In academe, mentors facilitate "learning the ropes" through provision of insider information, role modeling, advising, and coaching. Students in both undergraduate and graduate settings report that mentors facilitate the development of professional skills and behaviors (Koch & Johnson, 2000; Schlosser, Knox, Moskovitz, & Hill, 2003). Mentored students report engaging in teaching, research, and grant writing more often than nonmentored peers (Smith & Davidson, 1992). A study of 228 female graduate students at one university revealed that those reporting a mentorship also reported more active involvement in professional activities such as conference attendance and organizational participation (LeCluyse, Tollefson, & Borgers, 1985). Mentored graduate students are more likely to intentionally develop professional ethics and values, and more prone to hone applied/clinical skills as well (Atkinson et al., 1991; Ward, Johnson, & Campbell, 2005). In sum, there is early empirical evidence to support the notion that student–faculty mentoring facilitates inculcation of professional attitudes and skills in neophyte professionals. Protégés are more likely to adopt the professional demeanor of the mentor and sharpen many of the profession-specific skills crucial to eventual success.

Networking

In academic settings, protégés often describe feeling more "connected" or "engaged" with colleagues and power-holders – both in their local institution, and in the profession at large (Atkinson et al., 1991; Clark et al., 2000; Dixon-Reeves,

2003; Tenenbaum et al., 2001). Excellent mentors seek opportunities to introduce protégés to important colleagues; introductions often occur at professional conferences but may also occur through correspondence or e-mail (Johnson & Huwe, 2003). When a protégé is tied into the network of his or her mentor, he or she enjoys greater professional influence, more immediate access to power-holders, and greater allocation of resources (e.g., stipends, fellowships, grants). For example, among 250 early-career faculty from several universities, collaboration with a senior faculty member was predictive of active network involvement (Cameron & Blackburn, 1981). Although research findings in this area are preliminary and rely on self-report of engagement with colleagues, it appears that faculty mentors hold tremendous influence when it comes to connecting protégés; one might hypothesize that excellent mentoring is significantly correlated with securing funding, invitations to present or publish work, and eventual academic job offers.

Initial Employment

Another benefit of mentoring in academe concerns the protégé's prospects for initial employment following graduate school. In several studies of academic sponsorship and initial employment, findings reveal that working under an eminent or frequently cited scholar significantly increases the quality of both initial and subsequent jobs in academe (Reskin, 1979; Sanders & Wong, 1985). In at least one study of prestigious academic institutions, predoctoral productivity was less salient in predicting prestige of first job than the mentor's eminence in the field (Long, 1978). Among minority group sociologists and psychologists, protégés are specifically inclined to mention assistance in career development and job placement when reflecting on the benefits derived from graduate school mentorships (Atkinson et al., 1991; Dixon-Reeves, 2003). It appears that two distinct components of mentorship contribute to this beneficial outcome for graduate students. First, the mentor's reputation in the field is extended to the protégé and he or she benefits from positive attributions connected to the mentor. Second, the mentor's active advocacy, networking, and provision of insider job information likely contribute importantly to the protégé's job success.

Professional Confidence and Identity Development

One of the least tangible but perhaps most important benefits of being mentored is the enhancement of professional confidence and identity. In fact, this may be among the more enduring benefits of student–faculty mentorships (Johnson & Huwe, 2003; Schlosser et al., 2003). Undergraduates who were able to identify a role model in a faculty member reported that having a faculty role model helped them to formulate professional attitudes and values, and to establish both personal and professional priorities (Erkut & Mokros, 1984). Among graduate students, having a mentor is associated with enhancements in the protégé's confidence and sense of self in the profession (Atkinson et al., 1991; Clark et al., 2000). By offering several salient functions identified by Kram (1985), such as acceptance, affirmation, and emotional support, mentors help protégés to overcome perceived inadequacies and bolster confidence required for risk-taking and experimenting with new professional behaviors. Protégés are also prone to adopting a mentor's professional stance and theoretical commitments. Sammons and Gravitz (1990) found that clinical psychology graduate students were significantly more likely (than would be predicted by chance) to hold the psychotherapy orientation promulgated by their graduate school mentor.

Career Eminence

In academic settings, having a mentor during graduate school is associated with productivity, prestige of first job, and professional success in the early career years (Cameron & Blackburn, 1981; Reskin, 1979). Although there are very few studies of career success or eminence and its association with mentoring in academe, one investigation in this area was notably thorough and innovative. Zuckerman (1977) studied all US Nobel laureates (through 1972) and discovered that more than half of these (48) had worked, either as students, post-doctoral fellows, or junior collaborators, under older Nobel laureates. In interpreting these findings, Zuckerman described a process of "social heredity" in which promising students seek out genuine masters (potential academic mentors) in the field and the masters, in turn, select protégés from among the numerous promising students who seek training.

Satisfaction with Program and Institution

Although outcome research on student–faculty mentoring is generally sparse, a comparatively large number of studies have scrutinized the association between mentorship during graduate school and satisfaction with the academic program and the institution writ large (Clark et al., 2000; Cronan-Hillix et al., 1986; Fallow & Johnson, 2000; Johnson et al., 2000; Tenenbaum et al., 2001). Clark et al. (2000) found that mentored graduates were significantly more satisfied with their doctoral program, as well as significantly more likely to rate mentorship as extremely important in graduate education. Tenenbaum et al. (2001) discovered that among 189 graduate students, there was a significant positive correlation between level of satisfaction with the advisor and level of satisfaction with the graduate program itself, and that the more products (papers and articles) the dyad produced, the more satisfied they were with graduate school. There was a caveat, however, in that satisfaction with the advisor declined the longer the student remained in graduate school. This finding may indicate that protégés are most satisfied when the mentor keeps the protégé moving ahead through important program hurdles.

Two studies of satisfaction among undergraduates reveal similar trends. Among more than 500 Naval Academy students, there was a strong positive correlation between having a mentor and satisfaction with the Academy (Baker et al., 2003). In one university, Koch and Johnson (2000) found that psychology undergraduate alumni who reported a mentoring relationship with a professor were significantly more likely to report that the university had prepared them effectively for their current position. Satisfaction research at both the undergraduate and graduate levels supports the hypothesis that mentoring creates a population of satisfied graduates, and therefore institutional alumni that one might expect to be supportive and loyal in the long term. It appears that protégés can tolerate a number of program shortcomings as long as protégés feel connected to and supported by a significant faculty mentor.

Psychological Health Benefits

A final area of potential benefit from student–faculty mentorships is that of personal or psychological well-being. Although this arena is minimally explored, four studies from academe offer enticing results. Liang, Tracy, Taylor, and Williams (2002), in a sample of 296 undergraduate women with at least one mentorship, found that mentoring high in specific relational qualities (e.g., empathy, engagement, authenticity, empowerment) was associated with higher levels of self-esteem and lower self-ratings of loneliness. Frequency of contact within the mentorship was less predictive of positive health outcomes than quality of the relationship. Cannister (1999) found that religious undergraduate students who engaged in a year-long formal mentoring program were significantly more likely than non-mentored peers to report higher levels of spiritual well-being. And graduate students who had a peer mentor reported lower levels of stress at the end of their first year of graduate training (Grant-Vallone & Ensher, 2000). Finally, new faculty members who acknowledged having a mentor at the university reported less isolation and stress and more positive assessments of their ability to cope with the demands of academic life (Bode, 1999). Taken together, these preliminary findings suggest that protégés may reap psychological and emotional benefits from student–faculty mentorships. Such outcomes would be consistent with our forms of well-researched relationships (e.g., marriage, friendship, counseling).

Student–Faculty Mentoring: Benefits to Mentors

Do faculty who mentor students reap benefits from mentor relationships? Rheingold (1994) suggested that forming mentorships with students was at once among the most grave and rewarding decisions faculty can make:

> As for a student's electing you as an advisor, acceptance is even more serious. This academic relationship is one of the most important in your professional life. You will find yourself spending almost as much time on your student's research as on your own. Your efforts constitute the legacy you confer in terms of your ethical and scientific values, and the student constitutes your legacy in the future. (p. 29)

Although a number of authors offer anecdotal and reflective evidence for the benefits derived by mentors in academe, empirical support is nearly nonexistent. Only a study by Busch (1985) of 537 education professors specifically queried faculty regarding the personal outcomes associated with serving in the mentor role. Busch found that salient mentor benefits included a sense of excitement and fulfillment at seeing a protégé develop personally and professionally, incentive to stay on the cutting-edge in one's field, and enjoyment of the relationship as it became increasingly mutual and collegial.

In light of these enticing preliminary outcomes, and in light of consistent findings from mentoring research in organizations supporting numerous benefits accruing to mentors (Kram, 1985; Russell & Adams, 1997), it is reasonable to tentatively hypothesize the following benefits of mentorship for faculty mentors: a) personal satisfaction from witnessing growth and development in protégés; b) personal fulfill-ment and meaning (the mentor derives a sense of generativity from passing on skills and wisdom); c) creative synergy and professional rejuvenation from working with talented and creative students; d) networking (just as the protégé benefits from the mentor's connections, so too may the mentor subsequently benefit from affiliation with a network of loyal junior colleagues); e) motivation to remain current in one's field; f) friendship and support – as mentorships mature they become more collegial and reciprocal; and g) reputation for talent development; over time, institutions often recognize those faculty with a track record of successfully developing subsequent generations of scholars.

Student–Faculty Mentoring: Benefits to Institutions

Satisfied students are certainly more likely to become loyal and engaged alumni; one might predict a relationship between the availability of mentors and level of giving and support among graduates. Also, it can only be positive for an academic institu-tion when strong mentoring enhances academic success and lowers attrition among new students (Campbell & Campbell, 1997). Additionally, if well-mentored students are more likely to develop stronger professional skills and publish at higher rates, one might expect an acceleration in the institution's peer-rated prestige. Finally, if faculty are active mentors, if they are supported in this endeavor, and if they find satisfaction in the mentoring process, one might predict lower turnover and greater institutional commitment among faculty.

In fact, existing student–faculty mentoring literature offers consistent empirical support for only one consistent institutional and profession-wide benefit of mentoring. Numerous studies show a significant positive relationship between having been a protégé and the probability of subsequently serving as a mentor. In both graduate (Busch, 1985; Clark et al., 2000; Dohm & Cummings, 2003; Johnson et al., 2000) and undergraduate (Baker et al., 2003) samples, students who report being mentored are more likely to report mentoring others themselves – often during the educational program itself or very early in their own careers. Thus mentoring may beget men-toring in academe. By facilitating a culture conducive to mentorship, universities and entire professional fields may help ensure inertia in the cycle of active career develop-ment. In light of these trends, it is disconcerting that so few institutions of higher learning demonstrate intentional scrutiny of the advising and mentoring credentials and aptitude of prospective faculty members (Johnson & Zlotnik, 2005).

Benefits of Group or Team Mentoring in Academic Settings

Some consistent obstacles to traditional student–faculty mentoring help account for the fact that many undergraduate and graduate students are never mentored (Johnson & Huwe, 2003). Faculty are often so pressed with demands for teaching and scholarship that relationships with students are relegated to the status of ancillary duty. In undergraduate majors at large universities or professional graduate programs, large student–faculty ratios diminish the probability of individual mentorships. Further, a steady increase in part-time faculty in many institutions may also erode availability faculty for mentoring activities.

One promising solution to these obstacles is the advent of group, cohort, or team mentoring systems. Gradually accumulating theory and research bearing on team approaches suggest that they are associated with benefits such as professional development, student retention, team-building, and success in achieving curricular requirements (Mullen, 2003). Three preliminary studies of the benefits associated with group mentoring models bear mentioning here.

Mullen (2003) offered results of a qualitative analysis of a "Writers in Training" (WIT) cohort consisting of 25 doctoral students in a professionally oriented educational leadership doctoral program. In the WIT model, a single faculty mentor held biweekly research/writing mentoring sessions for all of the students she advised in the doctoral program. The primary focus of the group was dissertation success and development of professional writing skills. Qualitative data collected from a sample of 15 cohort members revealed the following student-reported benefits of the WIT experience: a) enhanced self-confidence, b) benefiting from the support and connection with other cohort members, c) opportunities for both vicarious and reciprocal learning, d) learning to value collegiality, and e) socialization into the world of academe and professional writing in particular.

In a research-oriented clinical psychology PhD program at Saint Louis University, Hughes et al. (1993) implemented a Research Vertical Team (RVT) model of dissertation supervision and mentoring designed to increase timely degree completion, generate more publications among students, expose students to more scholarly activity during graduate school, and promote the value of collaboration in research. In the RVT model, students meet weekly with faculty mentors (mentors were only assigned after the first year during which new students rotated among all the faculty-led RVTs and decided on the best match). RVTs offered a consistent source of emotional and professional support among student peers, increased student engagement in collaborative or "team" research products, and enhanced the formation of individual mentorships between the team leader and student members. After implementation of the RVT system, faculty in the program noted a decrease in the prevalence of "research vacations" among dissertation students, and an increase in timely completion of the PhD. Further, the proportion of students presenting papers at conferences increased from 30–40% to 70–80%.

Finally, Ward, Johnson, and Campbell (2005) extended the Hughes et al. (1993) RVT model to a practitioner-oriented clinical psychology doctoral program at George Fox University. Termed the Practitioner Research Vertical Team (PRVT) model, this team mentoring model involved groups of between 4 and 8 doctoral students meeting with a faculty mentor for 2 hours biweekly to focus on clinically relevant research, with particular emphasis on student dissertation projects. In contrast to the RVT model, PRVTs focus more broadly on preparation of competent clinical practitioners and the facilitation of mentorships between students and faculty.

A phone survey of doctoral program alumni, both prior to the implementation of the PRVT model ($n = 14$) and after the model was initiated ($n = 7$), was conducted by a trained rater with no affiliation to the doctoral program. Those who participated in the PRVT system were significantly more likely to report having a mentorship (versus merely an advisor) in the doctoral program. Further, those from the PRVT era were significantly more satisfied with the dissertation experience, the contribution of the research training to their professional development, and the graduate program in general.

It appears that team-oriented mentoring holds significant promise as one avenue for advancing the prevalence of student–faculty mentoring – both in research- and practitioner-oriented graduate programs. These preliminary findings also support evidence of the valuable role that peer mentoring may occupy in graduate school (Grant-Vallone & Ensher, 2000). Team or cohort mentoring models offer the advantage of the additive effects of blending traditional and peer mentoring.

Formal versus Informal Mentoring Outcomes

Nearly all the evidence bearing on student–faculty mentoring stems from studies exploring informally emerging mentorships. Although many mentorships in academe grow from formal advising assignments (Schlosser & Gelso, 2001), research on academic mentoring often assumes informal relationship development or fails to specify the context for relationship formation. In contrast to this trend, a few studies have explored the effects and outcomes of formally assigned mentorships. Campbell and Campbell (1997) and Thile and Matt (1995) found that formally assigned mentorships targeting ethnic minority undergraduates resulted in higher overall retention and slightly higher academic achievement. In a study of freshman and sophomore participants in the Undergraduate Research Opportunities Program (UROP) at the University of Michigan, Nagda, Gregerman, Jonides, von Hippel, and Lerner (1998) found a nonsignificant difference in attrition rates between students assigned to "research partnerships" with professors (7.2%) and nonpartnered control group students (9.6%). Additional research on formalized mentoring suggests that undergraduates assigned to faculty mentors as freshmen report greater confidence in their perceived ability to achieve goals and solve problems (Cosgrove, 1986), that new graduate teaching assistants give very positive ratings to an assigned teaching mentorship (Boyle & Boice, 1998), and that among School Psychologist alumni from one university, those who entered academic jobs following graduation were more likely to rank the relationship with their assigned advisor as the most important factor in their career choice (Shapiro & Blom-Hoffman, 2004).

Research bearing on formal mentoring in academe is preliminary at best and hampered by some consistent methodological problems. First, "mentoring" is often one of many components in these programs and conceptualizations of mentoring vary significantly; it cannot be assumed that research partnerships or group meetings with a faculty member result in traditional mentorships. Second, only a small percentage of those solicited tend to participate in these programs (e.g., Campbell & Campbell, 1997; Nagda et al., 1998); it is possible that formal program outcomes reflect the effects of self-selection as much as mentoring. Clearly, further research is required in the area of formal student–faculty mentoring.

Gender, Race, and Aptitude in Student–Faculty Mentoring Outcomes

Research bearing on student–faculty mentoring sometimes incorporates analyses of functions provided or outcomes reported in light of specific demographic variables. A significant proportion of the existing studies consider gender differences, while fewer studies analyze data for differences based on race. Many authors indicate that significant mentoring outcomes could be attributable, in part, to the effects of protégés' pre-mentoring personality traits or academic aptitude. In this section, I briefly summarize the relationship of gender, race, and aptitude to student–faculty mentoring outcomes. Although numerous student variables may influence mentorship, these are the only three that have been scrutinized with any consistency.

Gender

A significant amount of early scholarly writing on the mentoring experiences of women suggested that women had greater difficulty both securing and benefiting from mentorships in academe (cf. Bogat & Redner, 1985). Yet, research using a range of student–faculty samples largely disconfirms the hypothesized differences in outcomes for men and women. Research with graduate students consistently finds no gender differences in the prevalence of mentoring, method of mentorship initiation, relationship duration, mentoring functions received from the faculty member, or either the career or psychosocial benefits derived from the relationship (Clark et al., 2000; Dohm & Cummings, 2002, 2003; Green & Bauer, 1995; Tenenbaum et al., 2001). Even in programs where 90% of faculty are male, male and female protégés report equivalent prevalence and outcomes (Green & Bauer, 1995). The same appears to be true in undergraduate settings (Campbell & Campbell, 1997). In fact, one of the few studies with undergraduates revealed that women at a service academy were significantly more likely than men to be mentored (Baker et al., 2003).

The only research from academe suggesting gender differences utilized the role model, versus mentor, construct. Gilbert, Gallessich, and Evans (1983) found that female graduate students often identified female faculty role models (although no mentoring relationship may have existed), while men preferred male role models. Female students with female role models were more career-oriented, confident, and satisfied with the student role than those females with male role models. The authors acknowledged that students higher in these traits may select same-sex role models.

Race

Because minority group faculty are significantly underrepresented in most academic settings (Brinson & Kottler, 1993; Johnson & Huwe, 2003), it is reasonable to be concerned about both the prevalence and outcomes of mentoring for minority group students. Further, cross-cultural theory gives rise to concerns about potential sources of misunderstanding or dysfunction in cross-race relationships (Brinson & Kottler, 1993). These include: a) mistrust, b) power dynamics, c) differences in interpersonal style, and d) obstacles to requesting help. Further, Thomas (1993) found that when mentors and protégés differ with respect to a preferred method for addressing racial differences (direct engagement discuss versus avoidance), the potential for disconnection or conflict increases.

Existing research on the influence of race on academic mentoring outcomes is sparse. Studies of ethnic and racial minority students indicate that they are mentored at rates that equal (Clark et al., 2000; Johnson et al., 2000; Smith & Davidson, 1992) or exceed (Atkinson et al., 1991) those of majority group graduate students. Mentoring programs designed to reduce attrition and increase academic achievement among racial minority students (e.g., Thile & Matt, 1995) appear to be effective, but there is little evidence that race-matching makes them more efficacious.

Aptitude

A final variable worth noting in the context of student–faculty mentorship is that of protégés' pre-existing characteristics and capacities. Jacobi (1991) wisely observed that many authors inappropriately infer a casual relationship from observed correlations between mentoring and markers of protégé success. In fact, many of the features that make a student attractive as a protégé (e.g., previous academic achievement, intelligence, interpersonal skill, commitment to education, ambition, and creativity) are the very traits likely to make them successful with or without a faculty mentorship. Other authors have similarly expressed caution about causative assumptions regarding the benefits of mentoring (Erkut & Mokros, 1984; Green & Bauer, 1995; Reskin, 1979). It is now well established that productive and eminent professors engage in mentorships with those students in any cohort who show greatest aptitude, intense commitment to the academic program, interest the mentor's research area, and a strong work ethic (Green & Bauer, 1995; Johnson & Huwe, 2003; Zuckerman, 1977). Further, after mentorships form, faculty mentors rate relationships as more effective when protégés meet mentors' expectations (e.g., they are committed, organized, responsive to feedback) – also a function of protégé personality (Young & Perrewé, 2000b). In the current literature review, no study controlled for protégé aptitude or personality variables when measuring mentorship outcomes. It is reasonable to assume that characteristics students bring to academe make them more likely to become protégés and more likely to benefit from mentors.

Negative Outcomes in Student–Faculty Mentorship

Like all relationships, mentorships in any context are prone to conflict and dysfunction (Johnson & Huwe, 2002; Kalbfleisch, 1997). Negative outcomes in mentorships are seldom explored by researchers, yet narrative and retrospective accounts of bad outcomes suggest that they are both frequent and complex in origin (Kram, 1985; Merriam, 1983). For example, mentors may lose power in the organization, exit the institution suddenly, fail to adequately protect or assist a protégé, or demonstrate personal psychopathology. Far from always the responsibility of mentors, negative outcomes are often attributable to protégé behavior (Johnson & Huwe, 2002).

Protégés and mentors in academic contexts are prone to the occasional dysfunctional mentorship. Kalbfleisch (1997) found that one-half of both undergraduate and graduate students who were mentored reported at least one significant conflict event. Events frequently leading to conflict included: mentor requesting help with projects, mentor disagreeing with protégé, mentor becoming angry with protégé, mentor discounting protégé's ideas, or being critical of his or her work. Only one study evaluated negative experiences from the mentor's perspective. Busch (1985) found that when describing the negative aspects of mentoring from the professor's perspective, professors were most concerned about the significant time demands associated with mentoring and the extreme relational dependency demonstrated by some students. Mentorships in academe are likely to be dysfunctional if: a) the primary needs of one or both partners are not being met, b) the long-term costs for one or both partners outweigh the long-term benefits, or c) one or both partners are suffering distress as a result of being in the mentorship (Johnson & Huwe, 2002). In the balance of this section, I highlight the sparse empirical research bearing on negative outcomes and experiences in student–faculty mentorships.

Advisor/Mentor Neglect

Perhaps the most consistent problem with advising relationships in higher education is the failure of many to become genuine mentorships. Daniel Levinson made an observation about mentoring in academe nearly three decades ago that continues to have relevance today: "Our system of higher education, though officially committed to fostering intellectual and personal development of students, provides mentoring that is generally limited in quantity and poor in quality" (Levinson et al., 1978, p. 334). With faculty reaping promotion and tenure rewards primarily for funded research and teaching, it is no wonder that the majority of graduate students who are mentored are the ones who initiate the relationship (Clark et al., 2000). Depending on the sample, between one half and two thirds of graduate students report having a mentor (Atkinson et al., 1991; Clark et al., 2000; Cronan-Hillix et al., 1986; Johnson et al., 2000). The vast majority of those not mentored report regret at being unable to find a willing mentor. Among graduate students who do secure a mentorship, the most common complaint is mentor unavailability (Clark et al., 2000; Fallow & Johnson, 2000).

Mentor Incompetence

In academic settings, faculty mentors can suffer from ether relational or technical incompetence. Relational incompetence may stem from problematic personality features (e.g., rigidity, egocentrism, prejudice, disengagement) or psychopathology (Cronan-Hillix et al., 1986; Johnson & Huwe, 2002). While some faculty members may lack appropriate emotional intelligence, others fail to understand the developmental needs of students or how to deliver mentor functions (Johnson, 2003). Incompetence (or neglect) might explain why many graduate students report that terminating the mentorship was difficult or painful; termination led to conflict, misunderstanding, or perceived abandonment (Clark et al., 2000). Likewise, when graduate students fail to complete their program in a timely fashion and linger in a graduate program (perhaps at least partially a result of mentor's disengagement), satisfaction with the mentorship declines (Tenenbaum et al., 2001). Although competence in the roles of advisor and mentor is arguably essential in academe, less than 10% of academic job advertisements mention advising and less than 5% mention mentoring as salient job components (Johnson & Zlotnik, 2005).

Other Negative Mentoring Experiences

At times, mentors in academe may become symbiotically involved with students and over-invested in the student's career decisions and trajectory. Blackburn, Chapman, and Cameron (1981) found that graduate school professors tended to give preferential attention to protégés who follow the professor's career path most directly. The authors termed this *cloning*, and found that faculty mentors tended to nominate those protégés whose careers were most similar to their own as their "most successful." Because mentors hold significant power in the mentorship, and tend to influence protégé values and theoretical commitments (Sammons & Gravitz, 1990), it is important that they have awareness of this influence and use it without coercion.

A final area of concern in student–faculty mentorships is that of unethical behavior on the part of the mentor (Clark et al., 2000; Fallow & Johnson, 2000). Approximately 5% of graduate students note that a mentor took credit for the protégé's work or required them to do things about which they felt uncomfortable. Although only 2–3% of protégés report that a mentor sexualized the mentorship, 4% report that the mentor was seductive (Clark et al., 2000). Although graduate students describe mutuality (reciprocal support) and comprehensiveness (student and professor interact in a variety of contexts) as two of the most important ingredients in successful mentoring (Wilde & Schau, 1991), boundary violations do occur in mentorships and a small proportion of female graduate students report sexual contact with a faculty member (Johnson, 2003). The sparse research exploring negative student–faculty mentoring outcomes suggests that mentor neglect or unavailability are primary concerns, followed by relational or technical incompetence, conditional acceptance of protégés, and occasional boundary violations. Research in this area is, at best, in the exploratory phase.

Where Do We Go From Here?
Recommendations for Student–Faculty
Mentorship Outcome Research

Consistent with earlier critiques of student–faculty mentoring literature (Jacobi, 1991; Merriam, 1983), this review found very few empirical investigations of mentorship in academe. Studies that move beyond observation and anecdote to data collection in academic contexts are rare, generally limited to retrospective survey methodologies, and prone to utilizing poorly articulated constructs and variables. Although rough studies of prevalence and satisfaction in single departments (e.g., Kirchner, 1969) are giving way to more thorough evaluations of functions, relational characteristics, and outcomes in students from multiple programs (e.g., Clark et al., 2000; Tenenbaum et al., 2001), retrospective surveys remain the methodology of choice. Further, with rare exceptions (e.g., Busch, 1985), student–faculty mentoring relationships are evaluated exclusively from the protégé's perspective; empirical evidence for the value of mentoring for professors and academic departments is essentially nonexistent. In the brief concluding section below, I offer several reflections regarding the current state of student–faculty mentoring research and several recommendations for moving research in this area ahead.

- Evaluating the benefits of mentoring in academe would be facilitated by greater use of longitudinal, versus retrospective cross-sectional, designs. The best example of this approach was offered by Green and Bauer (1995) in their 2-year study of 233 entering PhD students from 24 academic departments at a single university. The authors assessed mentoring functions and outcomes during the initial weeks of the first semester, 3 weeks prior to the end of the first year, and 3 weeks prior to the end of year 2. Longitudinal research will provide a clearer sense of how mentorships evolve, which functions mentors deliver with what intensity at different phases in the relationship, and whether the benefits of mentoring change significantly during the life of the relationship.
- At present, student–faculty mentorship outcomes are confounded by lack of control for pre-relational protégé characteristics. It is essential that researchers begin collecting data on variables such as protégé achievement, motivation, personality, prior mentoring experience, number of current mentorships, and aptitude. These factors should be controlled or used to match subjects (in the case of formal mentoring programs) such that researchers can have greater confidence in interpreting outcome results (Jacobi, 1991). It is likely that self-selection accounts for at least some of the success of mentoring in academe.
- Although the distinction between formal and informal mentorship formation is substantial in organizational contexts (Russell & Adams, 1997), it is rarely, if ever, mentioned in academic settings. This may be because nearly all student–faculty mentorships begin with formally recognized advising assignments (Johnson et al., this volume; Schlosser & Gelso, 2001), which slowly evolve into mentorship. Because many academic accreditation guidelines require evidence of student advising, it is increasingly rare to find undergraduate or graduate degree programs in which no formal advisor is assigned. Thus many student–faculty mentorships begin with formally arranged advising – even though many never move beyond advising when it comes to functions offered, relational intensity, relational duration, and mutuality.
- It would be useful for researchers to begin focusing on aspects and qualities of the mentoring relationship itself instead of assuming that mentorships share the same qualities and produce equivalent results. Several authors have already made inroads in this area (Liang et al., 2002; Schlosser et al., 2003). It would be particularly helpful to better understand the characteristics and behaviors of mentors that correlate with both beneficial outcomes and negative experiences (Johnson, 2003).
- Finally, it is recommended that researchers evaluate and compare mentorship experiences and outcomes at specific phases of mentor relationship development (Kram, 1985). Using this approach, different outcome variables may be most relevant

to different relational phases (Gray & Johnson, 2005). For example, during the initiation phase, functions such as role modeling, affirmation, and direct coaching may be most relevant and outcomes such as retention, confidence, and risk-taking most salient. At the termination phase, mentor characteristics such as self-awareness and willingness to address endings would be important and protégé outcomes might include scholarly productivity, success securing post-doctoral training or employment, satisfaction with elements of the mentorship, and degree of collegiality achieved with the mentor.

Conclusion

This chapter reviewed existing outcome literature bearing on student–faculty mentorships in undergraduate and graduate settings. Although authors in this area are often effusive about the benefits of mentoring for students, extant empirical evidence suggests that a more cautious assessment and interpretation of the research is often hampered by inconsistent definitions of the mentoring construct. Both psychosocial and career mentoring functions are important to students. There is modest and preliminary evidence that mentoring may improve academic outcomes for undergraduates, enhance scholarly productivity, networking, and initial employment success for graduate students, and strengthen professional confidence and satisfaction with academic programs in both undergraduate and graduate student populations. There is comparatively little empirical research bearing on outcomes for mentors and institutions. While gender and race appear to exert little impact on academic mentorship outcomes, student aptitude may play a substantial role in determining mentorship efficacy. Future research in this arena will be enhanced by greater attention to methodological rigor, better control of pre-mentorship protégé characteristics, clearer distinctions between formal and informal mentorship outcomes, exploration of relationship quality, and clearer delineation of outcomes at distinct relationship stages.

References

Atkinson, D. R., Neville, H., & Casas, A. (1991). The mentorship of ethnic minorities in professional psychology. *Professional Psychology: Research and Practice, 22*, 336–338.

Baker, B. T., Hocevar, S. P., & Johnson, W. B. (2003). The prevalence and nature of service academy mentoring: A study of navy midshipmen. *Military Psychology, 15*, 273–283.

Blackburn, R. T., Chapman, D. W., & Cameron, S. M. (1981). "Cloning" in academe: Mentorship and academic careers. *Research in Higher Education, 15*, 315–327.

Bode, R. K. (1999). Mentoring and collegiality. In R. J. Menges & Associates (Eds.), *Faculty in new jobs: A guide to settling in, becoming established, and building institutional support* (pp. 118–144). San Francisco: Jossey-Bass.

Bogat, G. A., & Redner, R. L. (1985). How mentoring affects the professional development of women in psychology. *Professional Psychology: Research and Practice, 16*, 851–859.

Boyle, P., & Boice, B. (1998). Systematic mentoring for new faculty teachers and graduate teaching assistants. *Innovative Higher Education, 22*, 157–179.

Brinson, J., & Kottler, J. (1993). Cross-cultural mentoring in counselor education: A strategy for retaining minority faculty. *Counselor Education and Supervision, 32*, 241–253.

Busch, J. W. (1985). Mentoring in graduate schools of education: Mentors' perceptions. *American Educational Research Journal, 22*, 257–265.

Cameron, S. W., & Blackburn, R. T. (1981). Sponsorship and academic career success. *Journal of Higher Education, 52*, 369–377.

Campbell, T. A., & Campbell, D. E. (1997). Faculty/student mentor program: Effects on academic performance and retention. *Research in Higher Education, 38*, 727–742.

Cannister, M. W. (1999). Mentoring and the spiritual well-being of late adolescents. *Adolescence, 34*, 769–779.

Clark, R. A., Harden, S. L., & Johnson, W. B. (2000). Mentor relationships in clinical psychology doctoral training: Results of a national survey. *Teaching of Psychology, 27*, 262–268.

Cosgrove, T. J. (1986). The effects of participation in a mentoring-transcript program on freshmen. *Journal of College Student Personnel, 27*, 119–124.

Coulson, C. C., Kunselman, A. R., Cain, J., & Legro, R. S. (2000). The mentor effect in student evaluation. *Obstetrics and Gynecology, 95*, 619–622.

Cronan-Hillix, T., Gensheimer, L. K., Cronan-Hillix, W. A., & Davidson, W. S. (1986). Students' views of mentors in psychology graduate training. *Teaching of Psychology, 13*, 123–127.

Dixon-Reeves, R. (2003). Mentoring as a precursor to incorporation: An assessment of the mentoring experience of recently minted Ph.D.s. *Journal of Black Studies, 34*, 12–27.

Dohm, F. A., & Cummings, W. (2002). Research mentoring and women in clinical psychology. *Psychology of Women Quarterly, 26*, 163–167.

Dohm, F. A., & Cummings, W. (2003). Research mentoring and men in clinical psychology. *Psychology of Men and Masculinity, 4*, 149–153.

Ellis, H. C. (1992). Graduate education in psychology: Past, present, and future. *American Psychologist, 47*, 570–576.

Erdem, F., & Ozen, J. (2003). The perceptions of protégés in academic organizations in regard to the functions of mentoring. *Higher Education in Europe, 28*, 569–575.

Erkut, S., & Mokros, J. R. (1984). Professors as models and mentors for college students. *American Educational Research Journal, 21*, 399–417.

Fallow, G. O., & Johnson, W. B. (2000). Mentor relationships in secular and religious professional psychology programs. *Journal of Psychology and Christianity, 19*, 363–376.

Gibson, D. E. (2004). Role models in career development: New directions for theory and research. *Journal of Vocational Behavior, 65*, 134–156.

Gilbert, L. A., Gallessich, J. M., & Evans, S. L. (1983). Sex of faculty role model and students' self-perceptions of competency. *Sex Roles, 9*, 597–607.

Grant-Vallone, E. J., & Ensher, E. A. (2000). Effects of peer mentoring on types of mentor support, program satisfaction and graduate student stress: A dyadic perspective. *Journal of College Student Development, 41*, 637–642.

Gray, P. J., & Johnson, W. B. (2005). Mentoring and its assessment. In S. L. Tice, N. Jackson, L. Lambert, & P. Englot (Eds.), *University teaching: A guide for graduate students and faculty* (2nd ed., pp. 217–224). Syracuse, NY: Syracuse University Press.

Green, S. G., & Bauer, T. N. (1995). Supervisory mentoring by advisers: Relationships with doctoral student potential, productivity, and commitment. *Personnel Psychology, 48*, 537–561.

Hollingsworth, M. A., & Fassinger, R. E. (2002). The role of faculty mentors in the research training of counseling psychology doctoral students. *Journal of Counseling Psychology, 49*, 324–330.

Hughes, H. M., Hinson, R. C., Eardley, J. L., Farrell, S. M., Goldberg, M. A., Hattrich, L. G., et al. (1993). Research vertical team: A model for scientist-practitioner training. *The Clinical Psychologist, 46*, 14–18.

Jacobi, M. (1991). Mentoring and undergraduate academic success: A literature review. *Review of Educational Research, 61,* 505–532.

Johnson, W. B. (2003). A framework for conceptualizing competence to mentor. *Ethics and Behavior, 13,* 127–151.

Johnson, W. B., & Huwe, J. M. (2002). Toward a typology of mentorship dysfunction in graduate school. *Psychotherapy Theory, Research, Practice, Training, 39,* 44–55.

Johnson, W. B., & Huwe, J. M. (2003). *Getting mentored in graduate school.* Washington, DC: American Psychological Association.

Johnson, W. B., Koch, C., Fallow, G. O., & Huwe, J. M. (2000). Prevalence of mentoring in clinical versus experimental doctoral programs: Survey findings, implications, and recommendations. *Psychotherapy, 37,* 325–334.

Johnson, W. B., & Nelson, N. (1999). Mentor–protégé relationships in graduate training: Some ethical concerns. *Ethics & Behavior, 9,* 189–210.

Johnson, W. B., & Zlotnik, S. (2005). The frequency of advising and mentoring as salient work roles in academic job advertisements. *Mentoring and Tutoring, 13,* 95–107.

Kalbfleisch, P. J. (1997). Appeasing the mentor. *Aggressive Behavior, 23,* 389–403.

Kirchner, E. P. (1969). Graduate education in psychology: Retrospective views of advanced degree recipients. *Journal of Clinical Psychology, 25,* 207–213.

Koch, C., & Johnson, W. B. (2000). Documenting the benefits of undergraduate mentoring. *Council on Undergraduate Research Quarterly, 19,* 172–175.

Kram, K. E. (1985). *Mentoring at work: Developmental relationships in organizational life.* Glenview, IL: Scott, Foresman and Company.

LeCluyse, E. E., Tollefson, N., & Borgers, S. B. (1985). Differences in female graduate students in relation to mentoring. *College Student Journal, 19,* 411–415.

Levinson, D. J., Darrow, C. N., Klein, E. B., Levinson, M. H., & McKee, B. (1978). *The seasons of a man's life.* New York: Ballentine.

Liang, B., Tracy, A. J., Taylor, C. A., & Williams, L. M. (2002). Mentoring college-age women: A relational approach. *American Journal of Community Psychology, 30,* 271–288.

Long, J. S. (1978). Productivity and academic position in the scientific career. *American Sociological Review, 43,* 889–908.

Merriam, S. B. (1983). Mentors and protégés: A critical review of the literature. *Adult Education Quarterly, 33,* 161–173.

Mullen, C. A. (2003). The WIT cohort: A case study of informal doctoral mentoring. *Journal of Further and Higher Education, 27,* 411–426.

Nagda, B. A., Gregerman, S. R., Jonides, J., von Hippel, W., & Lerner, J. S. (1998). Undergraduate student–faculty research partnerships affect student retention. *Review of Higher Education, 22,* 55–72.

Peluchette, J. V. E., & Jeanquart, S. (2000). Professionals' use of different mentor sources at various career stages: Implications for career success. *Journal of Social Psychology, 140,* 549–564.

Reskin, B. F. (1979). Academic sponsorship and scientists' careers. *Sociology of Education, 52,* 129–146.

Rheingold, H. L. (1994). *The psychologist's guide to an academic career.* Washington, DC: American Psychological Association.

Russell, J. E. A., & Adams, D. M. (1997). The changing nature of mentoring in organizations: An introduction to the special issue on mentoring in organizations. *Journal of Vocational Behavior, 51,* 1–14.

Sammons, M. T., & Gravitz, M. A. (1990). Theoretical orientations of professional psychologists and their former professors. *Professional Psychology: Research and Practice, 21,* 131–134.

Sanders, J. M., & Wong, H. Y. (1985). Graduate training and initial job placement. *Sociological Inquiry, 55,* 154–169.

Schlosser, L. Z., & Gelso, C. J. (2001). Measuring the working alliance in advisor–advisee relationships in graduate school. *Journal of Counseling Psychology, 48*, 157–167.

Schlosser, L. Z., & Gelso, C. J. (2005). The Advisory Working Alliance Inventory – Advisor Version: Scale development and validation. *Journal of Counseling Psychology, 52*, 650–654.

Schlosser, L. Z., Knox, S., Moskovitz, A. R., & Hill, C. E. (2003). A qualitative study of the graduate advising relationship: The advisee perspective. *Journal of Counseling Psychology, 50*, 178–188.

Shapiro, E. S., & Blom-Hoffman, J. (2004). Mentoring, modeling, and money: The 3 Ms of producing academics. *School Psychology Quarterly, 19*, 365–381.

Smith, E. P., & Davidson, W. S. (1992). Mentoring and the development of African-American graduate students. *Journal of College Student Development, 33*, 531–539.

Swerdlik, M. E., & Bardon, J. I. (1988). A survey of mentoring experiences in school psychology. *Journal of School Psychology, 26*, 213–224.

Tenenbaum, H. R., Crosby, F. J., & Gliner, M. D. (2001). Mentoring relationships in graduate school. *Journal of Vocational Behavior, 59*, 326–341.

Terenzini, P. T., Pascarella, E. T., & Blimling, G. S. (1996). Students' out-of-class experiences and their influence on learning and cognitive development: A literature review. *Journal of College Student Development, 37*, 149–162.

Thile, E. L., & Matt, G. E. (1995). The ethnic minority undergraduate program: A brief description and preliminary findings. *Journal of Multicultural Counseling and Development, 23*, 116–126.

Thomas, D. A. (1993). Racial dynamics in cross-race developmental relationships. *Administrative Science Quarterly, 38*, 169–194.

Ward, Y. L., Johnson, W. B., & Campbell, C. D. (2005). Practitioner research vertical teams: A model for mentoring in practitioner-focused doctoral programs. *The Clinical Supervisor, 23*, 179–190.

Wilde, J. B., & Schau, C. G. (1991). Mentoring in graduate schools of education: Mentees' perceptions. *Journal of Experimental Education, 59*, 165–179.

Williamson, I. O., & Cable, D. M. (2003). Predicting early career research productivity: The case of management faculty. *Journal of Organizational Behavior, 24*, 25–44.

Young, A. M., & Perrewé, P. L. (2000b). What did you expect? An examination of career-related support and social support among mentors and protégés. *Journal of Management, 26*, 611–632.

Zuckerman, H. (1977). *Scientific elite: Nobel laureates in the United States.* New York: The Free Press.

Chapter 13

The Benefits Associated with Workplace Mentoring Relationships

Aarti Ramaswami and George F. Dreher

Expressed beliefs about the benefits associated with mentor–protégé relationships are now commonplace in the organizational literature. Early empirical studies typically reported that mentoring was associated with subjective and objective benefits for the protégé, such as higher promotion rates, income levels, and career satisfaction (Chao, 1997; Dreher & Ash, 1990; Fagenson, 1989; Kirchmeyer, 1998; Koberg, Boss, Chappell, & Ringer, 1994). A more limited academic literature also suggested that these types of relationships were associated with positive outcomes for the mentor – such as career revitalization, personal satisfaction, and organizational power (Burke & McKeen, 1997; Hunt & Michael, 1983; Ragins & Scandura, 1994). In addition to these academic studies, surveys show that managers strongly believe in the benefits associated with mentoring (Singh, Bains, & Vinnicombe, 2002). More recently, a comprehensive meta-analytic review concerning the career benefits associated with mentoring for the protégé confirmed a positive relationship (Allen, Eby, Poteet, Lentz, & Lima, 2004). Thus, it is understandable that seasoned organizational leaders have encouraged the establishment of mentoring relationships in their organizations and that organizational newcomers have sought out the advice and counsel of more senior managers.

Unfortunately, the empirical literature devoted to this topic has been dominated by cross-sectional, self-report field studies (Wanberg, Welsh, & Hezlett, 2003). It is very difficult to make any type of causal assertion linking mentoring to career benefits, owing to the weaknesses in these research designs. Granted, it would be very difficult to conduct highly controlled experiments with the random assignment of employees to various conditions of mentoring, but even more circumscribed attempts to isolate the effects of mentoring have been plagued with methodological deficiencies. For example, few studies exist that have capitalized on the temporal sequencing of data collection, and no studies have been able to satisfactorily control for the large number of individual characteristics that could act as third-variable explanations for the observed relationships between mentoring and career outcomes. Also, any causal inferences would be more defensible if the mechanisms through which mentoring can affect career outcomes had been fully specified and examined. To date, few studies have incorporated into their research designs the array of possible mediators between mentoring and distal outcomes like income attainment, hierarchical ascendancy, and career satisfaction (Wanberg et al., 2003).

It is to these possible mediators that we will focus the remainder of this chapter, along with the various outcomes of mentoring. While longitudinal research designs might make it possible to defend the notion that mentoring does indeed affect and benefit the career and personal prospects of protégés and mentors, it still is important to understand why. This is because different causal mechanisms would likely be associated with different (and inconsistent) organizational consequences – a theme to which we will be returning later in the chapter. The intent, then, of this presentation is to a) provide process-oriented frameworks for explaining how high-quality mentoring relationships could work to enhance the career and personal prospects of protégés and mentors, and how these processes may positively or negatively impact organizations; b) summarize the degree to which any of these proposed mechanisms have received empirical attention; and c) make recommendations regarding the most pressing themes that need to be addressed in new research devoted to mentoring.

In many ways our contribution will be incremental at best. That is, we will be drawing heavily from and putting into succinct form what has already been discussed and proposed in two comprehensive, detailed, and very well-thought-out reviews of the mentoring literature. The work of Noe, Greenberger, and Wang (2002) and Wanberg et al. (2003) serve as important resources to scholars interested in this area of inquiry, and it is to these two sources that we will repeatedly return for ideas and guidance. But our review will be primarily focused on the mechanisms that may explain why there are benefits associated with the establishment of mentoring relationships, will address mechanisms at the level of the individual protégé or mentor, and will attempt to identify and clarify which mechanisms are in the greatest need of empirical confirmation. We note, in particular, that it is beyond the scope of this chapter to address a variety of very plausible but negative and unintended effects that may be attributable to participating in a mentoring relationship. That is, our focus is on the proposed benefits of mentoring. Finally, presented frameworks represent our way of making sense of this complicated literature, so logical inconsistencies, errors of omission, or other conceptual inadequacies should be attributed only to us.

Models of the Consequences of Mentoring Relationships

We will structure the chapter's content mainly around the process linkages depicted in Figures 13.1 and 13.2. Figure 13.1 is a model of the consequences of a mentoring relationship for the protégé whereas Figure 13.2 focuses on outcomes for the mentor. In each model we have specified multiple causal paths or mechanisms that may link mentoring to career and personal outcomes, and have attempted to distinguish between the cognitive/affective and behavioral responses that are proposed to mediate the effects of mentoring on outcomes. Each figure also includes some positive and negative outcomes that may accrue to the organization. While our focus

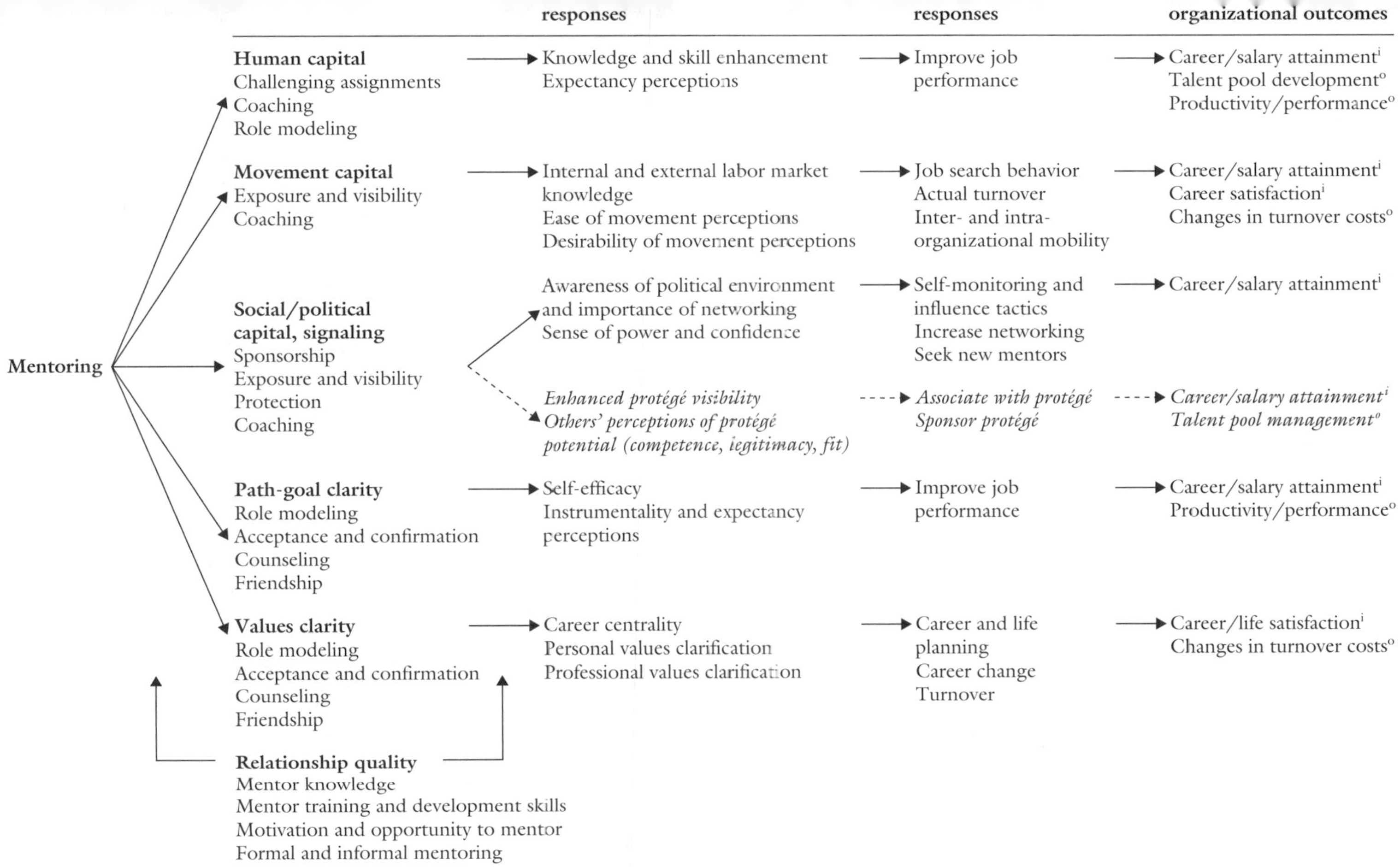

responses	responses	organizational outcomes

Human capital
Challenging assignments
Coaching
Role modeling
→ Knowledge and skill enhancement
Expectancy perceptions
→ Improve job performance
→ Career/salary attainment[i]
Talent pool development[o]
Productivity/performance[o]

Movement capital
Exposure and visibility
Coaching
→ Internal and external labor market knowledge
Ease of movement perceptions
Desirability of movement perceptions
→ Job search behavior
Actual turnover
Inter- and intra-organizational mobility
→ Career/salary attainment[i]
Career satisfaction[i]
Changes in turnover costs[o]

Social/political capital, signaling
Sponsorship
Exposure and visibility
Protection
Coaching
→ Awareness of political environment and importance of networking
Sense of power and confidence
→ Self-monitoring and influence tactics
Increase networking
Seek new mentors
→ Career/salary attainment[i]

Enhanced protégé visibility
Others' perceptions of protégé potential (competence, legitimacy, fit)
⇢ *Associate with protégé*
Sponsor protégé
⇢ *Career/salary attainment[i]*
Talent pool management[o]

Path-goal clarity
Role modeling
Acceptance and confirmation
Counseling
Friendship
→ Self-efficacy
Instrumentality and expectancy perceptions
→ Improve job performance
→ Career/salary attainment[i]
Productivity/performance[o]

Values clarity
Role modeling
Acceptance and confirmation
Counseling
Friendship
→ Career centrality
Personal values clarification
Professional values clarification
→ Career and life planning
Career change
Turnover
→ Career/life satisfaction[i]
Changes in turnover costs[o]

Relationship quality
Mentor knowledge
Mentor training and development skills
Motivation and opportunity to mentor
Formal and informal mentoring

Mentoring

Figure 13.1 A model of the consequences of a mentoring relationship for the protégé

i = individual outcome

o = organizational outcome

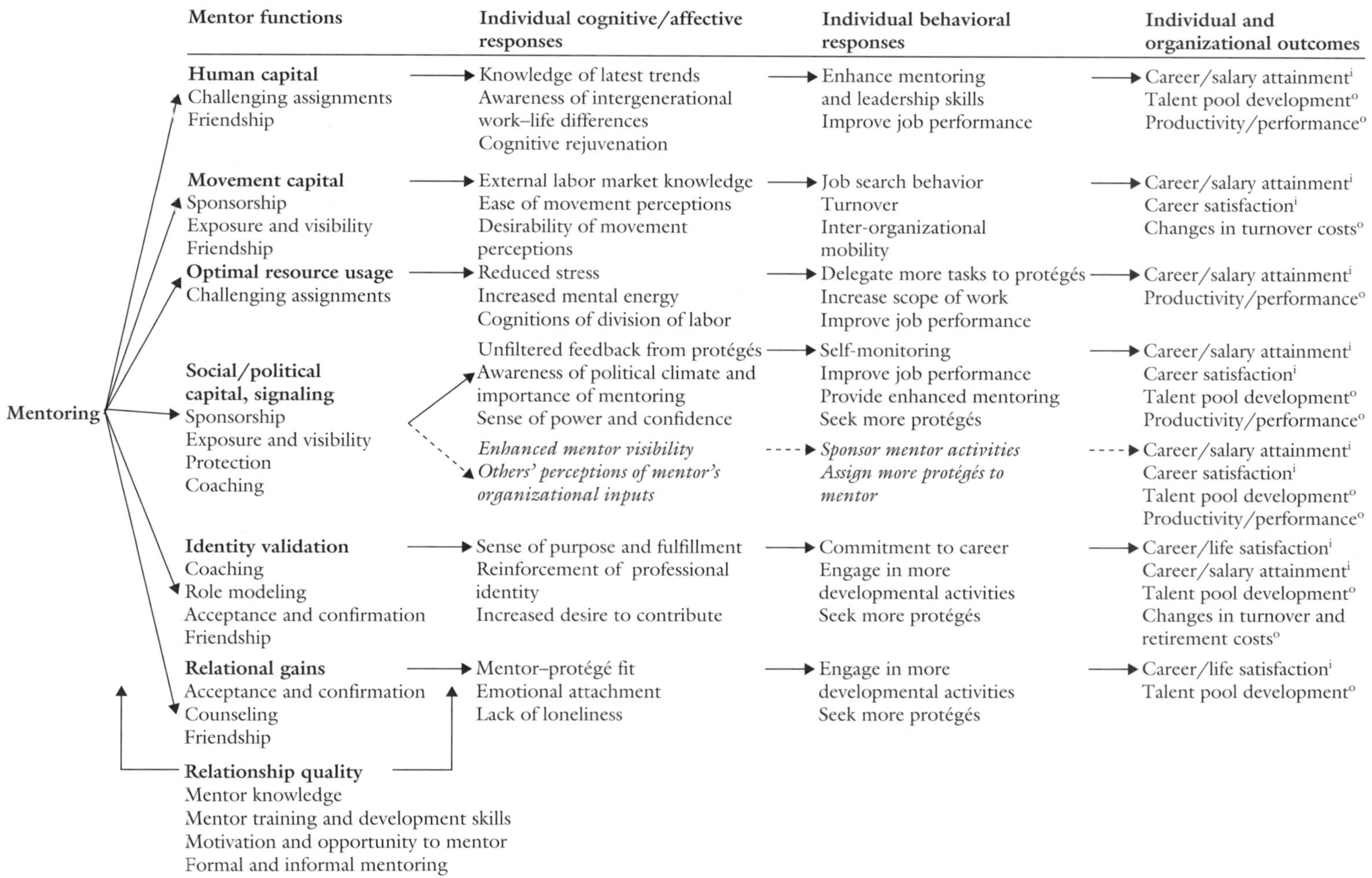

Mentor functions	Individual cognitive/affective responses	Individual behavioral responses	Individual and organizational outcomes
Human capital Challenging assignments Friendship	Knowledge of latest trends Awareness of intergenerational work–life differences Cognitive rejuvenation	Enhance mentoring and leadership skills Improve job performance	Career/salary attainment[i] Talent pool development[o] Productivity/performance[o]
Movement capital Sponsorship Exposure and visibility Friendship	External labor market knowledge Ease of movement perceptions Desirability of movement perceptions	Job search behavior Turnover Inter-organizational mobility	Career/salary attainment[i] Career satisfaction[i] Changes in turnover costs[o]
Optimal resource usage Challenging assignments	Reduced stress Increased mental energy Cognitions of division of labor	Delegate more tasks to protégés Increase scope of work Improve job performance	Career/salary attainment[i] Productivity/performance[o]
Social/political capital, signaling Sponsorship Exposure and visibility Protection Coaching	Unfiltered feedback from protégés Awareness of political climate and importance of mentoring Sense of power and confidence *Enhanced mentor visibility* *Others' perceptions of mentor's* *organizational inputs*	Self-monitoring Improve job performance Provide enhanced mentoring Seek more protégés *Sponsor mentor activities* *Assign more protégés to* *mentor*	Career/salary attainment[i] Career satisfaction[i] Talent pool development[o] Productivity/performance[o] Career/salary attainment[i] Career satisfaction[i] Talent pool development[o] Productivity/performance[o]
Identity validation Coaching Role modeling Acceptance and confirmation Friendship	Sense of purpose and fulfillment Reinforcement of professional identity Increased desire to contribute	Commitment to career Engage in more developmental activities Seek more protégés	Career/life satisfaction[i] Career/salary attainment[i] Talent pool development[o] Changes in turnover and retirement costs[o]
Relational gains Acceptance and confirmation Counseling Friendship	Mentor–protégé fit Emotional attachment Lack of loneliness	Engage in more developmental activities Seek more protégés	Career/life satisfaction[i] Talent pool development[o]
Relationship quality Mentor knowledge Mentor training and development skills Motivation and opportunity to mentor Formal and informal mentoring			

Mentoring

Figure 13.2 A model of the consequences of a mentoring relationship for the mentor

i = individual outcome

is at the individual level, some connection to organizational functioning seems in order. This is because one cannot assume that what is good for a particular mentor or protégé also is good for the employing organization. For each path, we will provide a description of the proposed mechanism and a summary of any associated empirical investigations. To maintain focus, we will emphasize the rows of each figure, but do acknowledge that the strength of any proposed mentoring effect will likely be a function of the mentoring relationship quality. The moderating effect of relationship quality is depicted in the figures, but will not be elaborated on in detail in this chapter. Also, note that these frameworks often are organized around Campbell, Dunnette, Lawler, and Weick's (1970, p. 11) notion that job performance and career achievement are a function of ability, motivation, and opportunity. When possible, we have considered the potential impact of mentoring on career outcomes from this perspective. That is, some of the linkages focus on the acquisition of knowledge, skills, and abilities (the human capital mechanism). Others address motivational states (e.g., the path-goal clarity mechanism), while others address opportunity (e.g., the social/political capital and signaling mechanism). The figures, and our discussion of them, also assume general familiarity with the mentoring functions or mentoring roles described by Kram (1985, pp. 22–46).

The Protégé Framework

The existence of a mentoring relationship would lead to the enactment of certain career and psychosocial functions by the mentor that elicit cognitive, affective, and behavioral responses from the protégé, ultimately affecting the latter's outcomes. Career functions such as coaching, sponsoring, providing challenging assignments, and exposure and visibility help the protégé learn the ropes, and prepare for advancement in an organization; psychosocial functions such as role modeling, acceptance and confirmation, friendship, and counseling enhance self-worth, sense of competence, clarity of identity, and in-role effectiveness. As Kram (1985) states, these functions are not mutually exclusive and an interaction could combine career and psychosocial functions. In the protégé framework, we propose five process paths, namely, Human Capital, Movement Capital, Social/Political Capital and Signaling, Path-Goal Clarity, and Values Clarity, that connect mentoring to career outcomes. For each of these paths, we explain what the mentoring functions entail, the cognitive, affective, and behavioral responses of the protégé, and how they may lead to individual and organizational outcomes. We do recognize that mentoring functions and processes other than what are modeled in the diagrams could also operate in each path.

Human Capital

The human capital path deals with the acquisition of knowledge, skills, and abilities (KSAs) that ultimately enhance the protégé's job performance. In turn, this leads to career benefits (Becker, 1975). A protégé can accumulate such human capital through challenging assignments, coaching, and role modeling provided by the mentor.

Apart from education, job, and organization tenure, the training provided by the mentor or employer is another form of investment that can enhance an individual's human capital (Wayne, Liden, Kraimer, & Graf, 1999). *Challenging assignments* involve providing challenging work and technical training with ongoing performance feedback that enables the protégé to develop specific competencies and to experience a sense of accomplishment in a professional role. *Coaching*, on the other hand, involves enhancing the protégé's knowledge and understanding of how to function in the corporate world through advice on role requirements and operational style. Protégés may avail themselves of job and organizational information that may not be available to employees without mentors (Schulz, 1995). Ostroff and Koslowski (1993) found that newly hired employees with mentors learned more about the job setting than those who relied on coworkers. They had more knowledge about the technical and organizational workings of the business than workers without mentors. Through *role modeling*, the mentor serves as a model of effective values, attitudes, and work behaviors for the protégé.

These mentor functions equip the protégé with strategies and information for accomplishing work objectives effectively. They also enhance skills and behaviors necessary to take advantage of opportunities presented by other mentor functions. The enhanced KSAs of the protégé could lead him or her to be successful at work tasks, which in turn influences expectancy perceptions (Dreher & Bretz, 1991; Porter & Lawler, 1968; Vroom, 1964). Wanberg et al. (2003) noted that there are well-established linkages between ability, conscientiousness, motivation, and job performance (Sackett, Gruys, & Ellingson, 1998; Schmidt & Hunter, 1998) and between ability, motivation, and objective career success (Tharenou, 1997). Thus, the effect of the three mentoring functions could either be fully or partially mediated by cognitive, affective, and behavioral responses of protégés. In support of this idea, Day and Allen (2004) found that career motivation fully mediated and self-efficacy partially mediated the relationship between mentoring and self-reported performance effectiveness. From the contest mobility perspective, training and development opportunities have been found to lead to enhanced salary (Tharenou, Latimer, & Conroy, 1994), promotability, and career satisfaction (Wayne et al., 1999). An organizational by-product of these protégé benefits is talent pool development, leading to organizational productivity and performance.

Numerous studies have tested the relationship between mentoring and career outcomes, and the effects of enhanced KSAs on job performance and subsequent work outcomes. However, these disparate process linkages have not been explicitly connected to mentoring. This knowledge gap needs to be filled by future research that tests the full causal linkages in the human capital path (i.e., mentoring functions leading to enhanced KSAs and expectancy perceptions, which are followed by improved job performance that ultimately leads to positive individual and organizational outcomes).

Movement Capital

This path deals with the extent to which exposure and visibility in the intra- and extra-organizational arena propel the protégé to seek new (and perhaps better) jobs within or outside the current organization. The main mentoring functions operating in this path are exposure and visibility, and coaching.

Exposure and visibility involves the mentor providing opportunities for the protégé to meet or correspond with key decision makers and senior managers – those who can judge the protégé's potential for further advancement. The mentor helps the protégé learn about and socialize in those parts of the organization that the protégé would like to enter. Labor market opportunities within and outside the organization are brought to the protégé's notice (Baugh & Scandura, 1999; Dreher & Ash, 1990). Once these internal and external labor market opportunities are identified, the mentor *coaches* the protégé regarding what may be the most appropriate or viable mobility option. As the knowledge of new labor markets and viable mobility options increases, the protégé may increasingly think of quitting the current position, and evaluate the expected utility of searching for another job versus the costs associated with leaving the present job (Rouse, 2001). If the probability of finding an acceptable option in the new labor markets is perceived to be high, the protégé may contemplate the desirability and ease of movement from the current position (March & Simon, 1958) leading to job search behaviors. As the number of job alternatives confronting an employee increases, attitudes regarding the current job become more negative (Pfeffer & Lawler, 1979). In fact, Gerhart (1990) found that perceptions of the job market predicted turnover much more than actual job search behavior. If the job search produces unsatisfactory alternatives then the protégé may intend on staying (Bretz, Boudreau, & Judge, 1994); else he or she may leave the current position. The individual outcome associated with increased labor market mobility may be higher compensation, particularly for Caucasian males (Dreher & Cox, 2000). Also, movement from one job to another may enhance the protégé's career satisfaction if the movement meets the protégé's career needs and expectations. However, as a result of protégé mobility the organization may encounter changes in turnover costs, which could be positive or negative. Moreover, along with the development of a high-quality talent pool, the organization faces a potential risk of losing talented employees.

The literature indicates that the movement capital path has also not been tested in its entirety. Although studies that link mentoring to some related processes in the mobility path such as turnover intentions, intentions to stay, and perceived job alternatives or opportunities (e.g., Barker, Monks, & Buckley, 1999; Baugh, Lankau, & Scandura, 1996; Fagenson, 1989; Mobley, Jaret, Marsh, & Lim, 1994; Prevosto, 2001) can be found in the literature, there are no studies that test linkages between the specific constructs we propose, such as desirability and ease of movement perceptions as a result of enhanced internal and external labor market knowledge. Within the same study, researchers should also test the relationships between these movement perceptions, job search behavior and turnover, and other outcomes of interest.

Social/Political Capital and Signaling

This path deals with the social and political processes involved in mentoring that help the protégé gain legitimacy and exposure. This path is bifurcated into the responses elicited from the protégé and those from key decision makers or other employees in the organization that ultimately lead to individual and organizational outcomes. The functions that operate here are sponsorship, exposure and visibility, protection, and coaching.

Sponsorship refers to the mentor's public support of the protégé during promotional decision meetings and conversations with other senior managers, as well as with the protégé's peers, superiors, and subordinates, which can critically influence organizational advancement (Kram, 1985). *Exposure and visibility*, as mentioned earlier, involves providing opportunities for the protégé to correspond with key decision makers and senior managers who can influence the protégé's career advancement. *Protection* involves shielding the protégé from potentially damaging contact with senior officials until the protégé has been completely socialized and knows when, how, and with whom to interact within the organization and outside. The mentor also *coaches* the protégé on how to establish rapport and credibility with other senior managers, thus paving the way to career attainment.

Protégé path. Gaining political information and exposure through the mentor enhances the protégé's awareness of the political environment and importance of networking. The protégé may also gain a sense of power and confidence by having a high-status primary developmental relationship, or a significant ally (Scandura, Tejeda, Werther, & Lankau, 1996), through which opportunities for challenging assignments and visibility among key players in the organization are provided. Having realized the importance of networking and strategically dealing with key organizational players, the protégé may engage in self-monitoring and other influence tactics, and also increase networking behavior. High self-monitors are more aware of the value of mentoring for career success (Turban & Dougherty, 1994) and hence may seek more mentoring relationships to tap new network resources. Ferris and Judge (1991) note that political influence behaviors could lead to increased positive affect (towards the protégé) and positive assessments of competence and fit (of the protégé), both of which impact human resources decisions and outcomes. Higgins, Judge, and Ferris's (2003) meta-analysis on the effects of influence tactics on work outcomes showed that ingratiation and assertiveness had positive effects on salary and promotions. We have not depicted any organizational outcomes for this path since we believe that this path benefits the protégé, and not the organization in any significant way.

Others' path. It is evident that the mentor functions noted above not only help in making protégés more visible and provide valuable information not available through formal channels (Dreher & Ash, 1990; Dreher & Bretz, 1991), but also signal and manage impressions of the protégé's legitimacy, competence, and fit among senior management, thus building the protégé's reputation. Higgins and Thomas (2001) state that having influential supporters may enhance an individual's perceived political power within an organization or profession. Decision makers may in turn be attracted to well-connected protégés (Kanter, 1977), seeking their services and enlisting them on their projects, thus sponsoring protégés by making favorable career decisions on their behalf. Such signaling helps senior managers make promotion and sponsorship decisions as they may not have any other way to judge a protégé's potential (Dreher & Bretz, 1991). Thus the mentor also helps in organizational talent pool management. However, whether such talent pool management has any positive or negative effect on organizational performance and productivity would depend on whether the mentor has promoted the "right" talent. Talent pool management can be a tricky area highly dependent on the knowledge, skills, and abilities of the mentor in identifying and sponsoring a deserving protégé who fits with the new role and organizational requirements. The criticality of mentor characteristics to the outcomes of all entities involved is further described in the section on moderating effects.

Although the usefulness of socialization, signaling, networking, and influence tactics in gaining positive outcomes for the employee has been established (e.g., Chao, Walz, & Gardner, 1992; Prevosto, 2001; Seibert, Kraimer, & Liden, 2001), the literature lacks studies that examine the antecedents to such cognitive, affective, and behavioral responses of protégés and others. A few studies, such as those of Dreher and Ash (1990) and Dreher and Bretz (1991), only theoretically illustrate how career outcomes could be attained through access to important informal networks that mentors provide, but there has been no measurement of the protégé's perceptions of the importance of politicking and networking, or others' perceptions of protégé competence, legitimacy, or fit. Thus, like the previous paths, no study has fully tested how mentoring can lead to outcomes by measuring the intervening social/political capital and signaling processes. This knowledge gap in the literature could also be fruitfully filled by future research.

Path-Goal Clarity

This route to career benefits deals with the processes of clarifying how a protégé can achieve career goals, and building the protégé's self-efficacy and motivation in achieving these goals. Mentor functions operating in this path are role modeling, acceptance and confirmation, counseling, and friendship.

Consciously or unconsciously, *role modeling* helps the protégé imbibe the mentor's attitudes, values, and behaviors that improve work life. Through role modeling, the protégé also learns how to manage work groups, relate to peers and superiors, balance work–family demands, and assume positions of greater responsibility (Kram, 1985). From the social learning perspective (Bandura, 1977), protégés attend to role models because they can be helpful in learning new skills, behaviors, and norms; from an identification perspective, role models influence motivational and self-definitional aspects of one's personality (Gibson, 2004). Through *acceptance and confirmation* from the mentor, the protégé feels free to experiment with new behaviors, and take risks in achieving his or her goals. *Counseling*, another psychosocial function operating in this path, helps the protégé explore personal concerns that undermine self-worth or interfere with productive behavior. The mentor helps the protégé alleviate anxieties, ambivalences, fears, and conflicts about the latter's competence in achieving career goals or even executing day-to-day tasks. *Friendship* between the mentor and protégé also helps in clearing the path to one's goal. Friendship arises from the social interactions that result in mutual liking and understanding, as well as from enjoyable informal exchanges about work and nonwork experiences (Kram, 1985). Friendship helps the protégé deal with difficult tasks of the early and middle career years, enhancing work experiences for all involved. Wanberg et al. (2003) note that mentor–protégé discussions on topics such as improved role clarity, how best to achieve one's career objectives or goals, and strategies for maintaining work–life balance have the potential to increase the protégé's job, career, and life satisfaction.

These mentor functions serve to enhance the protégé's self-efficacy in pursuing career goals. The protégé also begins to perceive enhanced behavioral instrumentality and expectancy in achieving outcomes. Instrumentality and expectancy perceptions in this path relate to how the mentor helps the protégé perceive that one's goals are attainable through perseverance. Path-goal clarity can be motivational if the mentor provides guidance, support, and rewards for effective performance, which in turn increase the protégé's effort and persistence on tasks at hand. As a result of improved protégé job performance, the organization also gains through enhanced overall productivity and performance.

Apart from Day and Allen (2004) who tested the mediating effects of career self-efficacy and career motivation on the relationship between mentoring functions and objective and subjective career outcomes, not many others have empirically tested the mediating effects proposed in the path-goal clarity route to career outcomes. The processes we modeled in this path are also yet to be empirically examined. Once again, we need more studies that can empirically establish the effects of mentoring functions on the protégé's self-efficacy and instrumentality perceptions, leading to better performance and subsequent individual or organizational outcomes.

Values Clarity

This path deals with the process of clarifying the status of the protégé's current work–life situation, the appropriateness of chosen career and life decisions, and whether they satisfy one's needs and preferences. The various psychosocial functions, such as role modeling, acceptance and confirmation, counseling, and friendship, impact the protégé at a more personal than professional level.

Apart from gaining technical knowledge from mentors, protégés also benefit by forming and understanding their professional identities and getting a sense of who they can become in a new role and work context. Since the mentor functions that operate in this path have been explained earlier, we will not elaborate here in detail the dynamics of these functions. Through *role modeling, acceptance and confirmation, counseling, and friendship*, the protégé identifies with the mentor and freely explores the meaning and importance of work–life balance, and relationships with the organization and other spheres of life (Kram, 1985). The processes in this path focus more on subjective outcomes such as career and life satisfaction, although objective career outcomes may also accrue to the protégé.

These mentor functions, in sum, enable the protégé to gauge work centrality and consolidate one's personal and professional values. According to Schulz (1995), new employees, with the help of mentors, can decide whether the organizations they are working for can support their career goals, or whether they need to look for other opportunities. Such behavioral and value choices are critical in establishing one's identity. Linked to competence and identity is how committed to his or her career an individual will be, and the amount of time and energy he or she is willing to invest in it.

Protégés who perceive failure in leading a meaningful work and/or family life may decide to engage in career and life planning, opt for a change in career, and could eventually leave the organization. Career and life planning could help protégés decide on possible changes in career paths, guided by the knowledge or assumption that it would lead to more career and life satisfaction. The career and life planning process also helps a protégé become aware of the extent to which one's identity is derived from work roles. Thus turnover may result from a change in career path or even just quitting from work life. The employing organization in such a situation may also face positive or negative changes in turnover costs.

Although most studies on mentoring focus on objective career outcomes, some have tested how the existence of a mentor and some mentoring functions can lead to subjective outcomes such as career satisfaction and career commitment (Aryee & Chay, 1994; Colarelli & Bishop, 1990; Day & Allen, 2004; Ragins, Cotton, & Miller, 2000; Wayne et al., 1999; Whitely & Coetsier, 1993). We are not aware of any studies that have examined the process linkages between mentoring and life satisfaction. Aryee, Wyatt, and Stone (1996) do study motivational variables such as the number of hours worked and career identity, but as independent (and not process) variables affecting salary, promotions, and career satisfaction. Thus the values-clarity path too needs to be studied in its entirety. Studies that simultaneously link mentoring to values clarity and perceptions of work centrality, and how they in turn lead to individual and organizational outcomes through career and life planning, career change, and turnover, are needed.

The Mentor Framework

Few studies have explicitly examined the benefits of mentoring for the mentors themselves (Burke & McKeen, 1997; Collins, 1994; Hunt & Michael, 1983; Johnson, Yust, & Fritchie, 2001; Ragins & Scandura, 1994). Noe et al. (2002) and Wanberg et al. (2003) note the gap in the literature on how mentoring can lead to increased career and social outcomes for the mentor. Although the primary outcome for a mentor has been purported to be psychosocial in nature, in this chapter we focus on the processes by which mentoring can also lead to *career* outcomes for the mentor, as well as outcomes for the organization. Some process paths in the mentor framework are similar to those in the protégé's, with the addition of a few others, such as Optimal Resource Usage and Relational Gains. Since research on mentor benefits has been very minimal, our discussion of the mentor framework will not be as extensive as that of the protégé framework. We were unable to find any study that tested the complete process paths described below. Nevertheless, wherever applicable, studies are noted that either mention the theoretical connection between process variables or empirically test part of the process linkages between mentoring and career outcomes.

Human Capital

Just as the protégé gains in human capital from the mentor, so too can the mentor benefit from the protégé. However, the focus here is not on the technical KSAs that mentors could learn from protégés but on the awareness of intergenerational differences in work–life demands and knowledge of the latest trends in one's field. Providing challenging assignments to protégés and developing a close bond through friendship brings to the mentor's notice new developments in the field and also encourages protégés to share information about issues that people of their generation face. Kram and Hall (1995) describe such a mentoring relationship as involving co-learning, in which the protégés also teach their mentors and share their ideas. Gaining new perspectives from this interaction with the protégé leads to cognitive rejuvenation and also enhancement of one's own mentoring and leadership. Increased diversity in mentoring relationships will help enhance the mentor's understanding and appreciation of, and empathy in relating to, multicultural, diverse protégés (Ragins, 1997a; Schulz, 1995). The mentor could thus improve his or her own job performance, ultimately leading to career attainment outcomes such as promotion and increased salary. At the organizational level this leads to further development of the mentor talent pool as well as improved organizational productivity and performance.

Movement Capital

Building a close friendship with the protégé could be beneficial to the mentor once the protégé moves from the present organization. The mentor's activities such as sponsoring, providing visibility and exposure, and investing time and energy in developing a friendship with the protégé could make the protégé feel indebted to the mentor. The protégé may then reciprocate by providing the mentor with knowledge about job opportunities in external labor markets. The mentor goes through the same process as does the protégé in such a situation, in terms of evaluating the ease and desirability of movement from the current position to those in other organizations. This leads to a series of behaviors such as job search and turnover, increasing the mentor's inter-organizational mobility. The new positions for the mentor could reap more career benefits in terms of career/salary attainment and career satisfaction. The organization in turn faces turnover cost issues.

Optimal Resource Usage

By providing challenging assignments to the protégé, the mentor can share the workload with the protégé and obtain relief from some technical responsibilities (Kram, 1985; Schulz, 1995). Such responsibility sharing can reduce the mentor's work stress, and increase mental energy to be invested in other organizational or personal tasks. The mentor thus begins to delegate more tasks to the protégé which enables the former to increase the scope and amount of work by taking on more projects. Working on multiple tasks with shared workload with the protégé could help the mentor improve job performance. This improved performance in terms of higher output could help the mentor gain career benefits such as increased salary and promotions, and the organization in turn benefits through improved overall performance and productivity.

Social/Political Capital and Signaling

Mentor functions that enhance the social/political gains for the protégé can also lead to the same benefits for the mentor. The career functions provided by the mentor may induce the protégé to reciprocate associated benefits in similar ways. This path is also bifurcated into the mentor's responses and other organizational members' responses. By providing sponsorship and exposure to protégés, mentors may gain an "informant" who can enhance both the mentor's awareness of the political climate in the organization and the importance of mentoring. The protégé may provide the mentor with unfiltered feedback on what others think of the mentor. High self-monitoring mentors may seek more information from their protégés (Mullen & Noe, 1999), improve job performance, and provide enhanced mentoring. As one continues to seek more protégés, one becomes the hub of a protégé network (Scandura et al., 1996). This network could serve in many capacities, from locating talent to providing information on behalf of the mentor (Ragins & Scandura, 1994). From the signaling and power perspectives, the protégé's performance and success will influence the mentor's visibility, reputation, and credibility (Noe, 1988; Ragins, 1997a), and this in turn increases the mentor's power base (Hunt & Michael, 1983) and sense of confidence. Others in the organization then become aware of the mentor's legitimacy, capability, and judgment in identifying and promoting talent. This leads to respect and admiration (Ragins & Scandura, 1994) from peers, subordinates, and superiors for the organizational inputs that the mentor provides through leadership and improved organizational talent. The mentor thus gains increased recognition which can make senior management more open to sponsoring the mentor's own activities. Acknowledging the mentor's ability to develop talent, senior management may assign more protégés to the mentor, increasing opportunities for improved performance. All these activities could open doors to outcomes such as career/salary attainment and career satisfaction for the mentor and improved talent pool development and productivity and performance for the organization.

Identity Validation

The mentoring relationship provides opportunity for the mentor to grow personally and professionally. While coaching a protégé, the mentor engages in a process of self-discovery that increases awareness of one's competence levels. This can lead to personal and professional satisfaction, and infuse a sense of motivation and revitalized interest in one's job (Schulz, 1995). Role modeling, acceptance and confirmation, and friendship with the protégé enable the mentor to satisfy the need for generativity (Levinson, Darrow, Klein, Levinson, & McKee, 1978; Schulz, 1995), and obtain a sense of purpose, fulfillment, and confirmation of the value of work experiences (Kram, 1985). The mentor becomes aware of the central aspects of his or her self-image and this reinforces a sense of professional identity. This identity reinforcement, accompanied by the increased desire to contribute to the development of the next generation, may increase the mentor's career commitment and desire to engage in more developmental activities. Thus, the mentor may seek more protégés to ensure continued personal and professional development. Making meaningful contributions to one's and others' lives could improve the mentor's career satisfaction, life satisfaction, and career attainment. It may also have organizational effects on talent pool development, turnover costs, and retirement costs.

Relational Gains

Apart from gaining professionally, having a protégé may also benefit the mentor relationally. Through the process of providing mentor functions such as acceptance and confirmation, counseling, and friendship the mentor begins to assess fit with the protégé, and may also develop a sense of emotional attachment with the protégé. Such close relationships may also help the mentor counter loneliness, especially during a life stage when one's children "leave the nest," and the mentor has no one "to take care of." The protégé provides the mentor with company that enables the latter to maintain emotional health and well-being. Such fit, emotional attachment, and lack of loneliness perceptions may lead the mentor to engage in more developmental activities and seek more protégés to help perpetuate the benefits of mentoring to oneself and others. The benefits gained from such experiences are primarily increased career and life satisfaction for the mentor, and talent pool development for the organization.

The dearth of studies on career benefits of mentoring to mentors cannot be over-stated. In their research on mentors, Ragins and Scandura (1994, 1999) studied the perceptions of costs and benefits of mentoring, but not the actual benefits accrued to mentors. Moreover, few studies have tested the actual benefits of mentoring to mentors. Johnson et al. (2001) found that being a mentor increased mentors' career satisfaction, and Collins (1994) found that mentoring led to self-reported career suc-cess, career satisfaction, and also increased income. There is a clear need for studies testing the mentoring–career outcomes relationship through the process paths we propose (as well as other processes that may operate in the outlined paths). The scope for research on mentor benefits is wide and future research needs to capitalize on this glaring knowledge gap.

Moderating Effects of Relationship Quality

While it has not been the focus of our discussion, both Figures 13.1 and 13.2 depict a set of potential moderators of the mentoring–outcome relationships. As shown in these figures, these variables may determine whether the relationship includes the enactment of all or only a subset of the major mentoring functions originally iden-tified by Kram (1985) and whether or not the mentoring relationship is of sufficient quality to affect the proposed cognitive, affective, and behavioral responses. This is a complex issue that has not received sufficient attention in the mentoring literature (Wanberg et al., 2003). Mentoring relationships can vary dramatically in terms of quality. We propose that only high-quality relationships will generate the proposed responses and outcomes. That is, quality moderates the relationship between having a mentor and the types of mentoring functions provided as well as the relationship between mentoring functions provided and subsequent processes. The problem, of course, is how to define and measure quality. In the figures we suggest that certain attributes of mentoring relationships are likely to be related to quality. However, our list is certainly incomplete and serves only to introduce the topic. Some likely determinants of quality include the following.

Mentor Knowledge

High-quality mentoring relationships would certainly depend on whether or not the mentor possesses accurate and meaningful knowledge about the organization and career path the protégé is participating in. Misinformed mentors or mentors who find themselves outside the networks of powerful decision makers are not as likely as their more informed and connected counterparts to be able to provide protégés with needed information and organizational perspective. While the organizational level of the mentor may serve as a useful proxy for this dimension, a more direct measure of mentor knowledge and connectivity is what we have in mind here.

Mentor Training and Development Skills

It would seem that high-quality mentoring relationships would require mentors who are skillful in developing, training, and coaching other individuals. Attributes such as communication and listening skills and knowledge about the principles of learning would be important in understanding mentors' ability to develop strong relationships with protégés.

Motivation and Opportunity to Mentor

High-quality relationships will require mentors who have the energy and opportunity to spend time with their protégés. Considering this dimension opens a whole set of issues requiring further consideration. For example, is it important for mentors and protégés to be able to meet regularly, or will extensive e-mail exchanges substitute for person-to-person discussions? What are the relationships between such things as geographic location, mentor workload, and relationship quality? Are mentors likely to devote more time and attention to protégés who a) they feel comfortable spending time with, b) share their interests and values, or c) they believe are candidates for high-potential pools? Here, a whole set of issues that relate to the composition of the mentoring dyad become paramount (e.g., race and gender composition of the relationship, the processes mentors use to select protégés, etc.).

Formal and Informal Mentoring

Finally, we note that the distinction between *formal* and *informal* mentoring serves to highlight potential quality issues. According to Ragins and Cotton (1999), formal and informal relationships may differ on multiple dimensions. One key difference is the way the relationship is formed. Informal relationships occur naturally. That is, via naturally occurring exchanges at work or in social settings, a mentoring relationship is formed because of mutual attraction and interest on the part of both parties. Formal relationships are often the result of some type of matching process initiated within the context of a company-sponsored mentoring program. Just like in the informal realm, there can be great variation on the formal mentoring theme. Formal mentoring programs can vary with respect to how they are structured, their official duration, or funding and support levels. Research also indicates that in comparison to informal mentoring, formal mentoring programs are generally less effective. Formal protégés have been found to have lower-quality mentoring relationships (Allen, Day, & Lentz, 2005), receive lower levels of mentoring functions (Chao et al., 1992), and also lower compensation (Ragins & Cotton, 1999). Wanberg et al. (2003) suggest that although formal protégés reap fewer benefits from the mentoring relationship, the full potential of the formal mentoring program can be realized by ensuring that protégés are satisfied with their mentors. While it may be that the formal/informal dimension will covary with the previously defined attributes of the mentoring relationship, we think the most useful way to consider the effects of moderators is to focus directly on the dimensions of quality.

Summary and Insights

As one looks at the mentoring literature, one realizes that there are numerous studies that examine the relationships between mentoring and career benefits, beyond the 43 studies that Allen et al. (2004) included in their meta-analysis. Interestingly, most of these studies have focused on protégés' career benefits such as compensation, promotion rate, and career satisfaction. Although we cannot put a specific number on the studies that have tested the relationships between mentoring and career outcomes, it is evident from the literature that a negligible percentage of these studies have explicitly measured process variables to explain the mentor–benefits linkage. For example, out of the five process paths that we proposed in the protégé framework, none have been studied in their entirety. The studies that do test some process linkages either do not link mentoring functions to processes or do not link processes to outcomes. Thus, studies that test overall paths between mentoring and career benefits are virtually nonexistent. This is true not only for the protégé benefits area, but more so for the mentor and organization benefits area, where research on the direct links between mentoring and benefits is also scant. This lack of research on the mentoring benefits for entities other than the protégé seems characteristic not just of studies conducted in industry settings but also of those conducted in academic settings (see Johnson, this volume) and youth settings (see Blinn-Pike, this volume).

Limitations

The limitations of our chapter are fourfold. First, it should be noted that our protégé and mentor frameworks are generally speculative. We acknowledge that mentor functions, process variables, and outcomes other than those we have modeled could operate in the different paths we propose; perhaps there are even other process paths from mentoring to outcomes that we have not described.

Second, some variables that linked mentoring to outcomes in our frameworks could covary with other related constructs that we may not have indicated, and could very well be proxies for our variables. Owing to this we may not have cited studies that tested the relationships between mentoring and these alternative variables. For example, in the movement capital path, desirability of movement might be replaced by commitment or job satisfaction due to their close theoretical relationship (Jakofsky & Peters, 1983; Payne & Huffman, 2005) and by intentions to turnover, owing to their conceptual similarity. Ease of movement perceptions could also be highly related to the number of job alternatives one has (Mitchell & Lee, 2001). Moreover, research demonstrates that the presence of a mentor or mentoring functions is negatively related to intentions to quit or turnover intentions (Viator & Scandura, 1991) and positively related to intentions to remain in the organization (Higgins & Thomas, 2001) and commitment (Aryee & Chay, 1994; Baugh et al., 1996; Colarelli & Bishop, 1990; Payne & Huffman, 2005). Finally, Payne and Huffman (2005) found that commitment partially mediates the relationship between mentoring and turnover, similar to our proposition that desirability of movement perceptions mediates the relationship between mentoring and turnover. The specific variables depicted in Figures 13.1 and 13.2 were chosen on theoretical grounds. Nevertheless, in the light of studies noted above, we encourage researchers to study process variables and mentoring outcomes similar to the ones we have noted.

A third limitation of our chapter is that we do not describe the theoretical reasoning underlying our process relationships in great detail. We opted to focus readers' attention on a wide range of possible process variables that link mentoring to outcomes in a crisp and concise fashion, rather than hone in on one or two paths in detail.

Lastly, the frameworks that we propose are more complicated than depicted. As indicated in our section on moderators, there are numerous determinants of mentoring relationship quality that likely influence whether and how the different process paths play out. Although we briefly describe potential moderating effects in this chapter, we refer the reader to Noe et al. (2002) and Wanberg et al. (2003) to learn more about moderating effects in the mentoring literature.

Needed Research

We would like to end our chapter by directing readers to grossly understudied areas of research that need to be pursued. Research is needed which incorporates mediating processes into mentoring research. Although we know what outcomes mentoring can lead to, it is as important to know how and why. We need studies that describe mentoring benefits for the protégé, the mentor, and the employing organization, with clear process explanations. Also, most research on mentoring has focused on the effects of "ad hoc" career or psychosocial functions on outcomes. We do not know the relative effects of individual functions on process variables and outcomes. This is perhaps because few scales that measure each function separately exist. Most studies on mentoring functions have used Noe's (1988) scales, which seem to have limited the mentoring–outcomes relationships one can study. Thus scale development for mentoring functions is another area that needs more attention.

It is interesting to note that the assumption we make about the mentoring process – that the protégé (and mentor) will be fundamentally changed into a fuller person over time – need not hold true. The social/political and signaling path, described in the protégé and mentor frameworks, brings to our attention the benefits that can accrue to both protégé and mentor as a result of the background work and signaling process that they engage in for each other. The very fact of being associated with a high-level mentor can trigger positive signals to decision makers who in turn sponsor and make favorable decisions for the protégé. While all this happens, the protégé may neither be aware of such a signaling process nor be changed in any appreciable way as a result of having a mentor, and yet reap the benefits of mentoring. It would be interesting to study the extent to which protégés benefit from such background work without undergoing any noticeable personal change. Having said that, what if it were true that all the benefits that protégés get were due just to the background work that mentors do for them? Also, what is the relative impact of the different process paths on career outcomes? These questions are yet to be answered in the mentoring literature. Although the background work that a protégé engages in may not have as great a corresponding impact on the mentor's benefits, such actions could impact the reputation of, and demand for, the mentor.

Another assumption we make regarding the mentoring process is that it leads to better organizational capabilities through sponsorship and promotion of the "right" people. We have no way to ensure that the mentors are capable themselves of identifying the "right" talent. More research is needed on what skills a mentor needs to accurately identify talent in the organization, the consequences of wrong talent identification, such as missed opportunities for people who are truly talented in the organization, and the bearings it may have on the employee–organization contract. Another interesting issue related to the choice of employees for mentoring is their *need* for mentoring. Allen, Poteet, and Russell (2000) found that mentors choose protégés based on ability and motivation rather than perceived need for help. This may render the mentoring process redundant as employees who are already capable of maneuvering and succeeding in their careers may not need extra guidance from mentors. Although such guidance may be welcome, not much incremental individual or organizational benefit may be gained by "preaching to the converted." Instead, mentor and organizational resources may be better utilized for identifying employees who are genuinely in need of such guidance and support, and providing mentoring functions to develop them and further their careers. More research on protégé selection criteria and identification processes may help in fully understanding the dynamics of the mentoring process.

Related to this, another area of research that has not been adequately explored is the entire field of unintended positive and negative consequences of a mentoring relationship. In this chapter we have proposed only a few of the mentoring outcomes for the protégé, mentor, and organization, though we acknowledge that consequences of mentoring could go beyond what we have described, and could also be negative, for all entities involved. Take the case of a mentoring relationship leading to greater movement capital for the protégé. Whilst the protégé benefits by moving to a better-paying and higher-position job, such turnover could either be positive for the organization, especially if the protégé was a liability to the organization, or it could be negative if the protégé was an asset to the organization. There could be many such unintended consequences for the protégé, mentor, and organization that demand more research attention.

Conclusion

Although the mentoring literature spans over a few decades, we believe that there is scope to further enrich this literature. As indicated in this chapter, there are many knowledge gaps that need to be addressed with regard to the types of mentoring benefits, and also the processes that lead to those benefits for the protégé, and more so for other entities such as the mentor and the organization. While this chapter makes a conceptual start in that direction, it is clear that a substantial amount of empirical research is needed to test the process paths we propose. We hope that the frameworks and ideas presented in this chapter offer an agenda for future process-oriented mentoring benefits research.

References

Allen, T. D., Day, R., & Lentz, E. (2005). The role of interpersonal comfort in mentoring relationships. *Journal of Career Development, 31*(3), 155–169.

Allen, T. D., Eby, L. T., Poteet, M. L., Lentz, E., & Lima, L. (2004). Career benefits associated with mentoring for protégés: A meta-analysis. *Journal of Applied Psychology, 89*, 127–136.

Allen, T. D., Poteet, M. L., & Russell, J. E. A. (2000). Protégé selection by mentors: What makes the difference? *Journal of Organizational Behavior, 21*, 271–282.

Aryee, S., & Chay, Y. W. (1994). An examination of the impact of career-oriented mentoring on work commitment attitudes and career satisfaction among professional and managerial employees: An interactionist approach. *British Journal of Management, 5*, 241–249.

Aryee, S., Wyatt, T., & Stone, R. (1996). Early career outcomes of graduate employees: The effect of mentoring an ingratiation. *Journal of Management Studies, 33*, 95–118.

Bandura, A. (1977). *Social learning theory.* Englewood Cliffs, NJ: Prentice-Hall.

Barker, P., Monks, K., & Buckley, F. (1999). The role of mentoring in the career progression of chartered accountants. *British Accounting Review, 31*, 297–312.

Baugh, S. G., Lankau, M. J., & Scandura, T. A. (1996). An investigation of the effects of protégé gender on responses to mentoring. *Journal of Vocational Behavior, 49*, 309–323.

Baugh, S. G., & Scandura, T. A. (1999). The effects of multiple mentors on protégé attitudes toward the work setting. *Journal of Social Behavior and Personality, 14*, 503–521.

Becker, G. S. (1975). *Human capital.* Chicago: University of Chicago Press.

Bretz, R. D., Boudreau, J. W., & Judge, T. A. (1994). Job search behavior of employed managers. *Personnel Psychology, 47*, 275–301.

Burke, R. J., & McKeen, C. A. (1997). Benefits of mentoring relationships among managerial and professional women: A cautionary tale. *Journal of Vocational Behavior, 51*, 43–57.

Campbell, J. P., Dunnette, M. D., Lawler, E. E., & Weick, K. E. (1970). *Managerial behavior, performance and effectiveness.* New York: McGraw-Hill, Inc.

Chao, G. T. (1997). Mentoring phases and outcomes. *Journal of Vocational Behavior, 51*, 15–28.

Chao, G. T., Walz, P. M., & Gardner, P. D. (1992). Formal and informal mentorships: A comparison on mentoring functions and contract with nonmentored counterparts. *Personnel Psychology, 45*, 619–636.

Colarelli, S. M., & Bishop, R. C. (1990). Career commitment: Functions, correlates and management. *Group and Organization Studies, 15*, 158–176.

Collins, P. M. (1994). Does mentorship among social workers make a difference? An empirical investigation of career outcomes. *Work and Occupations, 18*, 431–446.

Day, R., & Allen, T. (2004). The relationship between career motivation and self-efficacy with protégé career success. *Journal of Vocational Behavior, 64*, 72–91.

Dreher, G. F., & Ash, R. A. (1990). A comparative study of mentoring among men and women in managerial, professional, and technical positions. *Journal of Applied Psychology, 75*, 539–546.

Dreher, G. F., & Bretz, R. D. (1991). Cognitive ability and career attainment: Moderating effects of early career success. *Journal of Applied Psychology, 76*, 392–397.

Dreher, G. F., & Cox, T. H. (2000). Labor market mobility and cash compensation: The moderating effects of race and gender. *Academy of Management Journal, 43*, 890–900.

Fagenson, E. A. (1989). The mentor advantage: Perceived career/job experiences of protégés versus non-protégés. *Journal of Organizational Behavior, 10*, 309–320.

Ferris, G. R., & Judge, T. A. (1991). Personnel/human resources management: A political influence perspective. *Journal of Management, 17*, 447–488.

Gerhart, B. (1990). Voluntary turnover and alternative job opportunities. *Journal of Applied Psychology, 75,* 285–297.

Gibson, D. E. (2004). Role models in career development: New directions in theory and research. *Journal of Vocational Behavior, 65,* 134–156.

Higgins, C., Judge, T. A., & Ferris, G. R. (2003). Influence tactics and work outcomes: A meta-analysis. *Journal of Organizational Behavior, 24,* 89–106.

Higgins, M. C., & Thomas, D. A. (2001). Constellations and careers: Toward understanding the effects of multiple developmental relationships. *Journal of Organizational Behavior, 22,* 223–247.

Hunt, D. M., & Michael, C. (1983). Mentorship: A career training and development tool. *Academy of Management Review, 8,* 475–485.

Jakofsky, E. F., & Peters, L. H. (1983). The hypothesized effects of ability in the turnover process. *Academy of Management Review, 8,* 46–49.

Johnson, K. K. P., Yust, B. L., & Fritchie, L. L. (2001). Views on mentoring by clothing and textiles faculty. *Clothing and Textiles Research Journal, 19,* 31–40.

Kanter, R. M. (1977). *Men and women of the corporation.* New York: Basic Books.

Kirchmeyer, C. (1998). Determinants of managerial career success: Evidence and explanation of male/female differences. *Journal of Management, 24,* 673–692.

Koberg, C. S., Boss, R. W., Chappell, D., & Ringer, R. C. (1994). Correlates and consequences of protégé mentoring in a large hospital. *Group and Organization Management, 19,* 219–239.

Kram, K. E. (1985). *Mentoring at work: Developmental relationships in organizational life.* Glenview, IL: Scott, Foresman and Company.

Kram, K. E., & Hall, D. T. (1995). Mentoring in a context of diversity and turbulence. In E. E. Kossek & S. Lobel (Eds.), *Managing diversity: Human resources strategies for transforming the workplace* (pp. 108–136). Cambridge, MA: Blackwell.

Levinson, D. J., Darrow, D., Klein, E., Levinson, M., & McKee, B. (1978). *Seasons of a man's life.* New York: Knopf.

March, J. G., & Simon, H. A. (1958). *Organizations.* New York: Wiley.

Mitchell, T. R., & Lee, T. W. (2001). The unfolding model of voluntary turnover and job embeddedness: Foundations for a comprehensive theory of attachment. In L. Cummings & B. Staw (Eds.), *Research in organizational behavior* (Vol. 23, pp. 189–246). Greenwich, CT: JAI Press.

Mobley, G. M., Jaret, C., Marsh, K., & Lim, Y. Y. (1994). Mentoring, job satisfaction, gender, and the legal profession. *Sex Roles, 31,* 79–98.

Mullen, E. J., & Noe, R. A. (1999). The mentoring information exchange: When do mentors seek information from their protégés? *Journal of Organizational Behavior, 20,* 233–242.

Noe, R. A. (1988). An investigation of the determinants of successful assigned mentoring relationships. *Personnel Psychology, 41,* 457–479.

Noe, R. A., Greenberger, D. B., & Wang, S. (2002). Mentoring: What we know and where we might go from here. In G. R. Ferris & J. J. Martocchio (Eds.), *Research in Personnel and Human Resources Management* (Vol. 21, pp. 129–173). Greenwich, CT: Elsevier Science/ JAI Press.

Ostroff, C., & Koslowski, S. W. (1993). The role of mentoring in the information gathering processes of newcomers during early organizational socialization. *Journal of Vocational Behavior, 42,* 170–183.

Payne, S. C., & Huffman, A. H. (2005). A longitudinal examination of the influence of mentoring on organizational commitment and turnover. *Academy of Management Journal, 48,* 158–168.

Pfeffer, J., & Lawler, J. (1979). *The effects of job alternatives, extrinsic rewards, and commitment on satisfaction with the organization: A field example of the insufficient justification paradigm.* Berkeley, CA: University of California.

Porter, L. W., & Lawler, E. E. (1968). *Managerial attitudes and performance*. Homewood, IL: Dorsey Press.

Prevosto, P. (2001). The effect of mentored relationships on satisfaction and intent to stay of company-grade U. S. Army reserve nurses. *Military Medicine, 166*, 21–26.

Ragins, B. R. (1997a). Diversified mentoring relationships in organizations: A power perspective. *Academy of Management Review, 22*, 482–521.

Ragins, B. R., & Cotton, J. L. (1999). Mentor functions and outcomes: A comparison of men and women in formal and informal mentoring relationships. *Journal of Applied Psychology, 84*, 529–550.

Ragins, B. R., Cotton, J. L., & Miller, J. S. (2000). Marginal mentoring: The effects of type of mentor, quality of relationship, and program design on work and career attitudes. *Academy of Management Journal, 43*, 1177–1194.

Ragins, B. R., & Scandura, T. A. (1994). Gender differences in expected outcomes of mentoring relationships. *Academy of Management Journal, 37*, 957–971.

Ragins, B. R., & Scandura, T. A. (1999). Burden or blessing? Expected costs and benefits of being a mentor. *Journal of Organizational Behavior, 20*, 493–509.

Rouse, P. D. (2001). Voluntary turnover related to information technology professionals: A review of rational and instinctual models. *International Journal of Organizational Analysis, 9*, 281–290.

Sackett, P. R., Gruys, M. L., & Ellingson, J. E. (1998). Ability–personality interactions when predicting job performance. *Journal of Applied Psychology, 83*, 545–556.

Scandura, T. A., Tejeda, M. L., Werther, W. B., & Lankau, M. J. (1996). Perspectives on mentoring. *Leadership and Organization Development Journal, 17*(3), 50–56.

Schmidt, F. L., & Hunter, J. E. (1998). The validity and utility of selection methods in personnel psychology: Practical and theoretical implications of 85 years of research findings. *Psychological Bulletin, 124*, 262–274.

Schulz, S. F. (1995). The benefits of mentoring. In M. W. Galbraith & N. H. Cohen (Eds.), *Mentoring: New strategies and challenges* (Vol. 66, pp. 57–68). San Francisco: Jossey-Bass.

Seibert, S. E., Kraimer, M. L., & Liden, R. C. (2001). A social capital theory of career success. *Academy of Management Journal, 44*, 219–237.

Singh, V., Bains, D., & Vinnicombe, S. (2002). Informal mentoring as an organisational resource. *Long Range Planning: International Journal of Strategic Management, 35*, 389–405.

Tharenou, P. (1997). Managerial career advancement. In C. L. Cooper & I. T. Robertson (Eds.), *International review of industrial and organizational psychology, 12* (pp. 39–93). Chichester, England: John Wiley & Sons.

Tharenou, P., Latimer, S., & Conroy, D. (1994). How do you make it to the top? An examination of influences on women's and men's managerial advancement. *Academy of Management Journal, 37*, 899–931.

Turban, D. B., & Dougherty, T. W. (1994). Role of protégé personality in receipt of mentoring and career success. *Academy of Management Journal, 37*, 688–702.

Viator, R. E., & Scandura, T. A. (1991). A study of mentor–protégé relationships in large public accounting firms. *Accounting Horizons, 5*(3), 20–30.

Vroom, V. H. (1964). *Work and motivation*. New York: Wiley.

Wanberg, C. R., Welsh, E. T., & Hezlett, S. A. (2003). Mentoring research: A review and dynamic process model. *Research in Personnel and Human Resources Management, 22*, 39–124.

Wayne, S. J., Liden, R. C., Kraimer, M. L., & Graf, I. K. (1999). The role of human capital, motivation and supervisor sponsorship in predicting career success. *Journal of Organizational Behavior, 20*, 577–595.

Whitely, W. T., & Coetsier, P. (1993). The relationship of career mentoring to early career outcomes. *Organization Studies, 14*, 419–441.

Chapter 14

Reflections on the Benefits of Mentoring

Angie L. Lockwood, Sarah Carr Evans,
and Lillian T. Eby

The chapters in this section reviewed the benefits associated with youth, student–faculty, and workplace mentoring and suggest that mentorships have the potential to benefit protégés, mentors, and others in the context in which the mentorship is embedded (e.g., families, communities, academic institutions, companies). While there are similarities that should be noted in the pattern of potential benefits, it is clear that researchers in each area of study have a different lens through which they view mentoring relationships. A unique lens is justified, in part, by the general differences in mentors' and protégés' operating assumptions across areas of study, which in turn influence mentor–protégé interactions, and ultimately the type and breadth of benefits obtained. In this reflection chapter we integrate the three chapters in this section, and in so doing isolate similarities and differences in mentoring benefits in youth, student–faculty, and workplace mentoring, as well as the commonly discussed drivers of such benefits.

In that mentoring relationships are oriented toward protégé development, it is not surprising that the greatest breadth of research in each of the aforementioned areas of study pertains to protégé outcomes. In order to buttress anecdotal and early empirical evidence, researchers have focused on measuring specific behavioral and affective protégé outcomes. The chapters in this section reveal some common benefits, such as improved psychological health, more positive attitudes, and achievement. However, the extent to which different behavioral and affective outcomes are investigated by researchers varies considerably by area of study. For instance, benefits related to emotional and psychological well-being (e.g., self-esteem, self-concept, coping, anxiety, depression) appear more prevalently in youth mentoring studies, while research on student–faculty and workplace mentoring relationships focuses heavily on career-related achievement (e.g., scholarly productivity, skill development, salary, promotion rate) and, perhaps to a lesser extent, attitudes (e.g., professional competence, work attitudes).

All three chapters in this section highlight key drivers of benefits actually realized by the protégé, to include: relationship type (informal vs. formal), goals and objectives of the mentoring relationship, and mentor/protégé expertise. First, a programmatic driver of realized benefits is whether or not the mentoring relationship is informal (naturally occurring) or formal (established by a third party), a distinction primarily explored in workplace mentoring research. As Ramaswami and Dreher (this volume) note, formal mentoring relationships typically result in fewer benefits for protégés, as compared to informal mentoring relationships (though these authors acknowledge the ability to narrow this gap through increased relational quality in a formal mentoring relationship). In the case of youth and academic mentoring relationships, protégé benefits remain relatively unexplored in either informal (for youth) or formal (for academic) mentoring. As a result, mentoring research in these areas may not provide a complete picture of potential protégé benefits. For example, Blinn-Pike (this volume) notes that some initial research on informal mentoring demonstrates behavioral benefits (e.g., decreased likelihood of involvement in drug use and minor delinquency) and affective benefits (e.g., increased satisfaction with level of support) for the protégé. Academic mentoring presents an interesting case, because as Johnson (this volume) notes, the relationship is assumed to be informal based on the process of relationship initiation and development; yet the most prevalent protégé benefits closely parallel those associated with formal mentoring relationships in the workplace (e.g., networking, productivity).

Differences in the benefits reaped across types of mentorships can also be understood in terms of the goals and objectives that mentoring serves for youth, students, and employees. For instance, youth mentoring is commonly used to facilitate academic achievement, enhance positive attitudes toward self, school, and others, reduce risky behaviors, and improve psychological well-being. As such, youth mentoring tends to target "at risk" children and adolescents who are then paired with adults who offer guidance, psychological support, and instrumental help to achieve these goals. In contrast, both student–faculty and workplace mentoring tend to have more circumscribed objectives. For student–faculty mentoring, the focus is on career preparation and professional training, and in workplace mentoring the primary objective is professional development. Thus, the scope of potential benefits examined is greatest for youth mentoring. This may be driven in part by the widespread use of formal youth mentoring programs which tend to target one or more specific youth outcomes (e.g., reduced teen pregnancy, reduced alcohol/drug use, academic improvement).

The goals and objectives of the mentoring relationship also play a large role in determining the type, breadth, and extent of expertise that a mentor needs to possess. The importance of mentor expertise is most evident in research on student–faculty and youth mentoring relationships, though it is perhaps equally as important, yet less often discussed, in workplace mentoring. For example, studies that Blinn-Pike (this volume) reviews demonstrate increased scholastic achievement among youth who participated in school-based, as compared to community-based, mentoring programs. This suggests that protégés benefit the most when objectives for the mentoring relationship (e.g., scholastic achievement) are closely aligned to the mentor's type of expertise (e.g., teaching). Further, Blinn-Pike (this volume) posits that emotional and psychological benefits may not occur frequently in youth mentoring relationships because mentors are not clinically trained to handle more severe social, psychological, and behavioral issues. In student–faculty mentoring relationships, many of the benefits (e.g., initial employment, networking, career eminence) hinge on the mentor's publication productivity, access to resources and influential colleagues, and reputation (Johnson, this volume). It is clear that the full spectrum of possible protégé benefits is dependent on the knowledge, skills, abilities, and resources that the mentor brings to the relationship; therefore a match between specific mentor competencies and goal(s) of the relationship can enhance the protégé benefits that are actually realized.

One aspect of benefits that is significant to all types of mentoring, yet well researched in only the student–faculty relationships, is sustainability. As Johnson (this volume) notes, several achievement-related benefits in academic mentorship continue to impact the protégé long after graduation (e.g., scholarly productivity, professional confidence, networking). For instance, career eminence measures sustainability of protégé benefits over time. Similarly, some benefits in organizational mentoring inherently have a long-term impact, such as career/salary attainment; however, the sustainability of positive effects on attitudes (e.g., career satisfaction, life satisfaction) and achievement (e.g., productivity) has not been examined (Ramaswami & Dreher, this volume). In contrast, there is little evidence of sustainability of youth mentoring relative to organizational and student–faculty mentoring. Blinn-Pike (this volume) describes one study demonstrating that positive attitudinal changes seem to diminish 6 months after the mentoring relationship ends. While further research is required prior to drawing any conclusions, it seems plausible that the positive impact of a mentor may dissipate after the mentoring relationship ends due to environmental factors that continue to impact the youth's life (e.g., poverty, drug use among peers).

While early research on mentoring focused primarily on how these relationships benefit protégés, researchers in all three areas have begun to investigate the benefits that mentors may receive from mentoring others. Studies on organizational mentoring demonstrate the most progress in the assessment of mentor benefits. This makes sense given that in youth and academic mentoring, protégés may have less to "give back" to the mentor, at least in the early stages of the relationship. In these latter areas of mentoring scholarship, the protégé is either disadvantaged (e.g., child of divorce, low socioeconomic status) or is just starting a new field of study. In fact, as Blinn-Pike (this volume) notes, negative outcomes seem to outweigh the benefits of mentoring at-risk youth for elderly mentors, mid-life mentors seem to break even, and adolescent mentors may grow from the experience, though short-term benefits are minimal. Likewise, in the early stages of an academic mentorship the mentor may have much to invest and little to gain professionally; personal fulfillment and gratification in seeing the protégé develop may be the primary benefits. Academic mentoring may provide greater mentor benefits as the student advances in the program and has skills and knowledge to contribute to the mentorship. Mentors in organizations may have the most to gain at the outset of the relationship given that protégés are often high-potential employees who have fresh skills and perspectives to share with their mentors. As Ramaswami and Dreher (this volume) note, such mentor benefits might include enhanced satisfaction with self, life, and career, as well as improved job performance, enhanced leadership skills, and career success.

Finally, mentoring relationships can also benefit the context in which the mentorship is embedded (e.g., families, communities, academic institutions). Within each area of study, it is fairly easy to extrapolate the benefits to the larger context; however, very few studies have directly measured these benefits. For example, a reduction in delinquent behavior among mentored youths would seem to benefit the community in terms of fewer crimes, and potentially enhanced feelings of safety among residents in close proximity to the youth. While community benefits remain largely hypothetical in the study of youth mentoring, Ramaswami and Dreher (this volume) build organizational benefits into their overall framework (e.g., talent pool development, overall employee retention), although little empirical research to date has examined such organizational gains. Student–faculty mentoring, however, has made the greatest strides in identifying benefits to the institution (e.g., trained mentors, student loyalty, peer-rated prestige of the institution). It is important that researchers continue to explore these benefits to reveal the potential value of mentoring to communities, academic institutions, and organizations.

In summary, there is mounting evidence supporting the benefits of mentoring for protégés in youth, workplace, and student–faculty areas. In addition, the type and magnitude of benefits actually realized are determined, in part, by whether or not the relationship is formal or formal, the goals and objectives of the mentoring relationship, and mentor/protégé expertise. There is also evidence that mentors benefit in workplace and student–faculty mentoring relationships. However, mentor benefits in youth mentoring relationships remain largely unexplored and the research that does exist reveals the potential for heightened stress among those who choose to become mentors. Finally, mentoring relationships may benefit the context in which the mentoring relationship occurs (e.g., family, company, community). Mentoring is an investment for the mentor, protégé, and often more distal members (e.g., funds from community members), therefore it is important that we continue to integrate findings from research conducted on workplace, youth, and student–faculty mentoring to ensure a *holistic* picture of benefits for *all* relevant parties.

Part V

Diversity and Mentoring

Chapter 15

Diversity and Youth Mentoring Relationships

Belle Liang and Jennifer M. Grossman

During the past decade, youth mentoring has become increasingly popular in the United States (Rhodes, 2002b). Some youth are mentored in formal programs, whereas others are mentored more informally by members of their existing social networks. Children and adolescents in mentor programs, as well as in informal mentoring relationships, represent diverse demographics, including boys and girls who differ by racial and ethnic minority background, socioeconomic status, sexual orientation, disability, and religion (Balcazar, Majors, Blanchard, & Paine, 1991; Blechman, 1992). Because the variables by which mentored youth differ are limitless, for the purposes of this chapter we will focus on how differences in gender, race, and ethnicity impact youth mentoring relationships.

The process or format by which we examine differences in gender, race, and ethnicity and their impact on mentoring relationships may be used as a model for examining other diverse groups of youth in future studies. Indeed, existing research demonstrates that mentoring youth from a diversity of populations may involve parallel considerations. For example, similar to the research on matching mentors and protégés by gender and ethnic minority status, research on youth with disabilities (MacDonald, Balcazar, & Keys, 2005) or religious backgrounds (Maton, Domingo, & King, 2005) has suggested potential benefits to matching on such dimensions. At the same time, programs for youth with disabilities and faith-based programs must be sensitive to the variety of interests and perspectives of youth with disabilities or religious backgrounds that originate from their multiple social identities, not just a disability-specific identity or a faith-specific identity. Thus, programs for youth from diverse backgrounds not only need to sensitize mentors to issues related to youths' diversity status, but also issues related to other aspects of youths' social identity (e.g., developmental status and familial background). Moreover, youth with a diversity of backgrounds, including those with disabilities and religious backgrounds, benefit from a "relational" approach to mentoring that emphasizes autonomy granting and trust building (MacDonald et al., 2005; Maton et al., 2005).

In this chapter, we aim to integrate theory and research relevant to the informal and formal mentoring relationships of diverse youth. First, we will consider differences across gender and ethnicity/race in *access* to mentoring relationships. Second, variations in *relational processes* across these groups will be discussed. Next, we will examine *benefits obtained* through mentoring relationships across gender and ethnicity/race. Finally, we will make several recommendations for future research and practice.

Access to Mentoring Relationships

This section focuses on the accessibility and availability of mentor relationships to youth of diverse backgrounds. Because the success of a mentoring relationship depends on the goodness of fit between a protégé and mentor (Rhodes, 2002b), the question to be answered is not merely "how accessible are mentors?" but "how accessible are the types of mentors that protégés are looking for?" Thus, in this section, we will first consider the gender- and race/ethnicity-related factors that may determine what protégés from different backgrounds look for in a mentor. Next, we will consider the accessibility or availability of the desired mentors.

What are Protégés Looking for in a Mentor?

Similarity.   Youth who are given the opportunity to choose their own mentors select people who share similar characteristics or backgrounds. In particular, research on natural mentors suggests that young people tend to seek mentors from the same racial or ethnic background. This preference for *same-race* mentors applies to protégés from diverse backgrounds, such as urban, Latino, and African American pregnant and parenting teens (Klaw & Rhodes, 1995; Sanchez & Colon, 2005), and White American (Cavell, Meehan, Heffer, & Holladay, 2002) and African American (Jackson, Kite, & Branscombe, 1996) college students. Indeed, Latino students who were matched with mentors of the same ethnicity perceived their mentors to be more helpful in furthering their personal and career development; and they were more satisfied with their mentor programs than were students who had mentors of different ethnicity (Santos & Reigadas, 2000). Moreover, Black mentors compared to White mentors more often tended to initiate connections with Black protégés, to play a beneficial role in their personal and professional development (Kalbfleisch & Davies, 1991), and to evoke perceptions of credibility and cultural competence (Grant-Thompson & Atkinson, 1997).

Similarly, girls and boys from various ethnic groups, including Latino American (Sanchez & Reyes, 1999), overseas Chinese, and White American (Chen, Greenberger, Farruggia, Bush, & Dong, 2003), tended to choose *same-sex* mentors. Indeed, perceived similarity has been associated with protégés' level of satisfaction with the relationship and mentors' liking of protégés (Ensher & Murphy, 1997).

Cultural fit.   Cultural values may also play a role in the types of mentors that are sought after by youth from diverse backgrounds. For example, Sanchez and Colon (2005) posit that the cultural values of collectivism and individualism may determine whether youth are more likely to seek familial vs. nonfamilial mentors, respectively.

These values may also influence youth's styles of interaction and help-seeking tendencies. Collectivism has been defined as a culturally held value where the needs of the collective (i.e., community or family) are prioritized over those of the individual (Marin & Marin, 1991); in contrast, individualism places the needs of the individual first. Research demonstrates that collectivism is associated with high levels of interdependence, conformity, and mutual responsibility (Marin & Triandis, 1985). In particular, those who are collectivistic tend to rely on family members for support. Individualism, on the other hand, has been associated with self-reliance. Thus, youth from individualistic backgrounds may be more open to one-to-one relationships with adults outside the family, whereas those from collectivistic backgrounds may feel more comfortable with multiple mentors who are members of their own extended family and close friendship networks, including older siblings, aunts, uncles, family friends, or community leaders.

In this vein, researchers have found that minorities and females are more likely to have a wide network of individuals who are from varied backgrounds both racially and organizationally, rather than one traditional mentor (Ensher & Murphy, 1997). Thus, mentoring programs that emphasize one-on-one relationships between youth and adult strangers may feel less accessible to youth from collectivistic backgrounds, such as Asian American, Latino(a) American, and other ethnic minority youth. Instead, such youth may be more drawn to programs that support mentoring from multiple individuals in their existing social networks (Sanchez & Colon, 2005).

Mutual chemistry. Regardless of a protégé's preferences for a certain type of mentor, whether she is able to attain one at all apart from a program may partly depend on mutual self-selection and "interpersonal chemistry" (Carroll, Feren, & Olian, 1987; Kalbfleisch & Davies, 1993). Voluntary mentoring relationships have been likened to love relationships (Levinson, 1978) and intimate peer friendships that evolve from initial interactions (Kalbfleisch, 1993). Indeed, research suggests that mentors and protégés in natural settings select each other: when mentors initiate these relationships, it is often because protégés have successfully attracted them through interpersonal skills or communication competence, and expressions of interest and self-esteem (Kalbfleisch & Davies, 1993; Missirian, 1982).

Given that personal attributes, such as styles of interaction with potential mentors, appear to play a vital role in forming mentoring relationships, it is important to examine potential cultural differences in these areas that may aid or inhibit the process of attaining a mentor. Culture dramatically influences norms and expectations regarding relationships between young people and their elders or respected, nonkin adults (Nakagawa, Lamb, & Miyaki, 1992; Posada et al., 1995). For example, Western cultural values encourage autonomy-seeking behavior in children (Taub, 1997), whereas Eastern cultural values foster more interdependent relationships between youth and attachment figures (e.g., Fuligni, 1998). In Asian girls, interdependency has been associated with decreased autonomy and assertiveness; each of these characteristics is consistent with Asian values, which emphasize interdependence and respect among in-group members (Harrison, Wilson, Pine, Chan, & Buriel, 1990).

Therefore, even if they are interested in a mentoring relationship, some Asian or Asian American youth may tend not to initiate or verbalize their wishes in mentor relationships, especially those they consider as hierarchical. Because of such cultural differences in the way that interest is or is *not* expressed among Asian or other ethnic minority youth, potential cross-race mentors may have trouble detecting a potential protégé's interest, need, and liking. Consequently, given the role of mutual self-selection in forming natural mentor relationships, Asian Americans, compared to their European American peers, may be less successful in forming such relationships.

How Available are Same-sex and Same-race Mentors?

The literature discussed thus far suggests reasons why youth who have the luxury of choosing their own mentors may gravitate toward those of the same sex, same race, or similar cultural background (Sanchez & Colon, 2005). However, in formal mentoring programs, same-race and same-sex matching is often limited by the pool of available mentors. Currently, while youth served in mentor programs represent diverse backgrounds, adults who volunteer to be mentors are predominately White women (Sanchez & Colon, 2005). Many programs report difficulties in recruiting mentors of color, particularly men (Rhodes, 2002b). Some studies indicate that the availability of ethnic minority mentors may vary by setting. Specifically, mentors of color may more often serve as natural mentors in schools, workplaces, and churches than as volunteers in formal mentoring programs (AOL Time Warner Foundation, 2002, as cited in Sanchez & Colon, 2005). Of the formal mentoring programs, school-based compared to community-based settings have been more successful in recruiting ethnic minority mentors (Herrera, Sipe, & McClanahan, 2000).

Relational Processes

Little research has explicitly focused on the *process* of mentoring (Rhodes, 2002b). Even less work has examined variations in this process in youth from diverse backgrounds (Langhout, Rhodes, & Osborne, 2004; Rhodes, 2002b). However, several existing theories provide some insight into gender and cultural differences in the way that mentors and protégés relate to each other. In the following sections, we discuss gender and race influences that affect relationship processes in general (e.g., ways of relating to peers, parents, or other significant relationships). These sections are followed by discussions of gender and race influences on mentoring processes in particular. That is, how do gender and race impact engagement, intimacy, and other aspects of relating among mentors and protégés?

Gender Influences on General Relationship Processes

Gender theories and research have suggested that social, institutional, and cultural influences in the United States foster independence and autonomy in boys but inter dependence and relatedness in girls (Bakan, 1966; Cross & Madson, 1997; Maccoby, 1990; Markus & Oyserman, 1989). Some feminist authors suggest that girls are much more relational than are boys and that they place greater emphasis on being connected or experiencing "we-ness" (Gilligan, 1982; Mansfield, McAllister, & Collard, 1992). Indeed, some research shows that girls' relationships, compared to those of boys, are characterized by greater intimacy (Buhrmester, 1990), empathy (Tannen,

1990), and attunement to differences (Grazyk & Henry, 2001). Moreover, boys and girls reported different expectations for their friendships, with the latter seeking more intimacy, empathy, and self-disclosure (Clark & Ayers, 1993).

Not only does research suggest gender differences in expressed expectations for close relationships, it also suggests differences in boys' and girls' help-seeking tendencies. In general, adolescents discussed personal problems with friends, but discussed other issues, such as academic difficulties, with their parents (Sullivan, Marshall, & Schonert-Reichl, 2002). Girls, however, tended to have a more positive view of help-seeking than boys (Garland & Zigler, 1994). Girls were also more likely to seek support to help solve a problem with a friend (Sullivan et al., 2002), or to deal with stressful situations (Greenberger & McLaughlin, 1998). Moreover, in times of need, girls relied more on *emotional* support than did boys, but did not differ in levels of seeking *instrumental* support (Greenberger & McLaughlin, 1998).

Even though boys and girls might differ in "relational styles," relationships may carry similar importance for each group. In one study, boys reported as much satisfaction in their closest relationships as did girls (Parker & Asher, 1993). Moreover, Bergman (1996) has suggested that, in theory, males may be just as likely as females to value engaged, authentic, and empowering relationships. The caveat is that these qualities may be expressed differently in males. For example, rather than simply "being together" or "talking about the relationship," boys may prefer "doing together" (Pollack, 1999); but the point remains that each of these different processes results in building relationships.

Gender Influences on Mentoring Processes

Although little research explicitly examines boys' and girls' relational styles with mentors, the existing work suggests possible gender differences in styles. Two styles of mentoring have been identified in the youth mentoring literature: instrumental and psychosocial (Flaxman, Ascher, & Harrington, 1988). The *instrumental* style of mentoring involves advising the protégé about practical issues that relate to his or her success (e.g., career advancement, academic, involvement in risky behaviors, etc.). The *psychosocial* style emphasizes the interpersonal relationship between the mentor and the protégé through which the latter receives emotional support. Thus, while instrumental mentoring is more problem focused, a psychosocial mentoring relationship focuses more on the process. In a similar vein, Morrow and Styles (1995) identified two styles of mentoring: *prescriptive* mentors typically approached the relationship by attempting to change the youth's behavior in concrete ways (e.g., improving study habits), whereas *developmental* mentors emphasized establishing a friendship with their protégés by being flexible and supportive.

Research on adolescent girls suggests that they highly value and benefit from relationships with mentors that are characterized by psychosocial qualities, such as empathy, authenticity, and intimacy (Liang, Tracy, Taylor, & Williams, 2002; Sullivan, 1996). However, despite the literature on relationships in general, and research on adult mentoring in corporate settings suggesting that instrumental mentoring may be more common in male matches and psychosocial mentoring in female matches, little research has explicitly examined gender differences in youth mentoring style. Interestingly, one study on Big Brothers Big Sisters programs showed that male matches were actually more likely than female matches to have developmental relationships (Morrow & Styles, 1995). Explanations for this finding have focused on the nature of the participants (e.g., girls in the program had more behavioral problems than did boys) and program structure (e.g., the program tends to emphasize activities over talking, which may foster more satisfying friendships for males than for females), rather than a lack of desire or interest in developmental relationships among females (Bogat & Liang, 2005).

Ethnicity/Race Influences on General Relationship Processes

It is unclear whether the gender differences in relationship processes discussed above generalize beyond middle-class, Euro-American youth to diverse populations. Very limited research on relationship processes in youth examines gender differences across cultures, and existing studies are equivocal. Some research suggests that gender differences apply to youth from different ethnic and cultural backgrounds. For example, in a study examining the relationships of American and Taiwanese youth, girls compared to boys in both countries showed more caring for others, and more connectedness in all types of relationships (Karcher & Lee, 2002). Similarly, in a study of Latino American, African American, and Asian American youth in the US, girls in all three ethnic groups reported closer friendships than did their male counterparts (Way & Chen, 2000). On the other hand, in the same study, gender differences in the *level of general support* from friends varied across ethnic groups; girls compared to boys reported more support in the Latino American group, whereas African American and Asian American youth showed no gender differences. In another US study, girls had more peer support than boys in the European American sample, but not in the African American sample (DuBois & Hirsch, 1990). Other studies that add socioeconomic status to gender and race comparisons further complicate the picture. For example, White American and African American girls from middle-class backgrounds showed higher levels of self-disclosure in peer relationships than did those from low-income backgrounds (Way & Pahl, 2001). Thus, these studies, taken together, suggest complex interactions between gender, race, and socioeconomic status as they shape relational processes.

Ethnicity/Race Influences on Mentoring Relationship Processes

The quality of mentoring relationships may be shaped by the way race-related issues are negotiated by mentor–protégé pairs. For example, cross-race matches may be affected by the degree of cultural sensitivity on the part of the mentor, cultural mistrust on the part of the protégé, and feedback provided to the protégé (Sanchez & Colon, 2005). One study of African Americans in late adolescence working with White mentors showed that the closeness and effectiveness of the match could be affected by *how* feedback from mentors is given to protégés (Cohen, Steele, & Ross, 1999). Critical feedback was interpreted negatively by protégés when not accompanied by comments about the high standards used in judging the work and general praise indicating a belief in the protégé's ability to meet such standards. This study suggests that an important dilemma for the mentor is how to give useful feedback in a way that is encouraging rather than discouraging. While this dilemma may be relevant in most mentoring relationships, it may have particular significance for minorities who often face negative stereotypes about their group's intelligence and ability to achieve. In turn, this stereotype threat may cause a decision about whether to increase or improve efforts at success seem risky. Whereas increased effort may improve the likelihood of better outcomes and success, it may also increase the cost of failure as such failure may suggest or confirm a lack of ability in the eyes of the mentor, as well as in the eyes of the protégé. As a result of such threat, instead of risking failure, protégés may withdraw from the task when they receive negative feedback. In addition, as further protection, protégés may begin to adopt the defense of disidentification.

Disidentification has been defined as a defense whereby one diminishes the importance of an area of achievement in order to protect one's self-esteem (Steele, 1997). For example, a teenager uncertain about his or her academic abilities may downplay the importance of attending school or doing his or her homework. Thus, disidentification can be helpful in temporarily maintaining self-esteem. Unfortunately, this defense can also limit future success that could have been brought about from improvements made in response to feedback, or limit positive risks taken that could generate feelings of competence and positive self-regard.

Cohen and colleagues (Cohen et al., 1999) proposed that in successful matches, mentors provide feedback to their protégés in a "wise" manner. The term "wise," coined by sociologist Erving Goffman (Goffman, 1963 as cited by Cohen et al., 1999), originally referred to the ability of individuals in the mainstream culture to see those in the subculture as full persons. Cohen and colleagues (Cohen et al., 1999) use this term to describe mentoring strategies that assure minority protégés that they will not be judged stereotypically, and that *assume*, rather than doubt, their competence and belonging.

On the other hand, mentors who are sensitive to a minority protégé's potential anxiety over evaluation and feedback might inadvertently over-praise him or her (Cohen et al., 1999). Although well intended, this unconditional positive regard, especially when coupled with lower expectations, may feel patronizing to the protégé and communicate a lack of confidence in the latter's ability to achieve more challenging goals. Thus, Cohen and colleagues (1999) proposed that a "wise" mentor should be encouraging while simultaneously maintaining high, yet achievable expectations.

Indeed, these theories and findings pertaining to ethnic minorities may have similar relevance for girls given stereotypes and societal expectations that assume lower levels of performance and career attainment among them relative to boys. Gender role expectations and stereotypes have often resulted in occupations and careers that are disproportionately represented by individuals in one gender. For example, the science fields are dominated by males. Conversely, occupations that emphasize nurturing or caring for others, such as nursing or social work, are dominated by females. These skews in gender may be related to stereotypes about the abilities of males and females. While gender role stereotypes may influence a protégé's career choice, the mentor's beliefs about gender roles may also impact on the protégé's career path as the mentor may unconsciously encourage or discourage certain careers based on the protégé's gender.

Benefits of Mentoring Relationships

Despite the intuitive appeal of mentoring for girls and boys from diverse backgrounds, many questions remain about its efficacy and how it achieves any beneficial outcomes. In a world of limited resources, proponents of mentoring have been increasingly challenged to substantiate the claims of effectiveness in mentoring programs, and to identify what types of mentoring relationships are beneficial. Indeed, research does not demonstrate that just *any* mentoring relationship or program is able to produce benefits for young people (Sipe, 1996).

Studies based on primarily minority youth show mixed results (Rhodes, 2002b). Specifically, Big Brothers Big Sisters of America (BB/BS) data revealed that mentored youth compared to waitlist controls had lower levels of truancy, substance abuse, aggression, and better scholastic competence, as well as parent and peer relationships; however, it was later determined that effect sizes were small (.02 for the degree of change over time and .05 for the post-program difference between the treatment and control groups) (DuBois, Holloway, Valentine, & Cooper, 2002). In yet another reanalysis of these data, wide variations in effect size were noted when the *quality* of relationships was taken into account (Grossman & Rhodes, 2002). Similarly, other studies have linked the benefits of mentoring programs to the success and quality of the mentor–protégé match (Grossman & Johnson, 1998; Rhodes, Roffman, & Grossman, 2005). Such findings suggest the need to go beyond evaluations of treatment and control group differences and pre–post differences toward distinguishing between effective and ineffective mentor matches.

In general, research has shown that quality mentoring relationships are associated with important benefits in ethnic minority populations. Mentors can help youth from diverse backgrounds grow in socially accepted ways and influence their cognitive, interpersonal, and identity development (Galbo, 1986; Rhodes, 2002b). For example, mentored youth demonstrate improved school attendance (Grossman & Tierney, 1998) and academic achievement (Linnehan, 2001), and likelihood of graduating from high school (Klaw, Rhodes, & Fitzgerald, 2003). Moreover, they show reductions in delinquent behavior (Aseltine, Dupre, & Lamlein, 2000; Beam, Chen, & Greenberger, 2002; Davidson & Redner, 1988; Zimmerman, Bingenheimer, & Notaro, 2002) and increases in psychological well-being (McPartland & Nettles, 1991; Rhodes, Ebert, & Fischer, 1992). They also reveal improved relationships with their parents and peers (Rhodes, 2002b; Rhodes, Grossman, & Resch, 2000).

The success of mentoring programs, however, may vary across gender and race. Some studies indicate that the mentor relationships of girls and minorities do not last as long as those of boys and White youth in general. Specifically, in a large BB/BS study (Grossman & Rhodes, 2002), same-race minority matches did not last as long as same-race White matches, but these findings did not hold with respect to minority dyads that were matched explicitly for race. Similarly, although cross-race minority matches did not last as long as same-race White matches, these findings did not hold when dyads were matched for similarity of interests. The authors suggest that such findings may be due to the greater stress associated with being a female or a minority which may make relationships harder to sustain. Fortunately, in this study it appeared that some of these risks might be overcome by carefully matching minority youth and mentors. Another theory regarding matching by sex and/or race relates to the degree of perceived or actual similarity between mentor and protégé. This concept is explicated in the similarity-attraction paradigm (Byrne, 1971), which links the probability of individuals liking each other to perceptions of similarity. This theory was supported in relation to both sex and race by a study of summer interns and their staff protégés in a career mentoring setting, although perceived similarity was not necessarily based on demographic characteristics (Ensher & Murphy, 1997).

Benefits for Same-race vs. Cross-race Matches

Some research has examined the relative benefits of same-race and cross-race matches. Most of this work is based on formal mentor versus natural mentor relationships. Further, existing studies fail to compare various combinations of dyads, such as minority mentor–White protégé vs. White mentor–minority protégé and minority mentors paired with protégés from different minority backgrounds (e.g., Asian mentor–African American protégé). In a study of 190 African American, Latino, American Indian, and Asian American youth, Rhodes and colleagues (Rhodes, Reddy, Grossman, & Lee, 2002) compared same-race and cross-race matches (where mentors were White American). When matches were based on shared interests, geographic proximity, and the youth's and her parents' preferences for same-race pairs, no differences were found for the same-race and cross-race groups in the frequency of meetings and duration of relationships. Another study revealed that youth in same-race matches compared to those in cross-race matches reported receiving more instrumental support, but not more psychosocial support (Ensher & Murphy, 1997). Also, matching by race was not associated with youth's satisfaction with their mentors. Instead, this study suggested that protégés in cross-race matches might be just as satisfied as those in same-race matches if they perceive themselves to be similar to mentors in other ways.

Interestingly, when gender was taken into account, greater benefits for same-race matches were found (Rhodes et al., 2002). Specifically, compared to their counterparts in cross-race matches, boys in same-race matches were more likely to demonstrate increases in academic competence and self-esteem; girls in same-race matches were more likely to show increases in school value and self-esteem. There is no definitive evidence, however, of the superiority of same-race matches; the reported results may be due to differences in the benefits of same-sex versus cross-race relationships.

Benefits of Same-sex vs. Cross-sex Matches

Little research exists regarding the relative benefits of same-sex vs. cross-sex pairs in naturally occurring mentoring relationships. Mentoring program research provides only slightly more evidence regarding these issues. Indeed, most community-based mentoring programs match youth with a same-sex mentor (DuBois et al., 2002; Herrera et al., 2000). Owing to the shortage of male mentors, those that allow cross-sex matches tend to pair female mentors with male protégés, but not male mentors with female protégés. Thus, it is difficult to assess the benefits of same-sex pairs relative to different combinations of cross-sex pairings. Findings from a few existing studies comparing these benefits show mixed results. In two meta-analyses, there was no difference in outcomes based on sex matching. The first meta-analysis revealed that matching on sex was *not* a moderator of program effect size (DuBois et al., 2002). The second one showed no differences in ratings of closeness and supportiveness when protégés in community-based and school-based programs were paired with cross-sex vs. same-sex mentors (Herrera et al., 2000). It is important to note, however, that the percentage of cross-gender matches was small in both the community- and the school-based programs (11% and 23%, respectively) and male mentors were rarely matched with female protégés in each type of program (1% and 3%, respectively).

In contrast, another study (in which the number of male mentor–female protégé matches was too small to analyze) showed evidence of potential benefits associated with same-sex matching for boys (Novotney, Mertinko, Lange, & Baker, 2000). Specifically, male mentors in same-sex mentoring relationships, compared to female mentors in cross-sex mentoring relationships, were more likely to report that the mentoring relationship had helped boys to avoid drugs, alcohol, fights, gangs, weapons, and poor peer influences. Nevertheless, there were no differences in how well same-sex vs. cross-sex paired boys liked their mentors or felt understood by them.

In the national evaluation of the BB/BS program (in which only same-sex matches are made), ethnic-minority youth in same-race and same-sex matches had less deterioration in scholastic indicators and self-worth than did those in cross-race matches over the course of a year (Rhodes, Reddy, Grossman, & Lee, 2003). Thus, for youth in same-sex matches, equally positive outcomes from mentoring result when the match is also same-race. It is important to note, though, that given the study's methodology (set by program practices), one cannot be sure whether the effects were related to the sex of the mentor, sex of the protégé, or the same-sex match. Thus, although programs may prefer to match youth to same-race and same-sex mentors (especially when parents or their children request them), when these are not available, cross-matching may be a viable alternative to wait-listing youth for long periods of time. Cross-matched mentors, however, may require additional preparation and ongoing supervision to ensure a satisfying and rewarding result.

Gender- and Culturally-sensitive Mentor Programs

Although many programs that consider gender and race important attempt to match mentors and protégés on these variables, several programs go beyond simply matching by sex and race by integrating information related to culture and gender into their program curricula. In this section, three such programs are described. The Rural After-School Program represents a culturally sensitive mentoring program that expressly integrates cultural values as part of its framework. The Brothers Project (Royse, 1998) and the Girl World Builders (GWB) are single-sex mentoring programs that are explicitly designed to address the gender-specific needs of young people.

Rural After-School Program

Despite the fact that many matches were cross-race and cross-sex, the Rural After-School Program for Latino(a) youth described by Diversi and Mecham (2005) represents a culturally sensitive program that closely analyzed the potential pitfalls of cross matching and worked to integrate cultural values into mentor training and the program curriculum. All protégés in this program were immigrant Latino eighth and ninth graders, and most mentors, with the exception of three Latino college men, were White American college women. Specifically, this program was designed to address school failure, identified behavioral difficulties, and language and cultural issues among Latino(a) youth in a predominately White area.

As described by Diversi and Mecham (2005), this mentoring program was theoretically grounded in an empowerment model, based on models of conscientization (Freire, 1970), and reconstructing cultural narratives and ethnic identity toward bicultural success (Collins, 1991; Richardson, 1990). Therefore, mentors were trained in cultural and developmental issues, such as immigration, adolescent development, acculturation, and ethnicity. Together mentors and protégés not only worked on school projects and tests, but also on acculturation issues and awareness of biculturalism (e.g., code switching, Spanglish, rap cultures, racism in the community, and social perspective taking). Protégés had positive perspectives on the program, enjoying the camaraderie of mentors and other peers in the program, and crediting their mentor relationships for positive influences on their academic and personal lives. Mentors, for the most part, were gratified by the academic gains of the protégés, as well as the trusting relationships experienced with many of them. Interestingly, however, some described cultural differences to be a source of tension and misunderstanding. For example, the public display of affection among Latino(a)s made some mentors uncomfortable. Also, cultural differences in the concept of property became an issue in some matches. Specifically, some youths would "borrow" something from their mentors without asking permission, assuming that what was "out on the table" was openly available for sharing in the group.

Youth participating in this program also identified cultural tensions in their assessment of their mentoring relationships. Cultural tensions can occur on both individual and systemic levels. For example, mentors who had protégés facing extensive racism, poverty, or violence were more likely to take on crisis management roles, which contributed to rapid mentor burnout and increased stress in the mentor relationship (Ginwright, 2005). Ginwright also discussed cultural influences on working-class youth's decision-making roles in their own families, which may involve youth taking on adult responsibilities given the changes in welfare regulation, etc. For these youth, progressive mentoring models of shared youth responsibility may be perceived as stressful and burdensome, rather than as empowering. Another challenge recognized within the Rural After-School Program related to mentoring efforts to empower Latino(a) students by fostering a bicultural identity (i.e., supporting ties to youths' native language, rituals, and history, while encouraging youth to learn to navigate their host culture) (Phinney, Horenczyk, Liebkind, & Vedder, 2001). Although individual mentors supported these practices, the mentoring program was not structurally designed to address these cultural issues or structural inequities within youth's schools and other social systems. This program shortcoming carried the potential for perpetuating isolation among participating youth (Diversi & Mecham, 2005). Together, the individual and systemic difficulties exemplified by the Rural After-School Program highlight the need to understand and address youth's multiple contexts in order to provide culturally responsive mentoring interventions.

Brothers Project

The Brothers Project (Royse, 1998) matched at-risk, African American males between the ages of 14 and 16 with volunteer male mentors. Most matches lasted around 15 months. The program involved individual meetings with mentors, as well as group activities for all participants. Besides emphasizing the program purpose of providing youth with a good role model, there is little published information describing the mentoring process or goals. Results from a program evaluation indicated no significant differences between the mentored boys and those in the control group.

Girl World Builders (GWB)

GWB, designed specifically for girls by BB/BS in Chicago, has clearly delineated processes and goals. For example, that this program is coordinated entirely by women leverages the relational strengths of adolescent girls by engaging them in one-on-one mentoring with women volunteers. Moreover, the program places these relationships in a supportive group context through engaging mentor pairs in regular workshops. The GWB program also focuses on fostering self-worth and self-efficacy in an attempt to prevent common psychological risks among girls (Davis, Paxton, & Robinson, 1997). DuBois and colleagues (DuBois, personal communication, July 27, 2004) are working to increase GWB's potential for building self-esteem through the development of activities for both mentors and protégés that expressly target self-worth (e.g., workshop activities emphasizing girls' self-esteem, body, image, and gender identity). Through training workshops for mentors, the latter learn strategies and gain confidence in working with girls around gender-specific issues.

   Programs such as those described above may be important and relevant for either girls or boys. Program staff should be trained in sex equity so that they do not inadvertently deliver cues consistent with sex stereotypes. Nicholson (1991) argues that differential treatment in youth development programs may serve to perpetuate sex differences in interests and skills. Thus, program staff must be aware of the potential risks inherent in single-sex programs for undermining gender equity and perpetuating gender differences (Hughes, 2000; O'Neill, Horton, & Crosby, 1999).

Future Directions

Synthesis

In this chapter, based on literature in and out of the field of mentoring, we have shown that race and gender might affect: a) the accessibility and availability of best-fitting mentor relationships, b) the relational processes or ways of relating between protégés and their mentors, and c) the benefits obtained in same-race, same-sex matches vs. cross-race, cross-sex matches. We also have proposed that even when same-race, same-sex matches may be desired, they may not be necessary to achieve satisfying and beneficial mentoring relationships. For example, some research shows that having similar interests and attitudes may be an even better predictor of protégés' satisfaction with, and support received from, their mentors than is demographic similarity

(Ensher, Grant-Vallone, & Marelich, 2002; Ensher & Murphy, 1997; Grossman & Rhodes, 2002). Thus, research should be done to examine the impact of mentoring programs that prioritize cultural and gender competency training and culturally specific and gender specific program practices. Currently, gender-, race- and culture-sensitive approaches to mentoring are in short supply. The gender-, race- and culture-based trends noted in this chapter may not necessarily generalize to programs that are designed to meet the unique needs of youth across gender and race or ethnicity.

Moreover, most of the extant research on same-sex, cross-sex, and same-race, cross-race dyads fails to compare various dyadic combinations of mentor–protégé race and gender. For example, cross-race mentorships in which the minority is the mentor may be very different from cross-race mentorships in which the minority is the protégé. Likewise, same-sex mentorships comprised of two females are likely to differ from same-sex mentorships comprised of two males.

These caveats suggest the need for closer examination of various combinations of demographic variables that may affect the goodness of fit between youth and their mentors. Specifically, research methodologies may do well to include more comprehensive designs with observations in all cells: female minority mentor–female minority protégé, female white mentor–female white protégé, male minority mentor–male minority protégé, male white mentor–male white protégé, etc. In sum, the chapter suggests increasing attention to issues having to do with gender and race/ethnicity or other aspects of diversity in the design and evaluation of mentoring programs.

Recommendations for Research

Based on existing research in and out of the field of mentoring discussed thus far, we highlight the following three major areas for future study.

Beyond sex, ethnicity, and race, study how mentoring relationships vary by other demographic and diverse characteristics (e.g., socioeconomic status, immigrant status, sexual orientation, physical disability). While this chapter focuses on the effects of sex and race in mentoring relationships, other areas of difference may be equally important to consider. Unfortunately, little research has explored the effects of other diverse characteristics on mentoring relationships. Initial exploration of these issues suggests complex interactions between demographic characteristics and multiple aspects of a youth's identity (Rhodes, 2002b). These findings highlight the importance of understanding the unique interplay of intrapersonal and interpersonal characteristics. Indeed, variables beyond gender and ethnicity and race may interact with individuals' identity development and psychosocial health to determine the formation of, ways of relating in, needs within, and benefits of mentoring relationships. For example, research indicates that immigrant adolescents struggle with acculturative stress and discrimination, which in turn negatively relate to self-esteem and psychological adjustment (Jasinskaja-Lahti & Liebkind, 2001; Rumbaut, 1994). An understanding of the unique struggles of immigrant youth may thus enable mentors to target areas of vulnerability in this population. Moreover, the same understanding may help mentors to be sensitive to differences in protégés' expectations related to seeking and engaging mentors (Liang, Tracy, Kauh, Taylor, & Williams, 2006).

Identify aspects of the mentoring relationship that are important across diverse populations of youth. In general, research indicates that positive youth outcomes in psychological, social, and academic domains are associated with *quality* mentoring relationships (Beam et al., 2002; Klaw et al., 2003; McPartland & Nettles, 1991). Although the nature and benefits of quality mentoring relationships vary to some degree across gender and race, research suggests that some characteristics of mentoring relationships may be universally beneficial. For example, relational qualities, including mutual engagement, authenticity, empowerment, and learning to cope with conflict, have been identified as critical to growth-fostering relationships (Jordan, 1992, 1997; Miller & Stiver, 1997). Indeed, such qualities have been associated with positive outcomes among adolescent females (Liang et al., 2002; Sullivan, 1996), but may also be relevant for their male counterparts (Bergman, 1996). Moreover, the duration of mentoring relationships also predicts mentoring outcomes, with longer matches leading to greater benefits and reduced harm among youth (Rhodes, 2002b). Perceived similarity represents a third critical category associated with successful mentoring relationships. Similarity may be indicated by qualities such as shared interests and geographic proximity, both of which predict the longevity of matches (Rhodes et al., 2002). These characteristics represent an initial exploration of universal characteristics of quality mentoring relationships and support the importance of relationship characteristics beyond demographic matching of mentor and protégé. More research is needed to identify additional aspects of effective mentoring relationships and their application to diverse youth populations.

Develop new assessment instruments that are valid for youth from diverse backgrounds. The lack of research assessing gender, racial/ethnic, and other group differences may in part be due to limitations in the measurement of mentoring processes and constructs. With few exceptions (Liang et al., 2002; Rhodes, 2002b), most mentoring relationship measures rely on a global index or a few, atheoretical dimensions (for a review, see Nakkula & Harris, 2005). Thus, although such measures may reflect many activities or qualities that seem to be salient in youth mentoring, because they tend not to be theory-based they are at risk for missing aspects important for comparing different populations. Indeed, it would be useful to explore whether mentoring comprises separate dimensions that differentially relate to outcomes depending on gender or ethnic background. For example, giving youth choice over activities might be more important when mentoring youth from individualistic vs. collectivistic cultures, in light of cross-cultural theory that emphasizes differing levels of emphasis on autonomy and agency across cultures.

Recommendations for Practice

Design mentoring programs that are sensitive to theory and research on the gender and cultural characteristics of youth populations served. Studies indicate that a one-size-fits-all approach is not always effective for mentoring relationships (Grossman & Johnson, 1998; Rhodes et al., 2005). While many qualities of mentoring relationships may generalize across race, gender, and other diverse characteristics, these diverse characteristics may also present unique needs and opportunities for mentoring relationships. For example, girls and youth of color face challenges of sexism and racism, as well as other gender and culture-specific struggles that may negatively affect their school success and psychological well-being (Gonzales & Kim, 1997; Jasinskaja-Lahti & Liebkind, 2001), issues commonly targeted through mentoring programs (Linnehan, 2001). Thus, mentoring that takes into account gender, cultural, and racial issues may support these youth in ways that may be less relevant to majority youth. The Girl World Builders program, for instance, specifically targets psychological risk factors for girls, focusing on body image, gender identity, and self-esteem (DuBois et al., in press). Combining traditional aspects of mentoring programs with responsiveness to the diverse backgrounds and needs of mentored youth may enhance the applicability and effectiveness of mentoring relationships.

Provide training and ongoing support to mentors characterized by special attention to gender and cultural issues. Research documents that mentoring outcomes reflect more than simply the race and gender match between mentor and protégé; they reflect the ways in which mentors respond to multiple characteristics of the protégé. This includes aspects of a protégé's racial and gender identity. Research indicates that cross-race and cross-gender pairs can be successful when mentors are culturally competent (Sanchez & Colon, 2005). Without training in specific competencies, the most well-intentioned mentors may make critical errors that negatively impact these relationships (Rhodes, 2002b). However, ongoing training and support can help mentors better understand and relate to protégés of diverse backgrounds, and create more positive protégé outcomes, as demonstrated by the Rural After-School Program for Latino/a youth (Diversi & Mecham, 2005). Mentor training is critical given the shortage of same-sex, same-race mentors, particularly for males and youth of color (Rhodes, 2002b).

Foster close and satisfying mentor matches, regardless of the diverse backgrounds of mentors and protégés. Consistent with research identifying characteristics associated with quality mentoring relationships, the practice of mentoring should include attention to developmental and relational processes, enduring mentor commitments, and exploration of similarities between mentor and protégé. Relational aspects of mentoring include mutual engagement, authenticity, empowerment, and learning to cope with conflict (Jordan, 1992, 1997; Miller & Stiver, 1997). To foster these types of relationships, mentors must recognize and thoughtfully engage with both the strengths and struggles of their protégés, in ways that promote their growth and development, as in Cohen and colleagues' description of a "wise" mentor (Cohen et al., 1999). Mentoring relationships may also benefit from a developmental rather than a prescriptive approach to mentor relationships: one that allows for protégé self-exploration, goal-setting, and mutual relationship development, rather than imposing goals for the mentoring relationship. One aspect of mutuality involves shared characteristics and interests. Exploration of commonalities can serve as an early and central step in connecting with a protégé, and may form a base for lasting relationship development (Ensher & Murphy, 1997; Rhodes et al., 2002). Recruitment of mentors should target individuals who possess these relational qualities, value developmental aspects of mentor–protégé relationships, and are willing and able to invest time and energy in the mentoring process (for example, mentors with limited participation of only one semester related to a course or other context may have limited potential to engage in a meaningful relationship with their protégés). Mentor training would be enhanced by exploration of relational constructs and guidance regarding their practical application to mentor–protégé relationships.

References

AOL Time Warner Foundation (2002). *Mentoring in America.* New York: Author.

Aseltine, R. H. Jr., Dupre, M., & Lamlein, P. (2000). Mentoring as a drug prevention strategy: An evaluation of *Across Ages. Adolescent & Family Health, 1,* 11–20.

Bakan, D. (1966). *The duality of human existence.* Chicago: Rand McNally.

Balcazar, F. E., Majors, R., Blanchard, K. A., & Paine, A. (1991). Teaching minority high school students to recruit helpers to attain personal and educational goals. *Journal of Behavioral Education, 1,* 445–454.

Beam, M. R., Chen, C., & Greenberger, E. (2002). The nature of adolescents' relationships with their "very important" nonparental adults. *American Journal of Community Psychology, 30,* 305–325.

Bergman, S. (1996). Men's psychological development: A relational perspective. In R. F. Levant & W. Pollack (Eds.), *A new psychology of men* (pp. 68–90). New York: Basic Books. Blechman, E. A. (1992). Mentors for high-risk minority youth: Effective communication to bicultural competence. *Journal of Clinical Child Psychology, 21,* 160–169.

Bogat, G. A., & Liang, B. (2005). Gender in mentoring relationships. In D. L. DuBois & M. J. Karcher (Eds.), *Handbook of youth mentoring* (pp. 205–217). Thousand Oaks, CA: Sage.

Buhrmester, D. (1990). Intimacy of friendship, interpersonal competence, and adjustment during preadolescence and adolescence. *Child Development, 61,* 1101–1111.

Byrne, D. (1971). *The attraction paradigm.* New York: Academic Press.

Carroll, S., Feren, D., & Olian, J. (1987). Reactions to the new minorities by employees of the future: An experimental study. *Psychological Reports, 60,* 911–920.

Cavell, T. A., Meehan, B. T., Heffer, R. W., & Holladay, J. J. (2002). The natural mentors of adolescent children of alcoholics (COAs): Implications for preventive practices. *Journal of Primary Prevention, 23,* 23–42.

Chen, C., Greenberger, E., Farruggia, S., Bush, K., & Dong, Q. (2003). Beyond parents and peers: The role of important non-parental adults (VIPS) in adolescent development in China and the United States. *Psychology in the Schools, 40,* 35–50.

Clark, M. L., & Ayers, M. (1993). Friendship expectations and friendship evaluations: Reciprocity and gender effects. *Youth & Society, 24,* 299–313.

Cohen, G. L., Steele, C. M., & Ross, L. D. (1999). The mentor's dilemma: Providing critical feedback across the racial divide. *Personality and Social Psychology Bulletin, 25,* 1302–1318.

Collins, P. (1991). *Black feminist thought: Knowledge, consciousness, and the politics of empowerment.* New York: Routledge.

Cross, S. E., & Madson, L. (1997). Models of the self: Self-construals and gender. *Psychological Bulletin, 122,* 5–37.

Davidson, W. S. II, & Redner, R. (1988). The prevention of juvenile delinquency: Diversion from the juvenile justice system. In R. H. Price & E. L. Cowen (Eds.), *Fourteen ounces of prevention: A casebook for practitioners* (pp. 123–137). Washington, DC: American Psychological Association.

Davis, T., Paxton, K. C., & Robinson, L. (1997). *After school action programs: Girl World Builders summary report.* Unpublished manuscript, Department of Psychology, DePau University, Chicago.

Diversi, M., & Mecham, C. (2005). Latino(a) students and Caucasian mentors in a rural after-school program: Towards empowering adult–youth relationships. *Journal of Community Psychology, 33,* 31–40.

DuBois, D. L., & Hirsch, B. J. (1990). School and neighborhood friendship patterns of Blacks and Whites in early adolescence. *Child Development, 61,* 524–536.

DuBois, D. L., Holloway, B. E., Valentine, J. C., & Cooper, H. (2002). Effectiveness of mentoring programs for youth: A meta-analytic review. *American Journal of Community Psychology, 30*, 157–197.

DuBois, D. L., Silverthorn, N., Pryce, J., Reeves, E., Sanchez, B., Silva, A., Ansu, A. A., Haqq, S., & Takehara, J. (in press). Mentorship: The GirlPOWER! Program. To appear in C. W. Leroy & J. E. Mann (Eds.), *Handbook of preventive and intervention programs for adolescent girls*. Hoboken, NJ: Wiley.

Ensher, E. A., Grant-Vallone, E. J., & Marelich, W. D. (2002). Effects of perceived attitudinal and demographic similarity on protégés' support and satisfaction gained from their mentoring relationships. *Journal of Applied Social Psychology, 32*, 1407–1430.

Ensher, E. A., & Murphy, S. E. (1997). Effects of race, gender, perceived similarity, and contact on mentor relationships. *Journal of Vocational Behavior, 50*, 460–481.

Flaxman, E., Ascher, C., & Harrington, C. (1988). *Youth mentoring: Programs and practices.* New York: ERIC Clearinghouse on Urban Education, Institute for Urban and Minority Education, Teachers College, Columbia University.

Freire, P. (1970). *Pedagogy of the oppressed* (Myra Bergman Ramos, Trans; 29th anniversary ed.). New York: Continuum.

Fuligni, A. J. (1998). Authority, autonomy, and parent–adolescent conflict and cohesion: A study of adolescents from Mexican, Chinese, Filipino, and European backgrounds. *Developmental Psychology, 34*, 782–792.

Galbo, J. J. (1986). Adolescents' perceptions of significant adults: Implications for the family, the school and youth serving agencies. *Children & Youth Services Review, 8*, 37–51.

Garland, A., & Zigler, E. (1994). Psychological correlates of help-seeking attitudes among children and adolescents. *American Journal of Orthopsychiatry, 64*, 586–593.

Gilligan, C. (1982). *In a different voice: Psychological theory and women's development.* Cambridge, MA: Harvard University Press.

Ginwright, S. A. (2005). On urban ground: Understanding African American intergenerational partnerships in urban communities. *Journal of Community Psychology, 33*, 101–110.

Goffman, E. (1963). *Stigma: Notes on the management of a spoiled identity.* Englewood Cliffs, NJ: Prentice Hall.

Gonzales, N. A., & Kim, L. S. (1997). Stress and coping in an ethnic minority context: Children's cultural ecologies. In S. A. Wolchik & I. N. Sandler (Eds.), *Handbook of children's coping: Linking theory and intervention. Issues in clinical child psychology* (pp. 481–511). New York: Plenum Press.

Grant-Thompson, S., & Atkinson, D. (1997). Cross-cultural mentor effectiveness and African-American male students. *Journal of Black Psychology, 23*, 120–134.

Grazyk, P. A., & Henry, D. B. (2001). *A developmental perspective on the qualitative aspects of adolescent best friendships.* Paper presented at the Biennial meeting of the Society for Research in Child Development, Minneapolis, MN.

Greenberger, E., & McLaughlin, C. S. (1998). Attachment, coping, and explanatory style in late adolescence. *Journal of Youth and Adolescence, 27*, 121–140.

Grossman, J. B., & Johnson, A. W. (1998). Assessing the effectiveness of mentoring programs. In J. B. Grossman (Ed.), *Contemporary issues in mentoring* (pp. 25–47). Philadelphia: Public/Private Ventures.

Grossman, J. B., & Rhodes, J. E. (2002). The test of time: Predictors and effects of duration in youth mentoring relationships. *American Journal of Community Psychology, 30*, 199–219.

Grossman, J. B., & Tierney, J. P. (1998). Does mentoring work? An impact study of the Big Brothers Big Sisters program. *Evaluation Review, 22*, 403–426.

Harrison, A. O., Wilson, M. N., Pine, C. J., Chan, S. Q., & Buriel, R. (1990). Family ecologies of ethnic minority children. *Child Development, 61*(2), 347–362.

Herrera, C., Sipe, C. L., & McClanahan, W. S. (2000). *Mentoring school-age children: Relationship development in community-based and school-based programs.* Philadelphia: Public/Private Ventures.

Hughes, K. L. (2000). Gender and youth mentoring. *Advances in Gender Research, 4,* 189–225.

Jackson, C. H., Kite, M. E., & Branscombe, N. R. (1996). *African-American women's mentoring experiences.* Paper presented at annual meeting of the American Psychological Association, Toronto, Canada, August. (ERIC Document Reproduction Service No. ED 401 371)

Jasinskaja-Lahti, I., & Liebkind, K. (2001). Perceived discrimination and psychological adjustment among Russian-speaking immigrant adolescents in Finland. *International Journal of Psychology, 36,* 174–185.

Jordan, J. V. (1992). The relational self: A new perspective for understanding women's development. *Contemporary Psychotherapy Review, 7,* 56–71.

Jordan, J. V. (1997). A relational perspective for understanding women's development. In J. V. Jordan (Ed.), *Women's growth in diversity: More writings from the Stone Center* (pp. 9–24). New York: Guilford Press.

Kalbfleisch, P. (1993). *Interpersonal communication: Evolving interpersonal relationships.* Hillsdale, NJ: Lawrence Erlbaum Associates, Inc.

Kalbfleisch, P., & Davies, A. (1991). Minorities and mentoring: Managing the multicultural institution. *Communication Education, 40,* 266–271.

Kalbfleisch, P., & Davies, A. (1993). An interpersonal model of participation in mentoring relationships. *Western Journal of Communication, 57,* 399–415.

Karcher, M. J., & Lee, Y. (2002). Connectedness among Taiwanese middle school students: A validation study of the Hemingway Measure of Adolescent Connectedness. *Asia Pacific Education Review, 3,* 95–114.

Klaw, E. L., & Rhodes, J. E. (1995). Mentor relationships and the career development of pregnant and parenting African-American teenagers. *Psychology of Women Quarterly, 19,* 551–562.

Klaw, E. L., Rhodes, J. E., & Fitzgerald, L. F. (2003). Natural mentors in the lives of African American adolescent mothers: Tracking relationships over time. *Journal of Youth and Adolescence, 32,* 223–232.

Langhout, R. D., Rhodes, J. E., & Osborne, L. N. (2004). An exploratory study of youth mentoring in an urban context: Adolescents' perceptions of relationship styles. *Journal of Youth and Adolescence, 33,* 293–306.

Levinson, D. (1978). Major tasks of the novice phase. In *The seasons of a man's life* (pp. 97–101). New York: Knopf.

Liang, B., Tracy, A., Kauh, T., Taylor, C., & Williams, L. M. (2006). Mentoring Asian and White American College Women. *Journal of Multicultural Counseling and Development, 34,* 143–154.

Liang, B., Tracy, A. J., Taylor, C. A., & Williams, L. M. (2002). Mentoring college-age women: A relational approach. *American Journal of Community Psychology, 30,* 271–288.

Linnehan, F. (2001). The relation of a work-based mentoring program to the academic performance and behavior of African American students. *Journal of Vocational Behavior, 59,* 310–325.

Maccoby, E. E. (1990). Gender and relationships: A developmental account. *American Psychologist, 45,* 513–520.

MacDonald, K. E., Balcazar, F. E., & Keys, C. B. (2005). Youth with disabilities. In D. L. DuBois & M. J. Karcher (Eds.), *Handbook of youth mentoring* (pp. 493–508). Thousand Oaks, CA: Sage.

Mansfield, P., McAllister, F., & Collard, J. (1992). Equality: Implications for sexual intimacy in marriage. *Sexual & Marital Therapy, 7,* 213–220.

Marin, G., & Marin, B. V. (1991). *Research with Hispanic populations.* Newbury Park, CA: Sage.

Marin, G., & Triandis, H. C. (1985). Allocentrism as an important characteristic of the behavior of Latin Americans and Hispanics. In R. Diaz-Guerrero (Ed.), *Cross-cultural and national studies in social psychology* (pp. 85–104). Amsterdam: Elsevier Science.

Markus, H. R., & Oyserman, D. (1989). Gender and thought: The role of the self-concept. In M. Crawford & M. Gentry (Eds.), *Gender and thought: Psychological perspectives* (pp. 100–127). New York: Springer-Verlag.

Maton, K. I., Sto. Domingo, M. R. S., & King, J. (2005). Faith-based organizations. In D. L. DuBois & M. J. Karcher (Eds.), *Handbook of youth mentoring* (pp. 376–391). Thousand Oaks, CA: Sage.

McPartland, J. M., & Nettles, S. M. (1991). Using community adults as advocates or mentors for at-risk middle school students: A two-year evaluation of Project RAISE. *American Journal of Education, 99,* 568–586.

Miller, J. B., & Stiver, I. P. (1997). *The healing connection: How women form relationships in therapy and in life.* Boston: Beacon Press, Inc.

Missirian, A. K. (1982). *The corporate connection: Why executive women need mentors to reach the top.* Englewood Cliffs, NJ: Prentice-Hall.

Morrow, K. V., & Styles, M. B. (1995). *Building relationships with youth in program settings: A study of Big Brothers/Big Sisters.* Philadelphia: Public/Private Ventures.

Nakagawa, M., Lamb, M. E., & Miyaki, K. (1992). Antecedents and correlates of the Strange Situation behavior of Japanese infants. *Journal of Cross Cultural Psychology, 23,* 300–310.

Nakkula, M. J., & Harris, J. T. (2005). Assessment of mentoring relationships. In D. L. DuBois & M. J. Karcher (Eds.), *Handbook of youth mentoring* (pp. 100–117). Thousand Oaks, CA: Sage.

Nicholson, H. J. (1991). *Gender issues in youth development programs.* New York: Carnegie Council on Adolescent Development.

Novotney, L.C., Mertinko, E., Lange, J., & Baker, T. K. (2000). *Juvenile mentoring program: A progress review.* Washington, DC: US Department of Justice, Office of Justice Programs, Office of Juvenile Justice and Delinquency Prevention. Retrieved February 5, 2004, from http://www.ojjdp.ncjrs.org/jump/.

O'Neill, R. M., Horton, S., & Crosby, F. J. (1999). Gender issues in developmental relationships. In A. J. Murrell, F. J. Crosby, & R. J. Ely (Eds.), *Mentoring dilemmas: Developmental relationships within multicultural organizations. Applied social research* (pp. 63–80). Mahwah, NJ: Lawrence Erlbaum.

Parker, J. G., & Asher, S. R. (1993). Friendship and friendship quality in middle childhood: Links with peer group acceptance and feelings of loneliness and social dissatisfaction. *Developmental Psychology, 29,* 611–621.

Phinney, J., Horenczyk, G., Liebkind, K., & Vedder, P. (2001). Ethnic identity, immigration, and well-being: An interactional perspective. *Journal of Social Issues, 57,* 493–510.

Pollack, W. S. (1999). *Real boys: Rescuing our sons from the myths of boyhood.* Melbourne: Scribe Publications.

Posada, G., Gao, Y., Wu, F., Posada, R., Tascon, M., Schoelmersch, A., et al. (1995). The secure-base phenomenon across cultures: Children's behavior, mother's preferences, and experts' concepts. In E. Waters, B. Vaughn, G. Posada, & K. Kondo-Ikenura (Eds.), Caregiving, cultural, and cognitive perspective on secure-base behavior and working models. *Monographs of the Society for Research in Child Development, 60*(2–3), 27–48.

Richardson, L. (1990). *Writing strategies: Reaching diverse audiences.* Newbury Park, CA: Sage.

Rhodes, J. E. (2002b). *Stand by me: The risks and rewards of mentoring today's youth.* Cambridge, MA: Harvard University Press.

Rhodes, J. E., Ebert, L., & Fischer, K. (1992). Natural mentors: An overlooked resource in the social networks of young, African American mothers. *American Journal of Community Psychology, 20*(4), 445–461.

Rhodes, J. E., Grossman, J. B., & Resch, N. R. (2000). Agents of change: Pathways through which mentoring relationships influence adolescents' academic adjustment. *Child Development, 71,* 1662–1671.

Rhodes, J. E., Reddy, R., Grossman, J., & Lee, J. (2002). Volunteer mentoring relationships with minority youth: An analysis of same-versus cross-race matches. *Journal of Applied Social Psychology, 32,* 2114–2133.

Rhodes, J. E., Reddy, R., Grossman, J. B., & Lee, J. M. (2003). Same versus cross-race matches in mentoring programs: A comparison. *Journal of Applied Social Psychology, 32,* 2114–2133.

Rhodes, J. E., Roffman, J. G., & Grossman, J. B. (2005). Promoting successful youth mentoring relationships: A preliminary screening questionnaire, *Journal of Primary Prevention, 26,* 147–167.

Royse, D. (1998). Mentoring high-risk minority youth: Evaluation of the Brothers Project. *Adolescence, 33,* 145–158.

Rumbaut, R. (1994). The crucible within: Ethnic identity, self-esteem, and segmented assimilation among children of immigrants. *International Migration Review, 28,* 748–794.

Sanchez, B., & Colon, Y. (2005). Race, ethnicity, and culture in mentoring relationships. In D. L. DuBois & M. J. Karcher (Eds.), *Handbook of youth mentoring* (pp. 191–204). Thousand Oaks, CA: Sage.

Sanchez, B., & Reyes, O. (1999). Descriptive profile of the mentorship relationships of Latino adolescents. *Journal of Community Psychology, 27,* 299–302.

Santos, S., & Reigadas, E. (2000, February). *Evaluation of a university faculty mentoring program: Its effect on Latino college adjustment.* National Association of African American Studies & National Association of Hispanic and Latino Studies: 2000 Literature Monograph Series. Proceedings (Education Section). Houston, TX.

Sipe, C. (1996). *Mentoring: A synthesis of P/PV's research: 1988–1995.* Philadelphia: Public/Private Ventures. (ERIC Document Reproduction Service No. ED 404 410)

Steele, C. M. (1997). A threat in the air: How stereotypes shape the intellectual identities and performance of women and African Americans. *American Psychologist, 52,* 613–629.

Sullivan, A. M. (1996). From mentor to muse: Recasting the role of women in relationship with urban adolescent girls. In B. J. R. Leadbeater & N. Way (Eds.), *Urban girls: Resisting stereotypes, creating identities* (pp. 226–249). New York: New York University Press.

Sullivan, K., Marshall, S. K., & Schonert-Reichl, K. A. (2002). Do expectancies influence choice of help-giver?: Adolescents' criteria for selecting an informal helper. *Journal of Adolescent Research, 17,* 509–531.

Tannen, D. (1990). Gender differences in topical coherence: Creating involvement in best friends' talk. *Discourse Processes, 13,* 73–90.

Taub, D. J. (1997). Autonomy and parental attachment in traditional-age undergraduate women. *Journal of College Student Development, 38*(6), 645–654.

Way, N., & Chen, L. (2000). Close and general friendships among African American, Latino, and Asian American adolescents from low-income families. *Journal of Adolescent Research, 15,* 274–301.

Way, N., & Pahl, K. (2001). Individual and contextual predictors of perceived friendship quality among ethnic minority, low-income adolescents. *Journal of Research on Adolescence, 11,* 325–349.

Zimmerman, M. A., Bingenheimer, J. B., & Notaro, P. C. (2002). Natural mentors and adolescent resiliency: A study with urban youth. *American Journal of Community Psychology, 30,* 221–243.

Chapter 16

Mentoring in Academia: Considerations for Diverse Populations

William E. Sedlacek, Eric Benjamin, Lewis Z. Schlosser, and Hung-Bin Sheu

Mentoring has become widely accepted as an important process in professional development across a number of fields. In fact, theoretical and empirical research on mentoring has grown significantly in recent years. Some noteworthy areas include models of mentoring relationships, research on the mentor–protégé relationship, the process and outcomes of mentoring relationships, and dysfunctional mentoring, to name a few (Barnett, 1984; Bode, 1999; Healy & Welchert, 1990; Jacobi, 1991; Johnson & Huwe, 2003; Kram, 1985; Stafford & Robbins, 1991; Wilde & Schau, 1991). This increased attention to mentoring has improved the quantity and, more importantly, the quality of the research being conducted on mentoring. Therefore, it appears that mentoring is an important construct worthy of further discussion. In this chapter we will discuss research on mentoring in academic settings with an emphasis on diversity issues. We will then discuss a model for organizing and evaluating diversity-related mentoring, followed by examples of mentoring for African Americans and Asian Americans and conclude the chapter with some final comments.

Academic Focus

Because of the variety of arenas within which mentoring can occur, we believe that it is important to limit our work to retain a sharp focus. Hence, this chapter will concentrate on mentoring in academic settings, specifically the student–faculty relationship. Within academia, student–faculty relationships tend to be assigned, with the most common type being the advisor–advisee relationship in graduate school (Schlosser & Gelso, 2001; Schlosser, Knox, Moskovitz, & Hill, 2003; Schlosser, Talleyrand, Lyons, Kim, & Johnson, 2005). Research has shown that students almost always have an advisor (Schlosser & Gelso, 2001), but only 50 to 66% report having a mentor (Atkinson, Casas, & Neville, 1994; Clark, Harden, & Johnson, 2000; Cronan-Hillix, Davidson, Cronan-Hillix, & Gensheimer, 1986; Hollingsworth &

Fassinger, 2002; Johnson, Koch, Fallow, & Huwe, 2000). So, while our focus is on mentoring, it is important to note that many mentors are also advisors, and researchers have speculated that positive advising relationships and mentoring relationships are quite similar (Schlosser & Gelso, 2001; Schlosser & Gelso, 2005).

Graduate Training

In addition to focusing on academic settings, we are also limiting our review to mentoring relationships in graduate training. Although mentoring relationships can and do occur between student and faculty members at all levels of higher education, we are focusing on mentoring in graduate school for several reasons. First, the extant research on student–faculty mentoring is overwhelmingly focused on graduate-level mentoring relationships. Second, student–faculty mentoring relationships are an inherent part of graduate training models for many disciplines. Graduate school is typically viewed as an extension of the apprentice–master model of learning a trade; as such, it naturally follows that the relationship between mentor and protégé is of critical importance. Third, graduate-level mentoring relationships are qualitatively different than those at the undergraduate level. Mentors are likely to be more invested in their graduate student protégés than their undergraduate ones because a) the relationship will be longer with a graduate student protégé, b) many graduate student protégés will become colleagues with their mentors after graduation (Schlosser et al., 2003), and c) graduate student protégés come to their mentoring relationships with more complex and sophisticated thinking abilities than do their undergraduate counterparts. For all of these reasons, we are focusing on graduate-level mentoring relationships. That being said, some of our conclusions may be applicable to the undergraduate mentor–protégé relationship. Readers interested in undergraduate mentoring and diversity issues are directed to the relevant literature (e.g., Good, Halpin, & Halpin, 2000; Grant-Thompson & Atkinson, 1997; Kim, Goto, Bai, Kim, & Wong, 2001; Santos & Reigadas, 2002).

Mentoring and Advising

In preparing our work here, we reviewed relevant literature on both mentor–protégé and advisor–advisee relationships in graduate school. We chose this course because, as noted above and elsewhere, students are much more likely to have an advisor than they are to have a mentor, especially in academia where such relationships are formalized (Schlosser & Gelso, 2001). In addition, while advising and mentoring are not synonymous, they do share certain characteristics and thus the advising literature can be informative vis-à-vis mentoring. For example, a positive advising relationship is characterized by good advisor–advisee rapport and by the advisor facilitating the advisee's professional development (Schlosser & Gelso, 2001; Schlosser & Gelso, 2005), as well as the advisee feeling supported, respected, and valued by the advisor (Schlosser et al., 2003). The descriptions of the important aspects of advising relationships appear quite similar to how mentoring relationships are frequently described by the two-factor model (i.e., *psychosocial* and *career-related* functions). In the advising literature, these factors are typically referred to as *interpersonal* and *instructional* aspects, respectively. In fact, advisees might refer to their advisors as mentors, even if their formal relationship and means of coming together were for advising. It is unlikely, however, that someone who disliked their advisor would refer to that person as a mentor because of the inherent positive connotation associated with the word mentor (Schlosser & Gelso, 2001). Advising and mentoring, then, share some characteristics, but also diverge in certain areas. Material from both of these literatures can and will enhance our discussion of diversity issues in academic mentoring relationships.

Noncognitive Variables and Diversity

One way to understand the notion of developmental level, as well as other important contextual variables that can affect the student–faculty relationship, is through the use of noncognitive variables (Sedlacek, 1996, 2003a, 2004a). Briefly, the noncognitive variables include a) positive self-concept, b) realistic self-appraisal, c) understanding and dealing with racism and other "-isms," d) preference for long-range goals, e) availability of a strong support person, f) successful leadership experience, g) demonstrated community service, and h) knowledge acquired in a field. These noncognitive variables have been shown to assess the potential abilities of students from diverse backgrounds, specifically those whose racial and cultural socialization experiences differ from the "traditional" White, male, heterosexual, Christian, middle-to upper-middle-class Eurocentric experience (Sedlacek, 1996, 2003a, 2004a). For the purposes of our work here, we will refer to people from diverse backgrounds as *nontraditional students.*

Mentoring and Noncognitive Variables

There are several advantages to focusing on noncognitive variables in mentoring nontraditional students. First, because noncognitive variables have been shown to correlate with the academic success of nontraditional students, the mentor can emphasize the very attributes that relate to desirable protégé outcomes (Sedlacek, 2004a). Second, the noncognitive variables are developmental in nature and students can be evaluated on their progress along the dimensions (Sedlacek, 1991, 1994; Westbrook & Sedlacek, 1988). Third, there are methods available to assess each of the noncognitive variables in several ways (Sedlacek, 2004a). Fourth, using noncognitive variables allows for the training of mentors around a structure that can be practiced and duplicated for many mentors so they are operating in a similar and coordinated manner. Table 16.1 contains a description of the noncognitive variables suggested in this chapter.

Having defined the noncognitive variables, we can now examine ways that we might introduce them into a mentoring relationship. Students can be mentored by identifying behaviors associated with good or poor performance on each of the variables (see Table 16.2). Mentors can do a self-assessment on each of the variables to determine their own strengths and weaknesses in working on each dimension. For example, one advisor may be particularly effective at helping protégés set long-term goals while another might be better at assisting them in learning to negotiate the system. While most of the research with these noncognitive variables has been with

Table 16.1   Description of noncognitive variables

Variable #	Variable name
1	*Positive self-concept* • Demonstrates confidence, strength of character, determination, and independence.
2	*Realistic self-appraisal* • Recognizes and accepts any strengths and deficiencies, especially academic, and works hard at self-development. Recognizes need to broaden his/her individuality.
3	*Understands and knows how to handle racism (the system)* • Exhibits a realistic view of the system based upon personal experience of racism. Committed to improving the existing system. Takes an assertive approach to dealing with existing wrongs, but is not hostile to society, nor is a "cop-out." Able to handle racist system.
4	*Prefers long-range to short-term or immediate needs* • Able to respond to deferred gratification, plans ahead, and sets goals.
5	*Availability of strong support person* • Seeks and takes advantage of a strong support network or has someone to turn to in a crisis or for encouragement.
6	*Successful leadership experience* • Demonstrates strong leadership in any area of his/her background (e.g., church, sports, noneducational groups, gang leader, etc.).
7	*Demonstrated community service* • Participates and is involved in his/her community.
8	*Knowledge acquired in or about a field* • Acquires knowledge in a sustained and/or culturally related way in any field.

undergraduate students, Sedlacek (2003a, 2004a, 2004b) has discussed the value of the noncognitive variables in working with graduate and professional students of color, including a number of principles, techniques, and examples of working with the variables.

The noncognitive variables can be used along with any other variables, models, or techniques that are employed in whatever role or type of mentoring is involved. Teachers, advisors, or counselors who use the system can expect to obtain better student outcomes in terms of grades, retention, and satisfaction, as well as greater satisfaction themselves in employing something systematic with demonstrated utility in an area that often produces confusion and anxiety (Sedlacek, 2004a).

The noncognitive variables provide an important link between the two main foci of our chapter: that is, mentoring and issues related to cultural diversity. Our conception of diversity includes attending to issues faced by people of color, women, and lesbian, gay, bisexual, and transgender (LGBT) persons. The use of noncognitive variables with individuals from these groups is discussed in Sedlacek (2004a). While we also believe that other variables such as religion, social class, and ability status are important to consider vis-à-vis the mentoring relationship, the extant literature focuses more on issues pertaining to race, gender, and sexual orientation (Schlosser

Table 16.2 Positive and negative evidence of each noncognitive variable

---

VARIABLES 1 THROUGH 8
In the following, you will find the definition of the variable and a list of questions to guide you in the assessment of each variable

---

Variable #1: POSITIVE SELF-CONCEPT
This variable assesses the protégé's confidence, self-esteem, independence, and determination, all vital components of future achievement and success.

Positive evidence	Negative evidence
Does the protégé feel confident of making it through graduation?	Does the protégé express any reason he/she might not complete school or succeed and attain his/her goals?
Does the protégé make positive statements about him/herself?	Does the protégé express concerns that other students are better than he/she is?
Does the protégé expect to achieve his/her goals and perform well in academic and nonacademic areas?	Does the protégé expect to have marginal grades?
Does the protégé provide evidence on how he/she will attain his/her goals?	Does the protégé have trouble balancing his/her personal and academic life?
Does the protégé link his/her interests and experiences with his/her goals?	Does the protégé appear to be avoiding new challenges or situations?
Does the protégé assume he/she can handle new situations or challenges?	

Variable #2: REALISTIC SELF-APPRAISAL
This variable assesses the protégé's ability to recognize and accept his/her strengths and deficiencies, especially in academics, and works hard at self-development to broaden his/her individuality.

Positive evidence	Negative evidence
Is the protégé aware of his/her strengths and weaknesses?	Is the protégé unaware of how evaluations are done in school?
Does the protégé know what it takes to pursue a given career?	Is the protégé not sure about his/her own abilities?
Is the protégé realistic about his/her abilities?	Is the protégé uncertain about how his/her peers or superiors rate his/her performances?
Does the protégé show an awareness of how his/her service, leadership, extracurricular activities, or schoolwork has caused him/her to change over time?	Does the protégé overreact to positive or negative reinforcement rather than seeing it in a larger context?
Has the protégé learned something from these structured or unstructured activities?	Is the protégé unaware of how he/she is doing in classes until grades are out?

Table 16.2 *(Continued)*

Positive evidence	Negative evidence
Does the protégé appreciate and understand both positive and negative feedback?	Is the protégé unaware of positive and negative consequences of his/her grades, actions, or skills?
Does the protégé provide evidence of overcoming anger, shyness, and lack of discipline?	
Does the protégé face a problem, like a bad grade, with determination to do better?	

Variable #3: SUCCESSFULLY HANDLES THE SYSTEM (RACISM)
This variable assesses the protégé's ability to understand the role of the "system" in life and to develop a method of assessing the cultural/racial demands of the system and respond accordingly/assertively.

Positive evidence	Negative evidence
Is the protégé able to overcome challenges or obstacles he/she is confronted with as a result of racism in a positive and effective way?	Is the protégé unaware of how the "system" works?
Does the protégé understand the role of the "system" in his/her life and how it treats nontraditional persons?	Is the protégé preoccupied with racism or does not feel racism exists?
Does the protégé reveal ways that he/she has learned to "deal" with the "system" accordingly?	Does the protégé blame others for his/her problems?
	Does the protégé react with the same intensity to large or small issues concerned with race?
	Is the protégé's method for successfully handling racism that does not interfere with personal and academic development nonexistent?

Variable #4: PREFERENCE FOR LONG-TERM GOALS
This variable assesses the protégé's persistence, patience, long-term planning, and willingness to defer gratification and success in college.

Positive evidence	Negative evidence
Does the protégé reveal experience of setting both academic and personal long-term goals?	Does the protégé lack evidence of setting and accomplishing goals?
Does the protégé provide evidence that he/she is planning for the future?	Is the protégé likely to proceed without clear direction?

Table 16.2 (*Continued*)

Positive evidence	Negative evidence
Has the protégé determined a course of study and anticipated the type of career or path he/she might or could pursue?	Does the protégé rely on others to determine outcomes?
Is the protégé aware of realistic and intermediate steps necessary to achieve goals?	Does the protégé focus too much attention on the present?
Has the protégé participated in activities (volunteer work, employment, extra courses, community work) related to his/her anticipated career goal?	Is the protégé's plan for approaching a course, school in general, an activity, etc. nonexistent?
	If the protégé states his/her goals, are the goals vague or unrealistic?

Variable #5: AVAILABILITY OF STRONG SUPPORT PERSON
This variable assesses the protégé's availability of a strong support network, help, and encouragement, and the degree to which he/she relies solely on her/his own resources.

Positive evidence	Negative evidence
Does the protégé have a strong support system? (This can be a personal, professional, academic support as long as it is someone the protégé can turn to for advice, consultation, assistance, encouragement etc.)	Does the protégé avoid turning to a support person, mentor, or close advisors for help?
Is the protégé willing to admit that he/she needs help and able to pull on other resources, other than him/herself, to solve problems?	Does the protégé keep his/her problems to himself?
	Does the protégé state that he/she can handle things on his/her own?
	Does the protégé state that access to a previous support person may have been reduced or eliminated?
	Is the protégé unaware of the importance of a support person?

Table 16.2 (*Continued*)

Variable #6: LEADERSHIP EXPERIENCE
This variable assesses the protégé's skills developed or influence exercised from his/her formal and informal leadership roles.

Positive evidence	Negative evidence
Has the protégé taken leadership initiative, for example by founding clubs/organizations? What evidence is there?	Is the protégé unable to turn to others for advice or direction?
Does the protégé describe the skills he/she has developed as a leader, skills such as assertiveness, effectiveness, organizing, and time management?	Does the protégé lack confidence or leadership skills?
Has the protégé shown evidence of influencing others and being a good role model?	Is the protégé passive or does he/she lack initiative?
Is the protégé comfortable providing advice and direction to others?	Is the protégé overly cautious?
Does the protégé describe a commitment to being a role model for siblings, community members, or schoolmates?	Does the protégé avoid controversy?
Does the protégé show sustained commitment to one or two types of organizations with increasing involvement, skill development and responsibility?	
Does the protégé take action and initiative?	

Variables #7: COMMUNITY INVOLVEMENT
This variable assesses the protégé's identification with a cultural, geographic, or racial group and his/her demonstrated activity within that community grouping.

Positive evidence	Negative evidence
Does the protégé show sustained commitment to a service site or issue area?	Does the protégé lack involvement in cultural, racial, or geographical group or community?
Does the protégé demonstrate a specific or long-term commitment or relationships with a community?	Is the protégé involved in his/her community in name only?
Has the protégé accomplished specific goals in a community setting?	Does the protégé engage more in solitary rather than group activities (academic or nonacademic)?
Does the protégé's community service relate to career or personal goals?	

Table 16.2   (*Continued*)

Variable #8: KNOWLEDGE ACQUIRED IN A FIELD
This variable assesses the protégé's experiences gained in a field through study and experiences beyond the classroom. This variable pays particular attention to the ways the protégé gains nontraditional, perhaps culturally or racially based views of the field.

Positive evidence	Negative evidence
Does the protégé use his/her knowledge to teach others about the topic?	Does the protégé lack evidence of learning from the community or nonacademic activities?
Is the protégé working independently in his/her field? (Be sensitive to variations between academic fields and the experiences that can be gained. For example, if in the sciences, by doing independent research, or if in the arts or crafts, by participating in competitions or compositions.)	Is the protégé traditional in his/her approach to learning?
	Is the protégé unaware of his/her possibilities in a field of interest?

---

et al., 2005). In addition, our space limits a complete discussion of all diversity variables. Hence, we have used race as the primary cultural characteristic in the two groups focused on later in this chapter. We made this decision because of the ways that race informs culturally appropriate interpersonal interactions (Helms & Cook, 1999) and the extent that our understanding of race has historically served to advance our understanding of culture along other dimensions (e.g., sexual orientation identity development; Mohr, 2002). It is important to note that this discussion could be applied to other nontraditional student groups (e.g., LGBT individuals).

We believe that it is important to concentrate on diversity issues in mentoring for a number of reasons. First, nontraditional students have been historically underrepresented in academia, and as a result we do not know as much about mentoring for these groups of people, including what works for whom and under what set of circumstances. Second, students of color represent a small, but growing number of new doctorates in psychology (Kohout & Wicherski, 2003). If this trend holds true for other disciplines, then it appears critical for all academics to know how mentoring relationships with nontraditional students differ from those relationships with a traditional student, as well as knowing how to mentor nontraditional and traditional students with equal effectiveness. This latter issue is especially important because the existing research (e.g., Atkinson et al., 1994; Pope-Davis, Stone, & Neilson, 1997; Schlosser et al., 2005) suggests that mentoring experiences are different for those in socially privileged groups (e.g., Whites, men, Christians, heterosexuals) than those in socially oppressed groups (e.g., people of color, women, LGBT persons, religious minorities). This variation is likely to occur because of the unique intergroup experiences that people in diverse groups tend to have. Those in power positions (e.g., mentors) may assume that protégés are more similar than their varied experiences would warrant. In turn, protégés may have differing approaches to responding to those in power. Finally, we also know that the presence (or absence) of mentors of color is an important variable in the professional development of psychology doctoral students of color (Pope-Davis et al., 1997). The need for mentors for students of color has been stressed in other scholarly work as well (e.g., Blackwell, 1989; Brinson & Kottler, 1993). Therefore, it appears that addressing the underrepresentation of nontraditional students and faculty in academia is critical, and one in which mentoring can play an important role.

Research on Academic Mentoring

With regard to gender, it is somewhat surprising that no significant gender differences have been found in terms of finding a mentor (Clark et al., 2000; Cronan-Hillix et al., 1986) or initiating and maintaining mentoring relationships (Clark et al., 2000; Gilbert, 1985). This is important in that mentoring relationships can help women navigate obstacles to success that they often face, such as discouraging comments, differential opportunities, and sexual harassment (Ancis & Phillips, 1996; Brush, 1991). How well they learn to make the education system work for them is predictive of their grades in college (Ancis & Sedlacek, 1997) and mentoring can help women negotiate the sexism they encounter (Sedlacek, 2004a). Evidence also exists that women experience an academic climate that interferes with the ability to do realistic appraisals of their academic abilities (Ancis & Phillips, 1996; Brush, 1991). These difficulties bring about a corresponding decrease in academic and career aspirations from their first year to their last year in school (Ossana, Helms, & Leonard, 1992). Women who are able to make realistic self-appraisals have been shown to get higher university grades than those who have difficulty with such assessments (Ancis & Sedlacek, 1997). Again, mentoring can assist women in making more realistic appraisals of their abilities (Sedlacek, 2004a).

With regard to race, research reveals several obstacles for students of color to obtain mentoring. Some examples include a) a lack of faculty role models of color (Pope-Davis et al., 1997), b) differences in cultural values between mentor and protégé (Goto, 1999), c) not understanding the importance of good mentoring to success in one's career (Grant-Thompson & Atkinson, 1997), and d) reluctance to enter a cross-race advising or mentoring relationship (Brinson & Kottler, 1993). In addition, faculty members may believe one or more myths about mentoring students of color (see Brown, Davis, & McClendon, 1999), and faculty of color may be overwhelmed with requests for mentorship from students of color.

In order to elaborate on some of the points raised above, discussions of mentoring issues for African Americans and Asian Americans will be presented.

Mentoring African Americans

Traditionally, the selection of a mentor or a protégé has followed the dictum of shared interests, values, or traits (Olian, Carroll, Giannantonio, & Feren 1988). The rationale behind this is that the greater the commonality of the relationship, the greater the ability to foster empathy. The mentor–protégé relationship for African American students has tended to be defined racially (Collins, Kamya, & Tourse, 1997). However, as the enrollment of African Americans on college campuses increases, the ability to achieve same-group mentoring has decreased. According to the National Center for Education Statistics (2003), there are only 1.6 African American faculty members for every 100 African American students, although the ratio is better at historically Black colleges and universities (HBCUs) (Provasnik, Shafer, & Snyder, 2004). This is in contrast to the experience of White students who have 4.4 White faculty members for every 100 students. The ratio for African American students to African American faculty becomes even more disproportionate in math and empirical sciences.

Previous research has shown that the presence of a mentor is related to retention for African American students across majors and types of institutions (Lynch, 2002; Sedlacek, 2004a). However, it appears that same-race mentor–protégé relationships for students and academic faculty at predominantly White institutions (PWIs) require greater effort on the part of African American faculty and students than do their counterparts at HBCUs. This implied racial and cultural affirmation of HBCUs has traditionally been seen as an additional selling point for these institutions. According to research cited at the official website for the United Negro College Fund,

> HBCUs, because of their unique sensibility to the special needs of young African American minds, remain the institutions that demonstrate the most effective ability to graduate African American students who are poised to be competitive in the corporate, research, academic, governmental and military arenas (www.uncf.org/aboutus/hbcus.as).

The simple mathematic reality of same-race mentoring for African American students is that they will be waiting in a long line for the time and attention of a faculty member who will probably either be nontenured or not on a tenure track. This last demographic trend is important to note because it further demonstrates that the majority of available African American academic faculty mentors may be relatively young in their professional development, not seeking academic advancement, or have been unsuccessful at achieving academic advancement for whatever reasons. Collins et al. (1997) found that 79% of the African American students in their study had a mentor. Of those African American students who had a mentor, 80% of their mentors were African American. However, there were only 35 participants in their study. When the number of students increases, the ability of African American faculty to provide mentoring becomes not only onerous, but potentially detrimental to their scholarly productivity and professional advancement (Lynch, 2002). Many of the African American faculty members available to serve as mentors may be encountering the same issues of mentoring and professional development that their protégés are negotiating. Sedlacek and Brooks (1976) discuss this dilemma and provide a six-stage model to guide mentors in working with faculty and students of color. The noncognitive variables shown in Table 16.1 can be useful in mentoring Black students about graduate school opportunities (Sedlacek, 2003b), and their success while in graduate school (Davidson & Foster-Johnson, 2002). For example, in mentoring an African American female, consideration had to be given to her long-range goal of studying race-related career issues when this was not seen as an important area by her White male advisor. She "worked the system" by framing her interests as related to his and proceeded to do extensive work in the area during graduate school and beyond.

Psychosocial and Career Aspects of Mentoring African Americans

As was discussed earlier, a two-factor model of the relationship between mentor and protégé provides a useful, but limited framework. The psychosocial/interpersonal and career-related/instructional model does define very important aspects of the relationship, but there is also the interaction among interpersonal and instructional roles and identities. Benjamin (1995) found that African American students at PWIs construct bipartite identities that consist of a personal/cultural self and an academic/institutional self. However, one key area that both selves shared in common is how racism influences their identities on both a personal and institutional level. This appears consistent with the noncognitive variable of learning how to navigate the explicit and implicit values and practices of academic institutions, and by realizing that all institutions of higher education are firmly embedded in larger cultural systems.

Psychosocial Aspects

An important aspect of the professional development of the protégé may not be just his or her career development, but the role that race may or may not consciously play in his or her identity development. As was mentioned previously, the common trait between the otherwise discrete paths of career development and personal identity for African American college students is the experience of racism. More succinctly, the experiences of personal racism and institutional racism may be connected for many African American protégés. In order to understand the dynamics of race in the mentor–protégé relationship, the area of counselor training and therapeutic supervision may provide an instructive model. According to Bradley (as cited in Cook, 1994, p. 4), "supervision is intended to assist supervisees in integrating their personal and professional identities." In order to explore the supervisory relationship, Cook (1994) applied a *mainstream approach* (Constantine, Richardson, Benjamin, & Wilson, 1998) that is characterized by the development of ego statuses that reflect varying degrees of racial self-awareness ranging from internalized feelings of inferiority to feelings of cultural acceptance of one's self and others (Cross, 1995; Helms, 1994). According to Cook (1994), the combination of different racialized ego-statuses between mentor and protégé can be both predictive and descriptive of possible strengths and limitations of the dyad.

Although the mainstream approaches have become popular conceptualizations of racial identity for African Americans and people of color, there exist many other types of theories. For example, African-centered models (Akbar, 1979; Baldwin, 1984) do not focus on the process of identity development per se, but on the role of African and African American culturally defined values and practices. Applying African-centered theories to the mentor–protégé relationship would be based not only on understanding the beliefs and values of African American protégés and mentors, but also on understanding the role and relevance of African American culture in defining the sense of self for both the mentor and protégé. For example, an African American mentor at a conformist ego-status would place a different value on the role of African American cultural values in defining their professional identity than a protégé at the internalization status. This incongruity could be a source of conflict, but the process of negotiating and ameliorating the incongruity could be a necessary component for future professional development for the protégé.

Career Aspects

On a prima facie level this seems to be the most straightforward part of the relationship between mentors of any race and African American protégés. It would seem that the steps needed to become an engineer (for example) are clear and prescriptive. "In order to become an engineer, you should do this, this, and that at this time." However, the basis of noncognitive predictors of college student retention demonstrates that different groups of students employ different skills at different times to solve the same problem (Sedlacek, 2004a). Both the publishers of the most widely used career inventory, the Strong Interest Inventory (SII) (Prince, 1995), and subsequent empirical attempts to validate scores from the SII (Lattimore & Borgen, 1999) have produced reservations among counselors and researchers about the validity of SII scores for use with African American populations. According to Lattimore and Borgen (1999, p. 186), "The combination of the diverse research findings and numerous limitations makes final conclusions about cross-cultural validity difficult." They further assert more research needs to examine the effect that racial differences have on SII scores. Additionally, large within-group differences further complicate a mentoring relationship that includes use of the instrument.

Regardless of the race of the mentor, the belief that two people should make the assumption of similar career motivations, goals, and values, because they share the same demographic racial group, is naïve at best, and racist at worst. This is not to deny that within same-race mentor–protégé relationships there may be the benefit of the normalization of common racial experiences. However, this potential benefit is not without the possible cost of resource and time demands on both the mentor and protégé. Also, because the influence and role of race is a ubiquitous issue not just in career development, but in human development, it is benefited by the mentor understanding the racial transference and counter-transference that exists between mentor and protégé in terms of psychosocial development (Ladany, Constantine, Miller, Erickson, & Muse-Burke, 2000). The role of race may not be the primary issue within all mentor and protégé relationships, but the agreement on the role of race in the mentor–protégé relationship should be a function of the needs and role of the relationship. Additionally, the exploration of racial development should not be limited by unresolved issues of race, power, and entitlement.

Within all of the aforementioned theories of racial identity, the one core theme is that race can play a role in defining both same- and cross-race mentor–protégé relationships in both psychosocial and career development. Race may not be an overt feature of the relationship, but racial issues should not be ignored in order to explore career development for African American college students. Failure to address the role of race in the relationship can limit what the experience of supervision/mentoring has to offer. Concurrently, working through the parallel process of race may serve as a vehicle for both the protégé and mentor to better understand the interpersonal and career aspects of their own identity development.

Mentoring Asian Americans

As of 2001, 12.5 million US residents identified themselves as Asian Americans, which was 4.4% of the total population and represented an increase of more than 50% since 1990 (US Census Bureau, 2002, 2003). For individuals 25 years and older, Asian Americans hold the highest proportion of bachelor's degree or more (49.8%) in comparison with other racial groups (US Census Bureau, 2004). Furthermore, in 2001, more than 937,000 Asian Americans were enrolled in college, which represented a 54% increase since 1991 (American Council on Education, 2005). Despite these data, literature on mentoring Asian American students in educational settings is scarce. Researchers (e.g., Goto, 1999) have offered possible explanations for the lack of attention in this area, including the model minority myth and culturally incongruent mentorship. Nevertheless, Asian American college students do have their adjustment concerns and needs (Liang & Sedlacek, 2003b). Successful mentorship can help Asian American students in many ways, including easing difficulties in transition to college, improving their satisfaction with college life and a chosen major, and developing their professional skills, confidence, and personal and professional identity.

Model Minority Myth

For years, Asian Americans have been perceived as the "model minority" group, members of which are supposed to perform well in educational settings (Liang & Sedlacek, 2003a; Sedlacek, 2004a). This stereotype may perpetuate the impression that Asian Americans have encountered very few barriers in higher education and that mentoring programs should be targeting other minority students who do not perform as well (Kodama, McEwen, Liang, & Lee, 2002). Also, the academic success of Asian Americans may mask the complete picture of their college experiences, excluding issues related to psychosocial adjustment and psychological well-being (Sandhu, 1997; Kim et al., 2001).

However, a closer and deeper scrutiny of the status of Asian American students often yields a different story that contrasts sharply with popular views of their academic successes. Many writers have indicated the importance of recognizing the extreme diversity within the Asian American population as reflected by country of origin, language, socioeconomic status, and so forth (e.g., Maki & Kitano, 2002; Uba, 1994). Despite the high percentage of Asian Americans who hold a bachelor's degree, some Asian American subgroups constitute a large undereducated mass. For example, of those individuals over 25, 42.9% of all Asian Americans/Pacific Islanders had at least a bachelor's degree, whereas fewer than 10% of individuals from some Southeast Asian subgroups, such as Cambodians, Laotians, and Hmongs, had such degrees (Le, 2005a, 2005b). This bimodal distribution clearly indicates the enormous within-group differences among Asian Americans. It may also imply that Asian American students could benefit from mentoring and that mentoring programs should be tailored to fit the differing needs of Asian American subgroups.

Mentoring: A Culturally Incongruent Path to Success?

In her review, Goto (1999) suggested that cultural reasons (e.g., incompatibility between Asian and US mainstream cultures) might explain why some Asian Americans are reluctant to seek guidance and help from mentors, especially from those who are White. Through interviewing 25 first-year Asian American college students, Goto found that most interviewees believed that they would benefit from participation in a mentoring program for better adjustment, and 54% of them thought the program would help them develop cultural identity. However, several Asian American students later dropped out of the program because they worried that the program brought undesired attention to cultural differences and participation might result in separation and pressure from peers. A possible explanation is that a formal mentoring program as such might introduce the cultural conflict between individualism (seeking mentoring/help for oneself) and collectivism (fitting in with the ethnic group) for Asian American students. Another survey study showed that Asian American college students were more likely to participate in peer mentoring programs when these programs were designed to meet their needs (e.g., ease transition to college, strengthen ethnic identity, counter the model minority myth) (Kim et al., 2001). In spite of the paucity of empirical research, findings from the above two studies suggest that Asian American college students have their psychosocial needs, face unique adjustment issues, and can benefit from mentoring programs that are compatible with their cultural values.

Asian Cultural Values

Cultural values, such as collectivism versus individualism, have significant effects on social relationships (Chen, Brockner, & Chen, 2002). Research reviewed in the previous section and other literatures (e.g., counseling psychology) suggest the importance of considering the cultural values of Asian American students when developing mentoring programs (Atkinson, Lowe, & Matthews, 1995; Bui & Takeuchi, 1992). Therefore, it is imperative that non-Asian mentors familiarize themselves with Asian cultural values and understand the role these values might have on the mentoring relationship with Asian American students. Although the Asian American population is composed of many different subgroups, individuals who can trace their cultural roots back to Asia may share some cultural patterns and a sense of commonality (Chung, 1992; Sue & Sue, 2003). Below is an overview of core Asian cultural values and how they might influence the mentoring relationship.

Collectivism versus individualism as a cultural value. Major differences between US and Asian societies can be found in contrasting individualist versus collectivist cultures, in which individuals in collectivist cultures tend to value the needs and desires of the group over the needs and desires of the individual, whereas people in individualist cultures have the opposite tendency (Kim, Triandis, Kâğitçibaşi, Choi, & Yoon, 1994). Collectivist relationships are characterized by loyalty and obligation, and friendships are kept within the in-group, a set of people with whom one belongs and identifies (e.g., relatives, friends). On the other hand, individualists tend to see relationships opportunistically, and friendships are by personal choice, unconstrained by in-group ties (Myers, 1996). As suggested by Goto's (1999) study, Asian American students were reluctant to single themselves out of their cultural groups when participating in a mentoring program. Therefore, mentors and student service professionals should try to resolve this dilemma and develop new approaches to maintain the connection of Asian Americans to their cultural groups while offering necessary mentoring and guidance.

Hierarchical nature of relationships and well-defined social roles. Embedded in Asian cultures is a hierarchical social structure, where authority, leadership, and responsibility are at the top. Asian Americans tend to behave passively toward their superiors and show deference to their elders, which is often how mentors are perceived by their Asian American students. Every individual in this hierarchical structure has distinct obligations; and the role of each member in the hierarchical social structure is clear and apparent, and remains relatively stable (Paniagua, 1994). The hierarchical nature of relationships is in sharp contrast to the egalitarian and horizontal social structure of White American culture.

One-way communication from an authority figure to persons in a group is also more the norm in Asian society (Chung, 1992; Sue & Sue, 2003). Silence and lack of eye contact often occur when Asian American students listen or speak to someone higher in the hierarchy, such as parents, instructors, and mentors. Obedience and compliance may prompt Asian American students to await instructions from their mentors. Therefore, non-Asian/Asian American mentors should keep in mind that they may be expected to play a more active and directive role and should prepare themselves for the possibility of developing a more formal relationship with their Asian American students at the beginning stage of their mentoring relationship. Although it may be beneficial for non-Asian/Asian American mentors and Asian American students to find a middle ground in the collectivist–individualist continuum, failure to meet Asian American student cultural needs may result in the premature termination of the mentoring relationship.

Public repression of problems. In general, individuals heavily influenced by Asian cultural values tend to restrict any discussion of personal problems, including physical and mental illness (Paniagua, 1994). Members of the family are not encouraged to express their problems to people outside the group, especially to strangers. Also, one way to fulfill one's family obligations is not to create problems (Chung, 1992; Uba, 1994). This tendency plays an important role in prohibiting Asian American students from expressing and admitting their problems in settings outside their family, such as within a mentoring relationship. Non-Asian/Asian American mentors need to be culturally sensitive and develop their skills in creating a safe mentoring relationship in which Asian American students can feel free to seek help and explore themselves.

Acculturation and Ethnic Identity Development

In addition to cultural values, acculturation level appears relevant in developing an effective mentoring relationship with Asian Americans given that many are foreign born (Sue & Sue, 2003). The concept of psychological acculturation may be particularly useful as it emphasizes the effect of acculturation on individual adaptation (Berry, 1980; Szapocznik, Scopetta, Kurtines, & Aranalde, 1978). The four types of adaptation – assimilation, integration, separation, and marginalization – provide non-Asian/Asian American mentors a framework to understand the various issues that Asian American protégés might encounter in adjusting to college. Counseling research has supported the hypothesis that more acculturated Asian American college students perceived counseling professionals more favorably as sources of help for personal/emotional issues than less acculturated ones (Atkinson & Gim, 1989; Tracey, Leong, & Glidden, 1986; Zhang & Dixon, 2003). It seems reasonable that non-Asian/Asian American mentors could apply findings from the counseling literature and should take acculturation levels into consideration when mentoring Asian American students.

Another variable that might have an effect on the mentoring relationship is the racial/ethnic identity of mentors and protégés. As suggested by Helms and Cook (1999), where the therapist and the client stand in their own racial identity development process has a bearing on the nature and quality of the therapeutic relationship, which, in turn, would predict therapy outcomes. The same logic could be argued for the cross-cultural mentoring relationship as it represents one form of various helping relationships. It would be most helpful when non-Asian/Asian American mentors are at a more advanced (or at least equal) status of racial/ethnic identity development than their Asian American students. The mentoring relationship could be problematic if Asian American students were at a more mature identity status than their mentors, as this disparity might create tension in the relationship and it might be difficult for students to receive useful guidance on their identity development from mentors. Therefore, it is important for mentors to understand themselves as racial/ethnic beings and attend to how their own racial and cultural socialization experiences might play a positive or negative role in developing an effective mentoring relationship with Asian American students (Schlosser et al., 2005). Furthermore, several racial/ethnic identity development models have been proposed specifically for Asian Americans (e.g., Lee, 1989; Kim, 1981; S. Sue & Sue, 1971). These models may provide guidance for mentors to help their students explore who they are as Asian Americans and help mentors better understand the process that Asian American students go through to achieve a clear racial identity.

The Big Bang or Another Universe?

Are we able to use general references on the mentoring/advising/counseling process and apply them to people of color, or do we need research and models unique to those students? As with conceptions of diversity, we feel that both are useful. By examining the evidence on the mentor–protégé relationship for all groups, we set a context to study and analyze useful ideas and limitations in those studies and models. In turn, as we examine some of the issues specific to students of color, we find research evidence and theory that go beyond the overall models. We feel that by employing the noncognitive variable approach discussed above and shown in Tables 16.1 and 16.2, mentors of any race or gender and protégés from any nontraditional group can come together for mutual development. It is a bicultural experience for both to consider general and specific principles in that relationship.

Author Note

The order of authorship for the second, third, and fourth authors was determined alphabetically; each of the second, third, and fourth authors contributed equally to the chapter.

References

Akbar, N. (1979). African roots of Black personality. In W. D. Smith, K. Burlew, M. Mosely, & W. Whiteney (Eds.), *Reflections on Black psychology* (pp. 79–87). Washington, DC: University Press of America.

American Council on Education (2005). *Annual ACE report shows minority college enrollment continues to climb, but gaps still persist*. Retrieved February 27, 2005, from www.acenet.edu/hena/readArticle.cfm?articleID=1223.

Ancis, J. R., & Phillips, S. D. (1996). Academic gender bias and women's behavioral agency and self-efficacy. *Journal of Counseling and Development, 75*, 131–137.

Ancis, J. R., & Sedlacek, W. E. (1997). Predicting the academic achievement of female students using the SAT and noncognitive variables. *College and University, 72*(3), 1–8.

Atkinson, D. R., Casas, A., & Neville, H. (1994). Ethnic minority psychologists: Whom they mentor and benefits they derive from the process. *Journal of Multicultural Counseling and Development, 22*, 37–48.

Atkinson, D. R., & Gim, R. H. (1989). Asian-American cultural identity and attitudes toward mental health services. *Journal of Counseling Psychology, 36*, 209–212.

Atkinson, D. R., Lowe, S., & Matthews, L. (1995). Asian-American acculturation and willingness to seek counseling. *Journal of Multicultural Counseling and Development, 23*, 130–138.

Baldwin, J. A. (1984). African self-consciousness and the mental health of African Americans. *Journal of Black Studies, 15*, 177–194.

Barnett, S. K. (1984). The mentor role: A task of generativity. *Journal of Human Behavior and Learning, 1*, 15–18.

Benjamin, E. M. (1995). *The relationship between African-centered self-concept and the perceptions of socially based power for black students on predominantly White college campuses*. Unpublished doctoral dissertation, University of Texas at Austin.

Berry, J. W. (1980). Acculturation as varieties of adaptation. In A. M. Padilla (Ed.), *Acculturation: Theory, models, and some new findings* (pp. 9–25). Boulder, CO: Westview.

Blackwell, J. E. (1989). Mentoring: An action strategy for increasing minority faculty. *Academe, 75*, 8–14.

Bode, R. K. (1999). Mentoring and collegiality. In R. J. Menges & Associates (Eds.), *Faculty in new jobs: A guide to settling in, becoming established, and building institutional support* (pp. 118–144). San Francisco: Jossey-Bass.

Brinson, J., & Kottler, J. (1993). Cross-cultural mentoring in counselor education: A strategy for retaining minority faculty. *Counselor Education and Supervision, 32*, 241–253.

Brown, M. C., Davis, G. L., & McClendon, S. A. (1999). Mentoring graduate students of color: Myths, models, and modes. *Peabody Journal of Education, 74*, 105–118.

Brush, S. G. (1991). Women in science and engineering. *American Scientist, 79*, 404–419.

Bui, H. T., & Takeuchi, D. T. (1992). Ethnic minority adolescents and the use of community mental health care services. *American Journal of Community Psychology, 20*, 403–417.

Chen, Y. R., Brockner, J., & Chen, X. P. (2002). Individual–collective primacy and ingroup favoritism: Enhancement and protection effects. *Journal of Experimental Social Psychology, 38*(5), 482–491.

Chung, D. K. (1992). Asian cultural commonalities: A comparison with mainstream American culture. In D. K. Chung, K. Murase, & F. Ross-Sheriff (Eds.), *Social work practice with Asian Americans* (pp. 27–44). Newbury Park, CA: Sage.

Clark, R. A., Harden, S. L., & Johnson, W. B. (2000). Mentor relationships in clinical psychology doctoral training: Results of a national survey. *Teaching of Psychology, 27*, 262–268.

Collins, P. M., Kamya, H. A., & Tourse, R. W. (1997). Questions of racial diversity and mentorship: An empirical exploration. *Social Work, 42*(2), 145–152.

Constantine, M., Richardson, T., Benjamin, E., & Wilson, J. (1998). An overview of Black racial identity theory: Limitations and considerations for future theoretical change. *Applied and Preventive Psychology, 7*(2), 95–99.

Cook, D. A. (1994). Racial identity in supervision. *Counselor Education and Supervision, 34*(2), 1–7.

Cronan-Hillix, T., Davidson, W. S., Cronan-Hillix, W. A., & Gensheimer, L. K. (1986). Student's views of mentors in psychology graduate training. *Teaching of Psychology, 13*, 123–127.

Cross, W. E. (1995). The psychology of nigrescence: Revising the Cross model. In J. G. Ponterotto, J. M. Casas, L. A. Suzuki, & C. M. Alexander (Eds.), *Handbook of multicultural counseling* (pp. 93–122). Thousand Oaks, CA: Sage.

Davidson, M. N., & Foster-Johnson, L. (2002). Mentoring in the preparation of graduate researchers of color. *Review of Educational Research, 71*, 549–574.

Gilbert, L. A. (1985). Dimensions of same-gender student–faculty role-model relationships. *Sex Roles, 12*, 111–123.

Good, J., Halpin, G., & Halpin, G. (2000). A promising prospect for minority retention: Students becoming peer mentors. *Journal of Negro Education, 69*, 375–383.

Goto, S. (1999). Asian Americans and developmental relationships. In A. J. Murrell, F. J. Crosby, & R. J. Ely (Eds.), *Mentoring dilemmas: Developmental relationships within multicultural organizations* (pp. 46–62). Mahwah, NJ: Lawrence Erlbaum.

Grant-Thompson, S. K., & Atkinson, D. R. (1997). Cross-cultural mentor effectiveness and African American male students. *Journal of Black Psychology, 23*, 120–134.

Healy, C. C., & Welchert, A. J. (1990). Mentoring relations: A definition to advance research and practice. *Educational Researcher, 19*, 17–21.

Helms, J. E. (1994). Racial identity and career assessment. *Journal of Career Assessment, 2*, 199–209.

Helms, J. E., & Cook, D. A. (1999). *Using race and culture in counseling and psychotherapy: Theory and process.* Boston: Allyn & Bacon.

Hollingsworth, M. A., & Fassinger, R. E. (2002). The role of faculty mentors in the research training of counseling psychology doctoral students. *Journal of Counseling Psychology, 49*, 324–330.

Jacobi, M. (1991). Mentoring and undergraduate academic success: A literature review. *Review of Educational Research, 64*, 505–532.

Johnson, W. B., & Huwe, J. M. (2003). *Getting mentored in graduate school.* Washington, DC: American Psychological Association.

Johnson, W. B., Koch, C., Fallow, G. O., & Huwe, J. M. (2000). Prevalence of mentoring in clinical versus experimental doctoral programs: Survey findings, implications, and recommendations. *Psychotherapy, 37*, 325–334.

Kim, C. Y., Goto, S. G., Bai, M. M., Kim, T. E., & Wong, E. (2001). Culturally congruent mentoring: Predicting Asian American student participation using the theory of reasoned action. *Journal of Applied Social Psychology, 31*, 2417–2437.

Kim, J. (1981). The process of Asian American identity development: A study of Japanese-American women's perceptions of their struggle to achieve personal identities as Americans of Asian ancestry. *Dissertation Abstract International, 42*, 155 1A. (University Microfilms No. 81-18080)

Kim, U., Triandis, H. C., Kâğitçibaşi, Ç., Choi, S. C., & Yoon, G. (Eds.). (1994). *Individualism and collectivism: Theory, method, and applications.* Thousand Oaks, CA: Sage.

Kodama, C. M., McEwen, M. K., Liang, C. T. H., & Lee, S. (2002). An Asian American perspective on psychosocial development theory. In M. K. McEwen, C. M. Kodama, A. N. Alvarez, S. Lee, & C. T. H. Liang (Eds.), *Working with Asian American college students* (pp. 45–60). San Francisco: Jossey-Bass.

Kohout, J., & Wicherski, M. (2003). *1999 Doctorate employment survey.* Washington, DC: American Psychological Association.

Kram, K. E. (1985). *Mentoring at work: Developmental relationships in organizational life.* Glenview, IL: Scott, Foresman and Company.

Ladany, N., Constantine, M. G., Miller, K., Erickson, C. D., & Muse-Burke, J. L. (2000). Supervisor countertransference: A qualitative investigation into its identification and description. *Journal of Counseling Psychology, 47,* 102–115.

Lattimore, R. R., & Borgen, F. H. (1999). Validity of the 1994 Strong Interest Inventory with racial and ethnic groups in the United States. *Journal of Counseling Psychology, 146,* 185–195.

Le, C. N. (2005a). The model minority image. *Asian-Nation: The landscape of Asian America.* Retrieved April 8, 2005, from www.asian-nation.org/model-minority.shtml.

Le, C. N. (2005b). Socioeconomic statistics & demographics. *Asian-Nation: The landscape of Asian America.* Retrieved April 8, 2005, from www.asian-nation.org/demographics.shtml.

Lee, E. (1989). Assessment and treatment of Chinese American immigrant families. *Journal of Psychotherapy and the Family, 6,* 99–122.

Liang, C. T. H., & Sedlacek, W. E. (2003a). Attitudes of White student services practitioners toward Asian Americans. *National Association of Student Personnel Administrators Journal, 40*(3), 30–42. www.publications.naspa.org/naspajournal/vol40/iss3/art2.

Liang, C. T. H., & Sedlacek, W. E. (2003b). Utilizing factor analysis to understand the needs of Asian American students. *Journal of College Student Development, 44,* 260–266. www.publications.naspa.org/naspajournal/vol40/iss3/art2.

Lynch, R. V. (2002, November). *Mentoring across race: Critical case studies of African American students in a predominantly White institution of higher education.* Paper presented at annual meeting of the Association for the Study of Higher Education, Sacramento, CA.

Maki, M. T., & Kitano, H. H. L. (2002). Counseling Asian Americans. In P. B. Pedersen, J. G. Draguns, W. J. Lonner, & J. E. Trimble (Eds.), *Counseling across cultures* (5th ed., pp. 109–131). Thousand Oaks, CA: Sage.

Mohr, J. J. (2002). Heterosexual identity and the heterosexual therapist: Using identity as a framework for understanding sexual orientation issues in psychotherapy. *The Counseling Psychologist, 30,* 532–566.

Myers, D. G. (1996). *Social psychology* (5th ed.). New York: McGraw Hill.

National Center for Education Statistics (2003). *Digest of education statistics, 2003: Chapter 3. Postsecondary education.* Retrieved December 3, 2004, from www.nces.ed.gov//programs/digest/d03/ch_3.asp.

Olian, J. D., Carroll, S. J., Giannantonio, C. M., & Feren, D. B. (1988). What do protégés look for in a mentor? Results of three experimental studies. *Journal of Vocational Behavior, 33,* 15–37.

Ossana, S. M., Helms, J. E., & Leonard, M. M. (1992). Do "womanist" identity attitudes influence college women's self-esteem and perceptions of environmental bias? *Journal of Counseling and Development, 70,* 402–408.

Paniagua, F. A. (1994). *Assessing and treating culturally diverse clients: A practical guide.* Thousand Oaks, CA: Sage.

Pope-Davis, D. B., Stone, G. L., & Neilson, D. (1997). Factors influencing the stated career goals of minority graduate students in counseling psychology programs. *The Counseling Psychologist, 25,* 683–698.

Prince, J. P. (1995). *Strong Interest Inventory resource.* Palo Alto, CA: Consulting Psychologists Press, Inc.

Provasnik, S., Shafer, L. L., & Snyder, T. D. (2004). *Historically Black colleges and universities, 1976 to 2001* (National Center for Education Statistics Publication No. NCES 2004062). Washington, DC: ED Pubs.

Sandhu, D. S. (1997). Psychocultural profiles of Asian and Pacific Islander Americans: Implications for counseling and psychotherapy. *Journal of Multicultural Counseling and Development, 25,* 7–22.

Santos, S. J., & Reigadas, E. (2002). Latinos in higher education: An evaluation of a university faculty mentoring program. *Journal of Hispanic Higher Education, 1,* 40–50.

Schlosser, L. Z., & Gelso, C. J. (2001). Measuring the working alliance in advisor–advisee relationships in graduate school. *Journal of Counseling Psychology, 48,* 157–167.

Schlosser, L. Z., & Gelso, C. J. (2005). The Advisory Working Alliance Inventory – Advisor Version: Scale development and validation. *Journal of Counseling Psychology, 52,* 650–654.

Schlosser, L. Z., Knox, S., Moskovitz, A. R., & Hill, C. E. (2003). A qualitative study of the graduate advising relationship: The advisee perspective. *Journal of Counseling Psychology, 50,* 178–188.

Schlosser, L. Z., Talleyrand, R. M., Lyons, H. Z., Kim, B. S. K., & Johnson, W. B. (2005). *Advisor–advisee relationships in counseling psychology doctoral programs: Toward a multicultural theory.* Manuscript submitted for publication.

Sedlacek, W. E. (1991). Using noncognitive variables in advising nontraditional students. *National Academic Advising Association Journal, 11*(1), 75–82.

Sedlacek, W. E. (1994). Advising nontraditional students: The big bang or another universe? *National Academic Advising Association Journal, 14*(2), 103–104.

Sedlacek, W. E. (1996). An empirical method for determining nontraditional group status. *Measurement and Evaluation in Counseling and Development, 28,* 200–210.

Sedlacek, W. E. (2003a). Alternative admission and scholarship selection measures in higher education. *Measurement and Evaluation in Counseling and Development, 35,* 263–272.

Sedlacek, W. E. (2003b). Negotiating admissions to graduate and professional schools. In V. L. Farmer (Ed.), *The Black student's guide to graduate and professional school success* (pp. 13–22). Westport, CT: Greenwood Publishing Group.

Sedlacek, W. E. (2004a). *Beyond the big test: Noncognitive assessment in higher education.* San Francisco: Jossey-Bass.

Sedlacek, W. E. (2004b). Why we should use noncognitive variables with graduate and professional students. *The Advisor: The Journal of the National Association of Advisors for the Health Professions, 24*(2), 32–39.

Sedlacek, W. E., & Brooks, G. C., Jr. (1976). *Racism in American education: A model for change.* Chicago: Nelson-Hall.

Stafford, B., & Robbins, S. P. (1991). Mentoring for graduate social work students: Real and ideal. *Journal of Applied Social Sciences, 15,* 193–206.

Sue, D. W., & Sue, D. (2003). *Counseling the culturally diverse: Theory and practice* (4th ed.). New York: Wiley.

Sue, S., & Sue, D. W. (1971). Chinese-American personality and mental health. *American Journal, 1,* 36–49.

Szapocznik, J., Scopetta, M. A., Kurtines, W., & Aranalde, M. A. (1978). Theory and measurement of acculturation. *Interamerican Journal of Psychology, 12,* 113–120.

Tracey, T. J., Leong, F. T. L., & Glidden, C. (1986). Help seeking and problem perception among Asian Americans. *Journal of Counseling Psychology, 33,* 331–336.

Uba, L. (1994). *Asian Americans: Personality patterns, identity, and mental health.* New York: The Guilford Press.

US Census Bureau (2002). *Census brief: Current population survey.* Retrieved February 27, 2005, from www.census.gov/prod/2002pubs/c2kbr01-16.pdf.

US Census Bureau (2003). *Factors for features (CB03-FF.05)*. Retrieved February 27, 2005, from www.census.gov/Press-Release/www/releases/archives/facts_for_features/001627.html.

US Census Bureau (2004). *Educational attainment in the United States: 2003*. Retrieved February 27, 2005, from www.census.gov/prod/2004pubs/p20-550.pdf#search='Educational%20attainment%20in%20the%20United%20States:%202003'.

Westbrook, F. D., & Sedlacek, W. E. (1988). Workshop on using noncognitive variables with minority students in higher education. *Journal for Specialists in Group Work, 13*, 82–89.

Wilde, J. B., & Schau, C. G. (1991). Mentoring in graduate schools of education: Mentees' perceptions. *Journal of Experimental Education, 59*, 165–179.

Zhang, N., & Dixon, D. N. (2003). Acculturation and attitudes of Asian international students toward seeking psychological help. *Journal of Multicultural Counseling and Development, 31*, 205–222.

Chapter 17

Diversity and Workplace Mentoring Relationships: A Review and Positive Social Capital Approach

Belle Rose Ragins

Workforce projections suggest that diversified mentoring relationships will become the norm rather than the exception in the future. People of color are expected to comprise 32% of the labor force by 2010 (Fullerton & Toosi, 2001) and 36% by 2025 (Fullerton, 1999). Women are 47% of the labor force (Bureau of Labor Statistics, 2004) and their workforce participation is expected to outpace increases in men's participation in the next decade (Fullerton & Toosi, 2001). Workplace diversity extends to other groups as well. People with disabilities are 12% of the workforce (US Census, 2000), gay men and lesbians constitute between 4 and 17% of the work force (Gonsiorek & Weinrich, 1991), and 42% of the workforce will be over the age of 45 by 2015 (Fullerton, 1999). Increased immigration contributes to increasing religious diversity in the workplace, and it is projected that Islam will be the second largest religion in the US by 2010 (Digh, 1998).

Although diversity has become deeply entwined with most aspects of organizational life, it is often framed as a "challenge" that needs to be "managed" in organizations (Ragins & Gonzalez, 2003). Without doubt, diversified mentoring relationships face unique challenges and dilemmas (cf. Clutterbuck & Ragins, 2002). However, what is missing from current dialogues is the unique capacity for learning, growth, and enrichment that may emerge from diverse mentoring relationships. Indeed, current movements involving positive psychology (Seligman & Csikszentmihalyi, 2000; Snyder & Lopez, 2002), positive organizational scholarship (cf. Cameron, Dutton, & Quinn, 2003; Dutton & Ragins, 2007), and positive organizational behavior (Luthans, 2002; Luthans & Youssef, 2004) offer fresh perspectives to the mentoring arena. Instead of emphasizing what is wrong with or lacking in individuals or relationships, these positive movements examine what individuals, relationships, and organizations look like when they are at their best. Using a positive perspective, work relationships are viewed not only in terms of their challenges, problems, and dilemmas, but also are seen as potential sites of vitality, energy, thriving, resilience, flourishing, and generativity (Cameron, Dutton, & Quinn, 2003; Dutton & Ragins, 2007).

This positive perspective widens our view of diversity, allowing us to "see the sun as well as its shadow." Organizational scholarship often takes a deficit approach and the study of diversity and mentoring is no exception. For example, many studies examine whether women and people of color experience the same benefits, processes, and outcomes of mentoring as their White male counterparts. This comparison essentially uses the experience of White males as the standard by which mentoring relationships are evaluated, and ignores the possibility that diverse relationships may produce a broader or entirely different array of processes and outcomes. As a consequence, diverse mentoring relationships may be viewed more in terms of their weaknesses than their strengths. For example, if researchers frame a study in terms of instrumental outcomes, finding that female mentors offer less career advancement to their protégés than male mentors, they may miss what the female mentor actually offers her protégé: relational outcomes involving personal learning, development, and growth (cf. Fletcher & Ragins, in press; Kram, 1996; Ragins & Verbos, 2007). A positive perspective therefore offers a more balanced perspective on the strengths and weaknesses of diversified mentoring relationships.

Accordingly, the primary purpose of this chapter is to break new ground by applying a positive organizational relationship perspective to the arena of mentoring and diversity. In particular, this chapter offers the proposition that mentoring can be a source of positive social capital that expands the generative capacity of its members and creates states of positive psychological capital involving self-efficacy, hope, optimism, and resilience in its members (Baker & Dutton, 2007; Dutton & Heaphy, 2003; Luthans & Youssef, 2004). Nested within this positive mentoring perspective is the examination of an extended range of positive social capital processes, experiences, and outcomes uniquely associated with diversified mentoring relationships.

The chapter is organized as follows. First, I define diversified mentoring relationships, briefly review what we know about these relationships, and identify key challenges in the study of these relationships. Next, I define positive social and psychological capital and apply these concepts to the study of mentoring relationships. I then examine diversified mentoring relationships using a positive social capital perspective. Finally, I conclude with a roadmap for future research in this new and exciting area of mentoring research.

Diversity and Mentoring in the Workplace: Research Findings and Limitations

What are Diversified Mentoring Relationships?

Diversified mentoring relationships are defined as mentors and protégés who differ on the basis of race, ethnicity, gender, sexual orientation, disability, religion, socio-economic class, or other group memberships *associated with power in organizations* (Ragins, 1997a). A power perspective holds that mentoring relationships are influenced by inter-group power relationships within the organizational context (Ragins, 1997a, 1997b). For example, a cross-race mentoring relationship in a historically Black college will differ in processes and outcomes from a relationship with the same demography in a primarily White academic institution. Similarly, significant differences are expected in cross-gender relationships involving male mentors and female protégés as compared to female mentors and male protégés (cf. O'Neill & Blake-Beard, 2002), and the gender composition of the organization should influence these relationships (Ragins, 1989). To emphasize this subtle but important distinction, this chapter uses the terms "dominant" and "nondominant" rather than "minority" and "majority." Unlike the term "minority," "nondominant" explicitly extends beyond race, ethnicity, and gender to include groups that typically have less power in organizations (e.g., gay men, lesbians, bisexuals and transgendered employees, employees with disabilities, and those in religious minorities).

Although the consideration of power and organizational context is critical, most studies of workplace mentoring define diversity in simple demographic terms. As discussed later, this approach has created a number of problems and limitations in the study of diversity and mentoring in organizations.

Race and Gender Effects in Mentoring Relationships

Most research on diversity and workplace mentoring has investigated race and gender differences in protégés' reports about whether they have a mentor, the mentoring functions provided, and the job attitudes and career outcomes associated with having a current or prior relationship. Because a number of comprehensive literature reviews on diversity and mentoring have been published recently (cf. Noe, Greenberger, & Wang, 2002; O'Neill, 2002; Ragins, 1999a, 1999b, 2002; Wanberg, Welsh, & Hezlett, 2003), this section offers a relatively succinct review of the literature.

Developing the mentoring relationship. A fair number of studies have examined whether race or gender affects the probability of having a mentor. Studies consistently find that women are as likely as men to have a mentor (Dreher & Ash, 1990; Dreher & Cox, 1996; Fagenson, 1989; Ragins & Cotton, 1999; Ragins & Scandura, 1994), though there is no consensus in studies of race. Some studies have found that Blacks are as likely as Whites to have a mentor (Blake, 1999; Dreher & Cox, 1996; Mobley, Jaret, Marsh, & Lim, 1994; Thomas, 1990), but at least one study found that Blacks are less likely to have a mentor than Whites (Viator, 2001). Although race and gender may have different effects on the probability of getting a mentor, both women (Ragins & Cotton, 1991) and African Americans (Viator, 2001) report more barriers to getting a mentor than their White male counterparts.

Existing research suggests that the protégé's race and gender may influence who becomes his or her mentor. While having a mentor of a different race or gender is commonplace for female protégés and protégés of color, few White male protégés have mentors of a different race or gender (Collins, Kamya, & Tourse, 1997; Dreher & Cox, 1996; Ragins & Cotton, 1999; Thomas, 1990). There are at least three reasons for this. First, nondominant protégés may have restricted access to nondominant mentors because of the relative shortage of women and people of color at higher organizational ranks (Ragins, 1989). However, the role modeling and support functions provided by nondominant mentors are critical, and protégés of color are likely to go outside their department to develop these vital relationships (Thomas, 1990).

Second, female mentors and mentors of color may seek relationships with protégés of the same race and gender because they identify with these protégés and want to help them overcome barriers to advancement (Ragins & Scandura, 1994, 1997; Ragins, Townsend, & Mattis, 1998). Finally, White male protégés may not be attracted to relationships with nondominant mentors since these mentors may not be viewed as role models (Ragins, 1997b; Ragins & McFarlin, 1990) and are often restricted in their access to power-related resources (Dreher & Cox, 1996; Ragins & Cotton, 1999). Taken together, this line of research supports the idea that dominant and nondominant groups differ in the development of their mentoring relationships.

Mentor behaviors in the relationship.   A number of studies have examined whether protégés' race or gender is related to their reports of the behaviors or functions exhibited by their mentors. This research yields inconsistent findings for both race and gender (cf. reviews by Ragins, 1999a; Wanberg et al., 2003). Some studies have found that male and female protégés do not differ in reports of mentor functions (Dreher & Ash, 1990; Ensher & Murphy, 1997; Noe, 1988), but other research has found gender effects (Burke, McKeen, & McKenna, 1990; Feldman, Folks, & Turnley, 1999a; Tharenou, 2005). Similarly, while some investigations have found that Blacks report fewer mentor functions than Whites (Koberg, Boss, & Goodman, 1998; Thomas, 1990; Viator, 2001), other research indicates that they are as likely as Whites to report that their mentors provide career support in the relationship (Blake, 1999) and one study found that African Americans and Latinos reported more mentoring functions than their White counterparts (Koberg, Boss, Chappell, & Ringer, 1994).

These inconsistent findings may be due to at least three reasons. First, these studies differ in the degree to which they control for the racial and gender composition of the relationship. Studies that examine the interaction of race and gender offer different and perhaps more accurate assessments than studies that only examine the main effects of race or gender (cf. Ragins, 1999a). Although relatively few studies have examined the racial or gender composition of the relationship, these studies have found that relationship composition influences reports of mentor functions. Protégés of color in same-race relationships report receiving more psychosocial (Koberg et al., 1998; Thomas, 1990) and career development support (Ensher & Murphy, 1997) than protégés of color in cross-race relationships. Similarly, female protégés with female mentors report receiving more psychosocial (Koberg et al., 1998; Sosik & Godshalk, 2000b; Tharenou, 2005; Thomas, 1990) and role modeling functions (Ragins & McFarlin, 1990) than female protégés with male mentors. Gender composition also affects the mentor's reports on the relationship; male mentors report providing equivalent psychosocial functions to both male and female protégés while female mentors report giving more psychosocial mentoring to female than male protégés (Allen & Eby, 2004).

Second, studies vary in their control for variables that influence protégé reports of mentor functions. These reports are associated with the duration of the relationship (Burke & McKeen, 1997), who initiated the relationship (Scandura & Williams, 2001), whether the mentor was formally assigned (Chao, Walz, & Gardner, 1992; Ragins & Cotton, 1999; Ragins, Cotton, & Miller, 2000), and whether the mentor was a supervisor (Burke, McKenna, & McKeen, 1991; Ragins & McFarlin,

1990; Sosik & Godshalk, 2005) or held a higher ranking position (Ragins, 2002; Struthers, 1995). The sex-role orientation of the protégé (Scandura & Ragins, 1993) and the interpersonal comfort in the relationship (Allen, Day, & Lentz, 2005) also influence reports of mentor functions.

Finally, the discovery of deep-level diversity may affect reports of mentoring functions. Deep-level diversity, which is the similarities and differences in attitudes, beliefs, and values (Harrison, Price & Bell, 1998), influences mentoring relationships; protégés who perceive their mentors as more similar report more support and greater satisfaction from the relationship than protégés who perceive their mentor as dissimilar (Ensher & Murphy, 1997). One study found that perceived attitudinal similarity was a better predictor of satisfaction with mentor and support received from mentors than racial or gender similarity (Ensher, Grant-Vallone, & Marelich, 2002). Time is also an important factor to consider; while demographic diversity has a strong initial impact on work relationships, over time this effect dissipates as similarities and differences in deep-level diversity are discovered (Harrison et al., 1998).

Outcomes for protégés.   Existing research indicates that employees with mentors report greater compensation, more promotions, and more positive work attitudes than those without mentors (cf. Allen, Eby, Poteet, Lentz, & Lima, 2004) and the protégé's gender does not moderate the career outcomes associated with the presence of a mentor (Baugh, Lankau, & Scandura, 1996; Dreher & Ash, 1990; Fagenson, 1989; Ragins et al., 2000). However, the mentor's gender plays a key role in predicting protégé outcomes. In support of a power perspective, some studies have found that the presence of a male mentor is associated with greater protégé compensation than the presence of a female mentor (Dreher & Cox, 1996; Dreher & Chargois, 1998; Ragins & Cotton, 1999; Wallace, 2001). Female protégés with male mentors earn more than female protégés with female mentors, and male protégés with male mentors receive greater compensation than any other gender combination (Ragins & Cotton, 1999).

Similar findings have been found for race; protégés with White mentors earn greater compensation than protégés with mentors of color. Dreher and Cox (1996) found that although Black and Hispanic MBAs were less likely than their White counterparts to establish relationships with White mentors, those who established relationships with White mentors received more compensation than those who had mentors of color. Strikingly, employees with female mentors or mentors of color did not receive more compensation than employees who did not have a mentor (Dreher & Cox, 1996). These findings were replicated in a sample of graduates of historically Black institutions of higher education; even after controlling for age and education, only the presence of a White male mentor was associated with an income advantage for Black protégés (Dreher & Chargois, 1998).

Limitations of Research on Diversified Mentoring Relationships

This review reveals at least five limitations or challenges to research on diversified mentoring relationships (see also: Ragins, 1999b, 2002). First, most studies have been limited to race or gender, and most of the race research compares Caucasians with African Americans. There is very little published research on the mentoring experiences of other nondominant groups in the workplace. Two studies have been published on age diversity, but the results are inconsistent; one study found older protégés reporting more mentoring functions (Scandura & Williams, 2001), but a second study found the opposite effect (Finkelstein, Allen, & Rhoton, 2003). A study of socioeconomic class revealed that career mentoring predicted early career promotions for employees with upper-class backgrounds but not for those from lower-class backgrounds (Whitely, Dougherty, & Dreher, 1991). There is a lack of published research on the effects of sexual orientation, disability, and religion on mentoring relationships in the workplace, but two unpublished studies on sexual orientation were discovered. In a study of 253 gay and lesbian employees in Texas, workers with mentors reported more job satisfaction, job involvement, and promotions than those lacking mentors, but differences in compensation were not found (Hebl, Lin, Tonidandel, & Knight, 2003). This study also found that protégés with mentors of the same sexual orientation reported more job satisfaction, job involvement, and psychosocial support than those with heterosexual mentors. Moreover, consistent with a power perspective, workers with heterosexual mentors received more promotions than those with gay or lesbian mentors. In his dissertation study of 617 gay and lesbian employees in Canada and the US, Church (2006) discovered that nationality affected the development of mentoring relationships. Organizational heterosexism was a barrier to gaining a mentor in the US but not in Canada. Moreover, stronger reports of heterosexism were associated with receiving more psychosocial support from Canadian mentors but less psychosocial support from American mentors. These studies offer a glimpse into some of the similarities and differences in mentoring experiences and support the caveat that mentoring experiences may or may not generalize across diverse groups.

Second, with few exceptions (e.g., Catalyst, 1999; Dreher & Cox, 1996; Goto, 1999; Kalbfleisch & Davies, 1991), most studies have examined single dimensions of diversity (i.e., race or gender), but fail to capture the effects of multiple group memberships or compare mentoring experiences among African American, Latino, Asian, Native Americans or multiracial groups. This monolithic approach to mentoring is problematic in that it assumes that individuals are not members of multiple groups (e.g., that individuals have a race or a gender but not both) and that nondominant or "minority" groups have the same mentoring experiences. In contrast to this assumption, Catalyst's (1999) study of 1735 women found that Asian American women were less likely than Latinas to have mentors and that African American women were more likely than other women of color to receive race-related job advice from their mentors.

Third, very little research has examined the effects of the composition of the mentoring relationship on processes and outcomes. There are four cells that represent the composition of the mentoring relationship on any given dimension of diversity: dominant mentor/nondominant protégé, dominant mentor/dominant protégé, nondominant mentor/nondominant protégé and nondominant mentor/dominant protégé. Research on race and gender consistently reveals one cell that is small or even missing from most samples: dominant group protégés (e.g., White or male protégés) with nondominant mentors (e.g., female mentors or mentors of color) (cf. O'Neill & Blake-Beard, 2002; Ragins & Cotton, 1999). As a consequence, mentoring researchers are often limited to a sample that allows them to compare homogeneous and diversified relationships for women and protégés of color but not for their White male counterparts. This can be a problem in studies that purport to measure same- and cross-race/gender relationships, but in actuality conduct this analysis only for women and protégés of color. In spite of the difficulty in obtaining a sample of White male protégés with nondominant mentors, assessing only race and gender effects for protégés without including information about the mentor's race or gender masks the possibility that the study is a biased comparison of dominant protégés in homogeneous relationships with nondominant protégés in homogeneous and diversified relationships.

Fourth, most mentoring research has been approached from the protégé's perspective; we know very little about how diversity affects the mentor or the dyadic processes in the relationship. Some research has examined the effect of mentors' gender on their decision to enter the relationship (Ragins & Cotton, 1993), their reports of the functions or behaviors they provide in their relationships (Allen & Eby, 2004; Burke, McKeen, & McKenna, 1993), and their reports of the costs and benefits associated with being a mentor (Ragins & Scandura, 1994). However, there has been a lack of research on how relationship diversity affects and is affected by mentors. Along similar lines, it is important to gather data from both members of the relationship to gain insight into the dynamics underlying the relationship. For example, Thomas (1993) found that mentors and protégés who shared similar strategies for dealing with racial differences in their relationship developed more effective relationships than members who used different strategies.

Fifth, many studies are plagued by assumptions of symmetrical effects. This refers to the assumption that heterogeneity and homogeneity in relationships mean the same thing for different groups. For example, a relationship involving two White employees and a relationship involving two Black employees may both be classified as "same race" and combined into a "homogeneous relationship" category. This practice fails to recognize that the experiences, issues, and challenges faced by Black mentors and protégés are quite different than their White counterparts (cf. Johnson-Bailey & Cervero, 2004). The assumption of symmetrical effects also distorts the study of heterogeneous mentoring relationships. For example, cross-gender mentoring relationships involving male mentors and female protégés are often combined with cross-gender relationships involving female mentors and male protégés, even though these relationships have very different processes and outcomes (cf. O'Neill & Blake-Beard, 2002).

In addition to addressing these limitations, research on diversity and workplace mentoring needs to detangle the complexities associated with identity and group membership. Group memberships vary in the extent to which they are important or salient to the individual, their partner, and their relationship (cf. Ragins & Gonzalez, 2003). Groups also differ in their current and prior experiences with discrimination; some groups have a stronger legacy of discrimination than others. Finally, the visibility of group membership should be considered. Individuals with invisible stigmas (e.g., sexual orientation, invisible disability, religion) face the challenge of whether or not to disclose their stigma even though their stigma affects their needs, behaviors, and expectations of the relationship (Ragins, in press).

These issues and limitations point to a much broader concern: the restricted perspective of the unique processes and outcomes in diversified mentoring relationships.

The Need for a Relational Perspective on Mentoring

Like other research on mentoring (cf. Ragins & Verbos, 2007), research on diversified mentoring suffers from a restricted perspective on what constitutes effective mentoring. Relationship effectiveness typically is assessed through a relatively narrow range of readily available work and career outcomes (e.g., compensation, promotion, and job attitudes). This leads to the situation in which mentoring is defined by the criteria used to measure its effectiveness, which restricts our view of the relationship. Perhaps it is natural that mentoring relationships in organizations are viewed first and foremost as work relationships that benefit the organization and its members in their roles as employees. However, although organizational outcomes are salient for many organizational scholars and practitioners, these outcomes may not capture the full meaning, value, and effectiveness of mentoring relationships (Ragins & Verbos, 2007). Although some individuals enter mentoring relationships for the instrumental outcomes that are offered (promotions, advancement, prestige), there exists the possibility of a fuller, deeper range of relational outcomes and processes in mentoring relationships that have yet to be studied or even fully articulated in the literature (cf. Fletcher & Ragins, in press; Ragins, 2005; Ragins & Verbos, 2007).

What is missing from current dialogues is a relational perspective that defines mentoring relationships in terms of their ability to foster mutual growth, learning, and development in personal, professional, and career domains that extend within and beyond organizational boundaries (Ragins, 2005; Ragins & Verbos, 2007). Moreover, this relational perspective allows us to consider a broader and richer array of processes and outcomes that may reflect the unique needs, values, and experiences of nondominant group members (cf. Fletcher & Ragins, in press). Let us now turn to expanding our view of mentoring by applying positive perspectives that are aligned with and enriched by diversity in mentoring relationships.

A Positive Social Capital Approach to Mentoring

Mentoring relationships fall along a continuum ranging from high-quality to marginal or even dysfunctional mentoring states (Ragins & Verbos, 2007). This section focuses on the positive side of the continuum and applies a positive organizational relationship perspective to broaden our view of mentoring and uncover some of the unique processes and outcomes of diversified mentoring relationships.

This section is organized as follows. First, a general overview of the positive organizational relationship field as it applies to mentoring relationships is presented. A key proposition advanced here is that positive perspectives on organizational relationships can illuminate core qualities and properties of high-quality mentoring relationships. Next, I examine positive social capital as a function and outcome of high-quality mentoring relationships. Mentoring is posited to be both a form of positive social capital and the means by which positive social capital is developed in organizations and careers. I explore the idea that mentoring can be a high-quality connection (e.g., Dutton & Heaphy, 2003) that produces positive states of psychological capital (Luthans & Youssef, 2004) for both mentors and protégés. Finally, I apply these positive relational perspectives to diverse mentoring relationships and offer the idea that a positive social capital approach provides a richer and more accurate assessment of the unique processes and outcomes of diversified mentoring relationships.

Positive Organizational Relationships and Mentoring

Positive organizational scholarship involves the study of positive outcomes, processes, and attributes of organizations and their members (Cameron et al., 2003). As a new area of inquiry nested within positive organizational scholarship, the field of positive organizational relationships (POR) builds on the positive psychology view that relationships are a central source of life satisfaction, enrichment, development, and personal growth for individuals (cf. Berscheid, 1999; Reis & Gable, 2003; Snyder & Lopez, 2002). The field of positive organizational relationships examines the conditions under which relationships bring out the very best in their members by increasing their capacity for growth, generativity, resilience, enrichment, and vitality within and across work settings (Dutton & Ragins, 2007).

Although mentoring relationships vary with respect to quality, at their best they personify positive relationships at work (cf. Ragins & Verbos, 2007). Positive organizational relationship theory therefore offers mentoring scholars a rich theoretical framework for conceptualizing positive relational states in mentoring relationships and for capturing variables and processes that have not been discussed or identified in the mentoring literature.

Although there are numerous vistas that are opened by POR, the new constructs of positive social capital and high-quality connections (Baker & Dutton, 2007; Dutton & Heaphy, 2003) offer core insights for capturing the construct of high-quality mentoring relationships and resonate with some of the unique processes and outcomes of diversified mentoring relationships.

Positive Social Capital and High-Quality Connections

Social capital and social networks.   Social capital is generally defined as resources or assets that are created within and flow through relationships (Burt, 1997; Coleman, 1988; Leana & Van Buren, 1999). Unlike human capital, which resides in the individual, social capital resides within relationships and includes such resources as influence, information, knowledge, support, advice, and goodwill (Adler & Kwon, 2002). Social capital flows through social networks (cf. Burt, 1997; Granovetter, 1973; Lin, Ensel, & Vaughn, 1981), and mentoring has been positioned within a broader framework of social networks (Higgins, 2007; Higgins, Chandler, & Kram, in press; Higgins & Kram, 2001) that provide social capital to both mentors and protégés (cf. Seibert, Kraimer, & Liden, 2001). However, what is missing from this discussion is the nature of social capital. Social capital is often assumed to be positive, but it can be negative when the resources provided in relationships are used in destructive, manipulative, or defeating ways (Baker & Dutton, 2007; Baker & Faulkner, 2004). The concept of positive social capital as a process and outcome of positive work relationships offers exciting new possibilities for the study of high-quality mentoring relationships.

Positive social capital and high-quality connections.   Baker and Dutton (2007) define positive social capital as the resources that expand the *generative capacity* of individuals in relationships, leading to their increased ability to grow, thrive, and flourish in organizations. They define capacity as the individual's ability to achieve personal and professional goals and propose that capacity is generative when it renews and reproduces itself, expanding the individual's abilities and enabling the combination and recombination of resources in novel and new ways. They stress that positive social capital needs to be viewed both in terms of the *means* by which it is created and the *end* to which it is used, and theorize that positive social capital helps individuals achieve personal and collective goals through high-quality connections and systems of generalized reciprocity involving mutual exchange, aid, and benefit.

As a form of positive social capital, high-quality connections capture the relational essence of high-quality mentoring relationships. High-quality connections (HQCs) involve short interactions or long-term relationships that have three key features (Dutton & Heaphy, 2003). First, HQCs have higher *emotional carrying capacity* than other relationships and interactions. Emotional capacity reflects both the expression of more emotions as well as a greater range of emotions in the relationship. These relationships represent a "safe place" for expressing a range of positive and negative emotions. Second, HQCs have greater levels of *tensility*, which is the relationship's ability to bend and withstand strain in the face of challenges or setbacks. These relationships are able to withstand stress, conflict, and tension. Finally, HQCs are distinguished from other relationships and interactions by their capacity for *connectivity*, which involves generativity and openness to new ideas and influences as well as the ability to deflect behaviors that will shut down generative processes.

Dutton and Heaphy (2003) propose that people in high-quality connections have three unique subjective experiences. First, they experience feelings of *vitality and aliveness*, which are aligned with feelings of positive arousal and heightened states of positive energy. Second, they experience feelings of *positive regard*, which are derived from a sense of emotional connection, attachment, and security in the relationship. Finally, individuals in HQCs experience a sense of *mutuality*, which involves a state of mutual empathy, vulnerability, and responsiveness.

According to Dutton and Heaphy (2003), high-quality connections have four outcomes for individuals and relationships (see also Fletcher, 1998; Fletcher & Ragins, in press). First, HQCs create *new and valued resources* (e.g., trust, power, commitment, and influence) that are exchanged within the relationship. Second, HQCs provide a safe environment for members to experiment with the expression and development of different possible selves, thus leading to the development of *valued, authentic, and expanded identities*. Third, HQCs yield *psychological growth* and are the contexts for secure bases of attachment that promote caregiving in organizations. Fourth, HQCs enable the creation of new *knowledge*, facilitate relational and tacit *learning*, and increase members' understanding of themselves, their relationship, and the organization. As discussed later, these outcomes may have particular relevance for diversified mentoring relationships.

Positive psychological capital.   HQCs are aligned with the concept of positive psychological capital. As part of a broader framework of positive organizational behavior, Luthans and Youssef (2004) define positive psychological capital as psychological capacities or states that can be developed, measured, and managed for the purpose of improving performance in organizations. They identify four dimensions of positive psychological capital: a) *self-efficacy and confidence*, which involves the belief that one can mobilize cognitive resources to achieve specific outcomes; b) *hope*, which involves the motivation, willpower, and pathways to achieve goals; c) *optimism*, which involves attributing positive events to stable and internal causes; and d) *resiliency*, which is the capacity to bounce back from adversity or failure. Luthans and Youssef (2004) propose that these positive psychological capital states can be nurtured, developed, and carried with individuals across organizational settings.

An integration of positive organizational scholarship and positive organizational behavior perspectives yields the idea that high-quality connections may produce outcomes of psychological growth involving the four dimensions of positive psychological capital discussed above. These psychological outcomes hold particular promise for the study of mentoring and diversity in organizations.

Mentoring as High-Quality Connections: New Visions for Research on Relational Processes and Outcomes

At its best, mentoring is a high-quality connection that involves the transfer of positive social capital within and across organizational and career contexts. As a high-quality connection that produces positive psychological capital, high-quality mentoring relationships constitute both a form of positive social capital and the means by which positive social capital is developed in organizations and careers.

A positive social capital approach offers four advantages for the study of workplace mentoring. First, it expands the lens for viewing the nature, processes, and outcomes of mentoring relationships. Traditionally, the quality of workplace mentoring has been assessed through the instrumental outcomes provided to the protégé (cf. Ragins & Verbos, 2007). Using a positive social capital approach, relationship quality could be assessed not only through organizational and career outcomes, but also through relational properties of high-quality connections, such as the relationship's emotional carrying capacity, tensility, and connectivity. Along similar lines, mentoring scholars could extend their focus beyond psychosocial and career development functions to incorporate subjective experiences associated with HQCs, such as feelings of vitality, aliveness, positive regard, and mutuality that spring from the mentoring relationship. Perhaps most important, a positive social capital approach offers a new array of outcomes that assess the quality and effectiveness of mentoring relationships. Specifically, mentoring scholars can examine the degree to which mentoring relationships offer HQC outcomes, such as the resources exchanged in the relationship, the development of authentic, valued, and expanded identities, psychological growth, and the creation of new knowledge and new ways of learning. In addition, mentoring relationships may be evaluated by their ability to produce positive psychological capital outcomes that include self-efficacy, confidence, hope, optimism, and resiliency. By expanding the range of characteristics, processes, and outcomes studied in mentoring relationships, mentoring scholars may achieve a more complete and accurate assessment of the full continuum of quality in the relationship.

Second, a positive social capital approach can explain processes underlying the relationships between mentoring and career outcomes. For example, although we know that the presence of a mentor is associated with increased job and career satisfaction (Allen et al., 2004), the processes responsible for these relationships have not been articulated or studied. Luthans and Youssef (2004) propose that positive psycho-logical capital variables lead to increased productivity and performance in organiza-tions. If so, positive psychological variables may not only be outcomes of effective mentoring relationships, but they may also mediate the relationship between men-toring and other outcomes.

Third, a positive social capital approach increases our understanding of the benefits mentors receive from the relationship. Existing theory and research on mentoring have focused primarily on the protégé's side of the relationship (cf. Ragins & Verbos, 2007). Because the benefits, processes, and experiences of high-quality con-nections hold for both members of the relationship, an examination of these pro-cesses can shed needed light on the mentor's experience in the relationship.

Finally, the relational aspect of positive social capital makes it particularly relevant to groups with cultural values aligned with collectivism, communal norms, inter-dependence, and mutuality (e.g., women, Asian Americans, and Latinos) (Ragins, 2005), thus allowing mentoring scholars a more complete and accurate perspective on the mentoring experiences of nondominant groups.

Positive Social Capital in Diversified Mentoring Relationships

The positive social and psychological capital produced in high-quality mentoring rela-tionships has unique implications for diversified relationships. As discussed earlier, an integration of the high-quality connection and positive psychological capital per-spectives (Dutton & Heaphy, 2003; Luthans & Youssef, 2004) reveals four distinct outcomes of high-quality relationships. Let us now examine how diversity in men-toring relationships shapes these four outcomes.

#1: Development of valued, authentic, and expanded identities. High-quality mentoring relationships can provide a safe haven for exploring, developing, and constructing authentic identities in the workplace. This function is particularly important for nondominant group members who struggle with identity issues in the workplace. Organizational norms reflect the identity of dominant groups (cf. Ely, 1995; Nkomo & Cox, 1996), and nondominant group identities are often invis-ible, marginalized, or even penalized in many work settings (cf. Creed & Scully, 2000; Ragins, 2004, in press). Consequently, members of nondominant groups often experience pressures to both assimilate and preserve their identities, which can lead to identity stress and conflict (Nkomo & Cox, 1996; Ragins, 2004). High-quality mentoring relationships can offer nondominant group members key insights and strategies for constructing and displaying marginalized, hidden, and devalued iden-tities. In addition, partners who are members of the same nondominant group are able to share strategies for developing authentic and balanced identities in the work-place. However, irrespective of group membership, high-quality mentoring relationships allow both mentors and protégés to bring their full identities to the relationship; even if these identities are not valued in their organization, they are valued in their

relationship. This provides an invaluable source of psychological validation and support.

#2: Psychological growth and positive psychological capital.   While important for most workers, the development of positive psychological capital is absolutely critical for employees facing exclusion, marginalization, prejudice, and discrimination in the workplace. Toxic work environments take a daily toll in depleting workers' positive psychological capital, and high-quality mentoring can compensate for this by restoring and expanding positive psychological states associated with self-efficacy, confidence, hope, optimism, and resilience.

Diversified mentoring relationships can also provide a unique source of psychological growth related to diversity (cf. Ragins, 2002). The intimacy, acceptance, and closeness of high-quality mentoring relationships provide a safe place for mentors and protégés to explore their own attitudes, attributions, and prejudices. Members can confront their own stereotypes and sources of privilege associated with group membership. Diverse relationships can also push members beyond their comfort zones, which can lead to a cognitive restructuring of stereotypes (Ragins, 2002) and a reevaluation of mentoring schemas or expectations derived from group stereotypes (Ragins & Verbos, 2007).

#3: New knowledge and ways of learning.   Diversified mentoring relationships can offer their members unique opportunities for acquiring new knowledge, information, skills, and ways of learning. These benefits may accrue to members of both dominant and nondominant groups.

Members of nondominant groups can gain two forms of knowledge from diversified mentoring relationships. First, these members are often denied access to the information, knowledge, and social capital provided in dominant-group networks (Ibarra, 1993; James, 2000), so their mentoring relationship with a dominant group member can provide critical access to important and otherwise unavailable sources of knowledge. Second, mentors and protégés with the same nondominant group status may share their strategies for thriving and surviving as nondominant members of organizations. *Thriving strategies* are defined here as positive strategies that members of nondominant groups use in the face of discrimination, prejudice, and ignorance in work environments. One example of a thriving strategy is "grasping teachable moments," which involves turning negative episodes into opportunities for education and enlightenment (cf. Creed & Scully, 2000). Other examples of thriving strategies include "staying the course and turning the cheek" behaviors exemplified by Mahatma Gandhi and Martin Luther King, and the concept of "it takes a village," based on an African proverb that emphasizes the importance of community in creating social change. Thriving strategies for obtaining work–life balance can also be offered in mentoring relationships (cf. Nielson, Carlson, & Lankau, 2001; Wallace, 2001), and diversified relationships may take this one step further by including the impact of identity on life roles and work–life balance.

Members of dominant groups may also gain unique opportunities for learning and knowledge from the relationship. Diversified relationships offer them the opportunity to learn about the culture, experiences, and values of nondominant groups and to gain insight into the everyday experience of being "the other" in organizations (Ragins,

2002). Close mentoring relationships can help dominant group members develop multicultural skills and competencies that they can use in other relationships and settings (Ragins, 1997a). The ability to learn and integrate knowledge about other cultures is a core competency associated with the effective management of diversity in workgroups and organizations (e.g., Ely & Thomas, 2001) and is also a life skill that is critical for members of a global community.

#4: Exchange of resources.   High-quality connections involve the exchange of new and valued resources, such as trust, power, commitment, and influence (Dutton & Heaphy, 2003). These resources are particularly important for members of groups that lack power in organizations (Ragins, 1997a; Ragins & Sundstrom, 1989). For these individuals, mentoring relationships with dominant partners can provide needed access to career and organizational resources associated with power (cf. Dreher & Cox, 1996; Ragins & Cotton, 1999; Thomas, 1999).

At its core, mentoring is a relationship that involves the mutual exchange of information, knowledge, and resources (Mullen, 1994; Young & Perrewé, 2000a). In addition to the benefits received by protégés (e.g., Wanberg et al., 2003), mentors report receiving such benefits as commitment, information, and a loyal base of support from their relationships (Ragins & Scandura, 1999). These benefits may be particularly useful to nondominant mentors, since they lack access to networks that provide many of these resources. In addition to these benefits, both dominant and nondominant mentors gain a unique sense of satisfaction and fulfillment through helping their nondominant protégés reach their full career potential.

In sum, diversified mentoring relationships may provide unique and important forms of positive social capital to their members. As a corollary proposition, positive social capital may also assume different forms in diversified mentoring relationships. A positive social capital perspective widens the lens used to view mentoring relationships and can offer a more accurate assessment of the processes and outcomes of diversified mentoring relationships. This approach not only captures more fully the experiences of nondominant members but also avoids the pitfall of using the experiences of dominant group members as a basis for evaluating the experiences of nondominant members in mentoring relationships.

Roadmap for Future Research

A positive social capital perspective offers at least three important avenues for future research. First, future research can test the propositions developed here by examining mentoring as a high-quality connection that can produce positive social and psychological capital. Specifically, this research could examine when and how mentoring relationships become high-quality connections. Using HQC theory (Dutton & Heaphy, 2003) as a template, mentoring scholars can examine the emotional carrying capacity, tensility, and connectivity of mentoring relationships, as well as the subjective experiences of vitality, positive regard, and mutuality that may be experienced in high-quality mentoring relationships. In addition to assessing the degree that these processes and experiences are present in mentoring relationships, future research can examine the conditions under which mentoring relationships become high-quality connections. What individual, dyadic, and organizational factors lead to the development of high-quality mentoring relationships in work settings?

Second, future research needs to employ a broader array of outcome variables in the study of high-quality mentoring relationships. A key point emphasized in this chapter is that our assessment of the quality and effectiveness of mentoring relationships has been unduly hampered by an over-reliance on instrumental outcomes of the relationship. A positive social capital perspective offers a fresh new array of variables and methods for assessing the quality and effectiveness of mentoring relationships from both the mentors' and the protégés' perspective. Future research could examine the psychological growth experienced by mentors and protégés, the relational resources that are exchanged in the relationship, and how the relationship helps members develop authentic and valued identities in the workplace. The creation of new knowledge and new ways of learning represents an important social capital outcome of high-quality mentoring, and new research on learning processes in mentoring relationships (cf. Allen & Eby, 2003; Godshalk & Sosik, 2003; Lankau & Scandura, 2002) makes important inroads into our understanding of learning as a form of positive social capital in mentoring relationships. Finally, we need research that examines the conditions under which mentoring produces such positive psychological capital outcomes as self-efficacy, confidence, hope, optimism, and resiliency. Future studies need to examine the outcomes associated with these psychological states and whether these states mediate the relationship between the presence of a mentor and other outcomes of the relationship.

Finally, future research needs to examine the unique outcomes associated with diversified mentoring relationships. This chapter provides an initial foray into some of these outcomes, but more processes and outcomes related to diversity can be incorporated. For example, it would be useful to explore how the organization's culture, diversity climate, and leadership demography affect the development, processes, and outcomes of diversified mentoring relationships.

In conclusion, a positive perspective on organizational relationships can help mentoring scholars uncover the true essence of mentoring relationships: relationships that help their members grow, thrive, and flourish within and outside of organizations.

References

Adler, P. S., & Kwon, S. W. (2002). Social capital: Prospectus for a new concept. *Academy of Management Review, 27*(1), 17–40.

Allen, T., Day, R., & Lentz, E. (2005). The role of interpersonal comfort in mentoring relationships. *Journal of Career Development, 31*(3), 155–169.

Allen, T. D., & Eby, L. T. (2003). Relationship effectiveness for mentors: Factors associated with learning and quality. *Journal of Management, 29*(4), 469–486.

Allen, T. D., & Eby, L. T. (2004). Factors related to mentor reports of mentoring functions provided: Gender and relational characteristics. *Sex Roles, 50*, 129–139.

Allen, T. D., Eby, L. T., Poteet, M. L., Lentz, E., & Lima, L. (2004). Career benefits associated with mentoring for protégés: A meta analysis. *Journal of Applied Psychology, 89*, 127–136.

Baker, W. E., & Dutton, J. (2007). Enabling positive social capital at work. In J. Dutton & B. R. Ragins (Eds.), *Exploring positive relationships at work: Building a theoretical and research foundation* (pp. 325–345). Mahwah, NJ: Lawrence Erlbaum and Associates.

Baker, W. E., & Faulkner, R. R. (2004). Social networks and loss of capital. *Social Networks,* *26*(2), 91–111.

Baugh, S. G., Lankau, M. J., & Scandura, T. A. (1996). An investigation of the effects of protégé gender on responses to mentoring. *Journal of Vocational Behavior, 49*(3), 309–323.

Berscheid, E. (1999). The greening of relationship science. *American Psychologist, 54*(4), 260–266.

Blake, S. (1999). The costs of living as an outsider within: An analysis of the mentoring relationships and career success of black and white women in the corporate sector. *Journal of Career Development, 26*(2), 21–36.

Bureau of Labor Statistics (2004). *BLS releases 2002–12 employment projections* (Report USDL 04-148). Washington, DC: United States Department of Labor.

Burke, R. J., & McKeen, C. A. (1997). Benefits of mentoring relationships among managerial and professional women: A cautionary tale. *Journal of Vocational Behavior, 51,* 43–57.

Burke, R. J., McKeen, C. A., & McKenna, C. (1990). Sex differences and cross-sex effects on mentoring: Some preliminary data. *Psychological Reports, 67,* 1011–1023.

Burke, R. J., McKeen, C. A., & McKenna, C. (1993). Correlates of mentoring in organizations: The mentor's perspective. *Psychological Reports, 72*(3), 883–896.

Burke, R. J., McKenna, C. S., & McKeen, C. A. (1991). How do mentorships differ from typical supervisory relationships? *Psychological Reports, 68,* 459–466.

Burt, R. S. (1997). The contingent value of social capital. *Administrative Science Quarterly, 42,* 339–365.

Cameron, K. S., Dutton, J. E., & Quinn, R. E. (2003). Foundations of positive organizational scholarship. In K. S. Cameron, J. E. Dutton, & R. E. Quinn (Eds.), *Positive organizational scholarship: Foundations of a new discipline* (pp. 3–13). San Francisco: Berrett-Koehler.

Catalyst (1999). *Women of color in corporate management: Opportunities and barriers.* New York: Author.

Chao, G. T., Walz, P. M., & Gardner, P. D. (1992). Formal and informal mentorships: A comparison on mentoring functions and contrast with nonmentored counterparts. *Personnel Psychology, 45,* 619–636.

Church, R. (2006). *The effects of organizational heterosexism on the mentoring relationships of gay and lesbian protégés.* Unpublished doctoral dissertation, University of Toronto, Toronto, Canada.

Clutterbuck, D., & Ragins, B. R. (2002). *Mentoring and diversity: An international perspective.* Oxford: Butterworth-Heinemann.

Coleman, J. S. (1988). Social capital in the creation of human capital. *American Journal of Sociology, 94*(Suppl.), S95–S120.

Collins, P. M., Kamya, H. A., & Tourse, R. W. (1997). Questions of racial diversity and mentorship: An empirical investigation. *Social Work, 42,* 145–152.

Creed, W., & Scully, M. (2000). Songs of ourselves: Employee's deployment of social identity in workplace encounters. *Journal of Management Inquiry, 9*(4), 391–413.

Digh, P. (1998). Religion in the workplace: Make a good-faith effort to accommodate. *HR Magazine, 43*(13), 85–91.

Dreher, G. F., & Ash, R. A. (1990). A comparative study of mentoring among men and women in managerial, professional, and technical positions. *Journal of Applied Psychology, 75*(5), 539–546.

Dreher, G. F., & Chargois, J. A. (1998). Gender, mentoring experiences, and salary attainment among graduates of an historically black university. *Journal of Vocational Behavior, 53,* 401–416.

Dreher, G. F., & Cox, T. H. (1996). Race, gender, and opportunity: A study of compensation attainment and the establishment of mentoring relationships. *Journal of Applied Psychology, 81,* 297–308.

Dutton, J. E., & Heaphy, E. D. (2003). The power of high-quality connections. In K. S. Cameron, J. E. Dutton, & R. E. Quinn (Eds.), *Positive organizational scholarship: Foundations of a new discipline* (pp. 263–278). San Francisco: Berrett-Koehler.

Dutton, J., & Ragins, B. R. (2007). *Exploring positive relationships at work: Building a theoretical and research foundation.* Mahwah, NJ: Lawrence Erlbaum and Associates.

Ely, R. J. (1995). The role of dominant identity and experience in organizational work on diversity. In S. E. Jackson & M. N. Ruderman (Eds.), *Diversity in work teams: Research paradigms for a changing workplace* (pp. 161–186). Washington, DC: American Psychological Association.

Ely, R. J., & Thomas, D. A. (2001). Cultural diversity at work: The effects of diversity perspectives on work group processes and outcomes. *Administrative Science Quarterly, 46,* 229–273.

Ensher, E. A., Grant-Vallone, E. J., & Marelich, W. D. (2002). Effects of perceived attitudinal and demographic similarity on protégés' support and satisfaction gained from their mentoring relationships. *Journal of Applied Social Psychology, 32,* 1407–1430.

Ensher, E. A., & Murphy, S. E. (1997). Effects of race, gender, perceived similarity, and contact on mentor relationships. *Journal of Vocational Behavior, 50,* 460–481.

Fagenson, E. A. (1989). The mentor advantage: Perceived career/job experiences of protégés vs. non-protégés. *Journal of Organizational Behavior, 10,* 309–320.

Feldman, D. C., Folks, W. R., & Turnley, W. H. (1999a). Mentor–protégé diversity and its impact on international internship experiences. *Journal of Organizational Behavior, 20,* 597–612.

Finkelstein, L. M., Allen, T. D., & Rhoton, L. A. (2003). An examination of the role of age in mentoring relationships. *Group & Organization Management, 28,* 249–281.

Fletcher, J. K. (1998). Relational practice: A feminist reconstruction of work. *Journal of Management Inquiry, 7,* 163–187.

Fletcher, J. K., & Ragins, B. R. (in press). Stone center relational theory: A window on relational mentoring. In B. R. Ragins & K. Kram (Eds.), *The handbook of mentoring: Theory, research and practice.* Thousand Oaks, CA: Sage.

Fullerton, H. N., Jr. (1999). Labor force participation: 75 years of change, 1950–98 and 1998–2025. *Monthly Labor Review, 122*(12), 3–12.

Fullerton, H. N., Jr., & Toosi, M. (2001). Labor force projections to 2010: Steady growth and changing composition. *Monthly Labor Review, 112*(11), 21–38.

Godshalk, V. M., & Sosik, J. J. (2003). Aiming for career success: The role of learning goal orientation in mentoring relationships. *Journal of Vocational Behavior, 63,* 417–437.

Gonsiorek, J. C., & Weinrich, J. D. (1991). The definition and scope of sexual orientation. In J. C. Gonsiorek & J. D. Weinrich (Eds.), *Homosexuality: Research implications for public policy* (pp. 1–12). Newbury Park, CA: Sage.

Goto, S. (1999). Asian Americans and developmental relationships. In A. Murrell, F. J. Crosby, & R. Ely (Eds.), *Mentoring dilemmas: Developmental relationships within multicultural organizations* (pp. 47–62). Hillsdale, NJ: Lawrence Erlbaum Press.

Granovetter, M. (1973). The strength of weak ties. *American Journal of Sociology, 78,* 1360–1380.

Harrison, D. A., Price, K. H., & Bell, M. P. (1998). Beyond relational demography: Time and the effects of surface- and deep-level diversity on work group cohesion. *Academy of Management Journal, 41*(1), 96–107.

Hebl, M. R., Lin, J., Tonidandel, S., & Knight, J. (2003, April). *Super models: The impact of like-mentors for homosexual employees.* Poster session presented at the Society for Industrial and Organizational Psychology annual conference, Orlando, FL.

Higgins, M. C. (2007). A contingency perspective on developmental networks. In J. Dutton & B. R. Ragins (Eds.), *Exploring positive relationships at work: Building a theoretical and research foundation* (pp. 207–224). Mahwah, NJ: Lawrence Erlbaum and Associates.

Higgins, M. C., Chandler, D., & Kram, K. E. (in press). Boundary spanning of developmental networks: A social network perspective on mentoring. In B. R. Ragins & K. E. Kram (Eds.), *The handbook of mentoring at work: Theory, research and practice*. Thousand Oaks, CA: Sage.

Higgins, M. C., & Kram, K. E. (2001). Reconceptualizing mentoring at work: A developmental network perspective. *Academy of Management Review, 26,* 264–288.

Ibarra, H. (1993). Personal networks of women and minorities in management: A conceptual framework. *Academy of Management Review, 18*(1), 56–87.

James, E. H. (2000). Race-related differences in promotions and support: Underlying effects of human and social capital. *Organization Science, 11,* 493–508.

Johnson-Bailey, J., & Cervero, R. M. (2004). Mentoring in black and white: The intricacies of cross-cultural mentoring. *Mentoring and Tutoring, 12*(1), 7–22.

Kalbfleisch, P. J., & Davies, A. B. (1991). Minorities and mentoring: Managing the multicultural institution. *Communication Education, 40,* 266–271.

Koberg, C. S., Boss, R. W., Chappell, D., & Ringer, R. C. (1994). Correlates and consequences of protégé mentoring in a large hospital. *Group & Organization Management, 19,* 219–239.

Koberg, C. S., Boss, R. W., & Goodman, E. (1998). Factors and outcomes associated with mentoring among health-care professionals. *Journal of Vocational Behavior, 53,* 58–72.

Kram, K. (1996). A relational approach to career development. In D. T. Hall (Ed.), *The career is dead – Long live the career: A relational approach to careers* (pp. 132–157). San Francisco: Jossey-Bass.

Lankau, M. J., & Scandura, T. A. (2002). An investigation of personal learning in mentoring relationships: Content, antecedents, and consequences. *Academy of Management Journal, 45,* 779–790.

Leana, C. R., & Van Buren, H. J., III. (1999). Organizational social capital and employment practices. *Academy of Management Review, 24*(3), 538–555.

Lin, N., Ensel, W. M., & Vaughn, J. C. (1981). Social resources and strength of ties: Structural factors in occupational status attainment. *American Sociological Review, 46,* 393–405.

Luthans, F. (2002). The need for and meaning of positive organizational behavior. *Journal of Organizational Behavior, 23,* 695–706.

Luthans, F., & Youssef, C. M. (2004). Human, social, and now positive psychological capital management: Investing in people for competitive advantage. *Organizational Dynamics, 33,* 143–160.

Mobley, G. M., Jaret, C., Marsh, K., & Lim, Y. Y. (1994). Mentoring, job satisfaction, gender, and the legal profession. *Sex Roles, 31,* 79–98.

Mullen, E. J. (1994). Framing the mentoring relationship as an information exchange. *Human Resource Management Review, 4,* 257–281.

Nielson, T. R., Carlson, D. S., & Lankau, M. J. (2001). The supportive mentor as a means of reducing the work–family conflict. *Journal of Vocational Behavior, 59*(3), 364–381.

Nkomo, S. M., & Cox, T. H., Jr. (1996). Diverse identities in organizations. In S. R. Clegg, C. Hardy, & W. R. Nord (Eds.), *Handbook of organization studies* (pp. 338–356). London: Sage.

Noe, R. A. (1988). An investigation of the determinants of successful assigned mentoring relationships. *Personnel Psychology, 41*(3), 457–479.

Noe, R. A., Greenberger, D. B., & Wang, S. (2002). Mentoring: What we know and where we might go from here. In G. R. Ferris & J. J. Martocchio (Eds.), *Research in Personnel and Human Resources Management* (Vol. 21, pp. 129–173). Greenwich, CT: Elsevier Science/JAI Press.

O'Neill, R. M. (2002). Gender and race in mentoring relationships: A review of the literature. In D. Clutterbuck & B. R. Ragins, *Mentoring and diversity: An international perspective* (pp. 1–22). Oxford: Butterworth-Heinemann.

O'Neill, R. M., & Blake-Beard, S. D. (2002). Gender barriers to the female mentor–male protégé relationship. *Journal of Business Ethics, 37,* 51–63.

Ragins, B. R. (1989). Barriers to mentoring: The female manager's dilemma. *Human Relations, 42*, 1–22.

Ragins, B. R. (1997a). Diversified mentoring relationships: A power perspective. *Academy of Management Review, 22*(2), 482–521.

Ragins, B. R. (1997b). Antecedents of diversified mentoring relationships. *Journal of Vocational Behavior, 51*(1), 90–109.

Ragins, B. R. (1999a). Gender and mentoring relationships: A review and research agenda for the next decade. In G. Powell (Ed.), *Handbook of gender and work* (pp. 347–370). Thousand Oaks, CA: Sage.

Ragins, B. R. (1999b). Where do we go from here and how do we get there? Methodological issues in conducting research on diversity and mentoring relationships. In A. Murrell, F. J. Crosby, & R. Ely (Eds.), *Mentoring dilemmas: Developmental relationships within multicultural organizations* (pp. 227–247). Mahwah, NJ: Lawrence Erlbaum Press.

Ragins, B. R. (2002). Understanding diversified mentoring relationships: Definitions, challenges and strategies. In D. Clutterbuck & B. R. Ragins, *Mentoring and diversity: An international perspective* (pp. 23–53). Oxford: Butterworth-Heinemann.

Ragins, B. R. (2004). Sexual orientation in the workplace: The unique work and career experiences of gay, lesbian and bisexual workers. *Research in Personnel and Human Resources Management, 23*, 37–122.

Ragins, B. R. (2005). *Towards a theory of relational mentoring.* Unpublished manuscript.

Ragins, B. R. (in press). Disclosure disconnects: Antecedents and consequences of disclosing invisible stigmas across life domains. *Academy of Management Review.*

Ragins, B. R., & Cotton, J. L. (1991). Easier said than done: Gender differences in perceived barriers to gaining a mentor. *Academy of Management Journal, 34*, 939–951.

Ragins, B. R., & Cotton, J. L. (1993). Gender and willingness to mentor in organizations. *Journal of Management, 19*, 97–111.

Ragins, B. R., & Cotton, J. (1999). Mentor functions and outcomes: A comparison of men and women in formal and informal mentoring relationships. *Journal of Applied Psychology, 84*(4), 529–550.

Ragins, B. R., Cotton, J. L., & Miller, J. S. (2000). Marginal mentoring: The effects of type of mentor, quality of relationship, and program design on work and career attitudes. *Academy of Management Journal, 43*(6), 1177–1194.

Ragins, B. R., & Gonzalez, J. (2003). Understanding diversity in organizations: Getting a grip on a slippery construct. In J. Greenberg (Ed.), *Organizational behavior: The state of the science* (2nd ed., pp. 125–163). Mahwah, NJ: Lawrence Erlbaum Press.

Ragins, B. R., & McFarlin, D. (1990). Perception of mentor roles in cross-gender mentoring relationships. *Journal of Vocational Behavior, 37*, 321–339.

Ragins, B. R., & Scandura, T. (1994). Gender differences in expected outcomes of mentoring relationships. *Academy of Management Journal, 37*, 957–971.

Ragins, B. R., & Scandura, T. A. (1997). The way we were: Gender and the termination of mentoring relationships. *Journal of Applied Psychology, 82*, 945–953.

Ragins, B. R., & Scandura, T. A. (1999). Burden or blessing? Expected costs and benefits of being a mentor. *Journal of Organizational Behavior, 20*, 493–509.

Ragins, B. R., & Sundstrom, E. (1989). Gender and power in organizations: A longitudinal perspective. *Psychological Bulletin, 105*(1), 51–88.

Ragins, B. R., Townsend, B., & Mattis, M. (1998). Gender gap in the executive suite: CEOs and female executives report on breaking the glass ceiling. *Academy of Management Executive, 12*(1), 28–42.

Ragins, B. R., & Verbos, A. K. (2007). Positive relationships in action: Relational mentoring and mentoring schemas in the workplace. In J. Dutton & B. R. Ragins (Eds.), *Exploring positive relationships at work: Building a theoretical and research foundation* (pp. 91–116). Mahwah, NJ: Lawrence Erlbaum and Associates.

Reis, H. T., & Gable, S. L. (2003). Toward a positive psychology of relationships. In C. L. M. Keyes & J. Haidt (Eds.), *Flourishing: Positive psychology and the life well-lived* (pp. 129–159). Washington, DC: American Psychological Association.

Scandura, T. A., & Ragins, B. R. (1993). The effects of sex and gender role orientation on mentorship in male-dominated occupations. *Journal of Vocational Behavior, 43*, 251–265.

Scandura, T. A., & Williams, E. A. (2001). An investigation of the moderating effects of gender on the relationships between mentorship initiation and protégé perceptions of mentoring functions. *Journal of Vocational Behavior, 59*, 342–363.

Seibert, S. E., Kraimer, M. L., & Liden, R. C. (2001). A social capital theory of career success. *Academy of Management Journal, 44*, 219–237.

Seligman, M. E. P., & Csikszentmihalyi, M. (2000). Positive psychology: An introduction. *American Psychologist, 55*, 5–14.

Snyder, C. R., & Lopez, S. J. (Eds.). (2002). *Handbook of positive psychology*. New York: Oxford University Press.

Sosik, J. J., & Godshalk, V. M. (2000b). The role of gender in mentoring: Implications for diversified and homogeneous mentoring relationships. *Journal of Vocational Behavior, 57*, 102–122.

Sosik, J. J., & Godshalk, V. M. (2005). Examining gender similarity and mentor's supervisory status in mentoring relationships. *Mentoring & Tutoring, 13*(1), 39–52.

Struthers, N. J. (1995). Differences in mentoring: A function of gender or organizational rank? *Journal of Social Behavior and Personality, 10*, 265–272.

Tharenou, P. (2005). Does mentor support increase women's career advancement more than men's? The differential effects of career and psychosocial support. *Australian Journal of Management, 30*(1), 77–110.

Thomas, D. A. (1990). The impact of race on managers' experiences of developmental relationships (mentoring and sponsorship): An intra-organizational study. *Journal of Organizational Behavior, 11*, 479–491.

Thomas, D. A. (1993). Racial dynamics in cross-race developmental relationships. *Administrative Science Quarterly, 38*, 169–194.

Thomas, D. A. (1999). Beyond the simple demography-power hypothesis: How blacks in power influence white-mentor–black-protégé developmental relationships. In A. Murrell, F. J. Crosby, & R. Ely (Eds.), *Mentoring dilemmas: Developmental relationships within multicultural organizations* (pp. 157–170). Mahwah, NJ: Lawrence Erlbaum Press.

US Department of Census 2000 (n.d.). *Americans with disabilities: Table 4*. Retrieved October 15, 2001 from: www.census.gov/hhes/www/disable/sipp/disab97t4.html.

Viator, R. E. (2001). An examination of African Americans' access to public accounting mentors: Perceived barriers and intentions to leave. *Accounting, Organizations and Society, 26*, 541–561.

Wallace, J. E. (2001). The benefits of mentoring for female lawyers. *Journal of Vocational Behavior, 58*, 366–391.

Wanberg, C. R., Welsh, E. T., & Hezlett, S. A. (2003). Mentoring research: A review and dynamic process model. *Research in Personnel and Human Resources Management, 22*, 39–124.

Whitely, W., Dougherty, T. W., & Dreher, G. F. (1991). Relationship of career mentoring and socioeconomic origin to managers' and professionals' early career progress. *Academy of Management Journal, 34*(2), 331–351.

Young, A. M., & Perrewé, P. L. (2000a). The exchange relationship between mentors and protégés: The development of a framework. *Human Resources Management Review, 10*(1), 177–209.

Chapter 18

Reflections on Diversity and Mentoring

Hazel-Anne M. Johnson, Xian Xu, and Tammy D. Allen

This chapter reflects upon the state of diversity and mentoring research as presented in the preceding chapters. Although diversity includes a wide range of factors, most of the research discussed in these chapters focused on gender and race. Therefore, we will focus on summarizing the similarities and differences in the ways that these two variables influence the initial stage, the process, and the outcomes of mentoring.

Initial Stage of Mentoring Relationships

Developing a mentoring relationship involves concerns such as mentor preferences, access to, and availability of mentors. These issues are addressed to different degrees across the three different areas of mentoring study.

Gender. Research regarding mentor preferences indicates that youth across various ethnic groups prefer same-sex mentors. With regard to the availability of mentors, youth mentoring studies found that in most formal programs the majority of volunteer mentors are White women. Therefore, it is likely that the same-sex mentor preferences of young males will rarely be fulfilled. In contrast, available mentors in both student–faculty and workplace mentoring tend to be White males. Consequently, within university and workplace settings, females are more likely to experience cross-gender mentoring than are males. Across areas, research shows that females are as likely as males to find a mentor; however, females report more barriers to obtaining a mentor than do males in the work setting.

Race. Workplace mentoring research suggests that White male protégés may be less likely to initiate a relationship with female or Black mentors due to less perceived similarity and because such mentors have less access to power-related resources. Likewise, youth tend to seek same-race mentors, pointing again to perceived similarity as an

important factor within the mentoring relationship. However, despite their preferences, the ability of minority protégés to have same-race mentoring is hampered by
the lack of mentors with similar demographic characteristics in the youth, academic,
and work arenas. For example, same-race mentors may be less accessible for Black
students who have to compete for the attention and time of the limited Black
faculty at predominantly White institutions. However, this fact may be mitigated
by the tendency for Black mentors to initiate relationships with similar protégés.
Similarly, youth mentoring research demonstrates that Black mentors are more likely
than White mentors to seek out Black protégés and to help further their personal
and professional development.

Culture.   In addition to gender and race, cultural values, specifically individualism
and collectivism, have been discussed as playing a role in youth and student–faculty
mentoring relationships. Youth from collectivistic cultures tend to rely on members
of the family and community. Consequently formal mentoring programs that
emphasize relationships with adults outside the family or community network may
not be as attractive to them as to youth with individualistic values. Research on
student–faculty mentoring echoes these findings, such that Asian American students
perceive mentoring programs as potentially beneficial to their adjustment and to the
development of a mainstream cultural identity. However, they also feel that participation may lead to separation and pressure from their peers for going against the
collectivist value of blending with the ethnic group.

The Mentoring Process

Although there are no obvious gender differences in finding a mentor, the mentoring process can differ across gender. Some research indicates that young girls value
and benefit more from psychosocial mentoring than from instrumental mentoring. In the workplace, female protégés with female mentors report receiving more
psychosocial and role modeling functions than do female protégés in cross-gender
relationship.

   When it comes to the role of race, workplace mentoring research suggests that
protégés of color in same-race dyads perceive more psychosocial and career development support than do protégés of color in cross-race dyads. However, there is also
research indicating that cross-race protégés may be just as satisfied as protégés in
same-race matches if perceived similarity with their mentor is high. This is a common
point across all three areas of research. Specifically, race per se may not be the primary issue in cross-race mentoring relationships. The members of the dyad may determine the extent to which race plays a role in their relationship. If both approach the
issue of race from the same perspective then the relationship should prosper.

Outcomes of Diverse Mentoring Relationships

Although mentoring appears to be beneficial for diverse populations, differences in
the mentoring process may lead to different outcomes across gender and race. Some
studies show that the mentoring relationship may not last as long for young girls or
minorities compared to White male youth. Although the youth mentoring literature

has not yet provided clear support for greater benefits for same-race matches versus cross-race matches, greater benefits were demonstrated when gender was considered in conjunction with race. That is, within same-gender relationships, boys in same-race matches benefit more than boys in cross-race matches, with similar findings for girls. Boys in same-race mentoring relationships demonstrated improved academic competence and self-esteem, and girls in same-race matches displayed increased "school value" and self-esteem. However, youth in cross-race mentoring relationships did not demonstrate similar increases. Within the workplace mentoring dyad, the mentor's gender and race are more closely related to career outcomes than the protégé's gender and race. Research indicates that those with a White male mentor tend to have higher compensation than do those with a female mentor or a mentor of color. These findings support the perspective of looking at diversified mentoring in terms of power differences in organizations.

Other Forms of Diversity

All three authors within this section advocate expansion beyond demographic diversity in the study of mentoring relationships. Although demographic characteristics may influence newly formed relationships, it is likely that it is deep-level diversity, the similarities and differences in attitudes, beliefs, and values, that ultimately shapes the course of the relationship. In fact, workplace and student–faculty research has indicated that perceived attitudinal similarity has been found to be a better predictor of satisfaction with mentor and support received from mentors than has racial or gender similarity.

Ragins (this volume) cautions against global definitions of group membership (e.g., White versus non-White) because this confounds our understanding of diversified mentoring relationships. This point is echoed by Sedlacek et al. (this volume) as they point out that within the Asian American population, which is often classified as homogenous, there are important differences based on country of origin, language, and socioeconomic status. Research also demonstrates the importance of consideration of multiple group memberships because there were significant differences across racial and ethnic groups of women. Latinas were more likely than Asian American women to have mentors, and African American women received job advice relating to their race from their mentors to a greater extent than other women of color. Consideration of individuals' multiple group memberships, as well as the importance of each to the members of the dyad, is essential to understanding diversified mentoring relationships. Consequently, mentoring and diversity researchers need to be cognizant of the differences that exist both within and across groups. Ragins also discusses invisible group memberships such as sexual orientation and religion that may be stigmatized, where disclosure of the stigmatized identity can influence the mentoring relationship.

Collectivist values such as blending with ethnic group and rigidity of social roles can impact the initiation and process of diversified mentoring relationships. The current structure of mentoring relationships can run counter to collectivist values because it encourages a one-on-one relationship often with someone outside the familial or ethnic group. Ragins (this volume) points out that a paradigm shift toward a relational perspective on mentoring may make mentoring particularly relevant to groups with cultural values aligned with collectivism, communal norms, interdependence, and mutuality (e.g., women, Asian Americans and Latinos).

Conclusions

Although different approaches have been used to study diversity and mentoring, a general theme emerges across areas. This theme is captured by the definition of positive social capital. That is, mentoring can provide resources that increase the generative capacity of individuals in relationships through the development of the protégé both internally (e.g., social identities) and externally (e.g., relationship building). Specifically, Liang and Grossman's relational approach to youth mentoring emphasizes autonomy and trust building. Similarly, Ragins highlights the need for a relational perspective on mentoring to expand the existing research that has focused on instrumental outcomes. Liang and Grossman also point out the need for mentors to pay attention to youths' social identities. Along the same line, Sedlacek et al. suggest looking at noncognitive variables such as positive self-concept. This resonates with Ragins in the sense that mentoring, as a high-quality connection, can lead to expanded identities and psychological growth. Therefore, a unifying call for future research across areas may be to expand our understanding of the benefits of diversified mentoring as a resource that helps individuals improve both themselves and their relationships.

Part VI

Best Practices for Formal Mentoring Programs

Chapter 19

Best Practices for Formal Youth Mentoring

Andrew Miller

The formal youth mentoring described in this chapter includes structured programs delivered in the community, outside of educational institutions, which have a range of social aims and target client groups. It is *formal* in that the programs are managed, often by a community or voluntary sector organization, rather than *informal* involving naturally occurring sets of mentoring relationships. The notion of "practices" refers to the several components or elements of the mentoring program. There are a set of factors that form the building blocks of a successful program, but in themselves they do not guarantee good outcomes. These factors include, for example: policies relating to health and safety and child protection; job descriptions for program managers; marketing materials aimed at mentor and protégé recruitment; program handbooks and procedures; and arrangements for mentor supervision. It is possible to describe a mentoring program in the form of a series of discrete activities. For the purposes of this chapter, research and evaluation evidence on best practices is discussed under four main headings: planning; mentor recruitment to matching; mentoring processes; and evaluation. In each section best practice principles are presented based on guidelines from established programs and quality standards. Research and evaluation evidence for each of 23 principles is discussed, drawing on US and UK evidence.

The rapid rise of youth mentoring programs raises issues about how to maintain the quality of programs. It is argued that guidelines for the creation of mentoring programs based on "what works" are needed because of the dramatic increase of mentoring programs (Sipe & Roder, 1999). There is a wealth of guidance on what constitutes good or best practice and these sources have been drawn on throughout the chapter (see especially Jucovy's (2001a–e) resources for Public/Private Ventures; National Mentoring Center, 2003a; National Mentoring Network, 2001). There has been, particularly in the UK, a drive to codify good practice in the form of quality standards or quality assurance frameworks promulgated by national organizations. Such standards are often derived from the examination of many case study examples or from groups of practitioners coming together to agree what constitutes good practice. These standards are, therefore, often theory-based rather than evidence-based. The UK's National Mentoring Network (NMN), an umbrella organization sponsored by government, has published good practice guidelines on the development and running of a program based on the study of 20 leading-edge youth mentoring programs for social inclusion (Skinner & Fleming, 1999).

Such codification of good practice tends to draw heavily on American experience, practice, and research. For example, the successful Mentoring Plus program developed by Crime Concern in the UK was built upon a model and practice drawn up by an American mentoring practitioner (Benioff, 1997). The UK version of Big Brothers Big Sisters of America, which was called Big Brothers and Sisters UK (BB&S UK), relied heavily on modified US manuals to guide its program practices. In 2004, BB&S UK was one of 35 members of Big Brothers Big Sisters International. However, the experience of BB&S UK, which closed in 2004 after 6 difficult years, suggests that not all "best practices" transfer between countries, partly because of cultural differences (Miller, Drury, Stewart, & Ross, 2005). Hall (2003), in his literature review of youth mentoring research, notes that it is as important to learn from "what does not work" as from "what does work."

The case study of the failure of Big Brothers and Sisters UK illustrates a range of poor program integrity (Hollin, 1995) and a failure to take into account cultural differences when borrowing mentoring program models from other countries. Key issues, according to the government-commissioned evaluation (Miller et al., 2005), were:

- The provision of head office staffing was prioritized over operational staffing in the (one-person) agencies.
- English parents proved more reluctant to accept strangers into their homes than their American counterparts.
- Money was wasted on national marketing aimed at mentor recruitment when there were agencies in only three cities in England.
- There was a failure to develop either a franchising model (as used in the US) or local partnerships which bring access to local or regional sources of funding.

The remit of this chapter is to review research and evaluation evidence of the relationship between program practices and successful outcomes. In comparing US and UK practice it is important to highlight differences, as well as similarities, in youth mentoring programs and in the context in which they operate. Some of the well-known American mentoring schemes tend to be franchised models, such as Big Brothers Big Sisters of America (BBBS). BBBS has established close links with the research organization, Public/Private Ventures (P/PV), which has conducted various evaluative and empirical assessments of its mentoring programs (see, for example, Sipe, 1996, 1998; Tierney et al., 1995). The most extensive study of what constitutes best practice in youth mentoring was conducted by DuBois et al. (2002). In a meta-analysis of evaluations of 55 mentoring programs from 1970 to 1988 they examined so-called theory-based and empirically based indices of best practice that were associated with increased impact.

In contrast, in the UK youth mentoring generally occurs within the poorly funded youth and community sector. Often youth mentoring programs are run by small charities or local voluntary sector organizations for the benefit of a particular client group in a small locality. Typically these organizations have limited funds to run a mentoring program, which means there is little funding for evaluation or empirical research. Resources for evaluation tend to be invested in programs that have been funded by the central government to meet a particular policy agenda, or programs that have been franchised. This is especially true where government has seen mentoring as a way of diverting youth from offending behaviors (see, for example, Shiner et al., 2004; Tarling, Burrows, & Clarke, 2001) or of tackling social exclusion, for example, for children leaving care homes. "Care homes" is a broad term that encapsulates young people in foster care, children's homes, or other forms of care. Those leaving care have compressed and accelerated transitions to adulthood, and typically encounter difficulties such as unemployment and homelessness, which can lead to social exclusion (Clayden & Stein, 2002).

There is a criticism of the guidelines published in the UK by organizations such as the NMN that they are entirely theory-based because of a lack of empirical research on the effectiveness of different program practices upon outcomes for protégés. As Hall (2003) noted, in general the field lacks regulation and a set of proven standards or benchmarks that could be used to guide the development of a mentoring program. Here lessons can be learned from the American mentoring field. What is needed is a link to a research organization, much like BBBS has to P/PV. This would allow for more external evaluation of the effectiveness of different mentoring programs in the UK and evidence-based policy making.

Best Practice Principles

Planning

Best practice principle 1.   Youth mentoring programs should have an infrastructure and organizational capacity to plan and operate an effective program. Freedman (1992), in an often quoted phrase, pointed out the dangers inherent in "fervour without infrastructure" which can lead to poorly managed programs with dubious outcomes. Sipe (1996) recommended that for any mentoring program to be successful it needs an infrastructure that fosters the development of effective mentoring relationships. DuBois et al. (2002) observed that poorly implemented programs can have an adverse effect on youth. Shiner et al. highlighted the importance of a high level of mentoring "program integrity" (Hollin, 1995) which includes employing skilled staff, congruence between stated program aims and processes and those actually implemented, and sound management. This infrastructure can be provided by an organization that has the capacity to plan and manage an effective mentoring program. High levels of interaction between mentors and protégés are facilitated by well-structured and planned mentoring programs (Jekielek et al., 2002). This includes having sufficient human, financial, and physical resources to run a successful program. Some mentoring programs may be a franchise of a larger youth-serving agency. If a program is part of such an agency, it is vital that there is a demonstrable, ongoing commitment from the senior management and board of the host organization. If there is not, then they may be just as susceptible to failure as other smaller programs (Garringer, 2002).

The external evaluation of BB&S UK illustrated a program that lacked "integrity." It showed that only 49 active matches were achieved over 74 months, and 16 of these were no longer active (Miller et al., 2005). BB&S UK closed in April 2004 after the failure to secure additional government or corporate funding. One of the main reasons for the failure of BB&S UK was that funding was weighted toward the central operations leaving insufficient funding for the local agencies; indeed its organization chart was described as an "upside-down pyramid." This meant that there were a series of one-person agencies operating across major cities and the local program staff were unable to manage the range of tasks required, including promotion, recruiting, and briefing mentors, whilst also supervising existing matches. The BB&S UK local projects lacked the capacity to run an effective mentoring scheme (Miller et al., 2005).

Best practice principle 2. Youth mentoring programs should have a program manual that includes key policies and procedures. Research into 38 community-based mentoring programs in the UK found that three-quarters stressed the importance of initial research and knowledge development, and for a third this initial phase took longer than expected (Miller et al., 2005). US guidance from the National Mentoring Center (2003b) recommended that programs should draw up policies and procedures in the form of a manual. The policies of a mentoring program are often in the form of statements that address, for example, the goals of the program, how to achieve effective and consistent program operations, and a definition of what constitutes good practice in achieving those aims. US guidance has recommended that the written mission statement should be concise, but it must still answer the fundamental question for all mentoring programs: why does the program exist (Garringer, 2002)? A criticism of BBBS, which might be leveled at most youth mentoring programs, is the lack of empirical research into the effectiveness of BBBS program management and policies (Sipe, 1996).

Best practice principle 3. Before establishing a new youth mentoring program it is important to undertake an audit and needs assessment in an area. Some examples of what to look for include juvenile crime statistics, school dropout rates, teen pregnancy rates, substance abuse estimates, gang activity, and existing youth services in the area (National Mentoring Center, 2003b). Programs should also consider groups where there is a need but limited provision, including foster children, gay and lesbian youth, children who have a mentally ill parent, and children who have a parent in jail (National Mentoring Center Bulletin, 1999). Miller (2002) has also suggested that other youth programs should be investigated to ensure that the proposed mentoring program complements other services in the locality. The NMN suggests that the first stage of any proposal should be to define who the target group is and then set out the outcomes the program wants to achieve. These outcomes should be specific, measurable, realistic, and achievable aims that are tailored to the client group (Miller, 2002).

Best practice principle 4. Mentoring programs should target specific issues and should base program practices around a theoretical understanding of how mentoring will address the issue. Some commentators are critical of mentoring programs such as BBBS that have a policy of targeting "disaffected" youth, arguing that programs that seek to affect more specific areas of change, for instance offending behavior, can be more successful (Davidson et al., 1987). UK researchers Piper and Piper (2000) have also suggested that for a program to be successful it must seek to address particular issues that are regarded as important by protégés and not vaguer or broader concepts such as "disaffection." A criticism of youth mentoring generally is that formal mentoring programs often lack a solid theoretical basis as to why mentoring should actually effect change (Colley 2003; Shiner et al., 2004).

Best practice principle 5.   Mentoring programs should build partnerships with other agencies working with the same client group. BB&S UK failed to develop partnerships with other local agencies and this contributed to a lack of referrals from, for example, local Social Services departments (Miller et al., 2005). Establishing links with other projects is a best practice because, as can be evidenced by the failure of BB&S UK, programs will leave themselves adrift from potential sources of both recruitment and funding (Miller et al., 2005). An evaluation of a mentoring scheme for 18-year-old youth leaving care homes highlighted how failing to build effective partnerships with potential referral agencies can limit the recruitment of protégés (Clayden & Stein, 2002). The evaluation found that one of the main problems facing such mentoring projects was the reluctance of Social Services to provide the projects with potential protégés. A study of young people in 20 careers service companies (Ford, 1998) found that for a program to achieve success it required both the development of partnerships with local agencies and the integration of mentoring with other services. The "harmonious multi-agency co-operation" of services such as local police, the youth and community department of the local council, and the Home Office also "undoubtedly assisted" the Dalston Youth Project program for disengaged youth at risk of offending (Audit Commission, 1996; Tarling et al., 2001).

Once the target group has been decided, programs can then decide if they want to create a steering or advisory group. This group is often made up of stakeholders from the community and helps to ensure that the program is meeting the needs of those most at risk (National Mentoring Center, 2003b). Such a group is also evidence of a partnership with local referral agencies. Programs should also seek to build partnerships with both public and private parts of the community. These links can provide additional sources of revenue and give access to individuals who could provide the program with donated management and technical skills (Padgette, 2003).

Best practice principle 6.   Mentoring programs need to develop effective funding strategies for sustainability. In terms of resourcing, mentoring programs in America have widely varying budgets ranging from just under $500 to $6.5 million, with an average of $324,000 per program (Fountain & Arbreton, 1999). Smaller mentoring programs are just as likely as larger programs to receive funds from corporations and other sources of funding separate from a parent organization (such as BBBS) and government funds. What seems vital for all mentoring programs to survive are best practice "finance strategies" (Padgette, 2003). These include making better use of existing resources, which can be achieved by streamlining resources to reduce administrative costs. This also involves managing the balance between budget and in-kind contributions such as volunteers' free time. Such contributions are vital to mentoring programs as the costs of operating a youth mentoring program often tend to exceed the funds available (Fountain & Arbreton, 1999).

Mentor Recruitment to Matching

Best practice principle 7. Mentoring programs need a written plan, effective marketing materials, and recruitment strategies aimed at their target mentors. Guidelines produced by P/PV on the recruitment of mentors recommend the creation of a written plan setting out the goals of the program's recruitment drive, how many mentors are needed, and when. Good practice manuals also recommend that programs should calculate the exact budget of the recruitment drive and figure in any additional costs involved, such as presentations or extra hours for staff (Jucovy, 2001a). Often presentations are recommended, including, for example, bringing in former mentors to discuss their experiences, and using videos and slides (Jucovy, 2001a). One successful aspect of the BBBS recruitment model is to trade on its name and reputation to draw in volunteers from big businesses through presentations. As BB&S UK was less well known in the UK, this method of recruitment did not "bear similar fruit" (Miller et al., 2005). A large amount of money was also wasted on a national advertising campaign that generated a lot of interest from potential mentors but there were only three agencies throughout the entire UK and many could not be matched.

A potential issue for research is whether a particular recruitment method or a range of methods is most effective. In the UK, NMN guidelines recommend that to reach particular minority groups advertisements should be placed in specialist newspapers and magazines (Skinner & Fleming, 1999). Because of the large proportion of protégés from Black and other ethnic backgrounds in the Dalston Youth Project and Mentoring Plus programs, advertisements were placed in minority publications such as *The Voice* (African Caribbean), *The Big Issue* (Homeless), and Turkish newspapers (Benioff, 1997; Shiner et al., 2004; Tarling et al., 2001). As a result, the majority of mentors recruited were people of color. In a study of UK community-based mentoring programs half advocated the use of multiple methods to promote their programs and the other half highlighted the importance of approaches targeting specific audiences (Miller et al., 2005).

In the US, minority youths who want mentors tend to outnumber minority volunteers in most communities (Sherman, 1999). More specifically, while 15 to 20% of volunteers wishing to be mentors come from a minority ethnic background, around 50% of protégés come from such a background (Rhodes, 2002c). It is recommended that programs should take the time to develop trust and credibility within minority communities (Sherman, 1999). Programs with minority chairpersons and outreach staff have the best track records in bringing in those from minority communities (Sherman, 1999; Shiner et al., 2004). To target minority communities, programs can use a number of avenues, including fostering links with faith-based organizations, professional associations, sports teams, neighborhood political organizations, minority-owned businesses, and minority-oriented media.

A related issue is the mismatch between the high proportion of male protégés and the generally much lower proportion of male mentors, which has made many programs test out ways of recruiting more male role models (for further discussion of diversity, gender, and youth mentoring relationships see Liang and Grossman (this volume)). While there is a lack of research on best practices for the recruitment of males, Garringer (2004) has made some recommendations based on theory and evaluations of mentoring programs. For example, the marketing strategy should be examined to make sure that it appeals to men through its use of images and language. Programs should also seek to employ some males in key project worker roles. A final recommendation is that programs consider the nature of the activities in the program, as many men may feel more comfortable if they are actually given something to do with protégés, for example, building projects or computer tasks (Garringer, 2004).

Best practice principle 8. Youth mentoring programs need processes for screening out unsuitable mentors. The screening of potential mentors is a core factor as it determines a volunteer's suitability for a difficult and time-consuming task, ensures the safety of protégés, and protects the reputation of the program (National Mentoring Working Group, 1991; Roaf et al., 1994). UK guidelines recommend rejecting volunteers based on criteria such as failing a police check, poor references, lack of motivation, and poor attitudes toward protégés (National Mentoring Network, 2001). Safety checks can also be carried out on mentors by examining criminal history records and child abuse registries (Jucovy, 2001a). The life commitments and work schedules that volunteers have must be reviewed to ascertain if they have the time to fit the responsibilities of being a mentor into their lives.

A study by Sipe and Roder (1999) revealed that 95% of BBBS programs used written applications, personal interviews, reference checks, and criminal record checks in their screening process. P/PV research into mentoring programs that were less structured than BBBS found that mentors were less prepared and less successful (Sipe, 1996). However, there were problems in transferring this model to BB&S UK. While the checks were rigorous, with initial screening supplemented by four reference checks, many mentors failed at the interview stage, which suggests that references should have been checked only after a successful interview. Further to this, of the mentors that did pass screening checks, a suitable match could not always be found because of the limited number of BB&S UK programs (Miller et al., 2005). A screening process that involves one or more interviews is often used to probe the mentor's orientation to the role. If mentors suggest that they want to completely change protégés, they should perhaps be placed only on projects that are tackling specific behaviors (e.g., substance use). However, empirical research shows that screening procedures are not a significant indicator of an effective mentoring program (DuBois et al., 2002). The same research indicated that a background in a helping role or profession aided individuals in taking on the role of mentor.

Best practice principle 9. Effective training (which should be ongoing) should enable mentors to understand the needs of the client group, to become familiar with the program's procedures, and to practice and develop the skills of mentoring. Perhaps because of the view that mentoring is a naturally occurring intervention, some programs give little consideration to training (Jucovy, 2001b) or offer minimal introductory briefings that only include explanations of program requirements. The training of mentors differs between programs (Sipe, 1996), which may be because there has been a lack of consensus on the need for training of mentors (Rhodes, 1994). Data supplied by 20 mentoring programs included in the Mentoring Fund evaluation indicated an average of 28 hours of mentor training, with the longest being 88 hours for mentors working with protégés with drug problems (Miller et al., 2005). Some programs offer extensive training that can involve teaching components about youth backgrounds, adolescent development, and potential problems that mentors may encounter (Sipe, 1996). UK evaluation research has recommended that mentors should be able to suggest topics that they would want to have in the training program; for example, 55% of mentors in the care leavers program felt that potentially useful topics that were not covered in training were drugs awareness, race and culture, mental illness, and counseling skills (Clayden & Stein, 2002).

Empirical research on the effectiveness of training procedures is mixed. Initial pre-relationship training is not associated with positive outcomes for mentoring programs (DuBois et al., 2002). However, a review of 10 mentoring studies in the US found that the only training program that appeared to have a positive effect was where mentors received training on giving praise and rewarding positive behavior changes (Fo & O'Donnell, 1974). DuBois et al. (2002) found that mentoring programs that provided opportunities for ongoing training throughout the mentoring relationship had larger positive effects on protégés than those that did not. Many mentors have noted that the best training they received was the mentoring experience itself and the opportunity to reflect with other mentors upon that experience (Sipe, 1996). Although UK guidance states that the best forms of training involve formal processes where mentors can be accredited, there is no research evidence that accredited training leads to better mentors than non-accredited training (Skinner & Fleming, 1999).

Best practice principle 10.   Clear selection criteria, induction, and ongoing training for protégés should enable them to gain more from the mentoring relationship. Most youth mentoring programs set out eligibility criteria to define the client group, for example, poor school attendance, special education needs, low level of literacy, and concern to other agencies such as the police (Tarling et al., 2001). Additional criteria can include factors such as parental conflict and alcohol and substance abuse (Shiner et al., 2004). Targeting only the most difficult protégés can create problems for programs that have target numbers linked to funding. For example, the evaluation of Dalston Youth Project found that one-half of protégés left the program early (Tarling et al., 2001), representing a substantial waste of scarce program resources. A third of program managers included in the UK Mentoring Fund evaluation had problems with inappropriate referrals and the time taken to sort these out (Miller et al., 2005). It is important, therefore, that program managers invest some time in briefing referral agencies and talking to potential protégés before they join the program. The selection of potential protégés should also be based on a number of positive interpersonal characteristics including motivation, leadership skills, determination, and a desire to participate in the project (Skinner & Fleming, 1999).

Good practice guidelines recommend inducting protégés so that they understand the potential benefits and are more likely to be fully engaged in mentoring. Pre-match training for protégés can help them to learn about the thinking behind mentoring, understand the roles of program staff, develop reasonable expectations for the mentoring relationship, understand their responsibilities as protégés, and know the boundaries and limits of confidentiality (Skinner & Fleming, 1999; Taylor, 2003). Ongoing training can feature topics that are related to the areas the program wants to change, for example, dealing with difficult subjects, peer pressure, setting goals, and skills for getting on in school, and with parents and peers (Taylor, 2003).

Best practice principle 11.   Mentors and protégés should have a say over their match and the matching process should involve opportunities to meet before a final match is made. Empirical research does not support the use of matching as a best practice principle. Matching by gender does not correlate strongly with either the number of mentoring meetings or the length of those meetings (Sipe, 1996). Gender is also unrelated to the effect size of mentoring programs in relation to emotional, behavioral, and academic outcomes, amongst others (DuBois et al., 2002; Sipe, 1996). Furthermore, matching by ethnicity is not supported by empirical research. Mentors perceive the same level of closeness and support in same- and cross-cultural matches (Herrera, Sipe, & McClanahan, 2000). Based upon findings such as these, Sipe (1996) has suggested that matching is "the least critical element" of best practice in mentoring programs (p. 11). But while matching by sex and race may be unimportant, the importance of matching by other less "apparent" factors should not be overlooked. BBBS programs have a rigorous matching process and place importance on matching mentors and protégés based on shared interests and geographic proximity. Programs should also pay particular attention to matching when pairs are from different ethnic backgrounds to ensure that they have at least some common ground. As best practice, protégés should at least be given the choice of being matched to a mentor from the same ethnic background. However, protégés should be informed that by expressing such a wish they may face a much longer wait for a mentor.

As in the BBBS model, no recommendations are made in UK guidance on the importance of matching by gender, ethnicity, or age. However, an evaluation of the care leavers mentoring program found that 38% of protégés expressed preferences relating to the characteristics of their mentor, with the majority of these relating to gender (Clayden & Stein, 2002). While most of the protégés in the care leavers program were matched within three weeks, those with more specific requests had to wait as long as three months for a suitable mentor to be found (Clayden & Stein, 2002). A matching process that allows mentors and protégés to express preferences against a range of criteria such as age, gender, and ethnicity is very likely to lead to a longer waiting period prior to matching. Half the program managers interviewed in the Mentoring Fund evaluation thought that a "holistic" knowledge of mentor and protégé was the key to successful matching (Miller et al., 2005).

Recommended UK best practice in the matching process includes letting potential matches meet before formal mentoring begins, allowing protégés to reject matches, and monitoring matches to ensure that they are working well (Skinner & Fleming, 1999). There is evidence that the use of residential experience as a matching strategy with disaffected youth can be problematic. In the Dalston Youth Project potential mentor and protégé matches were brought together over a weekend at an activity center. This not only served to start the program off with a "bang," but was used to assess the suitability of potential matches (Tarling et al., 2001). If the matches did not work, the weekend provided an opportunity for other matches to be tried out. However, the evaluation of Mentoring Plus found weekend residentials to be "inherently unpredictable" and some were marked by tension between adults and protégés, with evidence of drinking, drugs, and sexual activity (Shiner et al., 2004).

Mentoring Processes

Best practice principle 12.   Youth mentoring relationships should be sustained over a period of at least 6 months. Evaluations of several BBBS programs indicated that around 6 months of meetings were required for mentors and protégés to establish a relationship that can affect change (Sipe, 1996). Empirical research based upon data from Tierney et al. (1995) found that protégés mentored for 12 months showed significant changes in confidence toward school, skipped fewer school days, had higher grades, and were less likely to begin use of drugs or alcohol (Grossman & Johnson, 1998). This research also found that protégés mentored for 3 to 6 months showed no significant positive changes. Protégés in relationships lasting less than 3 months were significantly less confident about their school work and had a substantially lower sense of self-worth (Grossman & Johnson, 1998). A review of 10 youth mentoring programs found that the longer the mentoring relationship, the better the outcomes (Jekielek et al., 2002).

Best practice principle 13.   Mentors and protégés should meet regularly (probably weekly), and mentors should be proactive in making arrangements and initiating telephone contact. Successful mentors are those that regularly contact protégés and ensure that meetings are scheduled, as opposed to those who wait for protégés to contact them (Styles & Morrow, 1992). The expectation of frequency of contact is an empirically based best-practice indicator (DuBois et al., 2002). Very short mentoring meetings and long intervals of noncontact can have damaging effects on protégés (Skinner & Fleming, 1999). A way of making sure that mentors and protégés do regularly meet up is to produce meeting schedules for mentors and protégés and give transport assistance to both (Sipe, 1996). Correlations suggest that BBBS mentors and protégés who meet once a week have more positive outcomes than those with more or less contact (Grossman & Johnson, 1998). The same research showed that mentoring relationships that involved high or modest frequency of contact over the telephone had more positive outcomes, for example, in reducing drug and alcohol use, in reducing incidents of skipping school, and in improving competence in school (Grossman & Johnson, 1998).

Best practice principle 14.   Mentoring programs should provide ongoing support for and supervision of youth mentoring relationships. Mentors and protégés need time to get to know, like, and trust each other. During early meetings mentors may find protégés unresponsive and feelings of rejection by mentors could be increased if protégés begin to miss meetings and send out messages that they find the mentor to be unimportant (Jucovy, 2001c). The help, guidance, and moral support that program staff can provide by keeping in regular contact can ensure that matches last and flourish (Sipe, 1996). Guidelines recommend that program staff make contact in the first two weeks, every two weeks for the first few months, and monthly thereafter (Jucovy, 2001c). Some guidelines recommend that an action plan be agreed upon at the outset to guide the content of meetings and that a written record be kept of the content discussed at each meeting (Skinner & Fleming, 1999). Research also suggests that successful mentors are those that recognize they do not have all of the answers and so seek out such help (Sipe, 1996). Programs should also seek to reassure mentors that they are achieving some success by relating any positive feedback from protégés or any one else involved in the program (Jucovy, 2001c). Ongoing support for mentors can also ensure that mentors and protégés maintain regular meetings and that possible problems that may lead to the relationship breaking down are addressed. In spite of this, a third of program managers interviewed by Miller et al. (2005) complained that mentor nonattendance at support meetings and compliance with program procedures were problems. Important factors in mentor attendance at support sessions were flexibility, the attendance of their supervisor, and the interest value of the session.

The breakdown of matches can be caused by a variety of factors. These include failure to attend meetings, lack of interest in activities, and failure of mentors and protégés to discuss personal issues (Sipe, 1996). It is often the lack of shared values and beliefs that can lead to social distance and the feelings of a mismatched pair (Grossman & Garry, 1997).

Best practice principle 15. Mentoring programs should support mentors in arranging enjoyable and structured activities. These can include publishing monthly calendars of low-cost events or (if funding allows) offering tickets to various sporting and other events that may be of interest to protégés. This theory-based recommendation is supported by an evaluation of a mentoring program that found that mentors who did not have enough money to take protégés to such activities were more likely to be inconsistent in meeting with protégés (Network Training & Research Group, 1996). Having fun with protégés can also show that mentors are focused and committed to the relationship (Jucovy, 2001d). More successful mentors are those who try to involve protégés in deciding how the pair will spend their time together, rather than simply organizing activities without any input from protégés (Morrow & Styles, 1995). Programs that are driven by the needs and interests of young people are more likely to succeed than those where the mentors are driving the choice of activities (Jekielek et al., 2002). Pawson (2004a), reviewing US research on mentoring relationships by Parra, DuBois, Neville, Pugh-Lilly, and Povinelli (2002), concludes that "non-directive, mutual activities in the form of basketball, music and retail grazing are the starting points of relationship building."

A qualitative study on "engagement" mentoring for disaffected young people found that the program's emphasis on the goal of entry to employment led to resistance by protégés and a re-creation of the experiences of social exclusion (Colley, 2003). A meta-analysis of mentoring programs found that the provision of structured activities for mentors and protégés was a significant moderator of the positive effects of a mentoring program under both fixed and random effects (DuBois et al., 2002). Programs also sometimes arrange additional education and training activities for protégés. The evaluation of the Dalston Youth Project found that 87% of protégés with successful outcomes from the program attended such classes, but only 24% of young people not attending extra classes had successful outcomes (Tarling et al., 2001).

Best practice principle 16. Mentoring programs should develop a theory of how the mentoring process aims to impact on program outcomes, which can be used to guide mentors through training and through the relationship. Shiner et al. (2004) observed that the mentoring relationships in action did not fit the theory-based best practices that tend to stress linear progress from building rapport to joint problem-solving. Many meetings between mentors and protégés were based on ordinary social interaction that did not address challenging behavior or the causes of social exclusion. They identified three potential cycles: a) the basic cycle: contact–meeting–doing (e.g., having coffee, playing pool, bowling); b) the problem-solving cycle: contact–meeting–doing–fire-fighting (e.g., dealing with a crisis such as homelessness, family breakdown, or substance misuse); and c) the action-oriented cycle: contact–meeting–doing–fire-fighting–action.

The action-oriented cycle was closer to the ideal-typical mentoring relationship and the relationships that progressed to that stage did so later on, after trust had been developed and key issues identified. However, many relationships were cyclical, returning after a crisis to the same starting point. In reviewing the literature on mentoring relationships and disaffected youth, Pawson (2004b) concludes: a) that the process is likely to be "long and halting," b) that simple befriending can "create the essential ground conditions for further improvement," and c) that other organizations need to be involved with mentoring programs to deliver "higher grade functions" such as coaching and advocacy. Other conclusions are that youth mentoring: a) succeeds best at befriending, and is progressively less effective at direction-setting, coaching, and advocacy, b) tends to be disrupted by the ongoing problems facing disaffected young people so the mentoring needs to be buttressed by further waves of trust-, resilience- and confidence-building to repair the damage and then move on, and c) needs to look outward to the resources of family and peers, youth workers, and the education system in order to succeed in its higher objectives of direction-setting, coaching, and advocacy.

Best practice principle 17. Programs should seek the support of parents/carers but not their active engagement in mentoring processes (Skinner & Fleming, 1999). Such support is important because nonsupportive parents can sabotage the mentor–protégé relationship (Johnson, 1998). Guidelines recommend that programs contact parents within the first two weeks of mentoring, and then at least once a month for a year, to find out if they think their child is benefiting from the mentoring relationship (Jucovy, 2001e). Parental support increases the likelihood that the relationship will be sustained and mentors who have parental support may be more likely to achieve successful outcomes for protégés. A study that tested two separate models through which mentoring may work found that the positive effects achieved by mentoring fit significantly better into a model that places the parental relationship as a central factor that mentoring must effect in order to achieve positive outcomes (Rhodes et al., 2000). The meta-analysis conducted by DuBois et al. (2002) also found that parental support was an empirically based best-practice indicator of the positive effect of mentoring. However, program staff are advised not to allow parents to become actively involved in the mentoring process. Protégés may already have numerous issues with their families, and mentors must guard against having too much involvement with families to the point where protégés view their mentors as having sided with their parents (Morrow & Styles, 1995).

Best practice principle 18.   Mentors should seek to develop equality in the relationship through mutual respect, encouragement, and openness. Guidelines state that mentors must not act like a parent, attempt to be an authority figure, or preach values. Instead mentors should focus on creating a bond and a sense of equality in the relationship (Jucovy, 2001d). Such equality can be achieved through respecting the protégés' viewpoints, not attempting to transform or reform them, and involving protégés in deciding how time will be spent together (Sipe, 1996). Another key element is that the benefits to all partners are recognized so that mentors are perceived as also benefiting from the mentoring process (Philip & Hendry, 2000). Grossman and Johnson (1998) analyzed factors such as how the mentor made the protégé feel (e.g., making them feel stupid = negative quality factor), how activities were structured (e.g., activities centered on what the youth wants to do = positive factor), and the approach taken by the mentor (pushing protégés too hard = negative factor). The findings suggested that mentors with high to modest positive ratings on these three factors had more positive effects than less positively rated mentors in relation to competence in school, grades, drugs, and alcohol use (Grossman & Johnson, 1998).

Best practice principle 19.   The ending of the mentoring relationship should be carefully managed. Mentors and protégés need to be prepared by the program for the end of the relationship (Skinner & Fleming, 1999). Guidelines suggest that the ending of the relationship can become cathartic for both mentor and protégé if they discuss the good times they have had, and perhaps arrange a special activity for the last time they see each other (Jucovy, 2001c). Youth mentoring programs that are short-term should seek to equip protégés with knowledge of other support services that they can access after the end of the mentoring relationship (Skinner & Fleming, 1999). A Scottish study of mentoring programs for socially excluded young people found that the ending had the potential to undermine any benefits gained from the process and could leave the young person feeling rejected (Philip et al., 2004). At "graduation nights" in youth mentoring programs, certificates of commendation for efforts and performance are handed out. The graduation night also allows protégés to have a sense of finishing and moving away from the program. A recommendation for best practice in conducting graduation nights is to make sure that the specific contribution and commitments of individual protégés are recorded on any documents (Tarling et al., 2001).

Evaluation

Best practice principle 20.   Mentoring programs should be able to demonstrate that they represent value for money. The basic descriptive information about any youth mentoring program is its aims and services, budget information, staffing, levels of expenses, and allocation of staff time (Fountain & Arbreton, 1999). This information can be used to demonstrate how much time and money is being allocated to indirect services, such as administration, and how much is going into the direct mentoring services. It is important to consider how successful programs are in obtaining and increasing the level of involvement of the community, because this is an "off-budget" cost (i.e., one that does not involve using money from the program). Programs that are ineffective in generating community involvement will be more expensive because they will need to acquire additional funds (Fountain & Arbreton, 1999).

Probably the simplest measure of value for money is the cost per checked, trained, matched mentor (Fountain & Arbreton, 1999). This needs to be calculated in this way as it allows for the data to be compared to data from other programs that may have more protégés or higher initial budgets. Such data can be used to examine whether programs that are smaller in terms of the number protégés served are more cost-effective than larger-scale programs with higher budgets and more protégés. The often-cited benchmark figure of cost per mentoring match in BBBS programs is $1114 (Fountain & Arbreton, 1999). In a study of 38 mentoring programs Miller et al. (2005) found that programs targeting young offenders at an average cost of £2000 per matched mentor were double the cost of programs targeting youth at risk. The main factors in actual (as opposed to estimated) costs were project performance in recruiting mentors, the number of mentee referrals, and the number of matches made. New projects sometimes set out unrealistic targets in their funding bids, for example, by failing to take into account factors affecting the recruitment and retention of mentors or the long lead-in time before matching can occur. Some projects experienced difficulties recruiting mentors to work with a challenging client group, whereas others found it hard to get sufficient referrals from other agencies (Miller et al., 2005).

In the UK, the Volunteer Investment and Value Audit (VIVA) is a recognized method of judging the value of the contribution made by volunteers to a program (Gaskin & Dobson, 1996). The data needed to calculate the VIVA are the number of mentors matched, the average length of contact time with the protégé, and the average number of meetings during the year. The value of volunteers' time is calculated by multiplying the average hourly wage rate for community mentors by the total number of annual volunteers' hours. Using these data, the ratio of the total annual program budget to the annual value of volunteers' time gives the VIVA ratio. Thus a VIVA ratio of one means that the value of volunteers' time to the program is equal to the budget, and a ratio above one means that the volunteers' time is greater than the budget. In the UK, the average VIVA for youth-at-risk mentoring programs included in the Home Office study was two (Miller et al., 2005).

Best practice principle 21. Mentoring programs should conduct internal monitoring and evaluation, and use agreed national standards to benchmark and improve the quality of program management, operations, and outcomes (National Mentoring Network, 2001). Evaluation methods can be varied, including a) attendance by researchers at committee meetings and "away days," b) semi-structured interviews with staff, c) nonparticipant observation of training sessions, d) classroom observations, e) semi-structured interviews with protégés, mentors, and parents, f) visits to local schools, and g) extraction of data from the program and school records (Tarling et al., 2001). Miller et al. (2005) found that although mentoring programs had internal monitoring and evaluation systems, including the identification of success criteria and key performance indicators, little use was made of data collected to inform stakeholders, partner organizations, or the project team. Miller et al. (2005) also advocated the use of "empowerment evaluation" workshops as a participatory and formative approach to evaluation which seemed to fit well with the aims of mentoring programs (Fetterman, 2000).

Best practice principle 22.   The evaluation of youth mentoring programs should, where feasible, involve the use of control or comparison groups (see also Blinn-Pike, this volume). This allows for differences between protégés and nonmentored youth to be compared, and means that any observed differences in protégés can be more reliably attributed to the program (Tarling et al., 2001). However, using a control group in evaluations of mentoring can be difficult. The evaluators of Project Chance were not allowed to randomly assign youths to be mentored or not because of the views of staff and parents (St James-Roberts & Singh, 2001). The strict eligibility criteria used in some programs also mean that a comparison or control group cannot be found (Tarling et al., 2001). The evaluation of Mentoring Plus did use a comparison group made up of those who had expressed an interest in joining the program but did not follow through with their interest (Shiner et al., 2004). But while it is recommended as best practice that programs do use comparison groups, preferably those who have been randomly assigned to be mentored or not, the practicality of achieving this has often proved difficult. One practical recommendation is to use those protégés who dropped out of the program early as the comparison group (Tarling et al., 2001).

Best practice principle 23.   Mentoring programs should develop a range of measures to judge the impact of the mentoring on protégés and, where available, they should use benchmarks for comparison. Examples of measures of quality in mentoring include the length of the relationship, frequency of telephone contact, protégés' perception of closeness, and caseworker's assessment of whether the mentor took a negative approach (Grossman & Johnson, 1998). In the UK, NMN has promoted the use of key performance indicators as one approach to self-evaluation (Miller, 1999). In the US, P/PV have developed a Youth Survey questionnaire based on questions in Tierney et al.'s (1995) study that can be used to evaluate three aspects of mentoring relationships: a) the extent that the relationship is centered on youth; b) the youth's emotional engagement; and c) the extent that the youth is dissatisfied with the mentoring relationship (Jucovy, 2002). It is recommended that the survey be administered 3 months after the start of the relationship when closeness may have started to develop (Grossman & Rhodes, 2002), and then at 6, 9, and 12 months. A benchmark from the Youth Survey is that mentors score an average of 3.69 on the youth-centered relationship scale (Grossman & Johnson, 1998). Programs can also use the impact study for other benchmarks, such as mentors calling protégés 6.36 times per month (Grossman & Johnson, 1998). Again, such data can be used to find out where improvements need to be made while the program is running or to find out where changes need to be made for the next cycle of a mentoring program.

Conclusion

Much of the extensive good practice guidance in the world of youth mentoring is theory-based rather than evidence-based. Evidence-based guidance has largely originated in the US and this has had a strong influence on practice in other countries such as the UK. Large-scale empirical research is facilitated where there are well-funded, franchised programs with the same goals and similar program procedures. In the UK there are a small number of such franchised programs and hence rigorous research into program effectiveness is comparatively recent. The plethora of small-scale, under-funded local youth mentoring programs tend not to welcome such investigation, which could threaten to expose the "modest" outcomes of their programs. But the experience of importing BBBS to the UK shows that a large-scale, franchised model founded on evidence-based, best practice principles can fail to take root, partly because of cultural differences. It is important to learn as much from what did not work as what did, and this may vary between countries. This review has shown that the range and quality of evidence-based best practice in youth mentoring are patchy. The link between BBBS and P/PV in the US shows what can be achieved when youth mentoring and research organizations work together to develop best practice principles based on empirical evidence of what works. It is up to other countries developing youth mentoring to ensure that there is more evidence-based good practice guidance available founded on research into their own programs.

References

Audit Commission (1996). *Misspent youth.* London: HMSO.

Benioff, S. (1997). *A second chance: Developing mentoring and education projects for young people.* London: Dalston Youth Project/Crime Concern.

Clayden, J., & Stein, M. (2002). *Mentoring for care leavers: Evaluation report.* London: University of York/Prince's Trust.

Colley, H. (2003). *Mentoring for social inclusion: A critical approach to nurturing successful mentoring relations.* London: RoutledgeFalmer.

Davidson, W. S., Redner, R., Blakely, C. H., Mitchell, C. M., & Emshoff, J. G. (1987). Diversion of juvenile offenders: An experimental comparison. *Journal of Consulting and Clinical Psychology, 55*(1), 68–75.

DuBois, D. L., Holloway, B. E., Valentine, J. C., & Cooper, H. (2002). Effectiveness of mentoring programs for youth: A meta-analytic review. *American Journal of Community Psychology, 30,* 157–197.

Fetterman, D. M. (2000). *Foundations of empowerment evaluation: Step by step.* Thousand Oaks, CA: Sage.

Fo, W. S. O., & O'Donnell, C. R. (1974). The buddy system: Relationship and contingency condition in a community intervention program for youth with non-professionals as behavior change agents. *Journal of Consulting and Clinical Psychology, 42*(2), 163–169.

Ford, G. (1998). *Career guidance mentoring for disengaged young people.* Stourbridge, England: Institute of Careers Guidance.

Fountain, D. L., & Arbreton, A. (1999). The cost of mentoring. In J. B. Grossman (Ed.), *Contemporary issues in mentoring* (pp. 49–65). Philadelphia: Public/Private Ventures.

Freedman, M. (1992). *The kindness of strangers: Reflections on the mentoring movement.* Philadelphia: Public/Private Ventures.

Garringer, M. (2002). Strengthening your "agency capacity". *National Mentoring Center Bulletin, Issue* 11.

Garringer, M. (2004). Putting the "men" back into mentoring. *National Mentoring Center Bulletin* 2:2.

Gaskin, K., & Dobson, B. (1996). *The economic equation of volunteering: A pilot study.* Loughborough, England: Centre for Research in Social Policy.

Grossman, J. B., & Garry, E. (1997). *Mentoring: A proven delinquency prevention strategy.* Washington, DC: US Department of Justice.

Grossman, J. B., & Johnson, A. (1998). Assessing the effectiveness of mentoring programs. In J. B. Grossman (Ed.), *Contemporary issues in mentoring* (pp. 24–47). Philadelphia: Public/Private Ventures.

Grossman, J. B., & Rhodes, J. E. (2002). The test of time: Predictors and effects of duration in youth mentoring relationships. *American Journal of Community Psychology, 30*(2), 199–219.

Hall, J. (2003). *Mentoring and young people: A literature review.* Glasgow, Scotland: The SCRE Centre, University of Glasgow.

Herrera, C., Sipe, C. L., & McClanahan, W. S. (2000). *Mentoring school aged children: Relationship development in community-based and school-based programs.* Philadelphia: Public/Private Ventures.

Hollin, C. R. (1995). The meaning and implications of programme integrity. In J. McGuire (Ed.), *What works: Reducing reoffending* (pp. 195–208). Chichester, England: Wiley.

Jekielek, S. M., Moore, K. A., Hair, E. C., & Scarupa, H. J. (2002). *Mentoring: A promising strategy for youth development.* Washington, DC: Child Trends Research Brief.

Johnson, A. W. (1998). *An evaluation of the long-term impacts of the Sponsor-a-Scholar Program on student performance. Final report to the Commonwealth Fund.* Princeton, NJ: Mathematica Policy Research, Inc.

Jucovy, L. (2001a). *Recruiting mentors: A guide to finding volunteers to work with youth.* Philadelphia: Public/Private Ventures.

Jucovy, L. (2001b). *Training new mentors.* Philadelphia: Public/Private Ventures.

Jucovy, L. (2001c). *Supporting mentors.* Philadelphia: Public/Private Ventures.

Jucovy, L. (2001d). *Building relationships: A guide for new mentors.* Philadelphia: Public/Private Ventures.

Jucovy, L. (2001e). *Supporting mentors.* Philadelphia: Public/Private Ventures.

Jucovy, L. (2002). *Measuring the quality of mentor-youth relationships: A tool for mentoring programs.* Philadelphia: Public/Private Ventures.

Miller, A. D. (1999). *Mentoring: A guide to effective evaluation.* Salford, England: National Mentoring Network.

Miller, A. D. (2002). *Mentoring students and young people.* London: Kogan Page.

Miller, A. D., Drury, C., Stewart, L., & Ross, B. (2005). *An evaluation of the Home Office Mentoring Fund Initiative.* London: Home Office (forthcoming).

Morrow, K. V., & Styles, M. B. (1995). *Building relationships with youth in program settings. A study of Big Brothers/Big Sisters.* Philadelphia: Public/Private Ventures.

National Mentoring Center (2003a). *Foundations of successful youth mentoring: A guidebook for program development.* Portland, OR: Northwest Regional Educational Laboratory.

National Mentoring Center (2003b). *Generic mentoring program policy and procedure manual.* Portland, OR: Northwest Regional Educational Laboratory.

National Mentoring Center Bulletin (1999). *Remembering forgotten kids 3.*

National Mentoring Network (2001). *Generic quality standards for mentoring.* Salford, England: National Mentoring Network.

National Mentoring Working Group (1991). *Mentoring: Elements of effective practice.* Washington, DC: National Mentoring Partnership.

Network Training and Research Group (1996). *Evaluation of the Mentoring Center and Bay Area mentoring efforts. First Evaluation Report.* Redwood City, CA: Network Training and Research Group.

Padgette, H. C. (2003). *Finding funding: A guide to federal sources for out-of-school time and community school initiatives.* Washington, DC: The Finance Project.

Parra, G., DuBois, H., Neville, H., Pugh-Lilly, A. O., & Povinelli, N. (2002). Mentoring relationships for youth: Investigation of a process-oriented model. *Journal of Community Psychology, 30*(4), 367–388.

Pawson, R. (2004a). *Mentoring relationships: An explanatory review.* London: UK Centre for Evidence Based Policy and Practice.

Pawson, R. (2004b). *Mentoring relationships: An explanatory review – summary.* London: UK Centre for Evidence Based Policy and Practice.

Philip, K., & Hendry, L. B. (2000). Making sense of mentoring or mentoring making sense? Reflections on the mentoring process by adult mentors with young people. *Journal of Community and Applied Psychology, 10,* 211–223.

Philip, K., Shucksmith, J., & King, C. (2004). *Sharing a laugh? A qualitative study of mentoring interventions with young people.* York, England: Joseph Rowntree Foundation.

Piper, H., & Piper, J. (2000). Disaffected young people as the problem. Mentoring as the solution. Education and work as the goal. *Journal of Education and Work, 13*(1), 77–94.

Rhodes, J. E. (1994). Older and wiser: Mentoring relationships in childhood and adolescence. *Journal of Primary Prevention, 14,* 187–196.

Rhodes, J. E. (2002c). What's race got to do with it? *Research Corner.* Retrieved May 8, 2005, from the National Mentoring Partnerships website, www.mentoring.org/.

Rhodes, J. E., Grossman, J. B., & Resch, N. R. (2000). Agents of change: Pathways through which mentoring relationships influence adolescents' academic adjustment. *Child Development, 71,* 1662–1671.

Roaf, P. A., Tierney, J. P., & Hunte, D. E. I. (1994). *Big Brothers/Big Sisters of America: A study of volunteer recruitment and screening.* Philadelphia: Public/Private Ventures.

Sherman, L. (1999). *Reaching out for diversity: Recruiting minority mentors requires multiple strategies and long-term commitment.* National Mentoring Center Bulletin 2.

Shiner, M., Young, T., Newburn, T., & Groben, S. (2004). *Mentoring disaffected young people: An evaluation of Mentoring Plus.* York, England: Joseph Rowntree Foundation.

Sipe, C. L. (1996). *Mentoring: A synthesis of P/PV's research: 1988–1995.* Philadelphia: Public/Private Ventures.

Sipe, C. L. (1998). Mentoring adolescents: What have we learned? In J. B. Grossman (Ed.), *Contemporary issues in mentoring* (pp. 12–25). Philadelphia: Public/Private Ventures.

Sipe, C. L., & Roder, A. E. (1999). *Mentoring school-age children: A classification of programs.* Philadelphia: Public/Private Ventures.

Skinner, A., & Fleming, J. (1999). *Quality framework for mentoring with socially excluded young people.* Salford, England: National Mentoring Network.

St James-Roberts, I., & Singh, C. S. (2001). *Can mentors help school children with behavior problems?* Home Office Report 233. London: Home Office.

Styles, M. B., & Morrow, K. V. (1992). *Understanding how youth and elders form relationships: A study of four linking lifetimes programs.* Philadelphia: Public/Private Ventures.

Tarling, R., Burrows, J., & Clarke, A. (2001). Dalston Youth Project Part II (11–14) – An Evaluation, *Home Office Research Study 232.* London: Home Office.

Taylor, J. S. (2003). *Training new mentees.* Portland, OR: National Mentoring Center.

Tierney, J. P., Grossman, J. B., & Resch, N. L. (1995). *Making a difference: An impact study of Big Brothers/Big Sisters.* Philadelphia: Public/Private Ventures.

Chapter 20

Best Practices for Student–Faculty Mentoring Programs

Clark D. Campbell

Mentoring has been an integral part of education from the beginning of academia. Plato learned at the feet of Socrates in what could be described as a mentoring relationship. Throughout the history of the academy, close mentoring relationships between faculty and students have been described. Although education delivery may take many forms today (traditional classroom settings, one-on-one supervision, distance learning, etc.), mentoring appears to be a key ingredient.

Mentoring has become so popular that virtually all universities provide mentoring for undergraduate and graduate students. A quick review of many university websites indicates that a mentoring program is available to several constituents of the university. Shapiro and Blom-Hoffman (2004) describe three types of mentor relationships or networks in the academy: peer-to-peer, alumni-to-peer, and faculty-to-student. Although mentoring in academia may have different meanings to different constituent groups, the focus of this chapter will be on student–faculty mentoring. After reviewing the research literature on mentoring programs, best practices to consider in developing such programs will be presented.

The meaning of student–faculty mentoring and the format for its provision vary radically from institution to institution. Some institutions appear to provide the name of a faculty member to an incoming student and describe the ensuing relationship as mentoring. Another institution labels typical faculty advising as mentoring. In some universities mentoring clearly means something more personal, significant, and lengthy. Other institutions provide a more elaborate matching program between mentors and protégés as well as a structured design to the relationship. Specifics of mentoring programs will be addressed later in this chapter. However, the variability between programs and the lack of clarity regarding the nature of academic mentoring create difficulties in evaluating mentoring programs.

A review of the literature on best practices in student–faculty mentoring yields several problems in comparing programs. One problem concerns the definition of mentoring. The common purpose of mentoring in academia, at both the undergraduate and graduate levels, is increased success in the educational program. However, various definitions of academic mentoring are present in the literature, which complicates our understanding of this unique relationship. Jacobi (1991) found six different definitions of academic mentoring. One example is: "Mentoring as a function of educational institutions can be defined as a one-to-one learning relationship between an older person and a younger person that is based on modeling behavior and extended dialogue between them" (Lester & Johnson, 1981, p. 119).

Since Jacobi identified these various definitions over a decade ago, some authors have simplified their definitions. For example, Wallace, Abel, and Ropers-Huilman (2000) provide the following operational definition of mentoring in their program: "We use 'formal mentoring' to designate the deliberate matching of TRIO university personnel with students from historically underrepresented groups" (p. 88). Other authors have elaborated the definition of mentoring in academia. Johnson (2002) writes:

> Mentoring is a personal relationship in which a more experienced (usually older) faculty member or professional acts as a guide, role model, teacher, and sponsor of a less experienced (usually younger) graduate student or junior professional. A mentor provides the protégé with knowledge, advice, challenge, counsel, and support in the protégé's pursuit of becoming a full member of a particular profession. (p. 88)

The breadth of definitions of academic mentoring makes it difficult to adequately understand the meaning of this relationship in general. Most authors imply something greater than advising or friendship, but may not include all of the aspects captured in Johnson's (2002) definition provided above. Thus, his definition may be more aspirational than descriptive of how mentoring is operationalized in most academic institutions.

Kram (1985) described mentoring as an interpersonal process in which guidance, instruction, and support are provided by a more experienced colleague to a less experienced individual. Key mentoring functions include career-related ones such as coaching and providing visibility and exposure in the profession, as well as psychosocial functions such as role modeling, counseling, and friendship. Both the career and psychosocial functions appear to be important in the success of any mentoring program in academia. Although this description is based on a small sample of mentors and protégés in the workplace, it still appears to succinctly capture the salient features of academic mentoring.

Formal or structured relationships between students and faculty members are common in most academic institutions. Typically, these relationships are valued by students, faculty members, and the institutions because they facilitate success in academic pursuits. Student–faculty mentoring relationships develop at both the undergraduate and graduate level. Although there are many similarities in the nature of mentoring at both levels, there are significant differences as well.

The focus of the relationship at the undergraduate level is often on general success in academia which includes continuation in school and completing the requirements for a major. Mentoring relationships at this level typically focus on advising students in academic and career decisions. Using Kram's (1985) model, the career functions may be related more to choosing a career that best matches one's strengths, goals, and personality. Psychosocial functions of undergraduate mentoring may be related more toward supporting a student in adjusting to life apart from home and making wise personal decisions.

The focus of the relationship at the graduate level is often on preparing for professional success, which may involve a career in academia or another profession. While undergraduate mentoring may involve preparation for a general professional field, mentoring at the graduate level is typically more focused on a specific career choice. Johnson and Huwe (2003) write: "Graduate school mentorships are typically longer in duration, more focused on achieving professional competence and identity development, and more likely to yield a collegial friendship at graduation than the typical undergraduate mentorship" (p. 6). Using Kram's (1985) model, both the career and psychosocial functions in graduate school mentoring may acculturate a graduate student toward a specific professional career.

Prevalence of Mentoring in Academia

While virtually nothing is known about the prevalence of mentoring within formal academic mentoring programs, mentoring in colleges and universities appears to be a popular term describing faculty–student relationships. A few surveys report some findings on mentoring relationships in general on campuses. Johnson and Huwe (2003) surveyed the professional literature and wrote, "Good research on the prevalence of mentorships between graduate students and faculty members is sparse. Most graduate programs do not collect data regarding mentoring of their own students" (p. 9). A more recent review of the literature reveals the same result – we know very little about the nature or prevalence of mentoring in academia.

Some surveys of mentoring in psychology have been conducted, while similar surveys in other academic disciplines have been lacking (Johnson, Koch, Fallow, & Huwe, 2000). As reported in Johnson and Huwe (2003), three studies of psychology doctoral students found that approximately 50% of the students were mentored (Cronan-Hillix, Gensheimer, Cronan-Hillix, & Davidson, 1986; Kirchner, 1969; Mintz, Bartels, & Rideout, 1995). Additionally, Atkinson, Casas, and Neville (1994) found that 51% of ethnic minority graduate students received mentoring. More recently, Clark, Harden, and Johnson (2000) reported that 66% of clinical psychology doctoral students were mentored.

Johnson and Huwe (2003) concluded their review of the limited literature on the prevalence of mentoring in academia with the following findings: a) Not all graduate students get mentored, b) protégés often initiate the mentoring relationship, and c) university-based graduate programs (as compared to free-standing schools) with small student–faculty ratios appear to place a greater emphasis on mentoring. Given the much larger population of undergraduates, it is reasonable to estimate the prevalence of mentoring at that level as much lower than for graduate students.

Targeted Mentoring Groups

Student–faculty mentoring programs have been developed to facilitate the success of students in academia. Success can be defined differently in various institutions, but generally success implies continuing in a degree program, improving grades, or increasing the numbers of students in specific programs within the university. Although the empirical and theoretical research has not kept pace with the proliferation of mentoring programs (Jacobi, 1991), some support has been shown to facilitate success in these ways (Campbell & Campbell, 1997; Nagda, Gregerman, Jonides, von Hippel, & Lerner, 1998; Waldeck, Orrego, Plax, & Kearney, 1997; Wallace, Abel, & Ropers-Huilman, 2000). A review of the literature reveals that three student groups are the frequent target of mentoring programs.

One target of mentoring programs is undergraduate freshmen. Several programs exist to promote retention of students from their freshman year into their sophomore year. Approximately half of the students who enter college will not graduate (Tinto, 1993), and most of the attrition occurs in the first year of college when students have to make multiple adjustments. Universities appear to have turned to mentoring, both peer and faculty, as a mechanism to ameliorate high attrition rates. Nagda et al. (1998) found support for this use of mentoring. They utilized one form of mentoring, student–faculty research partnerships, and found that these partnerships resulted in improved retention rates of freshmen and sophomores.

Other researchers have looked at increased satisfaction with the university as one aspect of improving retention. This idea is based on the hypothesis that those who are satisfied are more likely to continue their academic program. Cosgrove (1986) found that a mentoring-transcript program was useful in increasing students' satisfaction with the university. Wallace et al. (2000) also found that mentoring facilitated students' initial decision to attend college and their subsequent positive experiences in college. Campbell and Campbell (1997) used a control group design without random assignment with a large group of ethnic minority undergraduates and found that the dropout rate was 14.5% in the mentored group compared to 26.3% in the control group over a one-year period.

A second group targeted for mentoring has been ethnic minority and female groups. For various reasons these groups have faced difficulties in adjusting to university settings typically developed and maintained by White males. Mentoring programs have been designed to facilitate academic success of these groups. Graduation rates for underrepresented groups such as Hispanics and African Americans are significantly below that of White students (Tinto, 1993). Additionally, minorities may face additional difficulties in accessing mentors (Blackwell, 1989; Kalbfleisch & Davies, 1991).

Nagda et al. (1998) found that their mentoring program was particularly beneficial for low achieving African American students. In other words, those African American students whose academic performance was below the median for their ethnic group, yet participated in a mentoring program, had an attrition rate in their freshman year that was almost half that of those who did not participate. Their results showed some hopeful findings for Hispanic students, but did not demonstrate the magnitude of the findings for African American students. The authors attribute the findings regarding Hispanic students to their low numbers at the university. Thus, these students had more difficulty forming a supportive community and may have been further away from their homes.

Although some studies suggest that females have difficulties accessing mentor relationships (Kalbfleisch & Davies, 1991), most studies indicate that males and females are mentored at about the same rate (Johnson & Huwe, 2003). Waldeck et al. (1997)

surveyed 145 graduate students at 12 universities and found that protégés were predominately female. Additionally, Campbell and Campbell (1997) found no differences between male and female students in various measures of grade point average (GPA), dropout rate, or number of units completed.

Although women and men may have similar access to mentoring, there are still gender issues that need to be addressed in these relationships – particularly cross-gender relationships. Fassinger and Hensler-McGinnis (2005) suggested that female protégés experience the psychosocial functions of mentoring, whereas male protégés experience more career functions of mentoring. They report also that women have experienced difficulties in the mentoring relationships including sexual harassment and exclusion from the mentor's professional network. Furthermore, Gilbert and Rossman (1992) report that male mentors are more likely than female mentors to assert power over protégés. Gender and minority status may play a larger role in specific training or educational programs. Females and minority students in a psychiatry residency program were more likely than males and nonminority students to state concerns about gender and ethnicity in their mentoring experiences (Williams, Levine, Malhotra, & Holtzheimer, 2004).

A third group targeted for mentoring includes those with particular majors or career aspirations. Several universities have utilized mentoring as a mechanism to attract and retain students in specific areas of study such as engineering, math, and the sciences. Sowan, Moffatt, and Canales (2004) developed a mentoring project designed to increase the number of students participating in pubic health nursing. Their program resulted in a 150% increase in the number of students participating in such clinical experiences. Several programs sponsored by the McNair Scholars Programs, discussed later in this chapter, involve students from disadvantaged backgrounds as a means of facilitating their entry into graduate school.

Overall freshmen retention, retention of females and ethnic minorities, as well as facilitation of increased enrollment in particular majors have been the successful targets of mentoring programs. Perhaps the career and psychosocial functions of mentoring (Kram, 1985) are partly responsible for the success of these programs in reaching target populations. Additionally, the modeling and powerful influence of having respected faculty members believe in protégés are likely components in the success of these mentoring programs.

Mentoring in Undergraduate and Graduate Programs

The National Education Association maintains a list of universities that offer formal mentoring programs (www2.nea.org/he/pgms.html). A review of the website indicates that mentoring is a popular activity on American college campuses. As discussed above, mentoring is one mechanism that universities have utilized to promote retention. One of the identified causes of attrition is a lack of integration into the college culture, and a significant component of this lack of connection is a weak student-with-faculty bond (Nagda et al., 1998). Integrating students into the mission of the university that goes beyond typical classroom interactions has been suggested as an important method to increase retention.

Nagda et al. (1998) describe an undergraduate research program that developed research partnerships between faculty and first and second year college students. The

Undergraduate Research Opportunity Program (UROP) was developed as a way to integrate underrepresented minority students into the academic mission of the university. Although all students are eligible, minority and women students are specifically recruited. The program meets during the regular academic year and is not a designated Honors Program. Several academic disciplines are represented by faculty who choose to be involved in the program. Prospective protégés review suggested projects offered by faculty and, after a mutual selection process, decide to work together one-on-one or in small groups with a mentor. Students are encouraged to present their research, and they receive academic credit for their work.

The UROP program was evaluated by comparing mentor groups of African American, Hispanic, and White students with nonparticipant control groups. The results indicated that participation in the UROP program increased retention rates for some students. The retention was greatest for African American students and sophomores rather than for freshmen. "The program appeared to benefit African-American students whose academic performance was below the median for their race/ethnic group. There were also positive trends for Hispanic and White students who participated in UROP during their sophomore year" (Nagda et al., 1998, p. 66). These results are very promising for the utility of a research mentoring program with undergraduate students. Not only did the program facilitate acculturation to the academic enterprise of research, but it enhanced retention of minority students as well.

Other examples of mentoring programs are the TRIO programs. These are student assistance programs developed and maintained by the US Department of Education's Office of Higher Education (www.ed.gov/about/offices/list/ope/trio/index.html). TRIO is not an acronym, but is a term coined in the 1960s to describe the first three federal programs designed to assist disadvantaged youth in achieving academic success. One of the purposes of the TRIO programs is to facilitate development of mentoring relationships in higher education at the undergraduate and graduate levels. The goals of the programs are to increase academic success, retention, and graduation rates, particularly for low-income students and students with disabilities. These programs utilize mentoring relationships as one method to achieve these goals. Programs such as Upward Bound, Student Support Services, McNair Scholars Program, and Educational Opportunity Centers are designed to enhance academic acculturation for students from disadvantaged backgrounds.

Wallace et al. (2000) interviewed 20 students, 10 of whom participated in the Student Support Services program, 4 in the Veterans Upward Bound program, and 6 in the Educational Opportunity Center program. Half of the students were White and the other 10 were minority students. The goals of these programs were to increase student retention, academic performance, and satisfaction with college. Students were matched with mentors based on their individual needs rather than matched with like gender or race mentors. Their findings showed that race and gender matching were not significant in the success of the mentoring process as determined by their academic continuation, performance, and satisfaction. Of particular interest was the finding that students who completed these programs did not identify one mentor relationship but rather multiple mentor relationships – "a network of mentors" (p. 100). Overall, their findings support the utility of mentoring in facilitating retention and satisfaction with college experiences.

Mentoring programs can be focused also on success in graduate school. The Ronald E. McNair Post-baccalaureate Achievement Program is one of the TRIO programs designated for graduate students. The purpose of the program is described as follows:

> The Ronald E. McNair Post-baccalaureate Achievement program awards grants to institutions of higher education for projects designed to prepare participants for doctoral studies through involvement in research and other scholarly activities. McNair participants are from disadvantaged backgrounds and have demonstrated strong academic potential. Institutions work closely with these participants through their undergraduate requirements, encourage their entrance into graduate programs, and track their progress to successful completion of advanced degrees. The goal of McNair is to increase the attainment of the Ph.D. by students from underrepresented segments of society. (www.ed.gov/programs/triomcnair/index.html)

These programs were named after the late Ronald McNair, who was an African American astronaut. The McNair Scholars Programs are funded by the Department of Education at 156 institutions in the US and Puerto Rico. Mentoring is a required and significant aspect of these programs, and is designed to facilitate the success of students in their graduate studies through adequate preparation at the undergraduate level.

University websites provide information on the specific McNair Scholars Program at their institution. Some websites are quite detailed in providing information for both mentors and protégés. For example, the University of Missouri website provides substantial information on mentoring in their McNair Scholars Program including information for both faculty and students who wish to participate (web.missouri.edu/~mcnair/). The responsibilities of faculty are explicit in requiring weekly meetings with their protégés, accompanying their protégés to a professional conference, and evaluation of the protégés' research performance.

Several universities have mentoring programs available for graduate students. Again, specific university websites can be useful in finding information relevant to particular program components. One mentoring program that appears to be well articulated is at Virginia Commonwealth University. Their mentoring website (www.vcu.edu/graduate/es/mentoring.html) includes a mentoring handbook and graduate student mentoring application. The handbook is clear in articulating core values, expectations, and responsibilities of mentors and protégés. Documents such as these can be useful to those interested in establishing similar mentoring programs.

Zanna and Darley (2004) describe ways to develop and manage research mentoring with graduate students which will enhance the satisfaction and productivity of mentor relationships. They recommend multiple lines of research with multiple roles for protégés depending on their level of training. They also recommend that students work with more than one faculty member on research, which forces faculty members to collaborate and take collective responsibility for the development of students rather than focusing only on their own students. Their *modified apprenticeship model* utilizes vertical integration of research teams so that students can work at multiple levels on research projects. This model blends the roles of mentor and protégé so that all students are being mentored by a faculty member, but some more advanced students serve as peer mentors as well.

Problems in Evaluating Academic Mentoring Programs

One of the main problems in evaluating academic mentoring programs is the variability in descriptions of mentoring. As indicated previously, mentoring is defined and operationalized in various ways in different programs, which leads to problems in researching these programs. Jacobi (1991) summarized her review of the literature, "variation in operational definitions continues to plague mentoring research and has almost certainly devalued the concept for application in 'hard' research" (p. 508). Unfortunately, this variation is still true today and leads to difficulty in evaluating mentoring programs.

Another problem encountered in evaluating mentoring programs is that poor research designs plague the studies reported in the literature. Most studies use small sample sizes, rely on self-report measures, and utilize correlational designs. Waldeck et al. (1997) describe several methodological problems in studies on mentoring programs. These problems include unmatched samples of mentors and protégés, small and non-representative samples, and "testimonials or opinion pieces in which definitive conclusions are drawn without empirical support" (p. 94).

Those studies that do report outcomes of mentoring programs tend to utilize satisfaction measures to demonstrate positive outcomes. Additionally, attrition or retention rates may be reported. These are not inappropriate outcome measures since many mentoring programs are designed to enhance retention, but additional measures such as impact on academic performance and success in entrance to graduate school are rarely reported.

In addition to weak outcome measures, few research studies provide comparison between control and experimental groups. This lack of experimental design creates difficulty in making causal inferences. Many research studies report retrospective findings based on surveys and interviews. There is little empirical data on formal mentoring programs using experimental or quasi-experimental research designs, thus we have little evidence for the effective components of mentoring. Campbell and Campbell (1997) provide this summary of the literature: "In fact, a review of the literature has failed to locate a single report of a control-group study dealing with the effects of a university mentoring program on undergraduate retention and performance" (p. 730). The thrust of their conclusion is still true today.

General Characteristics of Mentoring Programs

Mentoring programs can be evaluated on several salient characteristics. Every program addresses the following issues in some way, and so they are essential components to consider when evaluating or developing mentoring programs. A best practice recommendation will follow the brief summary of each program characteristic.

Formal versus informal mentoring programs. One of the primary factors that distinguish mentoring practices is the level of intentionality that is evident in the program. Some graduate programs provide an intentional matching of protégé and mentor, while mentoring relationships in other programs appear to be almost accidental. In a rather crass analogy, mentoring relationships in academia can be classified in a way similar to the classification of murder: premeditated, spontaneous, or accidental. Some mentoring programs involve carefully planned and intentional mentoring relationships. Other mentoring programs are more incidental in which mentoring is desired but not planned in an organized manner. Still other mentoring programs seem to allow mentoring, but not anticipate its development. Mentoring in these programs seems almost accidental.

Fassinger and Hensler-McGinnis (2005) refer to formal mentoring programs as those that provide assignment of mentors by a third party, while informal mentoring programs are those in which mentoring develops spontaneously. They offer a third option, facilitated mentorships, wherein the institution provides the structure and expectations for mentoring to occur, but leaves the selection of mentor relationships to the students and faculty to determine on their own.

It appears that the distinguishing nature of formal mentoring programs is that they are organized and intentional. These programs expect mentoring to occur, emphasize the importance of protégé–faculty matching, provide time and space in the academic program for these activities, and may provide faculty load credit for such endeavors. Informal mentoring programs seem to use the term "mentoring" to describe student–faculty relationships, but the programs lack the structure required of organized and intentional ones. In this chapter these programs are referred to as loosely structured mentoring programs since they are designed to facilitate mentoring but do not provide training, matching, recruiting of mentors, etc. that the formal mentoring programs tend to provide.

Best practice – intentional mentoring.   Although there is not yet outcome data to support a firm recommendation, it appears that mentoring programs that are formal, structured, and intentional are best designed to meet the goals of the programs such as retention, academic performance, or placement in graduate school. While informal or loosely structured mentoring programs may meet the needs of some students, more students will likely be served adequately through an intentional program that is clearly articulated. An intentional or formal program also lends itself to assessment and evaluation. Although formality and structure are valued, it is important that there not be too much formality so that faculty and students do not feel forced into a nongenuine relationship.

Recruiting and selecting mentors.   What are the characteristics of a good mentor and what does it take to provide effective mentorship to protégés? Mentors should be selected for qualities they possess and other qualities they do not possess (Johnson & Huwe, 2003). Positive qualities desirable in a mentor include personality characteristics such as warmth, empathy, self-awareness, balance of demands, integrity, and honesty. Desirable behavioral characteristics include productivity, respect by colleagues, effective communication, availability, and a strong mentoring history. Conversely, negative personality characteristics to be avoided in a mentor include narcissism, avoidance, detachment, low self-awareness, and sexist or racist attitudes. Behavioral characteristics to be avoided include lack of productivity, unethical behavior, poor communication or history of mentoring, and unsupportive availability.

In a thoughtful and detailed description, Johnson and Huwe (2002) provide a typology of graduate school mentor dysfunction. These dysfunctions include such issues as mentor technical and relational incompetence, faulty mentor–protégé matching, and boundary violations. Strategies for preventing and responding to mentorship dys-functions are provided. Although these dysfunctions are directed to graduate school mentorships, they would apply to any mentoring relationship in academia.

One aspect of mentoring involves modeling appropriate professional or academic behavior. Students benefit by seeing professional behaviors in action, and some of the most powerful teaching occurs through this strong but subtle mechanism. Modeling is a form of observational learning in which behaviors are acquired by an individual who is in a close or valued relationship with a person in a position of authority. Modeling occurs in virtually all relationships, and we have a tendency to take on the characteristics of others through this interpersonal process of imitation, identification, and introjection.

Modeling, however, is not the same as mentoring. Mentoring involves an active relationship in which a faculty member provides important knowledge, skill, and attitudes to a student with the goal of enhancing the student's chances of success in the institution or profession. In other words modeling is more likely to be a pas-sive process of learning, whereas mentoring is more likely to be an active process. "Mentoring should be viewed as an active process in which mentors and protégés engage in a personal and environmental assessment before they initiate a mentoring relationship" (Black, Suarez, & Medina, 2004, p. 47). Additionally, mentoring is seen as a broader concept that includes modeling as one aspect of interpersonal learning.

Mentor selection should be based in part on modeling – faculty who are good models may become excellent mentors. Modeling appropriate professional behavior, interpersonal skill, self-care, research productivity, and academic success should be qualities to screen for in selecting mentors in a formal mentoring program.

Little has been written about recruiting mentors other than encouraging protégés to carefully choose their mentors with the above qualities in mind. Most mentor relationships in academia assume that the mentor is already employed and committed to the institution as the senior member of the mentor dyad. Thus, the emphasis is on protégés matching up with the characteristics already present in the mentors. Some programs have developed recruiting strategies and detailed mentor applications. Some university programs also provide external benefits for being a mentor, such as faculty load credit for mentoring freshmen. However, it is unknown whether or not external benefits or incentives actually improve the quality of mentoring or the outcomes these programs desire for their students. Further research to evaluate the role of faculty incentives for mentoring would be helpful.

Best practice – recruiting and selecting mentors.   Not all faculty members make good mentors. Those that do have the requisite interest, demeanor, and inter-personal skill to facilitate development in another person should be encouraged to mentor students. Selecting faculty members with mentoring as part of the job descrip-tion would be helpful in clarifying the significance of the mentoring role for new faculty. Load credit or other incentives for such important activities that facilitate retention and enhance the mission of the institution may also be beneficial in select-ing appropriate mentors. It will be necessary, however, to limit the number of pro-tégés that a particular faculty member takes on. As with any professional activity, mentoring can be both energizing and draining.

Matching mentors and protégés.   Most authors describe the match between mentors and protégés as one of the most important decisions in the history of the relationship. Just as in any significant and personal association, the match of personality characteristics and goals is necessary for the survival and productivity of the relationship. "Compatibility – 'being on the same wavelength' or 'having the right chemistry' is as essential to the mentoring relationship as it is to other successful dynamic and reciprocal relationships" (Jackson et al., 2003, p. 333).

Just as mentors can exhibit characteristics that facilitate productive relationships, protégés can exhibit useful characteristics as well. Huwe and Johnson (2003) provide a list of personality characteristics and behavioral patterns that facilitate mentoring relationships. These personality characteristics include emotional stability, internal locus of control, coachability, emotional intelligence, and commitment to the profession. Effective behavior patterns include initiating the relationship, articulating the match, demonstrating achievement, career planning, and direct communication. Mentors tend to look for these personality and behavior qualities in prospective protégés.

As in any effective and ongoing relationship, shared interests, mutual enjoyment, value similarity, and shared expectations are important in sustaining the relationship. However, demographic characteristics, such as race and gender, can be important as well. Fassinger and Hensler-McGinnis (2005) write, "gender as well as race, class, and other cultural identities interacts with relational factors such as personal interests, values, and expectations to create considerable complexity in the mentoring process" (p. 148). Careful attention to matching along both demographic and personal interests is warranted in any effective mentoring program.

Formal mentoring programs either tend to match students and faculty members or provide a mechanism for a relational connection to occur. Although the match should be facilitated, it should not be forced. A forced match is unlikely to produce a mutually beneficial relationship, and therefore they are discouraged unless they are necessary for a temporary time period. Black et al. (2004) describe an intentional process in which students and faculty members are encouraged to conduct an in-depth self-assessment regarding a mentoring relationship. This probing self-appraisal is designed to facilitate a better mentor–protégé match.

In a similar vein, Rose (2003) developed the Ideal Mentoring Scale (IMS) as an instrument designed to assist graduate students seeking faculty mentors. This scale can enhance communication between mentor and protégé and further clarify the nature and expectations of the mentoring relationship. Although this may seem like an overly formal way to pursue a mentor match, the process may raise significant issues to consider such as expectations of productivity and the mentor relationship.

Best practice – matching.   Findings from naturally occurring mentor relationships imply that matching between mentor and protégé is essential to the quality of the relationship. Facilitating this relationship without forcing mentors and protégés into relationships appears to be the best practice described in the literature. These relationships can be facilitated by providing information about mentors to prospective protégés – their areas of research interest, preferences in working with students, personal interests, etc. – and then encouraging students to meet with potential mentors for casual conversations. This helps potential protégés to actively seek the kind of mentors with whom they would like to work. The *facilitated mentorship* described by Fassinger and Hensler-McGinnis (2005) may be a helpful matching model to consider. The research on gender and minority matching is mixed – some advocate similarity in gender and ethnicity and others do not. It seems that the best practice is to have adequate representation of gender and ethnicity among the faculty so that students can choose a similar or cross-gender/ethnicity relationship.

Training in mentorship. Little research speaks directly to the issue of training faculty members to be mentors. Graduate faculty members may find that they are expected to mentor graduate students as a part of their academic duties. Demands for research productivity may determine the necessity of mentoring, whether the faculty member is trained or not. Just as with teaching expectations, faculty members are often required to meet the expectations of the department in mentoring research. Similarly, undergraduate faculty members may face mentoring expectations regarding recruiting students for their majors, for retention purposes, or for assuring appropriate socialization to university life.

As with many expectations of faculty, there is little preparation for the tasks of mentoring at both the graduate and undergraduate levels. The rationale appears to be that faculty members know the expectations of academia and, since they are teachers, they should be able to serve as appropriate resources for students. Although there is likely truth to this rationale, it probably overstates the competence of faculty members to assume that they are readily prepared to facilitate an effective mentoring relationship. The psychosocial functions that Kram (1985) identifies may be more challenging for some faculty members than some institutions realize.

Boyle and Boice (1998) developed a mentoring program for undergraduate faculty that informed potential senior faculty mentors about the nature of mentoring and provided what appears to be on-the-job training. The mentors met as a group monthly during the mentoring project and learned from each other some of the specifics of the role. The mentors reported that these required monthly meetings were very important to the success of the program. Although faculty mentoring is different than student–faculty mentoring, there are helpful implications from this well-developed program.

Best practice – training in mentorship. In many regards most faculty members have the requisite knowledge to become excellent mentors. Provided that the accompanying personality and interpersonal skills exist also, relatively little training in mentoring should be necessary. Faculty members could benefit from information regarding the nature, benefits, requirements, and boundaries of outstanding mentor relationships. This information could come through reading, lecture, small group discussion, and email listserves. The monthly meetings recommended in the formal mentoring program described by Boyle and Boice (1998) appear to be very helpful in facilitating useful mentoring practices as well as support.

Length and boundaries of mentor relationships. As in any ethical relationship, there are boundaries that define the nature and limits of the association. One way to conceptualize boundaries is to think of them as the rules and expectations that define relationships. Thus, the question to address here is what rules and expectations should define a mentoring relationship? One of the boundary expectations relates to the length or ending of the mentoring relationship.

A natural ending point for a faculty–student mentor relationship occurs when the student graduates from his or her university program. It would be reasonable to expect most mentor relationships to either end or change significantly at the point of graduation. In many regards, the purpose of the mentorship ends when the protégé receives the degree for which he or she has been training. For undergraduates, graduation usually implies leaving the university for employment elsewhere or for a graduate program in another university. Some contact may continue as the protégé needs letters of recommendation or some occasional career advice.

Johnson and Huwe (2003) indicate that a similar boundary to ending the mentoring relationship may apply at the graduate level as well. "For most graduate students, a natural tie for separation and redefinition of the relationship is the completion of graduate education, successful defense of the dissertation, or landing that first job" (p. 107). However, since the mentoring relationship at the graduate level can be more intense and ongoing, such absolute boundaries may not always apply. The relationship may continue beyond graduation because career direction and facilitation is one of the goals of the relationship, and it is not unusual for a student's career to just be starting at the point of graduation. Another reason for the mentor relationship to continue beyond graduation is because of the personal and gratifying nature of these connections.

It is important for the mentor to initiate discussion of separation or diminishment of the mentoring relationship prior to graduation so that appropriate expectations can be maintained. It is difficult to talk about the ending or separation of any significant relationship, and thus the easiest path to follow is to avoid this discussion and continue the fantasy that the relationship does not have to end or change substantially. However, not clarifying the changed relationship can lead to misunderstanding and confusion.

The length of the relationship is one of many boundaries in the student–faculty mentor dyad. Boundary violations within mentor relationships are very real potential problems and should be considered carefully. Mentor–protégé relationships are inherently multiple relationships in which multiple role expectations operate. Biaggio, Paget, and Chenoweth (1997) describe the difficulties in navigating the overlapping roles professors have with graduate students, including teacher, supervisor, advisor, and potentially that of an employer. Thus, caution is appropriate in managing these multiple and sometimes competing roles.

Working in close proximity with someone who has similar interests can promote feelings of intimacy. Proximity (Festinger, Schacter, & Back, 1950) and similarity (Byrne, 1969) have been shown to be key ingredients in producing intimate relationships, and thus faculty members should be well aware of the potential for inappropriate or unethical relationships developing in the context of mentoring.

The key to managing multiple role relationships is to constantly clarify the expectations of each party and to openly discuss potential ethical dilemmas. Seeking consultation with peers and maintaining the value of ethical behavior are of utmost importance in the quality of these relationships. Since mentors are in positions of power and can derive satisfaction from watching their protégés develop, caution is important in maintaining appropriate expectations that are in the best interest of the protégé.

Best practice – boundaries.   Mentors have an obligation to maintain appropriate boundaries since they have the most power in the relationship. In addition to valuing respect and avoiding the misuse of power, mentors should initiate regular conversations about the nature of the mentoring relationship. Is the protégé getting what he or she wants from the relationship? Is he or she being prepared for the next step in their professional or educational journey? Is the protégé becoming independent rather than dependent on the mentor? What needs of mine (as a mentor) are being met in this relationship that would be better met in a different relationship that did not have a power differential? Initiating these conversations and seeking consultation from a trusted colleague are helpful ways of maintaining appropriate boundaries.

Frequency of interaction in mentor relationships.   Some mentor programs structure the interaction so that the frequency of meetings is predetermined. For example, Boyle and Boice (1998) required mentors to meet with protégés weekly for brief meetings. Campbell and Campbell (1997) allowed mentors and protégés to determine their own meeting frequency and schedule. Over a year period, protégés averaged 7.28 contacts with their mentors for an average total meeting time of 124 minutes. It is interesting to note that students met with their faculty mentors for about two hours per year, and yet that contact time was significant in their successful college experience. However, there were significant correlations between the amount of meeting time and GPA and number of units completed, so increased mentoring time was related to more success for the protégés.

There appears to be no standard regarding the frequency of interaction in academic mentor relationships. It is likely that the frequency of interaction is related to the needs of the protégé, whether those needs involve completion of the dissertation, advice regarding job opportunities, course selection, or help with time management. One important aspect of effective mentoring is the availability of the mentor to the protégé. Since the needs of the protégé are episodic and somewhat unpredictable, availability of the mentor is essential. As the study just described indicates, the actual amount of time spent mentoring a student may be relatively brief.

The episodic nature of the protégé's needs creates a situation in which the protégé should feel comfortable articulating his or her needs to the mentor, and the mentor should be sensitive to the needs of the protégé. Again, communication and clarification are essential aspects of the effective mentor relationship.

As the protégé develops it is reasonable that the intensity of the needs changes as well. "As the relationship develops, what was once hierarchical becomes collegial. Accountability to the relationship includes a commitment to communication, respect, and recognition of each other's needs" (Black et al., 2004, p. 53). One of the purposes of a mentoring relationship is to move a protégé from a position of dependence to independence. Mentor self-assessment can be helpful in assuring that mentoring relationships are not maintained simply for the ego needs of the mentor.

Best practice – frequency of meetings.   Meetings should be scheduled at regular intervals with protégés. This practice provides structure, predictability, and support, while not facilitating the urgent or crisis request for inopportune meetings. Although spontaneous meetings should be allowed, it is recommended that regular meetings be maintained as well. The frequency of these meetings may change over the course of the academic year or over the course of a program, and thus mutual input into the frequency of meetings should be encouraged.

Developing a Mentoring Program

Boyle and Boice (1998) advocate the development of structured mentoring programs as opposed to spontaneous or naturally occurring mentoring. They reported that those mentoring dyads in a program met more regularly over a longer period of time and experienced greater campus involvement than those dyads that were not in a mentoring program. Additionally, they reported that the mentors learned significantly from each other in the program, and this likely would not have happened without the formal structure of the program.

Boyle and Boice (1998) recommended a mentoring program model that could be implemented at other universities. Their program was set up for mentoring new faculty members and new graduate teaching assistants, but it appears that the model could be useful to a variety of student–faculty mentoring endeavors. The three phases of their model are planning, structure, and assessment. In the planning phase they recommended recruiting participants early. This allows those who are involved to make the mentoring program a central part of their academic life. The participants scheduled other responsibilities around the mentoring program. Assigning faculty–graduate student dyads within the department was the second aspect of the planning phase. Finally, the planning phase involved a clear articulation of program goals and expectations so that participants understood the mission of the mentoring program.

The second phase of the mentoring program model involved structure. Mentor–protégé dyads were required to meet weekly, but briefly, throughout the length of the program. Regular contact by the program directors assured that mentors and protégés were actually meeting as expected. An additional aspect to the structure phase was the inclusion of monthly group meetings. This allowed mentors and protégés from various dyads to share experiences and to sense involvement with the full mentoring program. These group meetings were described as the most beneficial part of the program by participants.

The third phase of the program was assessment. Boyle and Boice (1998) recommend collecting three types of data: program involvement data, pair bonding data, and mentoring context data. The program involvement data consisted of tracking the frequency and regularity of the mentor–protégé meetings. The pair bonding data consisted of collecting data on a 10-item mentoring index. This allowed the program directors to have a better idea of the bond between the mentor and protégé. The mentoring context data consisted of the records of the mentor–protégé meetings. A content analysis of these data revealed the themes and issues that were significant to the participants involved.

This model appears to be useful as a template for establishing similar programs on college campuses with various constituents. An added benefit of this model is the built-in assessment phase. This phase provides data which will assist in altering the program to meet local needs, and will also provide outcome assessment and program evaluation data so that similar programs potentially could be compared across campuses.

Beyond designing a mentoring model, it will be important to address issues that are likely to be present in the culture of the institution or department. These issues, if not addressed, will likely sink the implementation of any mentoring program. Johnson et al. (2000) recommend several methods designed to increase the prevalence of mentoring in graduate programs. These include creating a culture of mentoring, emphasizing mentoring as a criterion during faculty hiring and student selection, providing education regarding mentoring to students and faculty, monitoring the mentoring demands on faculty and explicitly rewarding them for this activity, creating mentoring programs that are consistent with particular local departmental needs, and collecting mentoring program data. Although these recommendations are intended for graduate psychology programs, it appears that many of the methods would be appropriate for undergraduate and graduate programs in a variety of disciplines.

Best practice – developing a mentoring program.   Careful planning, recruitment of appropriate faculty, and institutional support appear to be essential aspects of a successful mentoring program. Articulating the program structure and requiring some meetings between mentors and protégés as well as between mentors and other mentors are additional salient features. Anticipating data collection and assessment is vital to the ongoing administrative support of most programs, so this aspect of the mentoring program should be anticipated from the outset.

Barriers to Developing a Mentoring Program

Barriers to any academic program can occur at various levels including institutional, departmental, and individual. Barriers to mentoring at the institutional level may include an over-emphasis on faculty publication and funded research to the extent that teaching and mentoring suffer. The external benefits of funded research and publication are apparent, while the significance of student satisfaction and retention is perhaps less obvious. Additionally, funding an internal program such as a mentoring program may have low priority when compared to other more visible competing programs.

Barriers at the department or division level may occur in a local culture of competition. When limited student positions are available or when a "weeding out" process is the norm, then unhealthy competition can exist between students and between faculty members which may counter the efforts of a supportive or nurturing mentor environment. Alternatively, recognition for a mentoring team or group by the institution may shift some of the normal pressures for competition to more healthy outlets between groups rather than between individuals. Reduced class loads or some financial compensation for excellent mentors would perhaps set a new and positive standard in many academic departments.

Individual barriers to developing a mentor program include both intrapsychic and interpersonal issues. Some faculty members would not make good mentors. Intrapsychic characteristics such as inflexibility, low empathy, perfectionism, or high anxiety may preclude productive mentor relationships. Likewise, interpersonal characteristics such as poor communication skills, extreme introversion, poor personal boundaries, or poor conflict management skills may pose strained mentor–protégé relationships as well.

Directors of mentoring programs should assess their institutions and faculty members at each of these levels when considering implementation of a mentoring program. There will always be some issues to address on each of these levels, but awareness of the issues prior to program implementation will help assure the success of the program.

Best practice – addressing barriers.   Developers of mentoring programs should seek institutional support for such programs. This support must be actual and not only conceptual. Thus, time and space allocations for faculty must be addressed as well as the accompanying financial implications. Some funding for mentor expenses (perhaps for small research projects or for occasional social functions) would be helpful institutional supports. Confronting unhealthy forms of competition that create unobtainable standards or further alienate students must be addressed directly with faculty so that a nurturing and supportive environment can be facilitated.

Recommendations

Mentoring programs have proliferated rapidly in academic settings, and it appears that they are here to stay. Intuitively these programs make sense and therefore they appeal to various constituents in the university. Although the zeal to develop these programs is apparent, the research to support the development has been lacking. Few research studies utilize control groups with random assignment so that appropriate interpretations of findings can result. Thus, we know little about the effectiveness of mentoring programs versus naturally occurring mentoring. More outcome studies evaluating the effect of such programs on GPA, job procurement, or graduate school placement would be helpful.

Further research on the effective components of mentoring programs would be useful as well. What aspects of mentoring programs are particularly necessary? How much mentoring is needed, with whom, and under what circumstances? In academia, it is natural that mentoring occurs around research, but are there other professional activities that would be appropriately suited as well? Mentoring in field placements or real-life consultations with businesses, educational programs, or non-profit agencies may provide an alternate context for academic mentoring. Research into these areas would help shape programs that better prepare students for productive careers.

References

Atkinson, D. R., Casas, A., & Neville, H. (1994). Ethnic minority psychologists: Whom they mentor and benefits they derive from the process. *Journal of Multicultural Counseling and Development, 22*, 37–48.

Biaggio, M., Paget, T. L., & Chenoweth, M. S. (1997). A model for ethical management of faculty–student dual relationships. *Professional Psychology: Research and Practice, 28*, 184–189.

Black, L. L., Suarez, E. C., & Medina, S. (2004). Helping students help themselves: Strategies for successful mentoring relationships. *Counselor Education and Supervision, 44*, 44–55.

Blackwell, J. E. (1989). Mentoring: An action strategy for increasing minority faculty. *Academe, 75*, 8–14.

Byrne, D. (1969). Attitudes and attraction. In L. Berkowitz (Ed.), *Advances in experimental social psychology* (Vol. 4, pp. 35–89). New York: Academic Press.

Boyle, P., & Boice, B. (1998). Systematic mentoring for new faculty teachers and graduate teaching assistants. *Innovative Higher Education, 22*, 157–180.

Campbell, T. A., & Campbell, D. E. (1997). Faculty/student mentor program: Effects on academic performance and retentions. *Research in Higher Education, 38*, 727–742.

Clark, R. A., Harden, S. L., & Johnson, W. B. (2000). Mentor relationships in clinical psychology doctoral training: Results of a national survey. *Teaching of Psychology, 27*, 262–268.

Cosgrove, T. J. (1986). The effects of participation in a mentoring-transcript program on freshmen. *Journal of College Student Personnel, 27*, 119–124.

Cronan-Hillix, T., Gensheimer, L. K., Cronan-Hillix, W. A., & Davidson, W. S. (1986). Student's views of mentors in psychology graduate training. *Teaching of Psychology, 13*, 123–127.

Fassinger, R. E., & Hensler-McGinnis, N. F. (2005). Multicultural feminist mentoring as individual and small-group pedagogy. In C. Z. Enns & A. L. Sinacore (Eds.), *Teaching and social justice: Integrating multicultural and feminist theories in the classroom* (pp. 143–161). Washington, DC: American Psychological Association.

Festinger, L., Schacter, S., & Back, K. W. (1950). *Social pressure in informal groups*. New York: Harper.

Gilbert, L. A., & Rossman, K. M. (1992). Gender and the mentoring process for women: Implications for professional development. *Professional Psychology: Research and Practice, 23*, 233–238.

Huwe, J. M., & Johnson, W. B. (2003). On being an excellent protégé: What graduate students need to know. *Journal of College Student Psychotherapy, 17*, 41–57.

Jackson, V. A., Palepu, A., Szalacha, L., Caswell, C., Carr, P. L., & Inui, T. (2003). Having the right chemistry: A qualitative study of mentoring in academic medicine. *Academic Medicine, 78*, 328–334.

Jacobi, M. (1991). Mentoring and undergraduate academic success: A literature review. *Review of Educational Research, 61*, 505–532.

Johnson, W. B. (2002). The intentional mentor: Strategies and guidelines for the practice of mentoring. *Professional Psychology: Research and Practice, 33*, 88–96.

Johnson, W. B., & Huwe, J. M. (2002). Toward a typology of mentorship dysfunction in graduate school. *Psychotherapy Theory, Research, Practice, Training, 39*, 44–55.

Johnson, W. B., & Huwe, J. M. (2003). *Getting mentored in graduate school*. Washington, DC: American Psychological Association.

Johnson, W. B., Koch, C., Fallow, G. O., & Huwe, J. M. (2000). Prevalence of mentoring in clinical versus experimental doctoral programs: Survey findings, implications and recommendations. *Psychotherapy, 37*, 325–334.

Kalbfleisch, P., & Davies, A. (1991). Minorities and mentoring: Managing the multicultural institution. *Communication Education, 40*, 266–271.

Kirchner, E. P. (1969). Graduate education in psychology: Retrospective views of advanced degree recipients. *Journal of Clinical Psychology, 25*, 207–213.

Kram, K. E. (1985). *Mentoring at work: Developmental relationships in organizational life*. Glenview, IL: Scott Foreman and Company.

Lester, V., & Johnson, C. (1981). The learning dialogue: Mentoring. In J. Fried (Ed.), *Education for student development. New directions for student services* (No. 15, pp. 49–56). San Francisco: Jossey-Bass.

Mintz, L. B., Bartels, K. M., & Rideout, C. A. (1995). Training in counseling ethnic minorities and race-based availability of graduate school resources. *Professional Psychology: Research and Practice, 26*, 316–321.

Nagda, B. A., Gregerman, S. R., Jonides, J., von Hippel, W., & Lerner, J. S. (1998). Undergraduate student–faculty research partnerships affect student retention. *Review of Higher Education, 22,* 55–72.

Rose, G. (2003). Enhancement of mentor selection using the Ideal Mentor Scale. *Research in Higher Education, 44,* 473–494.

Shapiro, E. S., & Blom-Hoffman, J. (2004). Mentoring, modeling, and money: The 3 Ms of producing academics. *School Psychology Quarterly, 19,* 365–381.

Sowan N. A., Moffatt, S. G., & Canales, M. K. (2004). Creating a mentoring partnership model: A university-department of health experience. *Family and Community Health, 27,* 326–337.

Tinto, V. (1993). *Leaving college: Rethinking the causes and cures of student attrition* (2nd ed.). Chicago: University of Chicago Press.

Waldeck, J. H., Orrego, V. O., Plax, T. G., & Kearney, P. (1997). Graduate student/faculty mentoring relationships: Who gets mentored, how it happens, and to what end. *Communication Quarterly, 45,* 93–109.

Wallace, D., Abel, R., & Ropers-Huilman, B. (2000). Clearing a path for success: Deconstructing borders through undergraduate mentoring. *Review of Higher Education, 24,* 87–102.

Williams, L. L., Levine, J. B., Malhotra, S., & Holtzheimer, P. (2004). The good-enough mentoring relationship. *Academic Psychiatry, 28,* 111–115.

Zanna, M. P., & Darley, J. M. (2004). Mentoring: Managing the faculty–graduate student relationship. In J. M. Darley, M. P. Zanna, & H. L. Roediger (Eds.), *The compleat academic: A career guide* (2nd ed., pp. 117–131). Washington, DC: American Psychological Association.

Chapter 21

Best Practices in Workplace Formal Mentoring Programs

Lisa M. Finkelstein and Mark L. Poteet

Our working definition of a formal mentoring program is based on descriptions by several authors (e.g., Douglas & McCauley, 1999; Eddy, Tannenbaum, Alliger, D'Abate, & Givens, 2001; Forret, Turban, & Dougherty, 1996): *A formal mentoring program occurs when an organization officially supports and sanctions mentoring relationships. In these programs, organizations play a role in facilitating mentoring relationships by providing some level of structure, guidelines, policies, and assistance for starting, maintaining, and ending mentor–protégé relationships.* This definition distinguishes formal programs from *informal mentoring* where it is the primary responsibility of the mentor and/or protégé to initiate, maintain, and end a relationship, with little or no official organizational support.

Articles from both the practical and academic literature indicate that many companies had at one time or currently have a formal mentoring program in place. For example, Eddy et al. (2001) located 143 companies that had some form of mentoring program, including companies such as American Airlines, Lockheed-Martin, and Marriott International. Given the benefits of informal mentoring, formal programs can be seen as perks and as a recruiting advantage. Mentoring in general has been related to job satisfaction, commitment, expectations for advancement, compensation, and promotions (Allen, Eby, Poteet, Lentz, & Lima, 2004). Further, given the continuing need for companies to groom early-career employees for succession planning purposes, facilitate the upward mobility of underrepresented groups, and respond to structural changes, there is reason to believe that the use of such programs will flourish. But are formal programs really beneficial?

The extant literature (see Ramaswami & Dreher, this volume) is mixed. Some studies have found benefits to formal mentoring (e.g., Fagan, 1988) – others report that participants actually received less mentoring (cf. Wanberg, Welsh, & Hezlett, 2003). These findings beg the question – are mentorships best left to develop naturally? Ragins, Cotton, and Miller (2000) caution that categorizing mentoring relationships with broad strokes as formal or informal may cloud the specific aspects of formal

programs that may enhance their success. Additionally, the work of Eby and colleagues (e.g., Eby, Butts, Lockwood, & Simon, 2004; Eby & Lockwood, 2005) has
brought our attention to the dark side of mentoring, finding that abusive, neglectful,
or just mismatched relationships – formal or informal – can have negative outcomes
for those involved. So, although it appears that formal programs may be at a *potential* disadvantage, not all formal mentoring programs or mentorships are created equally,
and it is possible there are many formal relationships that have been far more successful than informal ones. We must closely examine the specific features of formal
mentoring programs to understand how to put a program together in a way that
will maximize its chances for success.

Our goal in this chapter is to trace the process of developing a formal mentoring
program from inception to evaluation. For each step, we first review the best practices recommended in the applied literature, and the descriptive research that has
identified what companies have been doing with respect to those recommendations.
After this, we turn to the more academically focused, empirical literature to see
if indeed there is any research evidence to support these best practice suggestions.
Ragins et al. (2000) lamented the lack of empirical research comparing features of
formal programs, and although a bit more has emerged the existing research base
is quite small. Because of this, where applicable we also consider other literatures
to see if there is indirect evidence to support best-practices claims. Following this,
we integrate what we know, what we need to know, and what we need to do to
get there.

Inception: Organizational Support for the Program

A consistent theme in the practitioner literature is that the sponsoring organization
must show a high level of support for a formal mentoring program to succeed. The
logic is that employees will be more committed to an initiative if they believe their
leaders value it or see their leaders practice it. Communication and visibility seem
to be the most frequently used methods for showing support (cf. Burke & McKeen,
1989a; Douglas & McCauley, 1999; Kizilos, 1990). Tyler (1998) described a program where top leaders actually serve as mentors. Phillips-Jones (1983) reported that
in some companies executives allow time away from the job for participants to meet.
As reported by Forret et al. (1996), one company holds semi-annual meetings as a
way of publicizing the mentoring programs.

There are other ways an organization can show its commitment to formal mentoring. Several authors have suggested using reward systems as a way to encourage
mentors to participate (e.g., Keele, Bucker, & Bushnell, 1987; Wilson & Elman,
1990). Granfield (1993) reports that one company links managerial bonuses to their
performance in hiring and promoting underrepresented groups. Burke and McKeen
(1989a) and Catalyst (1993) also recommend changing organizational structures
(e.g., the design of work) and systems (e.g., performance appraisal) to complement
mentoring. Gunn (1995), Keele et al. (1987), and Phillips-Jones (1983) suggest
making the mentoring program part of a company's overall employee/management
development initiative. Cunningham (1993) recommends that an organization should
create a philosophy statement around the mentoring program that links to its mission
statement.

Academic literature.   Empirical studies on formal programs have echoed the sentiment that upper management needs to support a program, yet no published studies have compared formal programs that have had more support to those that have had less support. However, a few studies have indirectly addressed the role of organizational support in successful mentoring.

Eby et al. (2006) investigated the role of perceived organizational support in predicting negative mentoring outcomes. They suggest that support can play a key role in both preventing negative mentoring behavior and encouraging positive mentoring exchanges by promoting a culture that models positive behavior. It is important to note that we are considering this research to be indirect evidence for the role of organizational support for two reasons: a) The focus was on perceptions of support, not actual support, and b) their data combine informal and formal mentorships, with the majority (71%) being informal. More specifically, they found that as perceptions of accountability for mentoring decreased in their sample of protégés, reports of three types of negative mentoring behaviors – manipulative behaviors (e.g., deceit, credittaking), distancing behaviors (e.g., neglect, inappropriate delegation), and lack of mentor expertise – increased. They also found that perceptions of management support for mentoring were positively related to the receipt of both career and psychosocial mentoring by protégés.

Koberg, Boss, and Goodman (1998) examined the effects on mentoring of several aspects of a supportive department climate. In a sample of 387 hospital employees, perceptions of leader trust and approachability were related to more positive perceptions of psychosocial mentoring behaviors. Note that this study focused on support not from the top but within one's immediate work group, and there is no clear indication that this study included any formal relationships.

Outside literature.   Much research has examined the role of perceived organizational support outside of the mentoring context. A meta-analysis by Rhoades and Eisenberger (2002) demonstrated that fair treatment (e.g., procedural justice), supervisor support (e.g., employees' achievements are valued), and rewards and favorable job conditions (e.g., job security) were significantly related to perceived organizational support. In terms of outcomes, perceived organizational support was positively related to affective commitment, job involvement, job satisfaction, and desire to remain with the organization, and negatively related to withdrawal behaviors. Additionally, Milne, Blum, and Roman (1994) found that top management support for EAP programs influenced employees' confidence in and usage of the programs.

Extrapolating these results, one can see that recommendations such as incorporating reward systems or altering the design of work can demonstrate organizational support. Further, given how strongly organizational support is related to general work outcomes and usage of EAP programs, it can be reasonably inferred that support for a mentoring program may result in increased commitment to and intention to use the program.

Structuring the Program: Setting Program Objectives

One of the first steps in creating a formal mentoring program involves determining the program's objectives and intended outcomes. The objectives will influence decisions about the structure of the program, such as who should participate and under what conditions. Drawing upon the organizational development literature, it seems logical that an organization would want to conduct a thorough needs assessment first to determine whether a formal mentoring program is required. For example, Catalyst (1993) recommended that organizations conduct a needs and culture assessment to better understand employee and business needs. Forret et al. (1996) also recommended that organizations evaluate their needs to determine which employees should receive mentoring.

The practical literature alludes to several possible purposes and objectives of mentoring programs. Eddy et al. (2001) found that the most common purposes included helping with succession planning, improving employees' skills, increasing retention, and increasing diversity in the workplace. Catalyst (1993) revealed purposes such as providing support mechanisms for newly hired women and minorities, grooming individuals for senior management positions, helping to increase women and minorities in management, helping acclimate new employees to the organization's culture, and building relationships throughout the organization. Given these findings, no one "best practice" emerges in terms of what objectives are best achieved by mentoring programs. What is clear is that an organization needs to set an objective for its program, objectives need to be based on organizational needs, and objectives need to be clearly communicated (e.g., Catalyst, 1993).

Academic literature. To our knowledge, only one published empirical study has directly compared formal programs based on overall objective. Ragins et al. (2000) investigated whether programs aimed at career development would be viewed as more effective than programs designed to provide a general job orientation. In a sample of 104 protégés, there was no significant relationship found between goal of program and overall effectiveness perceptions, but those in programs designed to promote careers had greater satisfaction with promotion opportunities. The researchers noted that the purpose of the programs, as stated by respondents, may not necessarily have been the main or sole purpose of the program as designed by the organization.

In their qualitative work on negative mentoring relationships, Eby and Lockwood (2005) found that mentors and protégés strongly recommended that organizations clarify program objectives as a means of improving formal relationships. This does not provide us with direct evidence that such communication would improve a program, but there is a perception that this would be the case.

Structuring the Program: Selecting Program Participants

In terms of who should be a mentor, Eddy et al. (2001) reported that most organizations used experienced professionals, managers, and executives. Other organizations allowed anyone to be a mentor or restricted mentor participation to certain groups depending upon the objectives of the program (e.g., minorities; functional managers). Programs reviewed by Phillips-Jones (1983) included top management, experienced technical personnel, and functional leaders as mentors. Catalyst (1993) reports that some companies used multiple mentors who differ in position, organizational level, gender, functional area, and race.

Several factors need to be considered when identifying mentors, such as their experience and expertise, their knowledge, skills, and abilities (KSAs), and their interest and motivation. Eddy et al. (2001) found that the two most common practices to identify mentors were to allow people to volunteer and to use some type of nomination process. Catalyst (1993) reviewed one program that sought referrals from previous mentors. Another program they reviewed allows volunteers, but requires them to complete a self-assessment questionnaire to evaluate their ability to be an effective mentor. The program described by Geiger-DuMond (1995) requires mentors to describe the assistance and expertise they can provide.

In terms of the required KSAs for effective formal mentors, Messmer (2001) suggested that mentors need to be empathetic and enjoy helping others. Other criteria include the mentor's ability to model the work styles and behaviors that the organization wants emulated by protégés (Catalyst, 1993; Messmer, 2001). Cunningham (1993) suggested that mentors need to be confident, patient, trusting, and communicate well. Tyler (1998) noted that mentors should be good listeners and questioners. Eddy et al. (2001) found that over two thirds of responding companies screen their potential mentors for several criteria, including technical knowledge, communication ability, organizational level and tenure, past performance, commitment to the mentoring process, credibility, and ability to be an effective role model.

Finally, several authors indicated that mentors need to have a high level of motivation to mentor (e.g., Burke & McKeen, 1989a). Logically, motivated mentors will make more effort to honor appointments, give protégés guidance, and make the relationship successful. Organizations should ensure that the mentor has enough time to commit to the relationship and that they are willing to participate for the "right" reasons (e.g., desire to help others develop; Eddy et al., 2001), rather than because of pressure from top management (Catalyst, 1993).

In terms of selecting protégés, two themes emerged from our review: a) Which overall group or group(s) of employees should be targeted, and b) within a particular group, which specific employees should participate? For programs that are focused on developing future leaders and managers, high-potential employees and those who are ready for a promotion may be identified as protégés (Geiger-DuMond, 1995; Tyler, 1998). Conversely, Forret et al. (1996) described a program that includes all employees with less than 2 years' experience, and another program that was restricted to professional women. However, Tyler (1998) argued that limiting a mentoring program to one race or gender can create resentment among excluded individuals. Eddy et al. (2001) found that the top four groups that organizations targeted programs for were new hires, anyone in the organization, high-potential employees, and those in professional and managerial ranks. Overall, organizations target a wide range of populations, such that it is difficult to conclude there is one "best practice." Essentially, an organization's decision as to who will be a protégé will depend on the program's objectives (cf. Eddy et al., 2001; Forret et al., 1996; Tyler, 1998).

After having determined which group or groups are to receive mentoring, attention turns to selecting individuals within those groups. Eddy et al. (2001) found that most organizations allow people to volunteer to become protégés, with a smaller number using a nomination process involving senior management, immediate supervisors, and program administrators. One program reviewed by Catalyst (1993) uses a cross-functional committee to review employees' development plans along with human resources and organizational planning information. In many programs, meeting basic entry requirements is enough for an employee to become a protégé. For example, as long as the person is a newly hired employee, he or she can become a protégé in a program targeted to this population. However, recognizing that there is often a small ratio of mentors to protégés, some authors have recommended that companies review additional criteria to ensure they have a manageable population of protégés. For example, Cunningham (1993) suggested that protégés have a strong achievement orientation, and high initiative and assertiveness. Further, protégés need to have a strong learning orientation. On this issue, Eddy et al.'s (2001) report obtained relevant information from 21 programs. Of those, just over 60% screen employees on such factors as potential for advancement, desire to participate, tenure, and interests and goals. Regardless of the criteria used to screen protégés, Gray (1988) stressed that the criteria need to be communicated openly and be fair and achievable.

Academic literature.   To our knowledge, there are no empirical studies that compare the success of general programs to those that target any particular groups. Thus, at this point we cannot conclude that programs with a targeted population help participants better than broad-based programs. Allen, Poteet, and Russell's (2000) work on what draws mentors to protégés indirectly speaks to this issue. They found that mentors generally are more drawn to protégés with high ability rather than those in need of help. Extracting from this, it may be that mentors in programs targeting fast-trackers have greater motivation than those in other types of programs. This remains an empirical question not yet directly investigated.

No studies have compared formal programs on which, if any, particular personal characteristics were used to screen participants into entry. However, some research has examined how personal characteristics might make for better mentors and protégés. Noe's (1988) investigation of an assigned mentoring program focused on locus of control, job involvement, time spent in career planning, and belief in the importance of work relationships in a sample of 139 formal protégés. Findings indicated that higher levels of career planning and job involvement were associated with more psychosocial mentoring, but did not appear to impact perceptions of the overall relationship quality. Noe called for an increased focus on protégé characteristics in future research toward the goal of a "readiness for mentoring" measure that could be used in participant selection. In the 15 years since this call was made, no such measure has appeared in the literature. However, other personal characteristics have been investigated.

Wanberg, Kammeyer-Mueller, and Marchese (2004) developed a conceptual model linking the antecedents and outcomes of formal mentoring. Protégé and mentor personal characteristics were included as important antecedents to successful formal mentoring. Initial tests of their model on a final sample of 224 protégés and 193 mentors (at the time of a third wave of data collection) in a formal program indicated mixed conclusions as to the importance of these various characteristics. Protégé proactivity was related to the amount of mentoring perceived by protégés part way through the program, protégé motivation was related to the amount of mentoring that mentors reported providing at the middle and end of the program, and openness to experience had no bearing on either party's reports of mentoring at either time. Turning to mentor characteristics, mentor proactivity was related to the amount of mentoring perceived by both mentors and protégés at both points in time. Wanberg and colleagues concluded that mentor proactivity might be one of the most central personal characteristics to success and that it should be considered in mentor selection.

Outside literature.   With respect to selecting protégés, the research literature on trainee motivation seems clear. A meta-analysis conducted by Colquitt, LePine, and Noe (2000) found that one's motivation to learn was positively associated with their skill and knowledge acquisition, reactions to the training, self-efficacy, and transfer of knowledge. Further, they found that having an internal locus of control, high achievement motivation, low anxiety, and positive valence was also related to motivation to learn. Clearly, these may be factors that companies could review in determining who will be protégés in mentoring programs.

Structuring the Program: Participation Guidelines

Regardless of which specific groups of people participate, many practitioner authors touched on the need to make participation voluntary for mentors (e.g., Burke & McKeen, 1989a; Kizolos, 1993). Other authors have noted that participation should be voluntary for both mentors *and* protégés (e.g., Catalyst, 1993; Gray, 1988), with no repercussion to those who do not participate or who withdraw. The argument supporting these recommendations is that people who participate voluntarily will be more committed to making the experience successful. Those who are forced to participate may harbor feelings of resentment at having their time and energy infringed upon, thus reducing their efforts and dedication. Organizations seem to be heeding these recommendations, as Forret et al. (1996) noted that mentor participation was voluntary in every program they reviewed. Eddy et al. (2001) found that only one out of 56 programs reviewed made mentor participation mandatory, whereas only three out of 50 programs made protégé participation mandatory.

Academic literature.   Chao et al. (1992) suggested that formal programs "without obligation or intimidating participation" (p. 633) would likely have a better chance for success, although this program characteristic was not accounted for directly in their study. Ragins et al. (2000) found that whether or not protégés' participation in a formal program was voluntary did not play a role in their effectiveness perceptions.

Allen, Eby, and Lentz (2006) investigated the underlying process by which voluntary participation could lead to more effective relationships by testing whether commitment to the relationship would mediate the relationship between voluntary participation and perceived program effectiveness. Allen's group did not find voluntary participation of protégés to make a difference regarding perceived program effectiveness. In another study using the same sample, protégés' voluntary participation was not related to mentor functions (career mentoring, role modeling, psychosocial mentoring) when it was considered in conjunction with other design characteristics (Allen, Eby, & Lentz, 2006). As there were too few nonvoluntary mentors in their sample, they were unable to test whether mentor voluntary participation made a difference.

Structuring the Program: The Match Process

One feature that distinguishes formal mentoring from informal mentoring is that mentors and protégés are usually matched with some involvement from the organization. However, the practice of matching protégés and mentors has been a common criticism of formal mentoring programs, in that no one can "force" the natural attraction and desire to work together that is essential for mentorships to be successful (cf. Clawson, 1985). Kizilis (1990) noted that forced pairing, if not done well, can contribute to resentment, hurt feelings, and suspicion. Thus, many researchers and practitioners have focused attention on the matching process, covering two distinct questions: a) Who has involvement in determining matches, and b) on what characteristics should matches be based?

Input into Matching

Organizations vary on the degree that they manage the pairing process versus how much control is given to participants. Out of 64 programs studied, Eddy et al. (2001) found that 75% used a structured matching procedure. Forret et al. (1996) described a program that matches protégés with mentors from the functional area in which the protégé wants to develop his or her skills. Tyler (1998) also described a company that matches partners based on the mentor's interests and the protégé's goals.

However, many authors contend that the mentor and protégé should have more input into selecting who will be their partner (e.g., Burke & McKeen, 1989a; Murray, 1991; Wilson & Elman, 1990). Eddy et al. (2001) noted that almost a quarter of 64 programs studied used natural pairing, whereby protégés and mentors are left on their own to form relationships. Some organizations provide assistance by holding social events, allowing participants to provide names of potential matches, or collecting and disseminating background information, yet still allow the mentor and protégé to choose (e.g., Eddy et al.; Forret et al., 1996; Tyler, 1998). Even when mentors and/or protégés have input, there are instances when the organization will make the final pairing recommendations.

Another possible method for pairing mentors and protégés is through random assignment. Several authors noted concerns with this approach, however, citing that a higher number of possible unsuccessful relationships (e.g., Forret et al., 1996). Eddy et al. (2001) were unable to locate any organization that used this practice.

Academic literature. Many reasons have been suggested as to why giving program participants some input into the match process should be an important program feature. Most obviously, allowing mentors and protégés some discretion likens the formal match more closely to an informal match that would develop naturally (cf. Ragins et al., 2000). Allen et al. (2006a, 2006b) also stressed that such a process may foster ownership and more commitment to the mentoring program.

Ragins et al. (2000) found no empirical support for their hypothesis that those in formal programs where participant match input occurred would be more satisfied than those in programs where no such input was allowed. Allen and colleagues (2006a), however, did find support for this prediction, and also found that enhanced mentor commitment and program understanding partially explained this relationship. Viator (1999) also found that protégés who had at least some input into the match process were significantly more satisfied with the relationship than those who had no say. What is noteworthy about these last two studies is that they both conclude that *some say* in the match process is helpful. What they are admittedly unable to pinpoint, however, is *how much* say is necessary. Is it enough to be able to choose from a few criteria to narrow down the pool from which one's partner will be drawn, or must one meet and get to know one's partner in advance? Furthermore, when participants get to choose the partner, on what characteristics are they most likely to base this choice, and are these the most important?

Matching Characteristics

Practice varies regarding the factors that are used to match protégés and mentors. Factors recommended or used include race or gender (Catalyst, 1993), organization level of the mentor (Phillips-Jones, 1983), type of work done/job function (e.g., Burke & McKeen, 1989a), geographical proximity and preferences (e.g., Catalyst, 1993; Eddy et al., 2001), talent and skill levels (Burke & McKeen, 1989a; Tyler, 1998), mentor work experiences (Catalyst, 1993), the protégé's development needs (Eddy et al., 2001; Geiger-DuMond, 1995), ability of the mentor to develop a protégé (Forret et al., 1996), motivations and goals for the mentorship (e.g., Burke & McKeen, 1989a; Forret et al., 1996), personality/personal chemistry (e.g., Kizilos, 1990; Tyler, 1998), and hobbies, interests, or background (e.g., Eddy et al., 2001; Messmer, 2001). Interestingly, Eddy et al. (2001) found a fairly close split between programs that matched protégés and mentors based on criteria similarity and those that matched based on dissimilarity. For example, depending on the program's objectives, some companies choose to have mentors and protégés from the same functional area, whereas other companies match protégés and mentors from different functions.

One of the primary factors discussed with respect to matching mentors and protégés is their difference in levels. Some have recommended that mentors be at least two organizational levels above the protégé (e.g., Tyler, 1998) and/or that the mentor not be in a direct reporting line to the protégé (Kizilos, 1990). Having a mentor of significantly higher rank may augment the likelihood that there will be a sufficient difference in experience and network breadth to be able to provide a protégé with a valuable experience. Mendleson, Barnes, and Horn (1989) stated that the best mentors were those who were only one level higher, as they would be better able to relate to their protégé's experiences. Keele et al. (1987) argued that using direct supervisors as mentors could result in inequities within the workgroup. Reviews of formal mentoring programs revealed that several programs used mentors who were two or more levels higher in the organization and who were outside the formal lines of report from the protégé (e.g., Catalyst, 1993; Geiger-DuMond, 1995). For example, Douglas and McCauley (1999) reported that 70% of programs they investigated used senior managers outside the direct report line as mentors for junior employees, and at least four of the programs reviewed by Catalyst (1993) stated that mentors were at least two levels above the protégé and/or outside a direct reporting line. Interestingly, Eddy et al. (2001) reported that only 6 out of 40 programs reviewed indicated that mentors and protégés were paired so as not to be in a direct reporting line.

Academic literature.   Several studies have examined the importance of objective characteristics as criteria for matching. Ragins et al. (2000) found no effect of the rank of a formal mentor on protégés' perceptions of relationship quality or their job attitudes. Allen et al. (2006b) did not find rank to have an impact on reports of career-related mentoring, but it did affect reports of role modeling. Interestingly, protégés reported greater modeling with lower-ranking mentors, while higher-ranking mentors were more likely to report providing higher levels of role modeling. The authors explain that the protégés may be able to relate to and emulate mentors who are closer to them in rank – they may seem a more realistic model for their immediate aspirations. The mentors, however, may not feel as if they are role models until they have garnered significant experience.

Another consideration in the match process is whether the mentor and protégé should be from the same department. Ragins and colleagues (2000) reported that protégés with mentors from different departments expressed marginally greater satisfaction with the relationship, lower intentions to quit, and higher levels of commitment and job satisfaction. The authors suggest that programs where mentors and protégés were restricted to the same department may be limiting the potential pool of mentors such that a good match is less likely. Further, a mentor from another department can add a fresh perspective. Allen et al. (2006b) added that conflicts can occur within a department if a special and exclusive relationship develops between a mentor and protégé. In their study, however, they found contradictory results to those of Ragins et al.; there were greater levels of psychosocial mentoring associated with protégés and mentors in the same department.

An additional variable that can factor into matching is the physical distance between mentor and protégé. In Eby and Lockwood's (2005) qualitative investigation, proximity emerged as an issue of concern for both protégés and mentors. This appeared to be largely a matter of logistics; close proximity increases the ease of meeting frequently. They also noted that it is possible that mentors in closer proximity to their protégés may be less likely to be neglectful of their mentoring duties if chance meetings with a protégé could serve as a reminder. Allen and colleagues (2006b) examined proximity in addition to department and rank, as mentioned above. However, in their study, although proximity had a small but statistically significant relationship to interaction frequency, it was not an independent predictor of relationship success.

In addition to objective criteria such as department and proximity, there are less objective but perhaps more psychologically meaningful characteristics that may be employed. Orpen (1997), for example, measured closeness of a formal relationship as a predictor of commitment, motivation, and work performance. Closeness was operationally defined as regard for, respect for, and enjoyment in sharing time with a formal mentor. As predicted, closeness predicted motivation and commitment, but not performance. However, we do not know what specific characteristics produced the closeness that yielded these positive results.

Wanberg et al.'s (2004) model of the formal mentoring process touts similarity perceptions as key relational features. Similarity is a broad concept. It may appear to be based on more surface-level, demographic characteristics, but could also be based on other shared qualities ranging from common leisure interests to compatible personality traits. Wanberg and associates' results supported the importance of similarity perceptions – protégés' perceptions of similarity led to higher reports of mentoring at times two and three of their investigation; mentors' reports were related to only time two reports of mentoring provided. Likewise, Finkelstein, Allen, and Montei (2002) found that formal protégés' perceptions of similarity to their mentor predicted their perceptions of relationship quality. Further, they found that similarity perceptions were not related to the gender and age composition of the pair. So, even though we may conclude that similarity perceptions foster more successful formal mentorships, no empirical studies have detailed the specific characteristics on which similarity perceptions are based.

Outside literature. Participative decision-making (PDM) has been defined by some as "the involvement of subordinates in decisions that are ordinarily the prerogative or responsibility of a manager" (Hespe & Wall, 1976, as cited in Parnell & Crandall, 2001, p. 48). Clearly, allowing participants a choice in their partner in a formal mentoring program *is* a type of PDM. After years of research and multiple reviews (cf. Wagner, 1994), one can reasonably conclude that there may be a significant, but small, relationship between PDM and organizational outcomes such as job performance and job satisfaction.

However, there are important moderators that should be considered before adopting a policy of involvement in selecting mentors or protégés. Tesluk, Vance, and Mathieu (1999) found that participative climates at multiple levels of an organization were important for maximizing PDM benefits. A second line of PDM research indicates that cultural differences may impact the acceptance of PDM. Organizations with multinational locations should be aware that not all cultures appear to be accepting of participation in decision-making, and that the form that PDM takes may also vary widely across culture (e.g., Parnell & Crandall, 2003). Finally, there is work suggesting that there may be individual differences in preference for PDM (e.g., Graham & Verma, 1991). Taken together, this research suggests that an organization consider its participative climate, the external culture, and employees' preferences for involvement before determining whether participants should have a say in selecting their mentoring partners.

A mentorship has the potential to be a close and important relationship in the life of both a protégé and mentor. Therefore, the literature on close relationships may offer some ideas for considering the match process. Although we are clearly not implying that there is nor should be a romantic component to mentorships, looking at the ways that potential romantic partners become matched may offer some insight into matching mentors and protégés. In some cultures the responsibility for mate selection often is in the hands of outside parties (Mullan, 1984). In some traditions compatibility or attraction among the partners is not considered a prerequisite to a match; in other cases, attraction plays a minor role in narrowing down selection.

Third-party mate selection has historically been present in Western society as well. Mullan (1984) describes various services that operate solely to create interpersonal matches, from the Shadkhan, or Jewish matchmaker, to marriage bureaus popular in England, to video dating services. Recently, a service called *eHarmony* has created a personality profile matching system to narrow down choices for each client, thereby taking a more active role in determining the user's choice. Clearly one must take a critical eye to success claims of "more marriages per match than any online dating service," but given that the psychological profile has been researched and tested, perhaps this type of model could be adapted and validated for use in matching mentorships.

The importance of similarity in dating relationships has been a mainstay in social psychology. Years of research supports the notion that "birds of a feather flock together," whereas the "opposites attract" argument has not been supported (Berscheid & Regan, 2005). Interestingly, perceived similarity is often more important than any objective measure of similarity (Acitelli, Douvan, & Veroff, 1993), implying that if perceived similarities between mentoring partners can be obtained, true differences may appear to be minimized.

Orientation and Training

A common recommendation in the field of organizational development is that individuals receive adequate training when they are about to assume a new role or assignment. In almost every practitioner article reviewed, some mention was made of the need to train mentoring program participants. Training topics mentioned in the literature include defining mentoring and outlining the program's objectives (Burke & McKeen, 1989a; Forret et al., 1996; Geiger-DuMond, 1995), reviewing roles and responsibilities for the mentor and/or the protégé (e.g., Eddy et al., 2001; Gray, 1988; Tyler, 1998), outlining what protégés and mentors can and cannot expect (e.g., Messmer, 2001; Phillips-Jones, 1983), setting expectations and understanding the program's limitations (e.g., Cunningham, 1993; Geiger-DuMond, 1995), and how to avoid typical mentoring problems (e.g., Forret et al., 1996; Kizilos, 1990). Eddy et al. revealed that some programs provide training on listening and communication skills.

Topics and skills taught by organizations specific to protégés included career assessment and goal-setting, action planning, career choices, and self-awareness (Eddy et al., 2001; Tyler, 1998). Geiger-DuMond (1995) described a program that holds a separation orientation session for protégés, allowing them to express their concerns and build networks with other participants. Topics and skills specific to mentors included outlining time requirements, providing behavioral guidelines, and coaching and feedback skills (Eddy et al., 2001; Geiger-DuMond, 1995; Tyler, 1998). Gray (1988) also recommended that mentors need training in conflict-resolution, role modeling, negotiation skills, and motivation techniques. In their report, Eddy et al. found no clear evidence as to whether it is advisable to train mentors and protégés together or separately.

Academic literature. Although a small number of academic research studies have included training in their recommendations (e.g., Noe, 1988; Orpen, 1997), very few have compared mentoring programs on whether or not training was provided, or what kind of training was provided to participants. Two recent studies by Allen and colleagues were the first to compare programs on the training dimension. Their research assessed three variables concerning training from the perspectives of 175 protégés and 110 mentors: 1) whether training was present or not; 2) the number of hours of training received; and 3) perception of training quality. In one study (Allen, Eby, & Lentz, 2006), protégés' receipt of training and their perceptions of the quality of training both significantly related to their perception of mentor commitment and program understanding, which in turn related to perceptions of program effectiveness. Training quality also directly impacted effectiveness (commitment and understanding were partial mediators). For mentors, receiving training positively impacted their commitment, and both receipt of training and perceptions of quality were related to program understanding. Both receipt of training and quality also were directly related to mentors' perceptions of effectiveness. Hours of training had no significant effects in any of their analyses.

In Allen and colleagues' second study using this sample (Allen et al., 2006b), the three training questions were related to reported psychosocial mentoring, career mentoring, and role modeling. Whether protégés received training and the length of training were both significantly related to psychosocial mentoring. Perceptions of training quality yielded relationships with all three mentoring functions. From the mentors' perspective, however, receipt of training was not related to reports of providing any of the mentoring functions. Surprisingly, receiving fewer hours of training was related to both mentorship quality and reports of providing greater role modeling. Reports of better training quality were related to mentors' reports of providing more psychosocial mentoring. Thus, high-quality training may include information that helps mentors and protégés develop an interpersonal connection. The authors note that this emphasizes the need for careful examination of training content.

Structuring the Mentoring Relationship

Another characteristic of formal mentoring programs is that they provide some degree of procedures, control, and oversight to the mentoring process covering such issues as creating a relationship, defining goals, meeting frequency, and the length of mentorships.

Setting Expectations

Several authors discussed the need for mentors and protégés to set expectations, goals, and responsibilities for their relationships (e.g., Cunningham, 1993). Eddy et al. (2001) found that over half of programs investigated ensured that mentors and protégés set expectations together. Cunningham (1993) and Phillips-Jones (1983) also suggested that mentors and protégés create a mentoring action plan containing activities, resources, and criteria for success. A program described by Forret et al. (1996) requires a mentoring contract that outlines the mentor and protégé's expectations and vision for the relationship. In some instances the roles and responsibilities may be set by the organization, based on the purposes of the program. Still, Phillips-Jones (1983) and Tyler (1998) recommended that organizations give leeway for mentors to determine how they can assist protégés best. Eddy et al. (2001) reported that confidentiality in the mentoring relationship is a common practice. For example, Kizilos (1990) described one organization that does not allow anyone to ask the mentor for feedback about the protégé for appraisal purposes.

Several authors touched on the need to include the protégé's supervisor in setting expectations and discussing responsibilities (e.g., Forret et al., 1996). Geiger-DuMond (1995) described a program where the protégé meets with her or his supervisor before meeting with the mentor, in order to discuss development needs. Phillips-Jones (1983) also recommended that a plan be developed to help deal with potential power struggles between the protégé, mentor, and protégé's supervisor. These actions can help ensure that the protégé's supervisor does not feel overlooked and that the protégé understands expectations around time, attention, and priority that he or she should give to the supervisor and the mentor (cf. Kizilos, 1990; Tyler, 1998).

Academic literature.   Many researchers have also touted the importance of clear expectations for the goals of the program, the roles of those involved in the program, and the potential benefits of the program. However, little research has examined programs as to whether these types of structural guidelines were put in place at inception. For example, in Klauss' (1981) conclusions based on interviews with participants in three programs, he suggested that expectations be made realistic as to the likely intensity of formal mentoring relationships, and that protégés and mentors be made to realize their role in the relationship's success. Specific roles for protégés and mentors are outlined in his article, yet no detail of his analysis strategy to determine the necessity of these roles is provided.

Viator (1999) provided some direct evidence regarding the importance of setting clear objectives. He looked at this in two ways – whether the organization required that the mentor and protégé set goals and objectives together, and whether or not the protégés reported that they actually adhered to these guidelines. Viator found that 69.2% of protégés reported that the program required such goal setting, and that only 8% reported not following these guidelines. Whether or not the program required these goal-setting events was not in itself predictive of protégé satisfaction, but actually taking part in goal-setting was.

Outside literature.   One of the more robust findings in the organizational behavior literature is the effectiveness of goal-setting for producing positive results. A classic review by Locke, Shaw, Saari, and Latham (1981) demonstrated that higher performance results from goals that are challenging, achievable, and specific. Further, higher performance is achieved when the individual accepts the goal and gets feedback about his or her progress. Applied to the current topic, this suggests that the mentoring intervention should result in more positive outcomes to the extent that the mentor and protégé set specific, clear, and achievable goals.

The literature on close relationships contributes here as well, as part of pre-marital training involves sharing and negotiating expectations for the relationship. Berscheid and Regan (2005) stressed the importance of expectancy in all human behavior, but noted its heightened importance in social relationships as "social interactions flow forward on a river of the partners' expectancies about each other's behavior" (p. 227). Our expectations continue to develop over time and experience, but we often begin a relationship with "one size fits all" expectations (p. 290) that suit our notions about the specific type of relationship rather than the individual person involved. Thus, we may have a "mentor" or "protégé" schema from which we build preconceived expectations before even meeting the actual mentoring partner. To the degree that their individual characteristics do not map onto that schema the relationship may start on shaky ground (cf. Olson, Roese, & Zanna, 1996). If the pair address those expectancies and shape new ones together, problems could be avoided.

Meeting Frequency and Method

Other components to address when structuring the formal mentoring relationship are the frequency of interaction and how protégés and mentors should meet. Mendleson et al. (1989) surveyed protégés and mentors and found that they preferred to have frequent face-to-face contact, and should have such contact early in the relationship. Eddy et al. (2001) found that of 30 programs studied, over half allowed for both face-to-face and distance relationships, with 40% more focusing mainly on face-to-face relationships. The most widely reported technology used for distance relationships was telephone and e-mail (90% and 80% respectively), with the Internet/intranet, faxes, and videoconferences used less frequently. These authors recommend that, even when distance relationships are used primarily, there be at least one face-to-face meeting in order to facilitate relationship building.

Most authors recommend some degree of formal interaction, but organizations vary in how often, if at all, they require their mentors and employees to meet. Eddy et al. (2001) reported that just under half of the 41 programs studied recommend monthly interactions, 15% suggest weekly meetings, 12% suggest meetings occur over a greater time period (e.g., every few months), some leave it up to participants themselves, and 7 programs do not specify or suggest any meeting frequency. Regardless of frequency and method of meeting, several authors recommend that this information be agreed-upon by the mentor and protégé (e.g., Forret et al., 1996; Phillips-Jones, 1983; Zey, 1985).

Academic literature.   Noe (1988) recommended that guidelines for meeting one time per week might be beneficial to overcome obstacles, yet meeting frequency (i.e., time spent together) was not a significant predictor of relationship outcomes. Orpen (1997) developed a scale to tap opportunities to interact that assessed physical proximity, time pressures, and conflicting work schedules. Orpen found that opportunities to interact were predictive of protégés' work motivation and organizational commitment. This finding does not directly assess the importance of structural guidelines for interaction frequency; in fact, the program in this study had in place a guideline for pairs to interact at least twelve times over the course of a year.

Viator (1999) found that 62.8% of protégés reported that their firm required "regular" meetings, and that 14% reported not sticking to these recommendations. As with the finding in regard to setting objectives, having a policy per se was not predictive of satisfaction, but actually meeting on a regular basis (whether policy in place or not) did show that relationship.

Ragins et al. (2000) found that having a guideline in place was predictive of perceived program effectiveness, but not predictive of any attitudinal variables (e.g., satisfaction). These authors did not report information regarding how often the guidelines suggested that participants meet, so these results do not speak directly to a suggestion for *what* frequency is optimal. Further, it is not clear whether the protégés in the sample actually followed the guidelines.

Finally, Allen et al. (2006b) considered interaction frequency as a mediator between various program characteristics and mentoring functions (reported by protégés and mentors). One significant mediation finding emerged in the protégé data: interaction frequency explained the relationship between whether the pair was in the same department and career mentoring. In the mentor data, a similar finding appeared, but with psychosocial mentoring provided as the criterion. Thus, although interaction frequency played a role in predicting mentoring functions, whether or not guidelines were in place for the amount of interaction was not assessed.

Duration of Relationship

Our review uncovered varying recommendations regarding how long mentorships should last. In their review of five programs, Forret et al. (1996) reported that companies typically structure the relationship to last anywhere from 6 months to 2 years. Just over half of the programs reviewed by Eddy et al. (2001) recommended that mentorships last 1 year, with the remaining companies recommending either 3-month, 6-month, 9-month, or greater than 1 year relationships. Further, 17 of 51 programs reviewed leave the duration of the relationship up to participants. Similar results were found in Catalyst's (1993) review, where programs lasted 6 months, 12 months, 18 months, 24 months, and 36 months, with some programs not specifying an endpoint and leaving it up to participants based on their desires and needs. Although no best practice emerged, it is logical that an organization should consider the goals of the program when determining how long a mentoring relationship should last and how often participants should meet (e.g., a mentoring program focused on providing technical skills to new hires may be shorter in length and higher in meeting frequency than a program designed to increase females' exposure to senior leadership positions).

Academic literature.   No studies were found that directly investigated differences between formal programs of varying durations. Ragins et al. (2000) included relationship duration as a control variable, citing Chao et al.'s (1992) suggestion that it may be important to control for in comparisons between formal and informal programs. Relationship duration demonstrated small but significant relationships with such outcomes as career commitment, organizational commitment, organizational-based self-esteem, procedural justice, and intention to quit (negative). Also, longer relationships were associated with informal relationships and less recognition given to mentors. The breakdown for formal vs. informal mentors was not provided.

Monitoring and Evaluation of the Program

Many practitioners recommend some degree of structured monitoring and evaluation of the mentoring program. Monitoring and evaluation can serve several purposes, such as identifying relationships that are "in trouble" and may need to be repaired or halted (e.g., Catalyst, 1993; Kizilos, 1990), seeing if the program is achieving its objectives (Catalyst, 1993; Eddy et al., 2001), evaluating the program's cost effectiveness (Gray, 1988), identifying benefits (Eddy et al., 2001), or generating improvement ideas (e.g., Eddy et al., 2001; Gray, 1988). Showing results from a formal mentoring program is an important step in obtaining and sustaining top management support (e.g., Forret et al., 1996). Perhaps it is not surprising, then, that many programs reviewed by Eddy et al. (2001) and Catalyst (1993) used some sort of formal evaluation process.

Monitoring

To monitor a program, authors have recommended that regular check-ups be conducted (e.g., Phillips-Jones, 1983). Our review revealed that the timing of these reviews ranges between weekly, monthly, quarterly, and semi-annually. Typical issues reviewed include what is working with the mentorship, what are the problems, and suggestions for how things might be improved (Catalyst, 1993). The method for these check-ups varies as well. Kizolos (1999) described a program where an administrator contacts mentors and protégés to discuss progress. A program reviewed by Catalyst (1993) has protégés submit experience reports quarterly. Most companies monitor their programs via regular meetings with participants. Eddy et al. (2001) reported that 19 out of 22 companies studied have procedures to help participants terminate their mentoring relationships, from having participants meet with their supervisors on the issue to having a program administrator handle the termination.

Academic literature.   Most of the discussion in the academic literature on program monitoring has occurred in the work on negative mentoring experiences. For example, Eby, Lockwood, and Butts (2006) inquired about monitoring in the context of an organization support measure that asked about mentor accountability. They discovered that perceived accountability (from protégés' perspective) related to fewer accounts of mentor manipulative and distancing behaviors. Accountability perceptions also related to fewer reports of mentors lacking expertise. Eby and Lockwood's (2005) qualitative work on negative mentoring indicated that monitoring emerged as a theme in interviews with both mentors and protégés as suggestions for improving formal programs. It is noteworthy that a larger number of mentors (20%) than protégés (9%) mentioned the importance of program monitoring.

Evaluation

Many companies use monitoring sessions as a way to evaluate overall success, but other companies supplement these with a more formal evaluation. Typical evaluation tools and information include questionnaires, interviews with participants, written reports, and 360° assessments (Catalyst, 1993; Eddy et al., 2001). One program reviewed by Catalyst uses performance appraisal reviews of protégés by HR personnel and mentors in order to determine if protégés actually developed their skills. With respect to the timing of the evaluation, Forret et al. (1996) suggested surveys anywhere from 6 months to 1 year into the relationship, while Catalyst (1993) suggested the end of the mentoring cycle.

Our review revealed a wide range of factors that are measured in the program evaluation. These include measures of career progress (Eddy et al., 2001; Phillips-Jones, 1983), frequency of meetings (Catalyst, 1993; Eddy et al., 2001), financial indicators (e.g., income) (Eddy et al., 2001), quality of the relationship (Catalyst, 1993), information on what did and did not work (Catalyst, 1993; Cunningham, 1993), skill and knowledge development (Catalyst, 1993), costs (Gray, 1988), participant satisfaction (Catalyst, 1993; Geiger-DuMond, 1995), and ideas on ways to improve the mentoring program (e.g., Catalyst, 1993; Cunningham, 1993). Eddy et al. found that the top two organizational criteria were turnover/retention rates and better succession planning, the top two mentor criteria were satisfaction with helping others and positive feedback, and the top protégé criteria were encouragement and support, improved skills, access to networks, and increased success. Interestingly, some programs reviewed by Catalyst (1993) used informal criteria, such as whether the mentorship continued beyond the required time and whether the program had expanded to other parts of the organization.

Academic literature.   There are no studies that specifically compared whether a program had a formal evaluation or not. Logistically, this would be quite challenging as the mere exercise of studying a program would constitute a type of evaluation. However, if this type of investigation was conducted retrospectively from an outside party, it may be considered independent of a typical program evaluation.

Outside literature.   With rare exception, the choice an organization makes regarding what type of results to measure will depend on the objectives of the mentoring program. A well-known framework for distinguishing between different types of outcome criteria was developed by Kirkpatrick (e.g., 1994). Kirkpatrick proposed four levels of measurement: a) *reactions* to the training; b) *learning* that resulted from the training; c) *behavior* or *performance* change; and d) *business results* for the organization. This model has been reviewed thoroughly (e.g., Alliger & Janak, 1989), with some authors making suggestions for modifications and enhancements. Still, it remains a useful way of categorizing different types of measurement that an organization can use to evaluate a formal mentoring program.

   With respect to how to research results, a variety of designs are available for the organization (e.g., Cook & Campbell, 1979). At a minimum, in order to conduct a true evaluation, an organization would want to employ a comparison control group of employees who did not have access to mentoring, as well as pre- and post-mentoring comparisons to determine the amount of attitudinal, behavioral, or knowledge change experienced. This pretest–posttest control group design is not without its problems, yet it can provide valid information about a program's effectiveness. The choice of what to measure will partly determine the methods used for data collection (e.g., surveys for reaction measures vs. observation to assess behavioral change).

Overall Summary and Conclusions

This review reveals that there are a variety of recommendations for designing and implementing a formal mentoring program that are being used by many companies. Unfortunately, across the board there is little direct research evidence suggesting which of these practices is more effective or relevant. This is not to say that what practitioners have suggested is not the best approach; rather, at this point few empirical studies have examined the specific features touted as the best, and so the scientific evidence to support or refute the claims is sparse. Still, we do have a start.

What We Know

- It seems clear that organizations need to stress their support for mentoring programs and that it is important for participants to *perceive* this support.
- It is conceivable that "one best" objective for mentoring programs will not emerge. However, it seems logical that the program should be tailored to the organization's needs, it should have a clear set of objectives, and its objectives should be clearly communicated.
- The benefits of voluntary participation have yet to be demonstrated unequivocally. Perhaps there are situations where nonvoluntary participation might be beneficial, such as when individuals who would typically not volunteer actually discover the value of being or having a mentor or when there are not enough people volunteering to serve as mentors.
- The applied literature indicates that organizations are using a variety of skill-based, motivation-based, and personality-based characteristics when selecting mentors and protégés. Some empirical work supports some of these selection criteria. For example, proactive personality is beginning to emerge as a beneficial characteristic for protégés and mentors. In the field of training and development, research has identified factors that relate to high training motivation and transfer that can be used to direct a company's search for potential protégés.
- We feel comfortable recommending against complete random assignment. Beyond that, we recommend basing the matching process on the program's objectives as well as the overall culture of the organization (e.g., if the objective is to provide engineers with marketing experience, the organization may proactively pair the engineer with a senior marketing executive).
- The best level of participation in the matching process is not yet clear. There may be moderators (e.g., culture, individual differences) as to when and for whom participation in the match will make an ultimate difference in satisfaction with a program.
- As far as matching characteristics, most of the literature has looked at objective characteristics such as rank, department, and location. Findings do not point in a clear direction. We located a few instances where companies had overcome problems surrounding the matching of mentors and protégés by using multiple mentors or groups from different levels. Eddy et al. (2001) found that peer mentoring, group mentoring, upward mentoring, or a combination of these was sometimes used. By having a protégé interact with more than one mentor (and vice versa), authors argue that the importance of (and problems with) "interpersonal chemistry" is lessened, and that the protégé has the benefit of being exposed to multiple viewpoints.
- Given the wide range of criteria that organizations use to match participants, four general observations can be made: a) There is nothing in the practical or research literature to indicate which factors are more or less important for ensuring a

successful relationship, b) given the complexity of relationships, it is recommended that organizations use multiple factors when matching, c) the selection of which factors to use will depend on the program's objectives, and d) what seems important, based on emerging research literature in formal mentoring and close relationships, is that the mentor and protégé *perceive* similarly between each other.

- Training is nearly universally recommended as a precursor to participation in a formal mentoring program.
- Expectations should be clear and agreed upon by both partners. Although allowing the partners to set expectations and goals may have some benefit, we do not know if that is because otherwise those expectations may not be clear or followed, or because participation itself provides some benefit. Perhaps participation is only beneficial for certain types of individuals.
- We feel comfortable recommending at a general level that evaluation of the formal mentoring program be done, but it is premature to recommend specific evaluation procedures or criteria. Again, these decisions should be based on the overall objectives of the program.

What We Need to Know

Despite what we know, several questions are still unanswered. Among these are:

- How much organizational support is *minimally necessary* for a program to be successful?
- Which matching characteristics are more or less important?
- Which matching characteristics are suitable for different types of program objectives?
- What level of participation in matching is most desirable?
- Can those who do not naturally possess the characteristics thought to make good participants in such a program be trained?
- Which characteristics most easily contribute to perceived similarity?
- When would dissimilarity in characteristics be a benefit?
- Are there real benefits to having multiple mentors at multiple levels, compared to more traditional mentoring?
- What training components lead participants to conclude that training was high quality?
- Which topics or components of training are most important?

With respect to future research, some of the program features described throughout this chapter could be manipulated and included in a thorough evaluation to provide clearer evidence of best or minimally necessary practices for worthwhile programs. If quasi-experimentation is not feasible, more studies that compare features across programs, controlling for other differences across organizations, are clearly needed. The only foreseeable way that scientific research can develop in this area is if more partnerships are established between coordinators of formal programs and scientists interested in conducting and disseminating this type of comparative research. We hope that after now realizing the current lack of systematic evidence that exists, many people from both parties will be further inspired to make that happen.

References

Acitelli, L. K., Douvan, E., & Veroff, J. (1993). Perceptions of conflict in the first year of marriage: How important are similarity and understanding? *Journal of Social and Personal Relationships, 10*, 5–19.

Allen, T. D., Eby, L. T., & Lentz, E. (2006a). The relationship between formal mentoring program characteristics and perceived program effectiveness. *Personnel Psychology, 59*, 125–153.

Allen, T. D., Eby, L. T., & Lentz, E. (2006b). Mentorship behaviors and mentorship quality associated with formal mentoring programs: Closing the gap between research and practice. *Journal of Applied Psychology, 91*, 567–578.

Allen, T. D., Eby, L. T., Poteet, M. L., Lentz, E., & Lima, L. (2004). Career benefits associated with mentoring for protégés: A meta-analysis. *Journal of Applied Psychology, 89*, 127–136.

Allen, T. D., Poteet, M. L., & Russell, J. E. A. (2000). Protégé selection by mentors: What makes the difference? *Journal of Organizational Behavior, 21*, 271–282.

Alliger, G. M., & Janak, E. A. (1989). Kirkpatrick's levels of training criteria: Thirty years later. *Personnel Psychology, 42*, 331–342.

Berscheid, E., & Regan, P. (2005). *The psychology of interpersonal relationships.* New York: Prentice-Hall.

Burke, R. J., & McKeen, C. A. (1989a). Developing formal mentoring programs in organizations. *Business Quarterly, 53*(3), pp. 76–79.

Catalyst (1993). *Mentoring: A guide to corporate programs and practices.* New York: Catalyst.

Chao, G. T., Walz, P. M., & Gardner, P. D. (1992). Formal and informal mentorships: Comparison on mentoring functions and contrast with nonmentored counterparts. *Personnel Psychology, 45*, 619–636.

Clawson, J. G. (1985). Is mentoring necessary? *Training and Development Journal, 39*(4), 36–39.

Colquitt, J. A., LePine, J. A., & Noe, R. A. (2000). Toward an integrative theory of training motivation: A meta-analytic path analysis of 20 years of research. *Journal of Applied Psychology, 85*, 678–707.

Cook, T. D., & Campbell, D. T. (1979). *Quasi experimentation: Design & analysis issues for field settings.* Boston: Houghton Mifflin Co.

Cunningham, J. B. (1993). Facilitating a mentorship programme. *Leadership & Organization Development Journal, 14*(4), 15–20.

Douglas, C. A., & McCauley, C. D. (1999). Formal developmental relationships: A survey of organizational practices. *Human Resource Development Quarterly, 10*(3), 203–220.

Eby, L. T., Butts, M., Lockwood, A., & Simon, S. A. (2004). Protégés' negative mentoring experiences: Construct development and nomological validation. *Personnel Psychology, 57*, 411–447.

Eby, L. T., & Lockwood, A. (2005). Proteges' and mentors' reactions to participating in formal mentoring programs: A qualitative inquiry. *Journal of Vocational Behavior, 67*, 441–458.

Eby, L. T., Lockwood, A., & Butts, M. (2006). Organizational support for mentoring: A multiple perspectives approach. *Journal of Vocational Behavior, 68*, 267–291.

Eddy, E., Tannenbaum, S., Alliger, G., D'Abate, C., & Givens, S. (2001). *Mentoring in industry: The top 10 issues when building and supporting a mentoring program.* Technical report prepared for the Naval Air Warfare Center Training Systems Division (Contract No. N61339-99-D-0012).

Fagan, M. M. (1988). Formal vs. informal mentoring in law enforcement. *Career Planning and Adult Development Journal, 4*(2), 40–48.

Finkelstein, L. M., Allen, T. D., & Montei, M. S. (2002, April). *Mentorship quality: The role of relational characteristics and expectations*. Paper presented at the 17th Annual meeting of the Society for Industrial and Organizational Psychology, Toronto, Canada.

Forret, M. L., Turban, D. B., & Dougherty, T. W. (1996). Issues facing organizations when implementing formal mentoring programmes. *Leadership & Organization Development Journal*, *17*, 27–30.

Geiger-DuMond, A. H. (1995). *Mentoring: A practitioner's guide*. Alexandria, VA: American Society for Training and Development, Inc.

Graham, J. W., & Verma, A. (1991). Predictors and moderators of employee responses to employee participation programs. *Human Relations*, *44*, 551–568.

Granfield, M. (March, 1993). Mentoring for money. *Working Woman*, 12–14.

Gray, W. A. (1988). Developing a planned mentoring program to facilitate career development. *Career Planning and Adult Development Journal*, *4*(2), 9–16.

Gunn, E. (August, 1995). Mentoring: The democratic version. *Training*, 64–67.

Hespe, G., & Wall, T. (1976). The demand for participation among employees. *Human Relations*, *29*, 411–428.

Keele, R. L., Bucker, K., & Bushnell, S. J. (1987). Formal mentoring programs are no panacea. *Management Review*, *76*(2), 67–68.

Kirkpatrick, D. (1994). *Evaluating training programs: The four levels*. San Francisco: Berrett-Koehler.

Kizilos, P. (April, 1990). Take my mentor please! *Training*, 49–55.

Klauss, R. (1981). Formalized mentor relationship for management and executive development programs in the federal government. *Public Administrative Review*, *July/August*, 489–496.

Koberg, C. S., Boss, R. W., & Goodman, E. (1998). Factors and outcomes associated with mentoring among health-care professionals. *Journal of Vocational Behavior*, *53*, 58–72.

Locke, E. A., Shaw, K. N., Saari, L. M., & Latham, G. P. (1981). Goal setting and task performance. *Psychological Bulletin*, *90*, 125–152.

Mendleson, J. L., Barnes, A. K., & Horn, G. (1989). The guiding light to corporate culture. *Personnel Administrator*, *34*(7), 70–72.

Messmer, M. (2001). *Human resources kit for dummies*. New York: Wiley.

Milne, S. H., Blum, T. C., & Roman, P. M. (1994). Factors influence employees' propensity to use an employee assistance program. *Personnel Psychology*, *47*, 123–145.

Mullan, B. (1984). *The mating trade*. London: Routledge & Kegan Paul.

Murray, M. (1991). *Beyond the myths and magic of mentoring*. San Francisco: Jossey-Bass.

Noe, R. A. (1988). An investigation of the determinants of successful assigned mentoring relationships. *Personnel Psychology*, *41*, 457–479.

Olson, J. M., Roese, N. J., & Zanna, M. P. (1996). Expectancies. In E. T. Higgins & A. W. Kruglanski (Eds.), *Social psychology: Handbook of basic principles* (pp. 211–238). New York: Guilford Press.

Orpen, C. (1997). The effects of formal mentoring on employee work motivation, organizational commitment, and job performance. *Learning Organization*, *4*, 53–60.

Parnell, J. A., & Crandall, W. (2001). Rethinking participative decision making: A refinement of the propensity for participative decision making scale. *Personnel Review*, *30*, 523–535.

Phillips-Jones, L. (1983). Establishing a formalized mentoring program. *Training and Development Journal*, *2*, 38–42.

Ragins, B. R., Cotton, J. L., & Miller, J. S. (2000). Marginal mentoring: The effects of type of mentor, quality of relationship, and program design on work and career attitudes. *Academy of Management Journal*, *43*, 1177–1194.

Rhoades, L., & Eisenberger, R. (2002). Perceived organizational support: A review of the literature. *Journal of Applied Psychology*, *87*(4), 698–714.

Tesluk, P. E., Vance, R. J., & Mathieu, J. E. (1999). Examining employee involvement in the context of participative work environments. *Group and Organization Management, 24,* 271–299.

Tyler, K. (April, 1998). Mentoring programs link employees and experienced executives. *HRMagazine, 43*(5), 98–103.

Viator, R. E. (1999). An analysis of formal mentoring programs and perceived barriers to obtaining a mentor at large public accounting firms. *Accounting Horizons, 13,* 37–53.

Wagner, J. A. (1994). Participation's effect on performance and satisfaction: A reconsideration of research evidence. *Academy of Management Review, 19,* 312–320.

Wanberg, C. R., Kammeyer-Mueller, J., & Marchese, M. (March, 2004). *Antecedents and outcomes of formal mentoring.* Paper presented at the Nineteenth Annual Meeting of the Society for Industrial and Organizational Psychology, Chicago, IL.

Wanberg, C. R., Welsh, E. T., & Hezlett, S. A. (2003). Mentoring research: A review and dynamic process model. *Research in Personnel and Human Resources Management, 22,* 39–124.

Wilson J. A., & Elman, N. S. (1990). Organizational benefits of mentoring. *Academy of Management Executive, 4*(4), 88–94.

Zey, M. G. (1985). Mentor programs: Making the right moves. *Personnel Journal, 64*(2), 53–57.

Chapter 22

Reflections on Best Practices for Formal Mentoring Programs

Kimberly E. O'Brien, Ozgun B. Rodopman, and Tammy D. Allen

Mentoring has been shown to be an effective method for enhancing individual growth and development. Formal mentoring programs have been developed to further capitalize on the benefits of mentoring. Best formal mentoring practices in different areas of mentoring research (youth, student–faculty, and workplace) have been investigated. Based on the existing empirical literature, it is clear that certain practices are associated with more effective mentoring programs; however, other practices require further investigation. Research on best practices regarding assessing program resources and needs, participant recruitment and selection, matching of mentor and protégé, mentor training, relationship structure, and program evaluation from each research area is discussed.

Assessing Program Resources

Before initiating a formal mentoring program, it is important to determine the availability of resources such as funding, the climate of the setting, and the support for the program. Specifically, youth mentoring emphasizes the need for assessing program capacity and infrastructure, obtaining stable funding sources, and creating partnerships with similar organizations. Institutional support is inherent in youth mentoring programs, but is also an important resource in student–faculty and workplace mentoring. The value of support from other parties has been demonstrated. For example, youth mentoring programs benefit from parental support, supervisor support is desired at the workplace, and peer support is useful in student–faculty mentoring. Workplace research has demonstrated that organizational support and commitment of top management to the program are beneficial.

Needs Assessment

A needs assessment is valuable to the development of a formal mentoring program. Research across areas has demonstrated that the needs of the organization, participants, and other constituents should be considered to determine the specific objectives of the programs (e.g., at-risk interventions, retention, training, or career development) and to determine program policy. For example, a needs assessment can be used to decide which groups should receive mentoring and to formulate criteria for evaluating the program. Moreover, a needs assessment can help a mentoring program develop clear, attainable, and realistic goals, which should be communicated to both the mentor and the protégé.

A needs assessment should also consider community and cultural factors. For example, economics, politics, and legal concerns (such as substance use or dropout rates) may influence the program's policies and objectives. Furthermore, the literature on workplace mentoring and student–faculty mentoring suggests assessment of the organizational or institutional culture, and evidence from youth mentoring programs indicates that assessment of national culture may be beneficial, particularly when cross-cultural programs are implemented.

Recruitment and Selection of Program Participants

All areas emphasize the importance of recruiting and selecting mentors and protégés, although each area acknowledges some ambiguity regarding the best way to do so. In terms of recruiting mentors, youth mentoring focuses on active strategies such as developing a written plan and targeted marketing, whereas workplace mentoring relies on internal recruitment. In the case of academic settings, mentoring is commonly viewed as inherent in the role of a faculty member. However, mentors may also be recruited for targeted formal university programs (e.g., McNair Scholars Program).

After potential mentors are identified, mentors likely to be effective are selected. In addition to common selection criteria for mentors such as motivation, experience, interest, and interpersonal skills, each context has demonstrated empirical support for other characteristics. Workplace mentoring research has found some evidence indicating that mentor empathy and a proactive orientation may facilitate effective mentoring, whereas youth mentoring research shows that a helping role or profession held by the mentor is advantageous. Furthermore, both student–faculty and workplace mentoring underscore the mentor's ability to model desired behaviors.

Each area also recognizes the potential detrimental effects of negative mentoring relationships and makes recommendations for screening out poor mentors. For example, workplace mentoring considers lack of accountability a potential problem; youth mentoring advises on elimination of mentors with criminal records or poor attitudes. Student–faculty mentoring research suggests guarding against selecting mentors who are racist, sexist, narcissistic, competitive, and inflexible.

Protégés are typically recruited and selected based on program objectives. For example, targeted workplace mentoring programs include those for protégés interested in management training, student–faculty mentoring programs may be geared toward the retention of freshmen, and youth mentoring often focuses on at-risk children. Each area emphasizes protégé motivation and interest for a successful and beneficial mentoring relationship to occur. In addition, workplace mentoring research suggests that the ability level of the protégé is important to attract mentors, and that proactive protégés attain more positive outcomes than their less proactive counterparts.

Matching of Program Participants

Once program participants are selected, matching is the next step. Whereas youth mentoring considers matching as the least critical element in the mentoring program, workplace and student–faculty mentoring place importance on the matching process to ensure a mutually beneficial mentoring relationship. Both workplace and youth mentoring research provide empirical evidence that perceived similarity in terms of interests and values relates to satisfaction with the relationship. However, the exact nature and components of similarity perceptions remain unknown. Student–faculty mentoring research, for example, shows that similarity in terms of gender and age may have an indirect effect on mentoring via shared interests and values, but no direct effects. Across all areas, the evidence of the value of matching based on participant ethnicity and gender is inconclusive.

Another issue across areas is that the match should include input from the participants. This finding has received empirical support in workplace mentoring. Likewise, youth mentoring suggests that potential partners should be allowed to meet and change their assignment if it is not mutually beneficial, and student–faculty mentoring emphasizes the importance of participant input to ensure that the relationship is perceived as natural and not forced.

Training of Program Participants

Each area emphasizes the importance of training for mentors, and specifies that training should include a discussion of the program requirements and procedures, and provide instruction on how to set expectations and boundaries of the relationship. Workplace mentoring research has shown that the receipt and quality of training are related to perceptions regarding the effectiveness of the mentoring program and mentoring provided. Furthermore, ongoing mentor training has been emphasized by both youth and student–faculty mentoring practices as important to program success.

Structure of the Program

A formal mentoring program may have specific policies regarding the frequency and method of interaction, duration of the relationship, and manner of ending the relationship; however, the extent that these policies are enforced and followed is not known. Likewise, there is little evidence to show which polices are best.

Regarding meeting frequency, all areas demonstrate the value of ongoing interactions between partners, depending on the nature of the relationship and the partner's availability. Student–faculty mentoring research emphasizes the importance of spontaneous meetings, whereas youth mentoring suggests an active role of the organization to sponsor activities that provide opportunities for partners to meet.

The literature in each area suggests that the mentoring relationship may last from 6 months to 2 years depending on the goals of the program. Although there is little evidence to support an ideal endpoint, youth mentoring research has shown that mentorships that lasted less than 6 months were not associated with positive protégé change. Furthermore, there is little research regarding the best method to end a relationship, but student–faculty mentoring advises a mentor-initiated meeting to discuss the end of the relationship in order to maintain appropriate expectations and good feelings.

Evaluation of the Program

Ongoing monitoring and program evaluation are important to demonstrate the effectiveness of the mentoring program, and provide further research in the area. Monitoring can help prevent negative mentoring experiences by influencing perceptions of accountability. Each area suggests that evaluation should assess the extent that the program accomplished its goals (as established by the needs assessment). Ideally, evaluation should be conducted through the use of an experimental design with multiple dependent variables. To date, the most rigorous evaluations that have been conducted involve youth mentoring programs (e.g., Big Brothers Big Sisters).

Concluding Comments

The three areas of mentoring research support assessing the resources and needs of the program prior to its inception, taking care to select and match partners, including mentor and protégé input regarding the relationship, providing guidelines to the participants, and evaluating the program. Specifically, it may be useful to have a handbook or manual stating program policies in order to show organizational support, help obtain funding, recruit and select program participants, provide training, and establish program structure. However, exact optimal practices regarding participant selection, partner matching, and program structure have not been well established. Consequently, each of the chapters in this section emphasizes a critical need for more empirical research to further determine best mentoring practices.

Part VII

Integrating Multiple Mentoring Perspectives

Chapter 23

New Directions in Mentoring

Steve Bearman, Stacy Blake-Beard, Laurie Hunt,
and Faye J. Crosby

One of the major benefits of the present book is its thrust toward integration. The book brings together knowledge from three domains of mentoring that have been largely kept separate – mentoring of youth; faculty mentoring of students; and mentoring in the workplace. It also sets the stage for increased collaboration between those in the academy and practitioners.

Like others in the volume, we strive in our chapter for yet a different integration: the knitting together of past, present, and future. The first part of the chapter concentrates on how social scientists have approached issues of mentoring and how they might approach these issues in the future. The second part of the chapter turns to the work of practitioners, noting why so many organizations and educational institutions today are interested in developing formal mentoring programs and also calling into question assumptions that underlie some of the programs.

Social Scientists Examine Mentoring

After 20 years of sustained intellectual effort, there are few in the social sciences today who would not recognize mentoring as a legitimate field of inquiry. Hundreds of studies exist on the antecedents, correlates, and consequences of mentoring. Some basic findings have been replicated numerous times; the positive impact of mentoring on outcomes such as salaries, promotions, feelings of competence, school attendance, and participation in extracurricular activities is well documented (Blake, 1999; Crosby, 1999; Dreher & Cox, 1996; Fagenson, 1989; Ragins & McFarlin, 1990; Scandura, 1992; Tierney, Grossman, & Resch, 2000; Whitely, Dougherty, & Dreher, 1991).

Certain persistent questions seem to organize much of the empirical work on mentoring. The first question is: What is mentoring? The natural next question: What are the effects of mentoring? And finally: How can individuals and organizations replicate mentoring successes when planning formal mentoring programs? We will reflect on each of these questions in turn. In addition, we believe that the progression from the second question about the effects of mentoring to the third and more applied question would be enhanced by interposing between them another question. As Dougherty, Turban, and Haggard (this volume) and Johnson (this volume) hint, and Ramaswami and Dreher (this volume) directly address, the time has come to ask about the reasons *why* mentoring proves effective. Examination of the causal mechanisms involved in mentoring is, in our view, the most pressing agenda item for future researchers.

What is Mentoring?

As Eby, Rhodes, and Allen (this volume) describe, and as Johnson, Rose, and Schlosser (this volume), Scandura and Pellegrini (this volume), Blinn-Pike (this volume), and Campbell (this volume) confirm, many different definitions of mentoring exist. In fact, Jacobi (1991) lists 15 distinct definitions in her review of the literature. One area of common disagreement among mentoring researchers is the necessity of emotional closeness as part of the definition of mentoring (Crosby, 1999).

How important is it to achieve consensus? On the one hand, it would seem as if consensus is needed if the field is to progress, especially if one considers mentoring to be a social *scientific* field of inquiry. Science can be productively understood as a set of practices for observing, describing, explaining, predicting, and controlling events in the natural world (Skinner, 1953). Kuhn (1970) indicates that the sign of an immature science is that its practitioners have not yet achieved consensus about basic definitions. It would seem that an agreed-upon definition is necessary if researchers are to know that they are looking at the same phenomenon. Surely, if scholars are to share their observations about X, they should agree on what X is.

Looking across the different chapters in the present book, however, one can also see reasons why researchers may not need to spend much effort looking for total agreement about the precise definition of mentoring, so long as: a) they all agree about the core components of a definition; and b) they are explicit about the divergent elements that comprise their own local definitions (Bowker & Star, 1999). The reason to avoid one universal definition is, stated simply, that mentoring is a social relationship. It always occurs in a social milieu and among specific people with different individual attributes. To impose overly specific and excessively rigid definitions on all investigations of mentoring does not adequately acknowledge the complexities of the real world.

Consider as an example the question of parents. Though parents are usually excluded from the definition of mentors, the potential overlap between parenting and mentoring is obvious enough that parents must be explicitly prohibited. Given any definition of what mentors do, it is certainly possible for parents to mentor their children, though they do not become mentors simply by virtue of parenthood. However, if a research team is trying to promote social dialogue about the value of nonparental adults in the lives of young people, excluding parents from the definition forwards their agenda, as does inviting "very important people" (VIPs) into the definitional domain.

What, then, should a research team do if they are interested in learning about parent mentors, perhaps investigating whether youth whose parents mentor them as part of their parenting style achieve similar outcomes to those in other mentoring relationships? What about a research team working to find out whether only some VIPs act as mentors, with others occupying the role of anti-mentor, modeling counter-productive habits, or undermining self-esteem for their protégés? These researchers will need to defy the growing consensus about how to define mentoring.

Must we thus claim that the field of mentoring cannot mature in the Kuhnian sense? Possibly, but even Kuhn acknowledges that the rules of social science differ in some particulars from the rules of physical science (Kuhn, 1989/2000). While physical sciences like astronomy and chemistry may study stars and molecules that have persisted in their current forms throughout long spans of history, the social sciences often set their sights on moving targets. Is the mentoring found in today's organizations the same mentoring studied by Kram (1985) 20 years ago? Perhaps not, because the surrounding social context has changed.

Indeed, part of the change in the ambient social milieu may be the result of the types of studies conducted by Kram and other social scientists. The rate of change in the physical world is glacial, and objects that are in "natural categories" have existed in their present forms for millennia (Quine, 1969). Perhaps the universe is expanding, but we do not expect the basic structure of atoms to change any time in the next hundred million years, let alone any time in the next decade. Chemists studying molybdenum do not make it a goal to change the number of protons in the element whose atoms, by definition, possess exactly 42 protons. As social scientists, however, if our research is influential enough to alter the very object of study, we take that as a sign of success. The social phenomena we study – already in flux as society evolves – change further as a result of our efforts. As the very phenomenon under study changes, definitions may change (Gergen, 1973).

Eschewing absolute agreement in definition does not mean that we should abandon all consensuses. On the contrary, as the present volume makes crystal clear, much is to be gained by noting the common core of all the various working definitions of mentoring (Eby et al., this volume). At the center of all the definitions is agreement that mentoring is a developmental process. Mentoring relationships, across all domains, bring protégés into new forms of participation in the meaningful activities of a cultural community. In, fact, all development can be conceptualized as changing participation within cultural communities (Rogoff, 2003). As a result of being in a mentoring relationship, the people who are seen as protégés are meant to change; and they are meant to change more than the other part of the dyad: mentors.

Even when mentors do change, the needs of the protégé must be predominant over the needs of the mentor. Good mentoring, furthermore, means that the mentor is attentive to and responsive to the changing needs of the protégé (Higgins & Kram, 2001; Miller, this volume). An excellent mentor is one who lets the capabilities and needs of the protégé, not his or her own needs, shape the interactions. The excellent mentor is the one, for example, who provides the protégé with a challenge that is age- and stage-appropriate for the protégé, not just with challenges that are convenient to or needed by the mentor.

The organization of the present volume facilitates the making of two very interesting observations. First, agreement about the central core of the definition of mentoring is not dependent on the domain of inquiry; the developmental aspect is as central to research in the workplace domain as to research in student–faculty relationships and to research in the domain of youth organizations. Second, variability concerning the peripheral aspects of the definition of mentoring – whether, for example, emotional connection is an essential part of mentoring – is equally pronounced in all three sub-fields.

What Are the Effects of Mentoring?

Most of the authors in the present volume agree with the accepted wisdom that mentoring produces positive outcomes (Allen, Eby, Poteet, Lentz, & Lima, 2003; Dougherty et al., this volume; DuBois, Holloway, Valentine, & Cooper, 2003; Eby et al., this volume; Johnson, this volume; Keller, this volume; Ramaswami & Dreher, this volume). Some of the authors (e.g., Blinn-Pike, this volume; Campbell, this volume; Mullen, this volume) see the research evidence about the positive effects of mentoring as slim. Yet others, like Scandura and Pellegrini (this volume), Mullen (this volume), Dougherty et al. (this volume), and Blinn-Pike (this volume), remind readers about possible negative outcomes. Even when some outcomes are positive, others may be troublesome.

Even as they differentiate among outcomes, none of the authors in the present volume seem to be attached to the assumption that we can always and easily differentiate between good outcomes and bad ones. Such a stance, we believe, is a sign of growing epistemological sophistication within our field.

Sometimes the assumption that one can tag a positive outcome seems warranted. Big Brothers Big Sisters of America is an outstanding example of a mentoring program which has produced desired outcomes for its protégé population: at-risk youth. External evaluators of the program find that youth who have regular contact with a volunteer mentor are less likely to use drugs, be violent, or skip school (Blinn-Pike, this volume; Grossman & Tierney, 1998). Differences in school attendance, drug use, and violence seem like excellent measures of the effectiveness of mentoring for at-risk youth.

Other times, the assumption of one definition of a good outcome seems problematic. Take, as an example, another potential mentoring environment for at-risk youth: street gangs. Gangs often provide community, belonging, protection, and a place to learn survival skills not available elsewhere. At-risk youth may be taken in by more experienced gang members and mentored in community activities that include generating income from illegal drugs or defending gang territory through acts of violence. These outcomes, opposite from what an organization like Big Brothers Big Sisters counts as measures of success, may still be the result of successful mentoring.

It is easy to imagine mentoring relationships with similarly questionable outcomes. Young people may be encouraged by adult mentors to link their self-esteem to overwork or perfect grades. New police recruits may be schooled in corrupt police practices by more experienced partners. Managers in training may be taken under the wing of those higher up in the company and taught to cheat customers. Graduate students may model their behavior after professors who gain their successes by denigrating the work of colleagues. If protégés become skilled in practices that, though valued locally, are detrimental to the wider community, are we to conclude that they were or that they were not mentored effectively?

And what if there is tension between what the protégé wants and what the mentor or the organization wants? As Crosby (1999) notes, organizations and the individuals within them face a dilemma when organizations seek to use mentoring programs as a way to diversify the organization. Newcomers may resist assimilation; this tension raises the issue of how much to school the newcomer in the established practices and how much to seek to change organizational practice (Liang & Grossman, this volume; Sedlacek, Benjamin, Schlosser, & Sheu, this volume).

Again, the point may be made by example. Consider that a medical school wishes to increase the number of women who train for surgery. Should the mentors of female students work with women to help them become skilled at spending time away from their children and partners? Or should those mentors instead advocate for their female protégés by urging the school to make modifications in its practice of subjecting medical residents in surgery rotation to days on end away from home and family?

We believe that answers to the questions about what makes for effective outcomes are not ultimately to be answered empirically (Crosby & Bearman, 2006). In advance of the empirical work, researchers need to specify what they consider to be good outcomes; and throughout the work, researchers need to remain sensitive to contrasting points of view. Several of the fine chapters in the present volume show by example how researchers can be receptive to complex issues about what constitutes good and bad outcomes. It is worth noting here that both faculty–student mentoring and workplace mentoring tend to occur within the structures of particular institutions, and the needs and goals of the institutions often govern what qualifies as good mentoring. Because youth mentoring is usually outside such well-defined bounds, it is our observation that researchers dealing with youth have the most sophisticated appreciation of contrasting moral orders and thus have a great deal to offer to researchers who concentrate on school success and on employment success.

How Can We Replicate Successes?

Even if we are to agree on the conservative strategy of progressing through the ranks without changing them, we still must ask: how can one extract the "active ingredients" of successful mentoring relationships for use in formal mentoring programs and mentor training? Organizations are hungry for recipes. Despite the enumeration of "best practices," researchers infrequently provide empirically driven answers (cf. Finkelstein & Poteet, this volume; Campbell, this volume) to the question of what makes for successful mentoring.

Part of the reluctance to extrapolate advice from studies has to do with the ever-changing and specific nature of the mentoring relationship. Learning from a more experienced mentor means learning from someone more experienced at something specific. The mentor's expertise in the domain is an essential ingredient in the mentoring relationship, a fact often glossed over in the attempt to find universal truths about mentoring. Though we assume that the form of mentoring relationships is the same across domains and that the main differences are differences of content, this assumption is an oversimplification. The very structure of mentoring factors in even the most rigorous factor analysis is bound to be different across contexts (Scandura & Pellegrini, this volume). In any given mentoring environment, mentoring functions are likely to be linked up in idiosyncratic ways. As a result, it is difficult to discern whether conclusions drawn from a given mentoring environment will be applicable in a different context.

Another source of reluctance to offer advice from empirical studies derives from the recognized gaps in our research-based knowledge (Johnson, this volume). For example, as Spencer (this volume) makes very clear, studies of naturally occurring mentoring relationships between adults and at-risk youth have ignored questions about the qualities of the mentors, even though answers to such questions would help people know how to design effective mentoring programs.

Over the years, researchers have gleaned a lot of information from practitioners, as is evident from the analyses of the Big Brothers Big Sisters program. Practitioners have, in turn, extracted some advice from academic scholars, mostly at the organizational level of best practices. We believe that practitioners will be able to reap a great deal more wisdom from academic studies only after the researchers have given serious attention to explaining why mentoring (whether naturally occurring or occurring through a formal mentoring program) produces the outcomes that it produces for individuals and organizations.

Interposed Question: Why Does Mentoring Work?

Practitioners who seek to create effective mentoring programs often look to the research literature for guidance, but until recently the research literature has not offered much guidance about how to create and sustain successful programs in the contexts of youth, student–faculty relationships, and the workplace. Part of the problem arises from the continuing skepticism about formal mentoring programs among those who, like Kram (1985), have been focused on naturally occurring relationships. But part of the problem arises from the inattention of researchers, who have traditionally been too preoccupied with demonstrating that mentoring works to pay much attention to questions of *why* mentoring works. As Liang and Grossman (this volume) note: "Little research has explicitly focused on the *process* of mentoring" (p. 242, italics in original).

We think that as a field of inquiry, mentoring is now ready to delve into causal questions. Three distinguishable paths lie open to researchers who wish to move beyond the descriptive assertion that mentoring works in order to emphasize why it works. The paths are not mutually exclusive.

Path 1: Specifying Causes and Effects

When predicting desired mentoring outcomes, it is possible to go beyond correlating overall mentoring with overall outcomes and to articulate which specific aspects of mentoring produce which specific outcomes. Liang and Grossman (this volume), Sedlacek et al. (this volume), Ramaswami and Dreher (this volume), and Finkelstein and Poteet (this volume) all take this approach, identifying specific components of arrangements that make a difference in the effectiveness of mentoring relationships. One might, for example, note that mentor consistency and follow-through are essential qualities in mentors of at-risk youth (Keller, this volume). Mentor reliability alone can make the difference between a mentoring relationship providing benefit or detriment to at-risk protégés. Such a conclusion is immediately useful to administrators developing training and selection criteria for youth mentors. One might note that socio-emotional help, but not instrumental help, predicts graduate students' satisfaction with their student–advisor relationship (Tenenbaum, Crosby, & Gliner, 2001). Again, such a specific prediction is of great potential use to advisors who want to develop positive relationships over time with their students. Recognizing specific relationships between causes and effects allows mentors and administrators to act accordingly.

At this stage in our progression as a scientific field, it is incumbent upon us to provide particulars. Though it may be necessary in any new mentoring context to establish first that mentoring leads to more desirable outcomes than no mentoring, it is equally necessary to take the next step. What about mentoring is making the difference? What specific components of mentoring interactions lead to which specific preferred (or, for that matter, undesired) outcomes?

Path 2: Probing-related Developmental Mechanisms

A second path toward understanding causal connections is to seek analogues to mentoring within developmental psychology. By looking at learning processes in a range of developmental relationships, researchers concerned with mentoring can gain new insights into the mechanisms that account for successful mentoring. Consideration of three developmental learning theories may help illuminate the causal mechanisms at play in mentoring: scaffolding, intent participation, and self-efficacy. Mentoring researchers need not limit themselves to these three theories, but each provides an example of how mentoring research and other areas of developmental research can interact.

Scaffolding. Originally proposed by Wood, Bruner, and Ross (1976), scaffolding is a metaphor for the process by which an individual's developmental capacity is raised by a more experienced other above the level it could achieve were the person left to their own devices. The more experienced other provides the temporary scaffold by which a learner can build up their knowledge and abilities. Though scaffolding and mentoring are not equivalent terms (Dennen, 2004), scaffolding may describe low-level interactions which occur within mentoring relationships.

For instance, mentors are likely to select tasks for their protégés which will challenge protégés to an extent appropriate to their developmental progress, but which will not overwhelm them. In addition, mentors may facilitate the learning of skills by bite-sizing projects into pieces more easily managed by protégés, sequencing tasks into a logical order that protégés, due to lack of experience, would be unable to determine on their own, direct protégés' attention away from superfluous activity and toward key areas, help protégés manage their frustration as they stretch beyond what is familiar, and demonstrate how to do what they want their protégés to do. All of these mentoring activities are enumerated in Wood et al.'s (1976) original description of scaffolding.

Scaffolding, however, is an imperfect metaphor for what actually happens in developmental relationships (Stone, 1993). Though all the activities listed above may occur, they are all examples of a mentor guiding and shaping the activity of a protégé. The even more important interactions may be ones in which mentor and protégé work together to develop a shared structure of meaning, a process that requires repeated contact. Scaffolding occurs as protégé and mentor develop a shared mental process that over time allows the protégé to integrate the mentor's cognitive structure of the world into their own. By sharing vocabulary, conceptual structures, and common practices, the protégé begins to see the world in a way that is congruent with the domain in which they are being mentored (Rogoff, 1990).

Mentoring researchers might productively explore the intersection of mentoring and scaffolding. As protégés progress from novice to adept, what specific kinds of supports do mentors provide at each step along the way? Are mentors more successful when they provide just enough, rather than too much, scaffolding? How do mentors and protégés determine when to take down scaffolding so that the protégé can learn to build on their own?

Intent participation.   The primary educational tradition in industrialized societies has been that of assembly line instruction (Rogoff, Paradise, Arauz, Correa-Chávez, & Angelillo, 2003), in which information is transmitted from experts to learners within environments specifically designed for teaching but segregated from the contexts in which productive community activities occur. Mentoring, on the other hand, may more closely resemble an alternative learning tradition: intent participation (Rogoff, 2003; Rogoff et al., 2003), often practiced in indigenous communities. In these communities, young people are far less segregated from meaningful community practices and as a result have more opportunities to observe adults engaged in productive activities. The quality of young people's observation is intensified by their knowledge that they will later be expected to participate in observed practices, often with little to no verbal instruction in how to do so. Learning through intent participation begins with keen observation in anticipation of engaging in an activity, progresses into a period of legitimate peripheral participation (Lave & Wenger, 1991), in which inexperienced individuals are included in roles of limited responsibility while they work to master needed community practices, and then phases into ongoing learning via full participation with gradually decreasing guidance.

Mentoring often resembles intent participation. Learning in mentoring relationships typically involves more learning by doing than is present in assembly line school environments. Protégés often have the opportunity to work shoulder to shoulder with their mentors, learning via the kind of keen observation that accompanies the protégé's expectation that they will soon be practicing what the mentor is doing. The mentoring relationship is a social structure that allows for protégés to become legitimate peripheral participants in meaningful community activities as they work to gain mastery in the domain in which they are mentored. The differences between the developmental environment of mentoring and the developmental environments typical in school settings may provide clues as to why learning can happen through mentoring which does not happen without it.

As with scaffolding, intent participation may illuminate some of the mechanisms that make mentoring work. Do protégés observe mentors with an intensity not present in other learning environments such as classrooms or job trainings? Is mentoring primarily effective not due to the mentoring relationship itself, but because it puts protégés into environments where they have the opportunity to participate actively in meaningful community activities? If the latter question turns out to be true, does this mean that mentors who are more integrated into their surrounding communities are of greater value to their protégés?

Self-efficacy.   As an extension of social learning theory (Bandura, 1986), Bandura's (1997) self-efficacy theory describes how a person's belief in their ability serves as an excellent predictor of actual ability. Like mentoring, self-efficacy is domain specific. For instance, academic self-efficacy, a belief in one's own academic ability, has been robustly demonstrated to predict academic success (Multon, Brown, & Lent, 1991).

Bandura (1997) identified a set of four interrelated sources contributing to the development of self-efficacy. The first source, graduated mastery, is in many ways analogous to scaffolding and refers to the acquisition of stage-appropriate skills on the way toward mastery. The second source, vicarious role modeling, which may serve a similar function to the keen observation present in intent participation, allows individuals to gain information about their own capabilities through witnessing others' capabilities. The third source of self-efficacy, social persuasion, enhances one's belief in one's abilities by providing positive feedback and encouragement. Finally, emotional experience is the fourth source of self-efficacy; feelings of anxiety or of enthusiasm, for instance, may impact a person's sense of their own abilities. Anxiety, enthusiasm, and related affects may of course be enhanced or diminished through interpersonal influence.

These four sources of self-efficacy – graduated mastery, vicarious role modeling, social persuasion, and emotional experience – are all potentially found in mentoring, suggesting that another way to understand the causal mechanism of mentoring is through its potential impact on self-efficacy. Of Bandura's four sources, only graduated mastery seems to tap directly into the instrumental component of mentoring, which highlights the importance of socio-emotional functions as adjuncts to instrumental help. It is through the mentor serving as a model and example, as a source of encouragement and feedback, and as a support in making the experience of learning feel better and easier, that self-efficacy develops.

Important research questions are implied here. While instrumental mentoring alone can lead to increased productivity for protégés in some contexts (Tenenbaum et al., 2001), does instrumental mentoring require a socio-emotional foundation in order to be effective? Which components of emerging self-efficacy are fed by which kinds of mentoring functions?

Path 3: Building Articulated Models

The third path to causality involves the articulation of causal models (Dutton & Ragins, 2007; Ragins, this volume). Not only do we believe that the time has come for researchers to concentrate on understanding why mentoring produces successful outcomes, we also believe that the field is ready to develop integrated models that incorporate fine-grained predictions and causal mechanisms suggested by related fields.

One good example of what we have in mind is Rhodes' (2002b) important model of the influence of mentoring on youth, especially those who are at risk (Keller, this volume; Rhodes, 2002b, 2005). According to Rhodes' model, mentoring achieves its positive outcomes through three interrelated processes. First, good mentoring enhances the social skills of the protégés, which in turn augments emotional well-being. Second, good mentoring enhances the cognitive skills of the protégés. Finally, good mentoring contributes to identity development such that youth's self-concepts change over the course of mentoring.

Another good example of a promising model is presented by Ramaswami and Dreher (this volume) concerning the effects of mentoring at work. These authors propose that certain mentor functions produce affective and cognitive responses in the protégé which then lead to behavioral responses, which in turn lead to outcomes for the individual and the organization. For example, they identify the mentoring functions of role modeling, acceptance and confirmation, counseling, and friendship as functions that concern path-goal clarity. They propose that such functions influence the protégé's feelings of self-efficacy and that enhanced self-efficacy leads to enhanced job performance which in turn leads to augmented productivity for the organization and increased salary for the individual. Ramaswami and Dreher propose a similar multistep process for mentors.

Self-efficacy is also central to a model of school achievement currently being developed and tested by Martin Chemers and his associates at the University of California, Santa Cruz (M. M. Chemers, personal communication, 2005). With funding from the National Institutes of Health,[1] Chemers and associates are seeking to map the dynamics of student enrichment experiences and student persistence in the sciences, particularly for ethnic minority students. Using both qualitative and quantitative approaches and both retrospective and prospective (longitudinal) designs, Chemers is looking at the school-related outcomes of students as a function of the laboratory experiences and the mentoring they receive.

Chemers found in a previous study (Chemers, Hu, & Garcia, 2001) that academic self-efficacy for entering college students was a significant predictor of academic performance in the first year of college, even after controlling for academic performance in high school. This finding led him to develop a model in which self-efficacy plays a mediating role (see Figure 23.1). In the model, mentoring, science research experiences in which students work closely with faculty and graduate students, and additional supports all contribute to self-efficacy in science inquiry skills and self-efficacy for participation in science teams. These in turn lead to the dual outcomes of competence in science skills and commitment to further science education and science research careers. It is hypothesized that these effects will exist for all students but will be stronger for minorities underrepresented in the sciences, for whom mentoring and additional support are needed to overcome structural inequalities built into the educational system.

The three models outlined above each situate mentoring in a larger system of which mentoring is only one component, albeit often an important one. Taken together, they demonstrate that fitting mentoring into complex causal models can be done in the contexts of youth, workplace, and student–faculty mentoring. Ongoing mentoring research should aim to discover in what kinds of systems mentoring must be embedded in order for it to be most useful. It should also work to sort out the effects of mentoring from the effects of other influences, a project which requires the measurement of more than just mentoring components and mentoring related outcomes.

Each of the three paths and their accompanying models for why mentoring works provides fruitful ground for future research. To integrate research and practice on

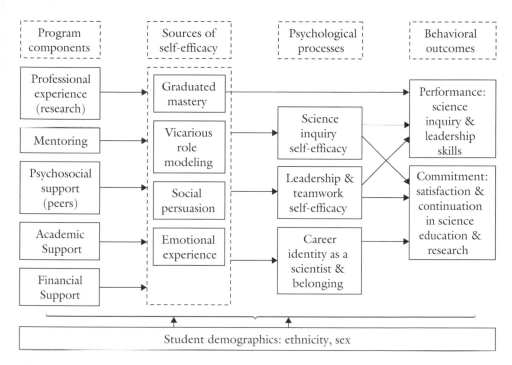

Figure 23.1 Working model for Chemers's research project: Assessing Scientific Inquiry and Leadership Skills. All effects are hypothesized to be stronger for minorities underrepresented in the sciences

mentoring, it is critical that we understand *why* mentoring works. If studying mentoring is a scientific enterprise, then determining its mechanisms is what allows us to develop mentoring technology. Only by understanding the dynamics of mentoring can we create programs and policies that are adapted to the needs of different organizations, institutions, and individuals.

Mentoring in Practice

Why the current interest in mentoring?

Today, many organizations and educational institutions show a strong interest in mentoring, often going so far as to develop formal mentoring programs. There are a number of factors driving the need for program planners to better understand and employ formal mentoring initiatives.

One factor is an increasingly diverse workforce (Cox & Blake, 1991; Thomas & Ely, 2001). In 1987, Johnston and Packer predicted that minorities were going to be an increasing percentage of the workforce. In fact, their forecasts have been realized; both organizations and universities are more diverse today than two decades ago and are now grappling with how to support/enable relationships among people who are engaged in some common enterprise but "who do not share a common history or culture" (Caproni, 2004, p. 269). One idea explored here is that mentoring may be a mechanism to facilitate positive interactions among the increasingly diverse individuals. Sedlacek et al. (this volume) describe this process in terms of graduate student development, noting how mentors of any race or gender can come together with protégés from any nontraditional group for mutual development.

Another factor is concern about the career outcomes and progression of this more diverse workforce. In spite of the increased number of women and people of color entering organizations and academic institutions, we still see a glass ceiling that effectively keeps the top levels absent of the same diversity that exists throughout the middle and lower levels. This glass ceiling has been recast as a concrete ceiling – an impermeable barrier that keeps women and people of color effectively locked out of the corridors of power in organizations across industries and professions (Catalyst, 2001; Tomlinson, 2001). And there are glass ceilings affecting women and people of color across all three domains investigated in this book. Granger (1993) and Marasco (2005b) discuss the continued under-representation and inequities in rank and salary facing women and minority faculty in higher education. In the academic environment, only 55% of Americans who start college manage to get degrees in 6 years (Mathews, 2004). Mentoring has been posed as a catalyst to shift the dynamics of power that keep women and people of color from advancing in organizations. For example, the Posse Foundation uses a model of peer mentoring to support urban students of color at the nation's top-ranked colleges and universities (Gee, 2005).

We are also faced with changing career dynamics (Arthur & Rousseau, 1996; Eddleston, Baldridge, & Veiga, 2004). Careers in today's organizations are often referred to as "boundaryless"; they do not correspond to any traditional career forms, patterns, or assumptions (Arthur & Rousseau, 1996). Old models of career progression called for vertical progression within large hierarchical firms driving employees to mold themselves into an image of the successful "organization man" (Whyte, 1956). Career advancement was expected to follow a predictable pattern of lock-step movement steadily up a defined organizational ladder. These traditional predictors of career outcomes are less normative within today's changing environment. For example, issues such as balancing work, family, and community (Clancy & Tata, 2005; Curtis, 2004) are more relevant given the demographic changes in our society. Firms are more decentralized than in the past, which increases the need for what Hall (1986) calls "meta-skills" or the ability to creatively adapt to new roles, processes, and experiences. Thus, traditional definitions of competence, merit, and ability are expanded; in fact, who moves ahead in an organization, as well as society at large, is determined by an interconnected set of factors. Mentoring is relevant because it has often been viewed as a tool for the development of youth and the socialization of both students and employees newly engaged in their career journeys. For example, Johnson (this volume) discusses how the professional skill development, networking, and confidence of a student protégé resulting from the presence of a faculty mentor better prepare the student for her or his career. Similarly, peer mentoring of first-year college students positively affects the social integration of the students into an educational process which is new territory for the student (Treston, 1999).

A final factor driving the need for formal mentoring initiatives is an increased focus on the retention and development of talent in organizations. This struggle with talent development begins with moving our youth from high school to completion of a 4-year college degree. Recent statistics indicate that one third of all first-year students who enrolled at postsecondary schools did not return to the same institution one year later (Lumina Foundation for Education, 2002). Futurists predict that one of the biggest challenges organizations will face is the war to retain their human talent or "wisdom" workers (Gornick, 2005; Herman, Olivo, & Gioia, 2003; Taylor, 2004). According to data from the US Bureau of Labor Statistics, we are facing an impending shortage of skilled workers; by 2010, there will be 10.3 million more jobs in the American workforce than skilled workers to fill them. In light of the predicted labor shortage, neither organizations nor educational institutions can afford to continue operating with a revolving door: recruiting and developing the best talent only to see them leave in frustration over challenges and barriers engendered by cultures that are not conducive to their personal and professional development. Mentoring has been suggested as a tool to increase the retention of skilled talent (Ramaswami & Dreher, this volume). In the same way, retention of students of color in academic institutions is positively affected by the presence of a mentor (Blinn-Pike, this volume; Sedlacek et al., this volume).

Each of these trends suggests that practitioners engaged in leading organizations and academic institutions through change should have mentoring on their radar screen. Recent statistics support the use of formal mentoring as an increasingly popular strategic intervention. In fact, a third of the nation's major companies have formal mentoring programs (Bragg, 1989) and 60% of *Fortune's* 100 best companies to work for in the US have formal mentoring programs (Branch, 1999). The long list of mentoring programs on the National Education Association (NEA) website is an indication of the prevalence of student mentoring programs at colleges and universities in the US (Campbell, this volume). The use of formal mentoring programs in the K-12 arena is also steadily increasing, as indicated by Sipe and Roder's (1999) study of 722 youth mentoring programs; they found that 40% of these programs had been operating for less than 5 years.

Practitioners have operated under a number of assumptions, based on outdated or possibly inaccurate information about formal mentoring, that warrant examination. Interestingly enough, just as we noted with the research on mentoring, we find that these assumptions related to the practice of mentoring apply to each of the three domains studied in this volume: youth, student–faculty, and workplace mentoring. In light of their presence across domains, understanding these assumptions becomes that much more important.

Challenging Assumptions About Formal Mentoring

Assumption 1: Formal mentoring evolves through the same phases as informal mentoring.   One assumption is that formal mentoring relationships evolve through the same four phases identified by Kram (1985) for informal mentoring. As Johnson (this volume) notes, nearly all of the research on formal mentoring in academia is derived from studies exploring informal mentoring relationships. The first phase of informal mentoring relationship in which the pairs are getting to know one another, Kram's (1985) Initiation Phase, has specific defining characteristics. In many informal mentoring pairs, this beginning phase is characterized by attraction to the other and excitement at the sense of possibility that the new relationship offers. Both mentors and protégés develop a sense of initial infatuation with the other and the possibilities that the relationship offers both.

McGowan's (2004) research on formal mentoring relationships in higher education, specifically within a faculty-to-faculty mentoring program, found important distinctions in the beginning of formal and informal mentoring relationships. Emotions accompanying the first phase of informal mentoring relationships are very different than those experienced by formal mentoring pairs. Unlike the sense of excitement and positive anticipation or fantasies that are associated with the beginning of informal mentoring relationships, formal mentoring pairs often express a sense of awkwardness in describing their initial interactions. Virtual strangers, identified as a pair, they are often thrown together at someone else's suggestion, with little information about their partner, their expectations, and how they hope to proceed. Thus, formal mentoring partners often enter the relationship "blind," knowing little or nothing about their assigned partner (Blake-Beard, O'Neill, & McGowan, in press). This is also the case for formal youth mentoring relationships (Miller, this volume).

Because of the unique challenges faced at the beginning of these relationships, formal mentoring may have an additional, fifth stage that we do not see in informal mentoring (McGowan, 2004). McGowan posits that formal mentoring partnerships actually begin prior to the Initiation Phase so often associated with the beginning of informal mentoring relationships (Kram, 1985) with an Orientation Phase during which mentors and protégés try to orient themselves in relationship to their new partner. They typically do this by negotiating the most basic of mentoring tasks – the balance between career and psychosocial functions. Understanding that formal mentoring relationships start with Orientation rather than Initiation should influence how practitioners develop mentoring partnerships as well as how these formal mentoring relationships are launched and supported.

Assumption 2: Participants should be matched based on similarity.   While formal mentoring programs hold a great deal of promise, inadequate attention is often paid to how mentoring partners are brought together – the match. In far too many cases, mentor–protégé pairs are formed in unreliable ways: at random, by geography, for convenience, or because there is a "hunch" that particular people will make a good pair. Researchers (Finkelstein & Poteet, this volume; Eby, McManus, Simon, & Russell, 2000) have noted that a badly managed matching process can contribute to a number of negative emotions, including resentment and suspicion. The manner in which participants are brought together is a critical component of effective formal mentoring programs.

One common assumption is that program coordinators should match participants based on similarity along a number of dimensions, including race and gender (Catalyst, 1993). The rationale is that it will be easier for relative strangers to forge a relationship with one another if they start with a level of similarity (Berscheid & Regan, 2005). This rationale may seem particularly attractive to planners who are using their programs to promote diversity efforts within their organizations (Hardy, 1998; Segal, 2005) or reach out to diverse youth (Liang & Grossman, this volume). Matching based on similarity, however, raises a number of questions and concerns.

One issue is around how similarity is determined. As Wanberg, Kammeyer-Mueller, and Marchese (2004) noted, similarity is a fairly broad concept. Should the program match on visible demographic characteristics, such as race and gender, or on factors that are not as readily apparent, such as values, personality, and common interests? Research from Harrison, Price, and Bell (1998) on the impact of surface-level (demographic) and deep-level (attitudinal) diversity on group social integration provides some insight in relation to this question. Harrison and his colleagues argued that deep-level variables are more important over time than surface-level variables in determining social integration within teams. For interactions with a lengthy time horizon, like mentoring relationships, this research suggests that similarity along deep-level or attitudinal variables may be more important than matching along surface-level or demographic dimensions of diversity. Youth mentoring research has shown that matching the mentors and protégés across differences can be satisfying if protégés perceive similarities beyond the surface-level differences (Liang & Grossman, this volume). Herrera, Sipe, and McClanahan (2000) found that youth mentor matches who share interests have stronger relationships than matches based only on ethnicity or gender.

Some programs have specifically matched across differences in order to bring participants together based on complementarity (Blake-Beard, O'Neill, & McGowan, in press). We see complementary matching used in a formal mentoring program implemented at Procter and Gamble (P&G). Zielinski (2000) describes P&G's *Mentor Up* program, which partnered mid- or junior-level female managers with senior-level male executives in an effort to raise consciousness about work-related issues affecting women. The program was offered because P&G wanted to reduce the "regrettable loss" of promising female managers. Zielinski did report some positive results. "Regretted losses" of female managers declined 25% and no longer exceeded attrition figures of male managers.

When program planners are determining how to do the matching, whether it is based on similarity or complementarity, program goals and objectives should be considered (Finkelstein & Poteet, this volume). As Hegstad and Wentling (2004) note, organizations should not put formal mentoring in place without it being tied to critical organizational goals.

Assumption 3: Training for mentors and protégés is "nice, but not necessary."

A third common assumption, particularly in workplace and educational mentoring, is that training for program participants is a nicety, rather than a critical component necessary for the success of formal mentoring initiatives. Not much attention in the empirical literature is dedicated to research on the structure and impact of training, an important gap in the extant body of research (Campbell, this volume; Finkelstein & Poteet, this volume; Jucovy, 2001; Miller, this volume). Miller indicates that while training should be an ongoing process, as many programs are implemented, little consideration is given to training. He suggests that the belief that mentoring is a naturally occurring intervention may account for the lack of attention given to this crucial aspect of formal mentoring programs.

This assumption is fed by a corollary belief that the purpose of training is to teach participants how to be effective mentors or protégés. We see this implicit assumption stated in Campbell's (this volume) review of best practices in student–faculty mentoring. Notes Campbell, "There is little preparation for the tasks of mentoring at both the graduate and undergraduate levels. The rationale appears to be that faculty members know the expectations of academia and since they are teachers, they should be able to serve as appropriate resources for students." (p. 336)

The assumption that mentors do not need training is also common in industry. Program planners may suggest that their mentors can forgo training because they are "naturals" in terms of their ability to mentor. This rationale overestimates the competence and preparedness of senior organizational members to act as mentors; it also misidentifies the purpose of training. While best practices for mentors and protégés are certainly offered as part of most training programs, dissemination of this information is not the only, or even the primary, purpose of these sessions.

Drawing on McGowan's Orientation phase, we suggest that the primary purpose of training is to provide a legitimate forum and structured process for participants to orient themselves to one another (Blake-Beard & Murrell, 2006). The initial training session prepares participants to step into the formal mentoring relationships on which they are about to embark and offers structured support for setting up their mentoring agreement and relationship guidelines and boundaries. Besides providing a space for Orientation to occur, training also serves additional purposes. It can be used to review mentor and protégé roles and responsibilities, set expectations, avoid typical formal mentoring problems, and offer guidance on listening and communication skills. Training may also be used to transmit or reinforce implicit messages and values. At a symbolic level, training signals that the sponsoring agency, be it an organization, university, or community, is serious about the formal mentoring initiative; the accompanying values communicated are that the agency values its human resources and is interested in supporting the development of program participants.

Results from some studies support the importance of training. Recent research in the context of workplace mentoring found significant effects for both mentors and protégés who participated in training (Allen, Eby, & Lentz, 2006a, 2006b). For mentors, receiving training impacted their commitment and understanding of the program. For protégés, Allen and her colleagues found that participation in training was significantly related to their perception of mentor commitment and their understanding of the program. They suggest that high-quality training may include information that helps mentors and protégés develop an interpersonal connection – in effect, to orient to one another. While the research evidence is somewhat mixed, youth mentoring programs may also benefit from the use of training (Miller, this volume). For example, in a meta-analysis of the effectiveness of youth mentoring programs, DuBois and colleagues (2002) found that programs with ongoing mentor training demonstrated more positive effects on youth than those without ongoing training. These findings speak to the need for more research on training as well as greater understanding among practitioners of the importance and varied roles of training in the formal mentoring process.

Challenging Assumptions as Mentoring Evolves

As the above discussion on common assumptions in the implementation of formal mentoring programs illustrates, the practice of mentoring will benefit as we learn more about these processes through continued research. We will also need to challenge our assumptions about mentoring as we research the processes and impacts of newer forms of mentoring that are emerging as the field continues to gain prominence.

Electronic mentoring.   Electronic mentoring, as a tool for formally bringing together people across geographic distances, is becoming more popular. MentorNet, a global electronic network for women in engineering and science, has grown steadily since its inception in 1997 (Marasco, 2005a; Single & Muller, 2001). This organization is focused on pairing students (undergraduate, graduate, and postdoctoral) with industry-based professionals for one-to-one electronic mentoring. As more global organizations take on e-mentoring as a form of delivery for their mentoring initiatives, it will be critical to take the learning from MentorNet's work with student–adult mentoring to better understand how. For example, Single and Muller (2001) note that early iterations of face-to-face formal mentoring programs often yielded poor results because they were implemented without enough structures and support systems in place. They suggest that as organizations move to electronic mentoring, having the necessary support systems in place will be even more important. Their work points to a clear area for additional research – what aspects of face-to-face formal mentoring will need to be changed to accommodate mentoring in a virtual medium?

Peer mentoring.   Yet another area where additional research would be beneficial is peer mentoring. The Posse Foundation's example of the potential of peer mentoring for young adults is compelling. This program started in 1989 with 5 students at Vanderbilt University. Fifteen years later, the Posse Program has placed groups or "posses" of multitalented youth at over two dozen of the nation's top-ranked colleges and universities. Institutions of higher education that have taken on these groups of students have also benefited. In addition to high retention and graduation rates (students are graduating at a rate of 90%), students involved in the Posse groups are also transforming the college campuses of which they are a part (Gee, 2005). The Vanderbilt posse was responsible for a host of change initiatives, ranging from founding of the university's first gospel choir to the development of an association for Hispanic students. The corporate sector has much to learn from the practices and outcomes related to peer mentoring that we see emerging from higher education.

Integration

Given the increasing popularity of formal mentoring, practitioners should be able to turn to the research literature to arm themselves as they roll out initiatives that can affect hundreds, or in large programs thousands, of people in their organizations. Researchers should be able to glean much information from actual attempts to create and sustain successful programs in the contexts of youth, student–faculty, and workplace environments. The collection of thought-provoking and illuminating papers presented in the present volume provides the ideal platform from which to launch the next, integrative, stage of thinking and acting in the field of mentoring.

Note

1   National Institutes of Health Grant #1 RO1 GM 71935, Assessing Scientific Inquiry and
    Leadership Skills, Martin M. Chemers, Principal Investigator.

References

Allen, T. D., Eby, L. T., & Lentz, E. (2006a). The relationship between formal mentoring pro-
    gram characteristics and perceived program effectiveness. *Personnel Psychology, 59*, 125–153.
Allen, T. D., Eby, L. T., & Lentz, E. (2006b). Mentorship behaviors and mentorship
    quality associated with formal mentoring programs: Closing the gap between research and
    practice. *Journal of Applied Psychology, 91*, 567–578.
Allen, T. D., Eby, L. T., Poteet, M. L., Lent, E., & Lima, L. (2004). Career benefits asso-
    ciated with mentoring protégés: A meta-analysis. *Journal of Applied Psychology, 89*, 127–136.
Arthur, M. B., & Rousseau, D. M. (1996). *The boundaryless career: A new employment
    principle for a new organizational era.* New York: Oxford University Press.
Bandura, A. (1986). *Social foundations of thought and action: A social cognitive theory.* Upper
    Saddle River, NJ: Prentice-Hall.
Bandura, A. (1997). *Self-efficacy: The exercise of control.* New York: W. H. Freeman.
Berscheid, E., & Regan, P. (2005). *The psychology of interpersonal relationships.* New York:
    Prentice-Hall.
Blake, S. D. (1999). The costs of living as an outsider within: An analysis of the mentoring
    relationships and career success of black and white women in the corporate sector. *Journal
    of Career Development, 26*(1), 21–36.
Blake-Beard, S. D., & Murrell, A. J. (2006). *Executive Leadership Council (ELC) guide to
    effective mentoring.* Washington, DC: ELC.
Blake-Beard, S. D., O'Neill, R. M., & McGowan, E. (in press). Blind dates?: The importance
    of matching in successful formal mentoring relationships. In K. E. Kram & B. R. Ragins
    (Eds.), *The handbook of mentoring at work: Theory, research and practice.* Thousand Oaks,
    CA: Sage.
Bowker, G. C., & Star, S. L. (1999). *Sorting things out: Classification and its consequences.*
    Cambridge, MA: MIT Press.
Bragg, A. (1989). Is a mentor program in your future? *Sales and Marketing Management,*
    141(September), 54–59.
Branch, S. (1999). The 100 best companies to work for in America. *Fortune, 139*(1),
    118–130.
Caproni, P. J. (2004). *Management skills for everyday life: The practical coach.* Englewood Cliffs,
    NJ: Prentice Hall.
Catalyst (1993). *Mentoring: A guide to corporate programs and practices.* New York: Catalyst.
Catalyst (2001). *Women of color executives: Their voices, their journeys.* New York: Catalyst.
Chemers, M. M., Hu, L., & Garcia, B. (2001). Academic self-efficacy and first-year college
    student performance and adjustment. *Journal of Educational Psychology, 93*, 55–65.
Clancy, M., & Tata, J. (2005). A global perspective on balancing work and family. *Inter-
    national Journal of Management, 22*(2), 234–241.
Cox, T. H., & Blake, S. (1991). Managing cultural diversity: Implications for organizational
    competitiveness. *Academy of Management Executive, 5*(3), 45–57.
Crosby, F. J. (1999). The developing literature on developmental relationships. In A. Murrell,
    F. Crosby, & R. Ely (Eds.), *Mentoring dilemmas* (pp. 3–20). Mahwah, NJ: Lawrence Erlbaum
    Associates.

Crosby, F. J., & Bearman, S. (2006). The uses of a good theory. *Journal of Social Issues, 62*, 415–438.

Curtis, J. W. (2004). Balancing work and family for faculty: Why it's important. *Academe, 90*(6), 21–24.

Dennen, V. P. (2004). Cognitive apprenticeship in educational practice: Research on scaffolding, modeling, mentoring, and coaching as instructional strategies. In D. H. Jonassen (Ed.), *Handbook of research on educational communications and technology* (2nd ed., pp. 813–828). Mahwah, NJ: Lawrence Erlbaum Associates.

Dreher, G. F., & Cox, T. H. (1996). Race, gender, and opportunity: A study of compensation attainment and the establishment of mentoring relationships. *Journal of Applied Psychology, 81*(2), 297–308.

DuBois, D. L., Holloway, B. E., Valentine, J. C., & Cooper, H. (2002). Effectiveness of mentoring for youth: A meta-analytic review. *American Journal of Community Psychology, 30*, 157–197.

Dutton, J. E., & Ragins, B. R. (2007). *Exploring positive relationships at work: Building a theoretical and research foundation.* Mahwah, NJ: Lawrence Erlbaum Associates.

Eby, L. T., McManus, S., Simon, S. A., & Russell, J. E. A. (2000). The protégé's perspective regarding negative mentoring experiences: The development of a taxonomy. *Journal of Vocational Behavior, 57*, 1–21.

Eddleston, K. A., Baldridge, D. C., & Veiga, J. F. (2004). Towards modeling the predictors of career success: Does gender matter? *Journal of Managerial Psychology, 19*(4), 360–385.

Fagenson, E. A. (1989). The mentor advantage: Perceived career/job experiences of protégés versus non-protégés. *Journal of Organizational Behavior, 10*, 309–320.

Gee, E. G. (2005). An investment in student diversity. *Trusteeship, 13*(2), 18–22.

Gergen, K. (1973). Social psychology as history. *Journal of Personality and Social Psychology, 26*, 309–320.

Gornick, M. (2005). A proactive approach to retaining "wisdom workers." *Benefits & Compensation Digest*, March, *42*(3), 18.

Granger, M. (1993). A review of the literature on the status of women and minorities in the professoriate in higher education. *Journal of School Leadership, 3*, 121–135.

Grossman, J. B., & Tierney, J. P. (1998). Does mentoring work? An impact study of the Big Brothers Big Sisters. *Evaluation Review, 22*, 403–426.

Hall, D. T. (1986). Career development in organizations: Where do we go from here? In D. T. Hall & Associates (Eds.), *Career development in organizations* (pp. 332–351). San Francisco: Jossey-Bass.

Hardy, L. C. (1998). Mentoring: A long term approach to diversity. *HR Focus*, July, S11.

Harrison, D. A., Price, K. H., & Bell, M. P. (1998). Beyond relational demography: Time and the effects of surface- and deep-level diversity on work group cohesion. *Academy of Management Journal, 41*, 96–107.

Hegstad, C. D., & Wentling, R. M. (2004). The development and maintenance of exemplary formal mentoring programs in fortune 500 companies. *Human Resource Development Quarterly, 15*(Winter), 421–448.

Herman, R. E., Olivo, T. G., & Gioia, J. L. (2003). *Impending crisis: Too many jobs, too few people.* Winchester, VA: Oakhill Press.

Herrera, C., Sipe, C., & McClanahan, W. S. (2000). *Mentoring school aged children: Relationship development in community-based and school-based programs.* Philadelphia: Public/Private Ventures.

Higgins, M. C., & Kram, K. (2001). Reconceptualizing mentoring at work: A developmental network perspective. *Academy of Management Review, 26*, 264–288.

Jacobi, M. (1991). Mentoring and undergraduate academic success: A review of the literature. *Review of Educational Research, 61*, 505–532.

Johnston, W., & Packer, A. (1987). *Workforce 2000: Work and workers for the 21st century.* Indianapolis, IN: Hudson Institute.

Jucovy, L. (2001). *Training new mentors.* Philadelphia: Public/Private Ventures.

Kram, K. E. (1985). *Mentoring at work: Developmental relationships in organizational life.* Glenview, IL: Scott, Foresman and Company.

Kuhn, T. S. (1970). *The structure of scientific revolutions.* Chicago: University of Chicago Press.

Kuhn, T. S. (1989/2000). The natural and the human sciences. In *The road since structure* (pp. 216–223). Chicago: University of Chicago Press.

Lave, J., & Wenger, E. (1991). *Situated learning: Legitimate peripheral participation.* New York: Cambridge University Press.

Lumina Foundation for Education (2002). *Enhancing student success. Annual report.* Indianapolis, IN: Lumina Foundation for Education.

Marasco, C. A. (2005a). Employment: MentorNet supports women in science. *Chemical & Engineering News, 83,* 38.

Marasco, C. A. (2005b). Women faculty make little progress. *Chemical & Engineering News, 83,* 38.

Mathews, J. (2004). Redefining scholarship: Search begins for college-bound "posse." *The Washington Post,* Metro Section, C1.

McGowan, E. M. (2004). *Relationship work: A descriptive theory of a faculty-to-faculty formal mentoring program in higher education.* Cambridge, MA: Harvard University.

Multon, K. D., Brown, S. D., & Lent, R. W. (1991). Relation of self-efficacy beliefs to academic outcomes: A meta-analytic investigation. *Journal of Counseling Psychology, 38,* 30–38.

Quine, W. V. O. (1969). Natural kinds. In *Ontological relativity and other essays* (pp. 114–138). New York: Columbia University Press.

Ragins, B. R., & McFarlin, D. B. (1990). Perceptions of mentor roles in cross-gender mentoring relationships. *Journal of Vocational Behavior, 37,* 321–339.

Rhodes, J. E. (2002b). *Stand by me: The risks and rewards of mentoring today's youth.* Cambridge, MA: Harvard University Press.

Rhodes, J. E. (2005). A theoretical model of youth mentoring. In D. L. DuBois & M. J. Karcher (Eds.), *Handbook of youth mentoring* (pp. 30–43). Thousand Oaks, CA: Sage.

Rogoff, B. (1990). *Apprenticeship in thinking: Cognitive development in social context.* New York: Oxford University Press.

Rogoff, B. (2003). *The cultural nature of human development.* Oxford: Oxford University Press.

Rogoff, B., Paradise, R., Arauz, R. M., Correa-Chávez, M., & Angelillo, C. (2003). Firsthand learning through intent participation. *Annual Review of Psychology, 54,* 175–203.

Scandura, T. A. (1992). Mentorship and career mobility: An empirical investigation. *Journal of Organizational Behavior,* 169–174.

Segal, J. A. (2005). Shatter the glass ceiling, dodge the shards. *HR Magazine,* April, 121–126.

Single, P. B., & Muller, C. B. (2001). When email and mentoring unite: The implementation of a nationwide mentoring program – MentorNet, the national electronic industrial mentoring network for women in engineering and science. In L. K. Stromei (Ed.), *Creating mentoring and coaching programs: Twelve case studies from the real world of training* (pp. 107–122). Alexandria, VA: American Society for Training and Development.

Sipe, C. L., & Roder, A. E. (1999). *Mentoring school-age children: A classification of programs.* Philadelphia: Public/Private Ventures.

Skinner, B. F. (1953). *Science and human behavior.* Oxford: Macmillan.

Stone, C. A. (1993). What is missing in the metaphor of scaffolding? In E. A. Forman, N. Minick, & C. A. Stone (Eds.), *Contexts for learning: Sociocultural dynamics in children's development* (pp. 169–183). New York: Oxford University Press.

Taylor, C. R. (2004). Retention leadership. *T&D,* March, 40–45.

Tenenbaum, H. R., Crosby, F. J., & Gliner, M. D. (2001). Mentoring relationships in graduate school. *Journal of Vocational Behavior, 59*, 326–341.

Thomas, D. A., & Ely, R. J. (2001). Making differences matter: A new paradigm for managing diversity. *Harvard Business Review, Sept/Oct*, 79–91.

Tierney, J. P., Grossman, J. B., & Resch, N. L. (2000). Making a difference: An impact study of big brothers big sisters. Philadelphia: Public Private Ventures.

Tomlinson, A. (2001, December 17). Concrete ceiling harder than glass to break for women of color. *Canadian HR Reporter*, pp. 7, 13.

Treston, H. (1999). Peer mentoring: Making a difference at James Cook University, Cairns – It's moments like these you need mentors. *Innovations in Education & Training International, 36*, 236–243.

Wanberg, C. R., Kammeyer-Mueller, J., & Marchese, M. (March, 2004). *Antecedents and outcomes of formal mentoring.* Paper presented at the Nineteenth Annual Meeting of the Society for Industrial and Organizational Psychology, Chicago, IL.

Whitely, W., Dougherty, T. W., & Dreher, G. F. (1991). Relationship of career mentoring and socioeconomic origin to managers' and professionals' early career progress. *Academy of Management Journal, 34*, 331–351.

Whyte, W. H. (1956). *The organization man.* New York: Simon and Schuster.

Wood, D., Bruner, J. S., & Ross, G. (1976). The role of tutoring in problem solving. *Journal of Child Psychology and Psychiatry, 17*, 89–100.

Zielinski, D. (2000). Mentoring up. *Training, October*, 136–140.

Chapter 24

Common Bonds: An Integrative View of Mentoring Relationships

Tammy D. Allen and Lillian T. Eby

As highlighted in this volume's previous chapters, the importance of mentoring relationships in developing individuals across the lifespan is well documented. Mentoring relationships have captured the attention of social scientists, communities, businesses, and the government (e.g., DuBois & Karcher, 2005; MENTOR/ National Mentoring Partnership, 2006; Rhodes, 2002b). Indeed, each January since 2002 has been designated as National Mentoring Month. The month-long outreach campaign has been designed to focus national attention on the power of mentoring and to encourage others to serve in this important role by including a Thank Your Mentor Day.

Our focus in this chapter is on identifying factors that are relevant to all mentoring relationships. In doing so, we develop a multidimensional, multilevel view of effective mentoring relationships in which fulfillment of the need to belong plays a central role. In the process of developing this framework, we examine areas of convergence, as well as points of departure, across the three areas of mentoring study discussed in this book: youth, student–faculty, and workplace mentoring. The overarching goal of this chapter is to develop a common framework for the study of mentoring that bridges the three mentoring research areas represented in this volume. This provides a fresh perspective on mentoring as well as an important integration of the mentoring literature. With such a foundation in place it will be easier to break down disciplinary silos, which should lead to a better appreciation and deeper understanding of mentoring relationships. We hope that the identification of cross-cutting themes in mentoring research and practice, and the corresponding development of a common lens by which to view mentoring relationships, will help unify the field of mentoring.

This chapter unfolds as follows. First we provide a definition of effective mentoring that focuses on fulfillment of the need to belong. This directly speaks to Bearman, Blake-Beard, Hunt, and Crosby's (this volume) plea to identify the mechanisms that account for successful mentoring relationships and development of causal models to

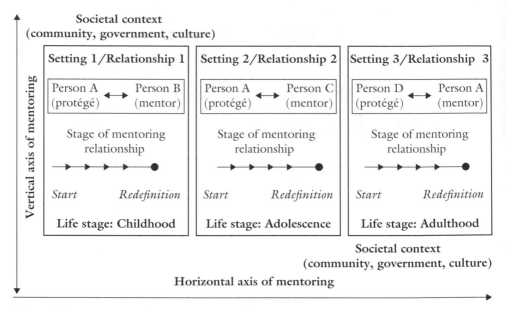

Figure 24.1 Horizontal and vertical axes of mentoring relationships

understand the effects of mentoring. Next we discuss what we refer to as the horizontal and vertical axes of mentoring, which are common across all types of mentoring relationships (see Figure 24.1). The horizontal axis is based on the developmental aspects of mentoring relationships and consists of two levels. One level references the developmental life stage of the individual (childhood, adolescence, adulthood) and the other level describes the developmental stage of the mentoring relationship (from start to redefinition). These two developmental levels are nested, as *mentoring relationships* exist within as well as across various *life stages*. For example, a mentoring relationship may occur when the protégé is in early adulthood and the mentor is in middle adulthood, and this relationship will progress through various stages. The vertical axis of mentoring reflects the four levels of context within which mentorships are embedded: individual, dyad, setting, and society. For example, a student–faculty mentoring relationship consists of *individuals* engaged in a *dyadic relationship* that exists within an academic *setting* in a particular *societal context*. Implications for fulfillment of the belongingness need are discussed throughout the presentation of the horizontal and vertical axes of mentoring. Integrative ideas regarding future research are also discussed as we summarize the horizontal and vertical axes of mentoring.

Fulfilling the Need to Belong and Effective Mentoring Relationships

The issue of defining a mentoring relationship is discussed throughout this volume (see especially Eby, Rhodes, & Allen) and thus is outside the scope of this chapter. Instead, we focus our attention on the defining characteristics of an *effective*

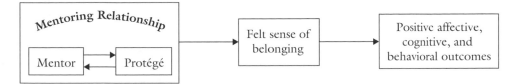

Figure 24.2   Belongingness model of mentoring relationships

mentoring relationship. We propose that the key hallmark of an effective mentorship is that it fulfills the "need to belong;" in other words, the need to form and maintain positive interpersonal relationships with others (Baumeister & Leary, 1995). The need to belong is fulfilled through affiliation and acceptance from others (Gardner, Pickett, & Brewer, 2000) and this is what makes mentoring relationships a powerful agent for individual growth and well-being. Our basic model is shown in Figure 24.2. As documented in Part IV of this volume, mentoring others has been associated with a variety of affective (e.g., life satisfaction), cognitive (e.g., self-esteem), and behavioral (e.g., school involvement) outcomes. We propose that fulfillment of the need to belong drives the relationship between mentoring and positive outcomes.

All types of mentoring relationships discussed in this volume have the potential to serve this role. Indeed, a mentoring program funded by the US Department of Education designed to help at-risk middle school students was given the title Project BELONG, which stands for Building Essential Life Options through New Goals (Blakely, Menon, & Jones, 1995). Our focus on the need to belong serves the purpose of identifying a concept that is universal to each of the areas of mentoring reviewed in this volume. It serves as a common underpinning process that unifies the mentoring literature and provides the basis for integrative research.

Baumeister and Leary (1995) propose that there are two main features associated with the need to belong. One is that an individual needs frequent interaction with the other person that is of a positive affective nature. The second is that the individual must perceive that the bond is marked by ongoing affective concern. Thus, an individual must believe that the relationship partner cares about his or her well-being and that the partner feels affection toward the individual. In situations where both of these criteria are met, there is a greater likelihood that the relationship will fulfill the belongingness need. Regardless of the type of mentoring relationship (youth, student–faculty, workplace), relational descriptors that are used to characterize successful mentorships focus on positive affective features of mentor–protégé interactions. Spencer, Jordan, and Sazama (2004) interviewed a diverse group of youth aged 7 to 18 years and found that youth placed a high value on respect, mutuality, and authenticity in their relationships with adults. Rhodes (2002b, 2005) identified mutuality, trust, and empathy as the keys to meaningful mentoring connections. A priority on creating an emotionally close and trusting relationship is also evident in the qualitative work of Morrow and Styles (1995; Styles & Morrow, 1992). Likewise, Ragins (this volume) notes that high-quality connections are those that involve feelings of vitality and aliveness, positive regard, and mutuality. Other workplace researchers also discuss how factors such as interpersonal comfort and trust are keys to mentoring relationship effectiveness (e.g., Allen, Day, & Lentz, 2005; Young & Perrewé, 2000b).

One of the key questions being asked in the mentoring literature at this time, and as reflected in the chapters in this volume (see Bearman et al., this volume, for a review and extension) is *why* mentoring relationships have the positive effects that they do. We suggest that fulfillment of the need to belong serves as a mechanism for positive outcomes (Karcher, Davis, & Powell, 2004). When protégés have this basic need met, they can develop self-esteem and feelings of personal competence, achieve in school, master work-related tasks, etc. Similarly, mentors can meet needs for belonging through mentoring others by experiencing "growth-in-connection" (Fletcher & Ragins, in press). This refers to the process by which basic human needs for affiliation are fulfilled by connecting with others through close relationships (Miller, 1976).

Support for viewing satisfaction of the need to belong as the catalyst for realizing beneficial mentoring outcomes can be drawn from each area of the existing mentoring literature. The effectiveness of formal youth mentoring programs has been attributed to the quality of the mentor–protégé relationship (e.g., Grossman & Rhodes, 2002). For example, as cited in Liang, Brogan, Corral, and Spencer (2005), Slicker and Palmer (1993) found no differences in grades or dropout rates between mentored and nonmentored high school students. However, when participants were differentiated by those who were effectively mentored versus those who were not, there was a significant improvement in achievement and return-to-school rates among those who had been effectively mentored. In a study of undergraduate student–faculty mentoring, LaRose, Tarabulsy, and Cyrenne (2005) found that students who reported strong feelings of relatedness following their mentoring relationships also reported better social adjustment. By contrast, those who reported weak feelings of relatedness were less adjusted and obtained lower grades. Finally, Ragins, Cotton, and Miller (2000) found that the characteristics of a formal workplace mentoring program were less important than the quality of the interaction with program mentors in determining the benefits that protégés accrued. In sum, a positive interpersonal connection between mentor and protégé is crucial to the effectiveness of the relationship.

Having established the need to belong as an underlying process in effective mentoring relationships, we now turn our attention to delineating the various dimensions associated with mentoring. We believe that these dimensions are unifying concepts applicable to all forms of mentoring relationships and that each has implications for meeting belongingness needs.

Horizontal Axis of Mentoring Relationships

The horizontal axis of mentoring concerns the developmental element of mentoring relationships, which is a common characteristic of all forms of mentoring. We view development as a normative, sequential process of maturation over time. As shown in Figure 24.1, there are two levels of development that are relevant to mentoring relationships. At the individual level is the developmental life stage of each mentoring partner (childhood, adolescence, adulthood). At the dyadic level is the developmental stage of the mentoring relationship (from start to redefinition). These two developmental aspects of mentoring are described in the following sections, with a focus on the role that belongingness plays in the developmental process of mentoring.

Developmental Life Stage

As shown in the chapters that comprise Part II of this volume, developmental theories are frequently used as a lens for understanding mentoring relationships. For example, youth mentoring researchers often reference Vygotsky's (1978) theory concerning the process of learning through social interaction (e.g., Keller, this volume; Rhodes, 2005). Johnson, Rose, and Schlosser (this volume) discusses Chickering's (1969) vector model of development as potentially useful for understanding student–faculty mentoring relationships. Levinson, Darrow, Klein, Levinson, and McKee's (1978) theory concerning adult development is also frequently cited in both the student– faculty and workplace literature (Johnson et al., this volume; Scandura & Pellegrini, this volume). Erikson's (1963, 1968) developmental stage theory has also been applied to workplace and youth mentoring (e.g., Ragins & Cotton, 1993; Rhodes, 2005).

Developmental theories suggest that individuals progress through relatively orderly periods of transition marked by specific developmental challenges (cf. Erikson, 1963, 1968; Levinson et al., 1978). During the transition periods an individual is particularly vulnerable and there is a danger that one's sense of belonging will be threatened. More specifically, if developmental transitions are not effectively navig ated individuals can feel isolated and socially disconnected. For example, failure to master the task of developing intimate relationships with others in early adulthood can lead to feelings of isolation and personal despair (Erikson, 1963).

Both Levinson's and Erikson's stage models are especially helpful in delineating the life stage aspect of mentoring relationships. These models are applicable to both protégés and mentors because individuals face developmental challenges throughout the life cycle, and the successful resolution of these challenges can often be facilit ated by effective mentoring relationships. Also consistent with both of these models, we propose that a given individual may engage in a series of mentoring relationships throughout his or her lifespan (see Figure 24.1). As the following discussion unfolds it is important to recognize that individuals may find themselves in both the pro tégé and mentor role simultaneously, perhaps across multiple life domains. For ex ample, a junior professor may be serving as a mentor to others within the bounds of a student–faculty mentorship while at the same time being mentored by a senior professor within the bounds of a workplace mentorship. This individual may also be serving as a volunteer mentor to an "at risk" youth as part of a community outreach program.

Infancy and early childhood.   Belongingness needs appear in infancy as babies act in ways to attract and sustain human contact. Erikson (1963) discusses the need to belong in infancy in terms of the developmental stage of *trust versus mistrust* (stage 1). During this stage infants are completely dependent upon their caregivers, and if their fundamental needs are met, a sense of trust develops which serves as the cor nerstone for later personality development. The need for social contact continues in early childhood and as a consequence children develop a sense of attachment with their primary caregivers (Bowlby, 1969). As children start to mature cognitively and emotionally they begin to develop a sense of how they fit into (belong) their family (Erikson, 1963). The challenge of figuring out one's unique role in the family and developing a sense of belongingness in the family is a fundamental developmental experience in the *initiative versus guilt* stage (stage 3) (Erikson, 1963). In infancy and early childhood, parents, nonfamily caregivers, and other family members are the primary role models and social referents. The types of mentoring relationships that are the focus of this volume are less relevant to this life stage, although early belongingness experiences are important to discuss because they influence one's close relationships later in life (Feeney, 1999; Kirkpatrick, 1999).

Middle childhood.   As individuals enter middle childhood their belongingness needs change. In the *industry versus inferiority* stage of Erikson's theory (stage 4), children must learn how to function socially outside their extended family and master challenges in their broader realm of school and society. Youth mentoring is valuable here as it can help children master challenging tasks, succeed in school, and develop effective social relationships (cf. Blinn-Pike, this volume). There is also considerable change in reasoning, social skills, and level of responsibility during this time period (cf. Weiten, 2005). Such rapid development may require adaptive skills on the part of the mentor to adjust to the child's changing needs (Keller, this volume).

Adolescence.   In adolescence, issues of belongingness center on fitting in with one's peer group. Erikson (1963) suggests that the primary issue here is *identity versus confusion* (stage 5) and belongingness is highly salient in this developmental stage. Several studies suggest that natural mentorships with nonrelated adults may occur with greater frequency as youth progress through adolescence (Beam, Chen, & Greenberger, 2002; Benson, 1993). Spencer (this volume) discusses the adolescence stage as a particularly important one where youth can greatly benefit from mentoring. She also notes that the relational processes associated with mentoring may differ across developmental time periods, a point echoed by Rhodes (2005). For example, in a study of youth in middle school, high school, and college, Liang et al. (2005) found that the different age groups tended to emphasize different aspects of the relationship. For example, older youth were more likely to emphasize mutuality within the relationship than were younger youth.

Early adulthood.   In Erikson's (1963) stage 6 the developmental transition is one of *intimacy versus isolation*, which also embodies belongingness. The task facing individuals here is developing close, intimate bonds with others. Erikson discusses this bonding primarily in terms of romantic relationships, but other types of relational bonding are also relevant during this time period. For example, during early adulthood individuals may be starting college or entering the world of work. These are new life experiences which require both detachments from one's parents and the forming of new social attachments. Student–faculty and workplace mentoring can meet young adults' need for belonging as they step out into these new arenas of life (Austin, 2002; Nagda, Gregerman, Jonides, von Hippel, & Lerner, 1998).

Interestingly, Johnson et al. (this volume) lament that there have been few efforts to investigate student–faculty mentoring in light of student developmental stages, tasks, or needs. This is important in that student needs and motivations evolve as they progress through their program of study. For example, Tinto (1993) described three stages of doctoral persistence, which include transition and adjustment, attaining candidacy, and completing the doctoral dissertation. Each of these stages requires different behaviors on the part of the mentor to help the protégé progress. Likewise, the workplace mentoring literature discusses how procuring the advice of a mentor is a critical step in a young adult's journey into adulthood (Levinson et al., 1978). It can also set in motion one's career trajectory, as evidenced by the relationship between mentoring received and both objective (e.g., pay, promotion rate) and subjective (e.g., career satisfaction) career success (cf. Allen, Eby, Poteet, Lentz, & Lima, 2004).

Middle to late adulthood.   Developmental theories suggest that the need to be mentored subsides later in life as the need to mentor others increases. This is consistent with normative societal expectations regarding roles and age in that it is assumed that older individuals need less mentoring support. For instance, older protégés in graduate school have been found to receive less professional development assistance than younger protégés (Wilde & Schau, 1991). Similarly, Finkelstein, Allen, and Rhoton (2003) found that older workplace protégés reported receiving less career mentoring than did younger protégés.

While the need to be mentored by others declines with age, belongingness needs do not. Erikson's theory proposes that in middle adulthood individuals must deal with *generativity versus self-absorption* (stage 7). The developmental tasks at this stage involve seeing that one has produced something of value and achieving a sense of immortality through others. Mentoring others is one way that this developmental challenge can be met (Kram, 1985; Levinson et al., 1978). In late adulthood the focus shifts to reflection on one's life and the assessment of whether or not one's life has meaning (Erikson's stage 8, *integrity versus despair*). Again, mentoring may be helpful in surmounting this transition. Through mentoring others, older individuals ensure the transfer and continuation of knowledge within organizations and help prepare junior organizational members for further responsibility (Kram & Hall, 1996). Finally, it is worth noting that Levinson's theory suggested that middle-aged individuals would be most willing to mentor others; however, this hypothesis has received little empirical support (Allen, Poteet, Russell, & Dobbins, 1997; Ragins & Cotton, 1993).

The intersection between life stage and relationship roles.   In discussing life stage as it relates to mentoring and the need to belong, it is important to recognize the different developmental needs of protégés and mentors. As has been noted previously, most mentoring research has focused on protégés. Individuals typically do not take on the role of mentor until they reach adulthood (there are exceptions such as cross-age peer mentoring between younger and older youth; see Karcher, 2005). Thus, as the life course unfolds individuals will be more likely to switch from the role of the protégé to the role of the mentor (see Figure 24.1 where Person A is a protégé in childhood and adolescence and then becomes a mentor in adulthood). This is supported by workplace research that indicates that those who have been mentored tend to go on to mentor others (e.g., Allen et al., 1997; Ragins & Cotton, 1993), reflecting a lifetime of mentoring activity.

Another important consideration is the developmental stage of the protégé *in comparison to* the mentor. It is generally thought that mentors need to be at a more advanced developmental stage in comparison to their protégés. For example, Levinson et al. (1978) noted that mentors should be 8–15 years older than their protégés. This is typically not an issue in youth mentoring relationships in which a considerable age difference between mentor and protégé is the norm. Age difference issues become more relevant in student–faculty relationships in which new faculty may be close in age to their protégés, and in workplaces in which older individuals make a career change and find themselves in the role of novice. Finkelstein et al.'s (2003) qualitative work revealed that concerns regarding mentor lack of experience and respect are issues for mentorships in which the protégé and mentor are similar in age. Clearly, these issues may detract from the quality of the relationship.

Developmental Stage of the Mentoring Relationship

Another developmental aspect common to all areas of mentoring research concerns the stages of the mentoring relationship (also see Bearman et al., this volume). That is, all mentoring relationships are thought to follow a natural progression. Although there are some differences across the three areas of study, there are general similarities in the models used to understand relationship stage. In her seminal qualitative research on workplace mentoring relationships, Kram (1985) suggested that mentoring relationships pass through four predictable stages: initiation, cultivation, separation, and redefinition (see Dougherty, Turban, & Haggard, this volume, for a review). Researchers investigating student–faculty mentoring relationships have also adopted Kram's stage model (Mullen, this volume). However, other stage models have also been developed to capture student–faculty mentoring. For example, O'Neil and Wrightsman (2001) described six stages of graduate student–faculty mentoring relationships, but did not tie them to specific time periods. Recently Keller (2005a) proposed a stage model of the development of the youth mentoring relationship, but he did not associate specific time periods with each of these stages. His model consists of five stages: contemplation, initiation, growth and maintenance, decline and dissolution, redefinition. Notably, in developing his model, Keller drew upon Hinde's (1997) work on periods of change during the course of relationships and Fehr's (2000) work on the life cycle of friendship. The stages of a mentoring relationship are inextricably tied with the issue of relationship duration. Thus, in the next section we consider research on relationship stage and relationship duration as related to belongingness.

Belongingness issues associated with relationship stage and duration. It seems likely that belongingness plays a key role in determining the course of a mentoring relationship. The degree that the mentoring relationship holds promise for a satisfying mentor protégé connection can influence whether or not the relationship progresses past the initial stage. A mentoring relationship that does not fulfill relatedness needs is likely to be discontinued or lead to dissatisfactory outcomes. A mentoring relationship that does provide participants with a sense of belonging is more likely to flourish and continue through the various developmental stages. The difficulty inherent in dissolving mentoring relationships, including those that may be considered dysfunctional, is also consistent with the belongingness hypothesis. Distress in response to the end of a relationship has been described as a nearly universal human tendency (Hazan & Shaver, 1994). Mentorship-specific research also indicates that termination of mentoring relationships is difficult (Clark, Harden, & Johnson, 2000).

Research regarding dysfunctional aspects of mentoring also points to the importance of belongingness. Eby, McManus, Simon, and Russell (2000) identified mentor neglect as the most common form of relationship dysfunction. This refers to mentoring experiences in which the protégé feels emotionally cut-off and neglected by his or her mentor. In other words, in this type of dysfunction belongingness needs are not met. Furthermore, Eby, Butts, Lockwood, and Simon (2004) found that mentor neglect was higher in the separation phase of mentoring than in other phases, suggesting that when protégés' needs for belongingness are not met, they may be more likely to exit the mentorship.

It is uncertain what length of time is needed for a relationship to mature into one that can meet individual needs such as belongingness and how well specific periods of time conform to the specific stages suggested by researchers. For instance, Spencer (this volume) discusses how the stages of a youth mentorship may differ for different types of mentors. Keller (2005a) also notes that mentoring relationships with extended family members may not as clearly pass through the contemplation and initiation stages proposed in his model. One consistency across the areas of mentoring research is that there has been limited empirical study of relationship phases. The few studies that exist have found mixed support for various stage models of mentoring (cf. Chao, 1997 and Bouquillon, Sosik, & Lee, 2005).

The extent that mentorship stages are tied to precise time frames is also unclear. Moreover, it seems likely that the time lengths within stages are accelerated for some relationships. Workplace mentoring research generally shows that formal mentoring is less effective than is naturally occurring mentoring, but better than no mentoring (Wanberg, Welsh, & Hezlett, 2003). One of the reasons why formal mentorships may be less effective is that they often have an established time limit that likely accelerates the cycling through of stages. For example, workplace formal mentoring programs are often structured to last 6 months or 1 year. This can clearly affect the nature in which the relationship develops and the needs that can be met by the relationship. For example, there may be some hesitation to form a close bond with someone in a situation in which the expectation is that the relationship will last for only a short time. Additionally, participants in short-term formally arranged mentoring relationships may feel the need to progress rapidly through the initiation phase and thus the mentoring partners may skip or rush through some of the important elements of getting to know someone that facilitates a close bond. This is relevant given that developing close relationships with others takes time (Sternberg, 1986) and belongingness needs are more likely to be met in relationships marked by intimacy, mutuality, and trust.

In addition to limited research support regarding evidence of distinct phases of mentoring relationships, there is mixed evidence regarding the relationship between duration of the mentorship and benefits realized. For example, Rhodes (2002b) indicates that short-term mentoring relationships that end prematurely can reduce youth feelings of self-worth and academic competence. To this point, Grossman and

Rhodes (2002) found that adolescents in formal mentoring relationships that lasted at least a year reported the greatest number of improvements. Fewer positive effects were found among youth who were in relationships that ended earlier, and youth who were in relationships that terminated within the first six months actually suffered significant declines in functioning. In a longitudinal study of adolescent mothers, Klaw, Rhodes, and Fitzgerald (2003) found that 35% of those who had mentoring relationships that lasted for at least 2 years dropped out of high school, compared with 48% of mothers who were in mentoring relationships that terminated sooner than 2 years in duration, and 64% of mothers who reported not having a mentor. On the other hand, it should be noted that in a meta-analytic review of youth mentoring programs, DuBois, Holloway, Valentine, and Cooper (2002) found no evidence that the length of the relationship made a difference in the outcomes realized.

There is scant research examining mentorship phases and duration from the perspective of the mentor; however, Grossman and Rhodes (2002) found that characteristics of the mentor were associated with mentorship duration. Volunteer mentors with higher incomes tended to be in longer-term matches than did lower-income volunteers. Additionally, married volunteers aged 26–30 were more likely to terminate their relationships early.

Summary

The horizontal axis of mentoring simultaneously considers the role of both individual development (developmental life stage) and relationship development (relationship stage and duration) in understanding the three types of mentoring relationships discussed in this volume. The developmental life stage aspect recognizes that while the need for belongingness exists from infancy to adulthood, the particular issues of relevance to mentoring vary across the lifespan. This suggests several ways that our knowledge of mentoring relationships could be extended.

Specifically, life stage likely plays a part in determining the saliency of belongingness needs. For example, individuals can be particularly vulnerable to isolation during periods of developmental transition. Identifying the specific developmental needs of individuals at different life stages and how these needs influence various aspects of the mentoring relationship could help in tailoring the design and delivery of formal mentoring programs, as well as the recruitment of mentors into these programs. Additionally, it would be informative to examine individuals' mentoring histories across time to assess how the dynamics of mentoring relationships at early developmental life stages influence the dynamics of mentoring relationships at later developmental stages.

The developmental relationship stage aspect of mentoring acknowledges that mentorships develop through various phases and that time in the relationship influences relational processes and outcomes. This leads to important questions that should be examined in an effort to move the field forward, such as the extent that there are in fact universal, orderly stages associated with mentoring relationships, the extent that belongingness needs are more or less relevant at various stages of the mentoring relationship, how belongingness needs relate to relationship duration, and whether there are fundamental differences in relationship phases as a function of the type of mentoring relationship (youth, student–faculty, workplace; formal versus informal). Finally, research that examines the intersection between life stage and relationship stage may yield greater insight into the varying needs and motivations of protégés and mentors across time. For example, it may be that individuals in certain life stages require mentorships of a longer duration in order to fulfill belongingness needs. In the next section we discuss the vertical axis of mentoring, which takes into consideration the various contexts in which mentoring relationships exist.

The Vertical Axis of Mentoring

One limitation of existing theories of mentoring is that there is little recognition of the multiple contexts within which mentoring relationships operate. We propose that mentoring relationships can be examined from four different levels of analysis, representing distinct contexts: individual, dyadic, setting, and society. Each level is situated within the other levels; individuals are nested within dyads, dyads are nested within settings, and settings are nested within society (see Figure 24.1). We acknowledge that although all mentoring relationships occur within these multiple levels, different levels are more or less relevant for some types of mentorships than others. Some of these differences are highlighted in the subsequent sections.

In this section we discuss the role of belongingness at each specific level of analysis and summarize pertinent mentoring research to illustrate how a multilevel perspective on the vertical axis can inform mentoring theory. By far, the majority of mentoring research and theory has focused attention on the individual level. Additionally, the primary emphasis has been on the protégé, which is reflected in most of the chapters in this volume.

Individual Level

The need to belong is a core individual need that drives emotional, cognitive, and behavioral responses and therefore it is an individual-level attribute. Although belonging is thought to be a fundamental human need, it is likely that there is individual variability in the need for belonging. In particular, Baumeister and Leary (1995) suggest that the form, intensity, and stability of the need to belong vary among individuals. The belongingness hypothesis suggests that people strive to achieve a certain minimum number and quality of social contacts. Beyond the minimum, the motivation to develop further relationships to fulfill the need to belong is reduced (Baumeister & Leary, 1995). Applied to mentoring theory, this suggests that mentoring relationships are most important for those who do not have other forms of satisfying interpersonal bonds. Examples may include youth from troubled family situations, first-generation college students who lack role models, and women and minorities in the workplace who have limited access to social networks. Therefore, the belongingness hypothesis suggests that individuals possess characteristics that may influence the likelihood that mentoring will occur (i.e., whether or not the belongingness need is salient and acted upon) as well as whether or not a mentoring relationship will be effective (i.e., whether or not the need for belonging will be fulfilled).

Individual differences in the experience of mentoring.   There are various individual-level attributes that influence whether or not individuals have the opportunity to have their belongingness needs met through mentoring. Moreover, there are fundamental differences in the type of individual that is likely to be mentored across various types of mentoring. With regard to youth mentoring, traditionally much of the focus has been on programs designed to help those "at risk" for difficulties (Keller, this volume), although there is growing movement toward positive youth development where the focus is on fostering competencies among youth rather than trying to remedy deficits (Keller, this volume; Rhodes, Grossman, & Roffman, 2002). In contrast, within the student–faculty and workplace literatures, those who are mentored are more likely to come from populations that might be considered as privileged. The focus in the student–faculty literature has been on undergraduate and graduate school populations. Typically, individuals who attend college are at a healthy level of functioning and are by definition well educated. Nonetheless, formal programs developed within educational institutions often target populations such as minorities that are "at risk" of attrition (see Campbell, this volume). Formal workplace mentoring programs have varied goals such as the development of those identified as high potentials or the development of women and minorities who may have less exposure to networking activities needed to gain access to higher-level organizational positions. Moreover, much of the workplace mentoring literature has focused on samples that consist of professional and managerial groups of employees. Individuals in blue-collar-type jobs are rarely investigated. Taken together, this suggests that the experience of mentoring may be more likely for certain types of individuals than for others.

There are also individual differences in the characteristics of those who choose to take on this important role. This is a major issue across all three mentoring areas as the need for mentors is substantial. One of the most significant challenges in youth mentoring is attracting and retaining qualified adult mentors (Stukas & Tanti, 2005). To understand the individual characteristics that influence the decision to mentor others, researchers in the youth mentoring literature are using conceptual frameworks based on volunteerism (Stukas & Tanti, 2005). Similarly, in the workplace literature, mentoring others has been viewed as a form of prosocial behavior (e.g., Allen, 2003). In the student–faculty literature, mentoring others is viewed more as a part of the faculty member's job (Austin, 2002). However, it seems likely that some faculty members take their role as mentor more seriously and engage in greater mentoring activity than do others.

Notwithstanding the different paradigms used to understand why individuals mentor others, there appear to be similarities in the dispositions and motives underlying this behavior. For instance, empathy has been found to relate to mentoring behavior in both the youth (Karcher & Lindwall, 2003) and the workplace (Allen, 2003) mentoring literature. Moreover, multiple motives for mentoring others with overlapping themes have been identified in the youth (Philip & Hendry, 2000) and the workplace (Allen, 2003; Allen, Poteet, & Burroughs, 1997) literatures. As noted by Keller (this volume), motivations for mentoring youth may differ among formal and informal mentors. Johnson et al. (this volume) also notes that research regarding prosocial or organizational citizenship behaviors may be useful for understanding faculty mentoring behavior. In a study of volunteer mentors of community programs geared toward helping lone parents, Cox (2000) found that individuals had different motives for volunteering. Specifically, 23 of 52 volunteers could be classified as altruistic, 22 career-oriented, and 6 compensatory. The career-oriented were most likely to successfully complete the program. In sum, it seems likely that mentor motives will relate to the extent that their own belongingness needs are met by a mentoring relationship and to the extent that their behaviors contribute to fulfilling the needs of their protégés.

Individual differences in social connectedness. Social connectedness reflects an internal sense of belonging and is a highly personalized, subjective awareness of being in close relationship with the social world (Lee & Robbins, 1998). A lack of connection with others has been described as a serious and pervasive social problem that can have detrimental psychological health consequences for the individual (Baumeister & Leary, 1995; Baumeister & Tice, 1990; Lee & Robbins, 1998; Prager & Buhrmester, 1998). This is consistent with the notion that affiliation with others allows at-risk populations to feel good about themselves and boosts self-image (e.g., Graziano & Musser, 1982).

Mentoring relationships can be an important social connection that provides a protective buffer to help individuals "maintain a sense of self." As noted by King, Vidourek, Davis, and McClellan (2002), the overarching goal of most youth mentoring programs is to reduce risky behavior while connecting the youth with someone who can serve as a positive role model. Similarly, Larose et al. (2005) suggest that mentoring facilitates the development of feelings of relatedness that can help academically at-risk students adjust to the transition to college. Parallels can be found in the workplace mentoring literature as mentoring is discussed as a way to help socialize new employees into an organization (Ostroff & Kozlowski, 1993).

Positive social connections through mentoring can influence important individual outcomes. With regard to youth, research has shown that a sense of positive connections with others protects youth from engaging in risky health behaviors (King et al., 2002). King et al. (2002) found that fourth-grade students who were part of a school-based mentoring program reported greater connectedness scores than did students in the nonmentored control group. Additionally, students assessed at post-intervention were less likely to engage in risky behavior such as weapon carrying and substance use than they were pre-intervention. Belonging is important to consider at the individual level within the context of student–faculty mentoring relationships because it has been associated with motivation in school. Enhanced sense of belonging in school has been associated with positive academic outcomes and less school absenteeism (e.g., Goodenow, 1993; Sanchez, Colon, & Esparza, 2005). Finally, mentoring has been discussed as a buffer of individual-level stress in the workplace (Kram & Hall, 1989; Sosik & Godshalk, 2000a) and the student–faculty (Larose et al., 2005) literature.

Dyad Level

The dyad level focuses on the mentoring pair as a unit. The hallmark of a close relationship is a shared sense of belongingness – a strong, mutual sense of connection between two individuals. A shared sense of belongingness (e.g., interconnectedness, mutuality, shared goals, reciprocity, sense of obligation to one another) is discussed in the social-psychological literature on close relationships (e.g., Huston & Burgess, 1979; Scanzoni, 1979) and the extent that both members of a dyad have a sense of belonging or are able to fulfill this basic need to affiliate determines relational depth and sustainability.

These ideas have been repeatedly applied to mentoring. O'Neil and Wrightsman (2001) note that important relationship qualities found in student–faculty mentoring include degree of mutuality or reciprocity, comprehensiveness or breadth of the relationships, and congruence (match between mentor and protégé needs and values). As another illustration, the approach that faculty mentors take to doctoral training can influence the extent that the mentorship is characterized by a shared sense of belongingness. In situations where faculty members approach the relationship as if graduate students exist to serve their own research needs, a sense of shared belongingness is not likely to emerge. In contrast, when faculty members view their role as one that should serve graduate students, the relationship may be more likely to be marked by a sense of mutual belongingness. Student–faculty researchers have invoked the concept of the working alliance to emphasize the notion that student–faculty relationships should be characterized by cooperation, mutuality, and collaboration (Schlosser & Gelso, 2001). The working alliance approach facilitates shared fulfillment of the belongingness need in that it reflects the connection between student and faculty member that results in collaboration toward common goals. Taken together, this suggests that there are strong dyadic factors at play which influence the likelihood that both members of the dyad will have their respective needs to belong fulfilled.

Considering the mentoring relationship at the dyadic level and the way in which belongingness factors into the relationship challenges some aspects of current thinking on mentoring relationships. For example, much of mentoring research in the workplace has been based on social exchange theory. Yet research has shown that indices of relationship costs are not consistently associated with ratings of relationship quality (Clark & Grote, 1998). An alternative view to social exchange is that people prefer to be in relationships characterized by mutuality. Communal relationships are relationships in which members feel a responsibility for meeting the needs of their relationship partners and in which the benefits provided to partners are not based on contingencies (e.g., Clark & Mills, 1979; Mills, Clark, Ford, & Johnson, 2004). Communal strength is characterized by the degree of costs or sacrifices the individual is willing to incur in order to benefit the other. Moreover, communal strength is also based on distress in not meeting needs. But perhaps social exchange and mutuality perspectives are not exclusive. One could argue that the primary "benefit" in a relationship is mutual fulfillment of the need to belong. If this need is not met for both individuals, commitment lessens and the relationship declines or dissolves. Regardless, the idea of mutuality within a relationship is consistent with the view that belongingness is the primary driver of positive mentoring outcomes.

Setting

The setting level focuses on the immediate context in which the mentoring relationship is enacted. For workplace and student–faculty mentoring relationships, the setting is clear. Workplace mentoring relationships occur within employment settings and student–faculty mentoring relationships occur within academic institutions. By contrast, there is considerable variability in the settings in which youth mentoring relationships occur (Rhodes, 2005). For example, formal mentoring youth programs take place within community agencies such as Big Brothers Big Sisters. Both formal and naturally occurring mentorships may occur through faith-based organizations where the setting is a church, synagogue, or mosque (Maton, Sto. Domingo, & King, 2005). Schools also can serve as a setting for youth mentoring for after-school programs. In discussing the setting, it is important to recognize that there are multiple layers within most organizational structures. As an example, within academia subspecialties (clinical psychology, organizational psychology) are embedded within departments, which are embedded within colleges, which are embedded within the specific university, which are embedded within the university system. Although we believe that each of these layers can influence the processes that occur in mentoring relationships, for the sake of parsimony we confine our discussion to the general rubric of the larger setting within which the mentoring relationship resides (e.g., school, organization).

Organized social structures (schools, communities, organizations) are important contributors to belongingness by providing members with a sense that they are part of something bigger than themselves. Individuals are "loyal" to and feel a sense of "place" in their school/academic institution, community, and organization because these social structures fulfill a need to belong and provide a sense of psychological safety to individuals. To illustrate, one could look at the literature on social embeddedness within organizational settings (e.g., Mitchell, Sablynski, Burton, & Holtom, 2004), organizational commitment (Allen & Meyer, 1996), and psychological sense of community (Sarason, 1974). In a similar way, college and graduate school can fulfill a need to belong and provide a place where individuals find a path, which helps them develop a sense of professional identity (Austin, 2002). Likewise, as individuals enter the workplace they may find that the organization and/or professional affiliations help crystallize their sense of belonging. Workplaces and academic institutions that facilitate formal mentoring programs can also foster the psychological sense of community that contributes to a felt sense of belongingness.

The setting is important to consider because it is likely to play some role in all aspects of the mentoring process, which in turn may influence whether or not belongingness needs are met through mentoring. For example, the setting itself may influence the decision to become a mentor (Keller, this volume). Similarly, aspects of an academic environment may be more or less conducive to the formation of effective mentoring relationships. As discussed by Johnson et al. (this volume), Clark et al. (2000) found that students who attended a traditional PhD program reported receiving more mentoring than did those who attended a practice-based PsyD program. Although we are not aware of research addressing this issue, it may be that smaller liberal arts colleges provide a greater opportunity for undergraduate student–faculty mentoring relationships to flourish than do larger research-oriented university settings where greater emphasis is placed on graduate education and research productivity than on teaching.

Although it has been recognized that the organization is important, within the workplace literature little research has been conducted on this issue (see Dougherty, Turban, & Haggard, this volume). A few workplace studies have examined how aspects of the organizational setting can influence mentoring behaviors. Allen (2004) demonstrated that organizational rewards for mentoring others related to the likelihood that mentors reported selecting high-potential employees as protégés. Aryee, Chay, and Chew (1996) found that the extent that the organization rewarded the development of junior employees related to the individuals' motivation to mentor others in the future. Finally, Eby, Lockwood, and Butts (2006) found that mentor and protégé perceptions of organizational support for mentoring influenced the quality of mentoring relationship (as reported by both mentors and protégés) and mentors' willingness to mentor in the future.

In the case of formal mentoring programs, the setting is critical because it establishes the stage for the mission, philosophy, and structure of the program (see Part VI of this volume), which in turn influences relational dynamics. For example, Herrera, Sipe, and McClanahan (2000) compared the characteristics of school-based youth mentoring programs versus community-based programs. School-based programs tend to focus more on academic activities while community-based programs focus more on social activities. Accordingly, it is possible that school-based programs provide less of an opportunity for the fulfillment of belongingness needs. Likewise, doctoral programs housed in universities that fail to reward faculty mentoring accomplishments may set the stage for dissatisfactory student–faculty mentoring relationships.

Society

The final level considered is that of society, in which we include the community where the mentoring parties reside, government, and culture. These three could be considered nested within each other, but for parsimony we consider all under the same umbrella.

Society at large plays a stabilizing role in individuals' lives and contributes to the fulfillment of belongingness needs. A sense of belongingness emerges as individuals with similar core characteristics in society bolster their self-esteem and self-identity through a sense of belonging with a particular social or cultural group. Durkheim's (1947, 1951) classic sociological work on *anomie* discussed how the lack of integration and connection among individuals, families, and communities contributes to a collective sense of isolation and normlessness in modern society. Merton (1957) also noted that the breakdown in social and cultural structure contributes to a sense of anomie. Psychologists have examined anomie as an individual rather than societal phenomenon, suggesting that it reflects "a psychological state which refers to the individual's generalized pervasive sense of self-to-others belonging . . . compared to self-to-others distance" (Srole, 1956, pp. 63–67).

The notion that society creates conditions that can influence individuals' sense of belongingness has been an impetus for many youth mentoring programs. Rhodes et al. (2002) discusses how changes in family structure, work demands, and community structure have led to greater numbers of children living in low-income families with smaller kinship networks and less parental contact. Likewise, Karcher et al. (2004) remark how changes in society such as disbursed family structures have contributed to a growing sense of disconnection among youth, which leads to a void to be filled by mentoring. Money is invested in government-sponsored mentoring programs because of the belief that there will be benefits not only to the individuals who are mentored but also to the community. As noted by Keller (this volume), youth mentoring has also been used as a tool for implementing social policy. That is, mentoring can be used as a mechanism for exerting social control.

Another way that society influences mentoring involves the availability of mentors for youth. Spencer (this volume) attributes the decline of available adults who can serve as natural mentors to youth to less cohesive communities. Furthermore, Keller (this volume) notes that some communities may be rich in role models while those communities that are often most in need of adult role models are those that are lacking in models. He further suggests that community factors such as size, population demographics, residential stability, and economic vitality may influence the rate of formal and informal mentoring.

Governments also play an important role in determining the prevalence of mentoring in terms of the funding they provide. Federally funded research programs designed to increase the number of students pursuing Science, Technology, Engineering, and Mathematics (STEM) careers include mentoring components. A report issued by the Government Accounting Office (GAO) (2005) indicated that mentoring was a key factor that influenced the decision of women and minorities to pursue STEM degrees. Specifically, a lack of role models and mentors has been cited as adversely affecting the pipeline and career path of women entering STEM fields. Funding from government agencies also determines the prevalence and form of mentoring programs within community-based agencies. For example, Congress appropriated $991.07 million for after-school programs in the 2005 fiscal year (US Department of Education, 2006).

Culture is another aspect of society that can influence the sense of belonging in society. A feeling of falling outside the mainstream of society puts individuals at risk for crime and other problems. The riots that occurred among the immigrant communities in France during October and November of 2005 illustrate the dangers of perceiving a lack of belonging to society. The riots are thought to have been fueled by the fact that minorities felt they were voiceless and disenfranchised by the French government (Valentine, 2005). Moreover, cultures that marginalize certain segments of society create conditions that threaten marginalized groups' sense of place within society and minimize their contribution to broader societal goals. This creates an unequal playing field in terms of access to important resources (e.g., housing, high-quality education, career opportunities) and perpetuates the marginalized status of certain groups. Mentoring initiatives in community, educational, and workplace settings often target marginalized populations in an effort to foster social justice among various cultural groups (see Blinn-Pike, this volume; Campbell, this volume; Finkelstein & Poteet, this volume).

Although culture often plays a role in identifying targets for mentoring programs, the impact of culture on mentoring relationships has been rarely studied (see Part V of this volume). We are only beginning to try to understand the effects of culture on mentoring relationships. Culture can have an impact on individual, dyadic, and setting processes. As described by Sedlacek, Benjamin, Schlosser, and Sheu (this volume), individuals in certain cultures may be more or less inclined to engage in a mentoring relationship. This is consistent with Baumeister and Leary's (1995) suggestion that culture influences the nature, strength, and stability of the need to belong.

Summary

The vertical axis of mentoring acknowledges that mentoring relationships exist in, and are influenced by, forces at the individual, dyad, setting, and societal level. Factors at each of these levels can influence the occurrence and course of mentoring, which in turn can influence how individuals feel connected to their environment. Moving the field forward will require examination of various issues related to the proposed vertical axis of mentoring. At the individual level this might include examining how the need to belong influences motives for engaging in mentoring as a protégé and as a mentor. At the dyadic level the issues center on efforts to understand how a shared sense of belonging within the mentor–protégé dyad may influence relational processes and outcomes such as overall effectiveness, relational depth, and sustainability. Because the behaviors of the mentor and the protégé are influenced by each other, more studies that include data at the dyadic level are critically needed in order to increase our understanding of both independent and joint effects on mentorship effectiveness. In terms of the setting, pressing questions focus on how the setting influences the likelihood that individuals' need for belonging are met and the specific aspects of the setting that provide an environment in which mentoring relationships can flourish. Finally, in terms of the societal context it seems important to explore how characteristics of the community and presiding government influence opportunities for mentoring to occur. Cross-cultural issues are also important to examine as one's culture establishes powerful norms related to interpersonal interactions (Weiten, 2005). Comparative cross-cultural research is also needed. As discussed by Miller (this volume), we cannot assume that formal mentoring programs that are successful in one culture will transfer or generalize to other cultures.

Conclusion

The research assembled in this book highlights the numerous benefits associated with the promotion of effective mentoring relationships among individuals at all developmental stages of life. In this chapter we synthesized some of the knowledge that exists across different mentoring contexts, examined factors that unify mentoring across the three main areas of study, and proposed ways to move the field forward. In so doing, we drew from the various substantive chapters in the present volume and extended Bearman et al.'s suggestions for future research in the preceding chapter by proposing an integrative model of mentoring. We do not contend that our approach captures all aspects of mentoring relationships. However, we believe it is a parsimonious beginning toward the development of models that can further establish the common bonds of all mentoring relationships. Although the concept of mentoring is often traced back to the early Greeks, relative to other areas of scientific inquiry the study of mentoring is still in the early stages. A great deal remains to be learned and we believe that much of this learning can occur through efforts by researchers studying mentoring from multiple perspectives. We hope we have woven the beginning strands of connective fiber that will continue to grow into a network of interconnections between the research domains of mentoring.

References

Allen, N. J., & Meyer, J. P. (1996). Affective, continuance, and normative commitment: An examination of construct validity. *Journal of Vocational Behavior, 49,* 252–276.

Allen, T. D. (2003). Mentoring others: A dispositional and motivational approach. *Journal of Vocational Behavior, 62,* 134–154.

Allen, T. D. (2004). Protégé selection by mentors: Contributing individual and organizational factors. *Journal of Vocational Behavior, 65,* 469–483.

Allen, T. D., Day, R., & Lentz, E. (2005). The role of interpersonal comfort in mentoring relationships. *Journal of Career Development, 31,* 155–169.

Allen, T. D., Eby, L. T., Poteet, M. L., Lentz, E., & Lima, L. (2004). Career benefits associated with mentoring protégés: A meta-analysis. *Journal of Applied Psychology, 89,* 127–136.

Allen, T. D., Poteet, M. L., & Burroughs, S. (1997). The mentor's perspective: A qualitative inquiry and agenda for future research. *Journal of Vocational Behavior, 57,* 70–89.

Allen, T. D., Poteet, M. L., Russell, J. E. A., & Dobbins, G. H. (1997). A field study of factors related to supervisors' willingness to mentor others. *Journal of Vocational Behavior, 50,* 1–22.

Aryee, S., Chay, Y. W., & Chew, J. (1996). The motivation to mentor among managerial employees in the maintenance career stage: An interactionist's perspective. *Group and Organization Management, 21,* 261–277.

Austin, A. E. (2002). Preparing the next generation of faculty. *Journal of Higher Education, 73,* 94–122.

Baumeister, R. F., & Leary, M. R. (1995). The need to belong: Desire for interpersonal attachments as a fundamental human emotion. *Psychological Bulletin, 117,* 497–529.

Baumeister, R. F., & Tice, D. M. (1990). Anxiety and social exclusion. *Journal of Social and Clinical Psychology, 9,* 165–195.

Beam, M. R., Chen, C., & Greenberger, E. (2002). The nature of adolescents' relationships with their "very important" nonparental adults. *American Journal of Community Psychology, 30,* 305–325.

Benson, P. (1993). *The troubled journey: A portrait of 6th–12th grade youth.* Minneapolis, MN: The Search Institute.

Blakely, C. H., Menon, R., & Jones, D. J. (1995). *Project BELONG: Final report.* College Station, TX: Texas A&M University, Public Policy Research Institute.

Bouquillon, E. A., Sosik, J. J., & Lee, D. (2005). It's only a phase: Examining trust, identification and mentoring functions received across the mentoring phases. *Mentoring and Tutoring, 13,* 239–258.

Bowlby, J. (1969). *Attachment and loss: Vol. 1. Attachment.* New York: Basic Books.

Chao, G. T. (1997). Mentoring phases and outcomes. *Journal of Vocational Behavior, 51,* 15–28.

Chickering, A. W. (1969). *Education and identity.* San Francisco: Jossey-Bass.

Clark, M. S., & Grote, N. K. (1998). Why aren't indices of relationship costs always negatively related to indices of relationship quality? *Personality and Social Psychology Review, 2,* 2–17.

Clark, M. S., & Mills, J. (1979). Interpersonal attraction in exchange and communal relationships. *Journal of Personality and Social Psychology, 37,* 12–24.

Clark, R. A., Harden, S. L., & Johnson, W. B. (2000). Mentor relationships in clinical psychology doctoral training: Results of a national survey. *Teaching of Psychology, 27,* 262–268.

Cox, E. R. J. (2000). The call to mentor. *Career Development International, 5,* 2002–210.

DuBois, D. L., & Karcher, M. J. (2005). *Handbook of youth mentoring.* Thousand Oaks, CA: Sage.

DuBois, D. L., Holloway, B. E., Valentine, J. C., & Cooper, H. (2002). Effectiveness of mentoring programs for youth: A meta-analytic review. *American Journal of Community Psychology, 30,* 157–197.

Durkheim, E. (1947). *The division of labor in society.* New York: The Free Press.

Durkheim, E. (1951). *Suicide* (John A. Spaulding & George Simpson, Trans.). New York: The Free Press.

Eby, L. T., Butts, M., Lockwood, A., & Simon, S. A. (2004). Protégés' negative mentoring experiences: Construct development and nomological validation. *Personnel Psychology, 57,* 411–447.

Eby, L. T., Lockwood, A., & Butts, M. (2006). Organizational support for mentoring: A multiple perspectives approach. *Journal of Vocational Behavior, 68,* 267–291.

Eby, L. T., McManus, S. E., Simon, S. A., & Russell, J. E. A. (2000). The protégé's perspective regarding negative mentoring experiences: The development of a taxonomy. *Journal of Vocational Behavior, 57,* 1–21.

Erikson, E. H. (1963). *Childhood and society.* New York: W.W. Norton and Company Inc.

Erikson, E. H. (1968). *Identity, youth, and crisis.* New York: Faber.

Feeney, J. A. (1999). Adult romantic attachment and couple relationships. In J. Cassidy & P. R. Shaver (Eds.), *Handbook of attachment: Theory, research and clinical applications* (pp. 355–377). New York: Guilford.

Fehr, B. (2000). The life cycle of friendship. In C. Hendrick & S. S. Hendrick (Eds.), *Close relationships: A sourcebook* (pp. 71–82). Thousand Oaks, CA: Sage.

Finkelstein, L. M., Allen, T. D., & Rhoton, L. (2003). An examination of the effects of age diversity in mentoring relationships. *Group & Organization Management, 28,* 249–281.

Fletcher, J. K., & Ragins, B. R. (in press). Stone Center Relational Theory: A window on relational mentoring. In B. R. Ragins & K. E. Kram (Eds.), *The handbook of mentoring at work: Theory, research and practice.* Thousand Oaks, CA: Sage.

Gardner, W. L., Pickett, C. L., & Brewer, M. B. (2000). Social exclusion and selective memory: How the need to belong influences memory for social events. *Personality and Social Psychology Bulletin, 26,* 486–496.

Goodenow, C. (1993). Classroom belonging among early adolescent students: Relationships to motivation and achievement. *Journal of Early Adolescence, 12,* 21–43.

Graziano W. G., & Musser, L. M. (1982). The joining and the parting of ways. In S. Duck (Ed.), *Personal relationships 4: Dissolving personal relationships* (pp. 75–106). London: Academic Press.

Grossman, J. B., & Rhodes, J. E. (2002). The test of time: Predictors and effects of duration in youth mentoring programs. *American Journal of Community Psychology, 30,* 199–219.

Hazan, C., & Shaver, P. R. (1994). Attachment as an organizational framework for research on close relationships. *Psychological Inquiry, 5,* 1–22.

Herrera, C., Sipe, C. L., & McClanahan, W. S. (2000). *Mentoring school-age children: Relationship development in community-based and school-based programs.* Philadelphia: Public/Private Ventures.

Hinde, R. A. (1997). *Relationships: A dialectical perspective.* Hove, England: Psychology Press.

Huston, T. L., & Burgess, R. L. (1979). Social exchange in developing relationships: An overview. In R. L. Burgess & T. L. Huston (Eds.), *Social exchange in developing relationships* (pp. 3–28). New York: Academic Press.

Karcher, M. J. (2005). Cross-age peer mentoring. In D. L. DuBois & M. J. Karcher (Eds.), *Handbook of youth mentoring* (pp. 266–285). Thousand Oaks, CA: Sage.

Karcher, M. J., Davis, C., & Powell, B. (2004). The effects of developmental mentoring on connectedness and academic achievement. *School Community Journal, 14,* 35–50.

Karcher, M. H., & Lindwall, J. (2003). Social interest, connectedness, and challenging experiences: What makes high school mentors persist? *Journal of Individual Psychology*, *59*, 293–315.

Keller, T. E. (2005a). The stages and development of mentoring relationships. In D. L. DuBois & M. J. Karcher (Eds.), *Handbook of youth mentoring* (pp. 82–99). Thousand Oaks, CA: Sage.

King, K. A., Vidourek, R. A., Davis, B., & McClellan, W. (2002). Increasing self-esteem and school connectedness through a multidimensional mentoring program. *Journal of School Health*, *72*, 294–299.

Kirkpatrick, L. A. (1999). Attachment and religious representations and behavior. In J. Cassidy & P. R. Shaver (Eds.), *Handbook of attachment: Theory, research and clinical applications* (pp. 803–822). New York: Guilford.

Klaw, E. L., Rhodes, J. E., & Fitzgerald, L. F. (2003). Natural mentors in the lives of African American adolescent mothers: Tracking relationships over time. *Journal of Youth and Adolescence*, *32*, 223–232.

Kram, K. E. (1985). *Mentoring at work: Developmental relationships at work*. Glenview, IL: Scott, Foresman and Company.

Kram, K. E., & Hall, D. T. (1989). Mentoring as an antidote to stress during corporate trauma. *Human Resource Management*, *24*, 493–510.

Kram, K. E., & Hall, D. T. (1996). Mentoring in a context of diversity and turbulence. In E. E. Kossek & S. Lobel (Eds.), *Managing diversity: Human resource strategies for transforming the workplace* (pp. 108–136). Cambridge, MA: Blackwell.

Larose, S., Tarabulsy, G., & Cyrenne, D. (2005). Perceived autonomy and relatedness as moderating the impact of teacher–student mentoring relationships on student academic adjustment. *Journal of Primary Prevention*, *26*, 111–128.

Lee, R. M., & Robbins, S. B. (1998). The relationship between social connectedness and anxiety, self-esteem, and social identify. *Journal of Counseling Psychology*, *45*, 338–345.

Levinson, D. J., Darrow, C. N., Klein, E. B., Levinson, M. H., & McKee, B. (1978). *The seasons of a man's life*. New York: Ballentine.

Liang, B., Brogan, D., Corral, M., & Spencer, R. (2005). *Youth mentoring relationships across three developmental periods: A qualitative analysis*. Unpublished manuscript.

Maton, K. I., Sto. Domingo, M. R., & King, J. (2005). Faith-based organizations. In D. L. DuBois & M. J. Karcher (Eds.), *Handbook of youth mentoring* (pp. 376–391). Thousand Oaks, CA: Sage.

MENTOR/National Mentoring Partnership (2006). *Legislative history*. Retrieved March 10, 2006, from www.mentoring.org/take_action/funding/legislative_history.php.

Merton, R. K. (1957). *Social theory and social structure*. Glencoe, IL: The Free Press.

Miller, J. B. (1976). *Toward a new psychology of women*. Boston: Beacon Press.

Mills, J., Clark, M. S., Ford, T., & Johnson, M. (2004). Measuring communal strength. *Personal Relationships*, *11*, 213–230.

Mitchell, T. R., Sablynski, C. J., Burton, J. P., & Holtom, B. C. (2004). The effects of job embeddedness on organizational citizenship, job performance, volitional absences, and voluntary turnover. *Academy of Management Journal*, *47*, 711–722.

Morrow, K. V., & Styles, M. B. (1995). *Building relationships with youth in program settings: A study of Big Bothers/Big Sisters*. Philadelphia: Public/Private Ventures.

Nagda, B. A., Gregerman, S. R., Jonides, J., von Hippel, W., & Lerner, J. S. (1998). Undergraduate student–faculty research partnerships affect student retention. *Review of Higher Education*, *22*, 55–72.

O'Neil, J. M., & Wrightsman, L. S. (2001). The mentoring relationship in psychology training program. In S. Walfish & A. Hess (Eds.), *Succeeding in graduate school: The career guide for the psychology student* (pp. 113–129). Hillsdale, NJ: Lawrence Erlbaum.

Ostroff, C., & Kozlowski, S. W. (1993). The role of mentoring in the information gathering process of newcomers during early organizational socialization. *Journal of Vocational Behavior, 42,* 170–183.

Philip, K., & Hendry, L. B. (2000). Making sense of mentoring or mentoring making sense? Reflections on the mentoring process by adult mentors with young people. *Journal of Community & Applied Social Psychology, 10,* 211–223.

Prager, K. J., & Buhrmester, D. (1998). Intimacy and need fulfillment in couple relationships. *Journal of Social and Personal Relationships, 15,* 435–469.

Ragins, B. R., & Cotton, J. L. (1993). Gender and willingness to mentor in organizations. *Journal of Management, 19,* 97–111.

Ragins, B. R., Cotton, J. L., & Miller, J. S. (2000). Marginal mentoring: The effects of type of mentor, quality of relationship, and program design on work and career attitudes. *Academy of Management Journal, 43,* 1177–1194.

Rhodes, J. E. (2002b). *Stand by me: The risks and rewards of mentoring today's youth.* Cambridge, MA: Harvard University Press.

Rhodes, J. E. (2005). A theoretical model of youth mentoring. In D. L. DuBois & M. J. Karcher (Eds.), *Handbook of youth mentoring* (pp. 30–43). Thousand Oaks, CA: Sage.

Rhodes, J. E., Grossman, J. B., & Roffman, J. G. (2002). The rhetoric and reality of youth mentoring. In J. E. Rhodes (Ed.), *New directions for youth development: Theory, practice, and research: A critical review of youth mentoring, 93,* 9–20. San Francisco: Jossey-Bass.

Sanchez, B., Colon, Y., & Esparza, P. (2005). The role of sense of school belonging and gender in the academic adjustment of Latino adolescents. *Journal of Youth and Adolescence, 34,* 619–628.

Sarason, S. B. (1974). *Psychological sense of community: Prospects for a community psychology.* San Francisco: Jossey-Bass.

Scanzoni, J. (1979). Social exchange and behavioral interdependence. In R. L. Burgess & T. L. Huston (Eds.), *Social exchange in developing relationships* (pp. 61–98). New York: Academic Press.

Schlosser, L. Z., & Gelso, C. J. (2001). Measuring the working alliance in advisor–advisee relationships in graduate school. *Journal of Counseling Psychology, 48,* 157–167.

Slicker, E. K., & Palmer, D. J. (1993). Mentoring at-risk high school students: Evaluation of a school-based program. *School Counselor, 40,* 327–334.

Sosik, J. J., & Godshalk, V. M. (2000a). Leadership styles, mentoring functions received, and job-related stress: A conceptual model and preliminary study. *Journal of Organizational Behavior, 21,* 365–390.

Spencer, R. A., Jordan, J. V., & Sazama, J. (2004). Growth-promoting relationships between youth and adults: A focus group study. *Families in Society, 85*(3), 354–362.

Srole, L. J. (1956). Anomie, authoritarianism, and prejudice. *American Journal of Sociology, 60,* 63–67.

Sternberg, R. (1986). A triangular theory of love. *Psychological Review, 93,* 119–135.

Stukas, A. A., & Tanti, C. (2005). Recruiting and sustaining volunteer mentors. In D. L. DuBois & M. J. Karcher (Eds.), *Handbook of youth mentoring* (pp. 235–250). Thousand Oaks, CA: Sage.

Styles, M. B., & Morrow, K. V. (1992). *Understanding how youth and elders form relationships: A study of four linking lifetimes programs.* Philadelphia: Public/Private Ventures.

Tinto, V. (1993). *Leaving college: Rethinking the causes and cures of student attrition* (2nd ed.). Chicago: University of Chicago Press.

US Department of Education (2006). 21st century community learning centers. Retrieved March 12, 2006 from www.ed.gov/programs/21stcclc/index.html

Valentine, V. (2005, November, 8). Economic despair, racism drive French riots. National Public Radio. Retrieved online March 13, 2006. www.npr.org/templates/story/story.php?storyId=5004897

Vygotsky, L. (1978). *Mind in society: The development of higher psychological processes.* Cambridge, MA: Harvard University Press.

Wanberg, C. R., Welsh, E. T., & Hezlett, S. A. (2003). Mentoring research: A review and dynamic process model. *Research in Personnel and Human Resources Management, 22*, 39–124.

Weiten, W. (2005). *Psychology: Themes and variations.* Belmont, CA: Wadsworth/Thompson Learning.

Wilde, J. B., & Schau, C. G. (1991). Mentoring in graduate schools of education: Mentees' perceptions. *Journal of Experimental Education 59*, 165–179.

Young, A. M., & Perrewé, P. L. (2000b). What did you expect? An examination of career-related support and social support among mentors and protégés. *Journal of Management, 26*, 611–632.

Bibliography

Aagaard, E. M., & Hauer, K. E. (2003). A cross-sectional descriptive study of mentoring relationships formed by medical students. *Journal of General Internal Medicine, 18,* 298–302.

Abbott, D. A., Meredith, W. H., Self-Kelly, R., & Davis, M. E. (1997). The influence of a Big Brothers program on the adjustment of boys in single-parent families. *Journal of Psychology, 131,* 143–156.

Acitelli, L. K., Douvan, E., & Veroff, J. (1993). Perceptions of conflict in the first year of marriage: How important are similarity and understanding? *Journal of Social and Personal Relationships, 10,* 5–19.

Adler, P. S., & Kwon, S. W. (2002). Social capital: Prospectus for a new concept. *Academy of Management Review, 27*(1), 17–40.

Ainsworth, M. D. S. (1989). Attachments beyond infancy. *American Psychologist, 44,* 709–716.

Akbar, N. (1979). African roots of Black personality. In W. D. Smith, K. Burlew, M. Mosely, & W. Whiteney (Eds.), *Reflections on Black psychology* (pp. 79–87). Washington, DC: University Press of America.

Allen, N. J., & Meyer, J. P. (1996). Affective, continuance, and normative commitment: An examination of construct validity. *Journal of Vocational Behavior, 49,* 252–276.

Allen, T. D. (2003). Mentoring others: A dispositional and motivational approach. *Journal of Vocational Behavior, 62,* 134–154.

Allen, T. D. (2004). Protégé selection by mentors: Contributing individual and organizational factors. *Journal of Vocational Behavior, 65,* 469–483.

Allen, T. D., Day, R., & Lentz, E. (2005). The role of interpersonal comfort in mentoring relationships. *Career Development Quarterly, 31,* 155–169.

Allen, T. D., & Eby, L. T. (2003). Relationship effectiveness for mentors: Factors associated with learning and quality. *Journal of Management, 29,* 469–486.

Allen, T. D., & Eby, L. T. (2004). Factors related to mentor reports of mentoring functions provided: Gender and relational characteristics. *Sex Roles, 50,* 129–139.

Allen, T. D., Eby, L. T., & Lentz, E. (2006a). The relationship between formal mentoring program characteristics and perceived program effectiveness. *Personnel Psychology, 59,* 125–153.

Allen, T. D., Eby, L. T., & Lentz, E. (2006b). Mentorship behaviors and mentorship quality associated with formal mentoring programs: Closing the gap between research and practice. *Journal of Applied Psychology, 91*, 567–578.

Allen, T. D., Eby, L. T., Poteet, M. L., Lentz, E., & Lima, L. (2004). Career benefits associated with mentoring for protégés: A meta-analysis. *Journal of Applied Psychology, 89*, 127–136.

Allen, T. D., Poteet, M. L., & Burroughs, S. (1997). The mentor's perspective: A qualitative inquiry and agenda for future research. *Journal of Vocational Behavior, 57*, 70–89.

Allen, T. D., Poteet, M. L., & Russell, J. E. A. (2000). Protégé selection by mentors: What makes the difference? *Journal of Organizational Behavior, 21*, 271–282.

Allen, T. D., Poteet, M. L., Russell, J. E. A., & Dobbins, G. H. (1997). A field study of factor related to willingness to mentor others. *Journal of Vocational Behavior, 50*, 1–22.

Allen, T. D., Russell, J. E. A., & Maetzke, S. B. (1997). Formal peer mentoring: Factors related to protégés' satisfaction and willingness to mentor others. *Group & Organization Management, 22*, 488–507.

Alliger, G. M., & Janak, E. A. (1989). Kirkpatrick's levels of training criteria: Thirty years later. *Personnel Psychology, 42*, 331–342.

Ambrose, L. (2003). Multiple mentoring. *Health Executive.* Retrieved June 30, 2005, from www.ache.org/newclub/CAREER/MentorArticles/Multiple.cfm.

American Council on Education (2005). *Annual ACE report shows minority college enrollment continues to climb, but gaps still persist.* Retrieved February 27, 2005, from www.acenet.edu/hena/readArticle.cfm?articleID=1223.

Ancis, J. R., & Phillips, S. D. (1996). Academic gender bias and women's behavioral agency and self-efficacy. *Journal of Counseling and Development, 75*, 131–137.

Ancis, J. R., & Sedlacek, W. E. (1997). Predicting the academic achievement of female students using the SAT and noncognitive variables. *College and University, 72*(3), 1–8.

Anderson, E. (1990). *Street wise: Race, class, and change in an urban community.* Chicago: University of Chicago Press.

Anderson, E. M., & Shannon, A. L. (1988). Toward a conceptualization of mentoring. *Journal of Teacher Education, 39*(1), 38–42.

AOL Time Warner Foundation (2002). *Mentoring in America.* New York: Author.

Applebaum, S. H., Ritchie, S., & Shapiro, B. T. (1994). Mentoring revisited: An organizational behaviour construct. *International Journal of Career Management, 6*, 3–10.

Arnett, J. J. (1999). Adolescent storm and stress reconsidered. *American Psychologist, 54*(5), 317–326.

Arthur, M. B., & Rousseau, D. M. (1996). *The boundaryless career: A new employment principle for a new organizational era.* New York: Oxford University Press.

Aryee, S., & Chay, Y. W. (1994). An examination of the impact of career-oriented mentoring on work commitment attitudes and career satisfaction among professional and managerial employees: An interactionist approach. *British Journal of Management, 5*, 241–249.

Aryee, S., Chay, Y. W., & Chew, J. (1996). The motivation to mentor among managerial employees in the maintenance career stage: An interactionist's perspective. *Group and Organization Management, 21*, 261–277.

Aryee, S., Lo, S., & Kang, I. L. (1999). Antecedents of early career stage mentoring among Chinese employees. *Journal of Organizational Behavior, 20*, 563–576.

Aryee, S., Wyatt, T., & Stone, R. (1996). Early career outcomes of graduate employees: The effect of mentoring an ingratiation. *Journal of Management Studies, 33*, 95–118.

Aseltine, R. H., Jr., Dupre, M., & Lamlein, P. (2000). Mentoring as a drug prevention strategy: An evaluation of *Across Ages. Adolescent & Family Health, 1*, 11–20.

Astin, A. W. (1977). *Four critical years: Effects of college on beliefs, attitudes, and knowledge.* San Francisco: Jossey-Bass.

Atkinson, D. R., Casas, A., & Neville, H. (1994). Ethnic minority psychologists: Whom they mentor and benefits they derive from the process. *Journal of Multicultural Counseling and Development*, 22, 37–48.

Atkinson, D. R., & Gim, R. H. (1989). Asian-American cultural identity and attitudes toward mental health services. *Journal of Counseling Psychology*, 36, 209–212.

Atkinson, D. R., Lowe, S., & Matthews, L. (1995). Asian-American acculturation and willingness to seek counseling. *Journal of Multicultural Counseling and Development*, 23, 130–138.

Atkinson, D. R., Neville, H., & Casas, A. (1991). The mentorship of ethnic minorities in professional psychology. *Professional Psychology: Research and Practice*, 22, 336–338.

Audit Commission (1996). *Misspent youth*. London: HMSO.

Austin, A. E. (2002). Preparing the next generation of faculty. *Journal of Higher Education*, 73, 94–122.

Bakan, D. (1966). *The duality of human existence*. Chicago: Rand McNally.

Baker, B. T., Hocevar, S. P., & Johnson, W. B. (2003). The prevalence and nature of service academy mentoring: A study of navy midshipmen. *Military Psychology*, 15, 273–283.

Baker, D. B., & Maguire, C. P. (2005). Mentoring in historical perspective. In D. L. DuBois & M. J. Karcher (Eds.), *Handbook of youth mentoring* (pp. 14–29). Thousand Oaks, CA: Sage.

Baker, W. E., & Dutton, J. (2007). Enabling positive social capital at work. In J. Dutton & B. R. Ragins (Eds.), *Exploring positive relationships at work: Building a theoretical and research foundation* (pp. 325–345). Mahwah, NJ: Lawrence Erlbaum and Associates.

Baker, W. E., & Faulkner, R. R. (2004). Social networks and loss of capital. *Social Networks*, 26(2), 91–111.

Balcazar, F. E., Majors, R., Blanchard, K. A., & Paine, A. (1991). Teaching minority high school students to recruit helpers to attain personal and educational goals. *Journal of Behavioral Education*, 1, 445–454.

Baldwin, J. A. (1984). African self-consciousness and the mental health of African Americans. *Journal of Black Studies*, 15, 177–194.

Bandura, A. (1977). *Social learning theory*. Englewood Cliffs, NJ: Prentice-Hall.

Bandura, A. (1982). Self-efficacy mechanism in human agency. *American Psychologist*, 37(2), 122–147.

Bandura, A. (1986). *Social foundations of thought and action: A social cognitive theory*. Upper Saddle River, NJ: Prentice-Hall.

Bandura, A. (1989). Human agency in social cognitive theory. *American Psychologist*, 44(9), 1175–1184.

Bandura, A. (1997). *Self-efficacy: The exercise of control*. New York: W. H. Freeman.

Banks, C. (2000). Gender and race as factors in educational leadership and administration. In Jossey-Bass Publishers (Ed.), *The Jossey-Bass reader on educational leadership* (pp. 217–256). San Francisco: Jossey-Bass.

Barker, P., Monks, K., & Buckley, F. (1999). The role of mentoring in the career progression of chartered accountants. *British Accounting Review*, 31, 297–312.

Barnett, S. K. (1984). The mentor role: A task of generativity. *Journal of Human Behavior and Learning*, 1, 15–18.

Barrera, M., & Bonds, D. D. (2005). Mentoring relationships and social support. In D. L. DuBois & M. J. Karcher (Eds.), *Handbook of youth mentoring* (pp. 133–142). Thousand Oaks, CA: Sage.

Bass, B. (1985). *Leadership and performance beyond expectations*. New York: The Free Press.

Batson, C. D., Ahmad, N., & Tsang, J. A. (2002). Four motives for community involvement. *Journal of Social Issues*, 58(3), 429–445.

Baugh, S. G., Lankau, M. J., & Scandura, T. A. (1996). An investigation of the effects of protégé gender on responses to mentoring. *Journal of Vocational Behavior*, 49, 309–323.

Baugh, S. G., & Scandura, T. A. (1999). The effects of multiple mentors on protégé attitudes toward the work setting. *Journal of Social Behavior and Personality, 14,* 503–521.

Baumeister, R. F., & Leary, M. R. (1995). The need to belong: Desire for interpersonal attachments as a fundamental human emotion. *Psychological Bulletin, 117,* 497–529.

Baumeister, R. F., & Tice, D. M. (1990). Anxiety and social exclusion. *Journal of Social and Clinical Psychology, 9,* 165–195.

Beam, M. R., Chen, C., & Greenberger, E. (2002). The nature of adolescents' relationships with their "very important" nonparental adults. *American Journal of Community Psychology, 30,* 305–325.

Bean, T. W., Readence, J. E., Barone, D. M., & Sylvester, T. (2004). An interpretive study of doctoral mentoring in literacy. *Mentoring & Tutoring, 12*(3), 371–381.

Becker, G. S. (1975). *Human capital.* Chicago: University of Chicago Press.

Beier, S. R., Rosenfeld, W. D., Spitalny, K. C., Zansky, S. M., & Bontempo, A. N. (2000). The potential role of an adult mentor in influencing high risk behaviors in adolescents. *Archive of Pediatric and Adolescent Medicine, 154,* 327–331.

Beiswinger, G. L. (1985). *One to one: The story of the Big Brothers/Big Sisters movement in America.* Philadelphia: Big Brothers/Big Sisters of America.

Benioff, S. (1997). *A second chance: Developing mentoring and education projects for young people.* London: Dalston Youth Project/Crime Concern.

Benjamin, E. M. (1995). *The relationship between African-centered self-concept and the perceptions of socially based power for black students on predominantly White college campuses.* Unpublished doctoral dissertation, University of Texas at Austin.

Bennouna, S. (2003). *Mentors' emotional intelligence and performance of mentoring functions in graduate doctoral education.* Unpublished doctoral dissertation, University of South Florida, Tampa.

Benson, P. L. (1993). *The troubled journey: A portrait of 6th–12th grade youth.* Minneapolis, MN: The Search Institute.

Bergman, S. (1996). Men's psychological development: A relational perspective. In R. F. Levant & W. Pollack (Eds.), *A new psychology of men* (pp. 68–90). New York: Basic Books.

Berk, R. A., Berg, J., Mortimer, R., Walton-Moss, B., & Yeo, T. P. (2005). Measuring the effectiveness of faculty mentoring relationships. *Academic Medicine, 80*(1), 66–71.

Berry, J. W. (1980). Acculturation as varieties of adaptation. In A. M. Padilla (Ed.), *Acculturation: Theory, models, and some new findings* (pp. 9–25). Boulder, CO: Westview.

Berscheid, E. (1999). The greening of relationship science. *American Psychologist, 54*(4), 260–266.

Berscheid, E., & Regan, P. (2005). *The psychology of interpersonal relationships.* New York: Prentice-Hall.

Berscheid, E., & Walster, E. H. (1969). *Interpersonal attraction.* Reading, MA: Addison-Wesley.

Beyene, T., Anglin, M., Sanchez, W., & Ballou, M. (2002). Mentoring and relational mutuality: Protégés' perspectives. *Journal of Humanistic Counseling, Education and Development, 41*(1), 87–102.

Biaggio, M., Paget, T. L., & Chenoweth, M. S. (1997). A model for ethical management of faculty–student dual relationships. *Professional Psychology: Research and Practice, 28,* 184–189.

Bierema, L. L., & Merriam, S. B. (2002). E-mentoring: Using computer mediated communication (CMC) to enhance the mentoring process. *Innovative Higher Education, 26,* 211–227.

Bigelow, J. R., & Johnson, W. B. (2001). Promoting mentor–protégé relationship formation in graduate school. *The Clinical Supervisor, 20*(1), 1–23.

Black, L. L., Suarez, E. C., & Medina, S. (2004). Helping students help themselves: Strategies for successful mentoring relationships. *Counselor Education and Supervision, 44,* 44–55.

Blackburn, R. T., Chapman, D. W., & Cameron, S. M. (1981). "Cloning" in academe: Mentorship and academic careers. *Research in Higher Education, 15,* 315–327.

Blackwell, J. E. (1989). Mentoring: An action strategy for increasing minority faculty. *Academe, 75,* 8–14.

Blake, S. D. (1999). The costs of living as an outsider within: An analysis of the mentoring relationships and career success of black and white women in the corporate sector. *Journal of Career Development, 26*(1), 21–36.

Blake-Beard, S. D., & Murrell, A. J. (2006). *Executive Leadership Council (ELC) guide to effective mentoring.* Washington, DC: ELC.

Blake-Beard, S. D., O'Neill, R. M., & McGowan, E. (in press). Blind dates?: The importance of matching in successful formal mentoring relationships. In K. E. Kram & B. R. Ragins (Eds.), *The handbook of mentoring at work: Theory, research and practice.* Thousand Oaks, CA: Sage.

Blakely, C. H., Menon, R., & Jones, D. J. (1995). *Project BELONG: Final report.* College Station, TX: Texas A&M University, Public Policy Research Institute.

Blau, P. M. (1964). *Exchange and power in social life.* New York: Wiley.

Blechman, E. A. (1992). Mentors for high-risk minority youth: From effective communication to bicultural competence. *Journal of Clinical Child Psychology, 21,* 160–169.

Blyth, D. A., Hill, J. P., & Thiel, K. S. (1982). Early adolescents' significant others: Grade and gender differences in perceived relationships with familial and nonfamilial adults and young people. *Journal of Youth and Adolescence, 11*(6), 425–450.

Bode, R. K. (1999). Mentoring and collegiality. In R. J. Menges & Associates (Eds.), *Faculty in new jobs: A guide to settling in, becoming established, and building institutional support* (pp. 118–144). San Francisco: Jossey-Bass.

Bogat, G. A., & Liang, B. (2005). Gender in mentoring relationships. In D. L. DuBois & M. J. Karcher (Eds.), *Handbook of youth mentoring* (pp. 205–217). Thousand Oaks, CA: Sage.

Bogat, G. A., & Redner, R. L. (1985). How mentoring affects the professional development of women in psychology. *Professional Psychology: Research and Practice, 16,* 851–859.

Bona, M. J., Rinehart, J., & Volbrecht, R. M. (1995). "Show me how to do like you": Comentoring as feminist pedagogy. *Feminist Teacher, 9*(3), 116–124.

Bordin, E. S. (1979). The generalizability of the psychoanalytic concept of the working alliance. *Psychotherapy: Theory, Research and Practice, 16*(3), 252–260.

Bordin, E. S. (1983). A working alliance based model of supervision. *The Counseling Psychologist, 11,* 27–34.

Bouquillon, E. A., Sosik, J. J., & Lee, D. (2005). It's only a phase: Examining trust, identification and mentoring functions received across the mentoring phases. *Mentoring and Tutoring, 13,* 239–258.

Bowker, G. C., & Star, S. L. (1999). *Sorting things out: Classification and its consequences.* Cambridge, MA: MIT Press.

Bowlby, J. (1969). *Attachment and loss: Vol. 1. Attachment.* New York: Basic Books.

Bowlby, J. (1969/1982). *Attachment and loss: Vol. 1. Attachment* (2nd ed.). New York: Basic Books.

Bowlby, J. (1973). *Attachment and loss: Vol. 2. Separation, anxiety and anger.* New York: Basic Books.

Boyle, P., & Boice, B. (1998). Systematic mentoring for new faculty teachers and graduate teaching assistants. *Innovative Higher Education, 22,* 157–179.

Bozionelos, N. (2004). Mentoring provided: Relation to mentor's career success, personality, and mentoring received. *Journal of Vocational Behavior, 64,* 24–46.

Bragg, A. (1989). Is a mentor program in your future? *Sales and Marketing Management, 141*(September), 54–59.

Branch, S. (1999). The 100 best companies to work for in America. *Fortune, 139*(1), 118–130.

Bretherton, I., & Munholland, K. A. (1999). Internal working models in attachment relationships: A construct revisited. In J. Cassidy & P. R. Shaver (Eds.), *Handbook of attachment: Theory, research, and clinical applications* (pp. 89–111). New York: Guilford Press.

Bretz, R. D., Boudreau, J. W., & Judge, T. A. (1994). Job search behavior of employed managers. *Personnel Psychology, 47*, 275–301.

Brinson, J., & Kottler, J. (1993). Cross-cultural mentoring in counselor education: A strategy for retaining minority faculty. *Counselor Education and Supervision, 32*, 241–253.

Brown, M. C., Davis, G. L., & McClendon, S. A. (1999). Mentoring graduate students of color: Myths, models, and modes. *Peabody Journal of Education, 74*, 105–118.

Bruffee, K. A. (1999). *Collaborative learning: Higher education, interdependence, and the authority of knowledge* (2nd ed.). Baltimore: Johns Hopkins University Press.

Brush, S. G. (1991). Women in science and engineering. *American Scientist, 79*, 404–419.

Bryant, A. L., & Zimmerman, M. A. (2003). Role models and psychosocial outcomes among African American adolescents. *Journal of Adolescent Research, 18*(1), 36–67.

Buhrmester, D. (1990). Intimacy of friendship, interpersonal competence, and adjustment during preadolescence and adolescence. *Child Development, 61*, 1101–1111.

Bui, H. T., & Takeuchi, D. T. (1992). Ethnic minority adolescents and the use of community mental health care services. *American Journal of Community Psychology, 20*, 403–417.

Bureau of Labor Statistics (2004). *BLS releases 2002–12 employment projections* (Report USDL 04-148). Washington, DC: United States Department of Labor.

Burke, R. J. (1984). Mentors in organizations. *Group and Organization Studies, 9*, 353–372.

Burke, R. J., & McKeen, C. A. (1989a). Developing formal mentoring programs in organizations. *Business Quarterly, 53*(3), pp. 76–79.

Burke, R. J., & McKeen, C. A. (1989b). Mentoring in organizations: Implications for women. *Journal of Business Ethics, 9*, 317–333.

Burke, R. J., & McKeen, C. A. (1997). Benefits of mentoring relationships among managerial and professional women: A cautionary tale. *Journal of Vocational Behavior, 51*, 43–57.

Burke, R. J., McKeen, C. A., & McKenna, C. (1990). Sex differences and cross-sex effects on mentoring: Some preliminary data. *Psychological Reports, 67*, 1011–1023.

Burke, R. J., McKeen, C. A., & McKenna, C. (1993). Correlates of mentoring in organizations: The mentor's perspective. *Psychological Reports, 72*(3), 883–896.

Burke, R. J., McKenna, C. S., & McKeen, C. A. (1991). How do mentorships differ from typical supervisory relationships? *Psychological Reports, 68*, 459–466.

Burnett, P. C. (1999). The supervision of doctoral dissertations using a collaborative cohort model. *Counselor Education and Supervision, 39*(1), 46–52.

Burt, R. S. (1997). The contingent value of social capital. *Administrative Science Quarterly, 42*, 339–365.

Busch, J. W. (1985). Mentoring in graduate schools of education: Mentors' perceptions. *American Educational Research Journal, 22*, 257–265.

Byrne, D. (1969). Attitudes and attraction. In L. Berkowitz (Ed.), *Advances in experimental social psychology* (Vol. 4, pp. 35–89). New York: Academic Press.

Byrne, D. (1971). *The attraction paradigm*. New York: Academic Press.

Byrne, D. (1997). An overview (and underview) of research and theory within the attraction paradigm. *Journal of Social and Personal Relationships, 14*, 417–431.

Cameron, K. S., Dutton, J. E., & Quinn, R. E. (2003). Foundations of positive organizational scholarship. In K. S. Cameron, J. E. Dutton, & R. E. Quinn (Eds.), *Positive organizational scholarship: Foundations of a new discipline* (pp. 3–13). San Francisco: Berrett-Koehler.

Cameron, S. W., & Blackburn, R. T. (1981). Sponsorship and academic career success. *Journal of Higher Education, 52*, 369–377.

Campbell, D. T., & Stanley, J. C. (1966). *Experimental and quasi-experimental designs for research.* Boston: Houghton Mifflin.

Campbell, J. P., Dunnette, M. D., Lawler, E. E., & Weick, K. E. (1970). *Managerial behavior, performance and effectiveness.* New York: McGraw-Hill, Inc.

Campbell, T. A., & Campbell, D. E. (1997). Faculty/student mentor program: Effects on academic performance and retentions. *Research in Higher Education, 38,* 727–742.

Cannister, M. W. (1999). Mentoring and the spiritual well-being of late adolescents. *Adolescence, 34,* 769–779.

Caplan, G. (1964). *Principles of Preventive Psychiatry.* New York: Basic Books.

Caproni, P. J. (2004). *Management skills for everyday life: The practical coach.* Englewood Cliffs, NJ: Prentice Hall.

Carroll, S., Feren, D., & Olian, J. (1987). Reactions to the new minorities by employees of the future: An experimental study. *Psychological Reports, 60,* 911–920.

Castro, S. L., & Scandura, T. A. (2004, November). *The tale of two measures: Evaluation and comparison of Scandura's (1992) and Ragins and McFarlin's (1990) mentoring measures.* Paper presented at the Southern Management Association Meeting, San Antonio, TX.

Catalano, R. F., & Hawkins, J. D. (1996). The social development model: A theory of anti-social behavior. In J. D. Hawkins (Ed.), *Delinquency and crime: Current theories* (pp. 149–197). New York: Cambridge University Press.

Catalano, R. F., Hawkins, J. D., Berglund, L. M., Pollard, J. A., & Arthur, M. W. (2002). Prevention science and positive youth development: Competitive or cooperative frameworks? *Journal of Adolescent Health, 31,* 230–239.

Catalyst (1993). *Mentoring: A guide to corporate programs and practices.* New York: Catalyst.

Catalyst (1999). *Women of color in corporate management: Opportunities and barriers.* New York: Author.

Catalyst (2001). *Women of color executives: Their voices, their journeys.* New York: Catalyst.

Cave, G., & Quint, J. (1990). *Career beginning impact evaluation.* New York: Manpower Demonstration and Research Corporation.

Cavell, T. A., Meeham, B. T., Heffer, R. W., & Holliday, J. (2002). The natural mentors of adolescent children of alcoholics (COAs): Implications for preventative practices. *Journal of Primary Prevention, 23,* 23–42.

Chao, G. T. (1997). Mentoring phases and outcomes. *Journal of Vocational Behavior, 51,* 15–28.

Chao, G. T., Walz, P. M., & Gardner, P. D. (1992). Formal and informal mentorships: A comparison on mentoring functions and contrast with nonmentored counterparts. *Personnel Psychology, 45,* 619–636.

Chemers, M. M., Hu, L., & Garcia, B. (2001). Academic self-efficacy and first-year college student performance and adjustment. *Journal of Educational Psychology, 93,* 55–65.

Chen, C., Greenberger, E., Farruggia, S., Bush, K., & Dong, Q. (2003). Beyond parents and peers: The role of important non-parental adults (VIPS) in adolescent development in China and the United States. *Psychology in the Schools, 40,* 35–50.

Chen, Y. R., Brockner, J., & Chen, X. P. (2002). Individual–collective primacy and ingroup favoritism: Enhancement and protection effects. *Journal of Experimental Social Psychology, 38*(5), 482–491.

Chickering, A. W. (1969). *Education and identity.* San Francisco: Jossey-Bass.

Chung, D. K. (1992). Asian cultural commonalities: A comparison with mainstream American culture. In D. K. Chung, K. Murase, & F. Ross-Sheriff (Eds.), *Social work practice with Asian Americans* (pp. 27–44). Newbury Park, CA: Sage.

Church, R. (2006). *The effects of organizational heterosexism on the mentoring relationships of gay and lesbian protégés.* Unpublished doctoral dissertation, University of Toronto, Toronto, Canada.

Cicchetti, D., & Aber, L. (1998). Contextualism and developmental psychopathology. *Development and Psychopathology, 10,* 137–141.

Clancy, M., & Tata, J. (2005). A global perspective on balancing work and family. *International Journal of Management, 22*(2), 234–241.

Clark, M. L., & Ayers, M. (1993). Friendship expectations and friendship evaluations: Reciprocity and gender effects. *Youth & Society, 24,* 299–313.

Clark, M. S., & Grote, N. K. (1998). Why aren't indices of relationship costs always negatively related to indices of relationship quality? *Personality and Social Psychology Review, 2,* 2–17.

Clark, M. S., & Mills, J. (1979). Interpersonal attraction in exchange and communal relationships. *Journal of Personality and Social Psychology, 37,* 12–24.

Clark, R. A., Harden, S. L., & Johnson, W. B. (2000). Mentor relationships in clinical psychology doctoral training: Results of a national survey. *Teaching of Psychology, 27,* 262–268.

Clary, E. G., Snyder, M., Ridge, R. D., Copeland, J., Stukas, A. A., Haugen, J., & Miene, P. (1998). Understanding and assessing the motivation of volunteers: A functional approach. *Journal of Personality and Social Psychology, 74*(6), 1516–1530.

Clawson, J. G. (1985). Is mentoring necessary? *Training and Development Journal, 39*(4), 36–39.

Clayden, J., & Stein, M. (2002). *Mentoring for care leavers: Evaluation report.* London: University of York/Prince's Trust.

Clutterback, D. (2004). What about mentee competences? In D. A. Clutterback & G. Lane (Eds.), *The situational mentor: An international review of competences and capabilities in mentoring* (pp. 72–82). Aldershot, England: Gower Publishing.

Clutterbuck, D., & Ragins, B. R. (2002). *Mentoring and diversity: An international perspective.* Oxford: Butterworth-Heinemann.

Coble, H. M., Gantt, D. L., & Mallinckrodt, B. (1996). Attachment, social competency, and the capacity to use social support. In G. R. Pierce, B. R. Sarason, & I. G. Sarason (Eds.), *Handbook of social support and the family* (pp. 141–172). New York: Plenum.

Cochran, A., Paukert, J. L., Scales, E. M., & Neumayer, L. A. (2004). How medical students define surgical mentors. *American Journal of Surgery, 187,* 698–701.

Cohen, G. L., Steele, C. M., & Ross, L. D. (1999). The mentor's dilemma: Providing critical feedback across the racial divide. *Personality and Social Psychology Bulletin, 25,* 1302–1318.

Cohen, J. (1988). *Statistical power analysis for the behavioral sciences* (2nd ed.). Hillsdale, NJ: Erlbaum.

Cohen, S., & Wills, T. A. (1985). Stress, social support, and the buffering hypothesis. *Psychological Bulletin, 98*(2), 310–357.

Colarelli, S. M., & Bishop, R. C. (1990). Career commitment: Functions, correlates and management. *Group and Organization Studies, 15,* 158–176.

Coleman, J. S. (1988). Social capital in the creation of human capital. *American Journal of Sociology, 94*(Suppl.), S95–S120.

Colley, H. (2003a). Engagement mentoring for "disaffected" youth: A new model of mentoring for social inclusion. *British Educational Research Journal, 29*(4), 521–542.

Colley, H. (2003b). *Mentoring for social inclusion: A critical approach to nurturing successful mentoring relations.* London: RoutledgeFalmer.

Collins, P. (1991). *Black feminist thought: Knowledge, consciousness, and the politics of empowerment.* New York: Routledge.

Collins, P. M. (1994). Does mentorship among social workers make a difference? An empirical investigation of career outcomes. *Work and Occupations, 18,* 431–446.

Collins, P. M., Kamya, H. A., & Tourse, R. W. (1997). Questions of racial diversity and mentorship: An empirical investigation. *Social Work, 42,* 145–152.

Colquitt, J. A. (2001). On the dimensionality of organizational justice: A construct validation of a measure. *Journal of Applied Psychology, 86,* 386–400.

Colquitt, J. A., LePine, J. A., & Noe, R. A. (2000). Toward an integrative theory of training motivation: A meta-analytic path analysis of 20 years of research. *Journal of Applied Psychology, 85,* 678–707.

Constantine, M., Richardson, T., Benjamin, E., & Wilson, J. (1998). An overview of Black racial identity theory: Limitations and considerations for future theoretical change. *Applied and Preventive Psychology, 7*(2), 95–99.

Cook, D. A. (1994). Racial identity in supervision. *Counselor Education and Supervision, 34*(2), 1–7.

Cook, T. D., & Campbell, D. T. (1979). *Quasi experimentation: Design & analysis issues for field settings.* Boston: Houghton Mifflin Co.

Cosgrove, T. J. (1986). The effects of participation in a mentoring-transcript program on freshman. *Journal of College Student Personnel, 27,* 119–124.

Coulson, C. C., Kunselman, A. R., Cain, J., & Legro, R. S. (2000). The mentor effect in student evaluation. *Obstetrics and Gynecology, 95,* 619–622.

Cowan, P. A. (1996). Meta-thoughts on the role of meta-emotion in children's development: Comment on Gottman et al. (1996). *Journal of Family Psychology, 10*(3), 277–283.

Cox, E. R. J. (2000). The call to mentor. *Career Development International, 5,* 2002–210.

Cox, M. J., & Paley, B. (1997). Families as systems. *Annual Review of Psychology, 48,* 243–267.

Cox, T. H., & Blake, S. (1991). Managing cultural diversity: Implications for organizational competitiveness. *Academy of Management Executive, 5*(3), 45–57.

Creed, W., & Scully, M. (2000). Songs of ourselves: Employee's deployment of social identity in workplace encounters. *Journal of Management Inquiry, 9*(4), 391–413.

Cronan-Hillix, T., Davidson, W. S., Cronan-Hillix, W. A., & Gensheimer, L. K. (1986). Student's views of mentors in psychology graduate training. *Teaching of Psychology, 13,* 123–127.

Crosby, F. J. (1999). The developing literature on developmental relationships. In A. J. Murrell, F. J. Crosby, & R. J. Ely (Eds.), *Mentoring dilemmas: Developmental relationships within multicultural organizations* (pp. 3–20). Mahwah, NJ: Lawrence Erlbaum.

Crosby, F. J., & Bearman, S. (2006). The uses of a good theory. *Journal of Social Issues, 62,* 415–438.

Cross, S. E., & Madson, L. (1997). Models of the self: Self-construals and gender. *Psychological Bulletin, 122,* 5–37.

Cross, W. E. (1995). The psychology of nigrescence: Revising the Cross model. In J. G. Ponterotto, J. M. Casas, L. A. Suzuki, & C. M. Alexander (Eds.), *Handbook of multicultural counseling* (pp. 93–122). Thousand Oaks, CA: Sage.

Csikszentmihalyi, M., & Larson, R. (1987). Validity and reliability of the Experience-Sampling Method. *Journal of Nervous and Mental Disease, 175*(9), 526–536.

Cunningham, J. B. (1993). Facilitating a mentorship programme. *Leadership & Organization Development Journal, 14*(4), 15–20.

Curtis, J. W. (2004). Balancing work and family for faculty: Why it's important. *Academe, 90*(6), 21–24.

D'Abate, C. P., Eddy, E. R., & Tannenbaum, S. I. (2003). What's in a name? A literature-based approach to understanding mentoring, coaching, and other constructs that describe developmental interactions. *Human Resource Development Review, 2,* 360–384.

Dansereau, F., Graen, G., & Haga, W. J. (1975). A vertical dyad approach to leadership within formal organizations. *Organizational Behavior and Human Performance, 13,* 46–78.

Darling, N., Hamilton, S. F., & Niego, S. (1994). Adolescents' relations with adults outside the family. In R. Montemayor, G. R. Adams, & T. P. Gullotta (Eds.), *Personal relationships during adolescence* (Vol. 6, pp. 216–235). Thousand Oaks, CA: Sage.

Darling, N., Hamilton, S. F., & Shaver, K. H. (2003). Relationships outside the family: Unrelated adults. In G. R. Adams & M. D. Berzonsky (Eds.), *Blackwell handbook of adolescence* (pp. 349–370). Malden, MA: Blackwell.

Darling, N., Hamilton, S., Toyokawa, T., & Matsuda, S. (2002). Naturally occurring mentoring in Japan and the United States: Social role and correlates. *American Journal of Community Psychology*, 30(2), 245–270.

Davidson, M. N., & Foster-Johnson, L. (2002). Mentoring in the preparation of graduate researchers of color. *Review of Educational Research*, 71, 549–574.

Davidson, W. S. II, & Redner, R. (1988). The prevention of juvenile delinquency: Diversion from the juvenile justice system. In R. H. Price & E. L. Cowen (Eds.), *Fourteen ounces of prevention: A casebook for practitioners* (pp. 123–137). Washington, DC: American Psychological Association.

Davidson, W. S., Redner, R., Blakely, C. H., Mitchell, C. M., & Emshoff, J. G. (1987). Diversion of juvenile offenders: An experimental comparison. *Journal of Consulting and Clinical Psychology*, 55(1), 68–75.

Davis, T., Paxton, K. C., & Robinson, L. (1997). *After school action programs: Girl World Builders summary report.* Unpublished manuscript, Department of Psychology, DePau University, Chicago.

Day, R., & Allen, T. D. (2004). The relationship between career motivation and self-efficacy with protégé career success. *Journal of Vocational Behavior*, 64, 72–91.

Dennen, V. P. (2004). Cognitive apprenticeship in educational practice: Research on scaffolding, modeling, mentoring, and coaching as instructional strategies. In D. H. Jonassen (Ed.), *Handbook of research on educational communications and technology* (2nd ed., pp. 813–828). Mahwah, NJ: Lawrence Erlbaum Associates.

Dickinson, S. C., & Johnson, W. B. (2000). Mentoring in clinical psychology doctoral programs: A national survey of directors of training. *The Clinical Supervisor*, 19(1), 137–152.

Digh, P. (1998). Religion in the workplace: Make a good-faith effort to accommodate. *HR Magazine*, 43(13), 85–91.

Dinham, S., & Scott, C. (2001). The experience of disseminating the results of doctoral research. *Journal of Further and Higher Education*, 25(1), 45–55.

Diversi, M., & Mecham, C. (2005). Latino(a) students and Caucasian mentors in a rural after-school program: Towards empowering adult–youth relationships. *Journal of Community Psychology*, 33, 31–40.

Dixon-Reeves, R. (2003). Mentoring as a precursor to incorporation: An assessment of the mentoring experience of recently minted Ph.D.s. *Journal of Black Studies*, 34, 12–27.

Dohm, F. A., & Cummings, W. (2002). Research mentoring and women in clinical psychology. *Psychology of Women Quarterly*, 26, 163–167.

Dohm, F. A., & Cummings, W. (2003). Research mentoring and men in clinical psychology. *Psychology of Men and Masculinity*, 4, 149–153.

Donaldson, S. I., Ensher, E. A., & Grant-Vallone, E. (2000). Longitudinal examination of mentoring relationships and organizational commitment and citizenship behavior. *Journal of Career Development*, 26, 233–248.

Dorn, S. M., & Papalewis, R. (1997). *Improving doctoral student retention.* Paper presented at the Annual Meeting of the American Educational Research Association, Chicago, IL.

Dorn, S. M., Papalewis, R., & Brown, R. (1995). Educators earning their doctorates: Doctoral student perceptions regarding cohesiveness and persistence. *Education*, 116(2), 305–310.

Douglas, C. A., & McCauley, C. D. (1999). Formal developmental relationships: A survey of organizational practices. *Human Resource Development Quarterly*, 10(3), 203–220.

Downey, G., & Feldman, S. I. (1996). The implications of rejection sensitivity for intimate relationships. *Journal of Personality and Social Psychology, 70*, 1327–1343.

Downey, G., Lebolt, A., Rincon, C., & Freitas, A. L. (1998). Rejection sensitivity and children's interpersonal difficulties. *Child Development, 69*(4), 1074–1091.

Dozier, M., & Tyrrell, C. (1998). The role of attachment in therapeutic relationships. In J. A. Simpson & W. S. Rholes (Eds.), *Attachment theory and close relationships* (pp. 221–248). New York: Guilford.

Dreher, G. F., & Ash, R. (1990). A comparative study of mentoring among men and women in managerial, professional and technical positions. *Journal of Applied Psychology, 75*, 539–546.

Dreher, G. F., & Bretz, R. D. (1991). Cognitive ability and career attainment: Moderating effects of early career success. *Journal of Applied Psychology, 76*, 392–397.

Dreher, G. F., & Chargois, J. A. (1998). Gender, mentoring experiences, and salary attainment among graduates of an historically black university. *Journal of Vocational Behavior, 53*, 401–416.

Dreher, G. F., & Cox, Jr., T. H. (1996). Race, gender and opportunity: A study of compensation attainment and the establishment of mentoring relationships. *Journal of Applied Psychology, 81*, 297–308.

Dreher, G. F., & Cox, T. H. (2000). Labor market mobility and cash compensation: The moderating effects of race and gender. *Academy of Management Journal, 43*, 890–900.

Dreher, G. F., & Dougherty, T. W. (1997). Substitutes for career mentoring: Promoting equal opportunity through career management and assessment systems. *Journal of Vocational Behavior, 51*, 110–124.

DuBois, D. L. (2005). Research methodology. In D. L. DuBois & M. J. Karcher (Eds.), *Handbook of mentoring* (pp. 44–64). San Francisco: Sage.

DuBois, D. L., & Hirsch, B. J. (1990). School and neighborhood friendship patterns of Blacks and Whites in early adolescence. *Child Development, 61*, 524–536.

DuBois, D. L., Holloway, B. E., Valentine, J. C., & Cooper, H. (2002). Effectiveness of mentoring programs for youth: A meta-analytic review. *American Journal of Community Psychology, 30*, 157–197.

DuBois, D. L., & Karcher, M. J. (2005). *Handbook of youth mentoring.* Thousand Oaks, CA: Sage.

DuBois, D. L., & Neville, H. A. (1997). Youth mentoring: Investigation of relationship characteristics and perceived benefits. *Journal of Community Psychology, 25*, 227–234.

DuBois, D. L., Neville, H. A., Parra, G. R., & Pugh-Lilly, A. O. (2000). Testing a new model of mentoring. In J. Rhodes (Ed.). *New directions for youth development: A critical view of youth mentoring* (pp. 21–55). San Francisco: Jossey-Bass.

DuBois, D. L., & Silverthorn, N. (2005a). Characteristics of natural mentoring relationships and adolescent adjustment: Evidence from a national study. *Journal of Primary Prevention, 26*(2), 69–92.

DuBois, D. L., & Silverthorn, N. (2005b). Natural mentoring relationships and adolescent health: Evidence from a national survey. *American Journal of Public Health, 95*(3), 518–524.

DuBois, D. L., Silverthorn, N., Pryce, J., Reeves, E., Sanchez, B., Silva, A., Ansu, A. A., Haqq, S., & Takehara, J. (in press). Mentorship: The GirlPOWER! Program. To appear in C. W. Leroy & J. E. Mann (Eds.), *Handbook of preventive and intervention programs for adolescent girls.* Hoboken, NJ: Wiley.

Dubowitz, H., Feigelman, S., & Zuravin, S. (1993). A profile of kinship care. *Child Welfare, LXXII*, 153–169.

Durkheim, E. (1947). *The division of labor in society.* New York: The Free Press.

Durkheim, E. (1951). *Suicide* (John A. Spaulding & George Simpson, Trans.). New York: The Free Press.

Dutton, J. E., & Heaphy, E. D. (2003). The power of high-quality connections. In K. S. Cameron, J. E. Dutton, & R. E. Quinn (Eds.), *Positive organizational scholarship: Foundations of a new discipline* (pp. 263–278). San Francisco: Berrett-Koehler.

Dutton, J. E., & Ragins, B. R. (2007). *Exploring positive relationships at work: Building a theoretical and research foundation*. Mahwah, NJ: Lawrence Erlbaum Associates.

Eby, L. T. (1997). Alternative forms of mentoring in changing organizational environments: A conceptual extension of the mentoring literature. *Journal of Vocational Behavior*, *51*, 125–144.

Eby, L. T., & Allen, T. D. (2002). Further investigation of protégés negative mentoring experiences: Patterns and outcomes. *Group and Organization Management*, *27*, 456–479.

Eby, L. T., Butts, M., Lockwood, A., & Simon, S. A. (2004). Protégés' negative mentoring experiences: Construct development and nomological validation. *Personnel Psychology*, *57*, 411–447.

Eby, L. T., & Lockwood, A. (2005). Proteges' and mentors' reactions to participating in formal mentoring programs: A qualitative inquiry. *Journal of Vocational Behavior*, *67*, 441–458.

Eby, L. T., Lockwood, A., & Butts, M. (2006). Organizational support for mentoring: A multiple perspectives approach. *Journal of Vocational Behavior*, *68*, 267–291.

Eby, L. T., & McManus, S. E. (2004). The protégé's role in negative mentoring experiences. *Journal of Vocational Behavior*, *65*, 255–275.

Eby, L. T., McManus, S. E., Simon, S. A., & Russell, J. E. A. (2000). The protégé's perspective regarding negative mentoring experiences: The development of a taxonomy. *Journal of Vocational Behavior*, *57*, 1–21.

Eccles, J., & Gootman, J. A. (Eds.). (2002). *Community programs to promote youth development*. Washington, DC: National Academy Press.

Eddleston, K. A., Baldridge, D. C., & Veiga, J. F. (2004). Towards modeling the predictors of career success: Does gender matter? *Journal of Managerial Psychology*, *19*(4), 360–385.

Eddy, E., Tannenbaum, S., Alliger, G., D'Abate, C., & Givens, S. (2001). *Mentoring in industry: The top 10 issues when building and supporting a mentoring program*. Technical report prepared for the Naval Air Warfare Training Systems Division (Contract No. N61339-99-D-0012).

Ellis, H. C. (1992). Graduate education in psychology: Past, present, and future. *American Psychologist*, *47*, 570–576.

Ely, R. J. (1995). The role of dominant identity and experience in organizational work on diversity. In S. E. Jackson & M. N. Ruderman (Eds.), *Diversity in work teams: Research paradigms for a changing workplace* (pp. 161–186). Washington, DC: American Psychological Association.

Ely, R. J., & Thomas, D. A. (2001). Cultural diversity at work: The effects of diversity perspectives on work group processes and outcomes. *Administrative Science Quarterly*, *46*, 229–273.

Ensher, E. A., Grant-Vallone, E. J., & Marelich, W. D. (2002). Effects of perceived attitudinal and demographic similarity on protégés' support and satisfaction gained from their mentoring relationships. *Journal of Applied Social Psychology*, *32*, 1407–1430.

Ensher, E. A., Heun, C., & Blanchard, A. (2003). Online mentoring and computer-mediated communication: New directions in research. *Journal of Vocational Behavior*, *63*, 264–288.

Ensher, E. A., & Murphy, S. E. (1997). Effects of race, gender, perceived similarity, and contact on mentor relationships. *Journal of Vocational Behavior*, *50*, 460–481.

Ensher, E. A., Thomas, C., & Murphy, S. E. (2001). Comparison of traditional, step-ahead, and peer mentoring on protégés' support, satisfaction and perceptions of career success: A social exchange perspective. *Journal of Business and Psychology*, *15*, 415–438.

Erdem, F., & Ozen, J. (2003). The perceptions of protégés in academic organizations in regard to the functions of mentoring. *Higher Education in Europe*, *28*, 569–575.

Erikson, E. H. (1950/1963). *Childhood and society* (2nd, reissued ed.). New York: W. W. Norton & Co.

Erikson, E. H. (1968). *Identity, youth, and crisis.* New York: Faber.

Erkut, S., & Mokros, J. R. (1984). Professors as models and mentors for college students. *American Educational Research Journal, 21,* 399–417.

Fagan, M. M. (1988). Formal vs. informal mentoring in law enforcement. *Career Planning and Adult Development Journal, 4*(2), 40–48.

Fagan, M. M., & Walter, G. (1982). Mentoring among teachers. *Journal of Educational Research, 76,* 113–118.

Fagenson, E. A. (1988). The power of a mentor: Protégés' and non-protégés' perceptions of their own power in organizations. *Group and Organization Studies, 13,* 182–194.

Fagenson, E. A. (1989). The mentor advantage: Perceived career/job experiences of protégés versus non-protégés. *Journal of Organizational Behavior, 10,* 309–320.

Fagenson, E. A. (1992). Mentoring – Who needs it? A comparison of protégés' and non-protégés' needs for power, achievement, affiliation, and autonomy. *Journal of Vocational Behavior, 41,* 48–60.

Fagenson-Eland, E. A., & Baugh, S. G. (2001). Personality predictors of protégé mentoring history. *Journal of Applied Social Psychology, 31,* 2502–2517.

Fagenson-Eland, E. A., Marks, M. A., & Amendola, K. L. (1997). Perceptions of mentoring relationships. *Journal of Vocational Behavior, 51,* 29–42.

Fallow, G. O., & Johnson, W. B. (2000). Mentor relationships in secular and religious professional psychology programs. *Journal of Psychology and Christianity, 19,* 363–376.

Fassinger, R. E., & Hensler-McGinnis, N. F. (2005). Multicultural feminist mentoring as individual and small-group pedagogy. In C. Z. Enns & A. L. Sinacore (Eds.), *Teaching and social justice: Integrating multicultural and feminist theories in the classroom* (pp. 143–161). Washington, DC: American Psychological Association.

Feeney, J. A. (1999). Adult romantic attachment and couple relationships. In J. Cassidy & P. R. Shaver (Eds.), *Handbook of attachment: Theory, research and clinical applications* (pp. 355–377). New York: Guilford.

Fehr, B. (2000). The life cycle of friendship. In C. Hendrick & S. S. Hendrick (Eds.), *Close relationships: A sourcebook* (pp. 71–82). Thousand Oaks, CA: Sage.

Feldman, D. C., Folks, W. R., & Turnley, W. H. (1999a). Mentor–protégé diversity and its impact on international internship experiences. *Journal of Organizational Behavior, 20,* 597–612.

Feldman, D. F., Folks, W. R., & Turnley, W. H. (1999b). The socialization of expatriate interns. *Journal of Managerial Issues, 10,* 403–418.

Ferris, G. R., & Judge, T. A. (1991). Personnel/human resources management: A political influence perspective. *Journal of Management, 17,* 447–488.

Festinger, L., Schacter, S., & Back, K. W. (1950). *Social pressure in informal groups.* New York: Harper.

Fetterman, D. M. (2000). *Foundations of empowerment evaluation: Step by step.* Thousand Oaks, CA: Sage.

Finkelstein, L. M., Allen, T. D., & Montei, M. S. (2002, April). *Mentorship quality: The role of relational characteristics and expectations.* Paper presented at the 17th Annual meeting of the Society for Industrial and Organizational Psychology, Toronto, Canada.

Finkelstein, L. M., Allen, T. D., & Rhoton, L. (2003). An examination of the effects of age diversity in mentoring relationships. *Group & Organization Management, 28,* 249–281.

Fishbein, M., & Ajzen, I. (1975). *Belief, attitude, intention, and behavior.* Reading, MA: Addison-Wesley.

Fitzsimons, D. J. (1991). From paternalism to partnership. *Journal of Compensation and Benefits, 6,* 48–52.

Flaxman, E., Ascher, C., & Harrington, C. (1988). *Youth mentoring: Programs and practices.* New York: ERIC Clearinghouse on Urban Education, Institute for Urban and Minority Education, Teachers College, Columbia University.

Fletcher, J. K. (1998). Relational practice: A feminist reconstruction of work. *Journal of Management Inquiry, 7,* 163–187.

Fletcher, J. K., & Ragins, B. R. (in press). Stone Center Relational Theory: A window on relational mentoring. In B. R. Ragins & K. E. Kram (Eds.), *The handbook of mentoring at work: Theory, research and practice.* Thousand Oaks, CA: Sage.

Fo, W. S., & O'Donnell, C. R. (1974). The buddy system: Relationship and contingency condition in a community intervention program for youth with non-professionals as behavior change agents. *Journal of Consulting and Clinical Psychology, 42*(2), 163–169.

Fo, W. S., & O'Donnell, C. R. (1975). The buddy system: Effect of community intervention on delinquent offenses. *Behavior Therapy, 6,* 522–524.

Ford, G. (1998). *Career guidance mentoring for disengaged young people.* Stourbridge, England: Institute of Careers Guidance.

Forret, M. L., Turban, D. B., & Dougherty, T. W. (1996). Issues facing organizations when implementing formal mentoring programmes. *Leadership & Organization Development Journal, 17,* 27–30.

Foster, L. (2001). *Effectiveness of mentor programs: Review of the literature from 1995 to 2000.* Sacramento, CA: California Research Bureau.

Fountain, D. L., & Arbreton, A. (1999). The cost of mentoring. In J. B. Grossman (Ed.), *Contemporary issues in mentoring* (pp. 49–65). Philadelphia: Public/Private Ventures.

Franke, A., & Dahlgren, L. O. (1996). Conceptions of mentoring: An empirical study of conceptions of mentoring during the school-based teacher education. *Teaching & Teacher Education, 12*(6), 627–641.

Freedman, M. (1992). *The kindness of strangers: Reflections on the mentoring movement.* Philadelphia: Public/Private Ventures.

Freedman, M. (1993). *The kindness of strangers: Adult mentors, urban youth, and the new voluntarism.* San Francisco: Jossey-Bass.

Freedman, M. (1994). *The kindness of strangers: The movement to mentor young people in poverty.* Berkeley, CA: Public/Private Ventures.

Freire, P. (1970). *Pedagogy of the oppressed* (Myra Bergman Ramos, Trans; 29th anniversary ed.). New York: Continuum.

Freire, P. (1997). A response. In P. Freire, with J. W. Fraser, D. Macedo, T. McKinnon, & W. T. Stokes (Eds.), *Mentoring the mentor: A critical dialogue with Paulo Freire* (pp. 303–329). New York: Peter Lang.

Friday, E., Friday, S. S., & Green, A. L. (2004). A reconceptualization of mentoring and sponsoring. *Management Decision, 42,* 628–644.

Fuligni, A. J. (1998). Authority, autonomy, and parent–adolescent conflict and cohesion: A study of adolescents from Mexican, Chinese, Filipino, and European backgrounds. *Developmental Psychology, 34,* 782–792.

Fullerton, H. N., Jr. (1999). Labor force participation: 75 years of change, 1950–98 and 1998–2025. *Monthly Labor Review, 122*(12), 3–12.

Fullerton, H. N., Jr., & Toosi, M. (2001). Labor force projections to 2010: Steady growth and changing composition. *Monthly Labor Review, 112*(11), 21–38.

Furstenberg, F. F. (1994). How families manage risk and opportunity in dangerous neighborhoods. In W. J. Wilson (Ed.), *Sociology and the public agenda* (pp. 231–258). Newbury Park, CA: Sage.

Galbo, J. J. (1986). Adolescents' perceptions of significant adults: Implications for the family, the school and youth serving agencies. *Children & Youth Services Review, 8,* 37–51.

Galbraith, M. W. (2003). Celebrating mentoring. *Adult Learning, 14*(1), 2–3.

Gallimore, R. G., Tharp, R. G., & John-Steiner, V. (1992). *The developmental and socio-cultural foundations of mentoring.* Columbia University, New York: Institute for Urban Minority Education (ERIC Document Reproduction Service No. ED 354292).

Garcia Coll, C. T., Meyer, E. C., & Brillon, L. (1995). Ethnic and minority parenting. In M. H. Bornstein (Ed.), *Handbook of parenting: Vol. 2. Biology and ecology of parenting* (pp. 189–209). Mahwah, NJ: Lawrence Erlbaum.

Gardner, W. L., Pickett, C. L., & Brewer, M. B. (2000). Social exclusion and selective memory: How the need to belong influences memory for social events. *Personality and Social Psychology Bulletin, 26,* 486–496.

Garland, A., & Zigler, E. (1994). Psychological correlates of help-seeking attitudes among children and adolescents. *American Journal of Orthopsychiatry, 64,* 586–593.

Garmezy, N. (1987). Stress, competence, and development: Continuities in the study of schizophrenic adults, children vulnerable to psychopathology, and the search for stress-resistant children. *American Journal of Orthopsychiatry, 57*(2), 159–174.

Garringer, M. (2002). Strengthening your "agency capacity". *National Mentoring Center Bulletin, Issue* 11.

Garringer, M. (2004). Putting the "men" back into mentoring. *National Mentoring Center Bulletin* 2:2.

Garvey, B. (2004). The mentoring/counseling/coaching debate: Call a rose by any other name and perhaps it's a bramble? *Development and Learning in Organizations, 18,* 6–8.

Garvey, B., & Alred, G. (2003). An introduction to the symposium on mentoring: Issues and prospects. *British Journal of Guidance and Counselling, 31,* 1–9.

Gaskin, K., & Dobson, B. (1996). *The economic equation of volunteering: A pilot study.* Loughborough, England: Centre for Research in Social Policy.

Gee, E. G. (2005). An investment in student diversity. *Trusteeship, 13*(2), 18–22.

Geiger-DuMond, A. H. (1995). *Mentoring: A practitioner's guide.* Alexandria, VA: American Society for Training and Development, Inc.

Gelso, C. J., Mallinckrodt, B., & Judge, A. B. (1996). Research training environments, attitudes toward research, and research self-efficacy: The revised Research Training Environment Scale. *The Counseling Psychologist, 24,* 304–322.

George, C., & Solomon, J. (1996). Representational models of relationships: Links between caregiving and attachment. *Infant Mental Health Journal, 17*(3), 198–216.

Gergen, K. (1973). Social psychology as history. *Journal of Personality and Social Psychology, 26,* 309–320.

Gerhart, B. (1990). Voluntary turnover and alternative job opportunities. *Journal of Applied Psychology, 75,* 285–297.

Germain, M. (2004, August). *Mentor learning: New constructs for mentoring research.* Southern Management Association Meeting, San Antonio, TX.

Gerstner, C. R., & Day, D. V. (1997). Meta-analytic review of leader–member exchange theory: Correlates and construct issues. *Journal of Applied Psychology, 82,* 827–844.

Gibb, S. (2003). What do we talk about when we talk about mentoring? Blooms and thorns. *British Journal of Guidance & Counselling, 31,* 39–49.

Gibson, D. E. (2004). Role models in career development: New directions for theory and research. *Journal of Vocational Behavior, 65,* 134–156.

Gilbert, L. A. (1985). Dimensions of same-gender student–faculty role-model relationships. *Sex Roles, 12,* 111–123.

Gilbert, L. A., Gallessich, J. M., & Evans, S. L. (1983). Sex of faculty role model and students' self-perceptions of competency. *Sex Roles, 9,* 597–607.

Gilbert, L. A., & Rossman, K. M. (1992). Gender and the mentoring process for women: Implications for professional development. *Professional Psychology: Research and Practice, 23,* 233–238.

Gilligan, C. (1982). *In a different voice: Psychological theory and women's development.* Cambridge, MA: Harvard University Press.

Gilligan, R. (1999). Enhancing the resilience of children and young people in public care by mentoring their talents and interests. *Child and Family Social Work, 4,* 187–196.

Ginwright, S. A. (2005). On urban ground: Understanding African American inter-generational partnerships in urban communities. *Journal of Community Psychology, 33,* 101–110.

Godshalk, V. M., & Sosik, J. J. (2003). Aiming for career success: The role of learning goal orientation in mentoring relationships. *Journal of Vocational Behavior, 63,* 417–437.

Goffman, E. (1963). *Stigma: Notes on the management of a spoiled identity.* Englewood Cliffs, NJ: Prentice Hall.

Gonsiorek, J. C., & Weinrich, J. D. (1991). The definition and scope of sexual orientation. In J. C. Gonsiorek & J. D. Weinrich (Eds.), *Homosexuality: Research implications for public policy* (pp. 1–12). Newbury Park, CA: Sage.

Gonzales, N. A., & Kim, L. S. (1997). Stress and coping in an ethnic minority context: Children's cultural ecologies. In S. A. Wolchik & I. N. Sandler (Eds.), *Handbook of children's coping: Linking theory and intervention. Issues in clinical child psychology* (pp. 481–511). New York: Plenum Press.

Good, J., Halpin, G., & Halpin, G. (2000). A promising prospect for minority retention: Students becoming peer mentors. *Journal of Negro Education, 69,* 375–383.

Goodell, G. E. (1985). Paternalism, patronage, and potlatch: The dynamics of giving and being given to. *Current Anthropology, 26,* 247–257.

Goodenow, C. (1993). Classroom belonging among early adolescent students: Relationships to motivation and achievement. *Journal of Early Adolescence, 12,* 21–43.

Gornick, M. (2005). A proactive approach to retaining "wisdom workers." *Benefits & Compensation Digest,* March, *42*(3), 18.

Goto, S. (1999). Asian Americans and developmental relationships. In A. J. Murrell, F. J. Crosby, & R. J. Ely (Eds.), *Mentoring dilemmas: Developmental relationships within multicultural organizations* (pp. 46–62). Mahwah, NJ: Lawrence Erlbaum.

Gottman, J., Katz, L. F., & Hooven, C. (1996). Parental meta-emotion philosophy and the emotional life of families: Theoretical models and preliminary data. *Journal of Family Psychology, 10*(3), 243–268.

Graen, G. B., & Scandura, T. A. (1987). Toward a psychology of dyadic organizing. *Research in Organizational Behavior, 9,* 175–208.

Graen, G. B., & Uhl-Bien, M. (1995). Relationship-based approach to leadership: Development of leader–member exchange (LMX) theory of leadership over 25 years: Applying a multi-level multi-domain perspective. *Leadership Quarterly, 6,* 219–247.

Graen, G. B., Liden, R. C., & Hoel, W. (1982). Role of leadership in the employee withdrawal process. *Journal of Applied Psychology, 67,* 868–872.

Graham, J. W., & Verma, A. (1991). Predictors and moderators of employee responses to employee participation programs. *Human Relations, 44,* 551–568.

Granfield, M. (March, 1993). Mentoring for money. *Working Woman,* 12–14.

Granger, M. (1993). A review of the literature on the status of women and minorities in the professoriate in higher education. *Journal of School Leadership, 3,* 121–135.

Granovetter, M. (1973). The strength of weak ties. *American Journal of Sociology, 78,* 1360–1380.

Granovetter, M. S. (1974). *Getting a job: A study of contacts and careers.* Cambridge, MA: Harvard University Press.

Grant-Thompson, S. K., & Atkinson, D. R. (1997). Cross-cultural mentor effectiveness and African American male students. *Journal of Black Psychology, 23,* 120–134.

Grant-Vallone, E. J., & Ensher, E. A. (2000). Effects of peer mentoring on types of mentor support, program satisfaction and graduate student stress: A dyadic perspective. *Journal of College Student Development, 41,* 637–642.

Gray, P. J., & Johnson, W. B. (2005). Mentoring and its assessment. In S. L. Tice, N. Jackson, L. Lambert, & P. Englot (Eds.), *University teaching: A guide for graduate students* and faculty (2nd ed., pp. 217–224). Syracuse, NY: Syracuse University Press.

Gray, W. A. (1988). Developing a planned mentoring program to facilitate career development. *Career Planning and Adult Development Journal, 4*(2), 9–16.

Graziano W. G., & Musser, L. M. (1982). The joining and the parting of ways. In S. Duck (Ed.), *Personal relationships 4: Dissolving personal relationships* (pp. 75–106). London: Academic Press.

Grazyk, P. A., & Henry, D. B. (2001). *A developmental perspective on the qualitative aspects of adolescent best friendships.* Paper presented at the Biennial meeting of the Society for Research in Child Development, Minneapolis, MN.

Green, S. G., & Bauer, T. N. (1995). Supervisory mentoring by advisers: Relationships with doctoral student potential, productivity, and commitment. *Personnel Psychology, 48,* 537–561.

Greenberger, E., Chen, C., & Beam, M. R. (1998). The role of "very important" nonparental adults in adolescent development. *Journal of Youth and Adolescence, 27,* 321–343.

Greenberger, E., & McLaughlin, C. S. (1998). Attachment, coping, and explanatory style in late adolescence. *Journal of Youth and Adolescence, 27,* 121–140.

Greenfield, P. M., Keller, H., Fuligni, A., & Maynard, A. (2003). Cultural pathways through universal development. *Annual Review of Psychology, 54,* 461–490.

Greig, R. (2004). *Natural mentors, ethnic identity, and adolescent mental health.* Unpublished doctoral dissertation, University of Florida.

Grineski, S. (2003). A university and community-based partnership: After-school mentoring for low income youth. *School Community Journal, 13,* 101–114.

Grossman, J. B., & Garry, E. (1997). *Mentoring: A proven delinquency prevention strategy.* Washington, DC: US Department of Justice.

Grossman, J. B., & Johnson, A. W. (1998). Assessing the effectiveness of mentoring programs. In J. B. Grossman (Ed.), *Contemporary issues in mentoring* (pp. 25–47). Philadelphia: Public/Private Ventures.

Grossman, J. B., & Rhodes, J. E. (2002). The test of time: Predictors and effects of duration in youth mentoring. *American Journal of Community Psychology, 30,* 199–219.

Grossman, J. B., & Tierney, J. P. (1998). Does mentoring work? An impact study of the Big Brothers/Big Sisters program. *Evaluation Review, 22,* 403–426.

Grube, J. A., & Piliavin, J. A. (2000). Role identity, organizational experiences, and volunteer performance. *Personality and Social Psychology Bulletin, 26*(9), 1108–1119.

Gunn, E. (August, 1995). Mentoring: The democratic version. *Training,* 64–67.

Hall, D. T. (1986). Career development in organizations: Where do we go from here? In D. T. Hall & Associates (Eds.), *Career development in organizations* (pp. 332–351). San Francisco: Jossey-Bass.

Hall, D. T. (1996). *The career is dead – long live the career.* San Francisco: Jossey-Bass.

Hall, J. (2003). *Mentoring and young people: A literature review.* Glasgow, Scotland: The SCRE Centre, University of Glasgow.

Hamilton, B. A., & Scandura, T. A. (2003). E-Mentoring: Implications for organizational learning and development in a wired world. *Organizational Dynamics, 31,* 388–402.

Hamilton, S. F., & Darling, N. (1989). Mentors in adolescents' lives. In K. Hurrelmann & U. Engle (Eds.), *The social world of adolescents* (pp. 121–139). New York: DeGruyter.

Hamilton, S. F., & Hamilton, M. A. (1990). *Linking up: Final report on a mentoring program for youth.* Cornell University: Department of Human Development & Family Studies.

Hamilton, S. F., & Hamilton, M. A. (1992). Mentoring programs: Promise and paradox. *Phi Delta Kappan, 73*(7), 546–550.

Hamilton, S. F., & Hamilton, M. A. (2004). Contexts for mentoring: Adolescent–adult relationships in workplaces and communities. In R. M. Lerner & L. Steinberg (Eds.), *Handbook of adolescent psychology* (2nd ed., pp. 395–428). New York: Wiley.

Haraven, T. K. (1989). Historical changes in children's networks in the family and community. In D. Belle (Ed.), *Children's social networks and social supports* (pp. 15–35). New York: Wiley.

Hardy, L. C. (1998). Mentoring: A long term approach to diversity. *HR Focus*, July, S11.

Harris, S. (2005). *Changing mindsets of educational leaders to improve schools: Voices of doctoral students.* Lanham, MD: Rowman & Littlefield Education.

Harrison, A. O., Wilson, M. N., Pine, C. J., Chan, S. Q., & Buriel, R. (1990). Family ecologies of ethnic minority children. *Child Development, 61*(2), 347–362.

Harrison, D. A., Price, K. H., & Bell, M. P. (1998). Beyond relational demography: Time and the effects of surface- and deep-level diversity on work group cohesion. *Academy of Management Journal, 41*, 96–107.

Harter, S. (1988). Developmental processes in the construction of the self. In T. D. Yawkey & J. E. Johnson (Eds.), *Integrative processes and socialization: Early to middle childhood* (pp. 45–78). Hillsdale, NJ: Lawrence Erlbaum.

Hartup, W. W., & Laursen, B. (1999). Relationships as developmental contexts: Retrospective themes and contemporary issues. In W. A. Collins & B. Laursen (Eds.), *Relationships as developmental contexts* (Vol. 30, pp. 13–35). Mahwah, NJ: Lawrence Erlbaum.

Hazan, C., & Shaver, P. R. (1994). Attachment as an organizational framework for research on close relationships. *Psychological Inquiry, 5*, 1–22.

Head, F. A., Reiman, A. J., & Thies-Sprinthall, L. (1992). The reality of mentoring: Complexity in its process and function. In T. M. Bey & C. T. Holmes (Eds.), *Mentoring: Contemporary principles and issues* (pp. 5–34). Reston, VA: Association of Teacher Educators.

Healy, C. C., & Welchert, A. J. (1990). Mentoring relations: A definition to advance research and practice. *Educational Researcher, 19*, 17–21.

Hebl, M. R., Lin, J., Tonidandel, S., & Knight, J. (2003, April). *Super models: The impact of like-mentors for homosexual employees.* Poster session presented at the Society for Industrial and Organizational Psychology annual conference, Orlando, FL.

Hegstad, C. D., & Wentling, R. M. (2004). The development and maintenance of exemplary formal mentoring programs in fortune 500 companies. *Human Resource Development Quarterly, 15*(Winter), 421–448.

Helms, J. E. (1994). Racial identity and career assessment. *Journal of Career Assessment, 2*, 199–209.

Helms, J. E., & Cook, D. A. (1999). *Using race and culture in counseling and psychotherapy: Theory and process.* Boston: Allyn & Bacon.

Henderson, D. W. (1985). Enlightened mentoring: A characteristic of public management professionalism. *Public Administration Review, 15*, 857–863.

Henrich, K. T. (1991). Loving partnerships: Dealing with sexual attraction and power in doctoral advisement relationships. *Journal of Higher Education, 62*(5), 514–538.

Henry, W. P., & Strupp, H. H. (1994). The therapeutic alliance as interpersonal process. In A. O. Horvath & L. S. Greenberg (Eds.), *The working alliance: Theory, research, and practice* (pp. 51–84). New York: Wiley.

Herman, L., & Mandell, A. (2004). *From teaching to mentoring: Principle and practice, dialogue and life in adult education.* London: RoutledgeFalmer.

Herman, R. E., Olivo, T. G., & Gioia, J. L. (2003). *Impending crisis: Too many jobs, too few people.* Winchester, VA: Oakhill Press.

Herrera, C., Sipe, C. L., & McClanahan, W. S. (2000). *Mentoring school-age children: Relationship development in community-based and school-based programs.* Philadelphia: P/PV.

Hespe, G., & Wall, T. (1976). The demand for participation among employees. *Human Relations, 29,* 411–428.

Higgins, C., Judge. T. A., & Ferris, G. R. (2003). Influence tactics and work outcomes: A meta-analysis. *Journal of Organizational Behavior, 24,* 89–106.

Higgins, M. C. (2007). A contingency perspective on developmental networks. In J. Dutton & B. R. Ragins (Eds.), *Exploring positive relationships at work: Building a theoretical and research foundation* (pp. 207–224). Mahwah, NJ: Lawrence Erlbaum and Associates.

Higgins, M. C., Chandler, D., & Kram, K. E. (in press). Boundary spanning of developmental networks: A social network perspective on mentoring. In B. R. Ragins & K. E. Kram (Eds.), *The handbook of mentoring at work: Theory, research and practice.* Thousand Oaks, CA: Sage.

Higgins, M. C., & Kram, K. (2001). Reconceptualizing mentoring at work: A developmental network perspective. *Academy of Management Review, 26,* 264–288.

Higgins, M. C., & Thomas, D. A. (2001). Constellations and careers: Toward understanding the effects of multiple developmental relationships. *Journal of Organizational Behavior, 22,* 223–247.

Hill, C. E., Thompson, B. J., & Williams, E. N. (1997). A guide to conducting consensual qualitative research. *The Counseling Psychologist, 25,* 517–572.

Hinde, R. A. (1997). *Relationships: A dialectical perspective.* Hove, England: Psychology Press.

Hollin, C. R. (1995). The meaning and implications of programme integrity. In J. McGuire (Ed.), *What works: Reducing reoffending* (pp. 195–208). Chichester, England: Wiley.

Hollingsworth, M. A., & Fassinger, R. E. (2002). The role of faculty mentors in the research training of counseling psychology doctoral students. *Journal of Counseling Psychology, 49,* 324–330.

Homans, G. C. (1958). Social behavior as exchange. *American Journal of Sociology, 63,* 597–606.

Horn, R. A. (2001). Promoting social justice and caring in schools and communities: The unrealized potential of the cohort model. *Journal of School Leadership, 11,* 313–334.

Horvath, A. O., & Luborsky, L. (1993). The role of the therapeutic alliance in psychotherapy. *Journal of Consulting and Clinical Psychology, 61*(4), 561–573.

Hughes, H. M., Hinson, R. C., Eardley, J. L., Farrell, S. M., Goldberg, M. A., Hattrich, L. G., et al. (1993). Research vertical team: A model for scientist-practitioner training. *The Clinical Psychologist, 46,* 14–18.

Hughes, K. L. (2000). Gender and youth mentoring. *Advances in Gender Research, 4,* 189–225.

Hunt, D. M., & Michael, C. (1983). Mentorship: A career training and development tool. *Academy of Management Review, 8,* 475–485.

Huston, T. L., & Burgess, R. L. (1979). Social exchange in developing relationships: An overview. In R. L. Burgess & T. L. Huston (Eds.), *Social exchanges in developing relationships* (pp. 3–28). New York: Academic Press.

Huwe, J. M., & Johnson, W. B. (2003). On being an excellent protégé: What graduate students need to know. *Journal of College Student Psychotherapy, 17,* 41–57.

Ibarra, H. (1993). Personal networks of women and minorities in management: A conceptual framework. *Academy of Management Review, 18*(1), 56–87.

Jackson, C. H., Kite, M. E., & Branscombe, N. R. (1996). *African-American women's mentoring experiences.* Paper presented at annual meeting of the American Psychological Association, Toronto, Canada, August. (ERIC Document Reproduction Service No. ED 401 371)

Jackson, V. A., Palepu, A., Szalacha, L., Caswell, C., Carr, P. L., & Inui, T. (2003). Having the right chemistry: A qualitative study of mentoring in academic medicine. *Academic Medicine, 78,* 328–334.

Jacobi, M. (1991). Mentoring and undergraduate academic success. A literature review. *Review of Educational Research, 61,* 505–532.

Jaffee, D. (2004, July 9). Learning communities can be cohesive – and divisive. *Chronicle of Higher Education, 50*(44), B16.

Jaffee, S. R., Moffitt, T. E., Caspi, A., & Taylor, A. (2003). Life with (or without) father: The benefits of living with two biological parents depend on the father's antisocial behavior. *Child Development, 74*(1), 109–126.

Jakofsky, E. F., & Peters, L. H. (1983). The hypothesized effects of ability in the turnover process. *Academy of Management Review, 8*, 46–49.

James, E. H. (2000). Race-related differences in promotions and support: Underlying effects of human and social capital. *Organization Science, 11*, 493–508.

de Janasz, S. C., & Sullivan, S. E. (2004). Multiple mentoring in academe: Developing the professorial network. *Journal of Vocational Behavior, 64*, 263–283.

Jasinskaja-Lahti, I., & Liebkind, K. (2001). Perceived discrimination and psychological adjustment among Russian-speaking immigrant adolescents in Finland. *International Journal of Psychology, 36*, 174–185.

Jekielek, S., Moore, K. A., & Hair, E. C. (2002). *Mentoring programs and youth development: A synthesis.* Washington, DC: Child Trends.

Jekielek, S. M., Moore, K. A., Hair, E. C., & Scarupa, H. J. (2002). *Mentoring: A promising strategy for youth development.* Washington, DC: Child Trends Research Brief.

Jennings, L., & Skovholt, T. M. (1999). The cognitive, emotional, and relational characteristics of master therapists. *Journal of Counseling Psychology, 46*, 3–11.

Johnson, A. W. (1997). *Mentoring at-risk youth: A research review and evaluation of the impacts of the Sponsor-A-Scholar Program on student performance.* Unpublished doctoral dissertation, University of Pennsylvania.

Johnson, A. W. (1998). *An evaluation of the long-term impacts of the Sponsor-a-Scholar Program on student performance. Final report to the Commonwealth Fund.* Princeton, NJ: Mathematica Policy Research, Inc.

Johnson, A. W. (1999). *An evaluation of the long-term impact of the Sponsor-a-Scholar (SAS) Program on student performance.* Princeton, NJ: Mathematica Policy Research.

Johnson, C. S. (1989). Mentoring programs. In M. L. Upcraft & J. Gardner (Eds.), *The freshman year experience: Helping students survive and succeed in college* (pp. 118–128). San Francisco: Jossey-Bass.

Johnson, K. K. P., Yust, B. L., & Fritchie, L. L. (2001). Views on mentoring by clothing and textiles faculty. *Clothing and Textiles Research Journal, 19*, 31–40.

Johnson, W. B. (2002). The intentional mentor: Strategies and guidelines for the practice of mentoring. *Professional Psychology: Research and Practice, 33*, 88–96.

Johnson, W. B. (2003). A framework for conceptualizing competence to mentor. *Ethics and Behavior, 13*, 127–151.

Johnson, W. B. (2006). *On being a mentor: A guide for higher education faculty.* Mahwah, NJ: Lawrence Erlbaum.

Johnson, W. B., & Huwe, J. M. (2002). Toward a typology of mentorship dysfunction in graduate school. *Psychotherapy: Theory/research/practice/training, 39*, 44–55.

Johnson, W. B., & Huwe, J. M. (2003). *Getting mentored in graduate school.* Washington, DC: American Psychological Association.

Johnson, W. B., Koch, C., Fallow, G. O., & Huwe, J. M. (2000). Prevalence of mentoring in clinical versus experimental doctoral programs: Survey findings, implications, and recommendations. *Psychotherapy, 37*, 325–334.

Johnson, W. B., & Nelson, N. (1999). Mentor–protégé relationships in graduate training: Some ethical concerns. *Ethics & Behavior, 9*, 189–210.

Johnson, W. B., & Ridley, C. R. (2004). *The elements of mentoring.* New York: Palgrave MacMillan.

Johnson, W. B., & Zlotnik, S. (2005). The frequency of advising and mentoring as salient work roles in academic job advertisements. *Mentoring and Tutoring, 13*, 95–107.

Johnson-Bailey, J., & Cervero, R. M. (2004). Mentoring in black and white: The intricacies of cross-cultural mentoring. *Mentoring & Tutoring, 12*(1), 7–21.

Johnston, W., & Packer, A. (1987). *Workforce 2000: Work and workers for the 21st century.* Indianapolis, IN: Hudson Institute.

Jordan, J. V. (1992). The relational self: A new perspective for understanding women's development. *Contemporary Psychotherapy Review, 7,* 56–71.

Jordan, J. V. (1997). A relational perspective for understanding women's development. In J. V. Jordan (Ed.), *Women's growth in diversity: More writings from the Stone Center* (pp. 9–24). New York: Guilford Press.

Jucovy, L. (2001a). *Recruiting mentors: A guide to finding volunteers to work with youth.* Philadelphia: Public/Private Ventures.

Jucovy, L. (2001b). *Training new mentors.* Philadelphia: Public/Private Ventures.

Jucovy, L. (2001c). *Supporting mentors.* Philadelphia: Public/Private Ventures.

Jucovy, L. (2001d). *Building relationships: A guide for new mentors.* Philadelphia: Public/Private Ventures.

Jucovy, L. (2001e). *Supporting mentors.* Philadelphia: Public/Private Ventures.

Jucovy, L. (2002). *Measuring the quality of mentor-youth relationships: A tool for mentoring programs.* Philadelphia: Public/Private Ventures.

Kalbfleisch, P. (1993). *Interpersonal communication: Evolving interpersonal relationships.* Hillsdale, NJ: Lawrence Erlbaum Associates, Inc.

Kalbfleisch, P. J. (1997). Appeasing the mentor. *Aggressive Behavior, 23,* 389–403.

Kalbfleisch, P. J., & Davies, A. B. (1991). Minorities and mentoring: Managing the multicultural institution. *Communication Education, 40,* 266–271.

Kalbfleisch, P., & Davies, A. (1993). An interpersonal model of participation in mentoring relationships. *Western Journal of Communication, 57,* 399–415.

Kanter, R. M. (1977). *Men and women of the corporation.* New York: Basic Books.

Karcher, M. J. (2005). Cross-age peer mentoring. In D. L. DuBois & M. J. Karcher (Eds.), *Handbook of youth mentoring* (pp. 266–285). Thousand Oaks, CA: Sage.

Karcher, M. J., Davis, C., & Powell, B. (2004). The effects of developmental mentoring on connectedness and academic achievement. *School Community Journal, 14,* 35–50.

Karcher, M. J., & Lee, Y. (2002). Connectedness among Taiwanese middle school students: A validation study of the Hemingway Measure of Adolescent Connectedness. *Asia Pacific Education Review, 3,* 95–114.

Karcher, M. J., & Lindwall, J. (2003). Social interest, connectedness and challenging experiences: What makes high school mentors persist? *Journal of Individual Psychology, 59,* 293–315.

Kaye, B., & Jacobson, B. (1996). Reframing mentoring. *Training & Development, 50,* 44–47.

Keashly, L., Trott, V., & MacLean, L. M. (1994). Abusive behavior in the workplace: A preliminary investigation. *Violence and Victims, 9,* 341–357.

Keele, R. L., Bucker, K., & Bushnell, S. J. (1987). Formal mentoring programs are no panacea. *Management Review, 76*(2), 67–68.

Keller, T., & Dansereau, F. (1995). Leadership and empowerment: A social exchange perspective. *Human Relations, 48,* 127–145.

Keller, T. E. (2005a). The stages and development of mentoring relationships. In D. L. DuBois & M. J. Karcher (Eds.), *Handbook of youth mentoring* (pp. 82–99). Thousand Oaks, CA: Sage.

Keller, T. E. (2005b). A systemic model of the youth mentoring intervention. *Journal of Primary Prevention, 26*(2), 169–188.

Keller, T. E., Pryce, J. M., & Neugebauer, A. (2004). *Observational methods for assessing the nature and course of mentor–child interactions.* Unpublished manuscript.

Kenny, D. A. (1996). Models of non-independence in dyadic research. *Journal of Personal and Social Relationships, 13,* 279–294.

Kim, C. Y., Goto, S. G., Bai, M. M., Kim, T. E., & Wong, E. (2001). Culturally congruent mentoring: Predicting Asian American student participation using the theory of reasoned action. *Journal of Applied Social Psychology, 31,* 2417–2437.

Kim, J. (1981). The process of Asian American identity development: A study of Japanese-American women's perceptions of their struggle to achieve personal identities as Americans of Asian ancestry. *Dissertation Abstract International, 42,* 155 1A. (University Microfilms No. 81-18080)

Kim, U., Triandis, H. C., Kâğitçibaşi, Ç., Choi, S. C., & Yoon, G. (Eds.). (1994). *Individualism and collectivism: Theory, method, and applications.* Thousand Oaks, CA: Sage.

King, K. A., Vidourek, R. A., Davis, B., & McClellan, W. (2002). Increasing self-esteem and school connectedness through a multidimensional mentoring program. *Journal of School Health, 72,* 294–299.

Kirchmeyer, C. (1998). Determinants of managerial career success: Evidence and explanation of male/female differences. *Journal of Management, 24,* 673–692.

Kirchner, E. P. (1969). Graduate education in psychology: Retrospective views of advanced degree recipients. *Journal of Clinical Psychology, 25,* 207–213.

Kirkpatrick, D. (1994). *Evaluating training programs: The four levels.* San Francisco: Berrett-Koehler.

Kirkpatrick, L. A. (1999). Attachment and religious representations and behavior. In J. Cassidy & P. R Shaver (Eds.), *Handbook of attachment: Theory, research and clinical applications* (pp. 803–822). New York: Guilford.

Kizilos, P. (April, 1990). Take my mentor please! *Training,* 49–55.

Klauss, R. (1981). Formalized mentor relationship for management and executive development programs in the federal government. *Public Administrative Review, July/August,* 489–496.

Klaw, E. L., & Rhodes, J. E. (1995). Mentor relationships and the career development of pregnant and parenting African-American teenagers. *Psychology of Women Quarterly, 19,* 551–562.

Klaw, E. L., Rhodes, J. E., & Fitzgerald, L. F. (2003). Natural mentors in the lives of African American adolescent mothers: Tracking relationships over time. *Journal of Youth and Adolescence, 32,* 223–232.

Knouse, S. B. (2001). Virtual mentors: Mentoring on the internet. *Journal of Employment Counseling, 38,* 162–169.

Knox, S., Schlosser, L. Z., Pruitt, N., & Hill, C. E. (2006). A qualitative study of the graduate advising relationship: The advisor perspective. *The Counseling Psychologist, 34,* 489–518.

Koberg, C. S., Boss, R. W., Chappell, D., & Ringer, R. C. (1994). Correlates and consequences of protégé mentoring in a large hospital. *Group and Organization Management, 19,* 219–239.

Koberg, C. S., Boss, R. W., & Goodman, E. (1998). Factors and outcomes associated with mentoring among health-care professionals. *Journal of Vocational Behavior, 53,* 58–72.

Koch, C., & Johnson, W. B. (2000). Documenting the benefits of undergraduate mentoring. *Council on Undergraduate Research Quarterly, 19,* 172–175.

Kochan, F. K., & Trimble, S. B. (2000). From mentoring to co-mentoring: Establishing collaborative relationships. *Theory Into Practice, 39*(1), 20–28.

Kodama, C. M., McEwen, M. K., Liang, C. T. H., & Lee, S. (2002). An Asian American perspective on psychosocial development theory. In M. K. McEwen, C. M. Kodama, A. N. Alvarez, S. Lee, & C. T. H. Liang (Eds.), *Working with Asian American college students* (pp. 45–60). San Francisco: Jossey-Bass.

Kohout, J., & Wicherski, M. (2003). *1999 Doctorate employment survey.* Washington, DC: American Psychological Association.

Kram, K. E. (1983). Phases of the mentor relationship. *Academy of Management Journal, 26,* 608–625.

Kram, K. E. (1985). *Mentoring at work: Developmental relationships in organizational life.* Glenview, IL: Scott, Foresman and Company.

Kram, K. E. (1996). A relational approach to career development. In D. T. Hall (Ed.), *The career is dead – Long live the career: A relational approach to careers* (pp. 132–157). San Francisco: Jossey-Bass.

Kram, K. E., & Hall, D. T. (1989). Mentoring as an antidote to stress during corporate trauma. *Human Resource Management, 24,* 493–510.

Kram, K. E., & Hall, D. T. (1995). Mentoring in a context of diversity and turbulence. In E. E. Kossek & S. Lobel (Eds.), *Managing diversity: Human resources strategies for transforming the workplace* (pp. 108–136). Cambridge, MA: Blackwell.

Kram, K. E., & Isabella, L. A. (1985). Mentoring alternatives: The role of peer relationships in career development. *Academy of Management Journal, 28,* 110–132.

Kring, J. P., Richardson, T. R., Burns, S. R., & Davis, S. F. (1999). Do mentors influence the appearance and content of student posters at regional and national conferences? *College Student Journal, 33,* 278–80.

Kuhn, T. S. (1970). *The structure of scientific revolutions.* Chicago: University of Chicago Press.

Kuhn, T. S. (1989/2000). The natural and the human sciences. In *The road since structure* (pp. 216–223). Chicago: University of Chicago Press.

Ladany, N., Constantine, M. G., Miller, K., Erickson, C. D., & Muse-Burke, J. L. (2000). Supervisor countertransference: A qualitative investigation into its identification and description. *Journal of Counseling Psychology, 47,* 102–115.

Langhout, R. D., Rhodes, J. E., & Osborne, L. N. (2004). An exploratory study of youth mentoring in an urban context: Adolescents' perceptions of relationship styles. *Journal of Youth and Adolescence, 33,* 293–306.

Lankau, M. J., & Scandura, T. A. (2002). An investigation of personal learning in mentoring relationships: Content, antecedents, and consequences. *Academy of Management Journal, 45,* 779–790.

Larose, S., & Tarabulsy, G. M. (2005). Academically at-risk students. In D. L. DuBois & M. J. Karcher (Eds.), *Handbook of youth mentoring* (pp. 440–453). Thousand Oaks, CA: Sage.

Larose, S., Tarabulsy, G., & Cyrenne, D. (2005). Perceived autonomy and relatedness as moderating the impact of teacher–student mentoring relationships on student academic adjustment. *Journal of Primary Prevention, 26,* 111–128.

Larson, R. W. (2000). Toward a psychology of positive youth development. *American Psychologist, 55*(1), 170–183.

Lattimore, R. R., & Borgen, F. H. (1999). Validity of the 1994 Strong Interest Inventory with racial and ethnic groups in the United States. *Journal of Counseling Psychology, 146,* 185–195.

Lave, J., & Wenger, E. (1991). *Situated learning: Legitimate peripheral participation.* New York: Cambridge University Press.

Le, C. N. (2005a). The model minority image. *Asian-Nation: The landscape of Asian America.* Retrieved April 8, 2005, from www.asian-nation.org/model-minority.shtml.

Le, C. N. (2005b). Socioeconomic statistics & demographics. *Asian-Nation: The landscape of Asian America.* Retrieved April 8, 2005, from www.asian-nation.org/demographics.shtml.

Leana, C. R., & Van Buren, H. J., III. (1999). Organizational social capital and employment practices. *Academy of Management Review, 24*(3), 538–555.

LeCluyse, E. E., Tollefson, N., & Borgers, S. B. (1985). Differences in female graduate students in relation to mentoring. *College Student Journal, 19,* 411–415.

Lee, E. (1989). Assessment and treatment of Chinese American immigrant families. *Journal of Psychotherapy and the Family*, *6*, 99–122.

Lee, J., & Cramond, B. (1999). The positive effects of mentoring economically disadvantaged students. *Professional School Counseling*, *2*, 172–178.

Lee, R. M., & Robbins, S. B. (1998). The relationship between social connectedness and anxiety, self-esteem, and social identify. *Journal of Counseling Psychology*, *45*, 338–345.

Lefkowitz, B. (1987). *Tough change: Growing up on your own in America*. New York: Free Press.

Lester, V., & Johnson, C. (1981). The learning dialogue: Mentoring. In J. Fried (Ed.), *Education for student development. New directions for student services* (No. 15, pp. 49–56). San Francisco: Jossey-Bass.

Levinger, G. (1979). A social exchange view on the dissolution of pair relationships. In R. L. Burgess & T. L Huston (Eds.). *Social exchange in developing relationships* (pp. 169–196). New York: Academic Press.

Levinson, D. (1978). Major tasks of the novice phase. In *The seasons of a man's life* (pp. 97–101). New York: Knopf.

Levinson, D. J., Darrow, C. N., Klein, E. B., Levinson, M. A., & McKee, B. (1978). *The seasons of a man's life*. New York: Knopf.

Lewicki, R. J., & Bunker, B. B. (1995). Trust in relationships: A model of trust development and decline. In B. B. Bunker & J. Z. Rubin (Eds.), *Conflict, cooperation, and justice* (pp. 133–173). San Francisco: Jossey-Bass.

Liang, B., Brogan, D., Corral, M., & Spencer, R. (2005). *Youth mentoring relationships across three developmental periods: A qualitative analysis*. Unpublished manuscript.

Liang, B., Tracy, A. J., Taylor, C. A., & Williams, L. M. (2002). Mentoring college-age women: A relational approach. *American Journal of Community Psychology*, *30*, 271–288.

Liang, B., Tracy, A., Kauh, T., Taylor, C., & Williams, L. M. (2006). Mentoring Asian and White American College Women, *Journal of Multicultural Counseling and Development*, *34*, 143–154.

Liang, C. T. H., & Sedlacek, W. E. (2003a). Attitudes of White student services practitioners toward Asian Americans. *National Association of Student Personnel Administrators Journal*, *40*(3), 30–42. www.publications.naspa.org/naspajournal/vol40/iss3/art2.

Liang, C. T. H., & Sedlacek, W. E. (2003b). Utilizing factor analysis to understand the needs of Asian American students. *Journal of College Student Development*, *44*, 260–266. www.publications.naspa.org/naspajournal/vol40/iss3/art2.

Liden, R. C., Sparrowe, R. T., & Wayne, S. J. (1997). Leader–member exchange theory: The past and potential for the future. *Research in Personnel and Human Resources Management*, *15*, 47–119.

Liden, R. C., Wayne, S. J., & Stilwell, D. (1993). A longitudinal study on the early development of leader–member exchanges. *Journal of Applied Psychology*, *78*, 662–674.

Lin, N., Ensel, W. M., & Vaughn, J. C. (1981). Social resources and strength of ties: Structural factors in occupational status attainment. *American Sociological Review*, *46*, 393–405.

Linnehan, F. (2001). The relation of a work-based mentoring program to the academic performance and behavior of African American students. *Journal of Vocational Behavior*, *59*, 310–325.

Lipsey, M. W., & Wilson, D. B. (2001). *Practical meta-analysis*. Thousand Oaks, CA: Sage.

Lock, E. (2002). *Examining the relationship between organizational ideologies and technology: The case of urban youth development programs*. Unpublished manuscript, University of Chicago.

Locke, E. A., Shaw, K. N., Saari, L. M., & Latham, G. P. (1981). Goal setting and task performance. *Psychological Bulletin*, *90*, 125–152.

Long, J. S. (1978). Productivity and academic position in the scientific career. *American Sociological Review, 43*, 889–908.

LoSciuto, L., Rajala, A. K., Townsend, T. N., & Taylor, A. S. (1996). An outcome evaluation of *Across Ages*: An intergenerational mentoring approach to drug prevention. *Journal of Adolescent Research, 11*, 116–129.

Lumina Foundation for Education (2002). *Enhancing student success. Annual report*. Indianapolis, IN: Lumina Foundation for Education.

Luna, G., & Cullen, D. (1998). Do graduate students need mentoring? *College Student Journal, 32*, 322–330.

Luthans, F. (2002). The need for and meaning of positive organizational behavior. *Journal of Organizational Behavior, 23*, 695–706.

Luthans, F., & Youssef, C. M. (2004). Human, social, and now positive psychological capital management: Investing in people for competitive advantage. *Organizational Dynamics, 33*, 143–160.

Lynch, R. V. (2002, November). *Mentoring across race: Critical case studies of African American students in a predominantly White institution of higher education*. Paper presented at annual meeting of the Association for the Study of Higher Education, Sacramento, CA.

Maccoby, E. E. (1990). Gender and relationships: A developmental account. *American Psychologist, 45*, 513–520.

MacDonald, K. E., Balcazar, F. E., & Keys, C. B. (2005). Youth with disabilities. In D. L. DuBois & M. J. Karcher (Eds.), *Handbook of youth mentoring* (pp. 493–508). Thousand Oaks, CA: Sage.

Maki, M. T., & Kitano, H. H. L. (2002). Counseling Asian Americans. In P. B. Pedersen, J. G. Draguns, W. J. Lonner, & J. E. Trimble (Eds.), *Counseling across cultures* (5th ed., pp. 109–131). Thousand Oaks, CA: Sage.

Malloy, T. E., & Albright, L. (2001). Multiple and single interaction dyadic research designs: Conceptual and analytical issues. *Basic and Applied Social Psychology, 23*(1), 1–19.

Mansfield, P., McAllister, F., & Collard, J. (1992). Equality: Implications for sexual intimacy in marriage. *Sexual & Marital Therapy, 7*, 213–220.

Marasco, C. A. (2005a). Employment: MentorNet supports women in science. *Chemical & Engineering News, 83*, 55.

Marasco, C. A. (2005b). Women faculty make little progress. *Chemical & Engineering News, 83*, 38–39.

March, J. G., & Simon, H. A. (1958). *Organizations*. New York: Wiley.

Marin, G., & Marin, B. V. (1991). *Research with Hispanic populations*. Newbury Park, CA: Sage.

Marin, G., & Triandis, H. C. (1985). Allocentrism as an important characteristic of the behavior of Latin Americans and Hispanics. In R. Diaz-Guerrero (Ed.), *Cross-cultural and national studies in social psychology* (pp. 85–104). Amsterdam: Elsevier Science.

Markus, H., & Nurius, P. (1986). Possible selves. *American Psychologist, 41*, 954–969.

Markus, H. R., & Oyserman, D. (1989). Gender and thought: The role of the self-concept. In M. Crawford & M. Gentry (Eds.), *Gender and thought: Psychological perspectives* (pp. 100–127). New York: Springer-Verlag.

Masten, A. S., Best, K. M., & Garmezy, N. (1990). Resilience and development: Contributions from the study of children who overcome adversity. *Development and Psychopathology, 2*, 425–444.

Masten, A. S., & Coatsworth, J. D. (1998). The development of competence in favorable and unfavorable environments: Lessons from research on successful children. *American Psychologist, 53*(2), 205–220.

Masten, A. S., & Garmezy, N. (1985). Risk, vulnerability, and protective factors in developmental psychopathology. In B. B. Lahey & A. E. Kazdin (Eds.), *Advances in child-clinical psychology* (pp. 1–52). New York: Plenum.

Mathews, J. (2004). Redefining scholarship: Search begins for college-bound "posse." *The Washington Post*, Metro Section, C1.

Maton, K. I., Sto. Domingo, M. R., & King, J. (2005). Faith-based organizations. In D. L. DuBois & M. J. Karcher (Eds.), *Handbook of youth mentoring* (pp. 376–391). Thousand Oaks, CA: Sage.

McAdams, D. P., Hart, H. M. H., & Maruna, S. (1998). The anatomy of generativity. In D. P. McAdams & E. de St. Aubin (Eds.), *Generativity and adult development: How and why we care for the next generation* (pp. 7–43). Washington, DC: American Psychological Association.

McGowan, E. M. (2004). *Relationship work: A descriptive theory of a faculty-to-faculty formal mentoring program in higher education.* Cambridge, MA: Harvard University.

McLaughlin, M. W., Irby, M. A., & Langman, J. (1994). *Urban sanctuaries: Neighborhood organizations in the lives and futures of inner-city youth.* San Francisco: Jossey-Bass.

McLearn, K. T., Colasanto, D., & Schoen, C. (1998). *Mentoring makes a difference: Findings from The Commonwealth Fund 1998 Survey of Adults Mentoring Young People.* The Commonwealth Fund. Retrieved March 23, 2005, from the World Wide Web: www.cmwf.org/publications/publications_show.htm?doc_id=230658

McLearn, K. T., Colasanto, D., Schoen, C., & Shapiro, M. Y. (1999). Mentoring matters: A national survey of adults mentoring young people. In J. B. Grossman (Ed.), *Contemporary issues in mentoring* (pp. 66–83). Philadelphia: Public/Private Ventures.

McManus, S. E., & Russell, J. E. A. (1997). New directions for mentoring research: An examination of related constructs. *Journal of Vocational Behavior, 51*, 145–161.

McPartland, J. M., & Nettles, S. M. (1991). Using community adults as advocates or mentors for at-risk middle school students: A two year evaluation of Project RAISE. *American Journal of Education, 99*, 568–586.

Meline, T., & Wang, B. (2004). Effect-size reporting practices in AJSLP and other ASHA journals, 1999–2003. *American Journal of Speech-language Pathology, 13*, 202–207.

Mendleson, J. L., Barnes, A. K., & Horn, G. (1989). The guiding light to corporate culture. *Personnel Administrator, 34*(7), 70–72.

MENTOR (2003). *Elements of effective practice* (2nd ed). Alexandria, VA: MENTOR/ National Mentoring Partnership.

MENTOR/National Mentoring Partnership (2006). *Legislative history.* Retrieved March 10, 2006, from www.mentoring.org/take_action/funding/legislative_history.php.

Merriam, S. B. (1983). Mentors and protégés: A critical review of the literature. *Adult Education Quarterly, 33*, 161–173.

Merton, R. K. (1957). *Social theory and social structure.* Glencoe, IL: The Free Press.

Mertz, N. T. (2004). What's a mentor anyway? *Educational Administration Quarterly, 40*, 541–560.

Messmer, M. (2001). *Human resources kit for dummies.* New York: Wiley.

Meyer, J. W., & Rowan, B. (1977). Institutional organizations: Formal structure as myth and ceremony. *American Journal of Sociology, 83*, 343–363.

Mezias, J. M., & Scandura, T. A. (2005). A needs-driven approach to expatriate adjustment and career development: A multiple mentoring perspective. *Journal of International Business Studies, 36*, 519–538.

Miller, A. D. (1999). *Mentoring: A guide to effective evaluation.* Salford, England: National Mentoring Network.

Miller, A. D. (2002). *Mentoring students and young people.* London: Kogan Page.

Miller, A. D., Drury, C., Stewart, L., & Ross, B. (2005). *An evaluation of the Home Office Mentoring Fund Initiative.* London: Home Office (forthcoming).

Miller, J. B. (1976). *Toward a new psychology of women.* Boston: Beacon Press.

Miller, J. B., & Stiver, I. P. (1997). *The healing connection: How women form relationships in therapy and in life.* Boston: Beacon Press, Inc.

Mills, J., Clark, M. S., Ford, T., & Johnson, M. (2004). Measuring communal strength. *Personal Relationships, 11,* 213–230.

Milne, S. H., Blum, T. C., & Roman, P. M. (1994). Factors influence employees' propensity to use an employee assistance program. *Personnel Psychology, 47,* 123–145.

Mintz, L. B., Bartels, K. M., & Rideout, C. A. (1995). Training in counseling ethnic minorities and race-based availability of graduate school resources. *Professional Psychology: Research and Practice, 26,* 316–321.

Missirian, A. K. (1982). *The corporate connection: Why executive women need mentors to reach the top.* Englewood Cliffs, NJ: Prentice Hall.

Mitchell, T. R., & Lee, T. W. (2001). The unfolding model of voluntary turnover and job embeddedness: Foundations for a comprehensive theory of attachment. In L. Cummings & B. Staw (Eds.), *Research in organizational behavior* (Vol. 23, pp. 189–246). Greenwich, CT: JAI Press.

Mitchell, T. R., Sablynski, C. J., Burton, J. P., & Holtom, B. C. (2004). The effects of job embeddedness on organizational citizenship, job performance, volitional absences, and voluntary turnover. *Academy of Management Journal, 47,* 711–722.

Mobley, G. M., Jaret, C., Marsh, K., & Lim, Y. Y. (1994). Mentoring, job satisfaction, gender, and the legal profession. *Sex Roles, 31,* 79–98.

Mohr, J. J. (2002). Heterosexual identity and the heterosexual therapist: Using identity as a framework for understanding sexual orientation issues in psychotherapy. *The Counseling Psychologist, 30,* 532–566.

Moon, T. R., & Callahan, C. M. (2001). Curricular modifications, family outreach, and a mentoring program: Impacts on achievement and gifted instruction in high-risk primary students. *Journal for the Education of the Gifted, 24,* 305–321.

Moore, K. M., & Amey, M. J. (1988). Some faculty leaders are born women. In M. A. D. Sagaria (Ed.), *Empowering women: Leadership development strategies on campus. New directions for student services: No. 44* (pp. 39–50). San Francisco: Jossey-Bass.

Morgan, D. L., Neal, M. B., & Carder, P. (1997). The stability of core and peripheral networks over time. *Social Networks, 19,* 9–25.

Morrow, K. V., & Styles, M. B. (1995). *Building relationships with youth in program settings: A study of Big Brothers Big Sisters.* Philadelphia: Public/Private Ventures.

Mullan, B. (1984). *The mating trade.* London: Routledge & Kegan Paul.

Mullen, C. A. (2003). The WIT cohort: A case study of informal doctoral mentoring. *Journal of Further and Higher Education, 27,* 411–426.

Mullen, C. A. (2005). *The mentorship primer.* New York: Peter Lang.

Mullen, C. A. (2006). *A graduate student guide: Making the most of mentoring.* Lanham, MD: Rowman & Littlefield Education.

Mullen, C. A., Cox, M. D., Boettcher, C. K., & Adoue, D. S. (Eds.). (2000a). *Breaking the circle of one: Redefining mentorship in the lives and writings of educators* (2nd ed.). New York: Peter Lang.

Mullen, C. A., Whatley, A., & Kealy, W. A. (2000b). Widening the circle: Faculty–student support groups as innovative practice in higher education. *Interchange: A Quarterly Review of Education, 31*(1), 35–60.

Mullen, E. J. (1994). Framing the mentoring relationship as an information exchange. *Human Resource Management Review, 4,* 257–281.

Mullen, E. J. (1998). Vocational and psychosocial mentoring functions: Identifying mentors who serve both. *Human Resource Development Quarterly, 9*(4), 319–339.

Mullen, E. J., & Noe, R. A. (1999). The mentoring information exchange: When do mentors seek information from their protégés? *Journal of Organizational Behavior, 20,* 233–242.

Multon, K. D., Brown, S. D., & Lent, R. W. (1991). Relation of self-efficacy beliefs to academic outcomes: A meta-analytic investigation. *Journal of Counseling Psychology, 38*, 30–38.

Murray, B. (2000, November). The growth of the new PhD. *Monitor on Psychology, 31*, 24–27.

Murray, M. (1991). *Beyond the myths and magic of mentoring.* San Francisco: Jossey-Bass.

Myers, D. G. (1996). *Social psychology* (5th ed.). New York: McGraw Hill.

Myers, D. W., & Humphreys, N. J. (1985). The caveats of mentorship. *Business Horizons, 28*, 9–14.

Nagda, B. A., Gregerman, S. R., Jonides, J., von Hippel, W., & Lerner, J. S. (1998). Undergraduate student–faculty research partnerships affect student retention. *Review of Higher Education, 22*, 55–72.

Nakagawa, M., Lamb, M. E., & Miyaki, K. (1992). Antecedents and correlates of the Strange Situation behavior of Japanese infants. *Journal of Cross Cultural Psychology, 23*, 300–310.

Nakkula, M. J., & Harris, J. T. (2005). Assessment of mentoring relationships. In D. L. DuBois & M. J. Karcher (Eds.), *Handbook of youth mentoring* (pp. 100–117). Thousand Oaks, CA: Sage.

National Center for Education Statistics (2003). *Digest of education statistics, 2003: Chapter 3. Postsecondary education.* Retrieved December 3, 2004, from www.nces.ed.gov//programs/digest/d03/ch_3.asp.

National Mentoring Center (2003a). *Foundations of successful youth mentoring: A guidebook for program development.* Portland, OR: Northwest Regional Educational Laboratory.

National Mentoring Center (2003b). *Generic mentoring program policy and procedure manual.* Portland, OR: Northwest Regional Educational Laboratory.

National Mentoring Center Bulletin (1999). *Remembering forgotten kids 3.*

National Mentoring Network (2001). *Generic quality standards for mentoring.* Salford, England: National Mentoring Network.

National Mentoring Working Group (1991). *Mentoring: Elements of effective practice.* Washington, DC: National Mentoring Partnership.

Network Training and Research Group (1996). *Evaluation of the Mentoring Center and Bay Area mentoring efforts. First Evaluation Report.* Redwood City, CA: Network Training and Research Group.

Nicholson, H. J. (1991). *Gender issues in youth development programs.* New York: Carnegie Council on Adolescent Development.

Nielson, T. R., Carlson, D. S., & Lankau, M. J. (2001). The supportive mentor as a means of reducing work–family conflict. *Journal of Vocational Behavior, 59*, 364–381.

Nkomo, S. M., & Cox, T. H., Jr. (1996). Diverse identities in organizations. In S. R. Clegg, C. Hardy, & W. R. Nord (Eds.), *Handbook of organization studies* (pp. 338–356). London: Sage.

Noe, R. (1988). An investigation of the determinants of successful assigned mentoring relationships. *Personnel Psychology, 41*, 457–479.

Noe, R. A., Greenberger, D. B., & Wang, S. (2002). Mentoring: What we know and where we might go from here. In G. R. Ferris & J. J. Martocchio (Eds.), *Research in personnel and human resources management* (Vol. 21, pp. 129–173). Greenwich, CT: Elsevier Science/JAI Press.

Northouse, P. G. (1997). *Leadership: Theory and practice.* Thousand Oaks, CA: Sage.

Novotney, L. C., Mertinko, E., Lange, J., & Baker, T. K. (2000). *Juvenile mentoring program: A progress review.* Washington, DC: US Department of Justice, Office of Justice Programs, Office of Juvenile Justice and Delinquency Prevention. Retrieved February 5, 2004, from http://www.ojjdp.ncjrs.org/jump/.

Nyquist, J. D., & Woodford, B. J. (2000). *Re-envisioning the PhD: What concerns do we have?* Seattle, WA: Center for Instructional Development and Research and the University of Washington.

O'Donnell, C. R., Lydgate, T., & Fo, W. S. O. (1979). The Buddy System: Review and follow-up. *Child Behavior Therapy*, *1*, 161–169.

O'Neil, J. M. (1981). Toward a theory and practice of mentoring in psychology. In J. M. O'Neil & L. S. Wrightsman (Chairs), *Mentoring: Psychological, personal, and career developmental implications*. Symposium presented at the American Psychological Association Annual Convention, Los Angeles.

O'Neil, J. M., & Wrightsman, L. S. (2001). The mentoring relationship in psychology training program. In S. Walfish & A. Hess (Eds.), *Succeeding in graduate school: The career guide for the psychology student* (pp. 113–129). Hillsdale, NJ: Lawrence Erlbaum.

O'Neill, R. M. (2002). Gender and race in mentoring relationships: A review of the literature. In D. Clutterbuck & B. R. Ragins, *Mentoring and diversity: An international perspective* (pp. 1–22). Oxford: Butterworth-Heinemann.

O'Neill, R. M., & Blake-Beard, S. D. (2002). Gender barriers to the female mentor–male protégé relationship. *Journal of Business Ethics*, *37*, 51–63.

O'Neill, R. M., Horton, S., & Crosby, F. J. (1999). Gender issues in developmental relationships. In A. J. Murrell, F. J. Crosby, & R. J. Ely (Eds.), *Mentoring dilemmas: Developmental relationships within multicultural organizations. Applied social research* (pp. 63–80). Mahwah, NJ: Lawrence Erlbaum.

Olian, J. D., Carroll, S. J., Giannantonio, C. M., & Feren, D. B. (1988). What do protégés look for in a mentor? Results of three experimental studies. *Journal of Vocational Behavior*, *33*, 15–37.

Olian, J. D., Carroll, S., & Giannantonio, C. M. (1993). Mentor reactions to protégés: An experiment with managers. *Journal of Vocational Behavior*, *43*, 266–278.

Olson, J. M. Roese, N. J., & Zanna, M. P. (1996). Expectancies. In E. T. Higgins & A. W. Kruglanski (Eds.), *Social psychology: Handbook of basic principles* (pp. 211–238). New York: Guilford Press.

Omoto, A. M., & Snyder, M. (1995). Sustained helping without obligation: Motivation, longevity of service, and perceived attitude change among AIDS volunteers. *Journal of Personality and Social Psychology*, *68*(4), 671–686.

Orpen, C. (1997). The effects of formal mentoring on employee work motivation, organizational commitment, and job performance. *Learning Organization*, *4*, 53–60.

Ossana, S. M., Helms, J. E., & Leonard, M. M. (1992). Do "womanist" identity attitudes influence college women's self-esteem and perceptions of environmental bias? *Journal of Counseling and Development*, *70*, 402–408.

Ostroff, C., & Kozlowski, S. W. (1993). The role of mentoring in the information gathering process of newcomers during early organizational socialization. *Journal of Vocational Behavior*, *42*, 170–183.

Packard, B. W-L., Walsh, L., & Seidenberg, S. (2004). Will that be one mentor or two? A cross-sectional study of women's mentoring during college. *Mentoring & Tutoring*, *12*(1), 71–85.

Padgette, H. C. (2003). *Finding funding: A guide to federal sources for out-of-school time and community school initiatives*. Washington, DC: The Finance Project.

Paludi, M. A., Waite, B., Roberson, R. H., & Jones, L. (1988). Mentors vs. role models: Toward a clarification of terms. *International Journal of Mentoring*, *2*, 20–25.

Paniagua, F. A. (1994). *Assessing and treating culturally diverse clients: A practical guide*. Thousand Oaks, CA: Sage.

Parker, J. G., & Asher, S. R. (1993). Friendship and friendship quality in middle childhood: Links with peer group acceptance and feelings of loneliness and social dissatisfaction. *Developmental Psychology*, *29*, 611–621.

Parnell, J. A., & Crandall, W. (2001). Rethinking participative decision making: A refinement of the propensity for participative decision making scale. *Personnel Review*, *30*, 523–535.

Parra, G. R., DuBois, D. L., Neville, H. A., & Pugh-Lilly, A. O. (2002). Mentoring relationships for youth: Investigation of a process-oriented model. *Journal of Community Psychology*,
30(4), 367–388.

Pasa, S. F., Kabasakal, H., & Bodur, M. (2001). Society, organizations, and leadership in
Turkey. *Applied Psychology: An International Review*, *50*, 559–589.

Pascarella, E. T. (1980). Student–faculty informal contact and college outcomes. *Review of
Educational Research*, *50*, 545–595.

Pascarella, E. T., Terenzini, P. T., & Hibel, J. (1978). Student–faculty interactional settings
and their relationship to predicted academic performance. *Journal of Higher Education*, *49*,
450–463.

Pawson, R. (2004a). *Mentoring relationships: An explanatory review*. London: UK Centre for
Evidence Based Policy and Practice.

Pawson, R. (2004b). *Mentoring relationships: An explanatory review – summary*. London: UK
Centre for Evidence Based Policy and Practice.

Payne, S. C., & Huffman, A. H. (2005). A longitudinal examination of the influence of
mentoring on organizational commitment and turnover. *Academy of Management Journal*,
48, 158–168.

Pellegrini, E. K., & Scandura, T. A. (2005). Construct equivalence across groups: An unexplored
issue in mentoring research. *Educational and Psychological Measurement*, *65*, 323–335.

Pellegrini, E. K., & Scandura, T. A. (2006). Leader–Member Exchange (LMX), paternalism and delegation in the Turkish business culture: An empirical investigation. *Journal
of International Business Studies*, *2*, 264–279.

Peluchette, J. V. E., & Jeanquart, S. (2000). Professionals' use of different mentor sources
at various career stages: Implications for career success. *The Journal of Social Psychology*, *140*,
549–564.

Penner, L. A. (2002). Dispositional and organizational influences on sustained volunteerism:
An interactionist perspective. *Journal of Social Issues*, *58*(3), 447–467.

Peper, J. B. (1994, April). *Mentoring, mentors, and protégés*. Paper presented at the annual
meeting of the American Educational Research Association, New Orleans, Louisiana.

Pfeffer, J., & Lawler, J. (1979). *The effects of job alternatives, extrinsic rewards, and commitment on satisfaction with the organization: A field example of the insufficient justification
paradigm*. Berkeley, CA: University of California.

Philip, K., & Hendry, K. L. (2000). Making sense of mentoring or mentoring making sense?
Reflections on the mentoring process by adult mentors with young people. *Journal of
Community and Applied Social Psychology*, *10*, 211–223.

Philip, K., Shucksmith, J., & King, C. (2004). *Sharing a laugh? A qualitative study of
mentoring interventions with young people*. York, England: Joseph Rowntree Foundation.

Phillips-Jones, L. (1982). *Mentors and protégés*. New York: Arbor House.

Phillips-Jones, L. (1983). Establishing a formalized mentoring program. *Training and
Development Journal*, *2*, 38–42.

Phinney, J., Horenczyk, G., Liebkind, K., & Vedder, P. (2001). Ethnic identity, immigration, and well-being: An interactional perspective. *Journal of Social Issues*, *57*, 493–510.

Pianta, R. C. (1999). *Enhancing relationships between children and teachers*. Washington, DC:
American Psychological Association.

Piantanida, M., & Garman, N. B. (1999). *The qualitative dissertation: A guide for students
and faculty*. Thousand Oaks, CA: Corwin.

Piper, H., & Piper, J. (2000). Disaffected young people as the problem. Mentoring as
the solution. Education and work as the goal. *Journal of Education and Work*, *13*(1),
77–94.

Pollack, W. S. (1999). *Real boys: Rescuing our sons from the myths of boyhood*. Melbourne: Scribe
Publications.

Pollock, R. (1995). A test of conceptual models depicting the developmental course of informal mentor–protégé relationships in the workplace. *Journal of Vocational Behavior, 46*, 144–162.

Pope-Davis, D. B., Stone, G. L., & Neilson, D. (1997). Factors influencing the stated career goals of minority graduate students in counseling psychology programs. *The Counseling Psychologist, 25*, 683–698.

Porter, L. W., & Lawler, E. E. (1968). *Managerial attitudes and performance.* Homewood, IL: Dorsey Press.

Portes, A. (1998). Social capital: Its origins and applications in modern sociology. *Annual Review of Sociology, 24*, 1–24.

Posada, G., Gao, Y., Wu, F., Posada, R., Tascon, M., Schoelmersch, A., et al. (1995). The secure-base phenomenon across cultures: Children's behavior, mother's preferences, and experts' concepts. In E. Waters, B. Vaughn, G. Posada, & K. Kondo-Ikenura (Eds.), Caregiving, cultural, and cognitive perspective on secure-base behavior and working models. *Monographs of the Society for Research in Child Development, 60*(2–3), 27–48.

Prager, K. J., & Buhrmester, D. (1998). Intimacy and need fulfillment in couple relationships. *Journal of Social and Personal Relationships, 15*, 435–469.

Prevosto, P. (2001). The effect of mentored relationships on satisfaction and intent to stay of company-grade US Army reserve nurses. *Military Medicine, 166*, 21–26.

Prince, J. P. (1995). *Strong Interest Inventory resource.* Palo Alto, CA: Consulting Psychologists Press, Inc.

Provasnik, S., Shafer, L. L., & Snyder, T. D. (2004). *Historically Black colleges and universities, 1976 to 2001* (National Center for Education Statistics Publication No. NCES 2004062). Washington, DC: ED Pubs.

Putnam, R. (2000). *Bowling alone: The collapse and revival of American Community.* New York: Simon & Schuster.

Quine, W. V. O. (1969). Natural kinds. In *Ontological relativity and other essays* (pp. 114–138). New York: Columbia University Press.

Raabe, B., & Beehr, T. A. (2003). Formal mentoring versus supervisor and coworker relationship: Differences in perceptions and impact. *Journal of Organizational Behavior, 24*, 271–293.

Ragins, B. R. (1989). Barriers to mentoring: The female manager's dilemma. *Human Relations, 42*, 1–22.

Ragins, B. R. (1997a). Diversified mentoring relationships in organizations: A power perspective. *Academy of Management Review, 22*, 482–521.

Ragins, B. R. (1997b). Antecedents of diversified mentoring relationships. *Journal of Vocational Behavior, 51*(1), 90–109.

Ragins, B. R. (1999a). Where do we go from here, and how do we get there? Methodological issues in conducting research on diversity and mentoring relationships. In A. J. Murrell, F. J. Crosby, & R. J. Ely (Eds.), *Mentoring dilemmas: Developmental relationships within multicultural organizations* (pp. 227–247). Mahwah, NJ: Lawrence Erlbaum.

Ragins, B. R. (1999b). Gender and mentoring relationships: A review and research agenda for the next decade. In G. N. Powell (Ed.), *Handbook of gender and work* (pp. 347–370). Thousand Oaks, CA: Sage.

Ragins, B. R. (2002). Understanding diversified mentoring relationships: Definitions, challenges and strategies. In D. Clutterbuck & B. R. Ragins, *Mentoring and diversity: An international perspective* (pp. 23–53). Oxford: Butterworth-Heinemann.

Ragins, B. R. (2004). Sexual orientation in the workplace: The unique work and career experiences of gay, lesbian and bisexual workers. *Research in Personnel and Human Resources Management, 23*, 37–122.

Ragins, B. R. (2005). *Towards a theory of relational mentoring.* Unpublished manuscript.

Ragins, B. R. (in press). Disclosure disconnects: Antecedents and consequences of disclosing invisible stigmas across life domains. *Academy of Management Review.*

Ragins, B. R., & Cotton, J. L. (1991). Easier said than done: Gender differences in perceived barriers to getting a mentor. *Academy of Management Journal, 34,* 939–951.

Ragins, B. R., & Cotton, J. L. (1993). Gender and willingness to mentor in organizations. *Journal of Management, 19,* 97–111.

Ragins, B. R., & Cotton, J. L. (1999). Mentor functions and outcomes: A comparison of men and women in formal and informal mentoring relationships. *Journal of Applied Psychology, 84,* 529–550.

Ragins, B. R., Cotton, J. L., & Miller, J. S. (2000). Marginal mentoring: The effects of type of mentor, quality of relationship, and program design on work and career attitudes. *Academy of Management Journal, 43,* 1177–1194.

Ragins, B. R., & Gonzalez, J. (2003). Understanding diversity in organizations: Getting a grip on a slippery construct. In J. Greenberg (Ed.), *Organizational behavior: The state of the science* (2nd ed., pp. 125–163). Mahwah, NJ: Lawrence Erlbaum Press.

Ragins, B. R., & McFarlin, D. (1990). Perception of mentor roles in cross-gender mentoring relationships. *Journal of Vocational Behavior, 37,* 321–339.

Ragins, B. R., & Scandura, T. (1994). Gender differences in expected outcomes of mentoring relationships. *Academy of Management Journal, 37,* 957–971.

Ragins, B. R., & Scandura, T. A. (1997). The way we were: Gender and the termination of mentoring relationships. *Journal of Applied Psychology, 82,* 945–953.

Ragins, B. R., & Scandura, T. A. (1999). Burden or blessing? Expected costs and benefits of being a mentor. *Journal of Organizational Behavior, 20,* 493–509.

Ragins, B. R., & Sundstrom, E. (1989). Gender and power in organizations: A longitudinal perspective. *Psychological Bulletin, 105,* 51–88.

Ragins, B. R., Townsend, B., & Mattis, M. (1998). Gender gap in the executive suite: CEOs and female executives report on breaking the glass ceiling. *Academy of Management Executive, 12*(1), 28–42.

Ragins, B. R., & Verbos, A. K. (2007). Positive relationships in action: Relational mentoring and mentoring schemas in the workplace. In J. Dutton & B. R Ragins (Eds.), *Exploring positive relationships at work: Building a theoretical and research foundation* (pp. 91–116). Mahwah, NJ: Lawrence Erlbaum and Associates.

Rauner, D. M. (2000). *"They still pick me up when I fall": The role of caring in youth development and community life.* New York: Columbia University Press.

Reis, H. T., Collins, W. A., & Berscheid, E. (2000). The relationship context of human behavior and development. *Psychological Bulletin, 126*(6), 844–872.

Reis, H. T., & Gable, S. L. (2003). Toward a positive psychology of relationships. In C. L. M. Keyes & J. Haidt (Eds.), *Flourishing: Positive psychology and the life well-lived* (pp. 129–159). Washington, DC: American Psychological Association.

Reskin, B. F. (1979). Academic sponsorship and scientists' careers. *Sociology of Education, 52,* 129–146.

Resnick, M., Bearman, P., Blum, R., Bauman, K., Harris, K., Jones, J., et al. (1997). Protecting adolescents from harm: Findings from the National Longitudinal Study on Adolescent Health. *Journal of the American Medical Association, 278*(10), 823–832.

Rheingold, H. L. (1994). *The psychologist's guide to an academic career.* Washington, DC: American Psychological Association.

Rhoades, L., & Eisenberger, R. (2002). Perceived organizational support: A review of the literature. *Journal of Applied Psychology, 87*(4), 698–714.

Rhodes, J. E. (1994). Older and wiser: Mentoring relationships in childhood and adolescence. *Journal of Primary Prevention, 14,* 187–196.

Rhodes, J. E. (2000). Mentoring programs. In A. E. Kazdin (Ed.), *Encyclopedia of psychology* (pp. 198–200). Washington, DC: American Psychological Association.

Rhodes, J. E. (2002a). Mentoring has become an extremely important aspect of youth program planning. In J. E. Rhodes (Ed.), *New directions for in youth development* (pp. 5–8). San Francisco: Jossey-Bass.

Rhodes, J. E. (2002b). *Stand by me: The risks and rewards of mentoring today's youth.* Cambridge, MA: Harvard University Press.

Rhodes, J. E. (2002c). What's race got to do with it? *Research Corner.* Retrieved May 8, 2005, from the National Mentoring Partnerships website, www.mentoring.org/.

Rhodes, J. E. (2005). A theoretical model of youth mentoring. In D. L. DuBois & M. A. Karcher (Eds.), *Handbook of youth mentoring* (pp. 30–43). Thousand Oaks, CA: Sage.

Rhodes, J. E., Contreras, J. M., & Mangelsdorf, S. C. (1994). Natural mentor relationships among Latina adolescent mothers: Psychological adjustment, moderating processes, and the role of early parental acceptance. *American Journal of Community Psychology, 22*(2), 211–227.

Rhodes, J. E., & Davis, A. B. (1996). Supportive ties between nonparent adults and urban adolescent girls. In B. J. Leadbeater & N. Way (Eds.), *Urban girls: Resisting stereotypes, creating identities* (pp. 213–225). New York: New York University Press.

Rhodes, J. E., Ebert, L., & Fischer, K. (1992). Natural mentors: An overlooked resource in the social networks of young, African American mothers. *American Journal of Community Psychology, 20*(4), 445–461.

Rhodes, J. E., Grossman, J. B., & Resch, N. L. (2000). Agents of change: Pathways through which mentoring relationships influence adolescents' academic adjustment. *Child Development, 71*, 1662–1671.

Rhodes, J. E., Grossman, J. B., & Roffman, J. G. (2002). The rhetoric and reality of youth mentoring. In J. E. Rhodes (Ed.), *New directions for youth development: Theory, practice, and research: A critical review of youth mentoring, 93*, 9–20. San Francisco: Jossey-Bass.

Rhodes, J. E., Haight, W. L., & Briggs, E. C. (1999). The influence of mentoring on the peer relationships of foster youth in relative and nonrelative care. *Journal of Research on Adolescence, 9*, 185–201.

Rhodes, J. E., Reddy, R., Grossman, J. B., & Lee, J. (2002). Volunteer mentoring relationships with minority youth: An analysis of same- versus cross-race matches. *Journal of Applied Social Psychology, 32*, 2114–2133.

Rhodes, J. E., Reddy, R., Grossman, J. B., & Lee, J. M. (2003). Same versus cross-race matches in mentoring programs: A comparison. *Journal of Applied Social Psychology, 32*, 2114–2133.

Rhodes, J. E., & Roffman, J. G. (2002). Nonparental adults as asset builders in the lives of youth. In R. J. Lerner & P. Benson (Eds.), *Developmental assets and asset-building communities. Implications for research, policy, and practice* (pp. 195–209). New York: Kluwer Academic Publishers.

Rhodes, J. E., Roffman, J. G., & Grossman, J. B. (2005). Promoting successful youth mentoring relationships: A preliminary screening questionnaire, *Journal of Primary Prevention, 26*, 147–167.

Rhodes, J. E., Spencer, R. A., Keller, T. E., Liang, B., & Noam, G. G. (2006). A model for the influence of mentoring relationship on youth development. *Journal of Community Psychology, 34*, 691–707.

Rice, M. B., & Brown, R. D. (1990). Developmental factors associated with self-perceptions of mentoring competence and mentoring needs. *Journal of College Student Development, 31*, 293–299.

Richardson, L. (1990). *Writing strategies: Reaching diverse audiences.* Newbury Park, CA: Sage.

Roaf, P. A., Tierney, J. P., & Hunte, D. E. I. (1994). *Big Brothers/Big Sisters of America: A study of volunteer recruitment and screening.* Philadelphia: Public/Private Ventures.

Roberts, A. (2000). Mentoring revisited: A phenomenological reading of the literature. *Mentoring and Tutoring, 8*, 145–170.

Roberts, A., & Cotton, L. (1994). Note on assessing a mentor program. *Psychological Reports, 75*, 1369–1370.

Roberts, P., & Newton, P. M. (1987). Levinsonian studies of women's adult development. *Psychology and Aging, 2*, 154–163.

Roche, G. R. (1979). Much ado about mentors. *Harvard Business Review, 57*, 14–28.

Rogers, A. M., & Taylor, A. S. (1997). Intergenerational mentoring: A viable strategy for meeting the needs of vulnerable youth. *Journal of Gerontological Social Work, 28*, 125–140.

Rogoff, B. (1990). *Apprenticeship in thinking: Cognitive development in social context.* New York: Oxford University Press.

Rogoff, B. (1998). Cognition as a collaborative process. In D. Kuhn & R. S. Siegler (Eds.), *Cognition, perception, and language* (5th ed., pp. 679–744). New York: Wiley.

Rogoff, B. (2003). *The cultural nature of human development.* New York: Oxford University Press.

Rogoff, B., Paradise, R., Arauz, R. M., Correa-Chávez, M., & Angelillo, C. (2003). Firsthand learning through intent participation. *Annual Review of Psychology, 54*, 175–203.

Rook, K. S. (1995). Support, companionship, and control in older adults' social networks: Implications for well-being. In J. F. Nussbaum & J. Coupland (Eds.), *Handbook of communication and aging research* (pp. 437–463). Mahwah, NJ: Lawrence Erlbaum.

Rose, G. L. (2003). Enhancement of mentor selection using the Ideal Mentor Scale. *Research in Higher Education, 44*, 473–494.

Rose, G. L. (2005). Group differences in graduate students' concepts of the ideal mentor. *Research in Higher Education, 46*, 53–80.

Roth, J. L., & Brooks Gunn, J. (2003). Youth development programs: Risk, prevention and policy. *Journal of Adolescent Health, 32*, 170–182.

Rouse, P. D. (2001). Voluntary turnover related to information technology professionals: A review of rational and instinctual models. *International Journal of Organizational Analysis, 9*, 281–290.

Royse, D. (1998). Mentoring high-risk minority youth: Evaluation of the Brothers Project. *Adolescence, 33*, 145–158.

Rumbaut, R. (1994). The crucible within: Ethnic identity, self-esteem, and segmented assimilation among children of immigrants. *International Migration Review, 28*, 748–794.

Russell, J. E. A., & Adams, D. M. (1997). The changing nature of mentoring in organizations: An introduction to the special issue on mentoring in organizations. *Journal of Vocational Behavior, 51*, 1–14.

Rutter, M. (1987). Psychosocial resilience and protective mechanisms. *American Journal of Orthopsychiatry, 57*, 316–331.

Ryan, R. M., Deci, E. L., & Grolnick, W. S. (1995). Autonomy, relatedness, and the self: Their relation to development and psychopathology. In D. Cicchetti & D. J. Cohen (Eds.), *Developmental psychopathology: Vol. 1. Theory and methods* (pp. 618–655). New York: Wiley.

Rychener, S. R. (2003). *The relationship between adolescent characteristics and the quality of their natural mentors.* Unpublished doctoral dissertation, Texas Tech University.

Rymer, J. (2002). "Only connect": Transforming ourselves and our discipline through co-mentoring. *Journal of Business Communication, 39*(3), 342–363.

Sackett, P. R., Gruys, M. L., & Ellingson, J. E. (1998). Ability–personality interactions when predicting job performance. *Journal of Applied Psychology, 83*, 545–556.

Sammons, M. T., & Gravitz, M. A. (1990). Theoretical orientations of professional psychologists and their former professors. *Professional Psychology: Research and Practice, 21*, 131–134.

Sanchez, B., & Colon, Y. (2005). Race, ethnicity, and culture in mentoring relationships. In D. L. DuBois & M. J. Karcher (Eds.), *Handbook of youth mentoring* (pp. 191–204). Thousand Oaks, CA: Sage.

Sanchez, B., Colon, Y., & Esparza, P. (2005). The role of sense of school belonging and gender in the academic adjustment of Latino adolescents. *Journal of Youth and Adolescence*, *34*, 619–628.

Sanchez, B., & Reyes, O. (1999). Descriptive profile of the mentor relationships of Latino adolescents. *Journal of Community Psychology*, *27*, 299–302.

Sanchez, B., Reyes, O., Potashner, I., & Singh, J. (2006). A qualitative examination of the relationships that play a mentoring function for Mexican American older adolescents. *Cultural Diversity and Ethnic Minority Psychology*, *12*, 615–631.

Sanders, J. M., & Wong, H. Y. (1985). Graduate training and initial job placement. *Sociological Inquiry*, *55*, 154–169.

Sandhu, D. S. (1997). Psychocultural profiles of Asian and Pacific Islander Americans: Implications for counseling and psychotherapy. *Journal of Multicultural Counseling and Development*, *25*, 7–22.

Sandler, I. N., Miller, P., Short, J., & Wolchik, S. A. (1989). Social support as a protective factor for children in stress. In D. Belle (Ed.), *Children's social networks and social support* (pp. 277–307). New York: Wiley.

Santos, S., & Reigadas, E. (2000, February). *Evaluation of a university faculty mentoring program: Its effect on Latino college adjustment.* National Association of African American Studies & National Association of Hispanic and Latino Studies: 2000 Literature Monograph Series. Proceedings (Education Section). Houston, TX.

Santos, S. J., & Reigadas, E. (2002). Latinos in higher education: An evaluation of a university faculty mentoring program. *Journal of Hispanic Higher Education*, *1*, 40–50.

Sarason, S. B. (1974). *Psychological sense of community: Prospects for a community psychology.* San Francisco: Jossey-Bass.

Scales, P. C. (2003). *Other people's kids: Social expectations and American adults' involvement with children and adolescents.* New York: Kluwer Academic.

Scales, P. C., & Gibbons, J. L. (1996). Extended family members and unrelated adults in the lives of young adolescents: A research agenda. *Journal of Early Adolescence*, *16*(4), 365–389.

Scandura, T. A. (1992). Mentorship and career mobility: An empirical investigation. *Journal of Organizational Behavior*, *13*, 169–174.

Scandura, T. A. (1997). Mentoring and organizational justice: An empirical investigation. *Journal of Vocational Behavior*, *51*, 58–69.

Scandura, T. A. (1998). Dysfunctional mentoring relationships and outcomes. *Journal of Management*, *24*, 449–467.

Scandura, T. A., & Hamilton, B. A. (2002). Enhancing performance through mentoring. In S. Sonnentag (Ed.), *The psychological management of individual performance. A handbook in the psychology of management in organizations* (pp. 293–308). Chichester, England: Wiley.

Scandura, T. A., & Pellegrini, E. K. (2003, November). *A multidimensional model of trust and LMX.* Southern Management Association Meeting, Clearwater Beach, FL.

Scandura, T. A., & Pellegrini, E. K. (2004). Competences of building the developmental relationship. In D. Clutterback & G. Lane (Eds.), *The situational mentor: An international review of competences and capabilities in mentoring* (pp. 83–93). Aldershot, England: Gower Publishing Limited.

Scandura, T. A., & Ragins, B. R. (1993). The effects of sex and gender role orientation on mentorship in male-dominated occupations. *Journal of Vocational Behavior*, *43*, 251–265.

Scandura, T. A., & Schriesheim, C. A. (1994). Leader–member exchange and supervisor career mentoring as complementary constructs in leadership research. *Academy of Management Journal*, *37*, 1588–1602.

Scandura, T. A., Tejeda, M. L., Werther, W. B., & Lankau, M. J. (1996). Perspectives on mentoring. *Leadership and Organization Development Journal, 17*(3), 50–56.

Scandura, T. A., & Viator, R. (1994). Mentoring in public accounting firms: An analysis of mentor–protégé relationships, mentoring functions, and protégé turnover intentions. *Accounting, Organizations & Society, 19,* 717–734.

Scandura, T. A., & Von Glinow, M. A. (1997). Development of the international manager: The role of mentoring. *Business and the Contemporary World, 9,* 95–115.

Scandura, T. A., & Williams, E. A. (2001). An investigation of the moderating effects of gender on the relationships between mentorship initiation and protégé perceptions of mentoring functions. *Journal of Vocational Behavior, 59,* 342–363.

Scanzoni, J. (1979). Social exchange and behavioral interdependence. In R. L. Burgess & T. L. Huston (Eds.), *Social exchange in developing relationships* (pp. 61–98). New York: Academic Press.

Schlosser, L. Z., & Gelso, C. J. (2001). Measuring the working alliance in advisor–advisee relationships in graduate school. *Journal of Counseling Psychology, 48,* 157–167.

Schlosser, L. Z., & Gelso, C. J. (2005). The Advisory Working Alliance Inventory – Advisor Version: Scale development and validation. *Journal of Counseling Psychology, 52,* 650–654.

Schlosser, L. Z., Knox, S., Moskovitz, A. R., & Hill, C. E. (2003). A qualitative study of the graduate advising relationship: The advisee perspective. *Journal of Counseling Psychology, 50,* 178–188.

Schlosser, L. Z., Lyons, H. Z., Talleyrand, R. M., Kim, B. S. K., & Johnson, W. B. (2005). *Advisor–advisee relationships in counseling psychology doctoral Programs: Toward a multicultural theory.* Manuscript submitted for publication.

Schlosser, L. Z., Talleyrand, R. M., Lyons, H. Z., Kim, B. S. K., & Johnson, W. B. (2005). *Advisor–advisee relationships in counseling psychology doctoral programs: Toward a multicultural theory.* Manuscript submitted for publication.

Schmidt, F. L., & Hunter, J. E. (1998). The validity and utility of selection methods in personnel psychology: Practical and theoretical implications of 85 years of research findings. *Psychological Bulletin, 124,* 262–274.

Schmidt, J., & Wolfe, J. (1980). The mentor partnership: Discovery of professionalism. *NASPA Journal, 17,* 45–51.

Schoeny, M. E. (2001). *An ecological model of adolescent risk and resilience: The influence of family, peers, and mentors.* Unpublished doctoral dissertation, DePaul University.

Schriesheim, C. A., & Castro, S. L. (1995, November). *A structural modeling investigation of leader–member exchange (LMX) and mentoring as complementary concepts.* Paper presented at the annual meeting of the Southern Management Association, Orlando, FL.

Schulz, S. F. (1995). The benefits of mentoring. In M. W. Galbraith & N. H. Cohen (Eds.), *Mentoring: New strategies and challenges* (Vol. 66, pp. 57–68). San Francisco: Jossey-Bass.

Schwab, D. P. (1980). Construct validity in organizational behavior. In L. L. Cummings & B. M. Staw (Eds.), *Research in organizational behavior* (Vol. 2, pp. 3–43). Greenwich, CT: JAI Press.

Sedlacek, W. E. (1991). Using noncognitive variables in advising nontraditional students. *National Academic Advising Association Journal, 11*(1), 75–82.

Sedlacek, W. E. (1994). Advising nontraditional students: The big bang or another universe? *National Academic Advising Association Journal, 14*(2), 103–104.

Sedlacek, W. E. (1996). An empirical method for determining nontraditional group status. *Measurement and Evaluation in Counseling and Development, 28,* 200–210.

Sedlacek, W. E. (2003a). Alternative admission and scholarship selection measures in higher education. *Measurement and Evaluation in Counseling and Development, 35,* 263–272.

Sedlacek, W. E. (2003b). Negotiating admissions to graduate and professional schools. In V. L. Farmer (Ed.), *The Black student's guide to graduate and professional school success* (pp. 13–22). Westport, CT: Greenwood Publishing Group.

Sedlacek, W. E. (2004a). *Beyond the big test: Noncognitive assessment in higher education*. San Francisco: Jossey-Bass.

Sedlacek, W. E. (2004b). Why we should use noncognitive variables with graduate and professional students. *The Advisor: The Journal of the National Association of Advisors for the Health Professions, 24*(2), 32–39.

Sedlacek, W. E., & Brooks, G. C., Jr. (1976). *Racism in American education: A model for change*. Chicago: Nelson-Hall.

Segal, J. A. (2005). Shatter the glass ceiling, dodge the shards. *HR Magazine, April*, 121–126.

Seibert, S. (1999). The effectiveness of facilitated mentoring: A longitudinal quasi-experiment. *Journal of Vocational Behavior, 54*, 483–502.

Seibert, S. E., Kraimer, M. L., & Liden, R. C. (2001). A social capital theory of career success. *Academy of Management Journal, 44*, 219–237.

Seidman, E., Yoshikawa, H., Roberts, A., Chesir-Teran, D., Allen, L., Friedman, J., et al. (1998). Structural and experiential neighborhood contexts, developmental stage, and antisocial behavior among urban adolescents in poverty. *Development and Psychopathology, 10*, 259–281.

Seligman, M. E. P., & Csikszentmihalyi, M. (2000). Positive psychology: An introduction. *American Psychologist, 55*, 5–14.

Shapiro, E. C., Haseltine, F. P., & Rowe, M. P. (1978). Moving up: Role models, mentors, and the "patron system". *Sloan Management Review, 19*(3), 51–58.

Shapiro, E. S., & Blom-Hoffman, J. (2004). Mentoring, modeling, and money: The 3 Ms of producing academics. *School Psychology Quarterly, 19*, 365–381.

Sheehan, K., DiCara, J. A., LeBailly, S., & Christoffel, K. K. (1999). Adapting the gang model: Peer mentoring to prevent violence. *Pediatrics, 104*, 50–54.

Sherman, L. (1999). *Reaching out for diversity: Recruiting mentors requires multiple strategies and long term commitment*. National Mentoring Centre Bulletin 2.

Shiner, M., Young, T., Newburn, T., & Groben S. (2004). *Mentoring disaffected young people: An evaluation of Mentoring Plus*. York, England: Joseph Rowntree Foundation.

Shweder, R., & LeVine, R. (1984). *Culture theory: Essays on mind, self, and emotion*. New York: Cambridge University Press.

Silverhart, T. A. (1994). It works: Mentoring drives productivity higher. *Managers Magazine, 69*, 14–15.

Singh, V., Bains, D., & Vinnicombe, S. (2002). Informal mentoring as an organisational resource. *Long Range Planning: International Journal of Strategic Management, 35*, 389–405.

Single, P. B., & Muller, C. B. (2001). When email and mentoring unite: The implementation of a nationwide mentoring program – MentorNet, the national electronic industrial mentoring network for women in engineering and science. In L. K. Stromei (Ed.), *Creating mentoring and coaching programs: Twelve case studies from the real world of training* (pp. 107–122). Alexandria, VA: American Society for Training and Development.

Sipe, C. (1996). *Mentoring: A synthesis of P/PV's research: 1988–1995*. Philadelphia: Public/Private Ventures. (ERIC Document Reproduction Service No. ED 404 410).

Sipe, C. L. (1998). Mentoring adolescents: What have we learned? In J. B. Grossman (Ed.), *Contemporary issues in mentoring* (pp. 12–25). Philadelphia: Public/Private Ventures.

Sipe, C. L. (2002). Mentoring programs for adolescents: A research summary. *Journal of Adolescent Health, 31*, 251–260.

Sipe, C. L. (2005). Toward a typology of mentoring. In D. L. DuBois & M. J. Karcher (Eds.), *Handbook of youth mentoring* (pp. 65–80). Thousand Oaks, CA: Sage.

Sipe, C. L., & Roder, A. E. (1999). *Mentoring school-age children: A classification of programs*. Philadelphia: Public/Private Ventures.

Skinner, A., & Fleming, J. (1999). *Quality framework for mentoring with socially excluded young people*. Salford, England: National Mentoring Network.

Skinner, B. F. (1953). *Science and human behavior.* Oxford: Macmillan.

Slicker, E. K., & Palmer, D. J. (1993). Mentoring at-risk high school students: Evaluation of a school-based program. *School Counselor, 40,* 327–334.

Smith, A. (2002). *Does mentoring really work? A meta-analysis of mentoring programs for at-risk youth.* Unpublished doctoral dissertation, Texas A&M University.

Smith, E. P., & Davidson, W. S. (1992). Mentoring and the development of African-American graduate students. *Journal of College Student Development, 33,* 531–539.

Snyder, C. R., & Lopez, S. J. (Eds.). (2002). *Handbook of positive psychology.* New York: Oxford University Press.

Sosik, J. J., & Godshalk, V. M. (2000a). Leadership styles, mentoring functions received, and job-related stress: A conceptual model and preliminary study. *Journal of Organizational Behavior, 21,* 365–390.

Sosik, J. J., & Godshalk, V. M. (2000b). The role of gender in mentoring: Implications for diversified and homogeneous mentoring relationships. *Journal of Vocational Behavior, 57,* 102–122.

Sosik, J. J., & Godshalk, V. M. (2004). Self-other rating agreement in mentoring: Meeting protégé expectations for development and career advancement. *Group and Organization Management, 29,* 442–469.

Sosik, J. J., & Godshalk, V. M. (2005). Examining gender similarity and mentor's supervisory status in mentoring relationships. *Mentoring & Tutoring, 13*(1), 39–52.

Sosik, J. J., Godshalk, V. M., & Yammarino, F. J. (2004). Transformational leadership, learning goal orientation, and expectations for career success in mentor–protégé relationships: A multiple levels of analysis perspective. *Leadership Quarterly, 15,* 241–261.

Sowan, N. A., Moffatt, S. G., & Canales, M. K. (2004). Creating a mentoring partnership model: A university department of health experience. *Family and Community Health, 27,* 326–337.

Speizer, J. J. (1981). Role models, mentors, and sponsors: The elusive concepts. *Journal of Women in Culture and Society, 6,* 692–712.

Spencer, R. (2006). Understanding the mentoring process between adolescents and adults. *Youth and Society, 37,* 287–315.

Spencer, R. A., Jordan, J. V., & Sazama, J. (2004). Growth-promoting relationships between youth and adults: A focus group study. *Families in Society, 85*(3), 354–362.

Spencer, R. A., & Rhodes, J. E. (2005). A counseling and psychotherapy perspective on mentoring relationships. In D. L. DuBois & M. J. Karcher (Eds.), *Handbook of youth mentoring* (pp. 118–132). Thousand Oaks, CA: Sage.

Sprague, R. L., Roberts, G. C., & Kavussanu, M. (1997). *Sources of ethical beliefs in their discipline: Faculty vs. graduate students.* Paper presented at the annual meeting of the Association for Practical and Professional Ethics, St. Louis, MO.

Srole, L. J. (1956). Anomie, authoritarianism, and prejudice. *American Journal of Sociology, 60,* 63–67.

Sroufe, L. A., & Fleeson, J. (1986). Attachment and the construction of relationships. In W. Hartup & Z. Rubin (Eds.), *Relationships and development* (pp. 51–71). Hillsdale, NJ: Erlbaum.

St James-Roberts, I., & Singh, C. S. (2001). *Can mentors help school children with behavior problems?* Home Office Report 233. London: Home Office.

Stafford, B., & Robbins, S. P. (1991). Mentoring for graduate social work students: Real and ideal. *Journal of Applied Social Sciences, 15,* 193–206.

Starks, F. I. (2002). *Mentoring at-risk youth: An intervention for academic achievement.* Unpublished doctoral dissertation, Alliant International University.

Steele, C. M. (1997). A threat in the air: How stereotypes shape the intellectual identities and performance of women and African Americans. *American Psychologist, 52,* 613–629.

Steinberg, L. (2001). We know some things: Parent–adolescent relationships in retrospect and prospect. *Journal of Research on Adolescence, 11*(1), 1–19.

Sternberg, R. (1986). A triangular theory of love. *Psychological Review, 93*, 119–135.

Stone, C. A. (1993). What is missing in the metaphor of scaffolding? In E. A. Forman, N. Minick, & C. A. Stone (Eds.), *Contexts for learning: Sociocultural dynamics in children's development* (pp. 169–183). New York: Oxford University Press.

Stripling, L. (2004). *All-But-Dissertation: Non-completion of doctoral degrees in education.* Unpublished doctoral dissertation, University of South Florida, Tampa.

Struthers, N. J. (1995). Differences in mentoring: A function of gender or organizational rank? *Journal of Social Behavior and Personality, 10*, 265–272.

Stukas, A. A., & Tanti, C. (2005). Recruiting and sustaining volunteer mentors. In D. L. DuBois & M. J. Karcher (Eds.), *Handbook of youth mentoring* (pp. 235–250). Thousand Oaks, CA: Sage.

Stumpf, S. A., & London, M. (1981). Management promotions: Individual and organizational factors affecting the decision process. *Academy of Management Review, 6*, 539–550.

Styles, M. B., & Morrow, K. V. (1992). *Understanding how youth and elders form relationships: A study of four Linking Lifetimes programs.* Philadelphia, PA: Public/Private Ventures.

Sue, D. W., & Sue, D. (2003). *Counseling the culturally diverse: Theory and practice* (4th ed.). New York: Wiley.

Sue, S., & Sue, D. W. (1971). Chinese-American personality and mental health. *American Journal, 1*, 36–49.

Sullivan, A. M. (1996). From mentor to muse: Recasting the role of women in relationship with urban adolescent girls. In B. J. R. Leadbeater & N. Way (Eds.), *Urban girls: Resisting stereotypes, creating identities* (pp. 226–249). New York: New York University Press.

Sullivan, K., Marshall, S. K., & Schonert-Reichl, K. A. (2002). Do expectancies influence choice of help-giver?: Adolescents' criteria for selecting an informal helper. *Journal of Adolescent Research, 17*, 509–531.

Swerdlik, M. E., & Bardon, J. I. (1988). A survey of mentoring experiences in school psychology. *Journal of School Psychology, 26*, 213–224.

Szapocznik, J., Scopetta, M. A., Kurtines, W., & Aranalde, M. A. (1978). Theory and measurement of acculturation. *Interamerican Journal of Psychology, 12*, 113–120.

Tannen, D. (1990). Gender differences in topical coherence: Creating involvement in best friends' talk. *Discourse Processes, 13*, 73–90.

Tarling, R., Burrows, J., & Clarke, A. (2001). Dalston Youth Project Part II (11–14) – An Evaluation, *Home Office Research Study 232.* London: Home Office.

Taub, D. J. (1997). Autonomy and parental attachment in traditional-age undergraduate women. *Journal of College Student Development, 38*(6), 645–654.

Taylor, A. S., LoSciuto, L., & Porcellini, L. (2005). Intergenerational mentoring. In D. L. DuBois & M. J. Karcher (Eds.), *Handbook of youth mentoring* (pp. 286–299). Thousand Oaks, CA: Sage.

Taylor, C. R. (2004). Retention leadership. *T&D, March*, 40–45.

Taylor, J. S. (2003). *Training new mentees.* Portland, OR: National Mentoring Center.

Tekian, A., Jalovecky, M. J., & Hruska, L. (2001). The impact of mentoring and advising at-risk underrepresented minority students on medical school performance. *Academic Medicine, 76*, 1264.

Tenenbaum, H. R., Crosby, F. J., & Gliner, M. D. (2001). Mentoring relationships in graduate school. *Journal of Vocational Behavior, 59*, 326–341.

Tepper, B. J. (1995). Upward maintenance tactics in supervisory mentoring and non-mentoring relationships. *Academy of Management Journal, 38*, 1191–1205.

Tepper, B. J. (2000). Consequences of abusive supervision. *Academy of Management Journal, 43*, 178–190.

Tepper, B. J., Brown, S. J., & Hunt, M. D. (1993). Strength of subordinates' upward influence tactics and gender congruency effects. *Journal of Applied Social Psychology*, 23, 1903–1919.

Tepper, K., Shaffer, B. C., & Tepper, B. J. (1996). Latent structure of mentoring function scales. *Education and Psychological Measurement*, 56, 848–857.

Terenzini, P. T., Pascarella, E. T., & Blimling, G. S. (1996). Students' out-of-class experiences and their influence on learning and cognitive development: A literature review. *Journal of College Student Development*, 37, 149–162.

Tesluk, P. E., Vance, R. J., & Mathieu, J. E. (1999). Examining employee involvement in the context of participative work environments. *Group and Organization Management*, 24, 271–299.

Tharenou, P. (1997). Managerial career advancement. In C. L. Cooper & I. T. Robertson (Eds.), *International review of industrial and organizational psychology*, 12 (pp. 39–93). Chichester, England: John Wiley & Sons.

Tharenou, P. (2005). Does mentor support increase women's career advancement more than men's? The differential effects of career and psychosocial support. *Australian Journal of Management*, 30(1), 77–110.

Tharenou, P., Latimer, S., & Conroy, D. (1994). How do you make it to the top? An examination of influences on women's and men's managerial advancement. *Academy of Management Journal*, 37, 899–931.

Tharp, R. G., & Gallimore, R. (1988/1999). *Rousing minds to life: Teaching, learning, and schooling in social context*. Boston: Cambridge University Press.

Thile, E. L., & Matt, G. E. (1995). The ethnic minority undergraduate program: A brief description and preliminary findings. *Journal of Multicultural Counseling and Development*, 23, 116–126.

Thoits, P. A. (1995). Stress, coping, and social support processes: Where are we? What next? *Journal of Health and Social Behavior*, 35, 53–79.

Thomas, D. A. (1990). The impact of race on managers' experiences of developmental relationships (mentoring and sponsorship): An intra-organizational study. *Journal of Organizational Behavior*, 11, 479–491.

Thomas, D. A. (1993). Racial dynamics in cross-race developmental relationships. *Administrative Science Quarterly*, 38, 169–194.

Thomas, D. A. (1999). Beyond the simple demography-power hypothesis: How blacks in power influence white-mentor–black-protégé developmental relationships. In A. Murrell, F. J. Crosby, & R. Ely (Eds.), *Mentoring dilemmas: Developmental relationships within multicultural organizations* (pp. 157–170). Mahwah, NJ: Lawrence Erlbaum Press.

Thomas, D. A., & Ely, R. J. (2001). Making differences matter: A new paradigm for managing diversity. *Harvard Business Review*, Sept/Oct, 79–91.

Thorpe, J. (2005, January). *APS Observer*, 18(1), 1–3. (Published interview with Robert Zajonc, Stanford University.) Online at http://www.psychologicalscience.org/observer.

Tierney, J., & Grossman, J. B. (2000). What works in mentoring. In M. P. Kluger, G. Alexander, & P. A. Curtis (Eds.), *What works in child welfare* (pp. 323–326). Washington, DC: Child Welfare League of America.

Tierney, J. P., Grossman, J. B., & Resch, N. L. (1995). *Making a difference: An impact study of Big Brothers/Big Sisters*. Philadelphia: Public/Private Ventures.

Tinto, V. (1993). *Leaving college: Rethinking the causes and cures of student attrition* (2nd ed.). Chicago: University of Chicago Press.

Tomlinson, A. (2001, December 17). Concrete ceiling harder than glass to break for women of color. *Canadian HR Reporter*, pp. 7, 13.

Tracey, T. J., Leong, F. T. L., & Glidden, C. (1986). Help seeking and problem perception among Asian Americans. *Journal of Counseling Psychology*, 33, 331–336.

Treston, H. (1999). Peer mentoring: Making a difference at James Cook University, Cairns – It's moments like these you need mentors. *Innovations in Education & Training International, 36*, 236–243.

Turban, D. B., & Dougherty, T. W. (1994). Role of protégé personality in receipt of mentoring and career success. *Academy of Management Journal, 37*, 688–702.

Turban, D. B., Dougherty, T. W., & Lee, F. K. (2002). Gender, race, and perceived similarity effects in developmental relationships: The moderating role of relationship duration. *Journal of Vocational Behavior, 61*, 240–262.

Turban, D. B., & Jones, A. P. (1988). Supervisor–subordinate similarity: Types, effects and mechanisms. *Journal of Applied Psychology, 73*, 228–234.

Twale, D. J., & Kochan, F. K. (2000). Assessment of an alternative cohort model for part-time students in an educational leadership program. *Journal of School Leadership, 10*(2), 188–208.

Tyler, K. (April, 1998). Mentoring programs link employees and experienced executives. *HRMagazine, 43*(5), 98–103.

Uba, L. (1994). *Asian Americans: Personality patterns, identity, and mental health.* New York: The Guilford Press.

Ugbah, S., & Williams, S. A. (1989). The mentor–protégé relationship: Its impact on Blacks in predominantly White institutions. In J. C. Elam (Ed.), *Blacks in higher education: Overcoming the odds* (pp. 29–42). Lanham, MD: University Press of America.

Uhl-Bien, M., & Maslyn, M. (2005). *Paternalism as a form of leadership: Differentiating paternalism from Leader–Member Exchange.* Academy of Management Meeting, Honolulu, Hawaii.

US Census Bureau (2002). *Census brief: Current population survey.* Retrieved February 27, 2005, from www.census.gov/prod/2002pubs/c2kbr01-16.pdf.

US Census Bureau (2003). *Factors for features (CB03-FF.05).* Retrieved February 27, 2005, from www.census.gov/Press-Release/www/releases/archives/facts_for_features/001627.html.

US Census Bureau (2004). *Educational attainment in the United States: 2003.* Retrieved February 27, 2005, from www.census.gov/prod/2004pubs/p20-550.pdf#search ='Educational%20attainment%20in%20the%20United%20States:%202003'.

US Department of Census 2000 (n.d.). *Americans with disabilities: Table 4.* Retrieved October 15, 2001 from: www.census.gov/hhes/www/disable/sipp/disab97t4.html.

US Department of Education (2006). 21st century community learning centers. Retrieved March 12, 2006 from www.ed.gov/programs/21stcclc/index.html

Vaillant, G. (1977). *Adaptation to life.* Boston: Little, Brown, & Company.

Valentine, J., Griffith, J., Ruthazer, R., Gottleib, B., & Keel, S. (1998). Strengthening causal inference in adolescent drug preventions studies: Methods and findings from a controlled study of the Urban Youth Connections program. *Drugs & Society, 12*, 127–145.

Valentine, V. (2005, November, 8). Economic despair, racism drive French riots. National Public Radio. Retrieved online March 13, 2006. www.npr.org/templates/story/story.php?storyId=5004897

Vertz, L. L. (1985). Women, occupational advancement, and mentoring: An analysis of one public organization. *Public Administrative Review, 45*(3), 415–423.

Viator, R. E. (1999). An analysis of formal mentoring programs and perceived barriers to obtaining a mentor at large public accounting firms. *Accounting Horizons, 13*, 37–53.

Viator, R. E. (2001). An examination of African Americans' access to public accounting mentors: Perceived barriers and intentions to leave. *Accounting, Organizations and Society, 26*, 541–561.

Viator, R. E., & Scandura, T. A. (1991). A study of mentor–protégé relationships in large public accounting firms. *Accounting Horizons, 5*(3), 20–30.

Vroom, V. H. (1964). *Work and motivation.* New York: Wiley.

Vygotsky, L. (1978). *Mind in society: The development of higher psychological processes.* Cambridge, MA: Harvard University Press.

Wagner, J. A. (1994). Participation's effect on performance and satisfaction: A reconsideration of research evidence. *Academy of Management Review, 19,* 312–320.

Wakabayashi, M., Graen, G. B., & Uhl-Bien, M. (1990). The generalizability of the hidden investment process in leading Japanese corporations. *Human Relations, 43,* 1099–1116.

Waldeck, J. H., Orrego, V. O., Plax, T. G., & Kearney, P. (1997). Graduate student/faculty mentoring relationships: Who gets mentored, how it happens, and to what end. *Communication Quarterly, 45,* 93–109.

Wallace, D., Abel, R., & Ropers-Huilman, B. (2000). Clearing a path for success: Deconstructing borders through undergraduate mentoring. *Review of Higher Education, 24,* 87–102.

Wallace, J. E. (2001). The benefits of mentoring for female lawyers. *Journal of Vocational Behavior, 58,* 366–391.

Wanberg, C. R., Kammeyer-Mueller, J., & Marchese, M. (March, 2004). *Antecedents and outcomes of formal mentoring.* Paper presented at the Nineteenth Annual Meeting of the Society for Industrial and Organizational Psychology, Chicago, IL.

Wanberg, C. R., Welsh, E. T., & Hezlett, S. A. (2003). Mentoring research: A review and dynamic process model. *Research in Personnel and Human Resources Management, 22,* 39–124.

Ward, Y. L., Johnson, W. B., & Campbell, C. D. (2005). Practitioner research vertical teams: A model for mentoring in practitioner-focused doctoral programs. *The Clinical Supervisor, 23,* 179–190.

Waters, L. (2004). Protégé–mentor agreement about the provision of psychosocial support: The mentoring relationship, personality, and workload. *Journal of Vocational Behavior, 65,* 519–532.

Way, N., & Chen, L. (2000). Close and general friendships among African American, Latino, and Asian American adolescents from low-income families. *Journal of Adolescent Research, 15,* 274–301.

Way, N., & Pahl, K. (2001). Individual and contextual predictors of perceived friendship quality among ethnic minority, low-income adolescents. *Journal of Research on Adolescence, 11,* 325–349.

Wayne, S. J., Liden, R. C., Kraimer, M. L., & Graf, I. K. (1999). The role of human capital, motivation and supervisor sponsorship in predicting career success. *Journal of Organizational Behavior, 20,* 577–595.

Weil, V. (2001). Mentoring: Some ethical considerations. *Science and Engineering Ethics, 7,* 471–482.

Weiten, W. (2005). *Psychology: Themes and variations.* Belmont, CA: Wadsworth/Thompson Learning.

Werner, E. E., & Smith, E. S. (1982). *Vulnerable but invincible: A study of resilient children.* New York: McGraw-Hill.

Westbrook, F. D., & Sedlacek, W. E. (1988). Workshop on using noncognitive variables with minority students in higher education. *Journal for Specialists in Group Work, 13,* 82–89.

Whitely, W., Dougherty, T. W., & Dreher, G. F. (1991). Relationship of career mentoring and socioeconomic origin to managers' and professionals' early career progress. *Academy of Management Journal, 34,* 331–351.

Whitely, W. T., & Coetsier, P. (1993). The relationship of career mentoring to early career outcomes. *Organization Studies, 14,* 419–441.

Whiting, B. B., & Whiting, J. W. M. (1975). *Children of six cultures: A psycho-cultural analysis.* Cambridge, MA: Harvard University Press.

Whyte, W. H. (1956). *The organization man.* New York: Simon and Schuster.

Wilde, J. B., & Schau, C. G. (1991). Mentoring in graduate schools of education: Mentees' perceptions. *Journal of Experimental Education, 59,* 165–179.

Williams, E. A. (2000). *Team mentoring: New directions for research on employee development in organizations.* Paper presented at the Academy of Management Meeting, Toronto, Canada.

Williams, E. A., Scandura, T. A., & Hamilton, B. A. (2001, November). Dysfunctional mentoring relationships and negative social exchange: Uncovering some unpleasant realities in mentoring relationships. *Southern Management Association Proceedings* (pp. 62–66). New Orleans: Southern Management Association Meeting.

Williams, L. L., Levine, J. B., Malhotra, S., & Holtzheimer, P. (2004). The good-enough mentoring relationship. *Academic Psychiatry, 28,* 111–115.

Williams, T., & Kornblum, W. (1985). *Growing up poor.* Lexington, MA: Lexington Books.

Williamson, I. O., & Cable, D. M. (2003). Predicting early career research productivity: The case of management faculty. *Journal of Organizational Behavior, 24,* 25–44.

Wills, T. A. (1991). Social support and interpersonal relationship. *Review of Personality and Social Psychology, 12,* 265–289.

Wilson J. A., & Elman, N. S. (1990). Organizational benefits of mentoring. *Academy of Management Executive, 4*(4), 88–94.

Wilson, J. (2000). Volunteering. *Annual Review of Sociology, 26,* 215–240.

Wilson, R. C., Gaff, J. G., Dienst, E. R., Wood, L., & Bavry, J. L. (1975). *College professors and their impact on students.* New York: Wiley.

Wilson, W. J. (1987). *The truly disadvantaged.* Chicago: The University of Chicago Press.

Winning, E. A. (1994). *Pitfalls in paternalism.* Retrieved February 22, 2005, from www.ewin.com/articles/paternal.htm.

Witte, J. E., & James, W. B. (1998). Cohort partnerships: A pragmatic approach to doctoral research. *New Directions for Adult and Continuing Education, 79,* 53–62.

Wood, D., Bruner, J. S., & Ross, G. (1976). The role of tutoring in problem solving. *Journal of Child Psychology and Psychiatry, 17,* 89–100.

Wrightsman, L. S. (1981, August). *Research methodologies for assessing mentoring.* Paper presented at the annual meeting of the American Psychological Association, Los Angeles, CA (ERIC Document Reproduction Service No. ED 209 339).

Young, A. M., & Perrewé, P. L. (2000a). The exchange relationship between mentors and protégés: The development of a framework. *Human Resources Management Review, 10*(1), 177–209.

Young, A. M., & Perrewé, P. L. (2000b). What did you expect? An examination of career-related support and social support among mentors and protégés. *Journal of Management, 26,* 611–632.

Young, C. Y., & Wright, J. V. (2001). Mentoring: The components for success. *Journal of Instructional Psychology, 28*(3), 202–206.

Young, J. P., Alvermann, D., Kaste, J., Henderson, S., & Many, J. (2004). Being a friend and a mentor at the same time: A pooled case comparison. *Mentoring & Tutoring, 12*(1), 23–36.

Youniss, J., McLellan, J. A., & Yates, M. (1997). What we know about engendering civic identity. *American Behavioral Scientist, 40*(5), 620–631.

Yukl, G. (1989). *Leadership in organizations.* Englewood Cliffs, NJ: Prentice Hall.

Zanna, M. P., & Darley, J. M. (2004). Mentoring: Managing the faculty–graduate student relationship. In J. M. Darley, M. P. Zanna, & H. L. Roediger (Eds.), *The compleat academic: A career guide* (2nd ed., pp. 117–131). Washington, DC: American Psychological Association.

Zellars, K. L., Tepper, B. J., & Duffy, M. K. (2002). Abusive supervision and subordinates' organizational citizenship behavior. *Journal of Applied Psychology, 87,* 1062–1076.

Zey, M. G. (1984). *The mentor connection.* Homewood, IL: Dow Jones-Irwin.

Zey, M. G. (1985). Mentor programs: Making the right moves. *Personnel Journal, 64*(2), 53–57.

Zhang, N., & Dixon, D. N. (2003). Acculturation and attitudes of Asian international students toward seeking psychological help. *Journal of Multicultural Counseling and Development, 31,* 205–222.

Zielinski, D. (2000). Mentoring up. *Training, October,* 136–140.

Zimmerman, M. A., Bingenheimer, J. B., & Behrendt, D. E. (2005). Natural mentoring relationships. In D. L. DuBois & M. J. Karcher (Eds.), *Handbook of youth mentoring* (pp. 143–157). Thousand Oaks, CA: Sage.

Zimmerman, M. A., Bingenheimer, J. B., & Notaro, P. C. (2002). Natural mentors and adolescent resiliency: A study with urban youth. *American Journal of Community Psychology, 30,* 221–243.

Zuckerman, H. (1977). *Scientific elite: Nobel laureates in the United States.* New York: The Free Press.

Name Index

Subject Index